VISUAL QUICKSTART GUIDE

PREMIERE ELEMENTS 2

FOR WINDOWS

Antony Bolante

Visual QuickStart Guide

Premiere Elements 2 for Windows

Antony Bolante

Peachpit Press
1249 Eighth Street
Berkeley, CA 94710
(510) 524-2178
(510) 524-2221 (fax)

Find us on the Web at www.peachpit.com.
To report errors, please send a note to errata@peachpit.com.

Peachpit Press is a division of Pearson Education.

Editor: Rebecca Gulick
Copy Editor: Liz Welch
Production Coordinator: Tracey Croom
Compositor: Chris Gillespie, Happenstance Type-O-Rama
Indexer: Rebecca Plunkett
Cover Production: George Mattingly

Notice of Rights

Notice of Liability

Trademarks

ISBN 0-321-38355-9

9 8 7 6 5 4 3 2 1

Printed and bound in the United States of America

In memory of my Uncle Phil,
Philip Shusterman
1925-2005

Thank You

Everyone involved creating the previous version of this book; I hope this one does you proud.

Rebecca Gulick and Liz Welch.

Simi Cover, Becky Winter, Tracey Croom, Myrna Vladic, Chris Gillespie, Happenstance Type-O-Rama, Rebecca Plunkett, and all the good people at Peachpit Press.

The brilliant folks at Adobe Systems, Inc., especially Charat Maheshwari, Stephen Inoue and Atsuko Yamagishi.

Stardust Video & Coffee.

Family and friends who've let me share their beautiful photos and faces.

The Big Craps Crew.

Shortstack.

My family, always.

Table of Contents

Back to Basics

In 1991, Adobe introduced an innovative video-editing program called *Premiere*. Even though technology at that time wasn't quite up to the task, Premiere hinted at the computer's potential for making video production and editing more accessible to all. What once could be achieved only on high-priced, high-end equipment would one day be done on a desktop. And sure enough, Premiere was an important player in what some call the desktop video revolution. Like any good revolution, it had a democratizing effect. Today, DV camcorders, digital cameras, and fast, capacious computers are within reach of the common folk.

Yet, as Premiere had kept pace with innovation, it had also become more complex. And as it had become more full-featured, it increasingly appealed to a professional elite. So after numerous revisions and improvements, Premiere finally made a break with its humble roots—becoming *Premiere Pro*, a video-editing program specifically geared toward the professional editor.

But what about the video revolution? What about technological democracy? As Premiere Pro, has the program rejected its heritage and betrayed its populist beginnings? Fortunately, out of the grassroots arose another, more approachable Premiere: *Premiere Elements.*

Make no mistake: Premiere Elements is neither "Premiere Lite" nor a "poor person's Premiere Pro." At its heart, Premiere Elements retains Premiere Pro's core strengths; but it sheds features you don't need and keeps the ones you want. Even as Premiere Elements matures, it retains its focus. It remains streamlined and intuitive, and helps you along with automated features and ready-to-use templates.

You've chosen Premiere Elements because you want a straightforward but powerful video-editing program. And you've chosen this book because you're ready to get started.

The VQS Series

Chances are that you're already familiar with Peachpit Press' *Visual QuickStart* series of books. They're known for their concise style, step-by-step instructions and ample illustrations.

Premiere Elements 2 for Windows: Visual QuickStart Guide distills a multifaceted program in the time-tested *QuickStart* tradition. If the book looks a little thick for a "concise" guide, consider that it contains literally hundreds of screen shots that clearly illustrate every task. Like other books in this series, *Premiere Elements 2 for Windows: Visual QuickStart Guide* strives to be quick without failing to guide.

Terminology: Digital and Analog

When you record audio and video, sound and light are converted to electrical signals. *Analog* media record these signals as continuously changing values. *Digital* media, on the other hand, record audio and video as a series of specific, discrete values. A playback device converts these values back to audio and video. The accuracy of each conversion greatly influences the picture and sound quality.

Because digital recordings use discrete values, it's easy to reproduce them exactly, time after time. In addition, you can take advantage of the computer's ability to manipulate these values—which means you can more easily alter the sound, color, and brightness, and add effects.

Using This Book

In this book, chapters are organized to present topics as you encounter them in a typical editing project, but the task-oriented format and thumb tabs let you jump to the topic that you need.

Although the text restricts itself to the task at hand, it doesn't hesitate to give you critical background information, usually in the form of *sidebars* that help you understand the concepts behind the task. If you're already familiar with the concept, feel free to skip ahead; if not, look to the sidebars for some grounding. Also keep an eye out for tips, which point out shortcuts, pitfalls, and tricks of the trade.

By explaining how to use Premiere Elements, this book inevitably touches on a multitude of related topics: file formats, editing aesthetics, special effects, DVDs, the Internet, and so on. Discussing the fundamentals and background of each of these areas is far outside the scope of this book (and even books that don't have the word *quick* in their title). Nevertheless, this guide tries to provide enough information to keep you moving and point you in new directions.

How Premiere Elements Works

Premiere Elements is digital nonlinear editing software. A breakdown of this description can give you clues about how it works:

Digital—Premiere Elements manipulates digital media: digital video and audio, scanned images, and digitally created artwork and animation stored in various formats. Regardless of the particular format, these materials are stored as files on your computer's hard disk. Strictly speaking, Premiere Elements doesn't convert analog images and audio to digital form. In other words, it won't help you scan a photo, but it will import the scanned image file.

Nonlinear—Editing in Premiere Elements is described as *nonlinear* because your sources aren't constrained to a linear medium, such as videotape. In other words, you can access any source clip instantly, without shuttling tape, and you can change the sequence of clips without rerecording.

Software—As a software-only package, Premiere Elements can be installed on any personal computer system that meets or exceeds the program's minimum requirements. Beyond the hardware that comes standard in most current computers, it doesn't require specialized hardware. But although the software isn't inextricably linked to particular system, it is sometimes offered together with a computer purchase, as part of the software *bundle*.

What You Can Do with Premiere Elements

The Premiere Elements workspace options reflect an incremental process, optimizing the interface for capture, editing and effects, titles, DVD layout, and export:

Capture DV footage—With DV and an IEEE 1394 or USB 2 connection, capture simply involves transferring video from your camera or deck to the hard drive. (Analog sources such as VHS require a capture device that can digitize the video, and separate software. Once they're digitized, though, you can import the files into Premiere Elements.)

Import digital files—At this point, you add to a Premiere Elements project the footage you want to use. You can import a variety of digital media: video, audio, stills, image sequences, and so on. Your project uses *references* to the source footage, not the footage itself.

Assemble a rough cut—Arrange and adjust the sequence of clips into an edited program using a variety of editing techniques. Because you're using file references, your decisions are nondestructive—that is, you can make as many changes as you want without permanently altering the source files.

Preview your sequence—Watch your sequence at any time, including transitions or special effects. Premiere Elements can render basic effects right away and at full playback speed using only your system's resources. You can also view your work on a connected television.

Fine-tune the sequence—Rearrange and fine-tune the clips in the sequence by dragging them in the timeline. You can also create freeze-frames, or slow- and fast-motion video and audio.

Add transitions—Control how each shot replaces the last using a wide range of transitions, from a basic cross-dissolve to a 3D page peel effect.

Add titles—Create onscreen titles or other graphics from scratch, or modify one of the many templates provided. You can even create professional-looking title rolls and crawls.

Add special effects—Superimpose clips, add motion or a wide variety of filters. Moreover, you can animate any effect, so that it changes over time.

Output—Export the finished sequence directly to tape or DVD, or save a file in any number of formats for playback on other computers, CD-ROM, or over the Web. You can even create a full-fledged DVD complete with a scene menu and motion backgrounds and buttons.

NTSC, PAL, and SECAM

You'll sometimes hear monitors and other video equipment referred to as NTSC, as in *NTSC monitor*. NTSC stands for National Television Standards Committee, a group that develops the television standards used in North America and Japan; its name describes everything that meets those standards.

Phase Alternation Line (PAL) is the standard used in most of Europe and other countries, whereas SECAM (Sequential Couleur avec Mémoire) is used primarily in France, the Middle East, and Eastern Europe.

Premiere Elements vs. Premiere Pro

As pointed out in the introduction, Premiere Elements is the offspring of a more mature and feature-rich application, Premiere Pro.

As its name indicates, Premiere Pro is geared toward the professional video editor and includes such features as multiple sequences, separate source and program monitors, advanced editing tools, multicamera editing, an advanced audio mixer, surround-sound support, robust media management—and arcane video tools like a waveform monitor and vectorscope.

Needless to say, the features of Premiere Pro are overkill for the casual editor of family events and work or school presentations. And although a side-by-side comparison of the two programs reveals Premiere Elements' lineage, it's far more streamlined, lean, and simple to use than the Pro version.

If you're not a professional editor (or an editor with lofty aspirations), you won't miss any of Premiere Pro's advanced features and more complex interface. In fact, you'll be glad they aren't there to overwhelm you—or your budget.

Premiere Elements and Photoshop Elements

Although Premiere Elements can bring together a range of digital media—video, audio, still images—its primary purpose is to edit them together as a movie. So even though Premiere Elements gives you a great way to *present* your digital photos, it's often better to *prepare* them in a program dedicated to the task. Photoshop Elements is that program.

Just as Premiere Elements is the more approachable, more affordable version of Premiere Pro, Photoshop Elements is the accessible version of Photoshop CS, the stalwart companion of photo professionals. Photoshop Elements makes it easy to retouch your photos, add text, crop, and doctor them in innumerable ways.

As you'll learn in this book, you can open Photoshop Elements from within Premiere Elements. It's easy to move files from one program to the other without performing intermediate steps or sacrificing elements of your work. Even the interfaces are quite consistent with one another.

In short, the two programs make great companions, and Adobe offers them together as a set for less than you would pay for them separately.

System Requirements

To use Premiere Elements 2, your system must meet these requirements:

- Intel Pentium 4, M, D, or Extreme Edition, or AMD Opteron or Athlon 64 (SSE2 support required)
- Microsoft Windows XP Professional, Home Edition, or Media Center with Service Pack 2 (SP2) or later
- 256 MB of RAM or more
- 4 GB of available hard disk space for installation
- 1024 x 768 16-bit display
- DVD-ROM drive
- DVD recordable drive required for exporting to DVD (go to Adobe.com for a list of compatible DVD burners)
- IEEE 1394 (aka FireWire or iLink) to connect a Digital 8 or DV camcorder, or a USB2 interface to connect a DV-via-USB-compatible DV camcorder
- You may import media from other devices using the appropriate connector and Premiere Elements 2's Media Downloader feature.

Suggested System

These features aren't required, but they can make working with Premiere Elements a lot more satisfying:

Faster processor—The faster your system can make calculations, the faster it can process frames of video and create effects.

Additional RAM—Premiere Elements relies partly on RAM for performance and stability. In addition, the number of frames you can watch with the RAM preview feature (which allows you to render sequences containing transitions and effects quickly) depends entirely on the amount of RAM you can allocate to Premiere Elements.

Larger hard drives—Video files are notoriously large. Five minutes of DV footage, for example, consumes more than a gigabyte of storage. Ample storage space allows you to work with more footage at once.

Faster hard drives—Your system's ability to play back footage smoothly relies partly on how quickly information can be read from the drives. To use DV footage your drives should sustain a data rate of around 5 MB per second. Most drives in a recent computer should be able to handle this.

Video monitor—Video monitors and computer monitors display images differently. So, since your work is destined for video, a television—preferably one with inputs compatible with your camcorder's connectors and with good color reproduction—allows you to judge it more accurately.

DVD recorder—DVD recorders are quickly becoming as commonplace in a desktop editing suite as video tape decks. (Thankfully, they're becoming more affordable as well.) You can use Premiere Elements to output your edited sequence DVD. Your DVD can even include a scene menu.

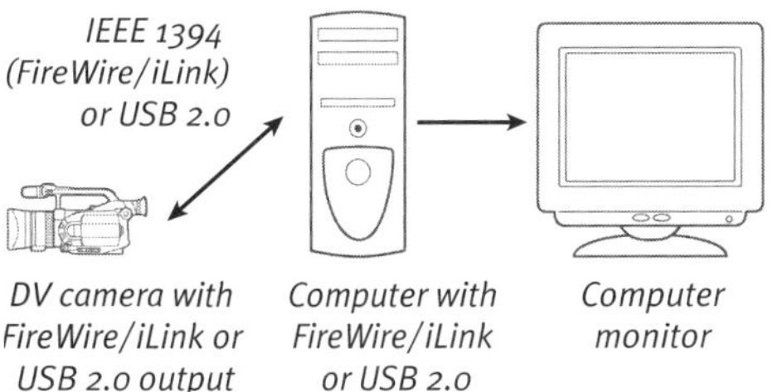

Figure i.1 This configuration includes a computer equipped with an IEEE 1394 (aka FireWire or iLink) and a DV camcorder.

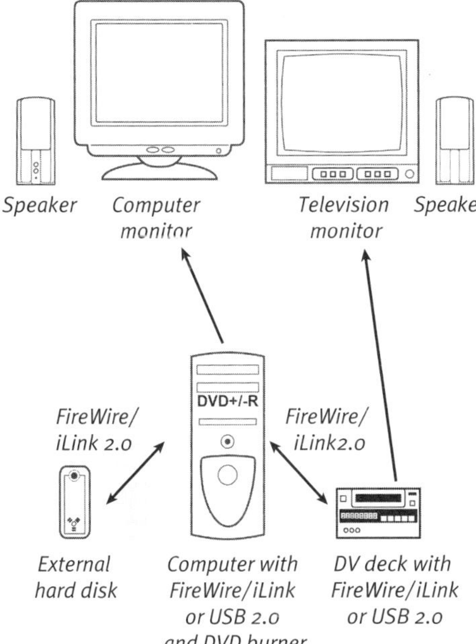

Figure i.2 This configuration uses several options, such as a television, speakers, an internal DVD burner, an external hard drive, and a dedicated deck.

System Configurations

As the preceding sections suggest, your Premiere Elements setup can be simple or elaborate. As long as your computer meets the minimum requirements, you can install Premiere Elements and start editing. On the other hand, your system might include a television monitor and a camera or deck. Here's how a couple of configurations might look:

DV camera configuration (Figure i.1)— In this setup, a DV camera is used to transfer source video to your computer's hard drive over an IEEE 1394 or USB 2.0 connection. The completed edited project can be played back and recorded to a tape in the camera.

Enhanced DV configuration (Figure i.2)— In this setup, several recommended options have been added to the system. A video monitor displays the program as it will appear on a television screen, and external speakers provide the audio. An external drive provides additional storage space for media (a secondary internal drive would work well, too). Inside the computer tower resides a DVD burner. The most extravagant option is a dedicated DV deck, which spares your camcorder the extra wear and tear from using it to capture footage.

1

Basic Elements

Before embarking on a journey, it can be useful to survey the landscape and learn a few local customs. In this chapter, you'll get oriented to Premiere Elements' interface and catch a glimpse of what's to come. In addition, you'll learn about the basic workings of the Premiere Elements interface: how to use context menus, keyboard shortcuts, and commands, and how to undo mistakes. Once you've familiarized yourself with this little travel guide, you can get your passport stamped in Chapter 2, "Starting a Project."

Using the Taskbar

When you start using Premiere Elements, one of the first things you'll notice is the *taskbar*, a row of handy buttons that's near the top of the screen but under the typical menu bar. Whereas the menu bar consists of categorized pull-down menus of nearly every command, the taskbar includes buttons to accomplish common tasks without scrolling through long menus.

Figure 1.1 Buttons on the left side of the taskbar accomplish some of the most common tasks.

Figure 1.2 Buttons on the right side of the taskbar switch the workspace, opening and arranging panels appropriate to the task.

The left side of the taskbar: common tasks

The left side of the taskbar includes buttons for the most common tasks: Open, Save, Add Media, Undo, Redo, and Export (**Figure 1.1**). Undo and Redo are explained later in this chapter; other buttons are discussed in the appropriate chapters later in the book.

The right side of the taskbar: workspaces

The right side of the taskbar includes buttons to change the arrangement of windows, or *workspace*, to suit a particular phase of the editing process. Workspaces configure panels for editing, or open panels you need to perform particular tasks, such as capturing video, creating titles, or creating a DVD menu. Workspace buttons include Capture, Edit, Titles, and DVD (**Figure 1.2**).

Later in this chapter, you'll learn about each workspace and about working with workspaces in general. Later chapters follow the workflow suggested by each workspace.

✔ Tip

- Premiere Elements 2's taskbar differs from the previous version of the program. The Export button appears on the left side (not the right side), because exporting invokes a dialog box, and not a workspace per se. Moreover, most users will opt to export to DVD. Also, the Effects workspace button is no longer included, because the enhanced, panel-based interface makes a special effects workspace less useful.

Using Workspaces

As you proceed through this book, you'll find that chapter topics follow the typical workflow of a project. Appropriately enough, the taskbar's workspace buttons also reflect the overall editing process.

To choose a workspace:

In the taskbar, *do either of the following:*

- To set the workspace or to set the first workspace listed in the Titles workspace button's pull-down menu, click the workspace button.
- To choose an option in the Titles workspace button's pull-down menu, click and hold the Titles workspace button, and choose the option you want (**Figure 1.3**).

  The panels open and arrange according to your choice (**Figure 1.4**). If you choose an option in the Titles workspace button's pull-down menu, Premiere Elements prompts you to select a template or specify the name of the title before the workspace is arranged for creating titles. (See Chapter 9, "Creating Titles," for more about creating titles.)

Figure 1.3 Click a workspace button; or, to choose an optional workspace, click and hold a workspace button, and choose an option (shown here).

Figure 1.4 The panels are arranged for the workspace automatically. Here, the panels are arranged according to the Editing workspace.

To customize a workspace:

- Rearrange the panels to suit your computer monitor, editing preferences, or personal taste.

  Henceforth, selecting the workspace arranges panels according to your choice (**Figure 1.5**).

Figure 1.5 Premiere Elements remembers any modifications you make to a workspace. Here, I've modified the default Editing workspace to optimize it for adjusting effects. Panels have been docked and resized, and the How To panel has been removed altogether.

Figure 1.6 Choose Window > Restore Workspace and choose the name of the workspace you want to reset to its default arrangement—in this case, the Editing workspace.

To restore a workspace to its default arrangement:

- Choose Window > Restore Workspace and choose the name of the workspace you want to reset (**Figure 1.6**).

  Henceforth, selecting the workspace arranges the panels in their default arrangement.

✔ Tip

- A particularly useful modification to a workspace involves docking panels. See the section "Customizing the Workspace," later in this chapter.

Looking at the Interface

Reviewing each panel should help orient you before you begin working in earnest. But because this book addresses each panel and tool as dictated by the editing process, this section groups the panels according to workspace.

Capture workspace

The Capture workspace opens the *Capture* panel, which lets you control a DV camera or deck and transfer, or *capture*, the video and audio to your hard drive so you can use them as clips in your movie project (**Figure 1.7**).

Figure 1.7 The Capture panel controls the capture of video and audio.

Editing workspace

Although it's the second workspace button, the Editing workspace is the one you'll see first. It includes all the basic panels you need to edit video, plus a *How To* panel and *History* panel (**Figure 1.8**). When editing, you might also want to use the *Audio Meters* panel and *Information* panel.

Figure 1.8 Most of your work takes place in the Editing workspace.

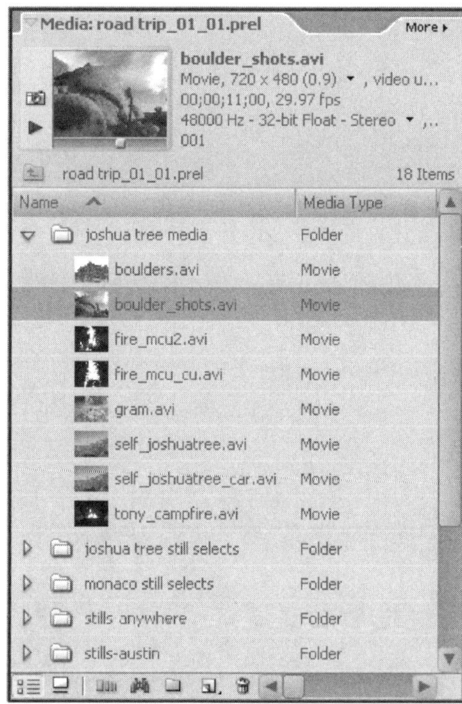

Figure 1.9 The Media panel lists all the footage you plan to use in your project.

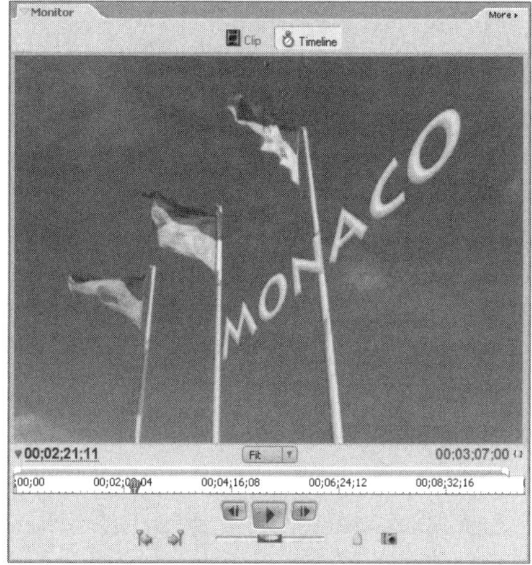

Figure 1.10 The Monitor panel shows source clips or the edited sequence, depending on the task at hand.

The *Media* panel lists and organizes the source clips you want to use (**Figure 1.9**). It displays important information about each clip that you can use to sort the clips. When you capture video using the Capture window, it's added to the Media panel as clips automatically. You can also import previously stored video, audio, or still-image files to list them as clips in the Media panel.

The *Monitor* panel displays the video much as it appears on a television (**Figure 1.10**). The Monitor panel toggles between two modes, or *views*, depending on the task at hand. To allow you to view and edit source clips, the Monitor panel switches to *Clip view*; to view the edited sequence, it switches to *Timeline view*.

The *Timeline* panel graphically represents your program as video and audio clips arranged in vertically stacked tracks (**Figure 1.11**). Time is measured along a horizontal ruler. You can adjust the length and arrangement of clips by dragging them in the Timeline panel. This panel also includes a few tools you can use to edit clips.

The *How To* panel includes an index of links to instructions and provides quick reference to Premiere Elements' help system (**Figure 1.12**). Once you gain some proficiency with the program, though, you can keep this panel closed or in the background to make room for other panels.

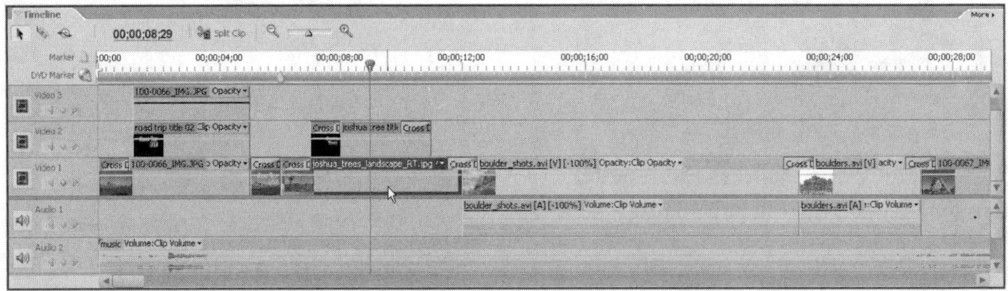

Figure 1.11 The Timeline panel shows the edited sequence as clips arranged in layered video and audio tracks along a horizontal timeline.

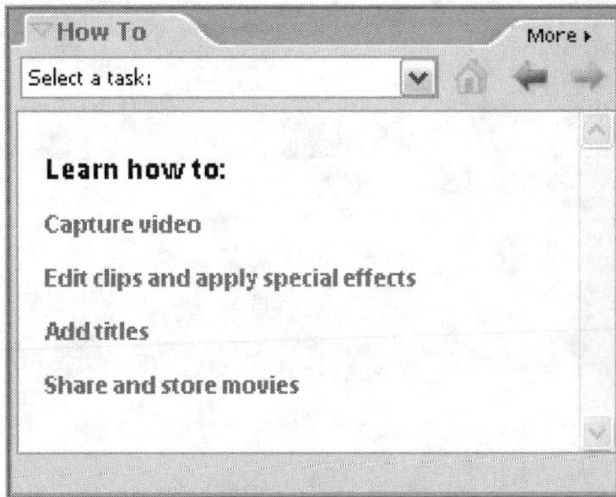

Figure 1.12 The How To panel lists an index of links that you can click to find out how to perform various tasks. When you no longer require its services, close it to make room for other panels.

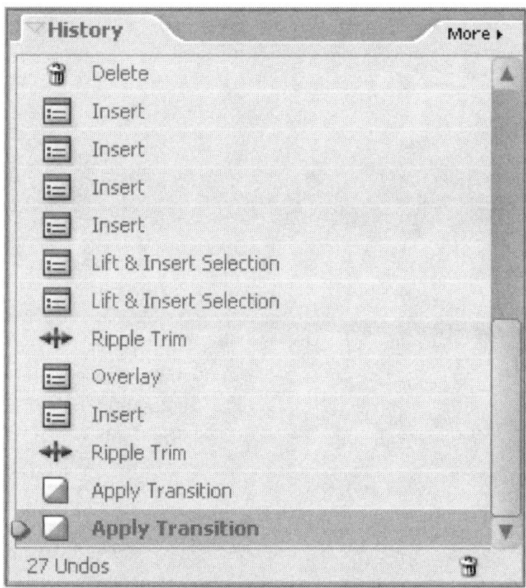

Figure 1.13 The History panel lets you return the project to an earlier state—to a point before you made a mistake, for example.

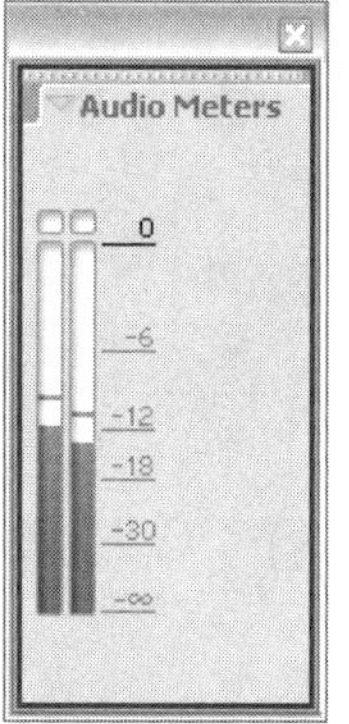

Figure 1.14 Open the Audio Meters panel to check the audio levels using a VU meter.

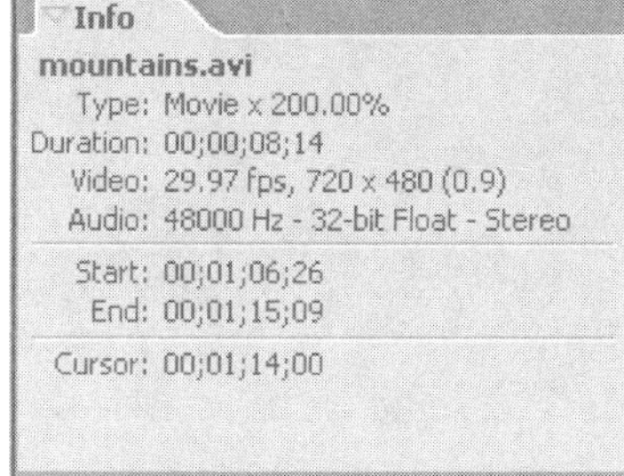

Figure 1.15 The Info panel provides all kinds of information about the task at hand.

The *History* panel, as in other Adobe programs, lists recent actions, allowing you to see where you made a mistake and return the project to an earlier state (**Figure 1.13**).

The *Audio Meters* panel displays a traditional VU (volume units) meter for measuring the audio levels of your edited movie (**Figure 1.14**).

The *Info* panel provides information pertinent to the task at hand—such as the vital statistics of the selected clip or the current position of the mouse pointer (**Figure 1.15**).

Effects editing

No, you won't find a separate workspace button for "effects editing." The panel-based interface incorporates what you need to add and adjust special effects. Even so, the panels devoted to effects merit a description set apart from the other panels included in the Editing workspace.

The *Effects and Transitions* panel lists and organizes video and audio transitions, as well as video and audio filters (**Figure 1.16**). The Properties panel automatically displays the appropriate controls for adjusting a selected transition (**Figure 1.17**) or for adjusting and animating a clip's effects—whether they're effects inherent to the clip (Image Control, Motion, Opacity, and Volume), or filters you add to it (**Figure 1.18**).

As you'll see in Chapter 10, "Adding Effects," you can also adjust and animate effects using controls in the Timeline. The method you choose depends on the effect and your preference.

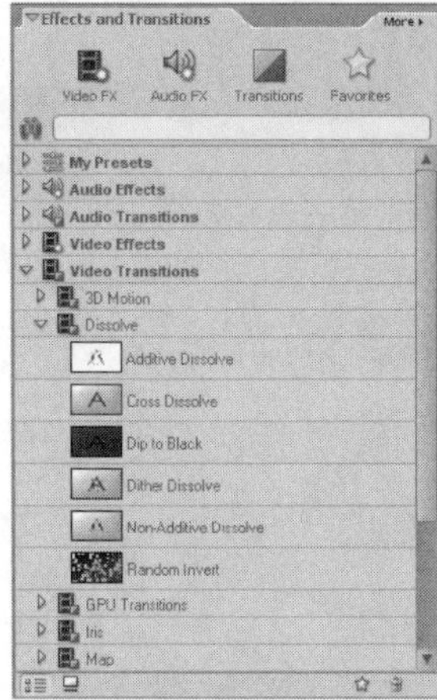

Figure 1.16 The Effects and Transitions panel lists and organizes transitions and filters.

Figure 1.17 The Properties panel provides controls for adjusting a selected transition.

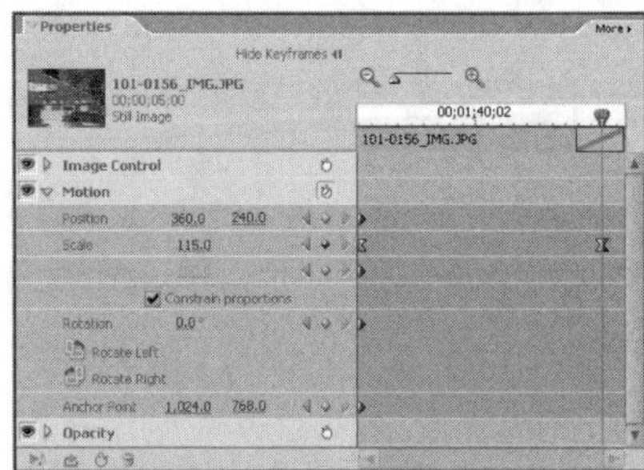

Figure 1.18 The Properties panel also helps you set and animate built-in effects like image control, motion, opacity, volume, as well as the filters you add to a clip.

Titles workspace

The Titles workspace rearranges panels to accommodate, a "suite" of several interrelated panels that allow you to create text and graphics for use in your program (**Figure 1.19**). If you're creating a new title, Premiere Elements prompts you to either specify a name for the title or select a title template before it invokes the Titles workspace.

Figure 1.19 The Title workspace opens the panels you need to create titles and graphics.

DVD workspace

The DVD button opens the *DVD Layout* panel, which lets you select and customize DVD menu templates and burn your edited movie project to a DVD (**Figure 1.20**). In the DVD layout, the Properties panel displays additional tools you can use to create a DVD (**Figure 1.21**).

✔ Tip

- You can adjust the brightness of the interface by choosing Edit > Preferences > General and dragging the User Interface Brightness slider.

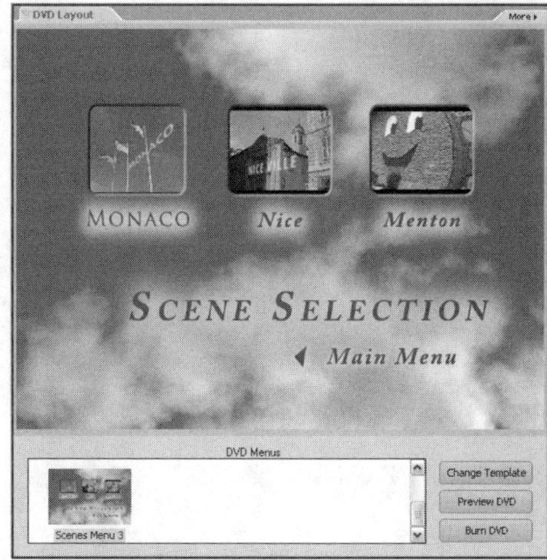

Figure 1.20 The DVD workspace opens the DVD Layout panel, which lets you turn your finished movie into a full-fledged DVD, complete with menus and scenes.

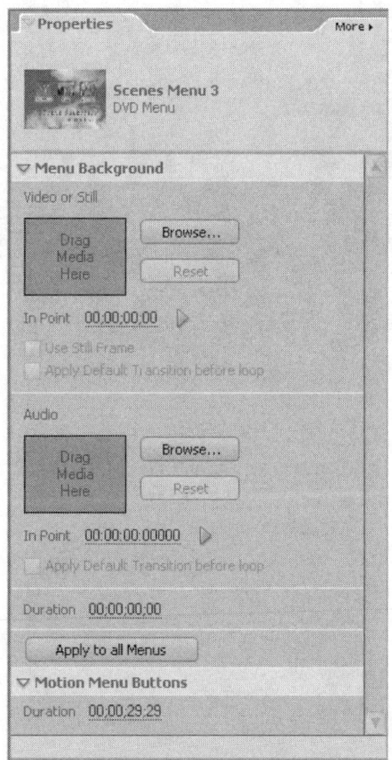

Figure 1.21 Invoking the DVD workspace also toggles the Properties panel to display other tools you may need to create your DVD.

Customizing the Workspace

Using the preset workspaces is convenient, not compulsory. By customizing the size and arrangement of the panels, you can optimize your workspace and your workflow. You just have to know a few things about panels and tabs.

The Premiere Elements interface consists of an interconnected system of *panels*. Unlike a collection of free-floating windows that can be arranged like playing cards on a tabletop, panels are joined together in such a way that the interface may remind you of a mosaic or stained glass. Resizing one panel affects the adjacent panels so that, as a whole, the panels always fill the screen (or more strictly speaking, the Premiere Elements' main application window, which most users maximize to fill the screen). With panels, it's easy to change the relative size of each part of the interface without wasting screen space. And you don't have to worry about one window disappearing behind another.

You can also customize a workspace by taking advantage of tabs. The tab that appears at the top of each panel looks a lot like its real-world counterpart in your office filing cabinet. By dragging a panel's tab into the same area as another panel, you *dock* the panels together. When panels are docked, it's as though they are filed one on top of the other. But like physical file folder tabs, the tabs of the panels in the back are always visible along the top edge of the stack; simply click a panel's tab to bring it to the front.

Just as docking reduces the number of spaces in the interface's "mosaic" of panels, dragging a panel between other panels creates an additional space.

Finally, you can separate a panel from the others, creating a free-floating window. A floating window might be useful for tasks you don't perform often, or when you can move it to a second computer screen. And unlike panels, you can close a floating window to remove it from the workspace.

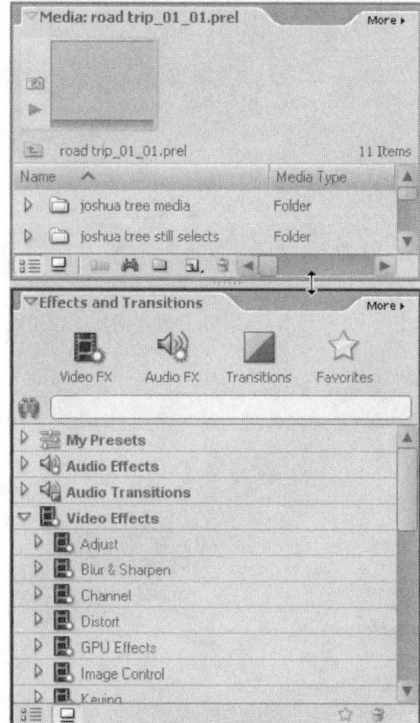

Figure 1.22 Position the mouse pointer over the border between panels so that the resize icon appears...

✔ Tips

- For the most part, you'll customize the Editing workspace to suit the task at hand, though you may find ways to tweak the other workspaces as well.
- As you progress through this book, you'll notice that many figures depict a customized workspace.
- A few panels are so narrow, they don't have a tab or label. Don't worry; they work like other panels. Instead of dragging them from a tab, you can drag them from the textured area at the top.

To resize panels:

- Position the mouse pointer on the border between panels, so that the resize icon ⟷ appears (**Figure 1.22**), and then drag. The size of adjacent panels change automatically, according to your adjustments (**Figure 1.23**).

Figure 1.23 ...and drag to resize the panels that share that border.

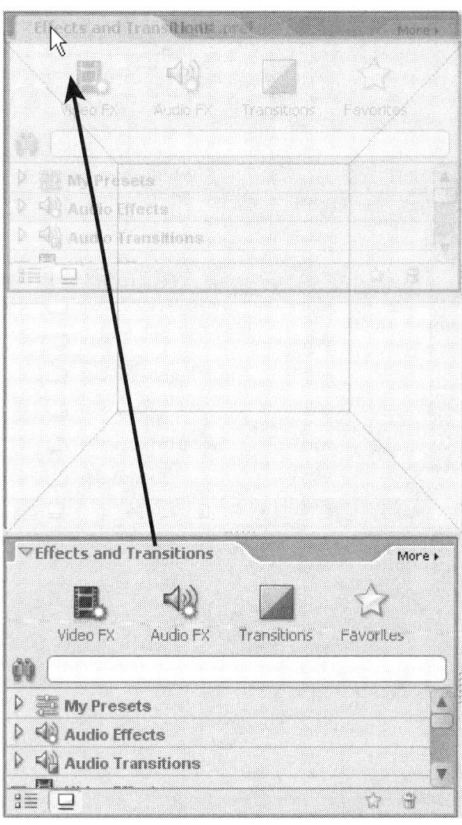

Figure 1.24 Dragging a panel into another panel...

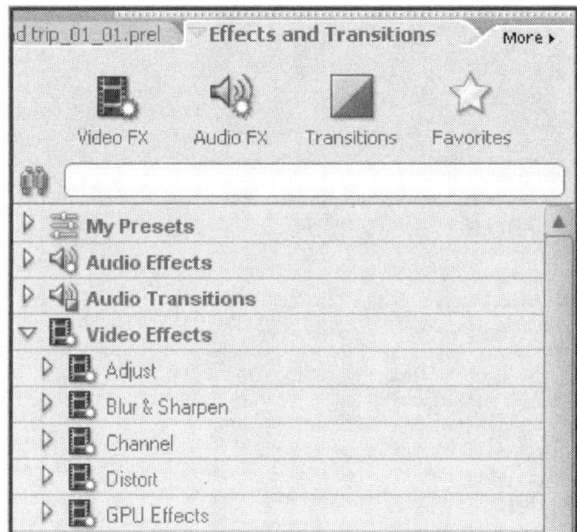

Figure 1.25 ...combines the two panels into a tabbed group.

To dock panels:

1. *Do either of the following:*
   - ▲ To dock a panel, drag its tab or the textured area at the top of the panel.
   - ▲ To dock a floating window, click and drag the top of the window.
2. Drag the mouse pointer within another panel, so that a highlighted area indicates the panel will appear docked as a tab (**Figure 1.24**), and then release the mouse.

   The panels are docked together, so that they occupy the same area in the interface's grid of panels (**Figure 1.25**). If the panel wasn't docked in its previous position, then docking it eliminates the space it had occupied in the grid of panels.

To view tabbed panels:

- To view a panel that's hidden behind another panel, click the tab of the panel you want to view (**Figure 1.26** and **Figure 1.27**).
- To view tabs that are don't fit within the width of the panel area, drag the thin scroll bar that appears above the tabs (**Figure 1.28** and **Figure 1.29**).

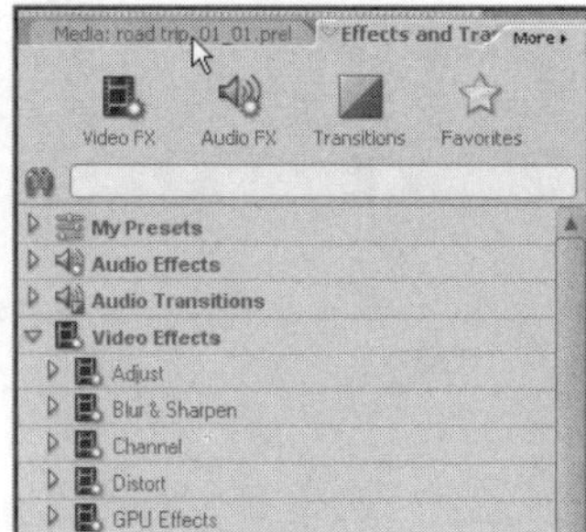

Figure 1.26 Clicking the tab of a panel in the back of the stack...

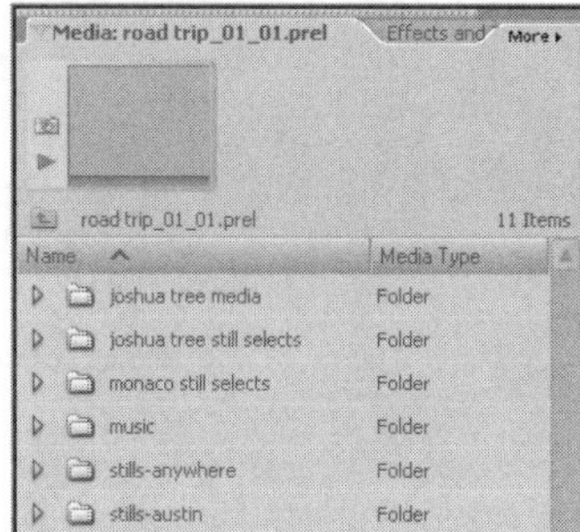

Figure 1.27 ...brings that panel to the front.

Figure 1.28 When the panel is too narrow to show all tabs, a thin scroll bar appears above the tabs.

Figure 1.29 Drag the scroll bar to bring the hidden tabs into view.

Figure 1.30 Dragging a panel between other panels...

To create a new panel area:

1. Do *either* of the following:
   - ▲ To move a panel, drag its tab or the textured area at the top of the panel.
   - ▲ To move a floating window, click and drag the top of the window.
2. Drag the mouse pointer near the side of any other panel, so that a highlighted area indicates where the panel will be inserted in the grid of panels (**Figure 1.30**), and then release the mouse.

   The panel occupies a new space in the grid of panels (**Figure 1.31**).

Figure 1.31 ...allows the panel to occupy a new space in the grid of panels.

To convert a panel into a floating window:

Drag a panel's tab or the textured area at the top of the panel to the empty space above the interface, so that the highlighted area indicates where the floating window will appear (**Figure 1.32**), and then release the mouse.

The panel becomes a floating window (**Figure 1.33**). If the panel wasn't docked in its previous position, then docking it eliminates the space it had occupied in the grid of panels.

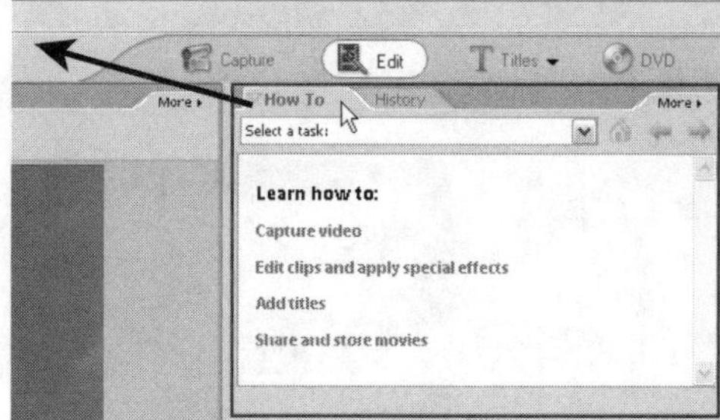

Figure 1.32 Dragging a panel to an empty area (such as the empty part of the taskbar)...

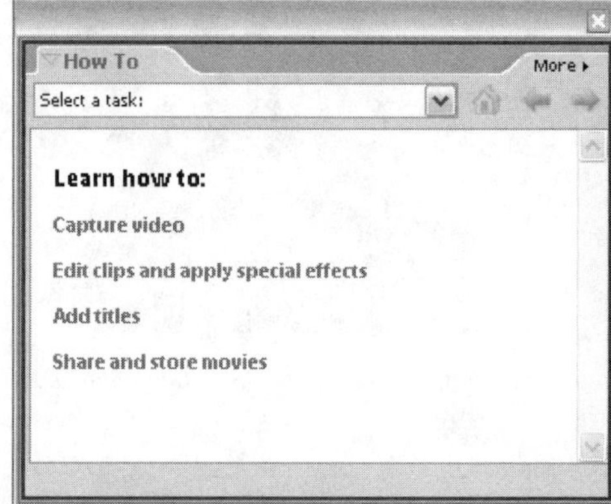

Figure 1.33 ...separates the panel from the others, converting it into a floating window.

✔ Tips

- Some panels—such as the Audio Meters and the Titler Actions—open as floating windows by default. You can incorporate them into the paneled interface using the methods described in the previous section.
- You can always open a panel (or bring it to the front of a tabbed group) by choosing its name in the Windows menu. Yes, the menu is still called "Windows," though the interface is based on interconnected "panels."
- Once you get the hang of the program, you might consider removing the "How To" panel. Just drag it off the grid to convert it into a floating window, and then close the window. The training wheels are off.

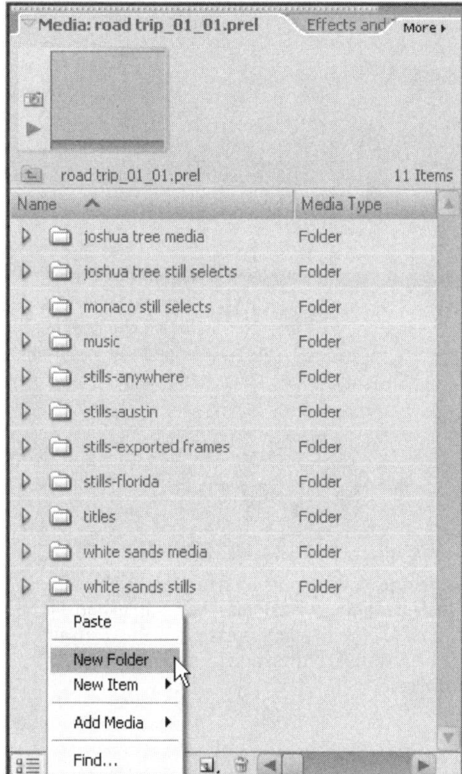

Figure 1.34 Right-click to view a context menu, which relates to the area where you're clicking.

Using Context Menus

In addition to accessing commands from the menu bar at the top of the screen, you can use context menus. As a Windows user, you're already aware that right-clicking, or *context-clicking*, reveals a context menu near the mouse pointer.

As the name suggests, *context menus* contain commands relevant in a particular context or area of the screen. In other words, context-clicking a clip in the Timeline panel reveals a menu similar to the one you'd see if you selected the clip and chose the Clip menu in the menu bar. The context menu for the Media panel contains commands that relate to it, such as the Import command. You get the idea.

Along with keyboard shortcuts, context menus can be a real time-saver. In fact, a few commands can only be accessed via a context menu.

To access a context menu:

1. Position the pointer on the appropriate panel or item, and right-click.

   A menu relating to the window or item appears (**Figure 1.34**).

2. Choose a command from the menu as you would from any other menu, and release the mouse button.

   Premiere Elements executes the command.

Using Keyboard Shortcuts

One way to increase your speed and efficiency is to take advantage of keyboard shortcuts. A standard set of keyboard shortcuts, the so-called Adobe Premiere Elements Factory Defaults, is built in. Premiere Elements doesn't ship with a Quick Reference Card for keyboard shortcuts, but the interface helps you learn them in other ways. The keyboard shortcut for a menu command appears across from the command in the right column (**Figure 1.35**). And you may have noticed that hovering the mouse pointer over a button or icon reveals a *tooltip*, a small box identifying not only the item's name but also its keyboard equivalent, if available (**Figure 1.36**). This book mentions the most common and useful shortcuts in the pertinent sections.

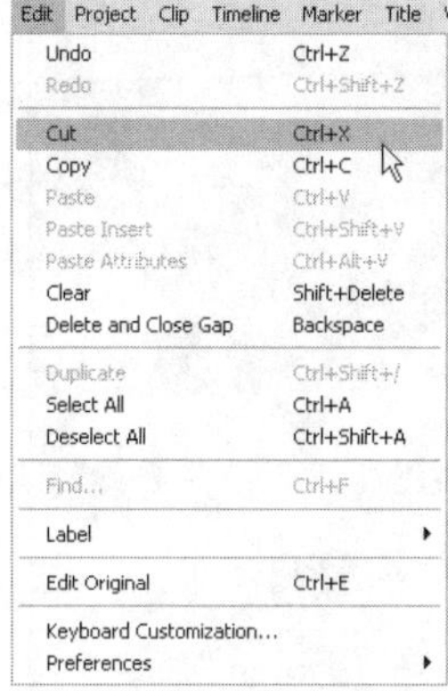

Figure 1.35 The keyboard shortcut for a menu command appears across from the command.

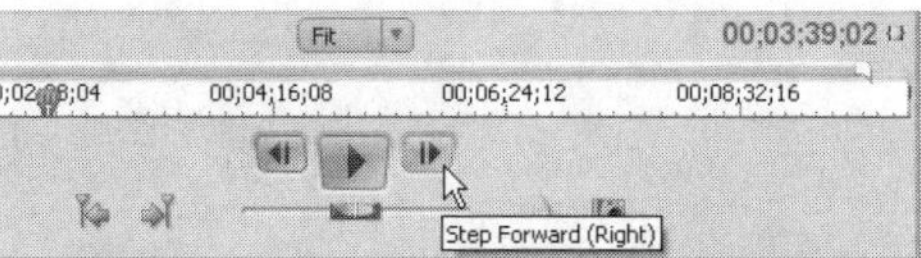

Figure 1.36 Hovering the mouse over a button or icon reveals a tooltip, which identifies the item and its keyboard shortcut—in this case, the Step Forward (Frame Advance) button and its shortcut, the right arrow key.

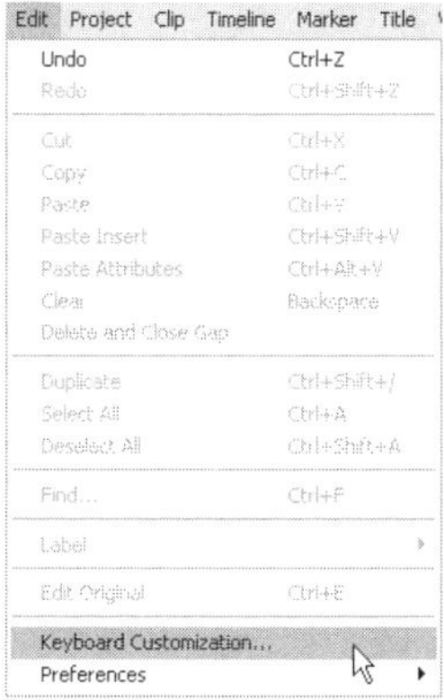

Figure 1.37 Choose Edit > Keyboard Customization.

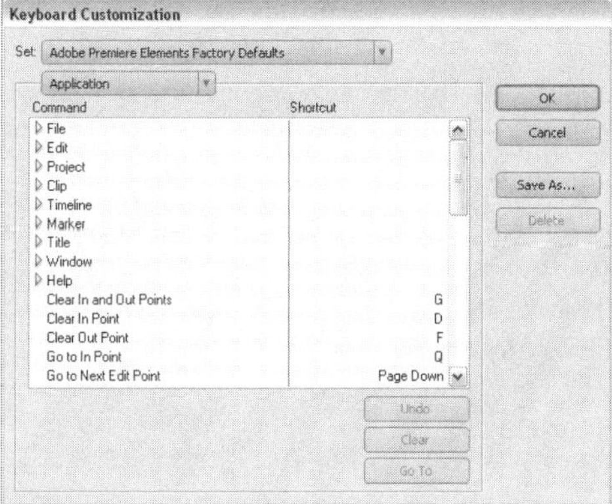

Figure 1.38 Create custom shortcuts using the Keyboard Customization dialog box.

Customizing Keyboard Shortcuts

In addition to offering a standard set of shortcuts, Premiere Elements lets you create your own shortcut for practically every button, tool, and command. Moreover, you can save sets of shortcuts and easily switch between the sets. Sets are great when more than one editor uses the same Premiere Elements system. (Of course, adjusting the chair height is still up to you.)

To assign custom keyboard shortcuts:

1. Choose Edit > Keyboard Customization (**Figure 1.37**).

   The Keyboard Customization dialog box appears (**Figure 1.38**).

2. In the drop-down menu under the set name, choose the category of shortcut you want to view and edit:

   Application—Displays menu commands and other general shortcuts

   Windows—Displays shortcuts related to specific panels and their drop-down menus

   Tools—Displays shortcuts assigned to tools

3. In the Command list area of the Keyboard Customization dialog box, select the command or tool to which you want to assign a shortcut. If necessary, first click the triangle next to a subcategory to expand it and reveal the commands it contains.

4. *Do one of the following:*
   - ▲ To assign a new shortcut to the selected item, type the shortcut.
   - ▲ To remove the current shortcut from the selected item, click Clear.

continues on next page

5. If you want, *do one of the following when prompted:*
   - ▲ To revert back to the previous shortcut assignment, click Undo.
   - ▲ To restore an undone shortcut, click Redo.
   - ▲ To find the command that already uses the shortcut you assigned to the selected item (if any), click Go To.
6. Repeat steps 2–5 as needed.

To save a custom set of keyboard shortcuts:

1. In the Keyboard Customization dialog box, click Save As (**Figure 1.39**).

   The Name Key Set dialog box appears.
2. In the Name Key Set dialog box, type the name for the key set, and click Save (**Figure 1.40**).

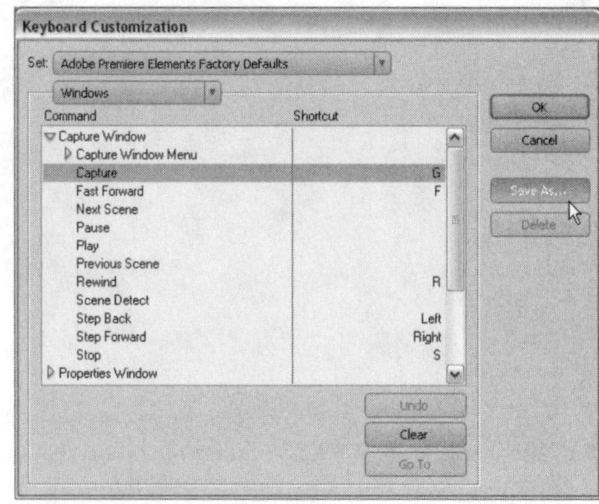

Figure 1.39 Click Save As to open the Name Key Set dialog box and save your custom set.

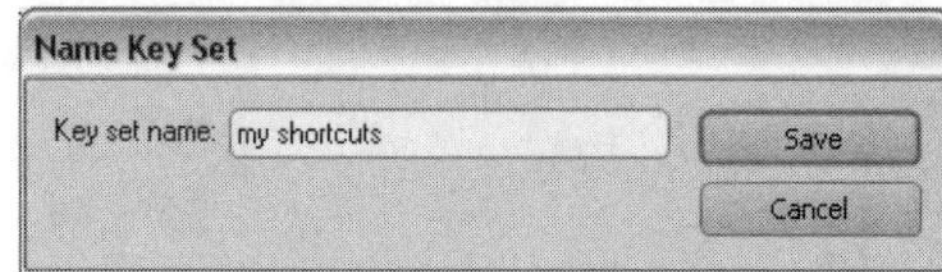

Figure 1.40 Specify the name for your set of shortcuts, and click Save.

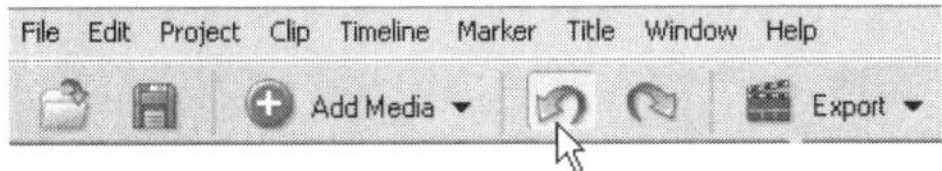

Figure 1.41 To negate the last action, click the taskbar's Undo button.

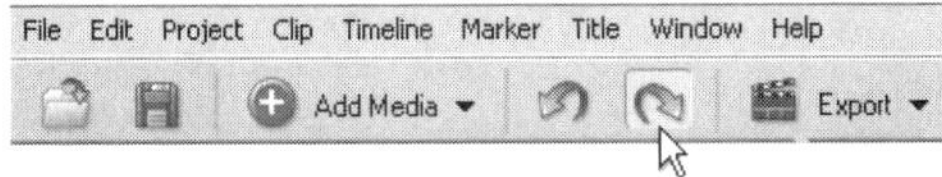

Figure 1.42 To reinstate an undone action, click the taskbar's Redo button.

Correcting Mistakes

Many people judge a program not only by how much it can do, but also by how much it can undo. The number of recent actions you can negate in Premiere Elements is limited only by the amount of available memory. If you change your mind again, you can redo the last undone action.

Premiere Elements also includes a History palette, another Adobe standard. The History palette lists your recent actions so it's easier to choose exactly how many steps back you'd like to take. This feature is covered in the following section.

When undoing can't solve the problem, you may want to revert to the last saved version of the project or open an archived version.

To undo an action:

- In the taskbar, click the Undo button (**Figure 1.41**).

  If the last action can't be undone, the button is dimmed.

To redo an action:

- In the taskbar, click the Redo button (**Figure 1.42**).

  If the last action can't be redone, the button is dimmed.

✔ Tip

- To cancel an action that Premiere Elements is processing (evidenced by a progress bar), press Esc.

Using the History Palette

If you're familiar with Adobe's other programs, you know that the History palette is like a super-undo or a time machine. The History palette lists your recent actions, and each new action is added to the bottom of the list. By looking at the list, you can see exactly what you did—and exactly where you went wrong. Clicking an action negates all the subsequent actions listed below it. When you resume editing, the undone actions are removed from the list, and history is rewritten.

To use the History palette:

1. If necessary, choose Window > History to make the History palette visible.

   The palette lists the most recent actions, with the latest action at the bottom of the list (**Figure 1.43**).

2. Click the last action you want to retain (**Figure 1.44**).

   Actions below the selected action become dimmed in the list. The project reverts to the state it was in at the time the selected action was taken. You can reselect different items.

3. If you're satisfied with your choice, resume other editing tasks.

   The dimmed actions disappear (**Figure 1.45**), and subsequent actions are added to the list.

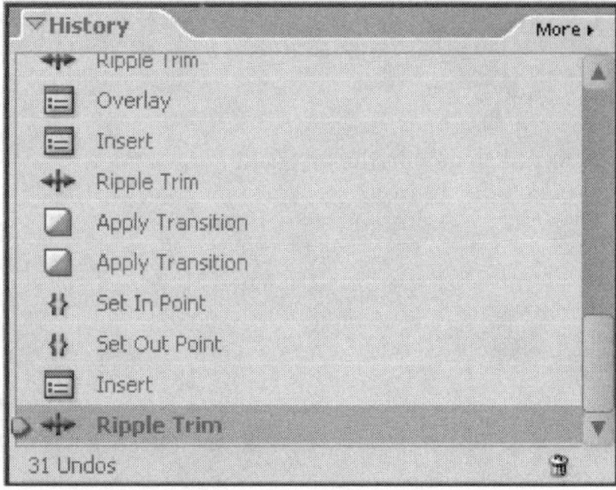

Figure 1.43 The History palette lists actions; the most recent appears at the bottom.

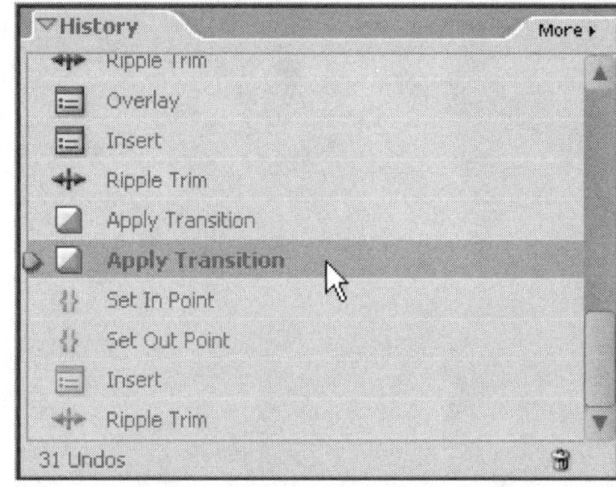

Figure 1.44 Click an action in the list to return the project to the state it was in when that action was performed.

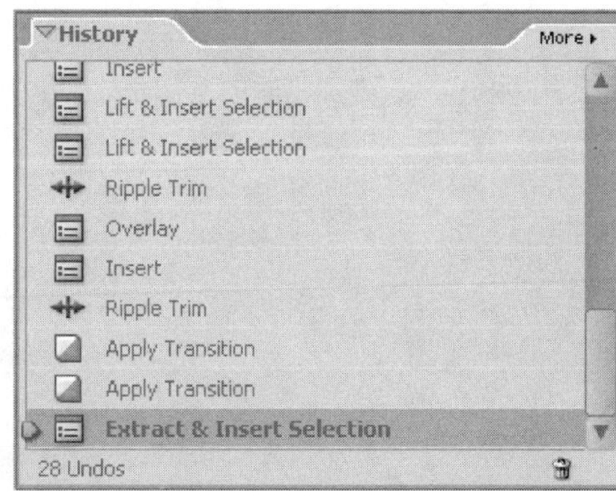

Figure 1.45 When you resume editing, the dimmed actions disappear, and your latest actions are added to the list.

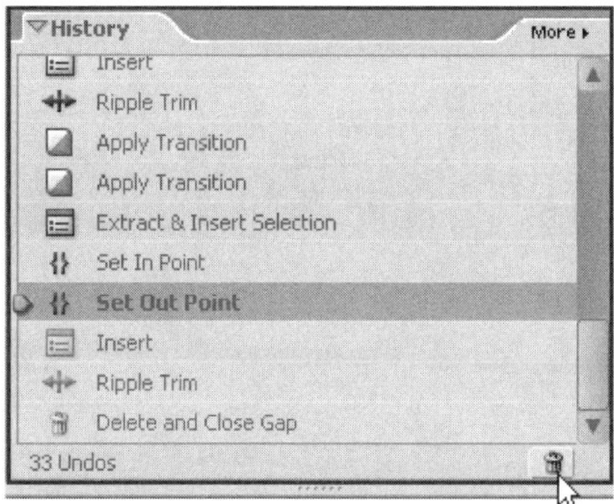

Figure 1.46 Select an action, and click the Delete Redoable Actions button.

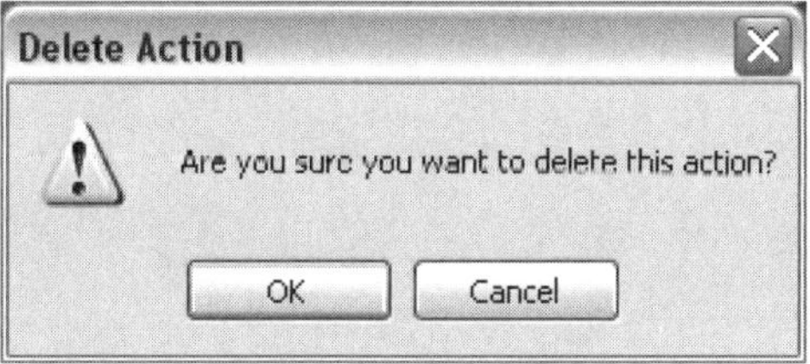

Figure 1.47 When you confirm your choice...

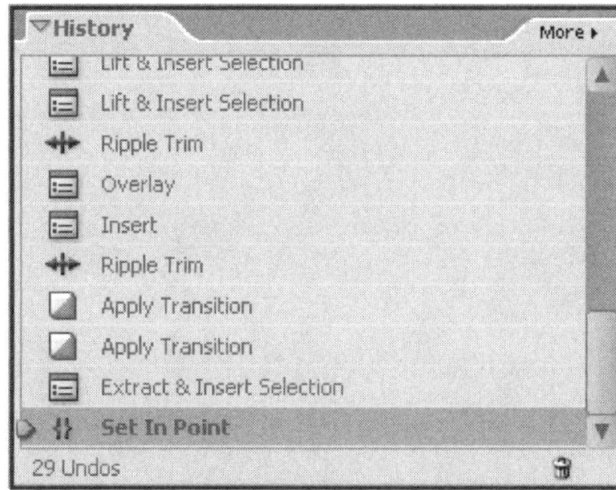

Figure 1.48 ...the action and subsequent actions are removed from the list, and the project returns to the state it was in prior to the deleted actions.

To undo and remove actions from the list:

1. In the History palette, select an action in the list.

   The project reverts to the state it was in at the time the selected action was performed.

2. *Do one of the following:*
   - ▲ Click the Delete Redoable Actions button (the Trash icon) (**Figure 1.46**).
   - ▲ From the History palette menu, choose Delete.

3. When prompted, click Yes (**Figure 1.47**).

   The action and subsequent actions are removed from the list, and the project returns to the state it was in prior to the deleted actions (**Figure 1.48**).

To clear the list without undoing actions:

- In the History palette menu, choose Clear History (**Figure 1.49**).

  All items are removed from the list, but the project remains unchanged.

✔ Tips

- The History palette doesn't list every move you make, but just actions that affect the project.
- Choosing File > Revert eliminates all the states listed in the History palette since the project was last saved.

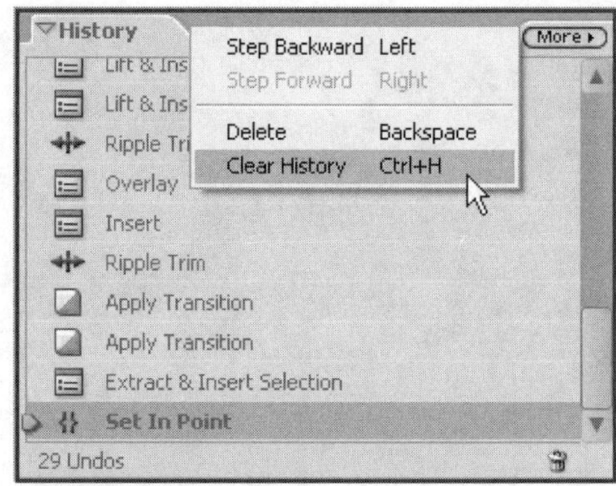

Figure 1.49 In the History palette menu, choose Clear History to clear the list without affecting the project.

2

Starting a Project

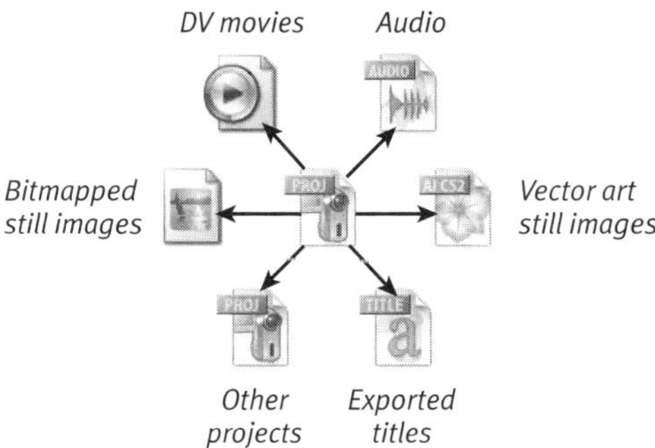

Figure 2.1 A project file is a detailed set of instructions that refers to—but doesn't contain—source files. Your hard drive must contain both the project (a small file) and the source files to which it refers (larger files).

When you're editing with Premiere Elements, you're creating a detailed set of instructions called a *project* (**Figure 2.1**). Each project can contain a single edited sequence, and you can have only one project open at a time. A project contains all your editing decisions: the arrangement of the video and audio, transitions, audio levels, titles, and effects. But although your project *lists* all the video and audio *clips* in your edited program, it doesn't actually *contain* them.

Just as sheet music refers to instruments and indicates when they should play, the project refers to media files and when they should play. You never alter the source files directly. Hence, editing in Premiere Elements is sometimes referred to as *nondestructive editing*. Because it's simply a detailed set of instructions, a project is a small file, usually only a few megabytes. The source files tend to take up a lot more hard drive space. For example, five minutes of DV footage with audio consumes more than 1 gigabyte of storage. In terms of the musical metaphor, you can slip sheet music into your pocket, but the actual orchestra is considerably more bulky. In this chapter, you'll focus on starting and saving a project (the sheet music); the next chapter deals with adding the source files (the orchestra).

Using the Welcome Screen

When you launch Premiere Elements, you're first greeted by—what else?—a welcome screen (**Figure 2.2**). Designed to get you started quickly and easily, the welcome screen is a panel of buttons. Whenever you close the project you're working on, Premiere Elements returns to this screen. Although the welcome screen is fairly straightforward, it's still worthwhile to take a closer look:

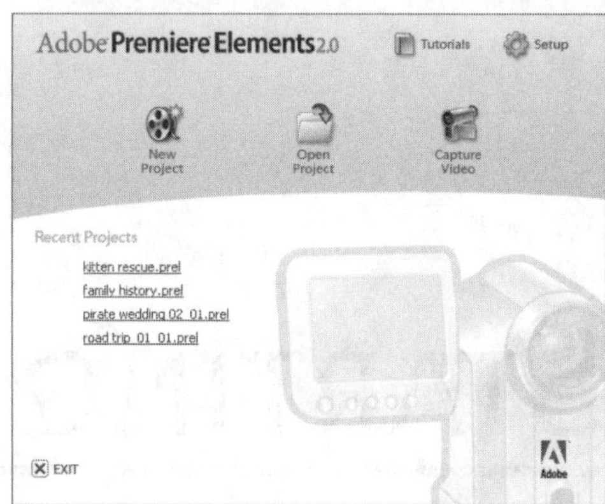

Figure 2.2 Premiere Elements first greets you with a welcome screen designed to get you started on a project quickly and easily.

Tutorials—Click this button to open the sample project that's installed with Premiere Elements. It also opens Premiere Elements' Help system to the section explaining how to re-create the project. Completing the tutorial is a good way to familiarize yourself with the program, especially if you don't have any footage of your own handy.

Setup—Click this button to open a Setup dialog box in which you choose preset project settings or specify custom settings. Because the default preset works for most users, it's unlikely you'll use this button often. Nevertheless, you'll learn exactly what the settings mean later in this chapter.

New Project—Click this button to open a New Project dialog box in which you specify the name and location of a new project file. Once you do, Premiere Elements opens a new project.

Open Project—Click this button to browse your system for a Premiere Elements project file to open. If you worked on the project recently, you'll also find a quick link to it listed in the Recent Projects section of the welcome screen.

Capture Video—Clicking this button starts a new project and opens the Capture panel automatically. Initially, it opens a New Project dialog box, just like when you click the New Project button. Once you specify the project's name and location, both a project and the Capture panel open. This book provides separate coverage of starting a new project and capturing video. But once you're familiar with those procedures, you may find that the Capture Video button makes a convenient shortcut.

Recent Projects—Clicking the name of a project file you worked on recently opens that project in Premiere Elements. This option spares you from having to search for recent projects manually.

Exit—Clicking this button closes Premiere Elements.

Adobe—Click this button to open your Web browser (such as Internet Explorer) to Adobe's Web site. You didn't suspect that the Adobe logo was also a button, did you?

✔ Tip

- Adobe programs—including Premiere Elements—each have a Help system that opens in a Web browser, such as Internet Explorer. Although the Help system looks and works like a Web site, the files are located on your hard disk, not on the Web. This way, you can browse through the Help system like a Web site, but you don't have to be online.

Starting a New Project

As you learned in the previous section, you can start a new project by clicking the button in Premiere Elements' welcome screen.

When you close a project (by choosing File > Close), Premiere Elements returns to the welcome screen. Alternatively, you can switch from an open project to another project or start a new one by choosing the appropriate command in the File menu at the top of the screen. Remember: you can have only one project open at a time.

The following steps explain how to start a project using the default *project settings*. Project settings match your project to the type of audio and video you're using. For more about choosing project setting presets or specifying custom presets, continue reading through the later sections.

To start a new project:

1. Launch Premiere Elements.
   A welcome screen appears.
2. In the welcome screen, click New Project (**Figure 2.3**).
   The New Project dialog box opens (**Figure 2.4**).
3. Enter a name for the project file in the Name field.

Figure 2.3 In the welcome screen, click New Project.

Figure 2.4 In the New Project dialog box, enter a name and location for the project file. Unless you like to use another organizational system, the default location should work fine.

4. For the Save In field, specify where you want to save the project file *by doing one of the following:*
   - ▲ Leave the file path unchanged to save the project file in the default location (in the Premiere Elements folder, within the My Documents folder).
   - ▲ Enter the file path manually.
   - ▲ Click Browse to navigate to the location where you want to save the project file.
5. Click OK.

   An untitled Project panel opens, as well as several associated panels, such as the Monitor panel and the Timeline panel.

✔ Tips

- Premiere Elements automatically appends the .prel extension to the file's name.
- When you launch Premiere Elements (or just about any program) for the first time, it creates a Preferences file in the Application Data folder. It's possible for the Adobe Premiere Elements Prefs file to become corrupted, causing the program to malfunction. Deleting the Preferences file forces the program to create a new, uncorrupted file. However, doing so also causes the program to "forget" minor settings, such as the recent projects listed in the welcome screen.

Saving Projects

Because your project file embodies all your editing decisions, protecting it from possible mishaps is crucial. As with any important file, you should save your project often and keep backups. Premiere Elements can help you protect your project by saving backup copies automatically (see the section "Saving Projects Automatically," later in this chapter).

To save a project using the taskbar:

- In the taskbar, click the Save Project button (**Figure 2.5**).

  Premiere Elements saves the project in the current state.

Figure 2.5 Click the Save Project button in the taskbar.

To save a project using a different name:

1. To save a project, *do one of the following:*
   - ▲ Choose File > Save As to save the project under a new name or location and continue working on the new copy of the project (**Figure 2.6**).
   - ▲ Choose File > Save a Copy to save a copy of the current project and continue working on the current project.
2. In the Save Project dialog box, specify a name and destination for the project (**Figure 2.7**).
3. Click Save to close the dialog box and save the file.

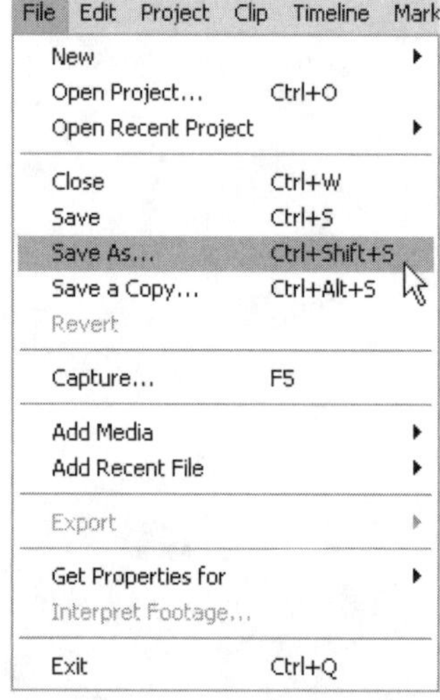

Figure 2.6 To save a project under another name, choose File > Save As.

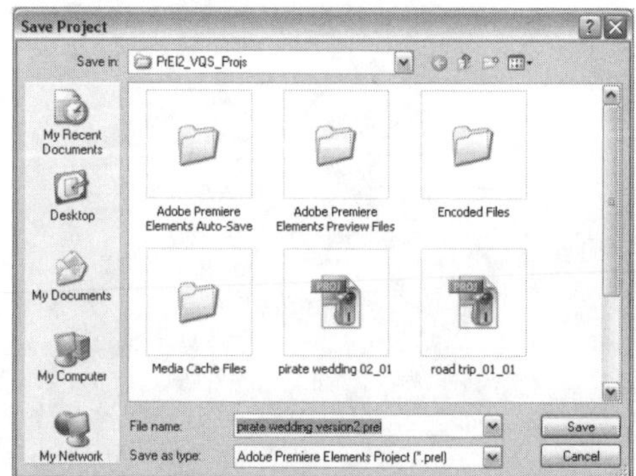

Figure 2.7 Specify a name and location in the Save Project dialog box.

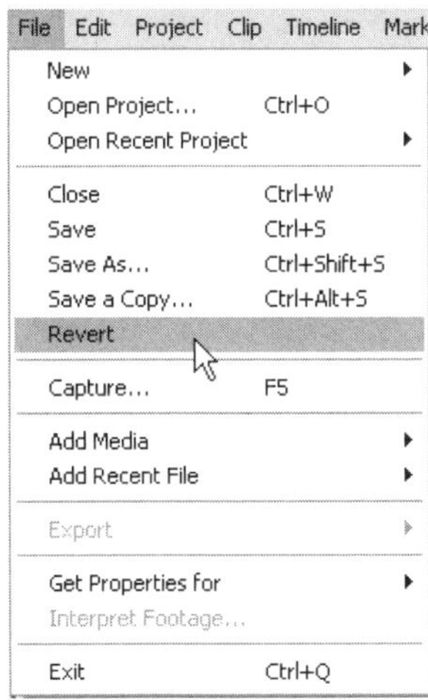

Figure 2.8 Choose File >Revert.

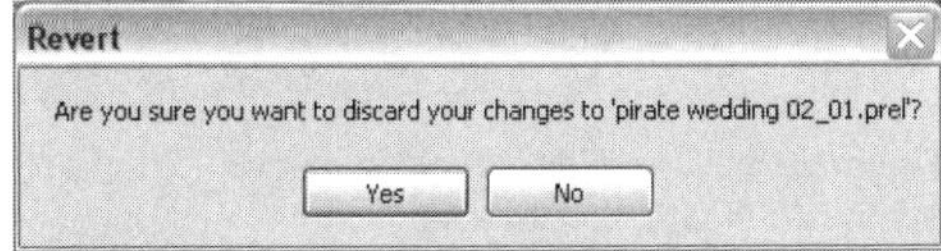

Figure 2.9 When prompted, click Yes to confirm your choice.

To revert to the last saved version of a project:

1. Choose File > Revert (**Figure 2.8**).

   Premiere Elements prompts you to confirm your choice (**Figure 2.9**).

2. Click Yes to confirm that you want to revert to the last saved version.

   The project returns to the state it was in when you last saved it.

Saving Projects Automatically

Premiere Elements can back up your project automatically as frequently as you choose. Backup files are saved in a folder called Adobe Premiere Elements Auto-Save, which is tucked inside the Premiere Elements folder. Backup files use the original project name followed by a dash and a number (filename-1.prel, filename-2.prel, and so on). In the event of a system crash or file corruption, you can retrieve one of the archived copies.

To set automatic save:

1. Choose Edit > Preferences > Auto Save (**Figure 2.10**).

   The Auto Save panel of the Preferences dialog box opens (**Figure 2.11**).

2. Select Automatically Save Projects.
3. In the Automatically Save Every field, enter the time interval at which you want Premiere Elements to save a backup of the current project, in minutes.
4. For Maximum Project Versions, enter the maximum number of versions of each project that you want Premiere Elements to automatically save.
5. Click OK to close the Preferences dialog box.

   Premiere Elements saves backups of the current projects at the interval you specified. When it has saved the maximum number of backups you specified, it replaces an older backup file with each new backup file.

Figure 2.10 Choose Edit > Preferences > Auto Save to set the automatic save option.

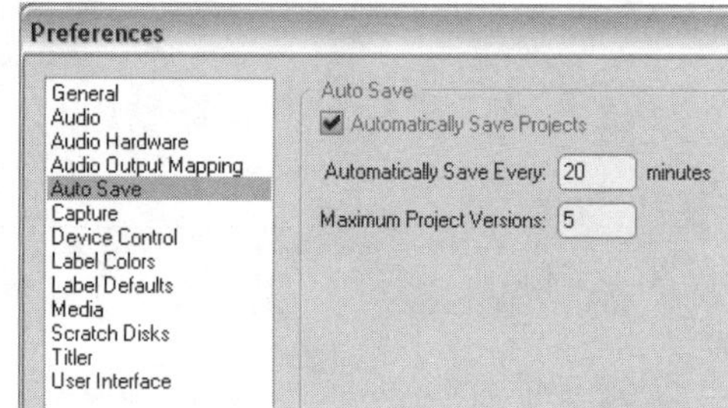

Figure 2.11 Select Automatically Save Projects and enter a time interval and the maximum number of project versions.

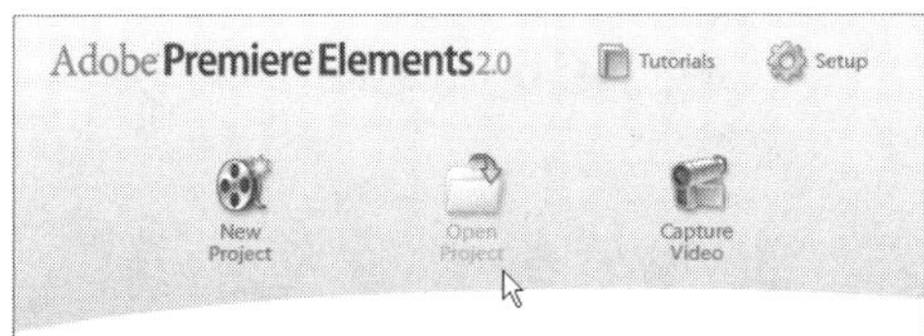

Figure 2.12 To open a project, click Open Project in the welcome screen...

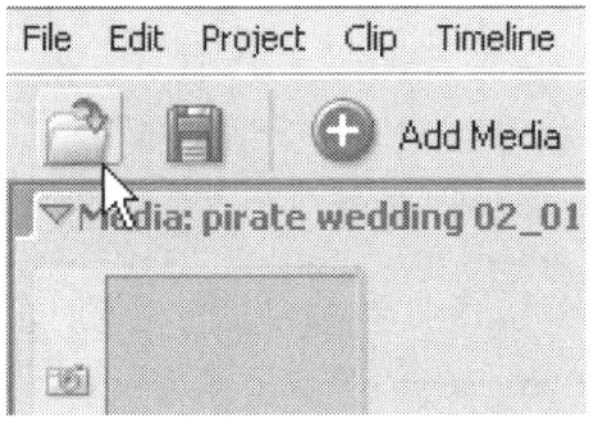

Figure 2.13 ...or, in an open project, click the taskbar's Open Project button.

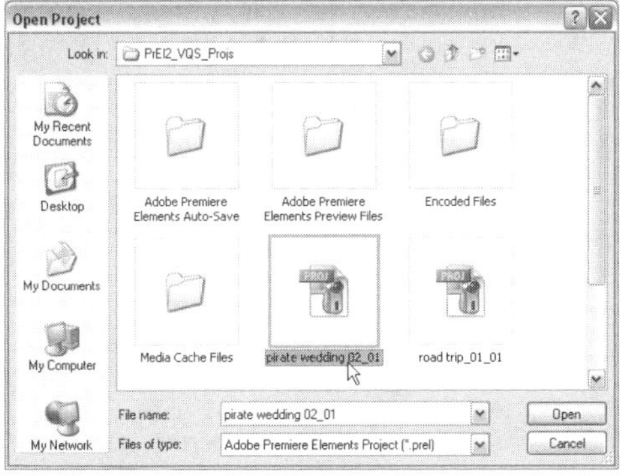

Figure 2.14 Navigate to the project you want to open, and select it.

Opening Projects

Premiere Elements' welcome screen makes it easy to open a project right after you launch the program. But, naturally, you can switch from an open project to another project at any time by using the appropriate command in the File menu.

To open a project:

1. *Do either of the following:*
   - ▲ In the welcome screen, click the Open Project icon (**Figure 2.12**).
   - ▲ With a project open, click the Open Project button in the taskbar (**Figure 2.13**).

   The Open Project dialog box appears.
2. Locate and select the project file that you want to open (**Figure 2.14**).

   Auto-saved projects are located in the Adobe Premiere Elements Auto-Save folder, which resides in the Premiere Elements folder.
3. Click Open.

To open a recent project:

- *Do either of the following:*
  - ▲ In the welcome screen, click the project's name in the Recent Projects list (**Figure 2.15**).
  - ▲ In an open project, choose File > Open Recent Project and choose the recently open project from the submenu (**Figure 2.16**).

  The project opens.

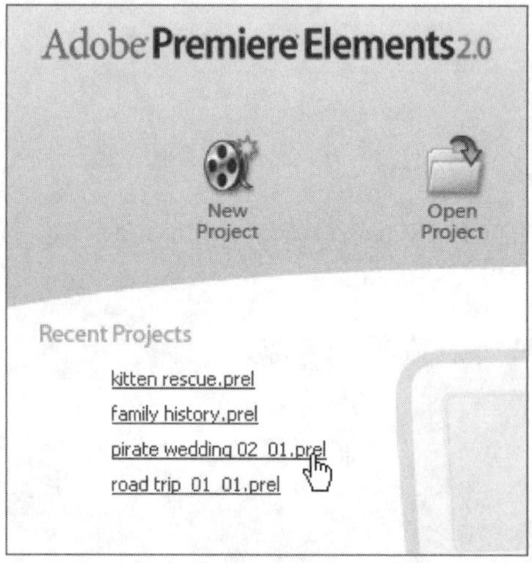

Figure 2.15 To open a recent project, click the name of the project in the welcome screen...

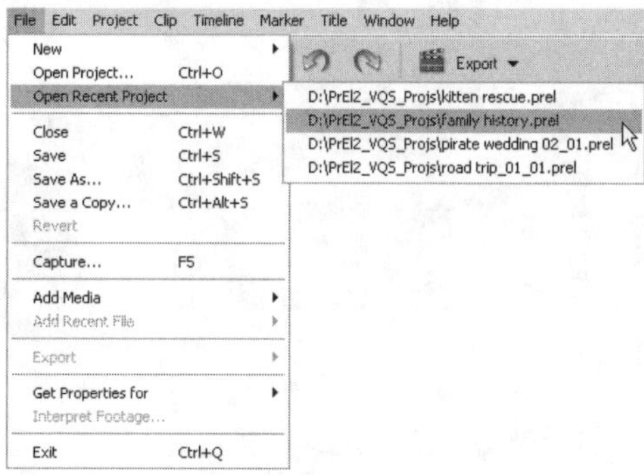

Figure 2.16 ...or, in an open project, choose File > Open Recent Project and choose the project you want.

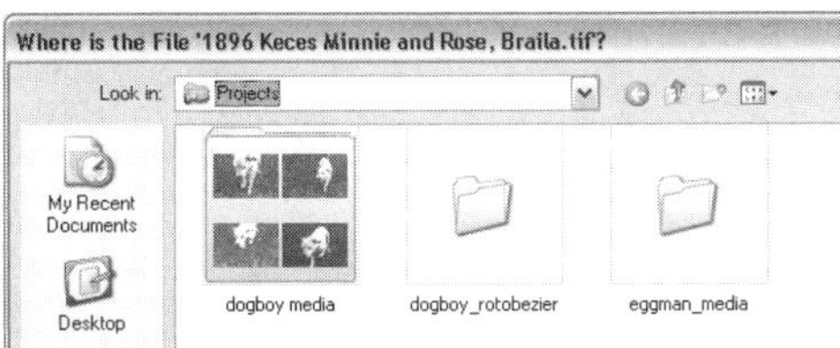

Figure 2.17 If source files have been moved or deleted since you last opened the project, you'll be prompted to account for them.

Figure 2.18 For each clip in the project whose source file is missing, Premiere Elements inserts a placeholder, or offline clip.

Locating Missing and Offline Files

As you learned at the beginning of this chapter, a project is a set of instructions that refers to files on a drive. When you open a project, Premiere Elements looks for the media files to which the project refers. Usually, they're where they were the last time you opened the project, and you can get right to work—and you can skip this section.

But if the source files have been moved, deleted, or renamed since the project was last saved, Premiere Elements will have trouble finding them and will prompt you to locate the missing media (**Figure 2.17**). When this is the case, the information in this section should come in handy.

If you moved the files, you can tell Premiere Elements their new location. Once you've accounted for the missing files, resave the project. From then on, the updated project will open without incident, because you've told Premiere Elements where to find the files.

If you open the project without locating the missing media files, Premiere Elements considers the media *offline*, or unavailable. Fortunately, Premiere Elements also inserts a blank placeholder, or *offline clip*, to stand in until you can get the media file back on your drive (or *online*) again (**Figure 2.18**). Naturally, an offline clip can't allow you to view the file it replaces, but it permits the project to remember the name of the file and recall how you used it in your project. This way, you still have a chance to restore or find the media file and use the Locate Media command to exchange the offline clip with a reference to the actual media file. (For more about locating offline media, see Chapter 4, "Managing Clips.")

continues on next page

✔ Tips

- Premiere Elements also attempts to find missing preview files, a kind of file Premiere Elements generates to create video effects; see Chapter 8, "Previewing a Sequence," for more information.
- In this context, the term *offline* means unavailable, or not on a hard disk. Professional video editors also use the term *offline editing*, which refers to the practice of creating a low-quality rough cut in preparation for *online editing*, which produces a high-quality final version.
- When the Media panel is set to list view, the Status column lists whether a clip is online or offline. The clip's icon also indicates whether it's online or offline. See Chapter 4 for more about the Media panel.

To open a project with missing files that are available:

1. Open a project using any of the methods described in the previous sections.

   If files are missing, a "Where is the File" dialog box opens. The name of the missing file appears in quotes as part of the name of the dialog box (**Figure 2.19**).
2. To find a file, *do either of the following:*
   - ▲ Locate the missing file or its replacement manually.
   - ▲ Click Find to launch the Windows search feature to help locate the file.
3. If the file you have located is the correct file, select it and click the Select button (**Figure 2.20**).

   Premiere Elements refers to the selected media file whenever it's used in the project.

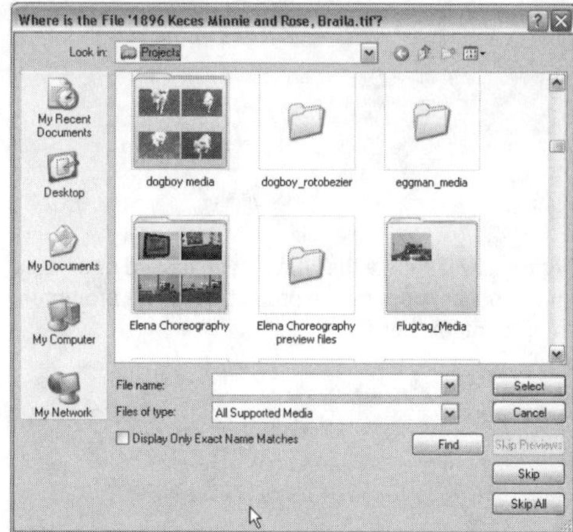

Figure 2.19 If files are missing, a "Where is the File?" dialog box appears.

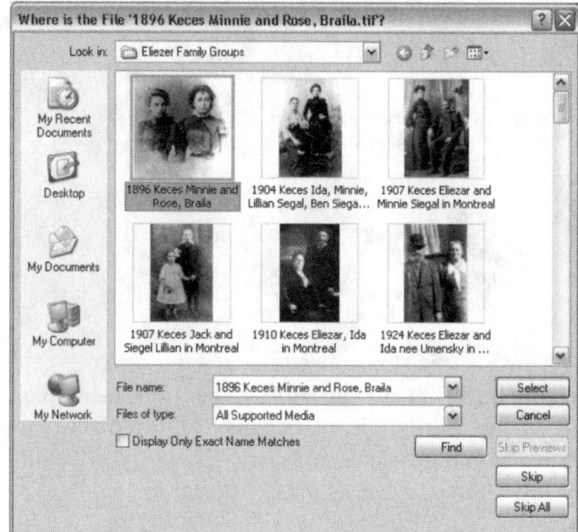

Figure 2.20 If you locate the correct file, select it and click Select.

4. If necessary, repeat steps 2 and 3 when you're prompted to locate other missing clips.

   If missing clips aren't available on your hard drive, follow the instructions in the next task, "To open a project with missing files that are unavailable." Once you specify the status of all the missing files, the project opens.

5. Save the project to update its file references.

   The project saves the current location of source media files, so that reopening the project doesn't prompt you with a "Where is the File" dialog box.

✔ Tips

- As a rule, use a consistent organizational method for your files, and avoid moving or renaming them until your project has been delivered and is ready to archive.
- Unless you're in the bad habit of moving, renaming, or deleting files, there are only a few good reasons Premiere Elements might prompt you for missing files. For example, you might have moved the project and media to another system, or restored the files from a backup. In these cases, the media probably aren't on the same drive as when you saved the project.
- If your source files are stored on a CD, copy the files to your hard disk before adding them to a project. This way, the files will be available without the CD. Also, CDs can't deliver data as quickly as the hard drive, and they're too slow to play DV video reliably.

To open a project with missing files that are unavailable:

1. Open a project using any of the methods described in the previous sections.

   If files are missing, a "Where is the File" dialog box opens. The name of the missing file appears in quotes as part of the name of the dialog box.

2. *Click one of the following buttons* (**Figure 2.21**):

   Cancel closes the dialog box without accounting for missing files. Premiere Elements will treat the files as missing the next time you open the project.

   Skip lists the missing file in the project as an offline clip.

   Skip All lists all missing files in the project as offline without prompting you for confirmation.

   Skip Previews removes all missing preview files from the project. Preview files are rendered audio and video effects, including transitions (see Chapter 8, "Previewing a Sequence").

3. If necessary, repeat step 2 each time you're prompted to locate a missing file.

   Once you account for all missing files, the project opens. In the Media panel, clips with missing media appear with an offline icon; in the Monitor panel, offline clips can't play back and instead display the message "media offline."

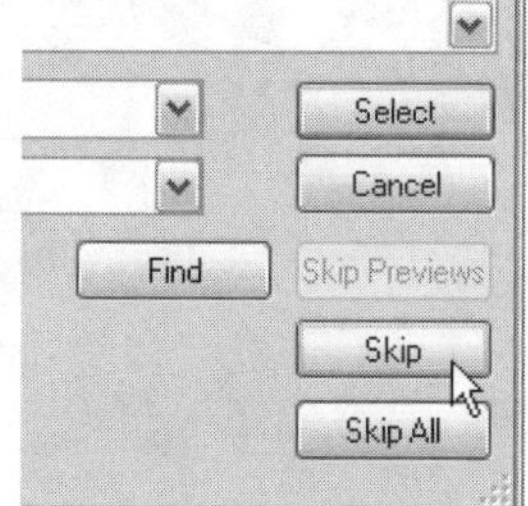

Figure 2.21 If the file is unavailable, skip the file or cancel the search.

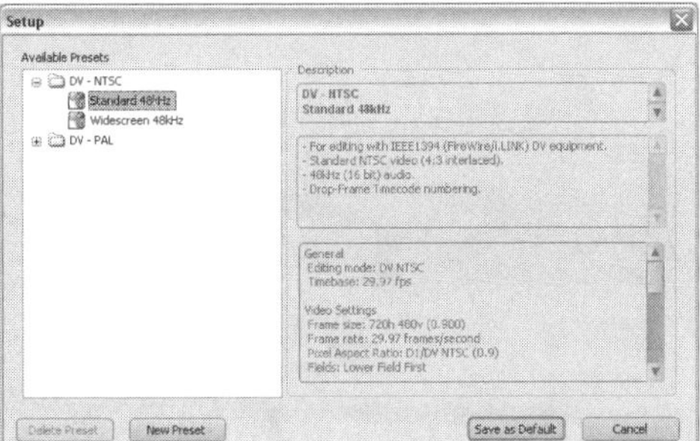

Figure 2.22 The Setup dialog box lets you view project settings but allows you to change only some of them.

Understanding Project Settings

Project settings determine how Premiere Elements processes audio and video as you edit. In other words, these settings determine the fundamental characteristics of the audio and video, such as the size of the image, the frame rate, the audio quality, and so on.

Because Premiere Elements is designed for DV, it processes video and audio in the DV format. For this reason, the project settings include few options you can customize. Except in rare cases, the default settings should already be tailored for your project; you won't need to set them, change them, or even look at them. Nevertheless, it's a good idea to have a basic understanding of the presets and how to change the default preset, if necessary.

As you learned at the beginning of the chapter, clicking the welcome screen's Setup button opens a Setup dialog box (**Figure 2.22**) in which you can view and specify project settings. The left side of the Setup dialog box lists preset project settings you can use. When you select a preset from the list, a description of the settings appears on the right side of the dialog box. The built-in presets include project settings optimized for the most common variations of DV:

DV – NTSC—DV footage shot in NTSC, the video standard used in North America, Japan, and other countries

DV – PAL—DV footage shot in PAL, the standard in most of Europe

continues on next page

These folders each contain the following two options:

Standard 48kHz—Used for DV footage shot in television's standard 4:3 aspect ratio (the ratio of the picture's width and height), using 48 kHz audio

Widescreen 48kHz—Used for DV footage shot in a 16:9 aspect ratio (the ratio of the picture's width and height), which is supported by some DV cameras and equipment, using 48 kHz audio

For some background on the NTSC and PAL video standards, see the sidebar "NTSC or PAL." To find out what 48 kHz means, see the sidebar "Audio Sample Rates."

NTSC or PAL

NTSC stands for the National Television Standards Committee. These folks develop the television standards used in North America, some parts of Central and South America, Japan, Taiwan, Korea, and other countries. But the acronym NTSC is more commonly used to describe everything that meets those standards. Generally speaking, the NTSC standard dictates that each video frame consists of 525 horizontal lines displayed at about 29.97 frames per second.

PAL stands for Phase Alternating Line, which is more descriptive of the technology than of those who developed it. PAL is the television standard used in much of the world, including most of Europe, China, India, Africa, and the Middle East. The PAL standard dictates that each video frame consists of 625 lines displayed at 25 frames per second.

As many world travelers know, differences between the two standards make NTSC and PAL equipment incompatible. If you're in an NTSC-dominant region, chances are Premiere Elements installed with the standard aspect ratio NTSC preset as the default; if you're in a PAL country, then it's set to the standard PAL preset. Globetrotters and ex-pats may have to switch to the appropriate project preset by clicking the welcome screen's Setup button.

Oh, by the way, there's one more standard out there: SECAM (Sequential Couleur Avec Memoire, which translates to Sequential Color with Memory). As the name suggests, it was developed in France. SECAM isn't as widespread as the other standards; it's used in France, Russia, Eastern Europe, and some parts of the Middle East. Like PAL, SECAM specifies a 625-line frame displayed at 25 frames per second. However, the color component of the image is implemented differently than in PAL.

Specifying Project Settings

For the vast majority of users, the default preset specifies the most appropriate settings. However, you might set a different default if you aren't using the dominant video standard for your region (see the sidebar "NTSC or PAL"). And although most folks shoot video in the standard format (4:3 aspect ratio), some cameras shoot in a widescreen format (16:9 aspect ratio). In these instances, go to the Setup dialog box to change the default preset.

You can also create your own setting presets, but because Premiere Elements is designed to work with DV projects, your choices are limited. Except for the video standard (NTSC or PAL) and the image aspect ratio (standard 4:3, or widescreen 16:9), you aren't permitted to set the fundamental characteristics of the video and audio—which could deviate from the DV standard.

Even so, you might want to create a preset that varies more superficial settings—such as the way video and audio frame rates are displayed, the title and action safe zones, or the initial number of video and audio tracks in the project's timeline. However, because you can change these options at any time, this book covers those options in the appropriate sections in later chapters.

Audio Sample Rates

Analog signals are described by a continuous fluctuation of voltage. An analog signal is converted to a digital signal by being measured periodically, or *sampled.* If you think of the original audio as a curve, the digital audio would look like a connect-the-dots version of that curve. The more dots (samples) you have, the more accurately you can reproduce the original curve. Therefore, an audio *sample rate* describes the number of times audio is sampled in a given period of time in order to re-create the original sound.

Audio sample rates are expressed in hertz (Hz), a measure of frequency equal to one cycle per second. It's often more convenient to express frequency in kilohertz (kHz), or 1,000 cycles per second.

DV cameras record audio at 32 kHz or 48 kHz or give you a choice between the two audio sample rates. Even if your footage was recorded at 32 kHz, Premiere Elements *upsamples* (converts it to a higher sample rate) and processes it at 48 kHz. You can create your own project preset, but you still aren't permitted to change a project's audio sample rate. Don't worry—your audio is compatible, and the processing shouldn't cause quality or playback problems.

To save a preset as the default:

1. In the welcome screen, click Setup (**Figure 2.23**).
   The Setup dialog box opens.
2. Select the preset you want to save as the default.
3. Click the Save as Default button (**Figure 2.24**).
   The settings specified by the selected preset are applied to all new projects.

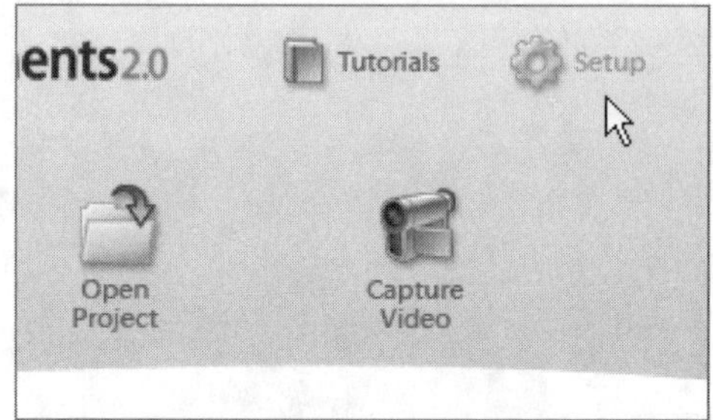

Figure 2.23 To specify the default project preset, click the Setup button in the welcome screen.

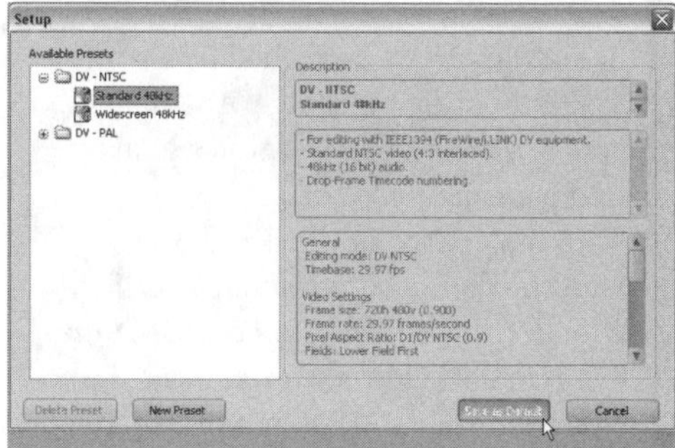

Figure 2.24 Select the preset you want, and click the Save as Default button.

✔ Tips

- You can also access an open project's settings by choosing Project > Project Settings > General. Doing so won't allow you to change the fundamental aspects of the project, such as how it processes video and audio. However, it does let you change how video and audio are displayed.
- Premiere Elements captures and processes video in the DV format in order to take advantage of the quality, efficiency, and simplified workflow DV offers. When you output your edited project, however, Premiere Elements can export to a DV tape or recompress the footage to another format—most notably, a format compatible for burning to a DVD.

Capturing and Adding Footage

Before you can begin editing, you need to get the video from a tape to your hard drive—a process known as video *capture*. In Premiere Elements, all the controls you'll need for capture are integrated into an easy-to-use Capture panel. The Capture panel lets you control a DV camera or deck, see and hear the video, and naturally, transfer the parts you want to your computer for editing in Premiere Elements.

But you don't have to shoot your own video footage to create a program in Premiere Elements. As explained in Chapter 2, "Starting a Project," you can import a wide range of digitally stored content: movie files in various formats, audio files, still images, and image sequences. Maybe you've already started using the files in Premiere Elements' tutorial. In addition, Premiere Elements generates commonly used footage items: black video, color fields, bars and tone, and even a countdown. You can even launch Photoshop Elements from within Premiere Elements. This way, you can create or retouch still images for your video project using a program dedicated to the job. You can also make titles, but this book covers that topic in Chapter 9, "Creating Titles."

Capturing DV Footage

Using the widely accepted DV format, the capture process couldn't get much easier. If your computer is equipped with the right port, you can easily transfer footage from a DV camera or deck to your hard disk in much the same way you'd copy files from one disk to another. Most cameras use a cable—known variously as FireWire, iLink, or IEEE 1394—to connect to your computer. But because an IEEE 1394 connection is often an optional addition to a computer, many cameras use a USB 2.0 (aka Fast USB) connection, which is a standard feature on most new computers. Both transfer methods can deliver DV video, audio, and timecode information to your hard disk over a single cable (**Figure 3.1** and **Figure 3.2**). Assuming your computer is fast enough to play back DV—and any relatively recent system is—you're in business. (See the sidebar "Why DV?")

The DV standard is just that: standard. It narrows what would otherwise be an intimidating selection of video and audio settings into a single set of options. This means you don't waste time choosing the video frame size, frame rate, and so on. Instead, you can choose the appropriate DV preset and get to work.

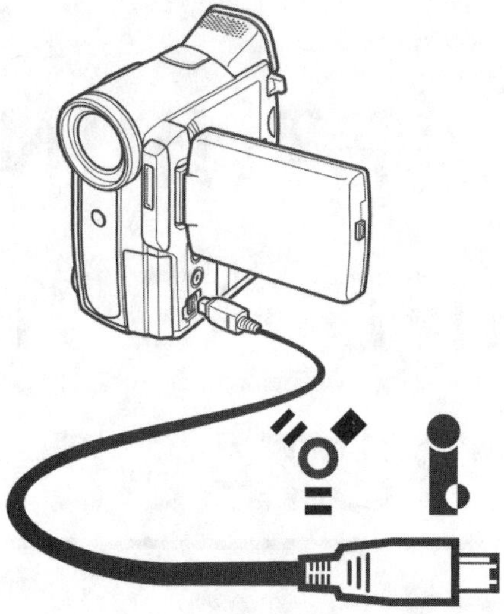

Figure 3.1 DV footage—including video, audio, and timecode—can be transferred over a single IEEE 1394 connection...

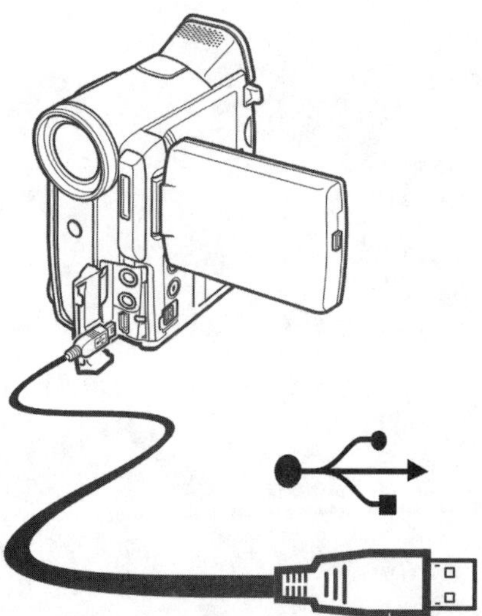

Figure 3.2 ... or USB 2.0 connection, depending on your camera and computer.

USB 2.0, Fast USB

For many, DV and IEEE 1394 are synonymous. The DV video standard emerged around the same time as the IEEE 1394 transfer protocol, and worked in tandem to make video acquisition and editing easier than ever before.

However, IEEE 1394 isn't the only way to move data—including video data—around quickly and easily. USB 2.0 (the second iteration of the Universal Serial Bus standard, aka Fast USB) is also up to the task. And in contrast to IEEE 1394, USB 2.0 connections are more often a standard feature of new computers. For this reason, manufacturers increasingly include a USB 2.0 port on DV camcorders.

IEEE 1394

IEEE 1394 provides simple, inexpensive, fast data exchange between electronic devices—most famously, between a video camera and computer. If your computer doesn't already have an IEEE 1394 controller card, you can install one yourself as long as your computer has an available expansion slot.

IEEE (pronounced "eye-triple-E") stands for the Institute of Electrical and Electronics Engineers, Inc., a nonprofit association of professionals who develop standards to foster compatibility between devices. They dubbed their 1,394th effort (what else?) IEEE 1394. However, the folks at Apple called it FireWire—a much snappier and more descriptive name. Sony uses name iLink for its IEEE 1394–capable devices. In the spirit of fairness, this book opts for the more generic (albeit more awkward) moniker, IEEE 1394.

✔ Tips

- If your camera uses IEEE 1394 (aka FireWire or iLink) but your computer doesn't, you can add an IEEE 1394 controller card to an empty expansion slot. Don't worry; controller cards are inexpensive and easy to install.
- When you're shopping for a computer to do DV editing, make sure you get enough drive space for your needs. In addition to the drive space for applications and other files, allocate 1 GB for every five minutes of DV footage you want to capture at a time.
- The maximum size for a single file isn't determined by Premiere Elements but by your operating system, capture device, and the file system used by your hard disk. Hard disks formatted using FAT32 limit files to 4 GB each. Disks formatted using NTFS don't limit file sizes. But you probably want to limit the length of a single clip for organizational purposes (after all, a 4 GB DV file would be 20 minutes long).

Digitizing Analog Footage

Despite the pervasiveness of DV, video and audio are still recorded, stored, and delivered using *analog* formats. Common consumer analog formats include VHS and Hi8 videotape and audiocassette tapes.

To use analog media, most computers require a video capture card—add-on hardware that you install in one of your computer's expansion slots. (Sometimes the capture card also includes a *break-out box*, an external component to which you connect audio and video cables.) The capture card *digitizes* analog video and audio, converting it to a digital form that can be stored on your computer (**Figure 3.3**). Digitizing analog video can be compared to using a scanner to convert a photograph into a format your computer can understand. In contrast to using DV, which uses a single IEEE 1394 (aka FireWire and iLink) or USB 2.0 (aka Fast USB) cable, analog capture cards typically use separate cables to deliver the video, audio, and timecode (data that identifies each video frame with a number, expressed in hours, minutes, seconds, and frames; see the sidebar "Timecode").

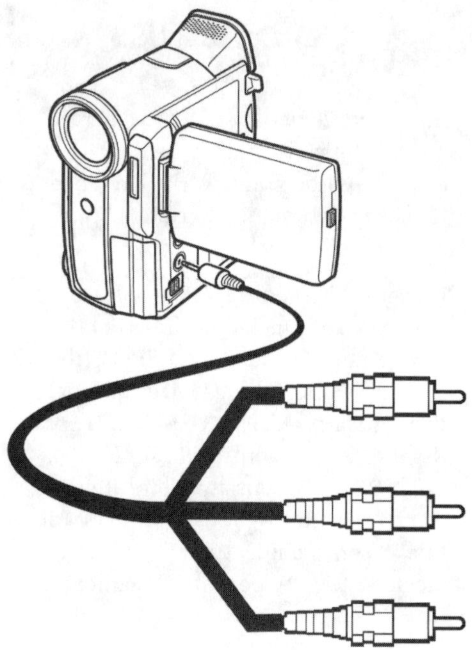

Figure 3.3 Analog footage is digitized with a capture card. Separate cables deliver the video and audio. A professional deck and a separate device-control cable are often required to deliver timecode.

Many capture devices convert analog sources into the DV format. This way, you can enjoy some of DV's editing advantages even if you didn't shoot or store the video in DV. One of those advantages is the ability to edit the footage using Premiere Elements. However, analog-to-DV converters can't be accessed directly within Premiere Elements. In other words, you won't be able to use Premiere Elements' Capture panel (explained shortly) to capture the footage. Instead, you'll have to use the software that comes with the capture card to digitize your footage, and then import the files—now in the DV format—into Premiere Elements.

Other (usually older) capture cards digitize video into other formats. For example, some digitize video using a format known as Motion-JPEG (MJPEG). Because these cards don't convert the analog footage into the DV format, you can't edit the captured footage using Premiere Elements.

Why DV?

It's not enough to have your video in a digital form; it must also be in a format that's practical to use for editing. As a digital file, every frame of standard (as opposed to high-definition) video consumes nearly 1 MB—that means every minute of footage consumes nearly 2 GB of storage space! Capturing and playing back approximately 30 frames per second (the standard video frame rate) is impossible for most processors and drives; the *data rate*, or flow of information, is simply too high (not to mention the storage capacity you'd need to hold such enormous files).

Some professionals use equipment that can process digital video in this relatively pristine, or *uncompressed*, form. However, most users either don't require or can't afford this level of quality; they use equipment that *compresses* the video for use on the computer. Compression is one way to reduce the file size (and thereby the data rate) of the video, making it easier to store, process, and play back. Other audio and video settings, such as frame size and frame rate, also affect the data rate.

A DV camera compresses the video as you record it—*in the camera*, if you will. Compared to raw, uncompressed video, DV's data rate is quite low: 3.6 MBps. Any moderately powerful computer manufactured in the last several years is more than capable of playing back DV footage (see "Minimum System Requirements" in the book's introduction). In terms of hard drive space, you can store about 5 minutes of DV footage using only 1 GB of storage. And one of the nicest things about DV is that although the video is compressed, it still looks really good. That's why DV is so common these days, and why Premiere Elements is designed for DV footage.

Digitizing Three Ways

If you want to use footage from analog sources, you have three options, explained in this section.

Dubbing to DV

In addition to an IEEE 1394 (aka FireWire or iLink) connector, most DV camcorders also have analog connections. Often, this connection is in the form of an adaptor cable. One end plugs into the camcorder (generally using a proprietary connector that works only with your brand of camcorder). The other end of the cable has analog connectors for video and audio (usually RCA connectors like the ones you use to hook up most consumer VCRs and audio equipment).

To view a DV tape on a TV or copy it to a VHS tape, you use the cable as an audio/video *output*. However, you can use the same cable as an *input* to record the audio/video signal coming from your television tuner or VCR. This way, you can copy, or *dub*, an analog source (such as a VHS tape) to a DV tape. Once your footage is on DV, you can use Premiere Elements to capture your footage in the manner described in the section "Capturing DV." As a plus, you'll have a copy of your (possibly precious) tape in a newer, more versatile, and more resilient format.

Converting to DV using a camcorder

Some DV camcorders can act as analog-to-DV converters. They accept video and audio from an analog source, convert the signals into the DV format, and output the DV signal directly to another device (such as your computer). This way, you can capture analog footage as DV in a single step, and (depending on your camera) without even using a DV tape. Not all DV camcorders have this feature, though. Check your camera's documentation for a *pass-through* feature or an *E-to-E* (electronic-to-electronic) mode. Pass-through lets you record and output DV simultaneously, whereas E-to-E converts and outputs the video and audio without recording to a tape.

Note that you'll have to use another program (such as Windows Movie Maker) to capture footage using this method. Once the footage is in DV form, however, you can import it into Premiere Elements (as explained later in this chapter).

Using an analog-to-DV converter

You can also convert analog video and audio to DV using—what else?—an analog-to-digital converter (sometimes called an *A-to-D* converter). Depending on the device, an A-to-D converter can also be a *D-to-A* (digital-to-analog) converter. These devices are small boxes with video and audio inputs and outputs appropriate to the formats being converted. In this case, one output is an IEEE 1394 (FireWire, iLink) connector.

A converter is an attractive option for those without a DV camcorder or with an overabundance of analog source tapes. Again, Premiere Elements isn't designed to work with converters directly, but you can use the DV files they create.

✔ Tip

- There's an old saying in video production: "Tape is cheap." In other words, the cost of videotape is typically the smallest expense in a video production. This adage holds true even for home productions. Although there's no need to waste tape, it's usually well worth using enough tape for your needs. Dubbing an old analog tape to DV also is often worth the expense—not only for the editing advantages you gain, but also to archive what is likely a rapidly deteriorating keepsake.

Capture and the Capture Panel

As you'll discover, capturing DV is almost as easy as watching it. Even so, several options deserve explanation, and this chapter breaks them into the following sections:

Watching Video During Capture explains how to specify whether you want to watch the video in the Capture panel or on a television, as well.

Controlling a Camera with the Capture Panel explains how to ensure that Premiere Elements' Capture panel controls your DV camera or deck.

Storing Captured Footage explains how to select where the files you capture are stored on your computer.

Using Playback Controls in the Capture Panel explains how to use the playback and capture controls in the Capture panel.

Capturing DV explains how to capture video and audio from a DV source—including how to capture shots automatically, and how to add captured clips into a sequence automatically.

Once you've read the first two sections, you'll rarely perform the tasks they contain. The next two sections are a more integral part of the capture process. But if you're eager to get started, it's OK to skip right to the final section, "Capturing DV," and refer back to the earlier sections as needed.

As long as you're getting an overview, take a moment to open and look at the Capture panel itself.

To open the Capture panel:

- In the Premiere Elements taskbar, click the Capture button (**Figure 3.4**).
  The Capture panel appears (**Figure 3.5**).

Capture
Edit
More ▸
▽History
New/Open

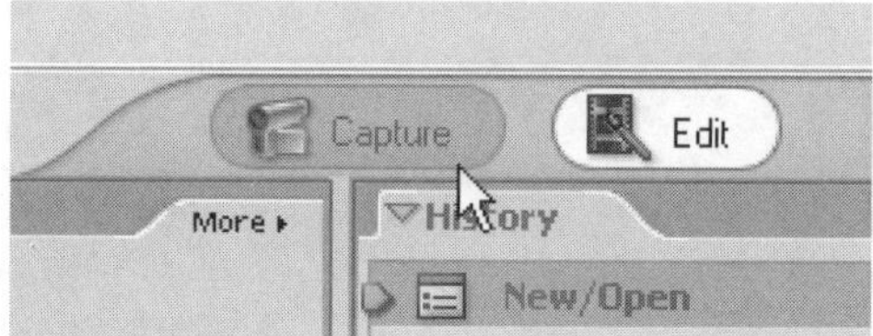

Figure 3.4 Clicking the Capture button in the taskbar...

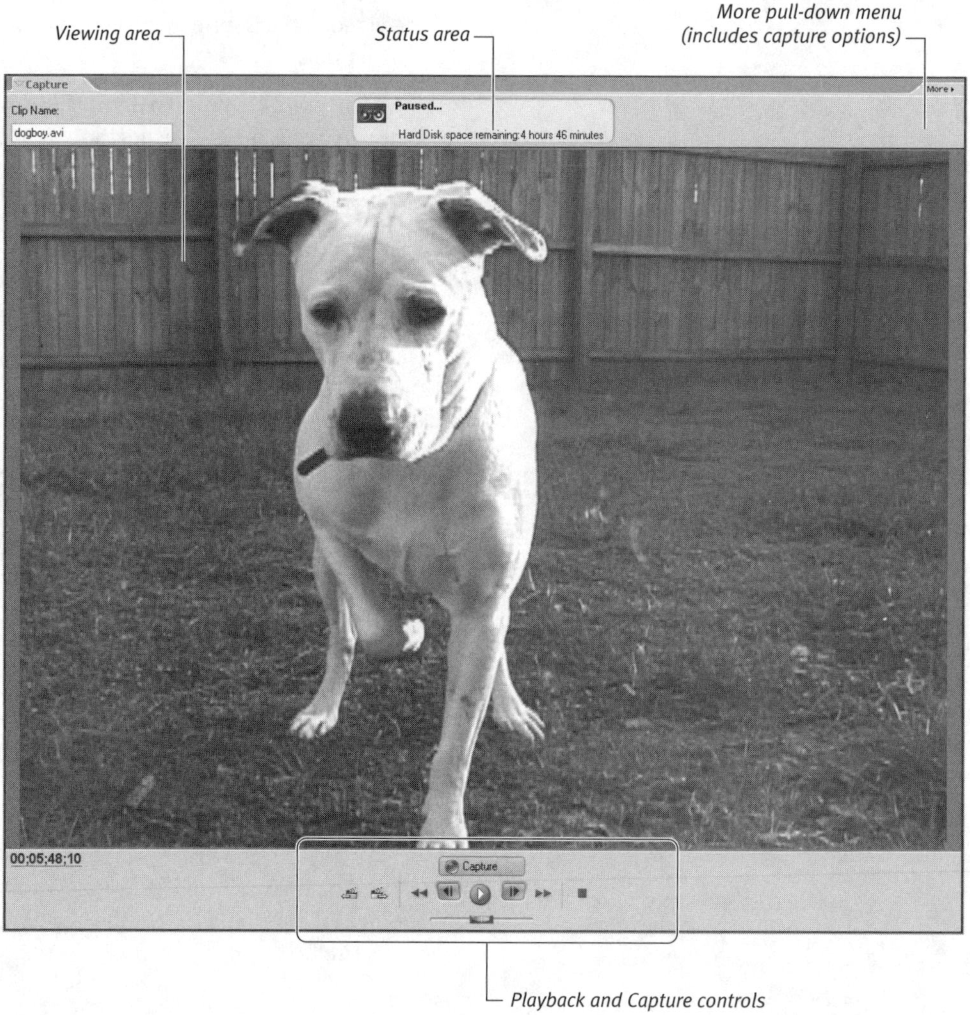
Viewing area
Status area
More pull-down menu
(includes capture options)
Capture
Clip Name:
dogboy.avi
Paused...
Hard Disk space remaining: 4 hours 46 minutes
More ▸
00;05;48;10
Capture
Playback and Capture controls

Figure 3.5 ...opens the Capture panel.

Watching Video During Capture

As you capture, you can play video and audio in the Capture panel only or through your camera to a television and external speakers as well. You can set your preference in the Project Settings dialog box, which you can access from the Capture panel.

To specify capture preview settings:

1. In the Capture panel's More pull-down menu, choose Capture Settings (**Figure 3.6**).

   The Capture panel of the Project Settings dialog box appears.

2. Click the DV Settings button (**Figure 3.7**).

   The DV Capture Options dialog box appears.

3. In the During Capture area of the DV Capture Options dialog box, select the options you want (**Figure 3.8**):

   ▲ Preview Video on Desktop

   ▲ Preview Audio on Desktop

   Selecting an item plays the video or audio in the Capture panel; leaving it unselected plays the video or audio on an external video monitor and speakers via the capture device only.

4. Click OK to close the DV Capture Options dialog box, and click OK again to close the Project Settings dialog box.

✔ Tips

- A television can represent video more accurately than a computer screen, and the display looks better, too. However, slower system performance (and dropped frames during capture) is a possible trade-off. If you experience problems, preview capture in the Capture panel only. Chances are, you can watch the captured video on a television during editing.

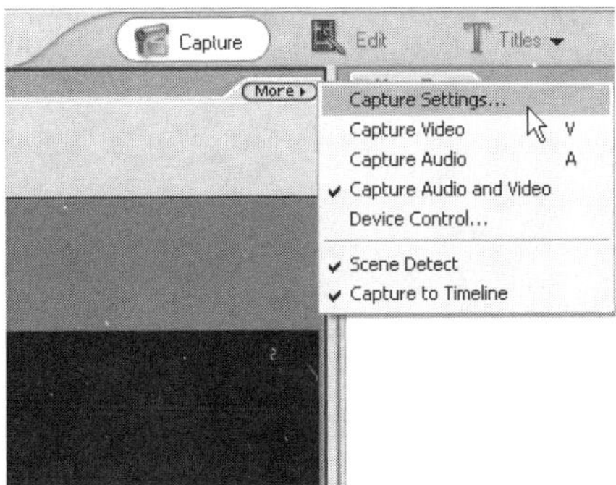

Figure 3.6 In the Capture panel's More pull-down menu, choose Capture Settings.

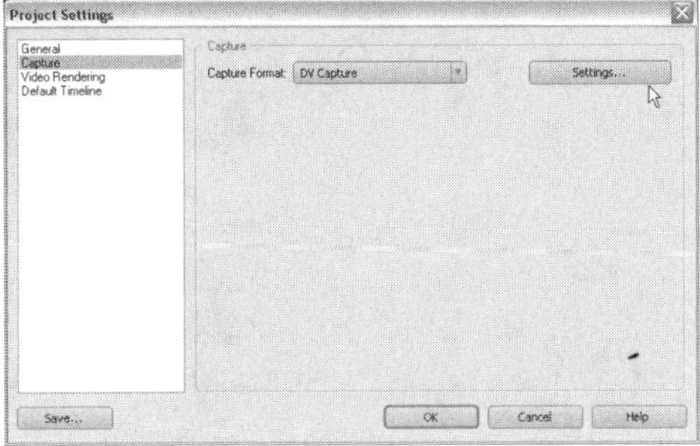

Figure 3.7 In the Project Settings dialog box, click the DV Settings button.

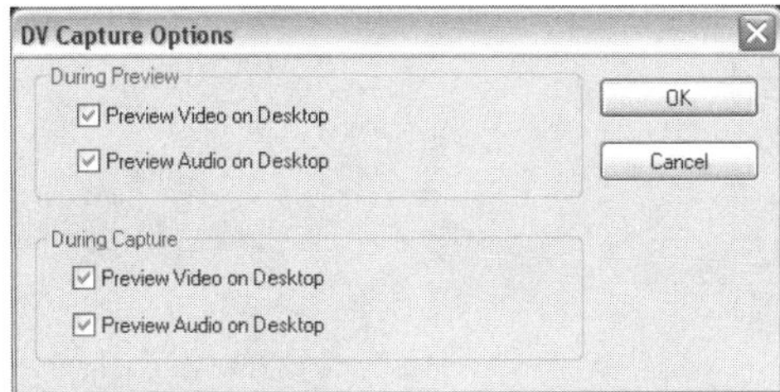

Figure 3.8 In the During Capture area of the DV Capture Options dialog box, check the options you want.

- Although the Capture area of the Project Settings dialog box includes a pull-down menu for Capture Format, Premiere Elements supports only DV–based capture devices. So, DV Capture is the only item in the pull-down menu.

Controlling a Camera with the Capture Panel

As the name indicates, *device control* gives a program a means of controlling an external device—in the case of Premiere Elements, it lets you control a DV deck or camera from within Premiere Elements' Capture panel. Device control can also activate a camera or deck to record your finished program (see Chapter 11, "Export").

DV devices can be controlled over the same IEEE 1394 or USB 2.0 cable that delivers the video and audio, and the plug-ins to control most DV cameras and decks come built into Premiere Elements. In most cases, the generic DV device-control settings work without tweaking. But you can specify your particular camera to ensure full functionality.

To set up device control:

1. In the Capture panel's More pull-down menu, choose Device Control (**Figure 3.9**).

   The Device Control pane of the Preferences dialog box appears (**Figure 3.10**).

2. In the Devices pull-down menu, *choose an option:*

   None—To capture without controlling a camera or deck

   DV/HDV Device Control—To control a DV or HDV camera or deck via IEEE 1394 / FireWire / iLink

   USB Video Class 1.0 – Device Control—To control a camera or deck via USB 2.0/Fast USB

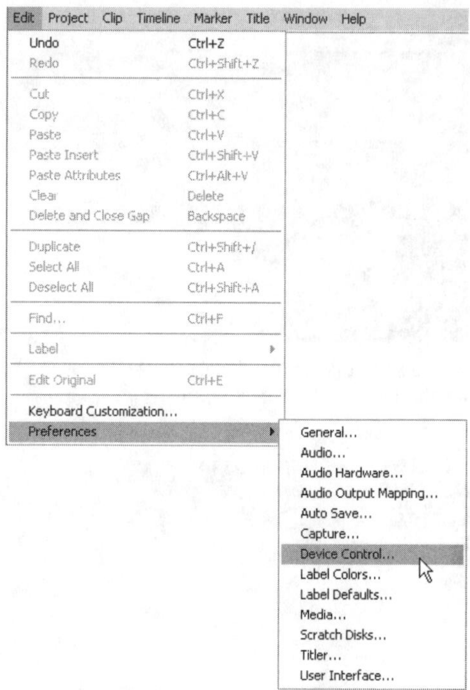

Figure 3.9 Choose Edit > Preferences > Device Control.

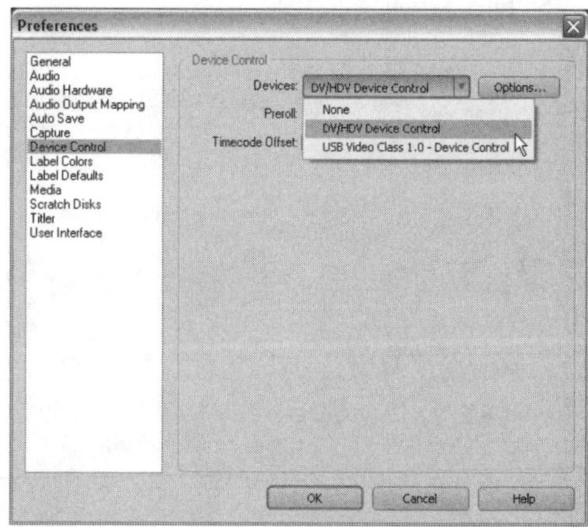

Figure 3.10 In the Device Control pane of the Preferences dialog box, specify whether you're using an IEEE 1394 or USB 2.0 connection.

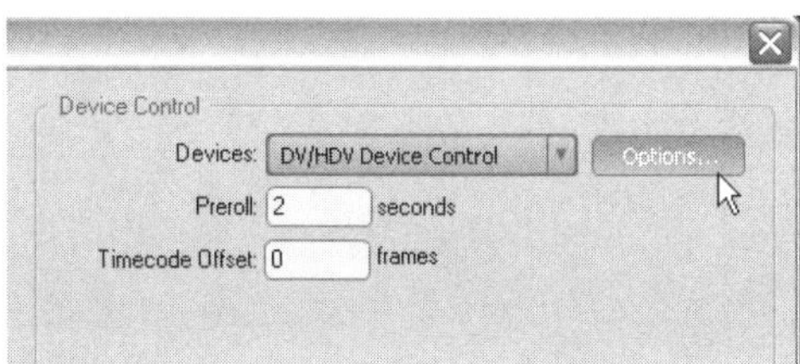

Figure 3.11 To specify a particular camera or deck, click the Options button.

Figure 3.12 The DV Device Control Options dialog box appears.

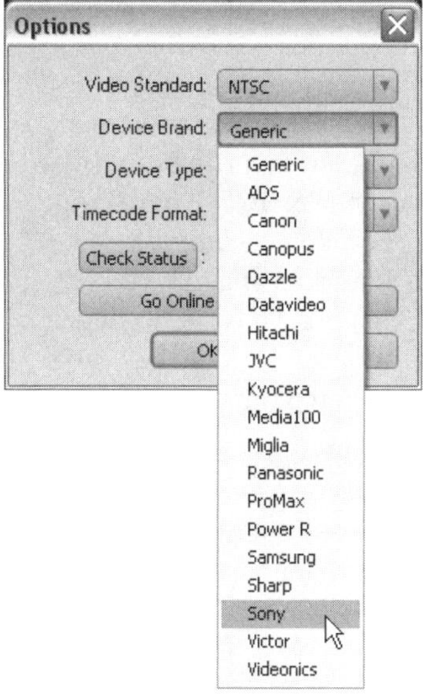

Figure 3.13 Choose the appropriate options from the drop-down menus, such as the brand of the device you're using.

3. To specify a particular camera or deck, click the Options button (**Figure 3.11**).

   The DV Device Control Options dialog box appears (**Figure 3.12**).

4. Select the options appropriate to your system from the drop-down menus:

   Video Standard—The video standard used by your equipment. NTSC is the standard used in North America and Japan. PAL is the standard used in most of Europe (see the sidebar "NTSC or PAL," in Chapter 2).

   Device Brand—The brand of the camera or deck you're using. If your brand doesn't appear on the menu, choose Generic (**Figure 3.13**).

   Device Type—The model of the camera or deck you're using. If your particular model doesn't appear in the menu, choose a closely related model, or choose Standard.

   Timecode Format—The counting method used by your tape and playback device. Consumer miniDV equipment records drop-frame timecode. More professional DV devices may offer a choice between drop-frame and non–drop-frame timecode.

5. Click the Check Status button to see if the device control is ready:

   Online—Indicates the device is connected and ready to use

   Offline—Indicates the device is not connected or not ready to use

6. Click Go Online for Device Info to open a browser and connect to Adobe's hardware guide for Premiere Elements.

7. Click OK to close the DV Device Control Options dialog box.

continues on next page

✔ **Tip**

- The software your computer needs to communicate with other devices, or *drivers*, for DV/HDV is built into Premiere Elements. The USB Video Class 1.0 Device Control driver must already be installed on your system. The proper driver is installed with Windows XP Service Pack 2 (SP 2), or may be included with your camcorder.

Preroll and Timecode Offset

The Device control pane of the Preferences dialog box includes a few items you may never use but still may be curious about: Preroll and Timecode Offset.

In Premiere Elements, *preroll* specifies the number of seconds the deck or camera rewinds before a specified point. This allows the deck to reach normal playback speed before capture begins when using the Scene Detect feature (see "Capturing using the Scene Detect feature," later in this chapter). When exporting your edited project to tape, the preroll helps the tape get up to speed before recording begins. (For more about exporting to tape, see Chapter 11, "Export".) If you're having trouble capturing successfully, you can try increasing the preroll time.

The Timecode Offset feature is designed to compensate for discrepancies between the timecode on the tape and on the captured clips. Although this is a highly unlikely event, you can check for a possible discrepancy the first time you capture and specify the number of 1/4 frames to correct it. For more about timecode, see the sidebar "Timecode."

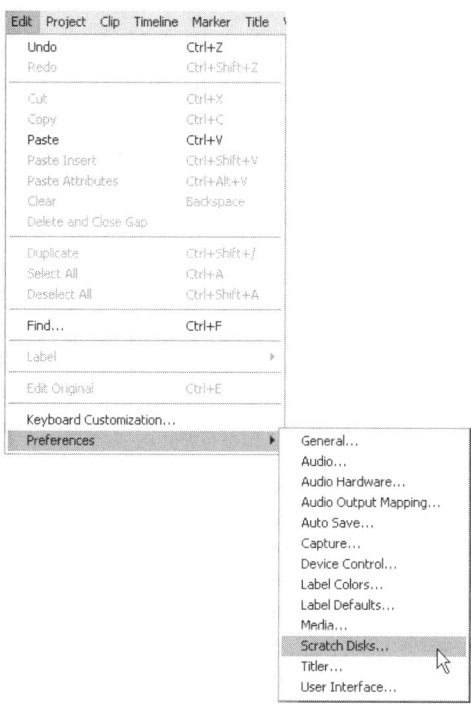

Figure 3.14 Choose Edit > Preferences > Scratch Disks.

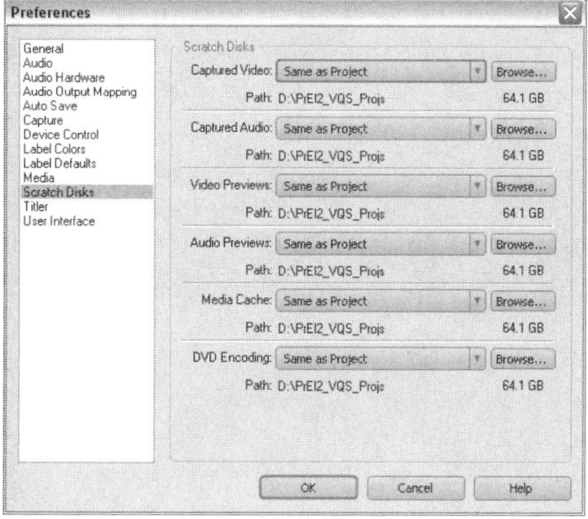

Figure 3.15 The Scratch Disks pane of the Preferences dialog box appears.

Storing Captured Footage

By default, Premiere Elements saves captured files to the same folder in which the current project is saved. However, this may not be the most convenient location for your captured video files. For example, your system may have a larger secondary drive better suited to storing large video files.

Before you capture, you can designate the disks that Premiere Elements uses to save video and audio media files. Given a choice, specify a fast disk with ample storage space; it will be the most capable of capturing all the frames successfully.

To set the capture location:

1. Choose Edit > Preferences > Scratch Disks (**Figure 3.14**).

   The Scratch Disks pane of the Preferences dialog box appears (**Figure 3.15**).

continues on next page

2. For Captured Video and Captured Audio, *do one of the following:*
   - ▲ To save captured video or audio in My Documents or the same folder as the project, choose the appropriate item in the pull-down menu (**Figure 3.16**).
   - ▲ To save captured video or audio in a folder you specify, click the Browse button, and specify a location in the Browse for Folder dialog box.
3. Click OK to close the Preferences dialog box.
   Captured video and audio files are captured to the location you specified.

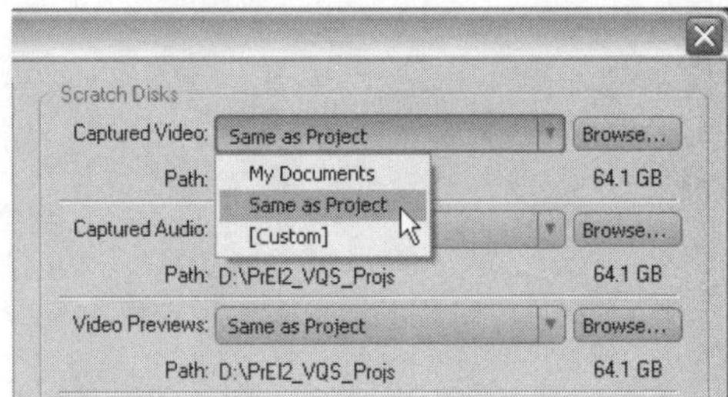

Figure 3.16 You can specify one of the preset scratch disks in the pull-down menu or click the Browse button to specify a custom location.

✔ Tips

- The location of the My Documents folder depends on which user is currently logged in. Remember, in Windows XP, you can specify different users, who each have their own directory and associated folders.
- To optimize your system for video editing, use your boot disk (C drive) for your system and software. Dedicate a different disk to storing media.
- A capture location is one type of scratch disk, a disk you designate for particular tasks. Later in the book, you'll learn how to specify scratch disks for video and audio preview files as well as conformed audio files.
- Avoid moving source footage files until after you've completely finished with a project and you're ready to archive the files. If you do move the files, your project won't be able to locate the source footage the next time you open the project. Consult the section "Locating Missing and Offline Files," in Chapter 2.

Using Playback Controls in the Capture Panel

Once device control is set up, you can control a camera or deck from the Capture panel. Although most of the Capture panel's controls should be familiar to you, they're still worth reviewing (**Figure 3.17**).

There are also a few buttons you won't find on other tape players: most notably, buttons to cue the tape to a *scene*, or *cut*—that is, the point at which the camera stopped and restarted recording. As you'll see later in this chapter, the *Scene Detect* feature not only makes it possible to quickly find different shots on the tape but also lets you capture an entire tape automatically—each shot becomes a separate clip.

You can also enter timecode numbers to set the current frame, In point, Out point, or duration.

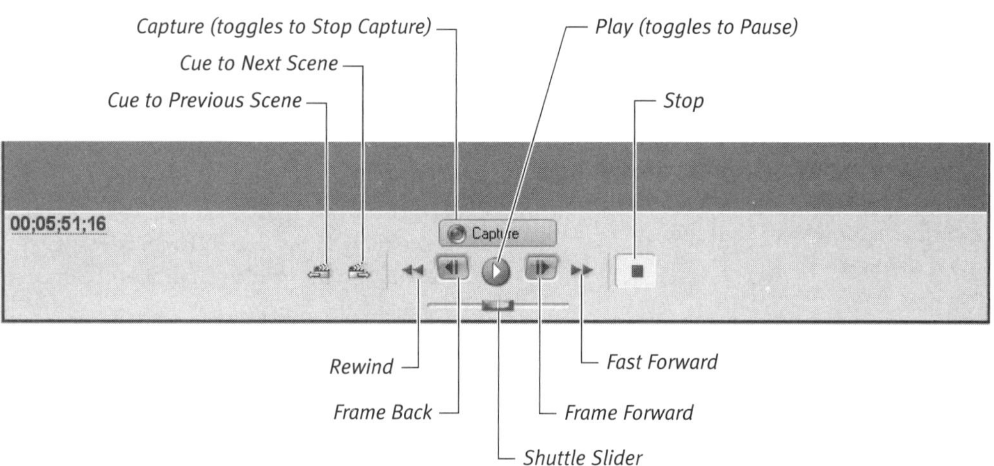

Figure 3.17 The Capture panel includes buttons for controlling the connected DV camcorder or deck.

To cue a tape to a scene break:

- In the Capture panel, *do either of the following:*
  - ▲ To cue to the previous cut point on the tape, click the Previous Scene button.
  - ▲ To cue to the next cut point on the tape, click the Next Scene button (**Figure 3.18**).

  The tape cues to the cut point you specified.

Figure 3.18 Cue to cut points on the tape by clicking the Previous Scene or Next Scene button (shown here).

To cue a tape to a specified timecode:

- In the Capture panel, click the current time display, enter a valid timecode number, and press Enter (**Figure 3.19**).

  The tape cues to the frame you specified.

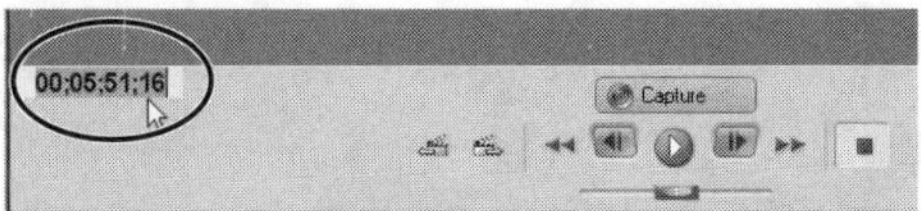

Figure 3.19 You can also cue to a particular timecode number by clicking the current time display, entering the number, and pressing Enter.

✔ Tips

- When the tape is stopped, the play head is no longer engaged, so that it rewinds and fast-forwards faster but doesn't scan the tape. Instead, the Capture panel displays the last frame you viewed until you engage the play head again by using another playback control.
- Many cameras and decks enter a standby mode after several minutes of inactivity and disengage the play head so as not to unnecessarily wear the tape.

Timecode

DV video is encoded with a signal called *timecode* that counts frames of video in hours, minutes, seconds, and frames. Timecode counts 30 frames per second (fps), from 0 up to 23:59;59;29, or just under one day. (Of course, widely available miniDV tapes for cameras are only 60 minutes in length, although 80-minute tapes are available.)

Timecode provides an *absolute* address for each frame of video—that is, each frame has a unique and unchanging number. Contrast that to the counter numbers found on some home VHS players, which merely count from any point and can be reset at any time.

Video professionals like timecode because it lets them identify each scene with a number and capture the footage they want automatically or repeatedly. But even amateurs can appreciate timecode. For example, when you have a lot of footage, you may want to create a paper log of shots with their corresponding timecode numbers. Using controls in the Capture panel, you can cue the tape to the exact points you want.

Figure 3.20 Click the taskbar's Capture button.

Figure 3.21 The Capture panel appears.

Capturing DV

Even though it takes the next several tasks to cover the capture process, don't be alarmed: Premiere Elements' Capture panel makes capture a simple and straightforward process. The following sections explain the variations.

You can capture clips on the fly, using the playback and capture controls manually. Or, you can use Premiere Elements' Scene Detect feature to capture clips automatically, so that each camera shot becomes a separate clip. Finally, you can have Premiere Elements add each clip you capture to the timeline automatically, creating a rough-cut sequence as you capture. Overall, the methods are similar and, for the most part, intuitive.

Whatever process you choose, remember that, by default, captured files are stored with the project file. Project files, in turn, are stored in your My Documents folder by default. To specify another location, follow the instructions in the section "Storing Captured Footage," earlier in this chapter.

To capture DV footage:

1. In the Premiere Elements taskbar, click the Capture button (**Figure 3.20**).

   The Capture workspace appears (**Figure 3.21**).

2. Make sure a DV camcorder or deck is connected to your computer (using an IEEE 1394 or USB 2.0 connection), is turned on, and is switched to VTR mode (not camera/recording mode); then insert the tape containing the footage you want to capture.

   An Enter New Tape Name dialog box appears.

continues on next page

3. In the Enter New Tape Name dialog box, type a unique name for the tape and then click OK (**Figure 3.22**).

   The name you enter is associated with each clip you capture, and appears in the Tape Name column of the Media panel (when set to list view).

4. In the More pull-down menu, select the tracks you want to capture (**Figure 3.23**):
   - ▲ Capture Video
   - ▲ Capture Audio
   - ▲ Capture Audio and Video

5. For Clip Name, type the name of the clip you're about to capture (**Figure 3.24**).

   If you don't enter a name, Premiere Elements uses the name of the project and appends a number (sequentially); for example, *project name* 01.avi, *project name* 02.avi, and so on.

6. Using the Capture panel's playback controls, play the portion of the tape you want to capture.

   See the section "Using Playback Controls in the Capture Panel," earlier in this chapter.

7. When the tape reaches the point at which you want to begin capturing, click the Capture button (**Figure 3.25**).

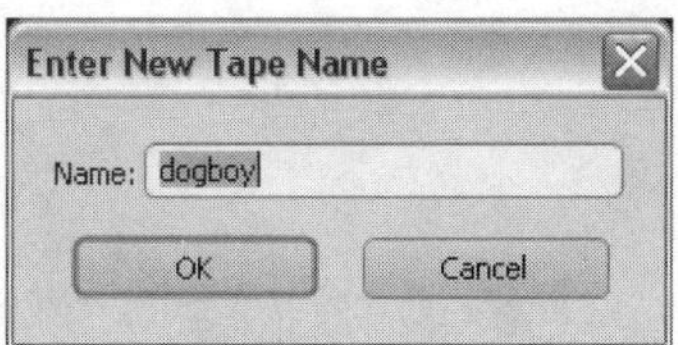

Figure 3.22 When you insert a tape, Premiere Elements prompts you to specify the tape's name.

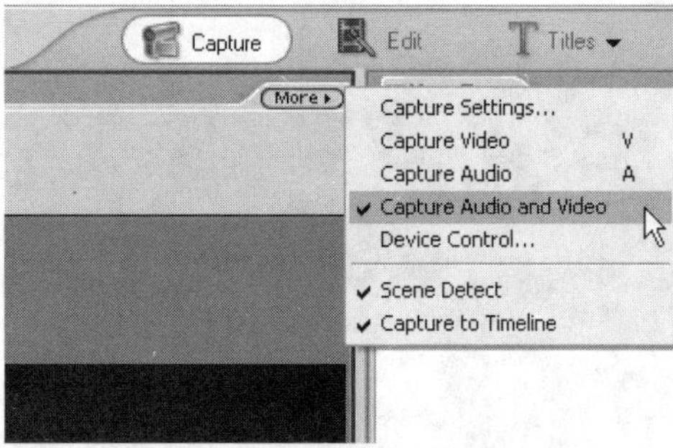

Figure 3.23 In the Capture panel's More pull-down menu, select whether you want to capture video, audio, or both.

Figure 3.24 Enter a name for the clip you want to capture (or use the default name).

Figure 3.25 When the tape reaches the point at which you want to begin capturing, click the Capture panel's Capture button.

Figure 3.26 Keep an eye on the video and on the status area (shown here) as you capture.

Figure 3.27 When the tape reaches the point at which you want to stop capturing, click the Stop Capture button.

The Capture button changes to the Stop Capture button. The status area of the Capture panel displays the elapsed time of the capture as well as the available time (based on the remaining hard disk space) (**Figure 3.26**).

8. When the tape reaches the point at which you want to stop capturing, click the Stop Capture button (**Figure 3.27**).

   The tape pauses, and the captured clip appears in the Media panel. For more about managing items in the Media panel, see Chapter 4, "Managing Clips." The captured file is stored in the location you specify, as explained in "Storing Captured Footage," earlier in this chapter.

✔ Tips

- It's impossible to record over a tape using the Capture panel, but it is possible to do so from your deck or camera controls. Play it safe by moving your DV tape's record inhibit slider from the Record to the Save position (which opens a small pit or hole in the cassette that your camera can detect). You'll find the slider on the front of the cassette, to the right of the label area.
- The status area at the top of the Capture panel displays information about the capture progress.
- If no image appears in the Capture panel, the problem is usually something embarrassingly simple. Make sure the camera or deck is on, check your cable connections, and be sure the tape contains (or is cued to) video.

Capturing using the Scene Detect feature

As you've seen, Premiere Elements can detect *scene breaks*, which are points on the tape where the camera stopped recording and then restarted—you know, where the director called "Roll camera" and "Cut!" You can use the Scene Detect feature to capture an entire tape automatically, so that each shot on the tape is captured as a separate media file. The clips use the name you specify plus a sequential number: filename01, filename02, and so on.

To enable Scene Detect:

1. In the Capture panel's More pull-down menu, select Scene Detect (**Figure 3.28**).

   When Scene Detect appears with a checkmark, the feature is enabled.

2. For Clip Name, type the name you want to use as the basis of each captured clip's name.

3. In the Capture panel, click Capture (**Figure 3.29**).

   Premiere Elements captures each shot on the tape as a separate file, and each file is listed in the Media panel as a clip, using the name you specified plus a sequential number (**Figure 3.30**).

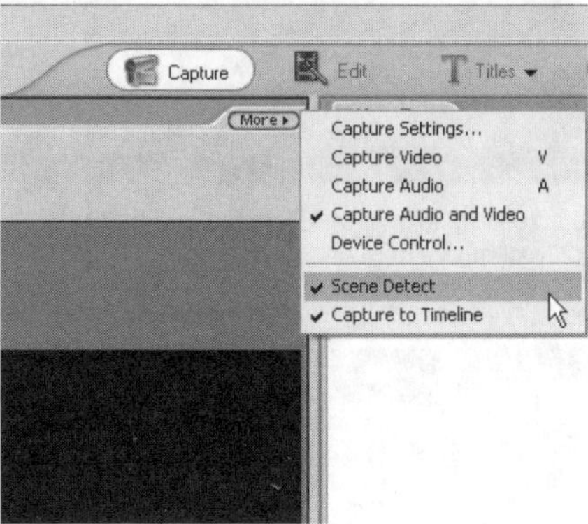

Figure 3.28 To capture each shot on the tape automatically, select Scene Detect in the Capture panel's More pull-down menu...

Figure 3.29 ...and then click Capture.

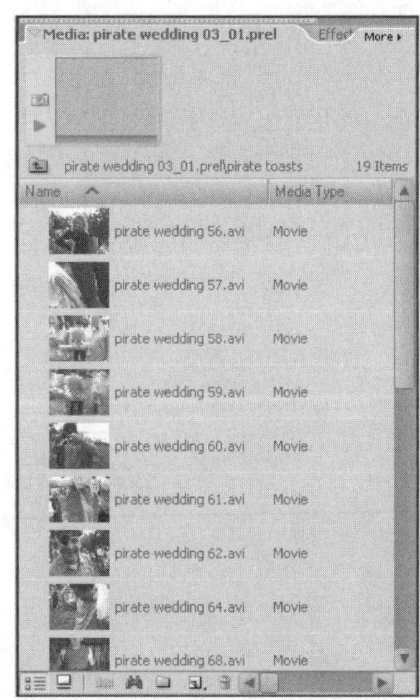

Figure 3.30 Premiere Elements captures each shot on the tape as a separate clip, naming them using a sequential numbering scheme.

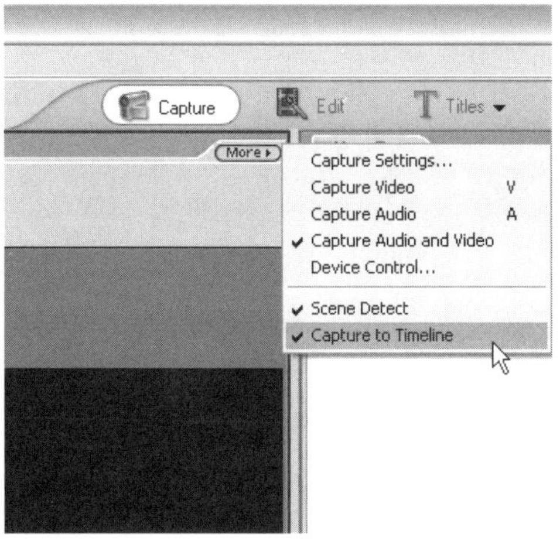

Figure 3.31 In the Capture panel's More pull-down menu, select Capture to Timeline.

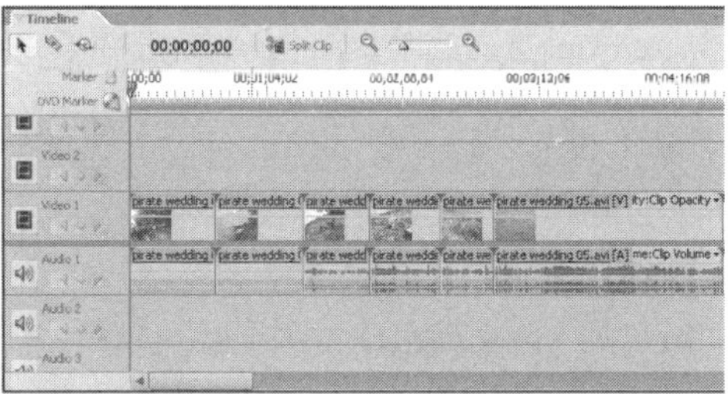

Figure 3.32 With Capture to Timeline enabled, each clip you capture is added to the Timeline automatically.

Adding captured clips to the timeline automatically

In Premiere Elements, you assemble an edited sequence in the Timeline panel. Future chapters cover editing in the Timeline panel in detail; for now, suffice it to say that one way to generate a rough cut is to enable the Capture panel's Capture to Timeline feature. With Capture to Timeline enabled, each clip you capture is added to the timeline automatically. If you capture footage in the order you want it to appear in the edited version, this can be a good way to generate a rough cut. When you've finished capturing, you can go right to refining the sequence.

To enable Capture to Timeline:

1. In the Capture panel's More pull-down menu, select Capture to Timeline (**Figure 3.31**).

   When Capture to Timeline appears with a checkmark, the feature is enabled.

2. Capture footage from the tape using the methods explained in "To capture DV footage" or "Capturing using the Scene Detect feature," earlier in this chapter.

   Each clip you capture appears in the Timeline panel, one after the other (**Figure 3.32**).

continues on next page

✔ Tips

- If you don't like the naming scheme, you can always change the name of the source clip (or an individual instance of the clip in the Timeline panel). See Chapter 4, "Managing Clips," for more details.
- A gap (unrecorded area) in the tape or a break (a discontinuity) in the tape's timecode can interrupt a capture, particularly when you're using the Scene Detect feature. Understand how your camera works in order to avoid these problems while you shoot. Otherwise, you can capture the items where the timecode is continuous and then cue the tape to the next continuous section manually to prevent Premiere Elements from encountering the gap or timecode break.
- It's a good practice to shoot about 30 seconds of black (or color bars, if your camera can generate them) at the very beginning of the tape. This way, you can capture the first shot with a handle at the beginning and not miss any footage. Also, the beginning of a tape is more prone to physical damage.

Tuning Up for Capture

Digital video thrives on a fast processor, speedy drives, and additional hardware. But if your system meets Premiere Elements' minimum requirements (listed in Chapter 1, "Basic Elements"), you should be able to capture video successfully without dropping frames. There's no reason to accept dropped frames when you can take certain steps to maximize your computer's performance:

- Quit all other applications.
- Turn off file-sharing software, at least temporarily.
- Disable other unnecessary operating-system features.
- Choose a fast, large disk or disk array as the disk used for capture (see "Storing Captured Footage").
- Defragment hard disks with a reliable disk utility to optimize their performance. (As usual, make sure important data is backed up beforehand!)

✔ Tip

- By default, Premiere Elements generates a report if any frames are missed, or dropped, during capture. To change this setting, choose Edit > Preferences > Capture.

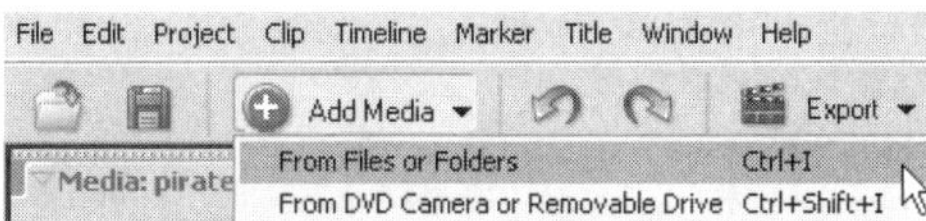

Figure 3.33 In the taskbar, click the Add Media button and choose From Files or Folders from the pull-down menu.

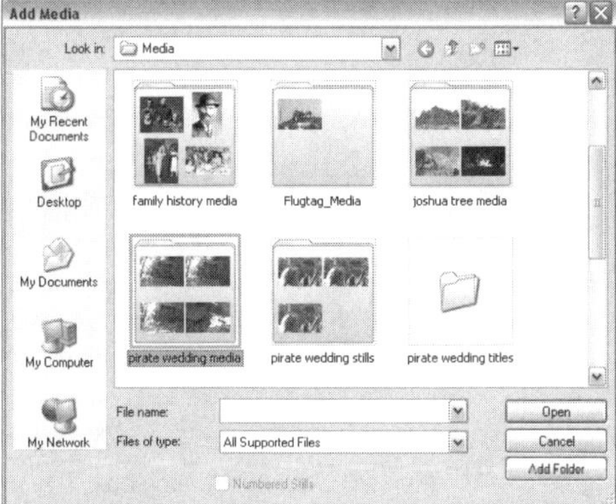

Figure 3.34 Select one or more files and click Open. Or, to import a folder of files, select it, and click Add Folder (shown here).

Figure 3.35 The selected files (or folder of files) appear as clips in the Media panel.

Adding Media

When you want to use a file in your project, you import the file as a clip. You can add one file at a time, several files at a time, or an entire folder of files. All the files you add appear as items in the Media panel.

The standard import method is designed to import files stored on a hard disk. However, you can use Premiere Elements' Media Downloader to import files stored on a DVD camera or removable drive, such as image files stored on a CD.

An imported still or video can be as big as 4,000 pixels tall by 4,000 pixels wide, and Premiere Elements can support a variety of video and audio formats.

To add files on a hard diskto a project:

1. In the Media panel, specify where you want to add the clip *by doing either of the following:*
   - ▲ Navigate to the folder into which you want to import or to the topmost level of the Media panel.
   - ▲ In list view, select the folder into which you want to import.
2. In the taskbar, click Add Media and choose From Files or Folders in the pull-down menu (**Figure 3.33**).
   The Add Media dialog box appears.
3. *Do one of the following:*
   - ▲ To import a single file, double-click the file.
   - ▲ To import multiple files, select the files and click Open.
   - ▲ To import a folder of files, select the folder and click Add Folder (**Figure 3.34**).

   The Add Media dialog box closes, and the clips appear in the Media panel (**Figure 3.35**). If you imported an entire folder, then the folder appears as a folder of clips in the Media panel.

To add files from a DVD camera or removable drive:

1. In the Media panel, specify where you want to add the clip *by doing either of the following:*
   - ▲ Navigate to the folder into which you want to import or to the topmost level of the Media panel.
   - ▲ In list view, select the folder into which you want to import.
2. In the taskbar, click Add Media and choose From DVD Camera or Removable Drive in the pull-down menu (**Figure 3.36**).
   The Media Downloader dialog box appears (**Figure 3.37**).
3. In the Media Downloader dialog box, choose a device in the Get Media From pull-down menu (**Figure 3.38**).
   Media files contained on the device you specify appear in the main viewing area.
4. For the Show option, select the button associated with the media type you want to display (**Figure 3.39**).
   You can resize the thumbnail images by using the slider under the images.
5. To specify the location where the files you select will be copied, click Browse and then specify a location on a hard disk.
   By default, Premiere Elements copies files to a folder called "Adobe," within your "My Videos" folder.

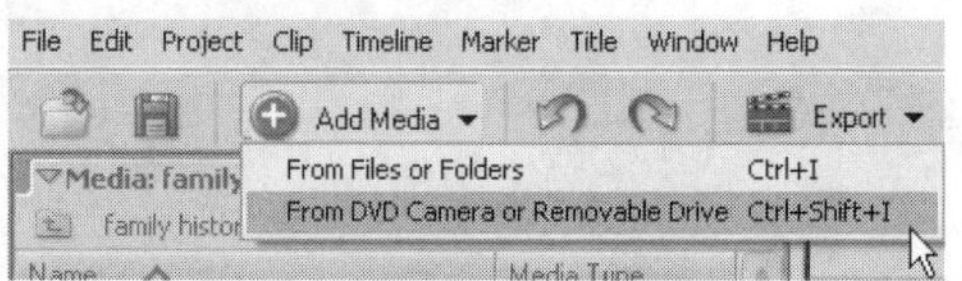

Figure 3.36 Click the Add Media and choose From DVD Camera or Removable Drive.

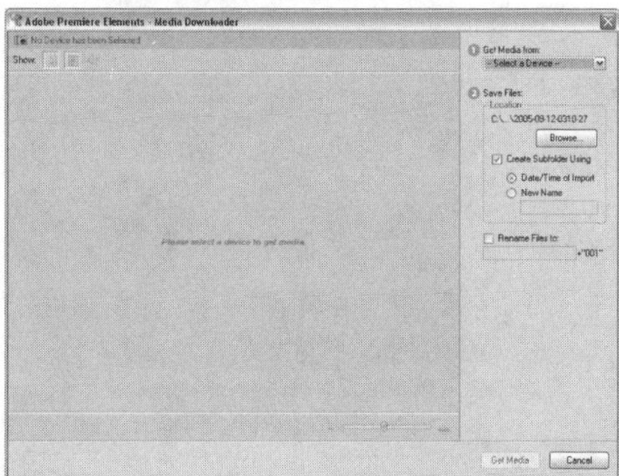

Figure 3.37 The Media Downloader dialog box appears.

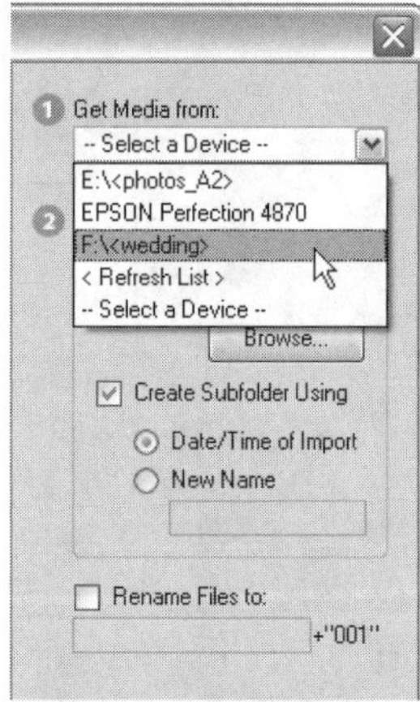

Figure 3.38 Choose the device containing the media files in the Get Media From pull-down menu.

Figure 3.39 Show or hide image, video, and audio files by clicking the appropriate button.

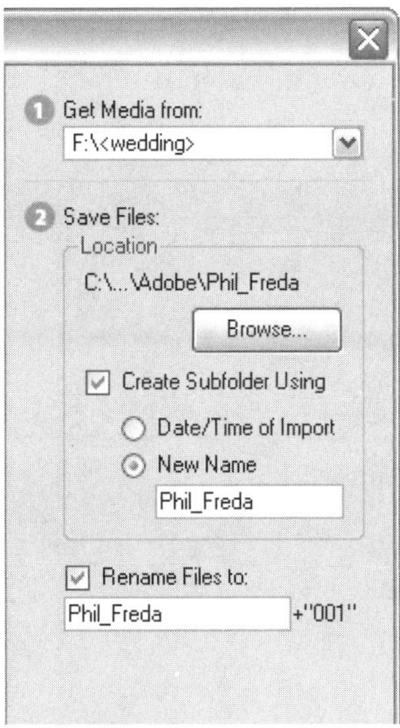

Figure 3.40 Specify where you want to store the copied files. You can also organize the files into subfolders, and specify a custom base filename.

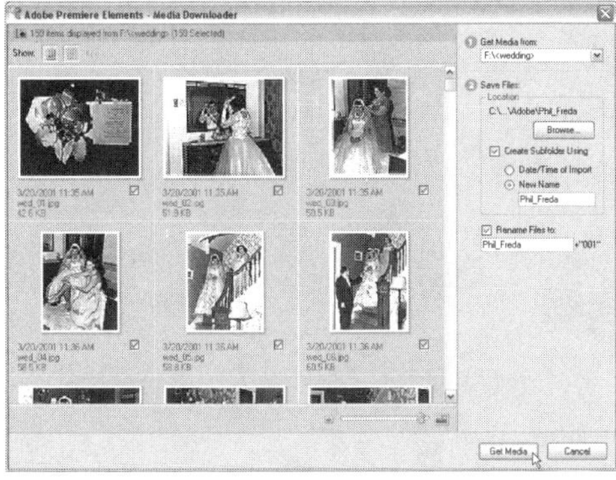

Figure 3.41 Check the items you want to copy and import and then click Get Media.

6. To store downloaded media in a folder within the folder specified in step 4, select Create Subfolder Using, and then select *either* of the following options:

   Date/Time of Import creates subfolders according to the date and time the files are imported.

   New Name allows you to enter a name for the subfolder in the field provided

7. To specify a custom name for the downloaded files, select Rename Files To (**Figure 3.40**).

   Files use the same base name, but are numbered incrementally.

8. Select the items you want to copy to the location you specified in step 5; deselect the items you want to exclude (**Figure 3.41**).

   You can check or uncheck multiple items by first selecting the items and then clicking any of the selected items' check box. You can select items in the Media Downloader as you do in an Import dialog box.

continues on next page

9. Click Get Media.

The selected files are copied to the location you specified, and renamed and organized into subfolders according to the options you set. The files copied to the hard disk are imported into the project automatically, and appear in the selected folder of the Media panel (**Figure 3.42**).

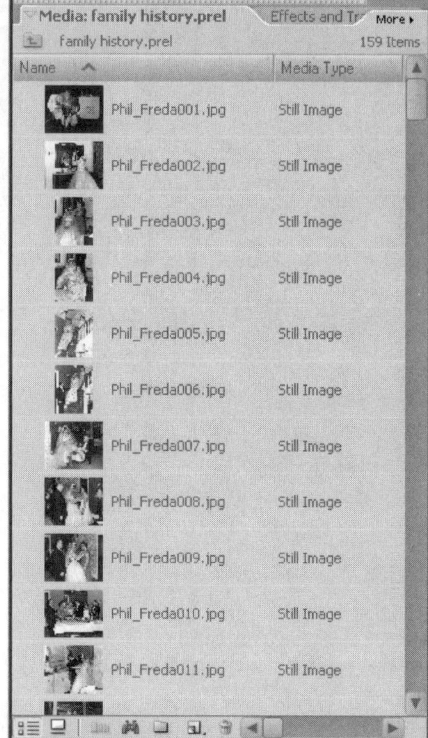

Figure 3.42 Checked items are copied to the location you specified, and the copies are imported automatically.

✔ Tips

- You can also open the Add Media dialog box by double-clicking in an empty area of the Media panel.
- Still images initially use the default duration you specify. See "Adding Stills," later in this chapter.
- Naturally, you can also copy files from an external drive to a hard disk manually, rename the files as you wish, and then import them using the standard method. The Media Downloader just simplifies the process.

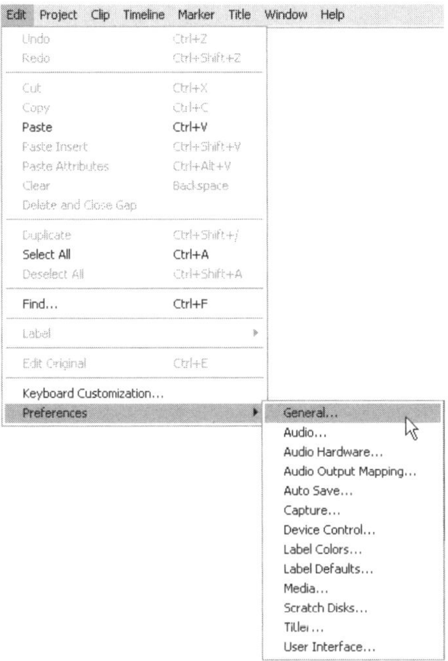

Figure 3.43 Choose Edit > Preferences > General.

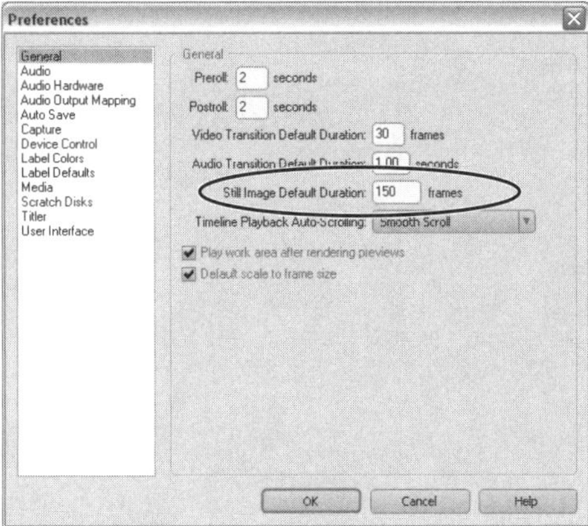

Figure 3.44 For Still Image Default Duration, type the initial duration of still images, in frames.

Adding Stills

Although individual images are only single frames, you can set them to play back in an edited sequence for any duration.

To set the default duration for still images before you add them:

1. Choose Edit > Preferences > General (**Figure 3.43**).

   The General pane of the Preferences dialog box opens.

2. For Still Image Default Duration, type the initial duration of still images, in frames (**Figure 3.44**).

   For NTSC video, enter 30 frames for a one-second duration; for PAL, 25 frames for one second. Hereafter, all still images imported into the project will use the default duration. Still images that are already in the project or program are unaffected. However, you can change the duration of a still-image clip at any time using techniques you'll learn in Chapter 6, "Editing in the Timeline."

Using Illustrator and Photoshop Files

Premiere Elements can *rasterize* Illustrator files—a process that converts the path-based (vector) art to Premiere Elements' pixel-based (bitmapped) format. The program *anti-aliases* the art, so that edges appear smooth; it also interprets blank areas as transparent.

Set crop marks in the Illustrator file to define the dimensions of the art that will be rasterized by Premiere Elements.

When you add a layered Photoshop file to Premiere Elements, it appears merged—in other words, all the visible layers are combined into a single layer, and any blank areas can be made transparent. For more about using transparency, see Chapter 10, "Adding Effects."

✔ Tips

- The term *aliasing* refers to the hard, jagged edges many objects show in digital, pixel-based images. Anti-aliasing subtly adds transparency to edges, making them appear smoother.
- The technically savvy may be interested to know that blank areas in an Illustrator file are interpreted by Premiere Elements as an alpha channel premultiplied with white. You can find out more about straight and premultiplied alpha channels in Illustrator or Photoshop's Help system.

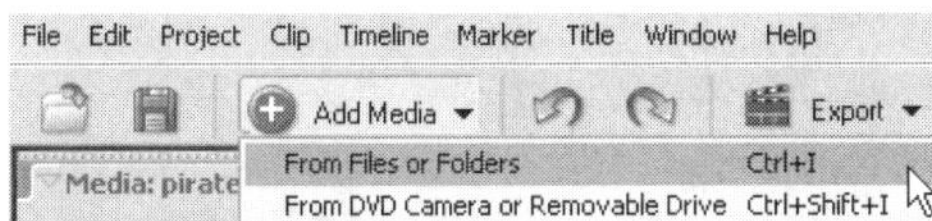

Figure 3.45 In the taskbar, click the Add Media button and choose From Files or Folders in the pull-down menu.

Figure 3.46 Select the first file in the sequence, select the Numbered Stills check box, and then click Open.

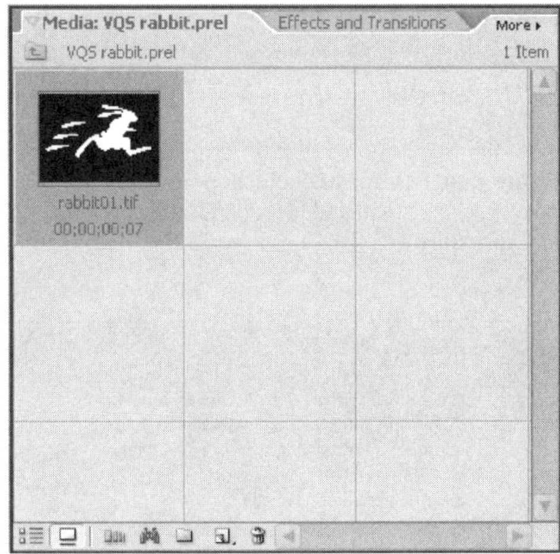

Figure 3.47 The image sequence appears in the Media panel as a single clip.

Adding Still-Image Sequences

Many programs export movies as a sequence of still images. Don't worry—Premiere Elements can add a numbered sequence as a single clip that acts just like a movie file.

To add numbered still images as a single clip:

1. Confirm that each image in the numbered sequence has the correct extension and that the filenames contain an equal number of digits at the end (seq000.bmp, seq001.bmp, and seq002.bmp, for example).
2. In the Media panel, specify where you want to add the clip *by doing either of the following:*
   - ▲ Navigate to the folder into which you want to import or to the topmost level of the Media panel.
   - ▲ In list view, select the folder into which you want to add the clip.
3. In the taskbar, click Add Media and choose From Files or Folders in the pull-down menu (**Figure 3.45**).

   The Add Media dialog box appears.
4. Select the first file in the numbered sequence.
5. Select the Numbered Stills check box (**Figure 3.46**), and click Open.

   The image sequence appears in the selected folder of the Media panel as a single clip (**Figure 3.47**).

✔ Tip

- By default, Premiere Elements assumes the image sequence uses the same frame rate as your project. To tell Premiere Elements that the footage uses a different frame rate, use the Interpret Footage command, explained in Chapter 4, "Managing Clips."

Creating a Still Image in Photoshop Elements

You can launch Photoshop Elements from within Premiere Elements. When you do, Photoshop Elements automatically opens a new file with the proper dimensions to create a full-screen image in a DV project. The image is added to the current Premiere Elements project automatically.

Naturally, your computer will require sufficient memory (RAM) to run both programs simultaneously.

To create a still image in Photoshop Elements:

1. Choose File > New > Photoshop File (**Figure 3.48**).
2. In the Save Photoshop File As dialog box that appears, make sure Add to Project (Merged Layers) is selected, and then specify a name and destination for the new file, and click Save (**Figure 3.49**).

   Photoshop Elements launches. An Adobe Photoshop Elements dialog box warns you that the image will appear distorted when displayed on a computer screen but will appear normally when viewed on a television (see the sidebar "PAR Excellence: Pixel Aspect Ratios").
3. In the Adobe Photoshop Elements dialog box, click OK to acknowledge and close the dialog box (**Figure 3.50**).

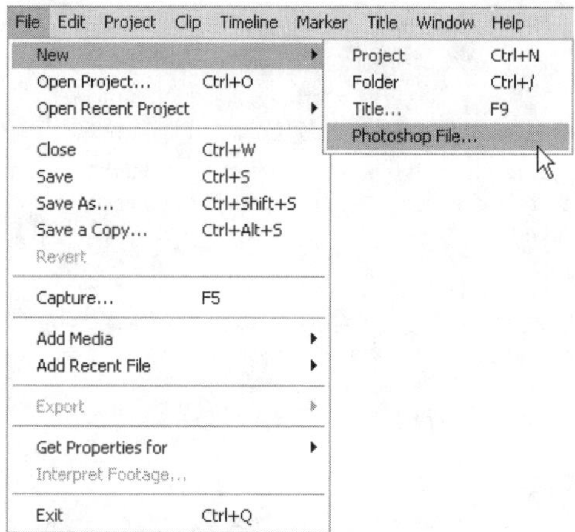

Figure 3.48 Choose File > New > Photoshop File.

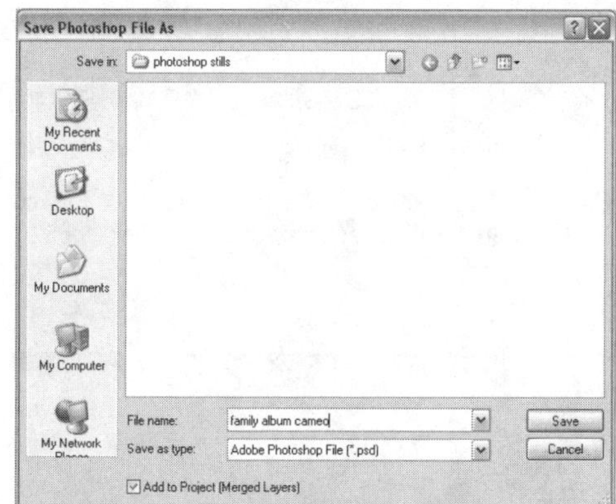

Figure 3.49 In the Save Photoshop File As dialog box, specify a name and location for the new file, and click Save.

Figure 3.50 Photoshop Elements points out the distortion caused by differences in pixel aspect ratios; click OK to close the dialog box.

Figure 3.51 In Photoshop Elements, create the still image you want, and then close the file.

Figure 3.52 The Photoshop Elements image file you created is added to Premiere Elements' Media panel automatically.

3. Create the still image you want (**Figure 3.51**).

   Consult the Adobe Photoshop Elements User Guide, Help System, or other instructional resources for more about using Photoshop Elements.

4. When you've completed the image, close Photoshop Elements.

   In the warning dialog box, confirm that you want to save and close the file. The image you created appears in the selected folder of the Premiere Elements Media panel (**Figure 3.52**).

✔ Tip

■ Instead of closing Photoshop Elements when you've finished with the image, you can also choose File > Save at any time. In this case, you'll be prompted to specify a name and location for the file or confirm the name and location you entered in step 3 of the task "To create a still image in Photoshop Elements."

PAR Excellence: Pixel Aspect Ratios

Pixel aspect ratio (PAR) refers to the dimensions of each pixel used to create the image frame. Although some formats share the same *image* aspect ratio, they use different *pixel* aspect ratios (**Figure 3.53** and **Figure 3.54**).

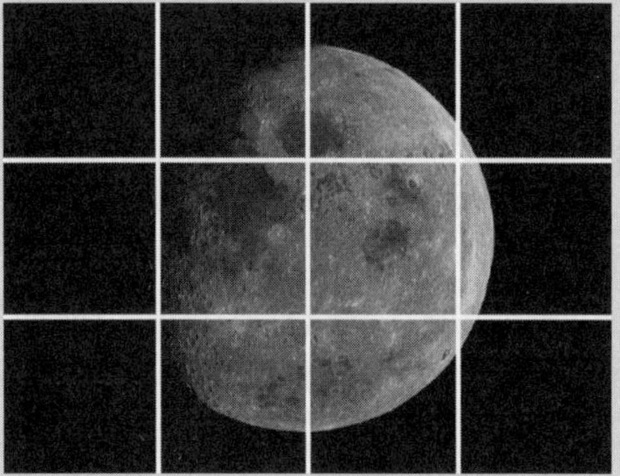

Figure 3.53 This example illustrates how square pixels can be used to form an image with a 43 aspect ratio.

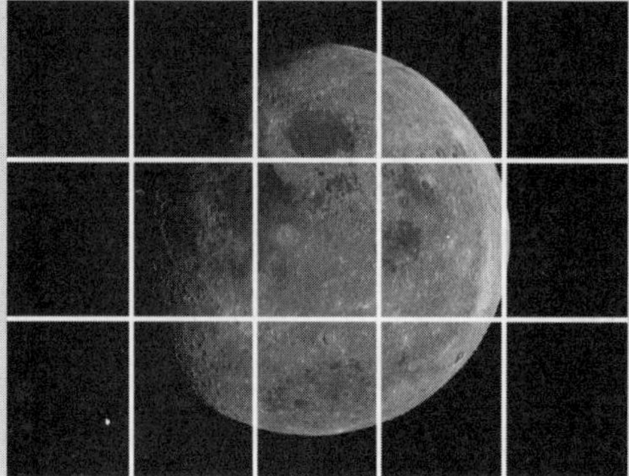

Figure 3.54 This example illustrates how nonsquare pixels form an image with a 43 aspect ratio.

Images appear distorted when the PAR of the footage doesn't match the PAR of the display. Footage in DV looks distorted when displayed on a typical computer monitor, which displays square pixels (**Figure 3.55**). Conversely, a square-pixel image appears distorted when viewed or output at DV resolution.

This is why Photoshop Elements warns you that the image you create appears distorted—squeezed 10% horizontally, as a matter of fact—when viewed on a computer screen. But don't worry; the distortion will disappear once the image is interpreted and displayed correctly.

When you create square-pixel footage for DV output, set the image size to 720×534 to compensate for the differences in PARs.

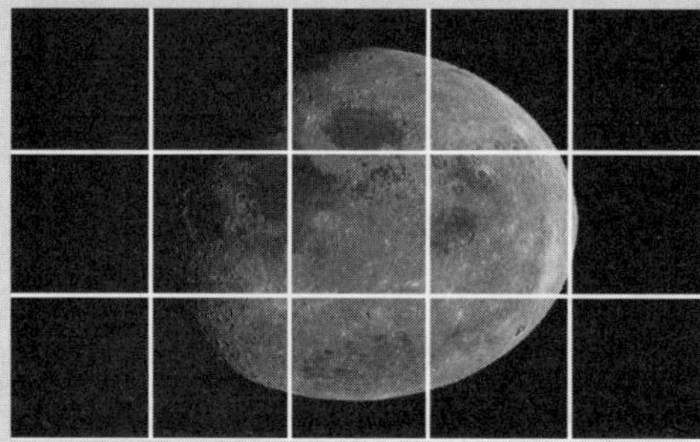

Figure 3.55 An image created with nonsquare pixels is distorted when displayed with square pixels.

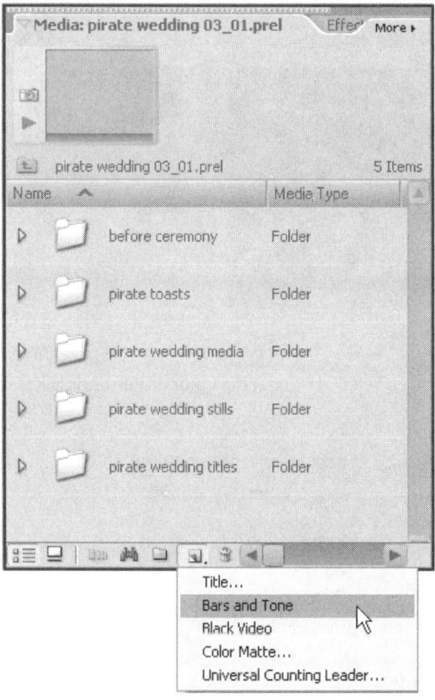

Figure 3.56 Click the Media panel's New Item button, and choose Bars and Tone or Black Video.

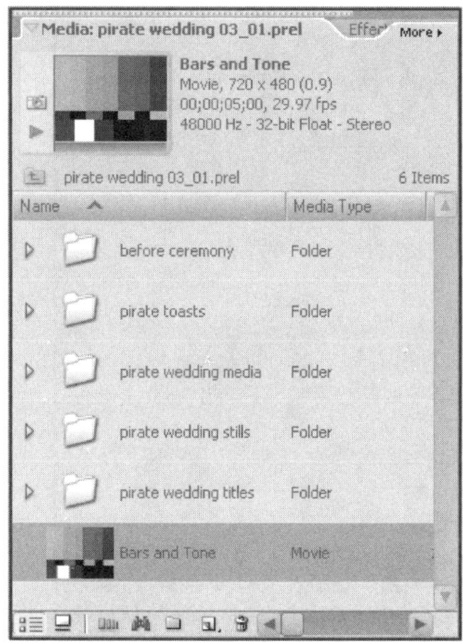

Figure 3.57 The item you selected appears in the Media panel.

Generating Synthetic Media

In addition to accepting a wide variety of source files, Premiere Elements can generate useful clips of its own. The Media panel's New Item button includes options for creating bars and tone (like the ones that TV stations broadcast after hours), black video, a color matte, and even a standard countdown. These files are called *synthetic* because they don't create a new file on your hard disk; they exist only as part of your project, not as independent files.

The New Item button also includes an option for creating titles. However, creating titles deserves a chapter all its own: Chapter 9.

To create bars and tone or black video:

1. In the Media panel, specify where you want to import the clip *by doing either of the following:*
   - ▲ Navigate to the folder into which you want to import or to the topmost level of the Media panel.
   - ▲ In list view, select the folder into which you want to import.
2. Click the New Item button, and *choose one of the following* (**Figure 3.56**):

   Bars and Tone creates a standard NTSC color bars pattern and 1 kHz audio tone.

   Black Video creates black video.

   The footage item you chose appears in the Media panel and uses the duration you specified for still images (**Figure 3.57**).

To create a color matte:

1. In the Media panel, specify where you want to import the clip *by doing either of the following:*
   - ▲ Navigate to the folder into which you want to import or to the topmost level of the Media panel.
   - ▲ In list view, select the folder into which you want to import.
2. Click the New Item button, and choose Color Matte from the drop-down menu (**Figure 3.58**).
   A Color Picker dialog box appears.
3. Choose a color, and click OK (**Figure 3.59**).
   A Choose Name dialog box appears.
4. Type a name for the color matte, and click OK (**Figure 3.60**).
   The color matte appears in the Media panel and uses the duration you specified for still images (**Figure 3.61**).

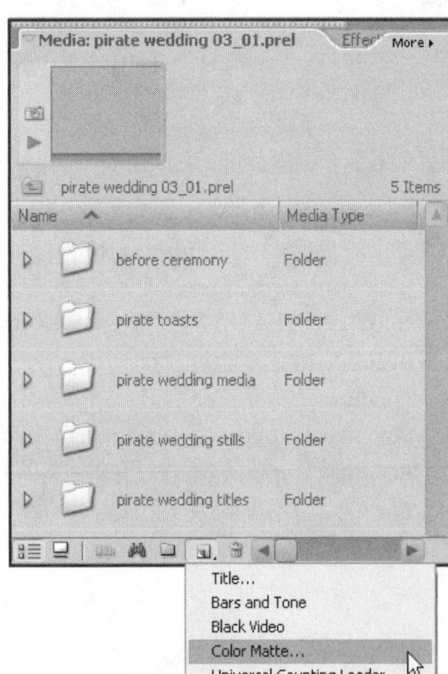

Figure 3.58 Click the Media panel's New Item button, and choose Color Matte.

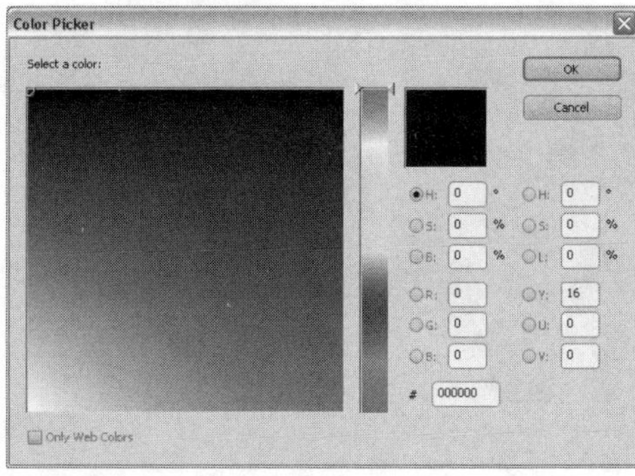

Figure 3.59 Select a color in the Color Picker, and click OK.

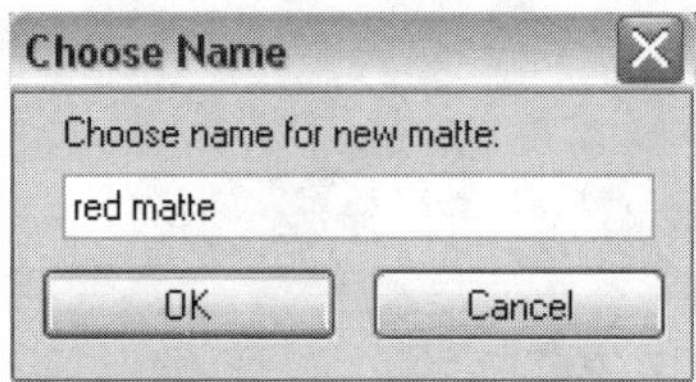

Figure 3.60 Type a name for the color matte, and click OK.

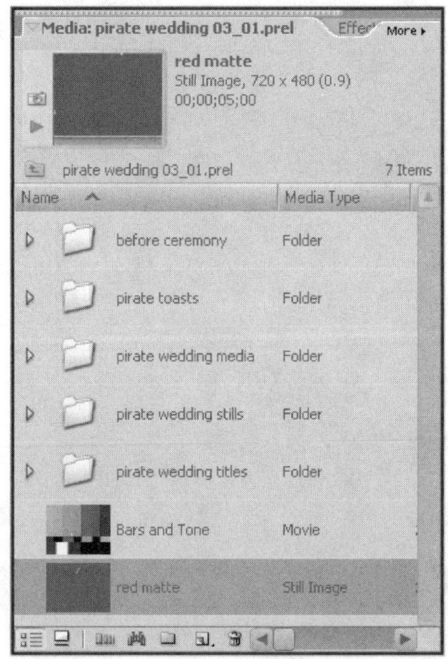

Figure 3.61 The color matte appears in the Media panel and uses the default duration for still images.

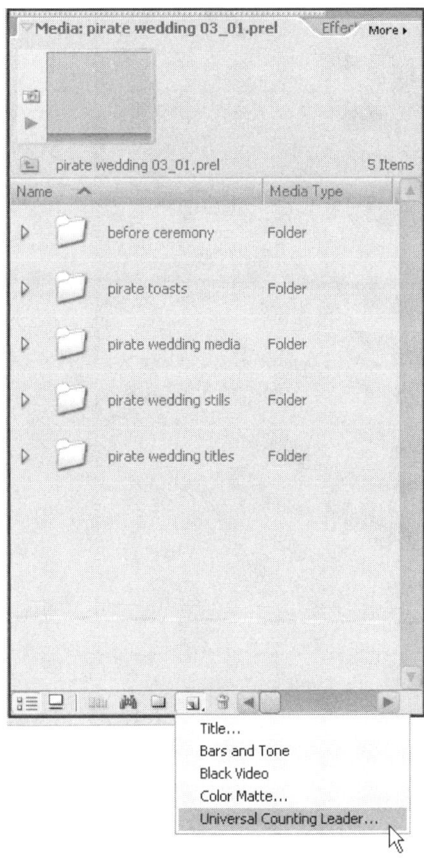

Figure 3.62 Click the Media panel's New Item button, and choose Universal Counting Leader.

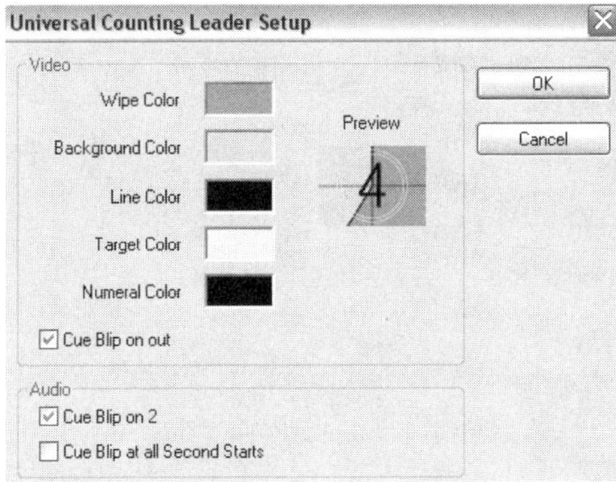

Figure 3.63 Specify options in the Universal Counting Leader Setup dialog box.

To create a countdown:

1. In the Media panel, specify where you want to import the clip *by doing either of the following:*
   - ▲ Navigate to the folder into which you want to import or to the topmost level of the Media panel.
   - ▲ In list view, select the folder into which you want to import.
2. Click the New Item button, and choose Universal Counting Leader from the pull-down menu (**Figure 3.62**).

   The Universal Counting Leader Setup dialog box appears.
3. *Specify the following options* (**Figure 3.63**):
   - ▲ To open the Color Picker for each element of the countdown, click the color swatch next to each element.
   - ▲ To display a small circle in the last frame of the leader, select the "Cue Blip on out" check box.
   - ▲ To play a beep at the two-second mark of the countdown, select the "Cue Blip on 2" check box.
   - ▲ To play a beep at each second of the countdown, select the "Cue Blip at all Second Starts" check box.

continues on next page

4. Click OK to close the dialog box.

   A Universal Counting Leader clip appears in the selected folder of the Media panel (**Figure 3.64**).

✔ Tips

- To make a slate (containing information such as program, producer, and total running time), you can create a title card, as explained in Chapter 9, "Creating Titles." For more about slates, see the sidebar "Creating a Leader."
- Double-clicking black video, color bars, or a counting leader opens the footage in the Clip view of the Monitor panel. However, double-clicking a color matte reopens the color picker.

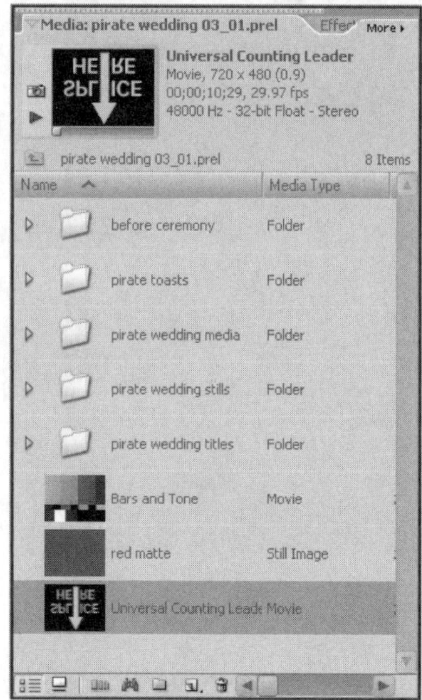

Figure 3.64 The countdown appears in the Media panel.

Creating a Leader

A *leader* is a series of shots that typically appears at the beginning of a master tape. The *master tape* is used to make duplicates (or *dubs*) and usually contains the following:

30 seconds of black—A black screen without sound keeps the program away from the *head*, or beginning, of the master tape, which is more prone to damage.

60 seconds of *bars and tone*—The color bars and reference tone are used by video technicians to faithfully reproduce your program's video and audio levels.

10 seconds of black—Here, black acts as a buffer between the bars and the slate.

10 seconds of a slate—A title screen appears, containing pertinent information about the program and the tape itself, such as the name of the program, the producer, whether the audio is mixed, and so on.

8 seconds of countdown—The visible countdown originally helped a film projectionist know when the program was about to start. It can serve a similar purpose for videotape operators. The standard countdown starts at 8 and ends at 2 (where there is usually a beep, or *2 pop*, to test the sound).

2 seconds of black—Black video immediately precedes the program.

Managing Clips

As you saw in the previous chapter, all the files you add to a project—video clips, audio clips, still pictures, and synthetic media like leaders and mattes—are listed in the Media panel. The more complex the project, the lengthier and more unwieldy this list becomes. Fortunately, the Media panel includes features that help you keep your clips organized and easy to find, as this chapter explains.

You'll also learn how to perform other media management tasks. For example, you can specify how Premiere Elements interprets aspects of a clip, such as its frame rate, pixel aspect ratio, and alpha channel. Finally, you'll learn how to restore an offline clip by reuniting it with its previously missing source file.

Working with the Media Panel

The Media panel is the receptacle of all the clips—video, audio, and still images—you intend to use. Accordingly, it's vital that the clips be organized, easy to find, and easy to evaluate. Premiere Elements' Media panel helps you achieve these goals (**Figure 4.1**).

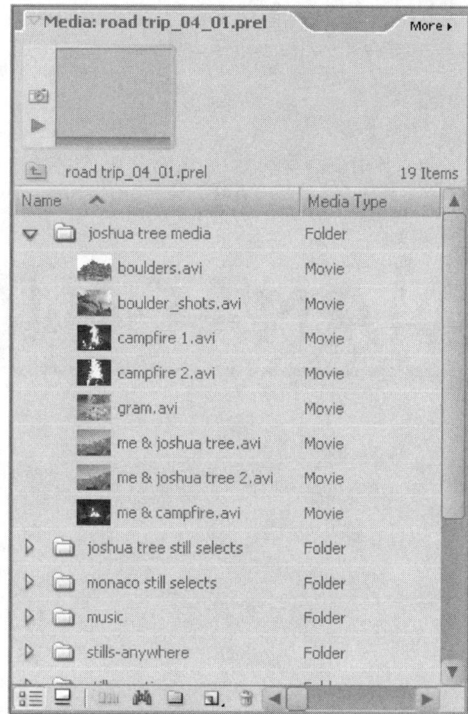

Figure 4.1 The Media panel helps you organize, find, and evaluate your clips.

To help you change the view options or access common commands quickly, several buttons are conveniently located at the bottom of the Media panel. As in all the primary panels, you can also access commands associated with the panel from an integrated menu that's labeled More.

The *preview area* displays vital information about selected items in the panel, as well as a sample image. You can play back movie files in the preview area. In addition, you can set any frame of a movie clip to represent the clip in the Media panel views.

You can change the appearance of the Media panel to the most efficient configuration, or according to your taste. Illustrations in this chapter depict the Media panel using various combinations of options: list view and icon view; thumbnails on and off; items at different sizes; with and without the preview area. You'll learn about all these options in the sections that follow.

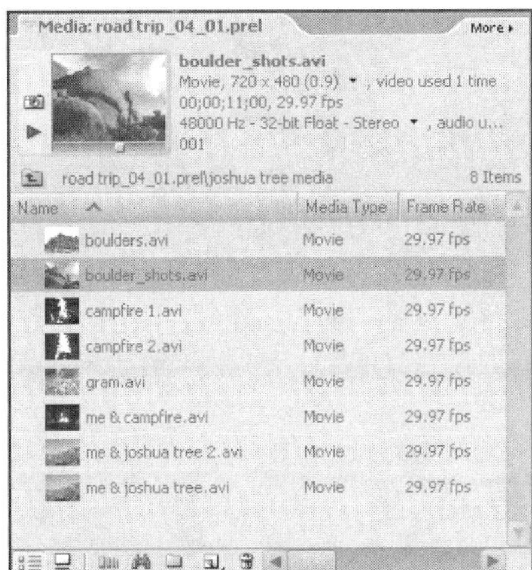

Figure 4.2 In list view, items are listed as rows and columns of information.

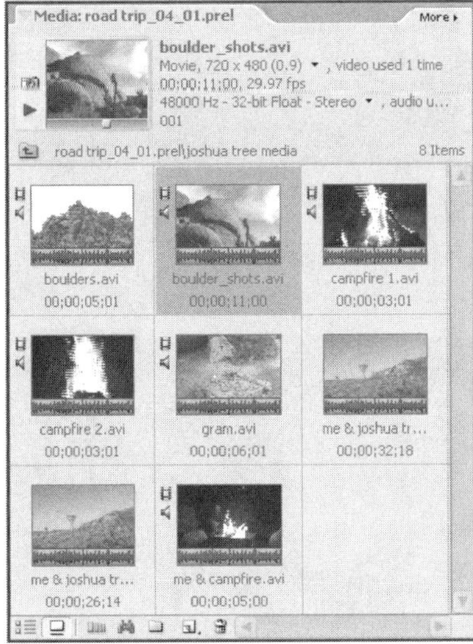

Figure 4.3 In icon view, Media panel items are arranged in a grid.

Viewing Items in the Media Panel

You can view the items in the Media panel two ways: as a list or as icons. In list view, items are listed with rows and columns of information, which can help you sort and organize your clips (**Figure 4.2**). Relatively speaking, list view can show more items at once, and its columns are key to managing a large number of clips. In icon view, on the other hand, items in the Media panel are arranged in a grid (**Figure 4.3**). This view tends to take up more space, but it lets you lay out the items like photos on a table. You can use icon view to create a kind of storyboard, which you can assemble into a sequence automatically (using the Create Slideshow feature, explained in Chapter 5, "Editing Clips into a Sequence").

Both view types let you choose whether to represent each item as a symbol representing the type of footage or as a thumbnail image of the footage. You can even set the size of the items.

The sections that follow explain how to work with each view, so you can customize the Media panel for the task at hand.

To change the Media panel view:

- At the bottom of the Media panel, click the button that corresponds to the view you want to use (**Figure 4.4**):
  - ▲ List
  - ▲ Icon

Figure 4.4 Click the appropriate button at the bottom of the Media panel to switch views.

To toggle thumbnails in the Media panel:

- In the Media panel's More menu, choose Thumbnails > Off (**Figure 4.5**).

  When Off is selected, items appear as icons (**Figure 4.6**); when Off is unselected, items appear as thumbnail images.

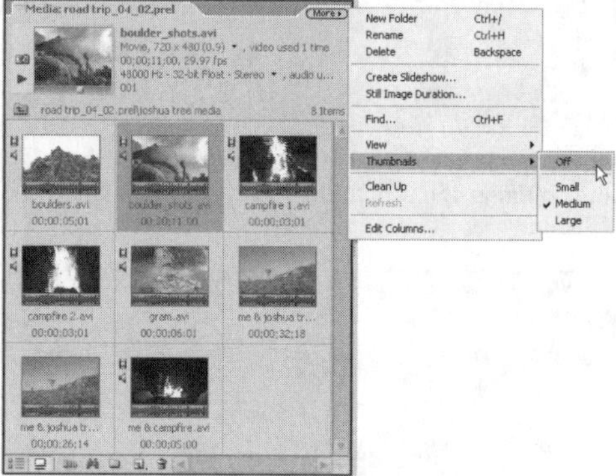

Figure 4.5 Choose Thumbnails > Off in the Media panel's More menu...

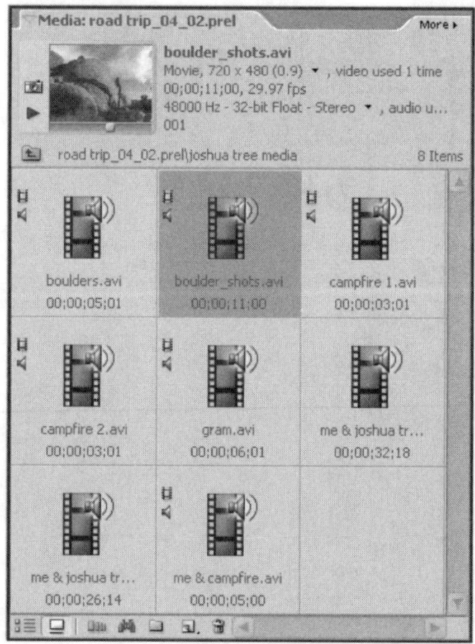

Figure 4.6 ...to make items appear as symbols.

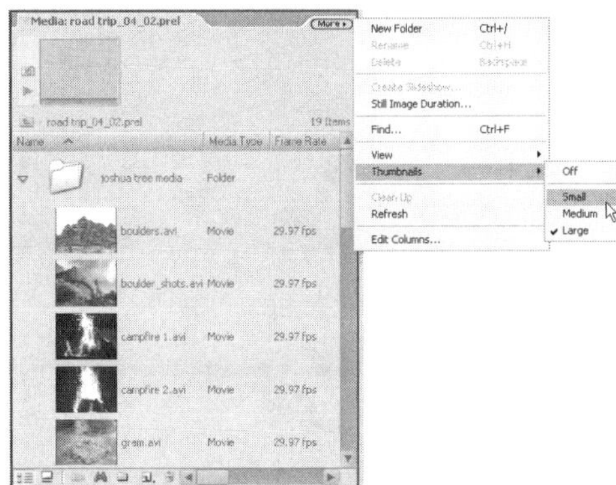

Figure 4.7 In the Media panel's More menu, choose Thumbnails and select a size.

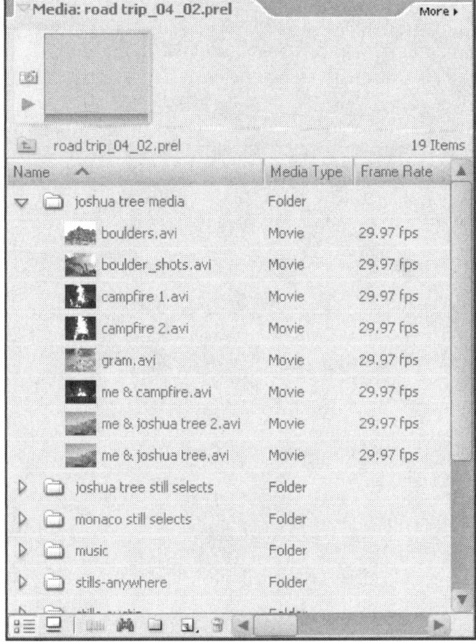

Figure 4.8 Items appear at the size you specify. Here, the thumbnails are set to the smallest size.

To change the size of items in the Media panel:

- In the Media panel's More menu, choose Thumbnails and select a size (**Figure 4.7**).

  Items in the Media panel appear at the relative size you specify (**Figure 4.8**).

Working with Icon View

In icon view, items in the Media panel appear as larger icons arranged in a grid (something like the tiles view in Windows XP).

Icon view also lends itself to a workflow you might call *storyboard editing*. You can arrange the clips in order, much like the sketches in a storyboard, and then assemble them into a sequence automatically using Premiere Elements' Create Slideshow command. (See Chapter 5 for more about the Create Slideshow feature.)

To arrange items in icon view:

1. With the Media panel set to icon view, select one or more items.
2. Drag the selected items to another cell in the grid.

   A bold line between grid cells indicates where the moved items will be inserted (**Figure 4.9**). When you release the mouse, subsequent items are shifted to the right to make room for the moved items (**Figure 4.10**).

Figure 4.9 When you select items to move to a new position in the grid, a bold line between grid cells indicates where the moved items will be inserted.

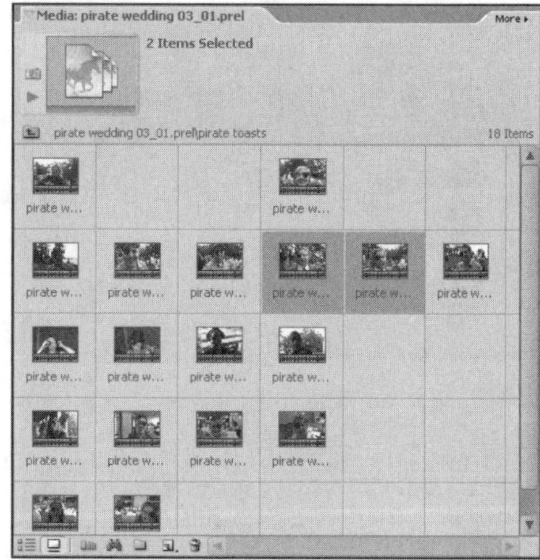

Figure 4.10 Subsequent items are shifted to the right to make room for the moved items.

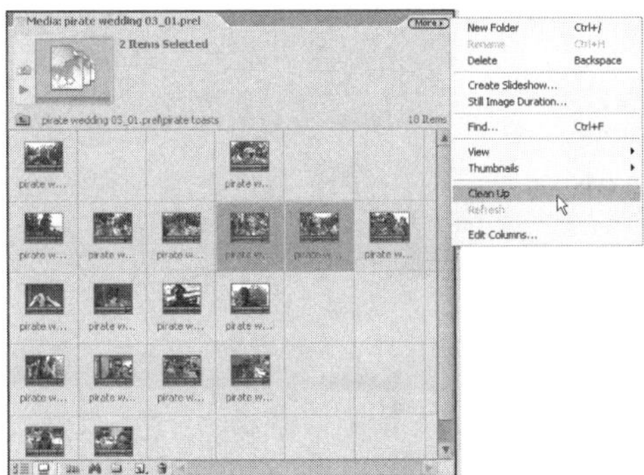

Figure 4.11 Choose Clean Up in the Media panel menu.

Figure 4.12 Items are rearranged so that there are no empty cells between them.

To clean up icon view:

- With the Media panel set to icon view, choose Clean Up in the Media panel menu (**Figure 4.11**).

  Items in the Media panel are arranged in the visible cells of the grid from left to right and from top to bottom, so that there are no empty cells between items (**Figure 4.12**).

Working with List View

List view lets you organize items according to a number of categories that appear as columns in the Media panel. You can select which columns you want to include and add your own custom columns. You can also resize and rearrange the columns to suit your organizational method. However, you can only rename or permanently remove custom columns, and the name column is always the first column.

To hide or show columns in list view:

1. In the Media panel's More menu, choose Edit Columns (**Figure 4.13**).

   The Edit Columns dialog box appears.

2. Select the headings for the type of information you want to view when the Media panel is set to list view (**Figure 4.14**).

3. Click OK to close the Edit Columns dialog box.

   Only the columns you specified appear in the Media panel.

To add custom columns in list view:

1. In the Media panel menu, choose Edit Columns.

   The Edit Columns dialog box appears.

2. Click Add (**Figure 4.15**).

   An Add Column dialog box appears.

Figure 4.13 In the Media panel's More menu, choose Edit Columns.

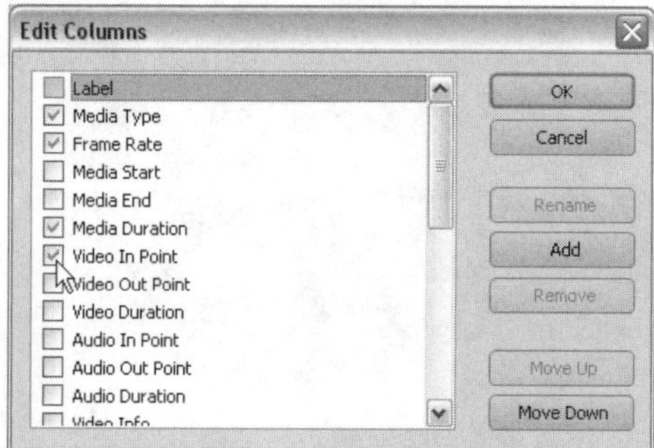

Figure 4.14 In the Edit Columns dialog box, select the headings for the type of information you want to view.

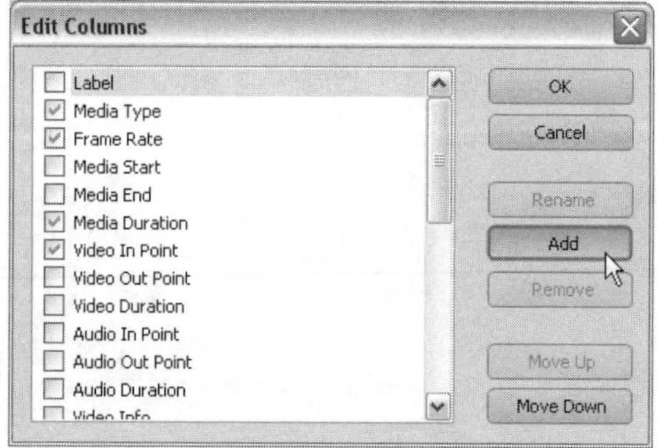

Figure 4.15 In the Edit Columns dialog box, click Add.

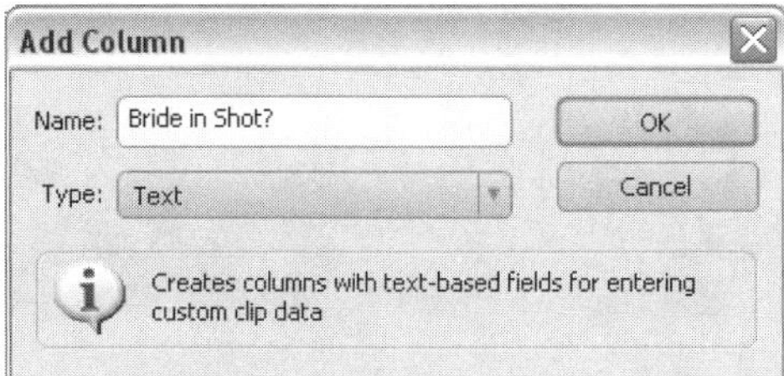

Figure 4.16 In the Add Column dialog box, type the name of the custom column.

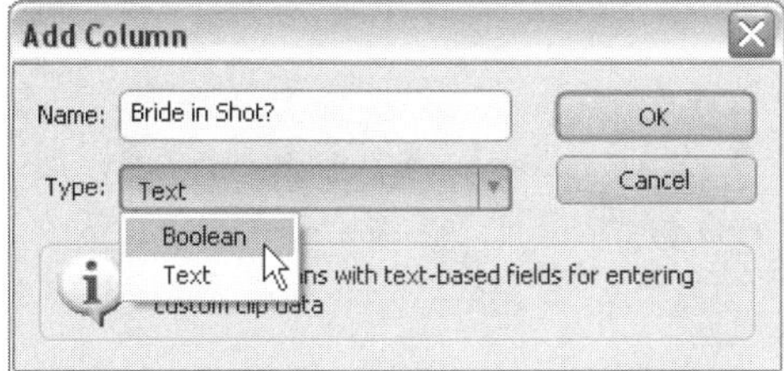

Figure 4.17 In the Type drop-down menu, specify whether the column will contain a text field or a check box.

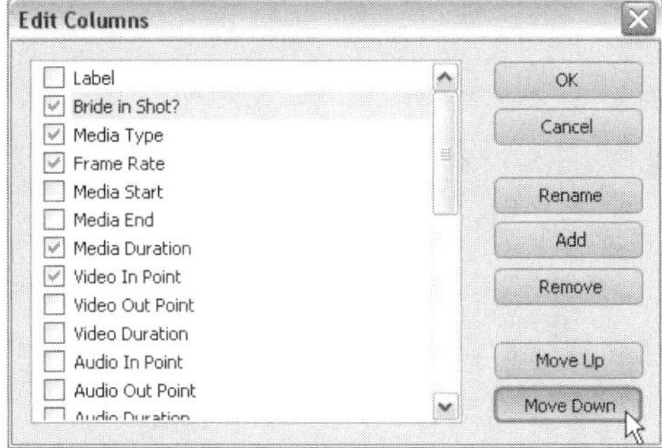

Figure 4.18 Select a column name, and choose to rename, remove, or move the column.

3. Type the name of the custom column (**Figure 4.16**).

4. Choose an option from the Type drop-down menu (**Figure 4.17**):

   Text creates a column of text fields in which you can enter information.

   Boolean creates a column of check boxes, which you can use to indicate a yes or no state.

5. Click OK to close the dialog box.

   The new column appears in the Edit Columns dialog box.

6. When you've finished editing columns, click OK to close the Edit Columns dialog box.

To edit columns in list view:

1. In the Media panel menu, choose Edit Columns.

   The Edit Columns dialog box appears.

2. Select a column name, and *click any of the following buttons* (**Figure 4.18**):

   Rename—To rename a custom column

   Remove—To remove a custom column

   Move Up—To move a column one item higher in the list, which moves it to the left in the Media panel

   Move Down—To move a column one item lower in the list, which moves it to the right in the Media panel

3. Click OK to close the dialog box.

   The Media panel reflects your choices.

✔ Tip

- You can't rename or remove any of the default columns, but you can hide them.

To rearrange headings in list view:

- With the Media panel set to list view, drag a heading in the Media panel to the left or right to place it where you want (**Figures 4.19** and **4.20**).

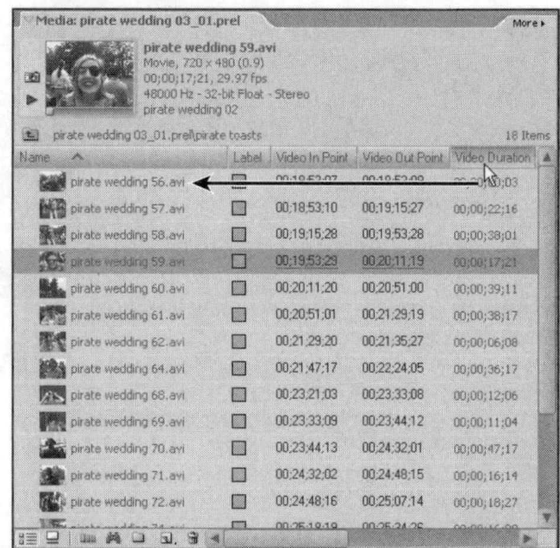

Figure 4.19 Dragging a heading to the left or to the right...

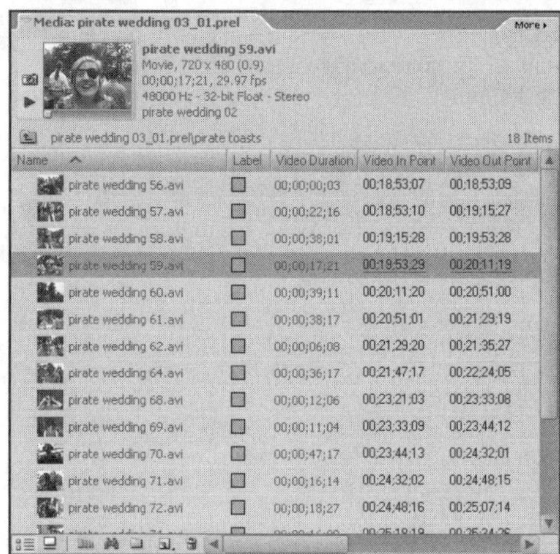

Figure 4.20 ...changes its relative position in the Media panel.

Figure 4.21 Drag the right edge of a heading to resize it.

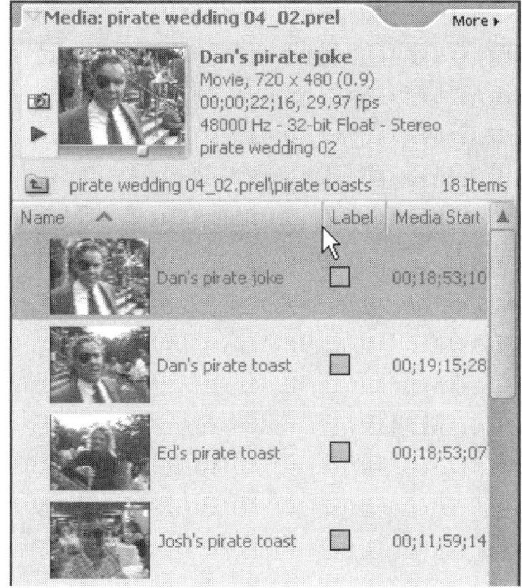

Figure 4.22 The heading appears narrower or (in this case) wider.

To adjust a column's width in list view:

- With the Media panel set to list view, drag the right edge of a heading in the Media panel to resize the heading (**Figures 4.21** and **4.22**).

To sort items in list view:

- With the Media panel set to list view, *do one of the following:*
  - ▲ Click a column heading to sort clips by that heading (**Figure 4.23**).
  - ▲ Click a column heading twice to reverse the sort order (**Figure 4.24**).

  A small triangle next to the column name indicates whether items are sorted in ascending or descending order.

✔ Tip

- List view can include a Label column. (See the task "To hide or show columns in list view," earlier in this chapter.) Instead of providing a text field or a check box, the Label column identifies each item by color. You can choose which colors represent different types of items in the Media panel by choosing Edit > Preferences > Label Colors.

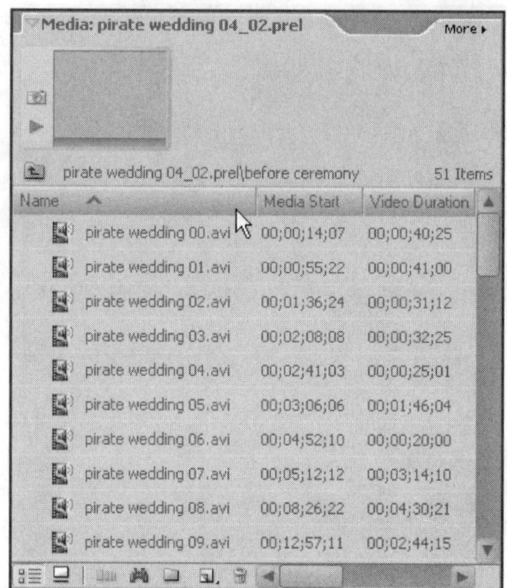

Figure 4.23 Click a column heading to sort clips by that heading.

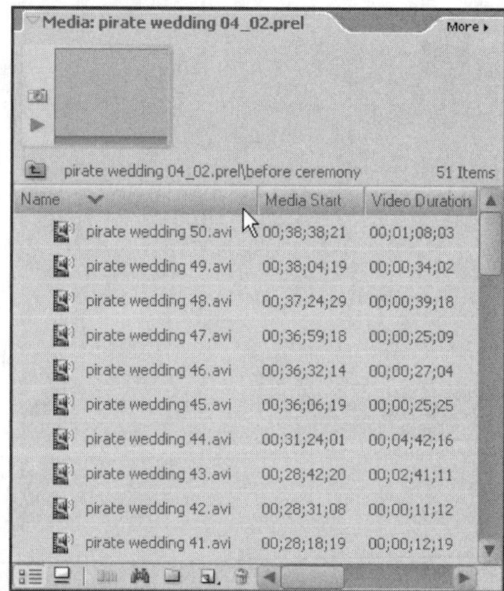

Figure 4.24 Click the same heading again to reverse the sort order.

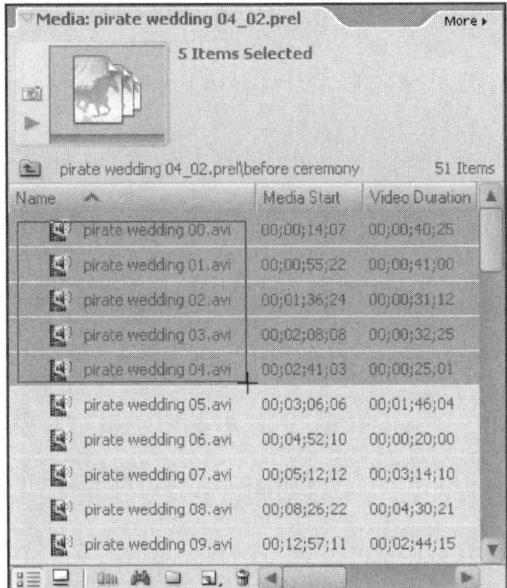

Figure 4.25 Select items by clicking, or select a range of items by dragging a marquee selection (shown here).

Selecting and Deleting Items in the Media Panel

You can select items in the Media panel in much the same way you select files in Windows XP. However, when you delete an item from the Media panel, bear in mind that you're only deleting a reference to a file on the hard disk, not the file itself. So, if you delete a clip, the project will no longer require that clip, but its source media remains on the hard disk. When you attempt to delete a clip that's in the timeline, Premiere Elements prompts you to confirm the action.

To select items in the Media panel:

1. If necessary, open the folder containing the clips you want to view.
2. To select a clip or clips, *do one of the following:*
   - ▲ Click an item.
   - ▲ Shift-click a range of items.
   - ▲ Ctrl-click several noncontiguous items.
   - ▲ Drag a marquee around two or more items (**Figure 4.25**).
   - ▲ Choose Edit > Select All to select all items.
   - ▲ Choose Edit > Deselect All to deselect all items.

To delete items from the Media panel:

1. In the Media panel, select one or more items.
2. Click the Delete button , or press Delete on your keyboard.

   Deleting a clip removes it from the project, but the source file remains on the hard disk (**Figure 4.26**). If the clip is used in a timeline, Premiere Elements prompts you to confirm your choice.

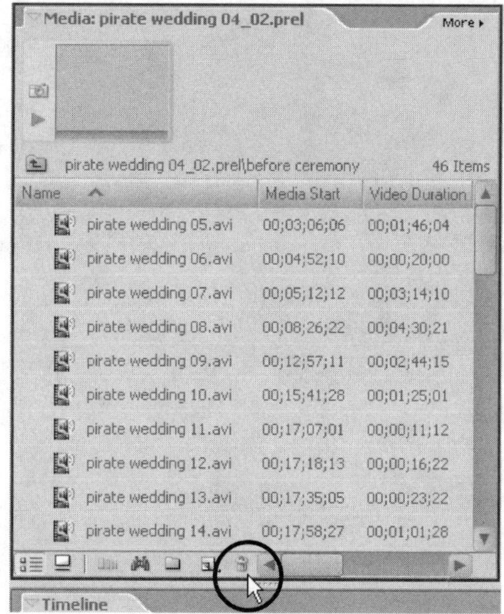

Figure 4.26 Clicking the Delete button removes selected items from the project but doesn't remove related media files from the disk.

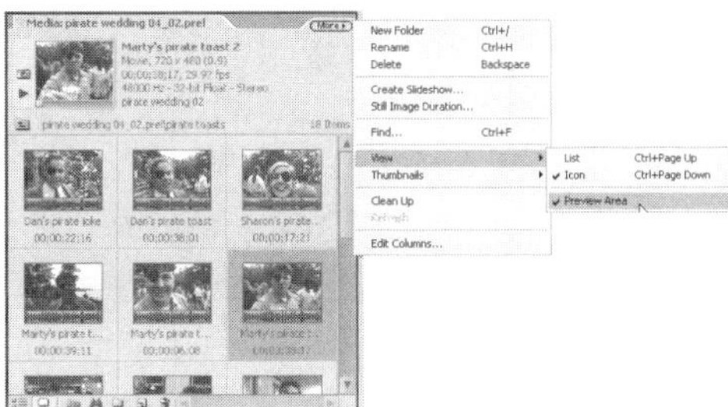

Figure 4.27 Here the preview area is visible. But choosing View > Preview Area in the Media panel's More pull-down menu...

Figure 4.28 ...deselects the option and hides the Media panel's preview area.

Using the Preview Area of the Media Panel

The preview area of the Media panel displays a sample image of the selected folder or clip. The preview area also displays the number of clips in a folder or the vital statistics of a clip—its name, file type, image dimensions, and so on.

If the selected clip is a movie file, you can play back the clip—with sound—directly in the Media panel. In addition, you can set any frame of the clip as the *poster frame,* the image used to represent the clip when you're viewing thumbnails of the clips in the Media panel. This way, you can choose the most appropriate image to represent the clip.

To show or hide the preview area of the Media panel:

- In the Media panel's More menu, select View > Preview Area (**Figure 4.27**).

  When Preview is selected, the preview area is visible; when Preview is deselected, the preview area is hidden (**Figure 4.28**).

To display a preview of an item in the Media panel:

◆ In the Media panel, click a clip to select it.

A sample frame and information appear in the preview area of the Media panel. Clip information can include the clip's name, file type, image size, duration, frame rate, data rate, and audio settings; the number of times the clip has been used in the Timeline; and so on (**Figure 4.29**).

To play back a movie clip in the preview area:

1. In the Media panel, click a movie clip to select it.

   A sample image and information appear in the preview area of the Media panel.

2. To play the preview image, *do either of the following:*

   ▲ To the left of the preview image, click the Play button (**Figure 4.30**).

   ▲ Press the spacebar.

3. Click the Play button or press the spacebar again to stop playback.

4. To cue the preview image, drag the slider below the image (**Figure 4.31**).

Figure 4.29 The preview area of the Media panel displays a thumbnail-sized version of the clip and other clip data.

Figure 4.30 Play the preview image by clicking its Play button...

Figure 4.31 ...or shuttle through the clip by dragging its slider.

Figure 4.32 Click the camera icon to set the clip's poster frame.

Figure 4.33 Click the small arrow to the right of the clip's video or audio usage information.

To set the poster frame for a movie clip:

1. In the Media panel, click a movie clip to select it.

   A sample image and information appear in the preview area of the Media panel.

2. Below the preview image, drag the slider to cue the preview to the frame you want to set as the poster frame.

3. To the left of the preview image, click the Set Poster Frame button (**Figure 4.32**).

   The current frame of the preview becomes the poster frame—the image used to represent the clip when you view thumbnail images of clips in the Media panel.

✔ Tips

- If you haven't set a poster frame for a clip by clicking the Set Poster Frame button, the poster frame is the clip's In point. If you have set the poster frame, and it's before the In point, it's changed to the In point. If you set it after the In point, then it remains where you set it. For more about edit points (In and Out points), see Chapter 5.

- In the Media panel, clicking the small arrow to the right of the clip's video or audio usage information opens a pull-down menu listing the starting time of each instance of the clip in the timeline. Selecting an item cues the current time in the timeline to that clip instance's In point (**Figure 4.33**).

Organizing Clips in Folders

Premiere Elements allows you to manage clips in the project in much the same way that you manage files on your computer operating system. You can specify whether to list imported clips in the topmost level of the Media panel's organizational hierarchy or nested inside a *folder*. Naturally, you can move clips in and out of folders at any time. But although using clips and folders in Premiere Elements is analogous to moving files and folders in the Windows XP operating system, there are important differences.

To create a folder:

1. In the Media panel, click the Folder button (**Figure 4.34**).

   A new folder appears in the Media panel. By default, new folders are named Folder 01, Folder 02, and so on. However, the name is highlighted and ready to change.

2. Enter a name for the folder (**Figure 4.35**).

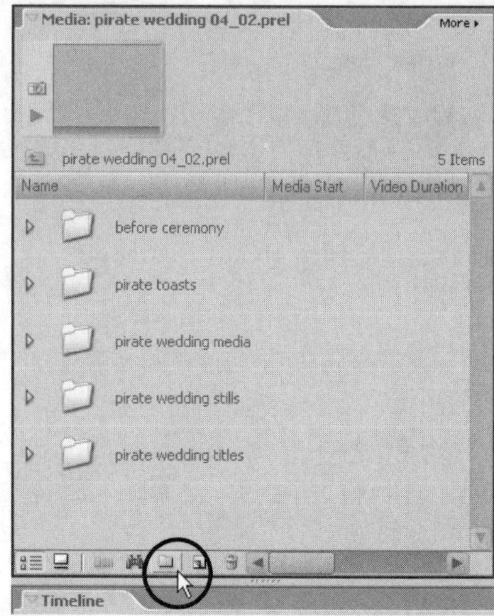

Figure 4.34 In the Media panel, click the Folder button.

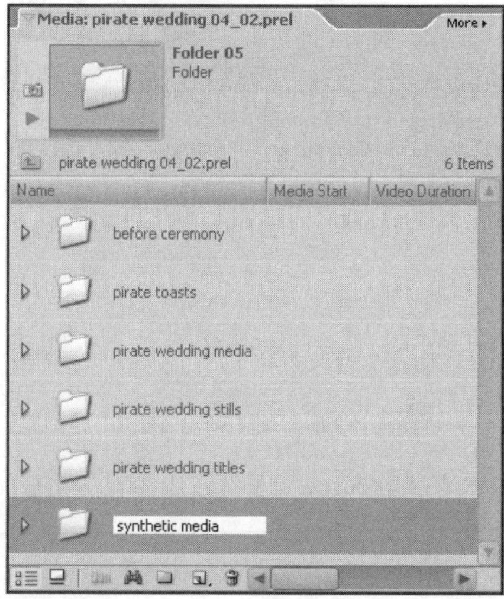

Figure 4.35 Enter a name for the folder.

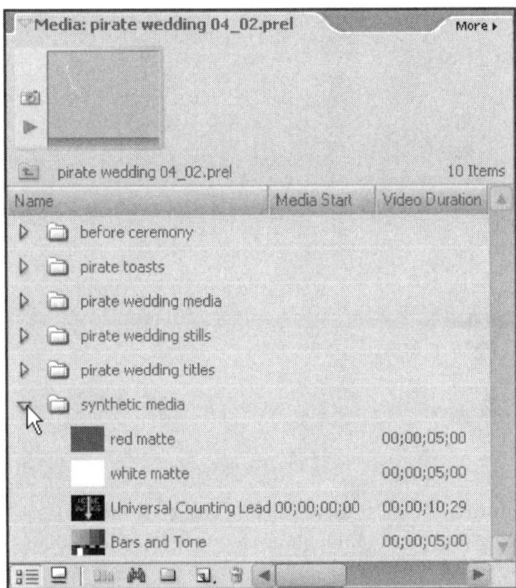

Figure 4.36 In list view, click the triangle next to the folder icon to expand the folder and view its contents in outline form.

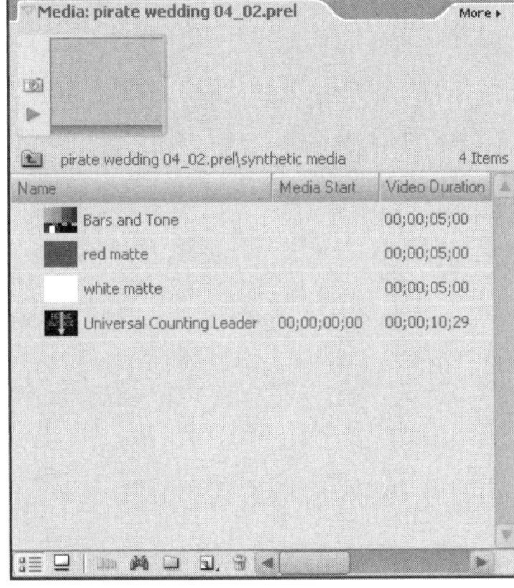

Figure 4.37 In list view or icon view, double-click the folder to open it and view its contents in the main clip area of the Media panel.

To view the contents of a folder:

- Do either of the following:
  - ▲ In list view, click the triangle next to the folder icon to expand the folder and view its contents in outline form (**Figure 4.36**).
  - ▲ In list view or icon view, double-click the folder to open it and view its contents in the Media panel's main clip area (**Figure 4.37**).

To hide the contents of a folder:

- *Do either of the following:*
  - ▲ In list view, click the triangle next to the folder icon so that the folder's contents are hidden.
  - ▲ In list view or icon view, click the Exit Folder button above the main clip area (**Figure 4.38**). The button looks and works like the Up One Level button in Windows XP.

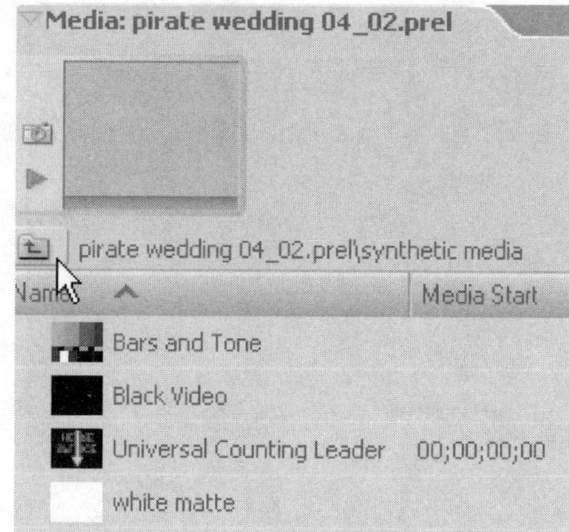

Figure 4.38 In list view or icon view, click the folder navigation icon to navigate up one level in the folder hierarchy.

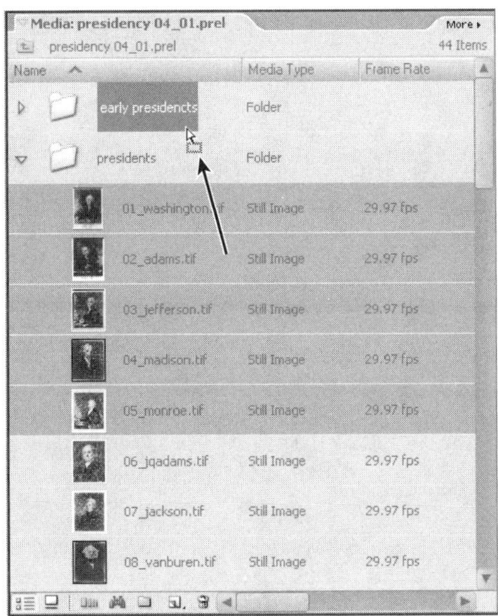

Figure 4.39 Dragging selected items into a folder...

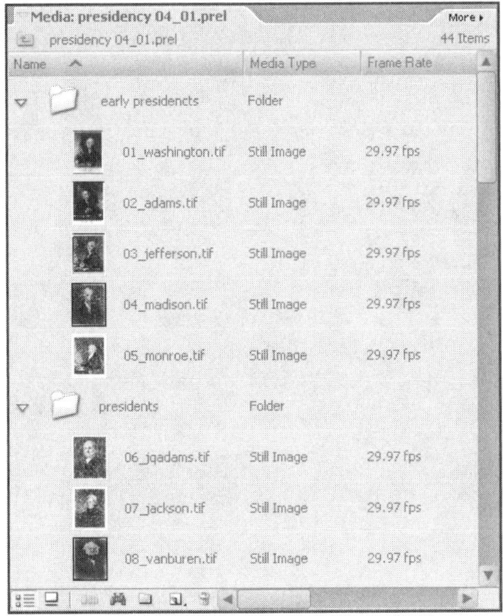

Figure 4.40 ...moves them into that folder.

To move items into a folder:

1. In list view or icon view, make sure the clips you want to move and the destination folder are both visible in the Media panel's main clip area.
2. Select one or more items.
3. Drag the selected items to another folder (**Figure 4.39**).

   The items are moved into the destination folder (**Figure 4.40**).

To move items out of a folder in list view:

1. Set the Media panel to list view.
2. Click the triangle next to a folder to expand the folder and view its contents.
3. Select the items you want to remove from the folder.
4. Drag the selected items down to an empty part of the main clip area (**Figure 4.41**).

   When you release the mouse, the selected items are moved out of the folder and placed one level up in the folder hierarchy (**Figure 4.42**).

Figure 4.41 When you drag items down to an empty part of the main clip area...

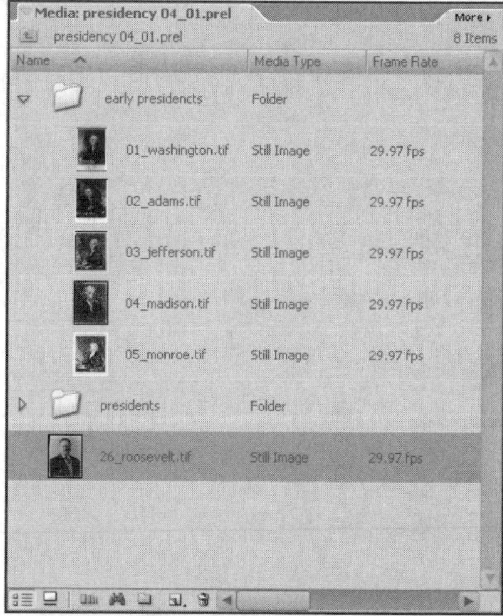

Figure 4.42 ...the selected items are moved out of the folder and placed one level up in the folder hierarchy.

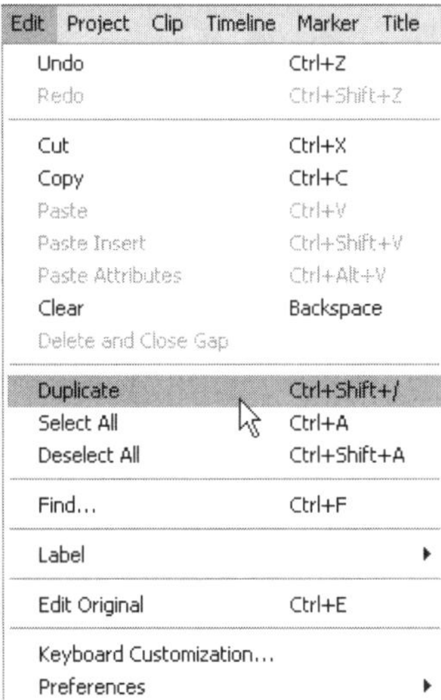

Figure 4.43 Choose Edit > Duplicate.

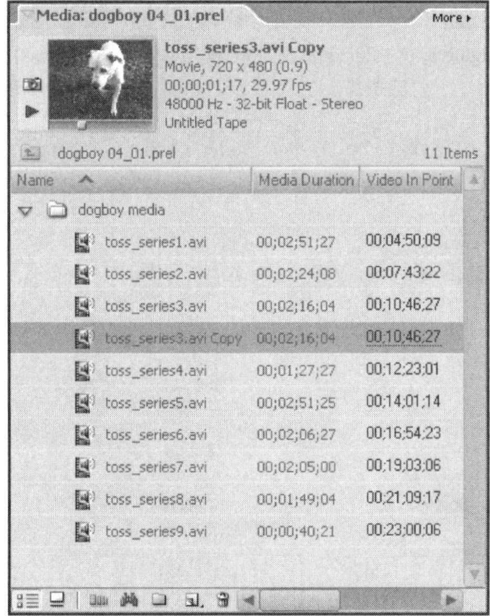

Figure 4.44 The duplicate uses the same name with Copy appended to it.

Duplicating and Copying Source Clips

You can duplicate any item in the Media panel. A duplicate item appears alongside the original, with *Copy* appended to its name.

Alternatively, you can use the cut, copy, and paste commands. This method is useful when you want to replicate a clip in a different folder. A pasted clip uses the same name as the original.

To duplicate clips:

1. Select one or more clips.
2. Choose Edit > Duplicate (**Figure 4.43**).

   A duplicate clip appears in the Media panel. It uses the name of the source clip with the word *Copy* appended to it (**Figure 4.44**).

To copy and paste clips:

1. Select one or more clips (**Figure 4.45**).
2. *Do either of the following:*
   ▲ Choose Edit > Cut.
   ▲ Choose Edit > Copy (**Figure 4.46**).
3. View the destination in the main clip area of the Media panel.
   If necessary, open the destination folder.

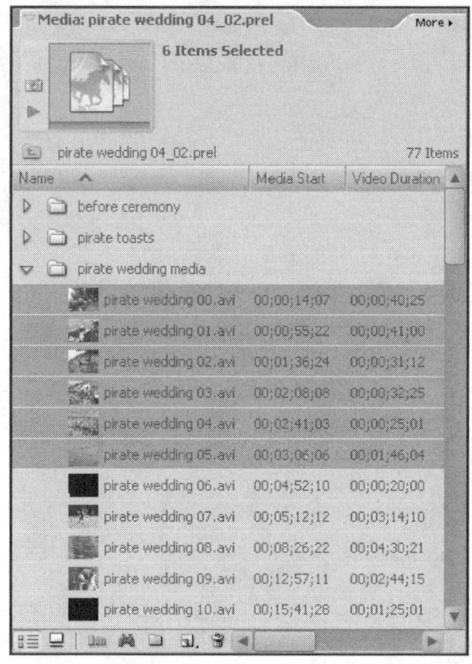

Figure 4.45 Select one or more clips in the Media panel.

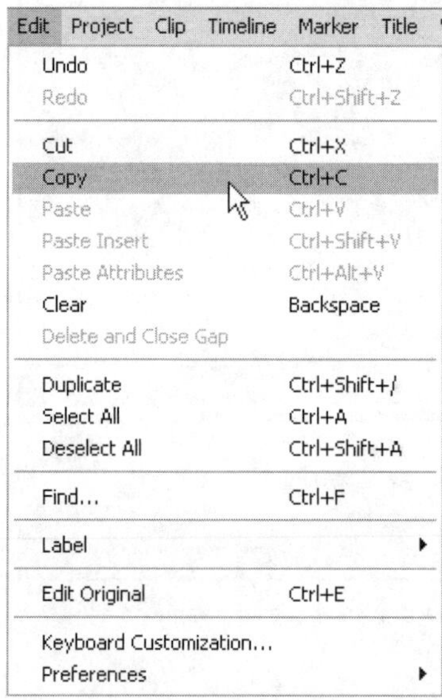

Figure 4.46 Choose Edit > Copy.

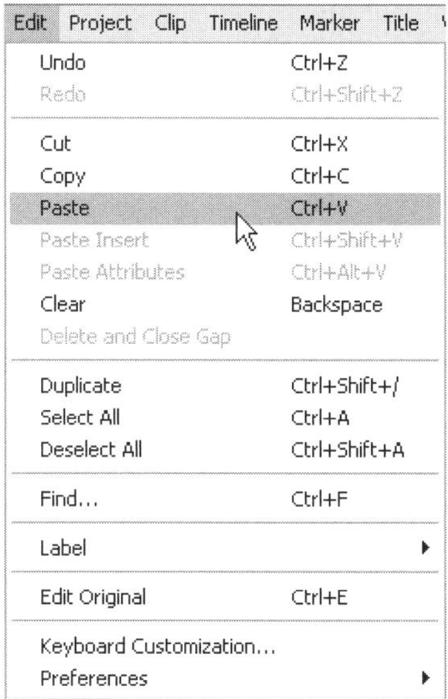

Figure 4.47 Navigate to a destination in the Media panel, and choose Edit > Paste.

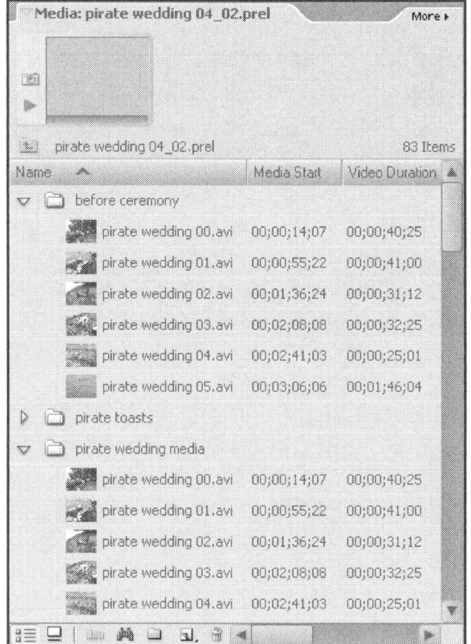

Figure 4.48 The pasted item uses the same name as the original.

4. Choose Edit > Paste (**Figure 4.47**).

   A duplicate of the clip appears in the selected destination. The clip uses exactly the same name as the original (**Figure 4.48**).

Using Duplicate Clips

In most cases, there's no need to copy a clip; you can add the same clip to any sequence again and again (changing its starting point and ending point each time, if you want). However, on some occasions, you may want the same clip listed more than once. For example, you might want to interpret each copy of a clip differently, such as ignoring the alpha channel for one and not the other (see "Interpreting Footage," later in this chapter). More commonly, you might make a copy for organizational purposes. For example, you could copy a lengthy clip to make it easier to work with. This way, you could give each copy its own name and keep them cued to the appropriate section. In addition, copies let you use parts of the same clip more than once in the Media panel, which could facilitate creating a storyboard and adding clips to the timeline all at once or by using the Create Slideshow command (see Chapter 5).

Although you might think of clip copies as *subclips*, they're full-fledged clips in their own right. Remember, each clip in the Media panel refers to a media file. A duplicate clip refers to the same media file; it isn't dependent on another clip. So, deleting one copy of a clip has no effect on other copies. (But, of course, deleting a source clip does delete any instance of that clip in the timeline.) In addition, clip copies access the same full range of source media; you can't limit them to a shorter segment.

Renaming Clips

After you import a file as a clip, you shouldn't rename the file on your hard disk. Doing so will ruin your project's reference to the file, and Premiere Elements won't be able to locate the file the next time you open the project (see the section, "Locating Missing and Offline Files" in Chapter 2, "Starting a Project"). Nevertheless, you may still need to identify a clip by another name. Fortunately, you can rename a clip in a project for the purposes of editing. Renaming the clip doesn't affect the source file's name or interfere with your project's references.

To rename a clip:

1. Select a clip.
2. *Do either of the following:*
   - ▲ Click the clip's name, and then click it again (don't double-click).
   - ▲ In the Media panel's More pull-down menu, choose Rename (**Figure 4.49**).

   The clip's name becomes highlighted.
3. Enter a new name (**Figure 4.50**).
4. Press Enter, or click away from the clip.

   The clip takes another name in the project. The source file on the drive isn't renamed, however.

✔ Tip

- If you want to know the original name of a renamed clip, you can right-click the clip and choose Properties from the menu. In the Properties panel, look at the File Path to discover the source media file's name, which is the default name of the clip.

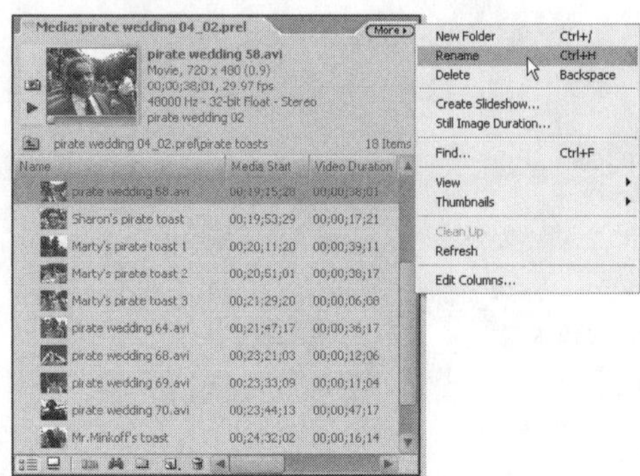

Figure 4.49 Choose Rename in the Media panel's More pull-down menu.

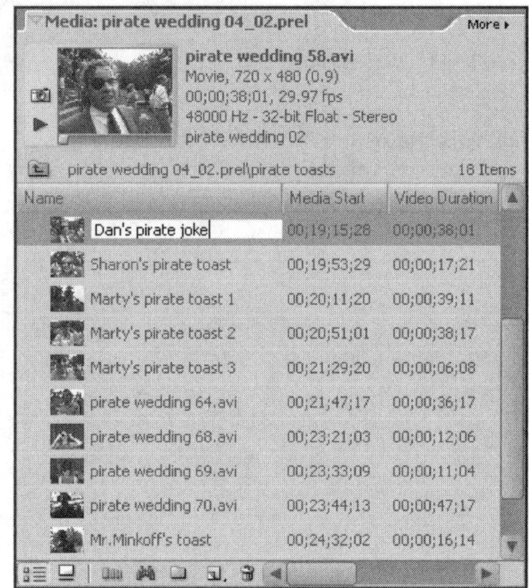

Figure 4.50 Enter a new name for the clip.

Figure 4.51 In the Media panel, click the Find button.

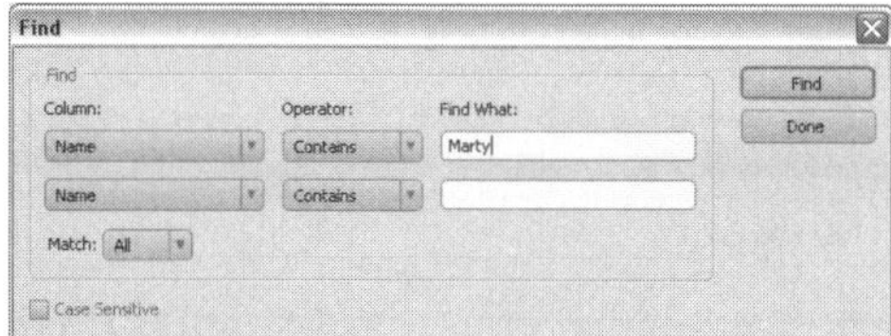

Figure 4.52 In the Find dialog box, enter search criteria.

Figure 4.53 If a clip meets your criteria, it's selected in the Media panel.

Finding Clips

Even the most organized person can lose track of a clip, particularly when a project contains a lot of clips. Here's how to find one from the Media panel.

To find a clip:

1. In the Media panel, click the Find button (**Figure 4.51**).

   The Find dialog box appears. It contains two lines of search criteria (**Figure 4.52**).
2. From the Column pull-down menu, choose a category by which to search.

   Find options match the columns of the Media panel's list view.
3. From the Operator pull-down menu, choose a limiting option.
4. In the Find What field, enter search content.
5. To narrow the search, specify another column, another operator, and more search content in the next line.
6. For Match, choose an option:
   - ▲ All
   - ▲ Any
7. To find only items that match the capitalization of the item you're searching for, select Case Sensitive.
8. Click Find.

   If a clip meets your criteria, it's selected in the Media panel (**Figure 4.53**).
9. To search for other clips that meet the search criteria, click Find again.

   If an additional clip meets your criteria, it's selected in the Media panel.
10. Repeat step 9 until you find the clip you're searching for or finish searching.
11. Click Done to close the Find dialog box.

Interpreting Footage

In most cases, Premiere Elements correctly *interprets* imported clips, accurately processing characteristics such as frame rate, pixel aspect ratio, and alpha channel. Nevertheless, sometimes you must override Premiere Elements' assessment and specify how these characteristics should be interpreted.

For example, a still image sequence may be designed to play back at a particular frame rate that you need to set. Or, an imported still image may appear distorted—a sure sign that its pixel aspect ratio (PAR) hasn't been interpreted correctly (see the sidebar "PAR Excellence," in Chapter 3, "Capturing and Adding Footage"). Finally, you may need to manually specify how to handle a clip's alpha channel. In these situations, use the Interpret Footage command to set things right. As usual, Premiere Elements doesn't alter the source media file; it just *processes* it differently.

Figure 4.54 Select a clip and choose File > Interpret Footage.

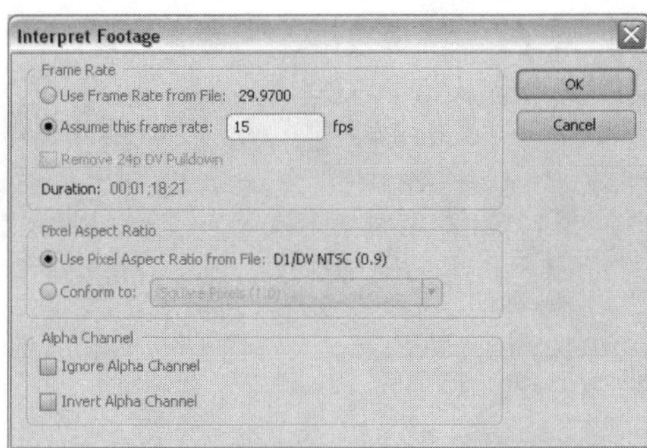

Figure 4.55 To use a frame rate different from that of the file, select "Assume this frame rate" and enter the rate expressed in frames per second.

To set the frame rate of a clip:

1. Select a clip, and choose File > Interpret Footage (**Figure 4.54**).

   An Interpret Footage dialog box appears.

2. Select an option:

   "Use Frame Rate from File"—To use the file's inherent frame rate

   "Assume this frame rate"—To enter a frame rate for the footage (**Figure 4.55**)

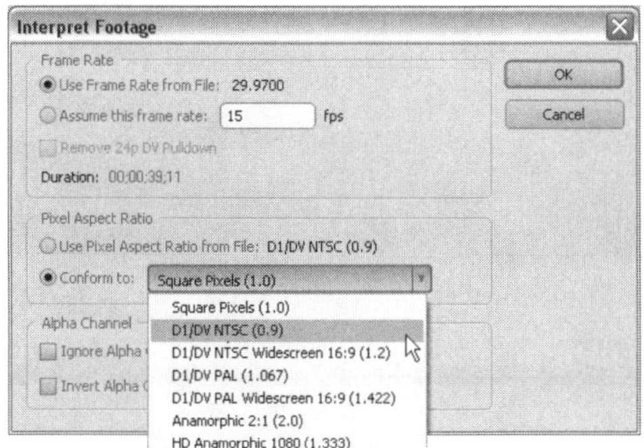

Figure 4.56 To change the PAR, select "Conform to" and select an option from the drop-down menu.

Figure 4.57 In the Interpret Footage dialog box, select whether to ignore or invert the clip's alpha channel.

To set the pixel aspect ratio of a clip:

1. Select a clip, and choose File > Interpret Footage.

   An Interpret Footage dialog box appears.

2. In the Pixel Aspect Ratio area of the Interpret Footage dialog box, select an option:

   "Use Pixel Aspect Ratio from File"—To use Premiere Elements' automatic interpretation of the file's PAR

   "Conform to"—To select an alternative PAR from a drop-down menu (**Figure 4.56**)

To ignore or invert a clip's alpha channel:

1. Select a clip, and choose File > Interpret Footage.

   An Interpret Footage dialog box appears.

2. In the Alpha Channel area of the Interpret Footage dialog box, select the options you want (**Figure 4.57**):

   Ignore Alpha Channel—To disregard the clip's alpha channel so that it doesn't define transparent areas when the clip is added to video track 2 and higher

   Invert Alpha Channel—To reverse the transparent and opaque areas defined by the clip's alpha channel

✔ Tips

- If you need more information about a clip than the Media panel provides, you can view detailed information by selecting the clip and choosing File > Get Properties For > Selection.
- For more information about superimposing clips, see Chapter 10, "Adding Effects."

Locating Files for Offline Items

By now, you should appreciate the relationship between the clips listed in the Media panel and source files on the hard disk. You know, for example, that deleting a clip doesn't remove the source file from the hard disk and, conversely, that deleting a source file results in clips with missing references.

Fortunately, Premiere Elements lets you restore the link between an offline clip and its source file at any time.

To locate missing media:

1. In the Media panel, select one or more offline clips (**Figure 4.58**).
2. Choose Project > Locate Media (**Figure 4.59**).

   An Attach Which Media to *clipname* dialog box appears.
3. Find and select the media file you want to attach to the clip, and click Select (**Figure 4.60**).

   If you selected more than one clip, Premiere Elements automatically relinks the other clips to matching media files in the same location.
4. Repeat step 3 for clips with media in other locations on the hard disk.

   When you've finished relinking clips and media, the dialog box closes. In the Media panel, the selected clip's icon indicates that it's linked to media. Make sure you resave the project in order to reestablish the locations of source files and avoid warnings about missing media the next time you open the project.

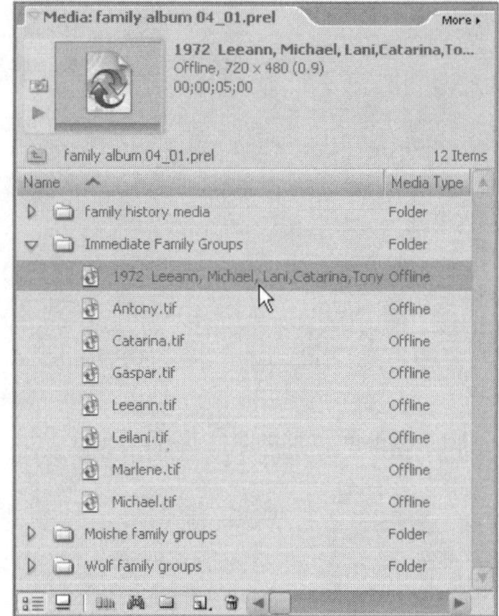

Figure 4.58 In the Media panel, select one or more offline clips...

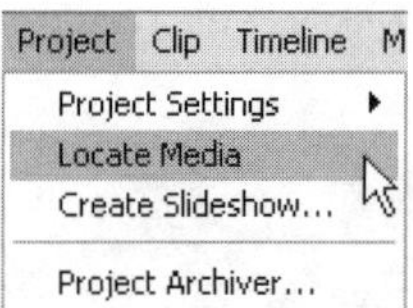

Figure 4.59 ...and choose Project > Locate Media.

Figure 4.60 In the Attach Which Media to clipname dialog box, find and select the media file you want to attach to the clip and click Select.

5 Editing Clips into a Sequence

You may have heard film editing referred to as *cutting* or *joining*. Before the days of digital video, strips of film were cut and spliced. The term you prefer might say something about your attitude toward editing. Literally speaking, of course, editing involves both cutting *and* joining clips.

Editing can be reduced to two simple tasks: defining the part of the clip you want to use, and adding it to a particular point in the sequence. To define the parts of the clip you want to use, you'll learn how to use the Monitor panel to view clips and set *edit marks*—important points in the clip, including where you want it to start and end. To assemble the clips into a sequence, you'll learn how to drag and drop clips to the timeline or employ an automated method. Keep this simple two-step model in mind as you progress through the tasks in this chapter. Sometimes, the number of choices can make the process seem more complex than it really is.

This chapter takes you through the *rough cut*—a relatively complete but still crude version of your final movie. The next chapter covers how to rearrange and adjust clips in the timeline, fine-tuning the sequence into what's known as the *fine cut*. In later chapters, you'll learn how to add transitions, titles, and special effects. But for now, concentrate on the heart of editing: cutting and joining.

Summarizing the Chapter

The first part of this chapter focuses on using the Monitor panel to view clips. With these features under your belt, you'll be prepared for the next part: using the Monitor panel to edit clips and add them to the sequence in the Timeline panel.

Viewing clips

The next several sections of the chapter are as follows:

Using the Monitor Panel explains two aspects of the Monitor panel: Clip view and Timeline view.

Viewing Clips in the Monitor Panel explains how to open clips for editing.

Opening Audio Clips explains unique characteristics of audio clips.

Using Playback Controls explains how to play and scan through clips.

Cuing the Monitor Panel Numerically explains how to find a frame by entering its timecode number.

Using the Monitor Panel's Time Ruler explains how to navigate through clips and the sequence using specialized controls.

Changing the Magnification explains how to change the size of the image in the monitor panel.

Adding clips to the timeline

The remaining sections are as follows:

Comparing Editing Methods explains the difference between manual and automatic ways to add clips to the timeline.

Setting In and Out Points explains how to define a clip's starting and ending points.

Setting Clip Markers explains how to tag other important frames in a clip.

Comparing Overlay and Insert Edits explains two ways that adding clips affect clips already in the timeline.

Adding Clips by Dragging explains how to add clips to the sequence manually.

Adding Clips to the Timeline Automatically explains how to use a command to add selected clips to the sequence automatically.

Figure 5.1 The Monitor panel toggles between Clip view, which shows the content of individual clips...

Using the Monitor Panel

The Monitor panel works like two panels in one. Buttons at the top indicate which mode, or *view*, the panel is in:

Clip view shows and controls the playback of individual clips (**Figure 5.1**). Double-clicking a clip in the Media panel opens the clip in the Monitor panel, switching it to Clip view automatically. This way, you can set the clip's starting and ending frames before adding it to the sequence in the Timeline panel. Similarly, double-clicking a clip already in the Timeline panel opens it in Clip view so you can change the clip's starting and ending points. Clip view also includes a button to tag important frames with a reference marker and a button that exports the current frame as a still-image file.

Opening Source Clips and Clip Instances

When you open a clip from the Media panel, you're opening a *source* clip. As you'll soon see, you open a source clip to view and edit it before adding it to the sequence in the timeline.

Each time you add a source clip to the sequence, you create a new *instance* of the source clip, also called a *sequence clip*. Opening a *clip instance* allows you to view that particular use of the clip in Monitor panel's clip view, and any edits you make are instantly reflected in the Timeline panel. But although you can always shorten a clip in the sequence this way, you can't always lengthen it: Subsequent clips may be in the way. Fortunately, there are numerous (and usually better) ways to edit sequence clips directly in the Timeline panel (instead of in clip view).

In this chapter, focus on opening source clips before adding them to the timeline. To fine-tune the clips in the sequence, use techniques covered in Chapter 6.

Timeline view shows and controls the playback of the edited sequence in the Timeline panel (**Figure 5.2**). The current time of the Timeline view directly corresponds with the current time of the Timeline panel; change one, and the other changes accordingly. Selecting the Timeline panel switches the Monitor panel to Timeline view automatically. The same playback controls found in the Clip view help you play back and cue the current frame of the edited sequence. In addition, buttons cue the current frame to cuts in the sequence—that is, to the points between clips. The Timeline view's Marker button tags important frames in the edited sequence (and has a corresponding button in the Timeline panel). Similarly, the Timeline view's Export Frame button exports the current frame of the sequence.

Figure 5.2 ...and Timeline view, which shows the edited sequence in the Timeline panel. Here you can see that a title has been superimposed over the clip in the timeline.

This chapter focuses on using the Clip view of the Monitor panel; Chapter 6, "Editing in the Timeline," explains using the Timeline view in more detail.

✔ Tip

- The Export Frame feature is covered in Chapter 11, "Export."

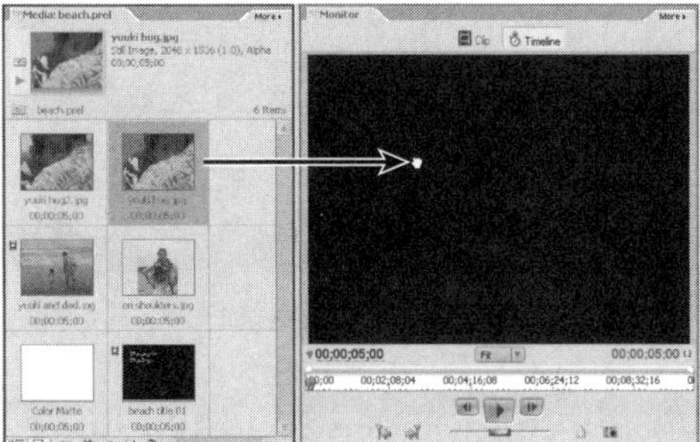

Figure 5.3 Double-click a clip or drag it to the Monitor panel, as shown here.

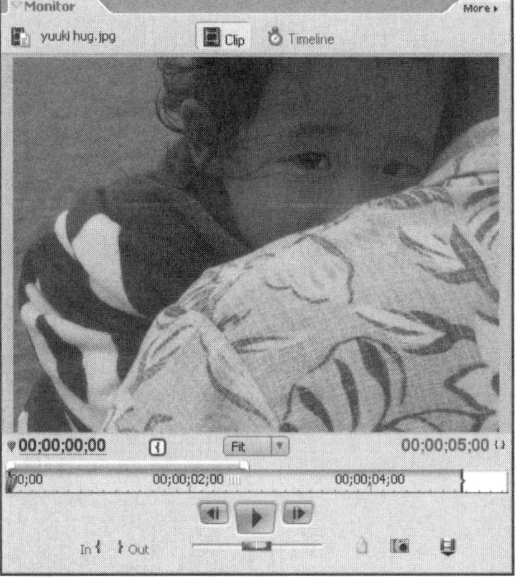

Figure 5.4 The clip appears in the Monitor panel, which toggles to Clip view automatically.

Viewing Clips in the Monitor Panel

When you open any kind of clip—a movie, a still image, or audio—it appears in the Clip view of the Monitor panel, where you can play it back and mark frames for editing.

To open a clip in the Clip view:

◆ *Do either of the following:*

▲ Double-click a clip in a Media panel, the thumbnail viewer, or the Timeline panel.

▲ Drag a clip from the Media panel or the thumbnail viewer into the Monitor panel (**Figure 5.3**).

The clip's image or audio waveform appears in the Clip view of the Monitor panel (**Figure 5.4**).

Opening Audio Clips

The source view works the same for audio clips as for movie clips—except that instead of showing the current frame of video, it depicts the audio as a *waveform*—a kind of graph of the audio's power over time. Monophonic tracks appear as a single waveform; stereophonic tracks appear as two waveforms (**Figures 5.5** and **5.6**). Often, you can identify particular sounds by examining the audio waveform. Powerful beats in a song are depicted as spikes in the waveform; silence or pauses between lines of dialogue result in flat horizontal lines in the waveform.

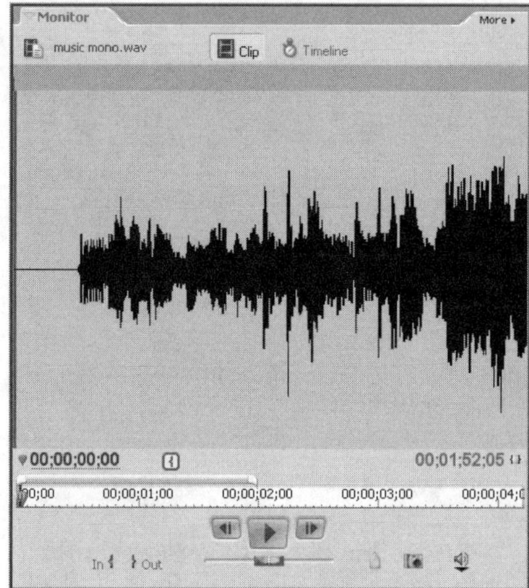

Figure 5.5 In the Monitor panel, monophonic audio clips appear as a single waveform...

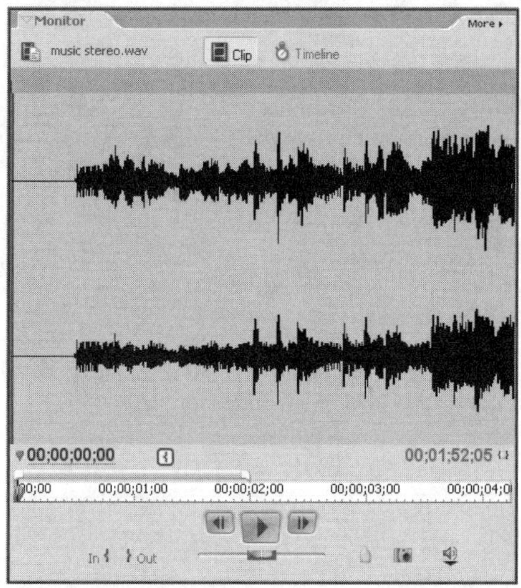

Figure 5.6 ...whereas stereophonic clips appear as a dual waveform.

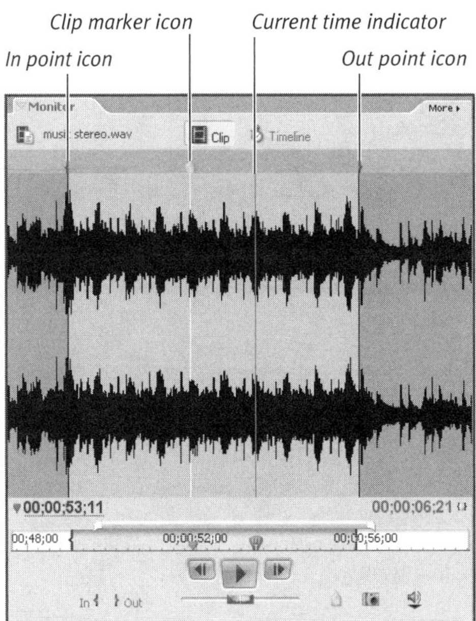

Figure 5.7 In addition to a waveform, the clip view shows other information for audio clips differently than it does for video.

Because the waveform depicts audio over a span of time (as opposed to a single video frame), the source view can display other information as well. A vertical line indicates the current time—the position of the playback head, if you will. In addition, icons for clip markers and In and Out points appear at the top of the source view, with vertical lines extending from them to help you see their positions in terms of the waveform. Furthermore, the area between the current In and Out points is shaded lighter so you can see your selection as well as hear it (**Figure 5.7**). (See the section "Setting In and Out Points," later in this chapter.)

To view the audio waveform of an audio/video clip:

1. Open a clip containing video and audio in the Monitor panel's Clip view.
2. Click the Toggle Source Tracks button until the Take Audio icon appears (**Figure 5.8**).

   The audio waveform linked to the video file appears in the image area of the source view (**Figure 5.9**).

✔ Tip

- If you add a clip to the Timeline panel with the Take Audio icon selected, only the clip's audio track is added to the sequence. To add both tracks, make sure the Take Both icon is selected before adding the clip.

Figure 5.8 Clicking the Toggle Source Tracks button...

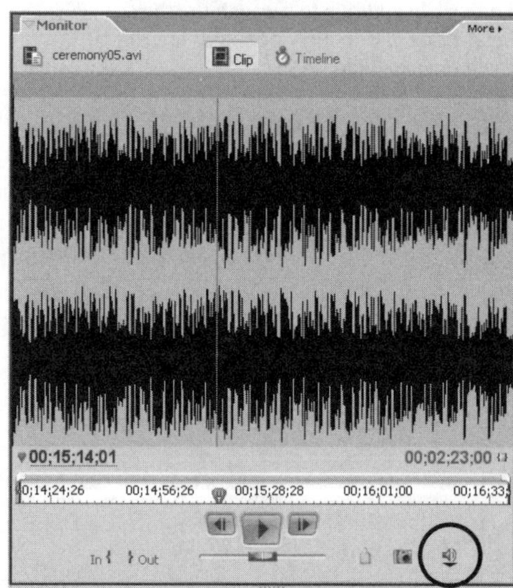

Figure 5.9 ...to the Take Audio icon allows you to see the waveform of a linked clip's (a clip containing video and audio) audio track.

Tracks

Video and audio are often described as discrete *tracks* of information due to the way they're physically stored on traditional media, such as magnetic tape. Digital files don't encode video and audio the same way tape does, of course. Nevertheless, it's helpful to think of video and audio as occupying tracks that you can manipulate separately.

Using Playback Controls

Whether you're playing back a clip in the Clip view or an edited sequence in the Timeline view, the basic playback controls work the same.

Most playback controls also have preset keyboard shortcuts, which are well worth learning. Before you use keyboard playback controls, however, be sure you first select the proper view of the Monitor panel.

Also bear in mind that the Timeline view of the Monitor panel corresponds to the sequence in the Timeline panel. As you change the current time in the Monitor panel's timeline view, watch how it affects the current time indicator in the Timeline panel (and vice versa). The same keyboard playback commands that work for the timeline view also work when the Timeline panel is selected.

To use the playback controls:

- Below the image in the Clip view and Timeline view, choose the appropriate playback control (**Figure 5.10**):

  Play/Pause plays the clip or sequence until it reaches the last frame. Click the control again to stop playback. The icon toggles accordingly.

  Frame advance moves the current view one frame forward in time.

  Frame back moves the current view one frame back.

  Shuttle scans through the clip or sequence more quickly, the further you drag the control from its center position; drag left to scan in reverse, and drag right to scan forward. Releasing the control returns it to its center position and stops playback.

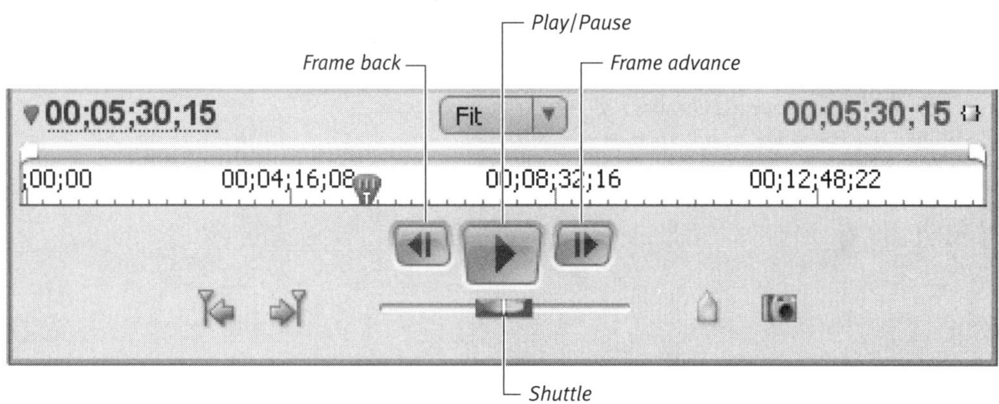

Figure 5.10 Most playback controls work the same in the Clip view and Timeline view (shown here).

To use keyboard shortcuts to control playback:

1. Make sure the appropriate view is active.
2. *Do one of the following* (**Table 5.1**):
   - ▲ To play in reverse, press J.
   - ▲ To stop playback, press K.
   - ▲ To play forward, press L.
   - ▲ To increase playback speed, press J or L again.
   - ▲ To play forward slowly, press Shift-L.
   - ▲ To play in reverse slowly, press Shift-J.
   - ▲ To toggle play and stop, press the spacebar.

✔ Tips

- ■ The J-K-L keyboard combination is worth getting used to. In Chapter 6, you'll see how you can use J-K-L along with other keyboard shortcuts for speedy keyboard-based editing. This keyboard combination has become standard in several popular editing programs. You can think of J-K-L as the home keys of nonlinear editing.
- ■ If you use a mouse with a scroll wheel, you can use the wheel to advance or reverse frames in the active view of the Monitor panel.

Table 5.1

Default Keyboard Shortcuts for Playback

Action	Result
Press L	Play
Press K	Pause
Press J	Play in reverse
Press J or L repeatedly	Increase speed (Clips play at 2x, 3x, and then 4x normal speed.)
Press Shift-J or Shift-L repeatedly	Play slowly (Clips play at .1x and then .2x normal speed.)

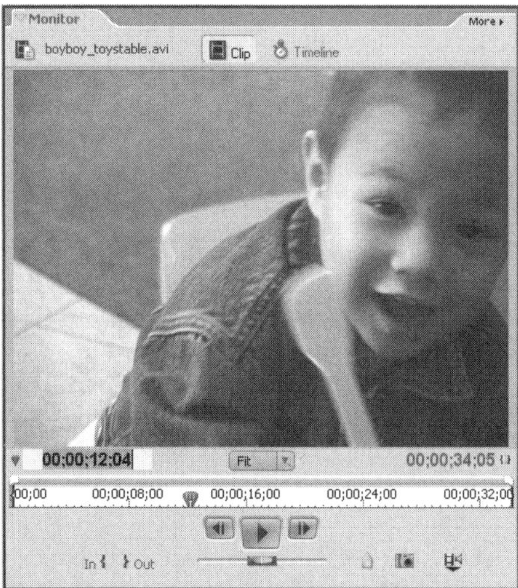

Figure 5.11 Click a view's current time display to highlight the number.

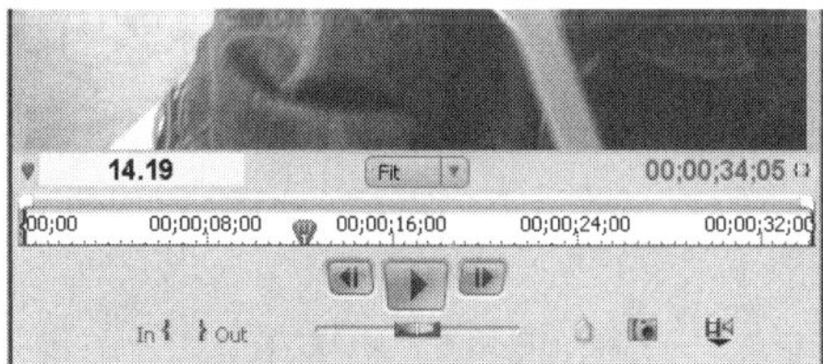

Figure 5.12 Type a valid timecode number, and press Enter...

Figure 5.13 ...and the view cues to that frame.

Cuing the Monitor Panel Numerically

You can use the time displays to cue the Clip and Timeline views to a particular frame number or *absolute time*. Or, you can cue to a *relative time*—in other words, add frames to or subtract frames from the current time. Like most user-defined values in Premiere Elements and other Adobe products, the time display is *scrubbable*—that is, you can adjust the value by dragging on the number.

To cue the view to an absolute time:

1. Click the current time display for a view to highlight the number (**Figure 5.11**).
2. Enter the number of the frame that you want to view, and press Enter (**Figure 5.12**).

   As long as the frame number you entered exists, the view displays that frame (**Figure 5.13**).

Entering Frame Values

Any duration number that you enter in Premiere Elements has a *threshold* of 100. That is, numbers 99 and below are interpreted as frames. Numbers 100 and above are expressed in the units of the selected time display. In a project that uses an NTSC timecode display; for example, the number 99 is interpreted as 99 frames, or 3 seconds and 9 frames; the number 100 is interpreted as seconds and frames, or 1 second and 00 frames.

To cue the view to a relative time:

1. Click the current time display for a view to highlight the number.
2. Type a plus (+) or a minus (–) sign and a number (**Figure 5.14**).

   To cue the clip 30 frames after the current frame, for example, type `+30`. To cue the view 60 frames before the current frame, type `-60`.

To cue the view by scrubbing the current time:

- Do either of the following:
  - Drag the current time display to the right to increase the number and advance the current time (**Figure 5.15**).
  - Drag the current time display to the left to decrease the number and reverse the current time.

✔ Tips

- You can highlight individual numbers in the current-time readout and change them to cue the current frame of the view.
- If the time you enter in the current-time readout doesn't exist, the view is cued to the nearest available frame—either the first or the last frame of the clip or sequence.

Figure 5.14 Here, the time display is set to cue the current time 60 frames forward.

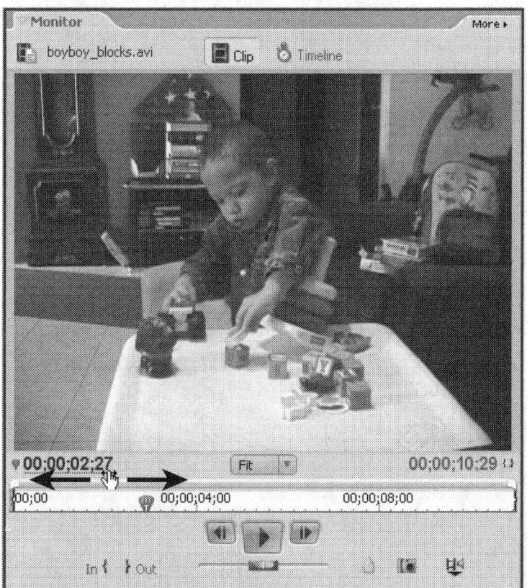

Figure 5.15 You can also drag the current time display to change its value. This is true for underlined values in all of Adobe's software.

Using the Monitor Panel's Time Ruler

Each view of the Monitor panel includes a *time ruler*, consisting of tick marks and timecode numbers. The time ruler not only measures time but also provides another way to navigate through a clip or sequence (**Figure 5.16**). The full width of the ruler represents the entire length of the clip in the Clip view or the entire length of a sequence in the Timeline view. The frame displayed in the view corresponds to a blue triangular marker in the ruler called the *current time indicator (CTI)*. Each time ruler also displays icons for its corresponding view's markers and In and Out points. You can move the current time, markers, and In and Out points by dragging the appropriate icon in the time ruler.

Just above each time ruler is a thin bar with curved ends, called the *viewing area bar*. By changing the width of the viewing area bar, you can control the scale of the time ruler. Expanding the bar to its maximum width reveals the entire span of its time ruler, and contracting the bar zooms into the ruler for a more detailed view. Dragging the center of the bar scrolls through the time ruler without changing its scale.

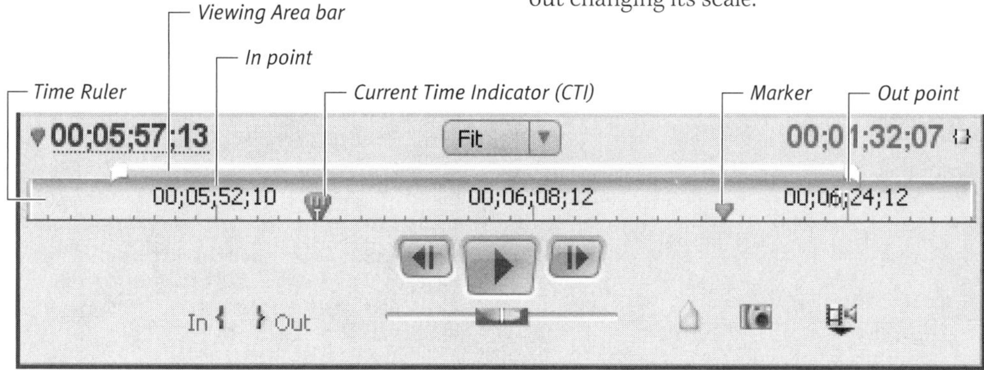

Figure 5.16 A time ruler in each view provides another way to navigate through a clip or sequence.

To view the time ruler in more or less detail:

- *Do either of the following:*
  - ▲ To show the view's time ruler in more detail, drag the ends of the viewing area bar closer together (**Figures 5.17** and **5.18**).
  - ▲ To show more of the view's time ruler, drag the ends of the viewing area bar farther apart.

  Dragging one end of the viewing area bar scales the bar from its center.

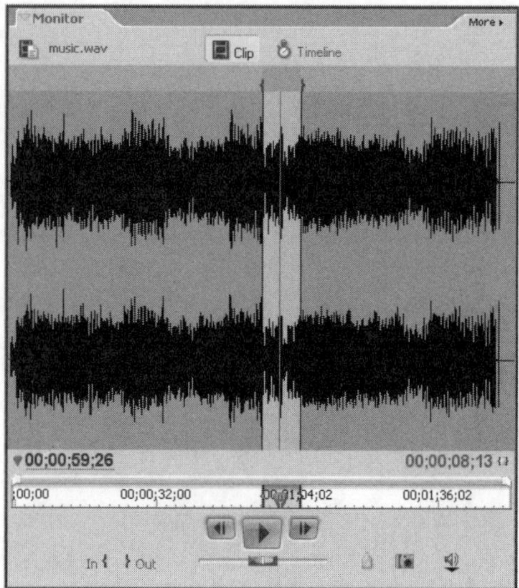

Figure 5.17 Here, the viewing area bar is set to show the full span of time. Note how the tick marks and icons appear at the current scale.

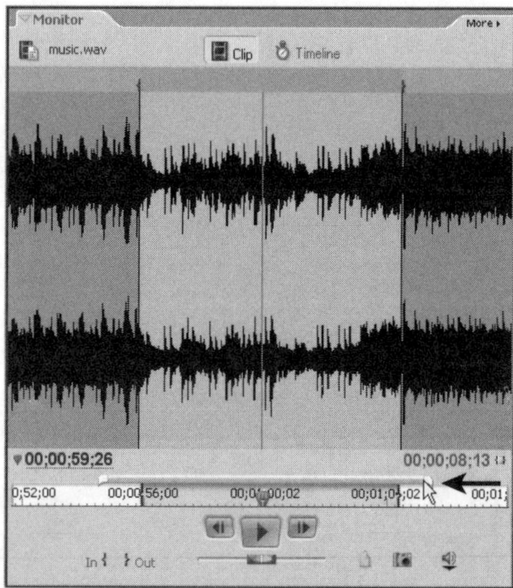

Figure 5.18 To view the ruler in more detail, drag the ends of the viewing area bar closer together. Again, note how the tick marks and icons look at the new scale.

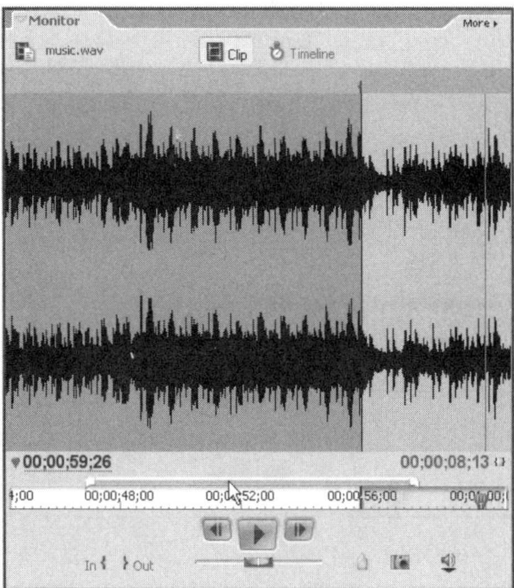

Figure 5.19 Drag the viewing area bar from the center to view a different part of the time ruler.

Figure 5.20 To set the current time, click the time ruler or drag the CTI.

To change the visible area of a view's time ruler:

- Drag the center of the viewing area bar to the left to see an earlier part of the time ruler or to the right to see a later part (**Figure 5.19**).

To set the current time in a time ruler:

- *Do either of the following:*
  - Click the time ruler to cue the current time.
  - Drag the blue CTI (**Figure 5.20**).

Changing the Magnification

Whatever size you make the Monitor panel, the video in each view automatically scales to fit in the available space. However, you can see the video in more detail by increasing a view's *magnification setting*. Alternatively, you can decrease the magnification setting to reduce the image relative to the pasteboard area around it—in order to adjust motion effects more easily, for example. The magnification setting is for viewing purposes only; it doesn't alter the video's appearance for output or change the source file in any way.

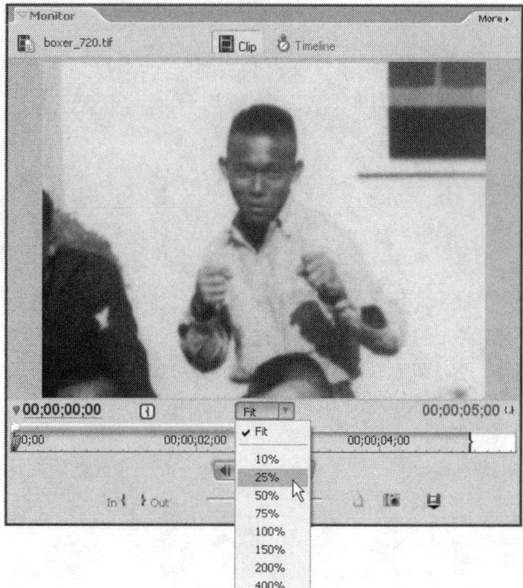

Figure 5.21 To magnify a view, choose a magnification setting from the pull-down menu.

To set the view's magnification:

- Under the source or timeline view's video image, click the magnification button, and choose an option from the pull-down menu:
  - ▲ To fit in the available area of the view, choose Fit.
  - ▲ To magnify the view, choose a percentage value (**Figure 5.21**).

Figure 5.22 Here, the image is reduced in order to adjust motion effects more easily.

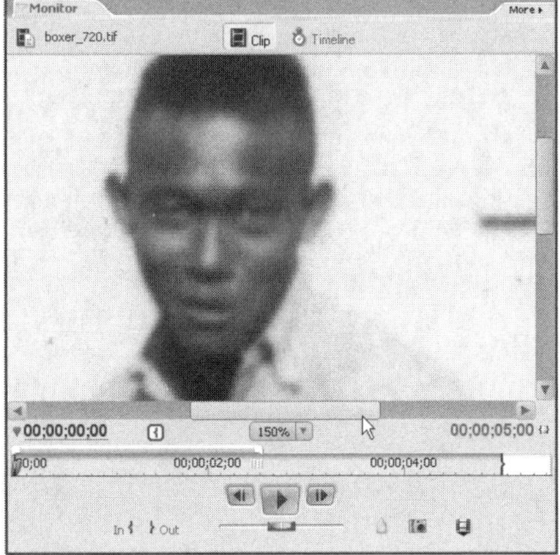

Figure 5.23 Scroll bars appear when a clip's magnified image doesn't fit in the confines of the Monitor panel.

Increasing the magnification setting zooms into the video image; using a lower magnification setting reduces the image relative to the view's pasteboard area (**Figure 5.22**).

Scroll bars appear when you magnify the view over 100%. You can use them to navigate around the view (**Figure 5.23**).

Comparing Editing Methods

You can add clips to a sequence in two ways. You can drag them to the Timeline panel and assemble a sequence in a manner akin to splicing film (albeit much faster). Alternatively, you can use the Media panel to plan the sequence in storyboard fashion, and have Premiere Elements execute your plan automatically. Or you can combine the two methods.

Drag-and-drop editing

The drag-and-drop method takes advantage of the computer's ability to display clips as objects that you can move and place using the mouse (**Figure 5.24**). You'll find that dragging and dropping clips to the timeline is both intuitive and reassuringly similar to the way the operating system works. Moreover, you can apply the same principles and techniques to refine and rearrange clips in the Timeline panel (fully explained in Chapter 6, "Editing in the Timeline").

Figure 5.24 Using the drag-and-drop method, you drag a clip from the Media panel or the Clip view (shown here) to the sequence in the Timeline panel.

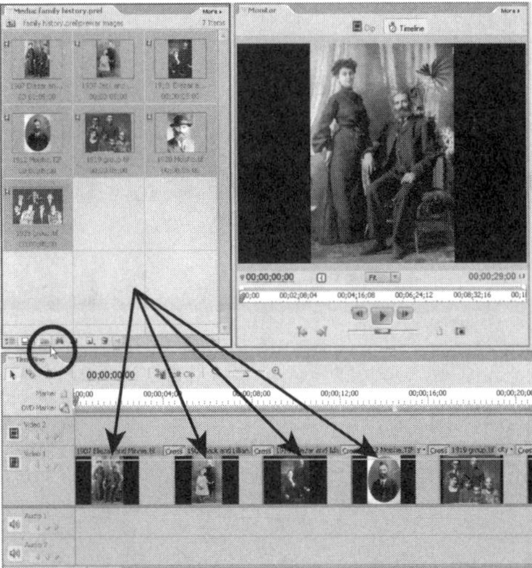

Figure 5.25 You can use the Create Slideshow command to quickly assemble clips—stills or audio/video clips—into a sequence automatically.

Automatic editing

Instead of adding clips to the timeline shot by shot, you can assemble an entire sequence automatically. As you saw in Chapter 3, "Capturing and Adding Footage," you can set the Capture panel to add each shot you capture to the Timeline panel, one after the other. Alternatively, you can create a rough cut according to how you've arranged the items in the Media panel—a technique often called *storyboard editing*. With the Media panel set to icon view, you can arrange the clips in storyboard fashion and use the Create Slideshow command to assemble them into a sequence (**Figure 5.25**). You can even have Premiere Elements apply a default transition between video and audio clips.

Even though the name Create Slideshow suggests this feature is designed for creating a sequence of still images, it works for video and audio as well. If your footage lends itself to storyboarding, this method provides a fast way to generate a rough cut. It's also well suited to people who prefer a storyboard's visual layout.

Setting In and Out Points

Setting In points and Out points is central to all editing. An *In point* is where you want the clip to start playing, and an *Out point* is where you want the clip to stop playing. The length of time between the In and Out points is called the *duration*.

When you edit, you start by setting the In and Out points for the clips to add them to the sequence in the timeline. The sections in this chapter focus on this part of the editing process.

Once a clip is in the sequence, you can rearrange and readjust its In and Out points. Chapter 6 explains how to refine the sequence this way.

To mark In and Out points:

1. Open a clip in the Monitor panel's Clip view.
2. Cue the current time to the frame where you want the clip to start, and click the Set In Point button In { or press I (**Figure 5.26**).

   An In point icon { appears at the CTI in the view's time ruler.
3. Cue the current time to the frame where you want the clip to end, and click the Set Out Point button } Out or press O (**Figure 5.27**).

   An Out point icon } appears at the CTI in the view's time ruler. In the view's time ruler, the area between the In point and Out point is shaded.

Figure 5.26 Cue to the starting frame, and click the Set In Point button.

Figure 5.27 Cue to the ending frame, and click the Set Out Point button.

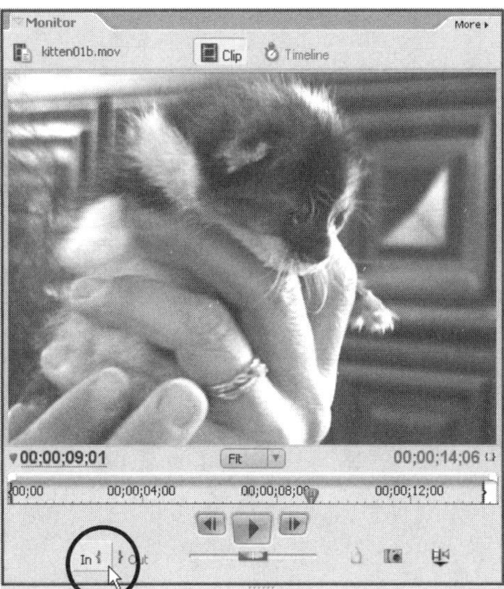

Figure 5.28 To clear an In or Out point, Alt-click the Set In Point (shown here) or Set Out Point button. In this figure, note how the In point set in Figure 5.26 has been removed, setting it back to the beginning of the clip media. (The CTI is still cued to the old In point.)

To clear an In or Out point:

- *Do any of the following:*
  - ▲ To clear an In point, Alt-click the Set In Point button (**Figure 5.28**).
  - ▲ To clear an Out point, Alt-click the Set Out Point button.
  - ▲ To clear both the In and Out points, select the appropriate view and press G.

To change In and Out points in the Monitor panel's time ruler:

◆ In a view's time ruler, *do any of the following:*
  ▲ To change the In point, drag the In point icon (the mouse pointer becomes a trim head icon .
  ▲ To change the Out point, drag the Out point icon (the mouse pointer becomes a trim tail icon) (**Figure 5.29**).
  ▲ To change both the In and Out points without changing the duration, drag the textured area between the In and Out points (**Figure 5.30**). (When the mouse is over the textured area, the Hand tool appears; otherwise, clicking cues the CTI.)

Figure 5.29 You can change an In or Out point by dragging the appropriate icon directly in the view's time ruler. Here, the Out point is being dragged to a different time. Note how the mouse pointer changes.

Figure 5.30 To change both the In and Out points by the same amount (maintaining the duration), drag the textured area between the In and Out points. The Hand icon appears when the mouse is over the textured area.

✔ Tips

- When you use the source view to change the In or Out point of a clip that's already in the sequence, adjacent clips may prevent you from extending the duration. In this case, adjust the clip directly in the Timeline panel using techniques covered in Chapter 6, "Editing in the Timeline."
- You can set a linked clip's video In and Out points separately from its audio In and Out points. This technique, called a *split edit*, can be accomplished by choosing Marker > Set Clip Marker > and selecting the appropriate edit point. However, because it's usually more effective to create split edit points in the timeline, a full discussion will wait until Chapter 6.
- Remember the technique of dragging the textured area between the In and Out point icons for Chapter 6. When you open a sequence clip in the Monitor panel, you can use the technique to adjust its In and Out points without changing its duration or placement in the sequence. This is called a *slip edit*.

Setting Clip Markers

During the editing process, you often need a way to mark important points in time. *Markers* allow you to visibly stamp these points both in individual clips and in the sequence (**Figures 5.31** and **5.32**). Markers help you visually identify beats in a song, synchronize video with a sound effect, or note where a title should fade up.

In each clip and in each sequence, you can add up to 100 numbered and any number of unnumbered markers. You can cue the CTI to markers in the source view, the Timeline view, or Timeline panel.

When you add markers to a source clip, its markers are included with the clip when you add it to a sequence. The markers aren't added to instances of the clip that are already in sequences. This means that each instance of the clip has a unique set of markers that aren't subject to unintentional changes.

This section concentrates on using the clip view to add clip markers. You'll use similar controls in the Timeline view and Timeline panel to add timeline markers. But because timeline markers appear in the timeline's time ruler and have a few special features, they'll be discussed in the next chapter.

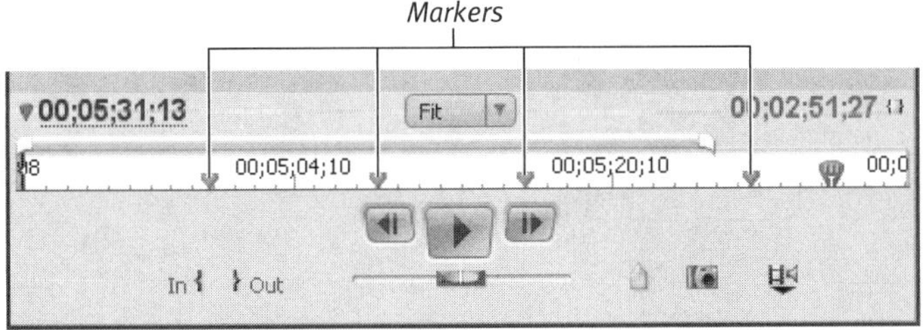

Figure 5.31 In the Monitor panel, clip markers appear in the Clip view's time ruler; sequence markers appear in the Timeline view's time ruler.

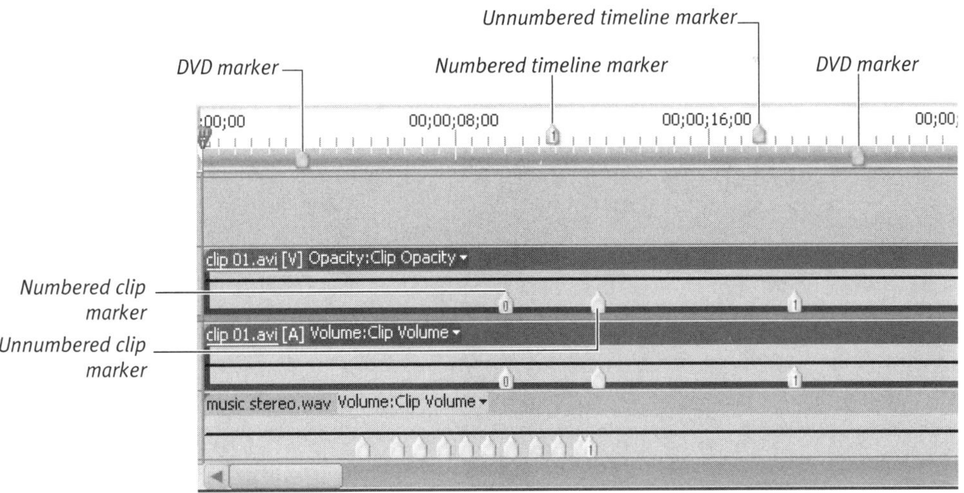

Figure 5.32 In the Timeline panel, clip markers appear in each clip; sequence markers appear in the sequence's time ruler.

To add an unnumbered clip marker in the Clip view:

1. Open a clip in the source view.
2. Cue the current frame to the point where you want to add a marker.
3. In the Monitor panel, click the Marker button (**Figure 5.33**).

   An unnumbered marker appears in the Clip view's time ruler. When the clip is added to a sequence, the marker also appears in the clip in the Timeline panel (provided the marker is between the clip's In and Out points).

Figure 5.33 In the Monitor panel, click the marker button.

To add numbered clip markers:

1. *Do either of the following:*
   - ▲ Open a clip in the Monitor panel's Clip view.
   - ▲ Select a clip in the Timeline panel.
2. *Do either of the following:*
   - ▲ For a clip in the source view, cue the CTI to the frame you want to mark.
   - ▲ For a selected clip in the Timeline panel, cue the CTI in the Timeline view of the Monitor or Timeline panel.
3. Choose Marker > Set Clip Marker, and choose either of the following (**Figure 5.34**):

   Next Available Numbered to mark the frame with the next consecutive number not already present in the clip. Skip to step 5.

   Other Numbered to mark the frame with the number of your choice.

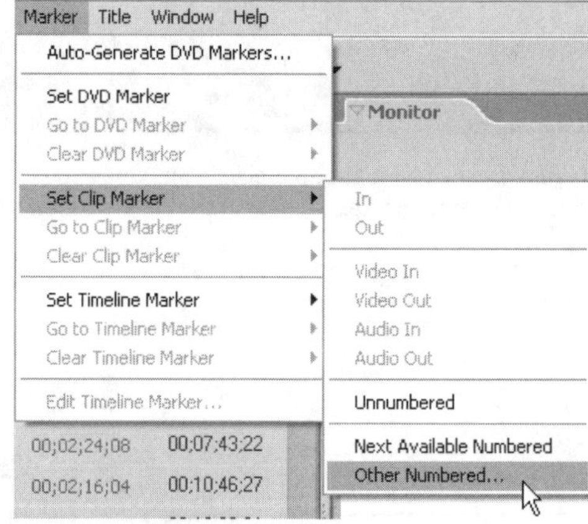

Figure 5.34 Choose Marker ⟶ Set Clip Marker, and choose an option. Here, Other Numbered is selected.

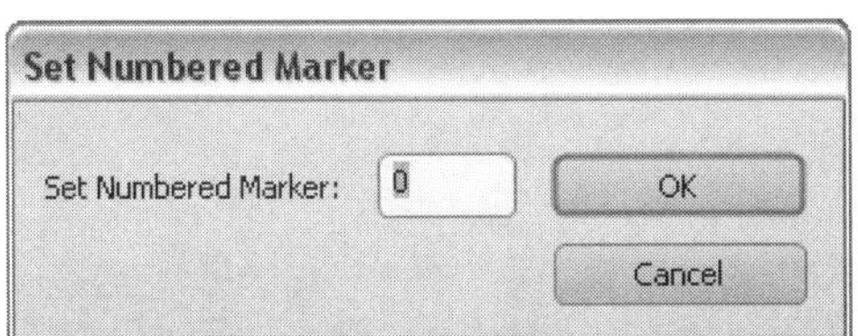

Figure 5.35 If you chose Other Numbered, a Set Numbered Marker dialog box appears. Enter the number, and click OK.

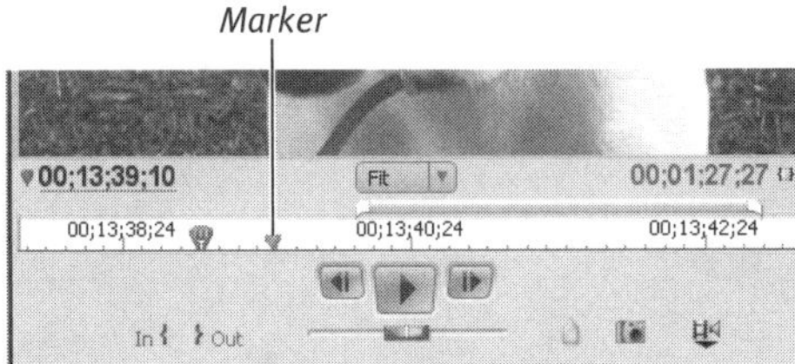

Figure 5.36 The marker you specified appears at the current time in the view's time ruler (here, the CTI has been moved aside so you can see the marker).

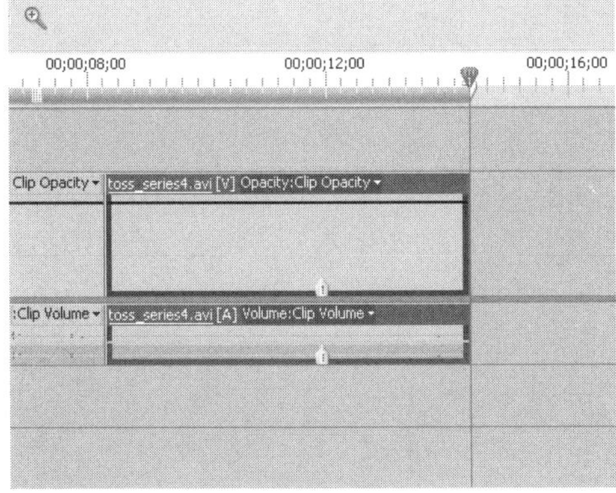

Figure 5.37 The clip marker appears with a number when added to the sequence in the Timeline panel.

4. Enter the number for the marker in the Set Numbered Marker dialog box, and click OK (**Figure 5.35**).
5. The marker you specified appears at the current time in the view's time ruler (**Figure 5.36**). In the Timeline panel, the clip marker's number is visible (**Figure 5.37**).

To add unnumbered clip markers on the fly:

1. Open a clip in the Monitor panel.
2. Play the clip.
3. Press the asterisk key (*) on the numeric keypad (not Shift-8 on the main keyboard).

   Each time you press the asterisk key, a marker appears in the source view's time ruler (**Figure 5.38**). If you opened a clip instance from a sequence, markers also appear in the clip as it appears in the Timeline panel.

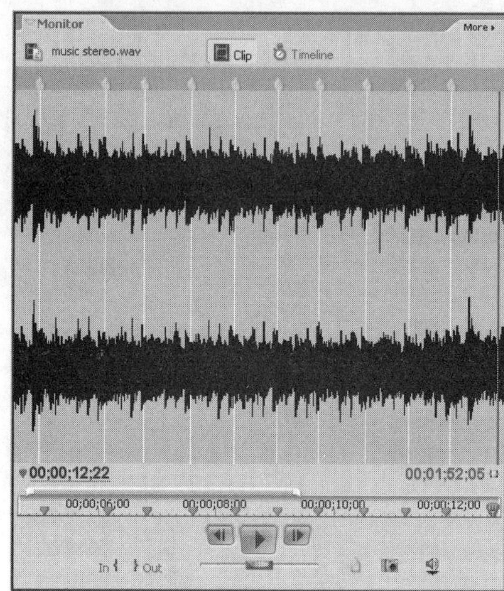

Figure 5.38 Each time you press the asterisk key (on the numeric keypad), an unnumbered marker appears. Here, the technique is being used to mark the beats of a music clip.

✔ Tips

- Applying a numbered marker to a different frame eliminates its original position.
- You can't set a marker on the same frame as an existing marker (the option appears dimmed in the menu). You must clear the marker first and then set the new marker.
- The 0 marker also has a special use with the frame-hold command. You may want to reserve the 0 marker for this purpose.

Cuing to and clearing edit marks

You can cue the CTI to any *edit mark*— In point, Out point, or marker—using menu commands. When the CTI is cued to an In or Out point, the corresponding icon appears under the image. Likewise, a marker icon appears when the CTI is on the same frame as a numbered or unnumbered marker. (The marker's number is only visible in the clip as viewed in the Timeline panel.)

Once the CTI is cued to an edit mark, a similar menu command can remove it from the clip. This method works best for clip markers, however; you can clear In and Out points more quickly by Alt-clicking (as explained in the section "Setting In and Out Points," earlier in this chapter).

This task focuses on cuing to and clearing edit marks in a clip, but you can use a similar procedure to cue to timeline markers.

To cue to any edit marks:

1. Open a clip in the Monitor panel's Clip view.
2. Choose Marker > Go to Clip Marker, and choose the appropriate option (**Figure 5.39**):

   Next cues the CTI to the clip marker later in time.

   Previous cues the CTI to the clip marker earlier in time.

   Video In cues the CTI to the clip's In point for its video track.

   Video Out cues the CTI to the clip's Out point for its video track.

   Audio In cues the CTI to the clip's In point for its audio track.

   Audio Out cues the CTI to the clip's Out point for its audio track.

   Numbered opens a Go to Numbered Marker dialog box.

   The CTI cues to the edit mark you specified. When the CTI is cued to an edit mark, the corresponding icon appears under the image in the Monitor panel (**Figure 5.40**).

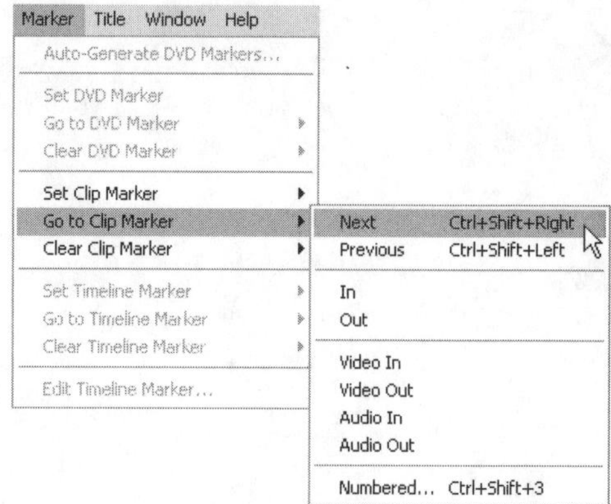

Figure 5.39 To cue the CTI to any edit mark, choose Marker > Go to Clip Marker, and select the mark you want.

Figure 5.40 When the CTI is cued to an edit mark, the corresponding icon—in this case, a clip marker icon—appears under the clip image.

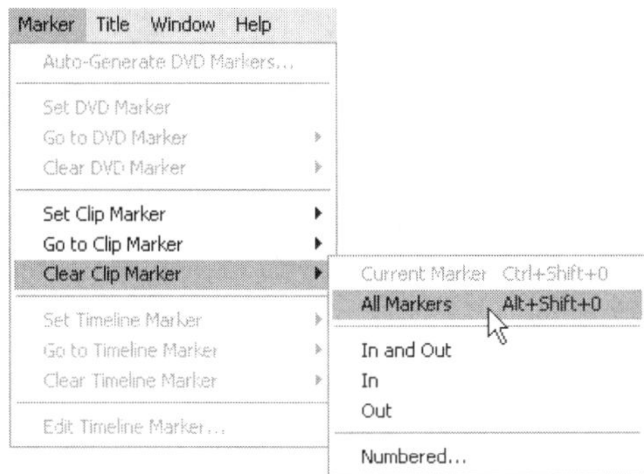

Figure 5.41 To clear all markers in the clip, choose Marker > Clear Clip Marker > All Markers.

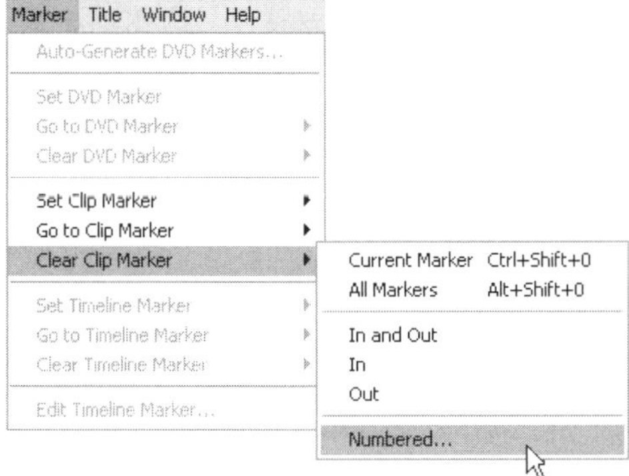

Figure 5.42 To clear a particular numbered marker, choose Marker > Clear Clip Marker > Numbered.

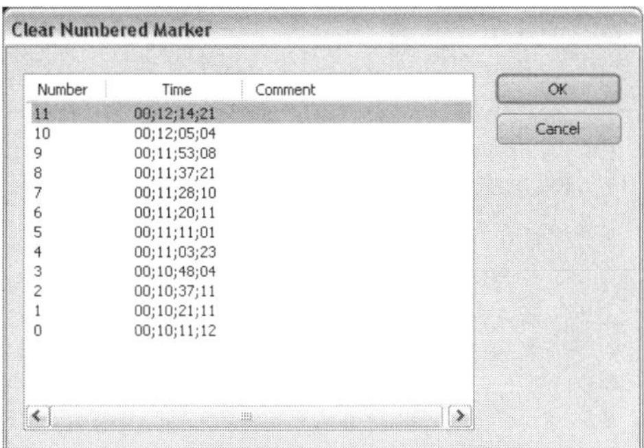

Figure 5.43 In the Clear Numbered Marker dialog box, select the marker you want to clear, and click OK.

To clear clip markers:

1. Open a clip in the Monitor panel's Clip view.
2. *Do either of the following:*
   - ▲ To clear a particular marker, cue the clip to a marker and choose Marker > Clear Clip Marker > Current Marker.
   - ▲ To clear all markers in the clip, choose Marker > Clear Clip Marker > All Markers (**Figure 5.41**).

   The clip markers you cleared disappear in the source view's time ruler (and in the Timeline panel, if the clip is in a sequence).

To clear specific numbered markers:

1. Open a clip in the source view.
2. Choose Marker > Clear Clip Marker > Numbered (**Figure 5.42**).

   A Clear Numbered Marker dialog box appears.
3. Select the marker you want to clear, and click OK (**Figure 5.43**).

   You may select only one marker at a time. The selected numbered marker disappears in the source view's time ruler (and in the Timeline panel, if the clip is in a sequence).

Comparing Overlay and Insert Edits

Whenever you add a clip to a sequence, you must determine how the new clip affects the clips already in the sequence. In particular, you must specify whether to replace material with an overlay edit or shift material with an insert edit.

An *insert edit* works much like adding a clip using film, inserting the new clip without removing material that is already in the program reel. When you *insert* a clip, the source clip is added at the designated point in the timeline, and subsequent clips are shifted later in time to make room for the new clip. If the insertion point in the sequence occurs at a point where clips already occupy the timeline, the clips in the timeline are split, and the portions after the edit are shifted later in time (**Figures 5.44** and **5.45**).

An *overlay edit* works like adding a clip using videotape, recording the new clip over any existing material on the master tape. When you *overlay* a clip, the source clip is added at the designated point in the timeline, replacing any material that was already there (**Figure 5.46**).

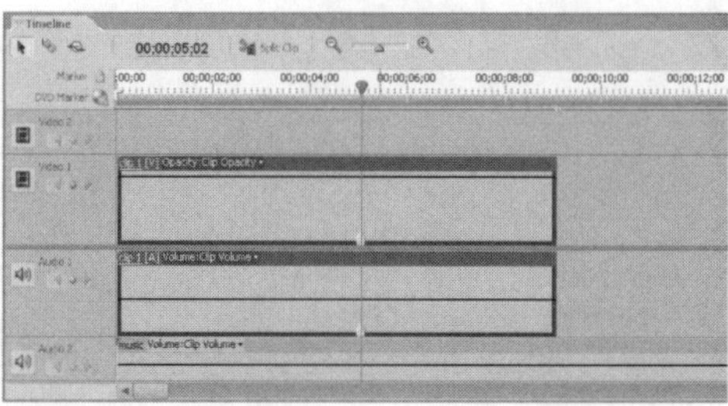

Figure 5.44 This figure shows a clip in a sequence. A new clip will be added, starting at the CTI (the vertical line).

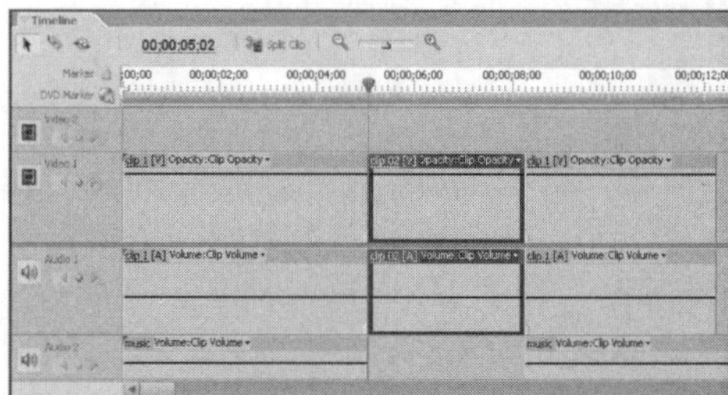

Figure 5.45 In an insert edit, everything after the edit point shifts forward in time to make room for the new material. If necessary, clips are split at the edit point.

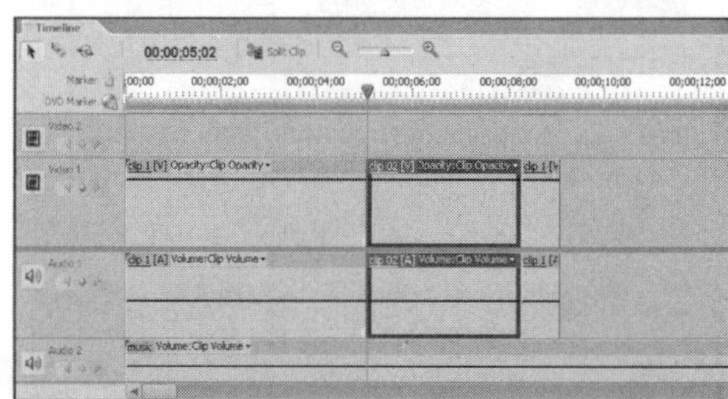

Figure 5.46 In an overlay edit, the new material replaces the old material.

Figure 5.47 In the Clip view, set In and Out points to define the part of the clip you want to add to the sequence.

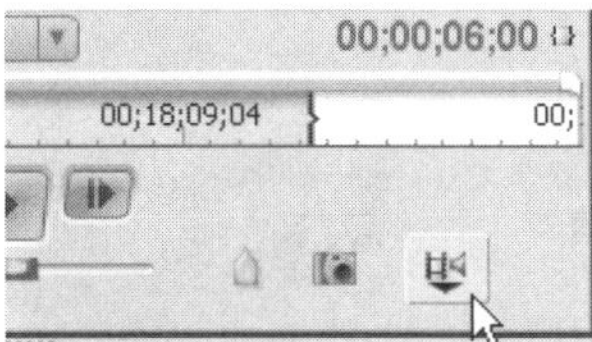

Figure 5.48 In the Clip view, click the toggle Take Audio and Video button to specify whether you want to use both video and audio...

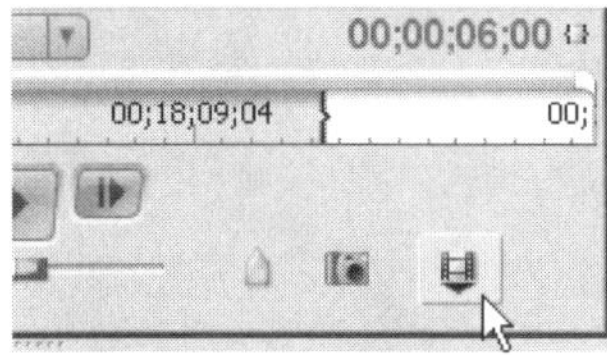

Figure 5.49 ...video only...

Figure 5.50 ...or audio only.

Adding Clips by Dragging

You can add a source clip to a sequence by dragging it to the appropriate track in the Timeline panel. Drag the clip from the Monitor panel's clip view if you want to set its edit marks (In point, Out point, markers) before adding it to a sequence. If you want to use the clip's most recent edit marks, you can drag it directly from the Media panel.

You can drag a linked clip (a clip containing both audio and video) to either a video or audio track. When you do, the video or audio components appear in a corresponding track. For example, dragging a clip to video 1 makes the linked audio appear in audio 1.

By default, clips tend to align with, or *snap* to, other clips in the sequence. As you drag a clip with snap on, a vertical line appears whenever In points, Out points, or markers align. This snapping behavior makes it easy to create a sequence without gaps between clips. For more on the snap feature, see Chapter 6.

To add a clip to a sequence by dragging:

1. Open a clip in the Monitor panel's Clip view.
2. Set the clip's In point and Out point (**Figure 5.47**).

   You may also want to set numbered or unnumbered markers. See "Setting Clip Markers," earlier in this chapter.
3. Click the toggle Take Audio and Video button so that it shows the icon for the source tracks you want:

   —Video and audio (**Figure 5.48**)

   —Video only (**Figure 5.49**)

   —Audio only (**Figure 5.50**)

continues on next page

If the source clip doesn't contain a track, the corresponding icon doesn't appear when you toggle the button.

4. Drag the clip from the Clip view to the appropriate track of the sequence in the Timeline panel, using one of the following methods:
   - ▲ To perform an insert edit, drag the clip so that the mouse pointer appears with the insert icon and arrows appear at the edit point in all tracks (**Figure 5.51**).
   - ▲ To perform an overlay edit, Ctrl-drag the clip so that the pointer appears with the overlay icon (**Figure 5.52**).

   A shaded area indicates where the clip will appear when you release the mouse.

Figure 5.51 To perform an insert edit, drag the clip to the track you want.

✔ Tips

- When you drag and drop a linked clip, be sure you're not inadvertently affecting material in one of the corresponding tracks. For example, if you only pay attention to where you're dragging the video, you might end up overwriting something in the audio track.
- To zoom into or out of a clip when you drag it to the timeline, continue to hold down the mouse button, and press the plus (+) key to zoom in or the hyphen (-) key to zoom out until you have zoomed as far as you want.
- You can also add one or more clips to the Timeline panel by dragging selected items directly from the Media panel (or by dragging a selected item's thumbnail in the Media panel's preview area). However, this method uses the In and Out points most recently set for the clips.

Figure 5.52 To perform an overlay edit, Ctrl-drag the clip to the track you want.

- You can change the speed of a clip after it's already in the timeline by using the Rate Stretch command or the Rate Stretch tool. For more information, see Chapter 6.
- You've lost sync between linked video and audio when a number appears before the clip's name in the Timeline panel. For now, use the Undo button to restore sync. To learn more about maintaining sync, see Chapter 6.

Overlay and Insert Keyboard Modifiers and Icons

As you gain experience editing in Premiere Elements, you'll notice a pattern in how you perform overlay and insert edits using the mouse: Insert edits are the default and never require a keyboard modifier; overlay edits are accomplished by pressing the Ctrl key. This is true not only when you add a new clip to a sequence but also when you rearrange clips already in a sequence (see Chapter 6, "Editing in the Timeline").

The editing conventions for overlay and insert edits are reinforced by visual feedback in the Timeline panel. When you perform overlay edits and insert edits with the mouse, a corresponding icon appears next to the mouse pointer (**Table 5.2**).

Similar icons are invoked when you move and rearrange clips by dragging them in the Timeline panel. You'll learn about that in Chapter 6, "Editing in the Timeline."

Table 5.2

Overlay and Insert Icons

Edit	Modifier	Icon
Insert (all tracks)	None	
Overlay	Ctrl	

Editing with the Home Keys, or Three-Finger Editing

As any typist will tell you, the basis for touch-typing is learning to keep your fingers over the home keys. Well, desktop editing programs have developed their own version of home keys: J, K, and L. Keeping one hand on your editing home keys and the other on the mouse is the secret to blazing-fast Monitor panel editing (**Figure 5.53**). This technique works in other popular editing programs as well. Learning it can produce joy and speed akin to typing 60 words per minute. But if you insist, you can use onscreen buttons for the equivalent of hunt-and-peck editing.

Figure 5.53 The home keys of editing. J plays in reverse; K pauses; and L plays forward. I sets the In point; O sets the Out point; a comma inserts the clip at the CTI; and a period overlays the clip at the CTI.

Adding Clips by Dragging

Adding Clips to the Timeline Automatically

Before shooting any footage, filmmakers usually create a *storyboard*—a series of sketches that depicts each shot in the finished program. Planning each shot in a storyboard can save you enormous amounts of time, money, and energy in production. In postproduction, you can use a similar storyboarding technique to plan a rough cut and instantly assemble it into a sequence, again saving time and energy.

As you learned in Chapter 3, "Capturing and Adding Footage," setting the Media panel to icon view allows you to arrange clips in a storyboard fashion. If you want, you can open the clips in the Monitor panel's clip view to set In and Out points, as well. Once your storyboard is complete, use the Create Slideshow command to assemble the selected clips into a sequence. You can also use it to add clips to a sequence according to the order in which you select them in the Media panel. Premiere Elements can even add the default video and audio transition between clips.

Although the name Create Slideshow implies that this feature was designed to assemble still images into a sequence, it works with any combination of still images, video, and audio clips.

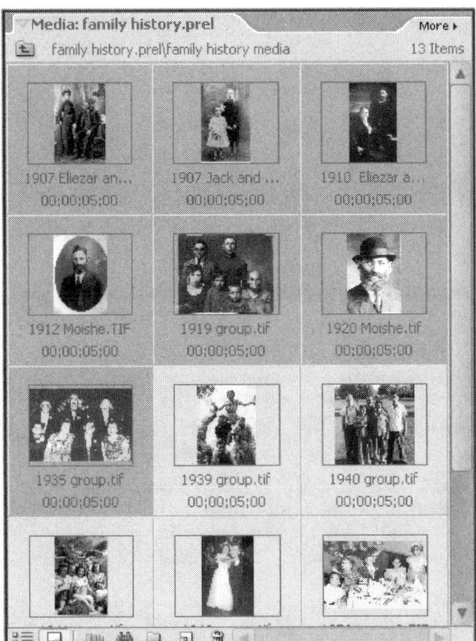

Figure 5.54 With the Media panel set to icon view, arrange the clips as in a storyboard, and select the ones you want to add to the sequence.

Figure 5.55 In the Media panel, click the Create Slideshow button.

To add clips using the Create Slideshow command:

1. In the Media panel, *do either of the following:*
   - ▲ Sort the clips in the order you want them to appear in the sequence (from left to right and top to bottom in icon view, or from top to bottom in list view), and select them (**Figure 5.54**).
   - ▲ Select the clips in the order you want them to appear in the sequence.
2. In the Media panel, click the Create Slideshow button (**Figure 5.55**).

   A Create Slideshow dialog box appears.

continues on next page

3. Choose an option from the Ordering pull-down menu (**Figure 5.56**):

   Sort Order arranges clips in the order in which they're sorted in the Media panel.

   Selection Order arranges clips in the order in which they're selected in the Media panel.

4. Specify which tracks of the selected clips you want to add to the timeline by choosing an option from the Media pull-down menu (**Figure 5.57**):

   Take Video and Audio

   Take Video Only

   Take Audio Only

   If none of the selected clips contain either video or audio, the corresponding option appears dimmed.

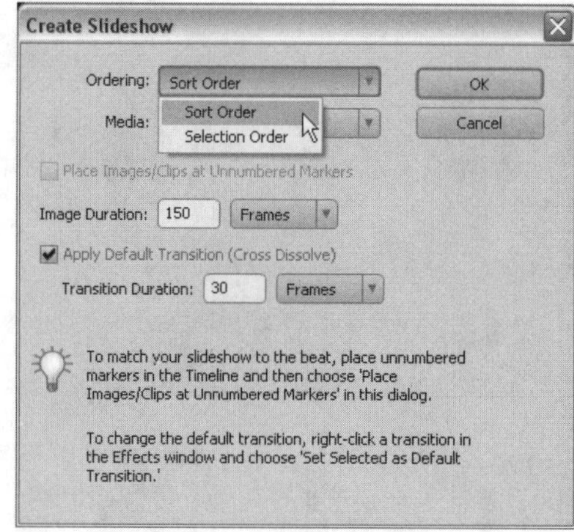

Figure 5.56 If you've arranged the clips in storyboard fashion, select Sort Order from the Sort Order pull-down menu.

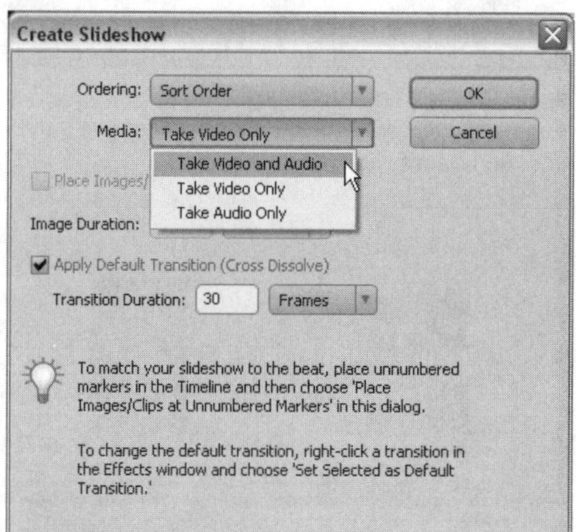

Figure 5.57 Specify the tracks of the selected clips you want to add.

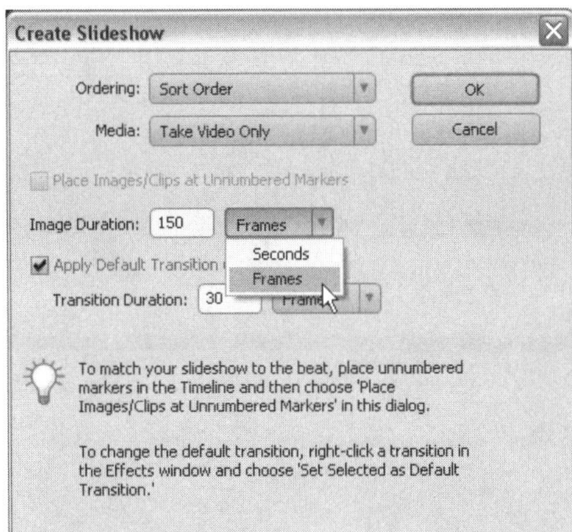

Figure 5.58 Specify the duration of the still images you're adding to the timeline.

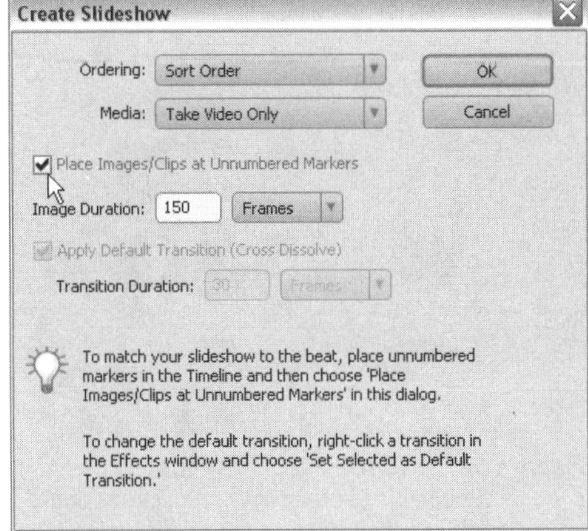

Figure 5.59 Selecting Place Images/Clips at Unnumbered Markers starts each clip at unnumbered markers in the timeline (a good way to cut shots to the beat of music).

5. To specify the duration of still images, enter a value for Image Duration and a unit of measurement in the corresponding pull-down menu (**Figure 5.58**).

   In NTSC projects, 30 frames are equivalent to 1 second.

6. Check either of the following options:

   Place Images/Clips at Unnumbered Markers places the beginning of each clip at an unnumbered timeline marker (**Figure 5.59**).

continues on next page

Apply Default Transition adds a transition between each clip (**Figure 5.60**). For more about setting the default transition, see Chapter 10, "Adding Effects."

7. If you checked Apply Default Transition in step 6, specify a value for the image or transition duration, and use the corresponding pull-down menu to specify the unit of measurement.
8. Click OK.
   The selected clips are added to the sequence beginning at the sequence's current time, according to the options you specified (**Figure 5.61**).

✔ Tips

- The Create Slideshow command always adds clips to video track 1 and audio track 1.
- If you have Photoshop Elements 3 (or later), you send one or more images directly to the current Premiere Elements timeline, using the equivalent of the Create Slideshow feature. In Photoshop Elements' Organizer, select the photos you want to add to the sequence and choose File > Send to Premiere Elements.

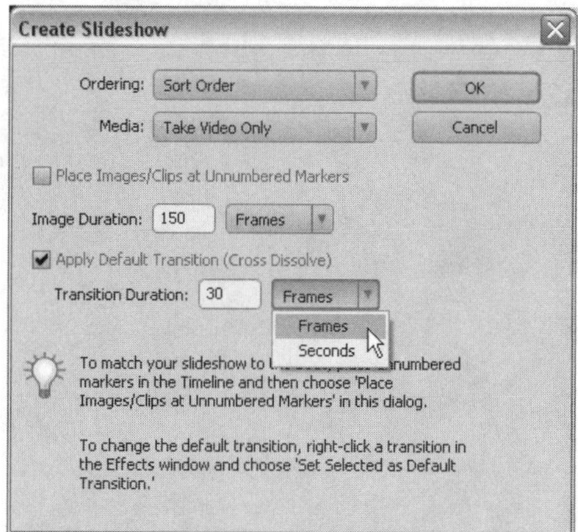

Figure 5.60 Selecting Apply Default Transition adds the default transition—a cross-dissolve or the transition you specify (as explained in Chapter 10)—between each clip automatically.

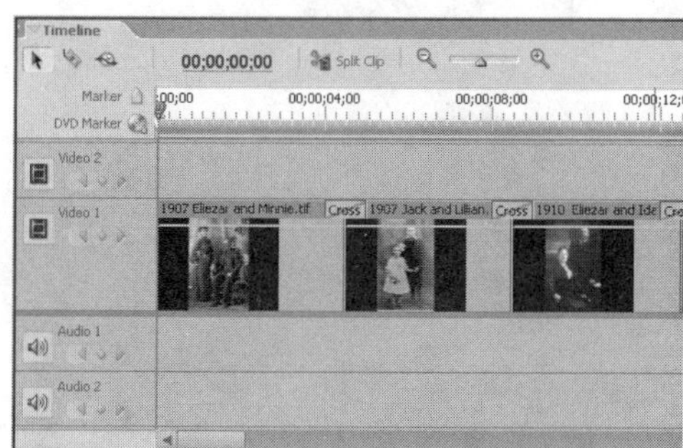

Figure 5.61 The selected clips are added to the sequence, beginning at the sequence's current time, and according to the options you specified. Here's a sequence of still images with cross-dissolves: a classic slideshow.

6

Editing in the Timeline

In the Timeline panel, the sequence looks a lot like edited film. Unlike film, however, the timeline allows you to view any segment of the sequence instantly or to view the entire sequence. The timeline isn't simply another way to look at or navigate through the sequence; it also gives you a way to edit. Editing in the timeline can feel almost as tactile as editing film but can be far more flexible and efficient than using razors and tape.

You'll start by concentrating on manipulating clips as discrete objects in the timeline. You'll learn how to select and group clips; move them; disable and delete them; split, copy, and paste them; and alter their playback speed. And just as you assembled the sequence using a combination of insert and overlay edits, you can rearrange and refine the clips in a sequence using comparable techniques—this time by dragging the sequence's clips in the Timeline panel. You'll further fine-tune edits by making adjustments to the In and Out points of the clips in the sequence—a process known as *trimming.*

In addition, this chapter covers techniques that deal with the connection between the audio and video components of linked clips. You'll learn how to override and break the link between video and audio so you can handle each component separately.

Summarizing the Chapter

Although this chapter is the lengthiest and covers numerous techniques, the sections fall into just three interrelated areas. As usual, you can progress through the chapter from beginning to end or jump to the sections you need.

Using the Timeline panel

The first part of the chapter includes these sections:

Viewing the Sequence explains how your sequence is displayed.

Customizing Track Views examines how to specify how video and audio clips appear in the timeline.

Resizing Tracks explores how to set the width of the tracks and their header, or label, area.

Adding, Deleting, and Renaming Tracks describes how to add, remove, and change the names of tracks in the timeline.

Getting Around the Timeline explains how to view clips in the sequence in more or less detail.

Playing the Sequence in the Timeline discusses how to play the sequence using controls in the timeline, and how to cue the CTI.

Using Sequence Markers explains how to mark important points in the sequence and add comments and links.

Manipulating clips in the timeline

The next part of the chapter includes these sections:

Understanding the Link Between Video and Audio explains how the video and audio components of linked clips are connected.

Selecting Clips in the Timeline examines how to select clips for editing purposes.

Cutting, Copying, and Pasting Clips describes how to use copy and paste functions with clips.

Removing Clips and Gaps from the Sequence explores how to clear clips and empty spaces from the sequence.

Enabling and Disabling Clips explains how to temporarily exclude a clip's contents from playback and export.

Grouping Clips describes how to treat multiple clips as a single clip.

Splitting Clips explains how to cut a clip into two separate clips.

Playing Clips at a Different Speed or in Reverse explores how to change a clip's playback speed, to create fast-motion, slow-motion, and reverse playback.

Creating a Freeze Frame explains how to use the Frame Hold command to create a freeze-frame effect.

Adjusting a Clip's Gain describes how to adjust the input audio levels manually and automatically using the Gain command.

Rearranging and trimming clips

The third part of the chapter includes these sections:

Using the Snapping Feature explains how the snapping feature helps you align clips, markers, and the CTI.

Editing by Dragging describes how to rearrange the order of clips in the timeline.

Understanding Trimming examines how adjusting clips' In and Out points works.

Trimming Clips in the Timeline explains how to adjust clips' In and Out points by dragging in the timeline.

Breaking and Creating Links explores how to disable the connection between the video and audio components of linked clips.

Keeping Sync describes how Premiere Elements indicates when linked video and audio are out of sync, and how to correct the problem.

Viewing the Sequence

As you saw in Chapter 5, "Editing Clips into a Sequence," you can view an edited sequence two ways: in the Monitor panel's Timeline view or in the Timeline panel. Before going any further, it's worthwhile to review the relationship between the two.

The Timeline view shows the frame at the current time, much as it would appear on a television display (**Figure 6.1**); the Timeline panel graphically represents all of the sequence's clips arranged in time (**Figure 6.2**). As you proceed through the chapter, bear in mind that you can cue the current time and control playback using either panel.

Figure 6.1 You can view a sequence in two ways. The Timeline view of the Monitor panel shows the frame at the current time, much as it would appear on a television...

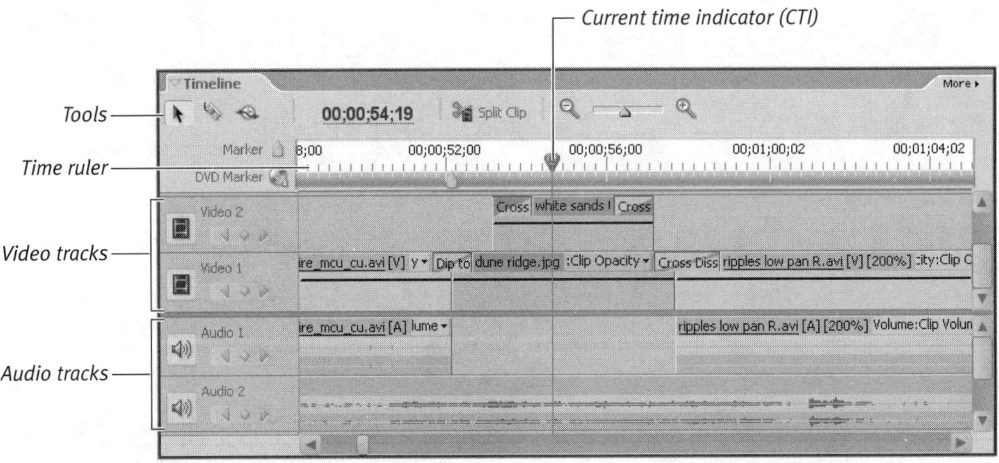

Figure 6.2 ...and the Timeline panel shows the edited sequence as clips arranged along a timeline.

Customizing Track Views

You can view the contents of each track in a sequence in more or less detail, according to your preferences or the task at hand.

In video tracks, each clip can appear as a bar (representing its duration) labeled with its name. Or, the clips in the track can contain *thumbnails*, small images taken from each clip's video content. Thumbnails can make it easier to identify each clip in the track. If you view the timeline in enough detail, thumbnails can even help you choose where to edit a clip. Similarly, you can set each audio track to show clips with or without a *waveform*, a kind of graph of the audio's power over time. Viewed in enough detail, it's possible to see particularly loud sounds as spikes in the waveform.

No matter what display style you choose, the clips in each track always contain a thin horizontal line. This line, sometimes called a *rubberband*, is used to control a clip's effects over time, such as a video clip's opacity, an audio clip's volume, or any special effect you add to a clip. See Chapter 10, "Adding Effects."

To set a video track's display style:

- Click a video track's display style button to toggle the appearance of clips in the track:

  Show Frames—Displays thumbnail images for each time unit in the clips in the track (the frequency of thumbnails depends on how closely you zoom into the timeline)

  Show Head and Tail—Displays a thumbnail image at the beginning and end of each clip in the track

  Show Head Only—Displays a thumbnail image at the beginning of each clip in the track

  Show Name Only—Displays the name of the clips in the track without thumbnail images

  The clips in the track use the display style you specify (**Figure 6.3**).

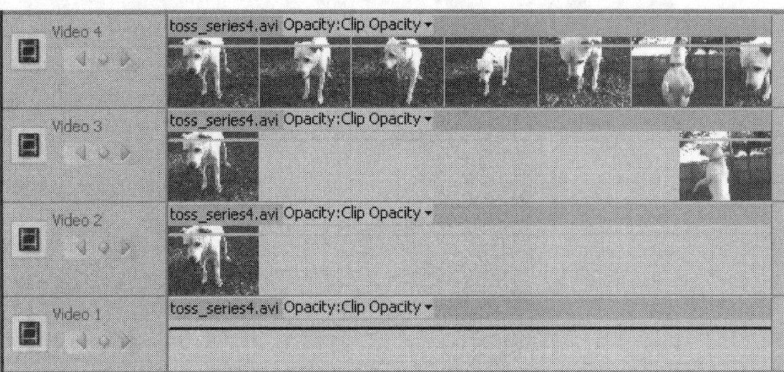

Figure 6.3 Each video track shown uses a different display style: (from top to bottom) Show Frames, Show Head and Tail, Show Head Only, and Show Name Only.

To set an audio track's display style:

- Click an audio track's display style button, to toggle the appearance of clips in the track:

  Show Waveforms—Displays an audio waveform for each clip in the track

  Show Name Only—Displays the name of the clips in the track without a waveform

  The clips in the track use the display style you specify (**Figure 6.4**).

✔ Tips

- When a track's display style is set to Show Name Only, its clips' rubberband (the horizontal graph of clip effects, such as opacity or volume) appears black; otherwise, the rubberband appears yellow.
- To maximize both screen space and performance, display only the information you need. Large icons and detailed track formats not only use up valuable screen space, they also take longer to display. Excessive detail can result in an overcrowded screen and slow scrolling in the timeline.

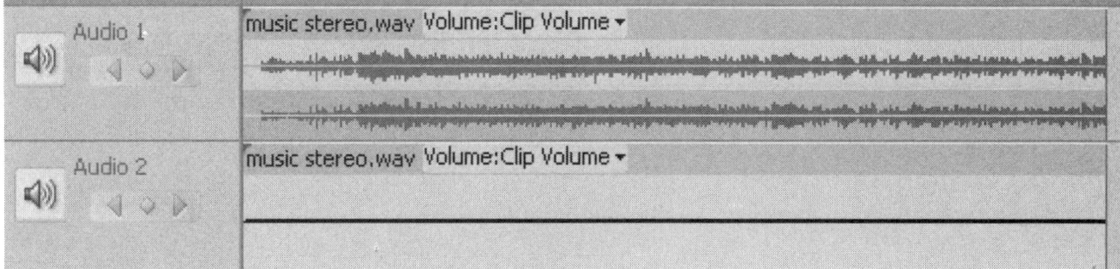

Figure 6.4 Audio track 1 is set to Show Waveform, whereas audio track 2 is set to Show Name Only.

Resizing Tracks

You can resize the height of each track to aid in the use of keyframes or other controls, or just to aid your eyesight. You can also resize the track header area to minimize its width or, more likely, to accommodate longer custom track names. When there are more tracks than the Timeline panel can show at once, you can adjust the border between the video and audio tracks to favor the tracks you need the most.

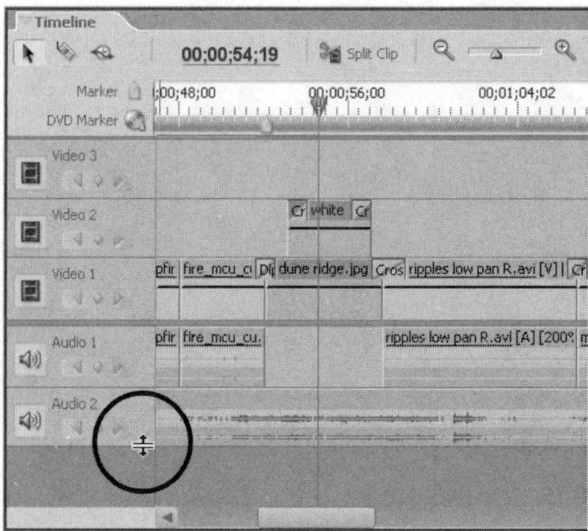

Figure 6.5 In the track header area, position the mouse over the top edge of a video track or the bottom edge of an audio track so an adjustment icon appears...

To resize the height of a track manually:

1. Position the mouse pointer at the top edge of a video track's header area or the bottom edge of an audio track's header area, so that the height-adjustment icon appears (**Figure 6.5**).
2. Drag up or down to adjust the width of the track (**Figure 6.6**).

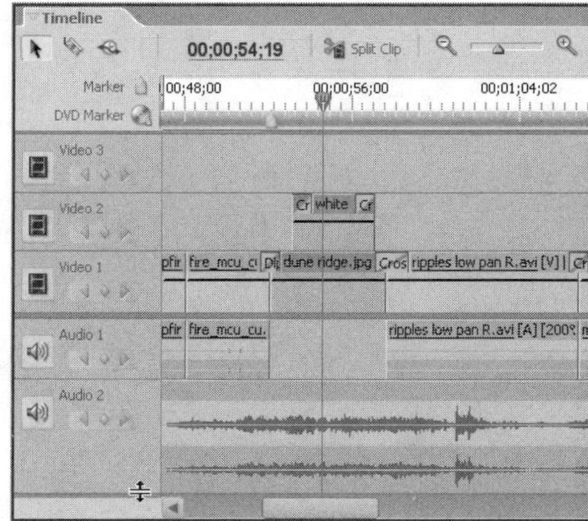

Figure 6.6 ...and drag to resize the track. Here, increasing the width of an audio track makes the waveform easier to see.

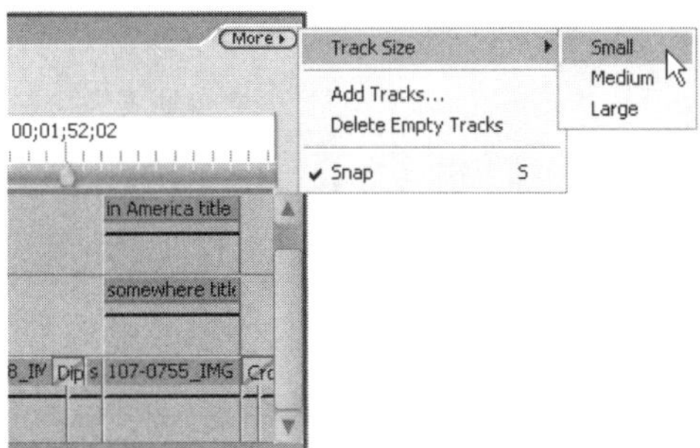

Figure 6.7 In the Timeline panel's More pull-down menu, choose Track Size, and select an option.

To resize the height of all tracks:

◆ In the Timeline panel's More pull-down menu, choose Track Size, and select an option from the submenu (**Figure 6.7**):

Small—Sets all tracks to their minimum height

Medium—Sets all tracks to about one and one half times the minimum height

Large—Sets all tracks to twice the minimum height

All tracks use the size you specify.

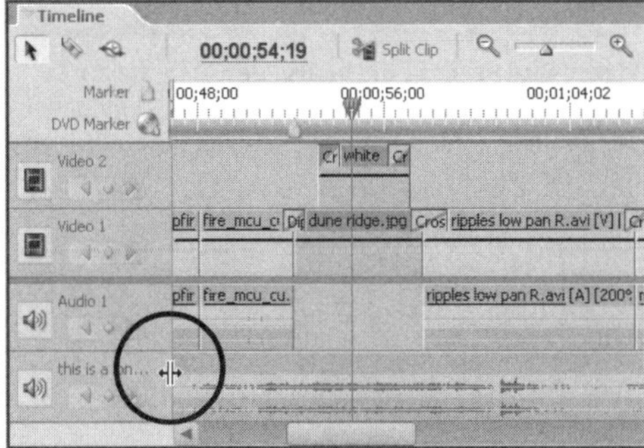

Figure 6.8 Dragging the right side of the track header area...

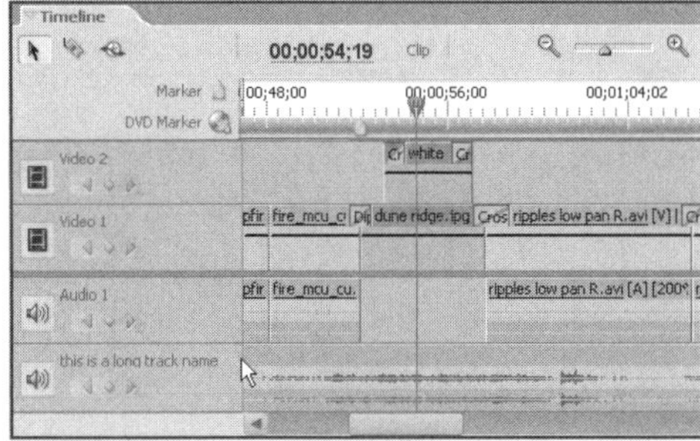

Figure 6.9 ...widens the track header area and makes room for longer track names.

To resize the track header area:

1. Position the mouse pointer over the right edge of the track header area so that the width-adjustment icon appears (**Figure 6.8**).
2. Drag right or left to change the track header width (**Figure 6.9**).

To change the proportion of video and audio tracks:

- Position the mouse pointer between the vertical scroll bars between the video and audio tracks (at the right of the Timeline panel) so the height-adjustment icon appears (**Figure 6.10**).
- Drag up or down to change the proportion of video and audio tracks visible in the Timeline panel (**Figure 6.11**).

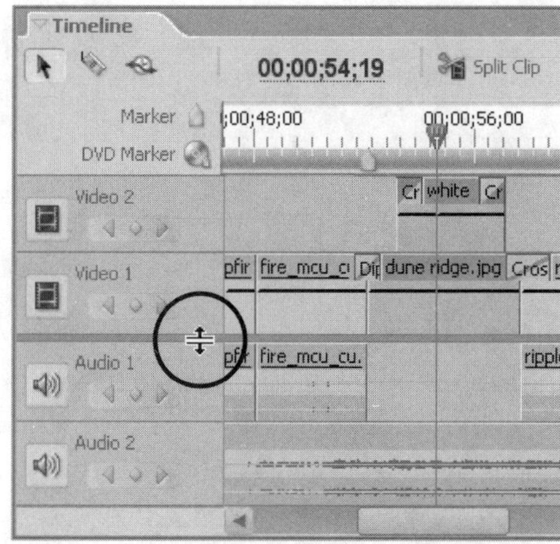

Figure 6.10 Position the mouse between the audio and video tracks on either end of the Timeline panel, so that the height-adjustment icon appears. Dragging up or down...

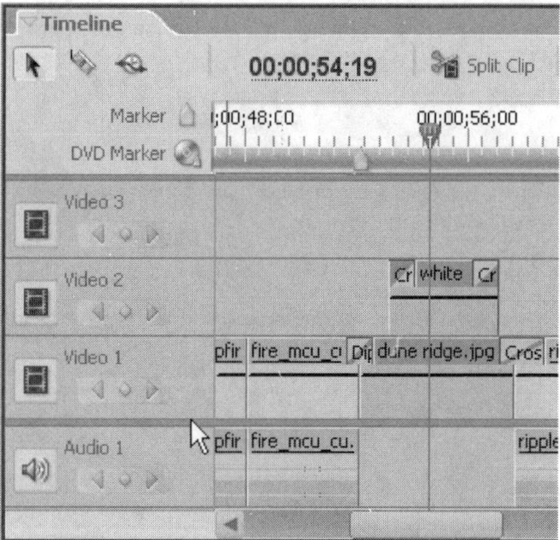

Figure 6.11 ...changes the proportion of video and audio tracks visible in the timeline.

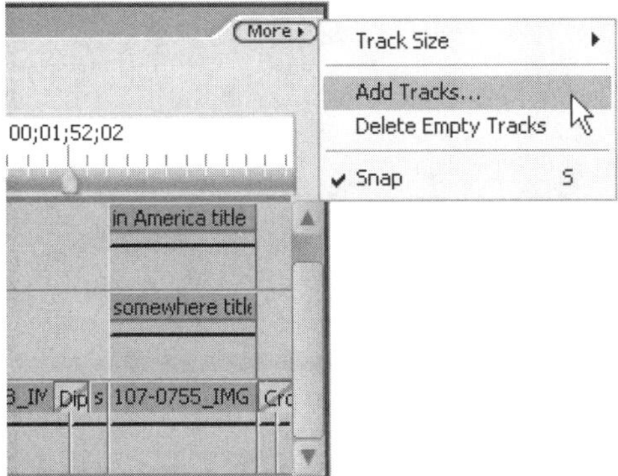

Figure 6.12 In the Timeline panel's More pull-down menu, choose Add Tracks.

Figure 6.13 In the Add Tracks dialog box, enter the number of video and audio tracks you want to add.

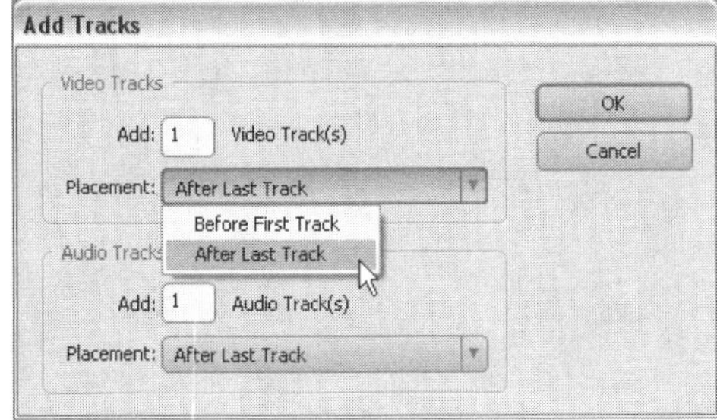

Figure 6.14 For each type of track you add, choose an option in the Placement drop-down menu.

Adding, Deleting, and Renaming Tracks

By default, the timeline initially contains three video tracks and three audio tracks. For most projects, this is the greatest number of tracks you'll ever need: a video track for the main content plus two more tracks for superimposing titles and other images; audio tracks for synchronized dialogue, sound effects, and music. However, Premiere Elements permits you to have as many as 99 video and 99 audio tracks in the timeline. What's more, you can name all those tracks, so it's much easier to discern the sound-effects track from the music and dialogue tracks, for example. Conversely, you can remove empty tracks you're not using.

To add tracks:

1. In the Timeline panel's More pull-down menu, choose Add Tracks (**Figure 6.12**).

   An Add Tracks dialog box appears (**Figure 6.13**).
2. In the Add Tracks dialog box, specify the number of video and audio tracks you want to add.
3. For each type of track you add, specify an option in the Placement pull-down menu (**Figure 6.14**).
4. When you've finished specifying the track options, click OK. The number and type of tracks you specified appear in the sequence.

✔ Tips

- To zoom out quickly to view the entire program in the timeline, press the backslash key (\).
- When you zoom into the time ruler closely enough for the ruler to measure video frames, a short blue line extends from the right side of the CTI. This represents the duration of the frame.

To delete empty tracks:

- In the Timeline panel's More pull-down menu, choose Delete Empty Tracks (**Figure 6.15**).

  Tracks containing no clips are removed from the Timeline panel.

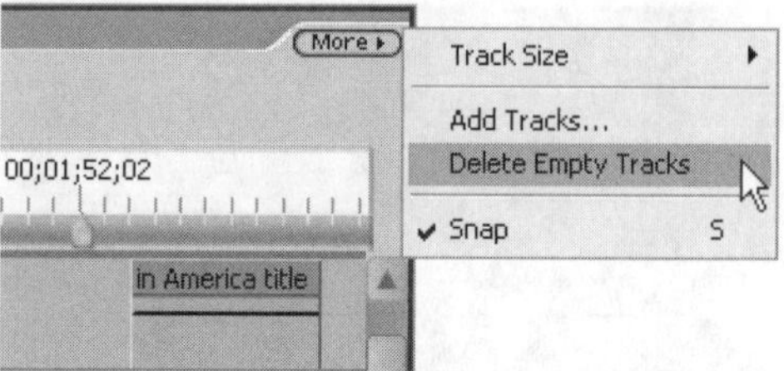

Figure 6.15 Choose Delete Empty Tracks from the timeline's More pull-down menu.

To rename a track:

1. Right-click the track's name, and choose Rename from the menu (**Figure 6.16**).

   The track's name is highlighted with a text-insertion cursor.

2. Type a new name for the track, and press Enter (**Figure 6.17**).

   The track uses the name you entered.

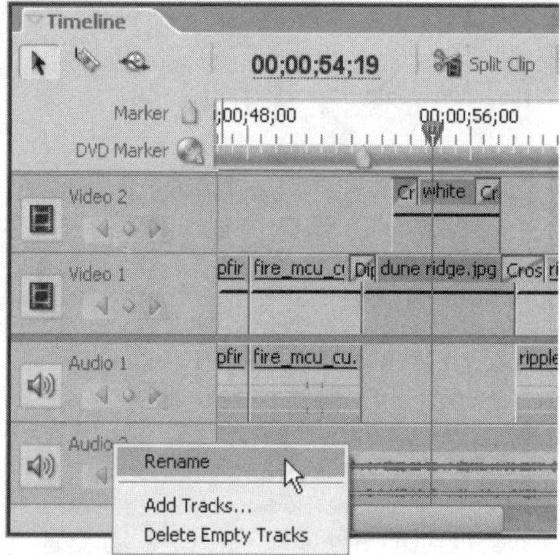

Figure 6.16 Right-click the track's header area and choose Rename from the context menu.

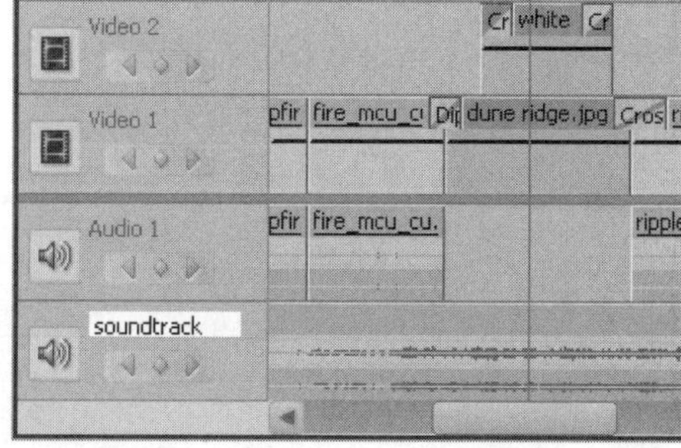

Figure 6.17 Type a new name for the track and press Enter.

✔ Tips

- You can also access the Add Tracks and Remove Tracks dialog boxes by right-clicking in the track header area and choosing the appropriate option in the context menu.
- When adding video tracks, keep in mind that you usually place clips in Video 2 and higher in order to superimpose or combine them with the image in lower tracks. See Chapter 10 for more information.
- You can change the default number of tracks by choosing Project > Project Settings > Default Timeline. The settings determine the initial number of tracks the sequence has.

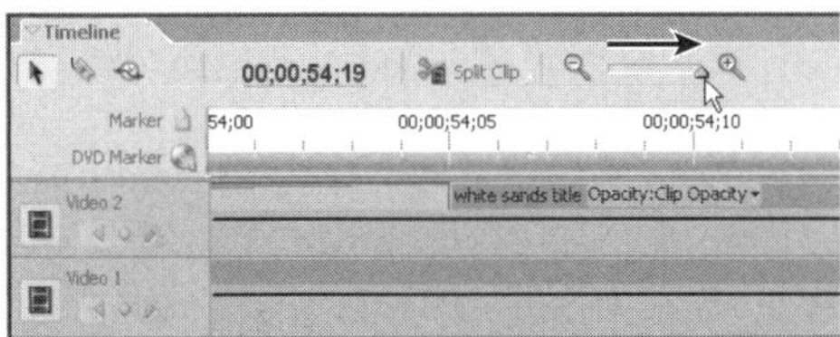

Figure 6.18 To view the sequence in more detail, drag the zoom slider to the right (shown here), or click the Zoom In button.

Figure 6.19 To view more of the sequence, drag the zoom slider to the left (shown here), or click the Zoom Out button.

Getting Around the Timeline

You can navigate through the sequence in the timeline in several ways. You can zoom in, zoom out, and scroll through the timeline.

To view part of the sequence in more detail:

- *Do one of the following:*
  - ▲ At the top of the Timeline panel, drag the zoom slider to the right (**Figure 6.18**).
  - ▲ To the right of the zoom slider, click the Zoom In button.

To view more of the sequence in the timeline:

- *Do one of the following:*
  - ▲ At the top of the Timeline panel, drag the zoom slider to the left (**Figure 6.19**).
  - ▲ To the left of the zoom slider, click the Zoom Out button.

To scroll through the timeline:

- *Do one of the following:*
  - ▲ At the bottom of the Timeline panel, click either the left or right scroll arrow to gradually move across a close view of the program.
  - ▲ Drag the scroll box right or left to view a different part of the program.
  - ▲ Click the scroll bar next to the scroll handle (not on it) to shift the view one width of the timeline.

Playing the Sequence in the Timeline

In the Timeline panel, a small blue triangle in the time ruler, the CTI, looks and works like its counterpart in the Monitor panel's Timeline view. However, a vertical line extends from the Timeline panel's CTI through the tracks of the sequence. This way, it's easy to see the current frame in relationship to the clips in the sequence. Furthermore, the vertical line makes it even easier to align clips with the CTI, and vice versa.

You can cue the Timeline panel's CTI by clicking or dragging in the time ruler or by using the Timeline panel's time display. If you press Shift while dragging the CTI, the CTI more readily aligns, or snaps to the edges of clips and with markers. (See "Using the Snapping Feature," later in this chapter.) Or, you can use buttons in the Monitor panel's Timeline view to cue the CTI to the previous or next edit, the point between two clips, or the point directly before or after a clip in a track.

Remember, the Timeline panel's CTI and the CTI in the Monitor panel's timeline view show the same frame of the sequence and move in tandem; however, their time rulers can show different parts of the same sequence at different scales.

Figure 6.20 Click the Timeline panel's time ruler to cue the CTI to that point.

Figure 6.21 Select the Timeline panel's time display, and enter an absolute time or a number relative to the current time. You can also drag the time display to change the number.

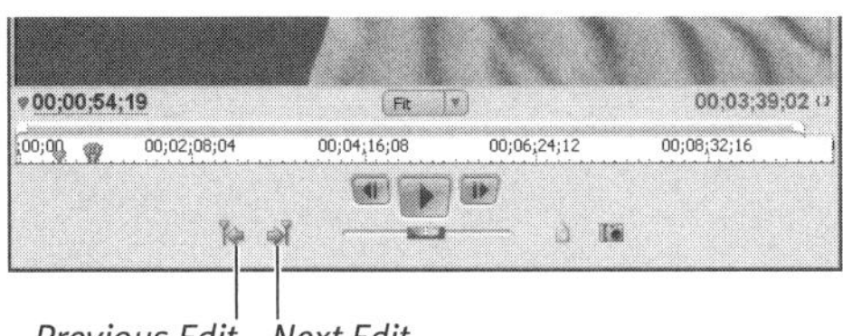

Figure 6.22 In the Monitor panel's Timeline view, click the Previous Edit or Next Edit button.

To cue the Timeline panel CTI:

- *Do one of the following:*
  - ▲ In the Timeline panel, click the time ruler to move the CTI to that point in the sequence (**Figure 6.20**).
  - ▲ In the Timeline panel, click the current time display to highlight it, and then type a relative or absolute time and press Enter (**Figure 6.21**).
  - ▲ In the Timeline panel, drag the current time display to change the number.
  - ▲ In the Timeline view of the Monitor panel, use the playback controls (or a keyboard shortcut) to cue the current program frame. (See "Using Playback Controls" in Chapter 5.)

To cue to the next or previous edit:

- In the Timeline view of the Monitor panel, *click either of the following buttons* (**Figure 6.22**):

  Previous Edit —Cues the edit line to the previous edit in a selected track

  Next Edit —Cues the edit line to the next edit in a selected track

✔ Tips

- Shift-dragging the CTI makes it snap to, or align with, clip edges and markers.
- You can also drag the vertical line extending from the Timeline panel's CTI, as long as there are no clips at the point where you grab the line.
- You can set whether the timeline's visible area shifts, or scrolls, to follow the current frame during playback by specifying an option in the General pane of the Preferences dialog box.

Using Timeline Markers

Just as clip markers can help you identify important frames in the source clips, *timeline markers* can specify important points in the sequence.

In most respects, timeline markers work exactly the same way as clip markers. The commands you use to set, delete, and cue to timeline markers are equivalent to the commands you use for clip markers. However, timeline markers appear in a timeline's time ruler, rather than in clips. Apart from these minor differences, the methods you learned in Chapter 5 can be applied to timeline markers and won't be repeated here.

However, timeline markers do have a few unique features that merit a separate explanation. First, timeline markers can include a text message. Comments are for your reference only and can only be accessed through the marker dialog box; they don't appear in playback or export.

Timeline marker comments can also be embedded into an exported movie of the sequence, if you export to the Microsoft AVI or DV AVI file type. In addition, timeline markers can contain a Web link or chapter link that's embedded in the exported movie file. When the movie reaches a Web link marker, it automatically opens a Web page in your browser. A chapter link specifies points to which you can cue the movie.

The Timeline panel also includes a button for DVD markers. Use these to mark scenes for a DVD you create in Premiere Elements. DVD markers are covered in Chapter 11, "Export."

Figure 6.23 In the Timeline panel, click the Marker button.

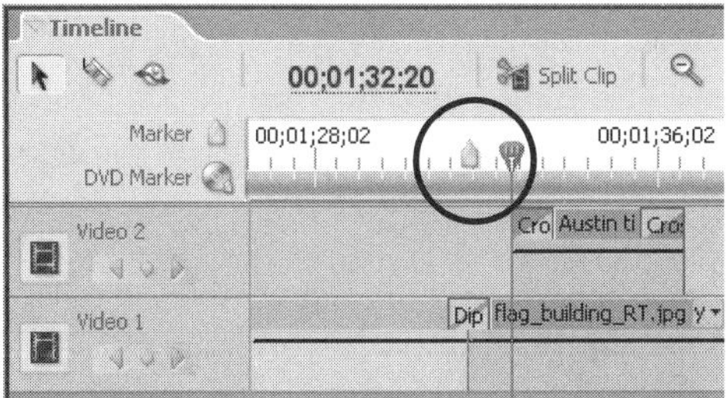

Figure 6.24 The marker appears at the CTI. Here, the CTI has been moved aside so it doesn't obscure the marker icon.

To add an unnumbered marker to the timeline:

1. Using controls in the Timeline view or Timeline panel, set the sequence's CTI to the frame you want to mark.
2. In the Timeline panel, click the Marker button (**Figure 6.23**).

   The unnumbered timeline marker appears at the CTI. However, the blue CTI marker obscures the marker initially; move the CTI to see the marker (**Figure 6.24**). The marker also appears in the time ruler of the Monitor panel's Timeline view.

To add comments or link information to a timeline marker:

1. Double-click a timeline marker.

   A dialog box for the marker appears.

2. To enter a comment, *enter information in the following fields* (**Figure 6.25**):

   Comments—A text message that appears in the Monitor panel's timeline view

   Duration—The amount of time the marker lasts, beginning at the marked time in the sequence

3. To create chapter or Web links, *do one of the following* (**Figure 6.26**):

   ▲ To set a chapter link, enter the name of the chapter in the Chapter field.

   ▲ To set a Web link, enter the Web address in the URL field.

   ▲ To activate a particular frame of the site in a Web link, enter the filename of the frame in the Frame Target field.

4. Click OK to close the dialog box.

✔ Tips

- DVD authoring guidelines restrict the proximity of chapter links. When you set markers for use as chapter links, make sure they are spaced at least 15 frames apart or by the number of frames your authoring software requires.
- Double-clicking the Marker button to the left of the timeline ruler allows you to set a marker and add a comment in one step.

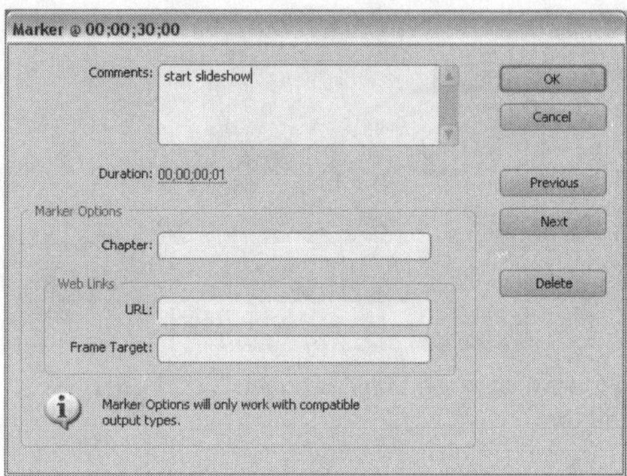

Figure 6.25 In the Marker dialog box, enter a comment and duration.

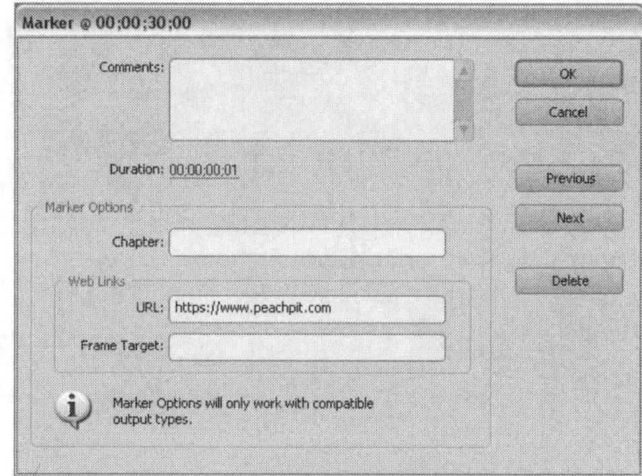

Figure 6.26 To set a chapter link, enter the name of the chapter in the Chapter field. To set a Web link, enter a URL and, if you want, a Frame Target filename.

Using Timeline Markers

Understanding the Link Between Video and Audio

When a clip contains both video and audio material, it's known as a *linked clip*. To perform the tasks described in this chapter, you need to understand how linked clips behave in the timeline.

When you move a linked clip in the timeline, the video and audio portions of the clip move together. Similarly, when you change a linked clip's edit marks, the video and audio tracks both change—unless you deliberately treat them separately. The link helps you keep the video and audio synchronized.

Nevertheless, it's possible to lose sync between the tracks of a linked clip. Fortunately, Premiere Elements alerts you to the loss of sync by tagging the affected clips in the timeline. Premiere Elements even tells you by exactly how much the clips are out of sync and provides easy ways to restore sync.

Even if your video and audio were recorded separately (as in a film shoot), you can create an artificial link between video and audio.

Although the link is usually an advantage, Premiere Elements permits you to override it if necessary. You can even break the link, if you want.

Selecting Clips in the Timeline

Not surprisingly, whenever you want to manipulate or affect a sequence clip in any way, you have to select it first.

Clicking a linked clip selects both the video and audio portions of the clip. To select or otherwise manipulate only the video or audio portion of a linked clip, press Alt when you select the clip.

To select clips in the Timeline panel:

- *Do any of the following:*
  - To select a clip, click it in the timeline (**Figure 6.27**).
  - To add or subtract from the selection, Ctrl-click clips.
  - To select a range of clips, drag a marquee selection around the range of clips (**Figure 6.28**).
  - To select only the video or audio portion of a linked clip, Alt-click the clip (**Figure 6.29**).

  When a clip is selected, it appears highlighted.

✔ Tip

- When you select multiple contiguous clips in the timeline, the Info panel indicates the number of clips selected and the total duration of the clips. If you select noncontiguous clips, the duration is calculated from the In point (beginning) of the first clip to the Out point (ending) of the last clip.

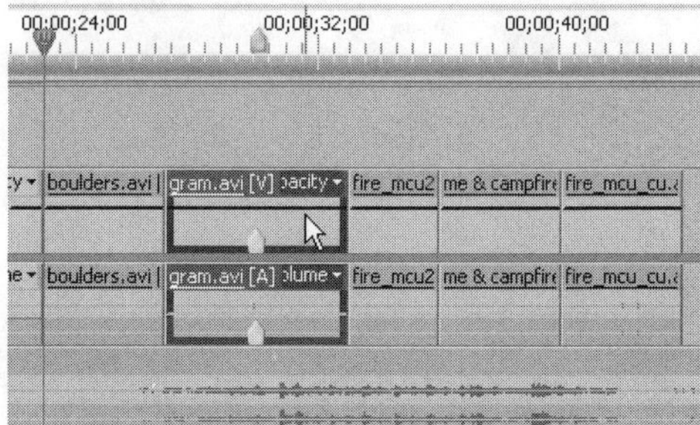

Figure 6.27 To select clips in the Timeline panel, you can click a clip...

Figure 6.28 ...or drag a marquee selection around multiple clips. Be sure you start the drag in an empty track; otherwise, you could move a clip.

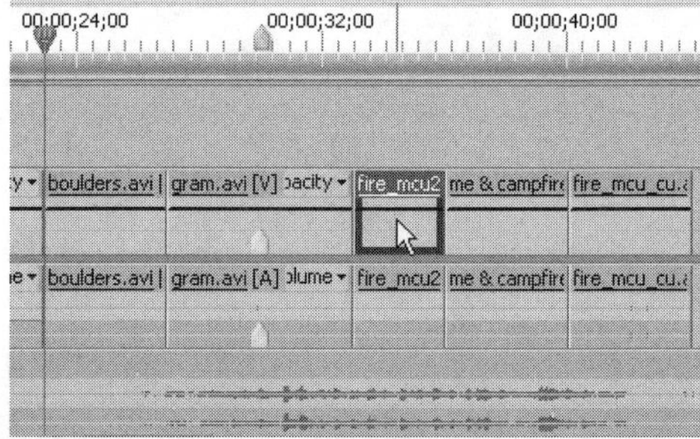

Figure 6.29 Alt-click to select only the video or audio portion of a linked clip.

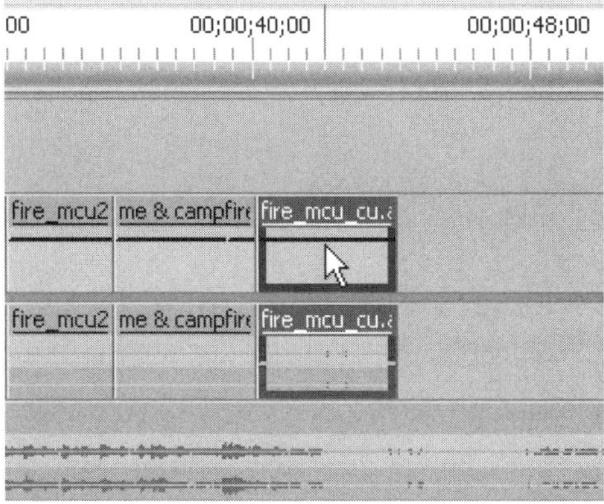

Figure 6.30 Select one or more clips in the sequence.

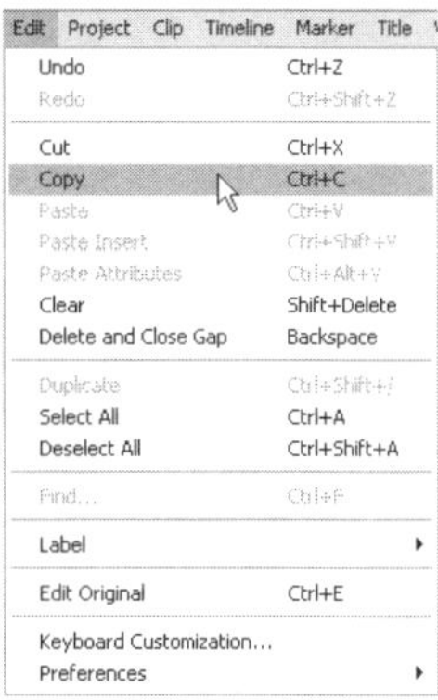

Figure 6.31 Choose Edit > Cut or Edit > Copy (shown here).

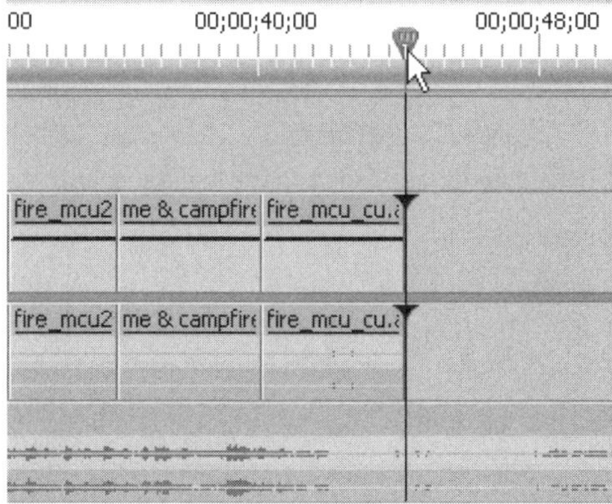

Figure 6.32 Position the CTI where you want the pasted selection to start.

Cutting, Copying, and Pasting Clips

As you would expect of any computer program, Premiere Elements uses copy and paste functions. The standard Paste command works like an overlay edit, whereas the Paste Insert command works like an insert edit. (For more about overlay and insert edits, see Chapter 5, "Editing Clips into a Sequence.")

To paste clips:

1. Select one or more clips in a sequence (**Figure 6.30**).
2. *Do either of the following* (**Figure 6.31**):
   - ▲ Choose Edit > Cut.
   - ▲ Choose Edit > Copy.
3. Position the CTI where you want the pasted clips to begin (**Figure 6.32**).

continues on next page

4. *Do either of the following* (**Figure 6.33**):
   - ▲ Choose Edit > Paste.
   - ▲ Choose Edit > Paste Insert.

   The selection appears in corresponding tracks beginning at the CTI (**Figure 6.34**).

✔ Tip

- Instead of copying and pasting a clip itself, you can copy its *attributes*—motion effects, opacity, volume, and other effects—and paste those to another clip. See Chapter 10, "Adding Effects," for more about effects.

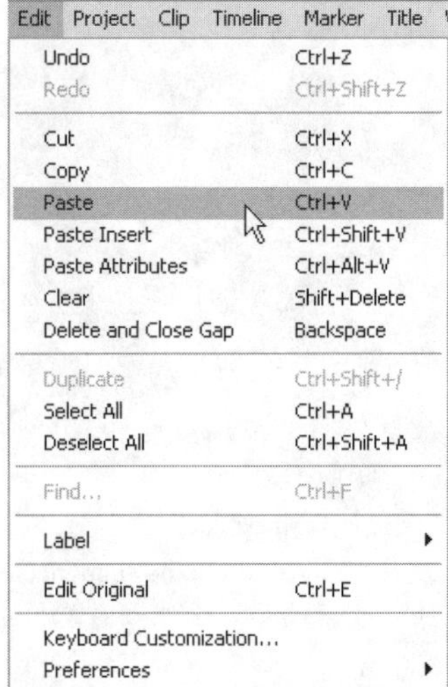

Figure 6.33 Choose Edit > Paste (shown here) or Edit > Paste Insert.

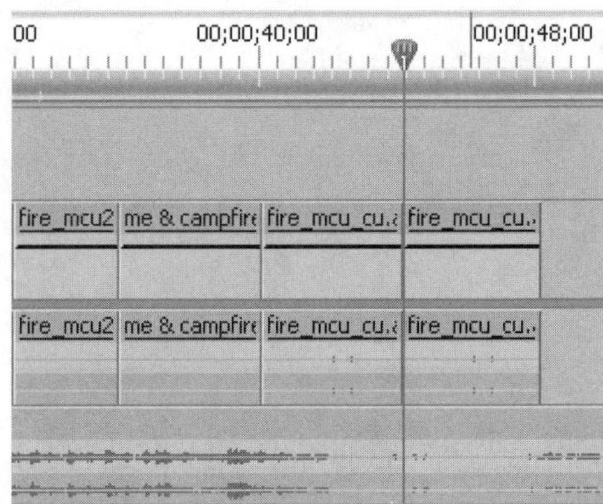

Figure 6.34 The selection appears in the sequence, starting at the CTI.

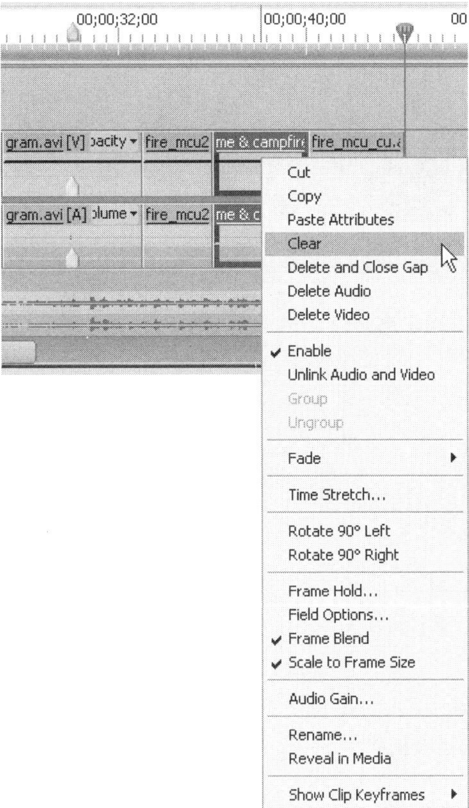

Figure 6.35 Select one or more clips in the Timeline panel, right-click the selection, and choose Clear from the context menu.

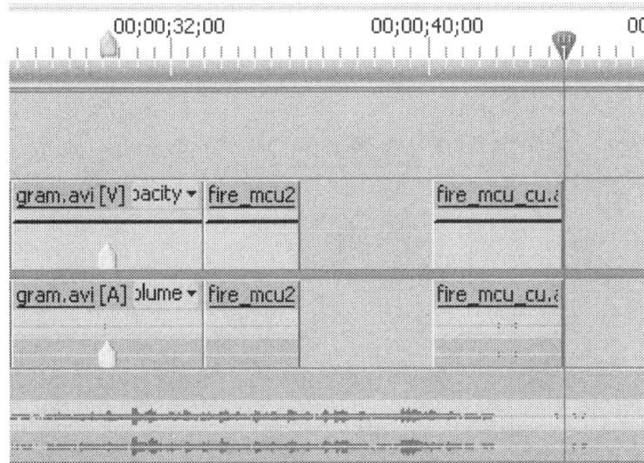

Figure 6.36 The selected clips are removed from the sequence, leaving a gap in the track.

Removing Clips and Gaps from the Sequence

Whatever you can select, you can delete. That includes both clips and empty gaps between clips. Just as the method you use to add clips to the sequence depends on whether you want subsequent material to shift forward in time, the method you use to remove material from the sequence depends on whether you want subsequent clips to shift back:

Clear removes the defined range from the timeline, leaving a gap in the timeline. You can think of Clear as the opposite of an overlay edit. *Clear* is sometimes referred to as *lift*.

Delete and Close Gap does just that: it removes the defined range from the timeline and shifts all the later clips earlier in the timeline, closing the gap. The Delete and Close Gap command is the opposite of an insert edit. In the previous version of Premiere Elements, it was known as *Ripple Delete*, and some editors refer to the technique as *extract*.

To remove clips without moving subsequent clips:

1. Select one or more clips in the Timeline panel.

   The selected clips appear highlighted.

2. Right-click the selection, and choose Clear from the context menu (**Figure 6.35**).

   The selected clips are removed from the sequence, leaving a gap in the track (**Figure 6.36**).

To remove clips or gaps and shift subsequent clips back:

1. *Do either of the following:*
   - ▲ To remove clips, select one or more clips in the Timeline panel.
   - ▲ To remove a gap, select a gap between clips.

   The selection appears highlighted. Selecting a gap highlights only the track you click, but the gap in both tracks will be extracted in step 2.

2. *Do one of the following:*
   - ▲ Press Backspace.
   - ▲ Press Delete (on an extended keyboard).
   - ▲ Right-click the selection, and choose Delete and Close Gap from the context menu (**Figure 6.37**).

   The selection is removed, and subsequent clips in the sequence are shifted back in time accordingly (**Figure 6.38**).

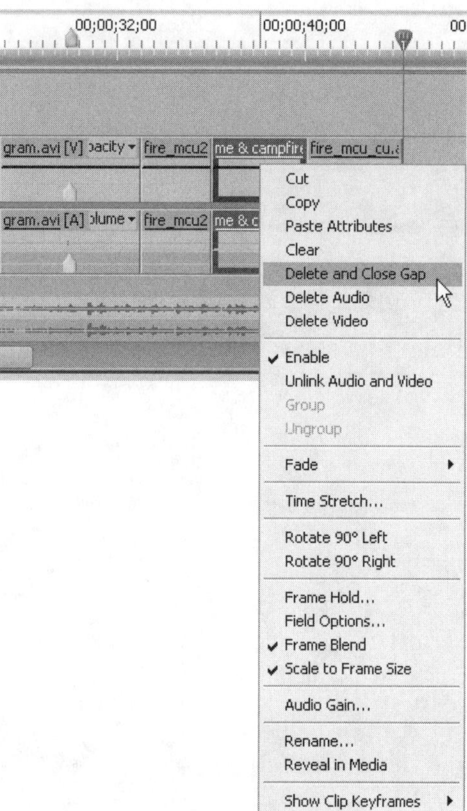

Figure 6.37 Right-click selected clips (or a gap between clips), and choose Delete and Close Gap.

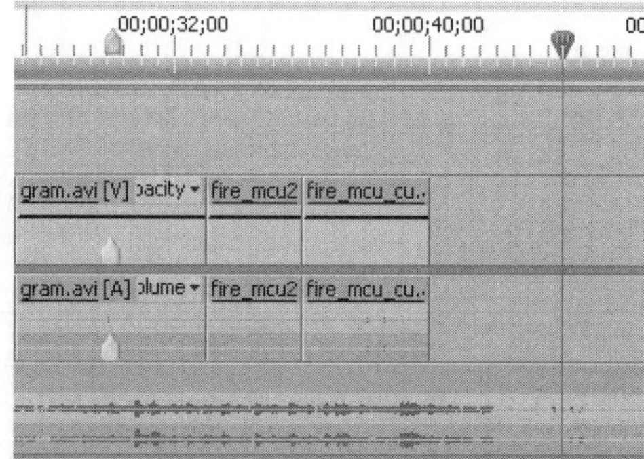

Figure 6.38 The selection is removed, and subsequent clips in the sequence are shifted back in time accordingly.

✔ Tips

- You can't select a gap and a clip simultaneously.
- Remember, you can Alt-click to select only the video or audio portion of a linked clip, and then clear that part.
- The Delete and Close Gap command appears dimmed (and can't be selected) if you try to use it on a single track (because it tends to shift linked clips out of sync). To move clips in one track without affecting clips in other tracks, select and drag them manually.
- The Clear and Delete and Close Gap options are great for removing *entire* clips or gaps. To remove portions of clips or to remove frames from several clips and tracks, first cut the clips using the Razor tool or Split Clips button, as explained in the section "Splitting Clips," later in this chapter.

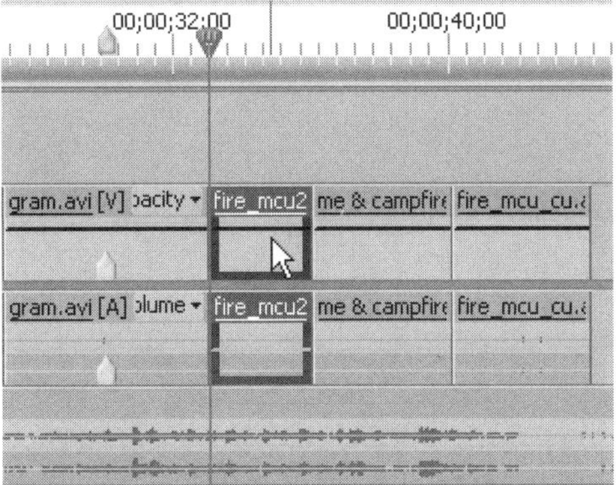

Figure 6.39 Select one or more clips in the Timeline panel.

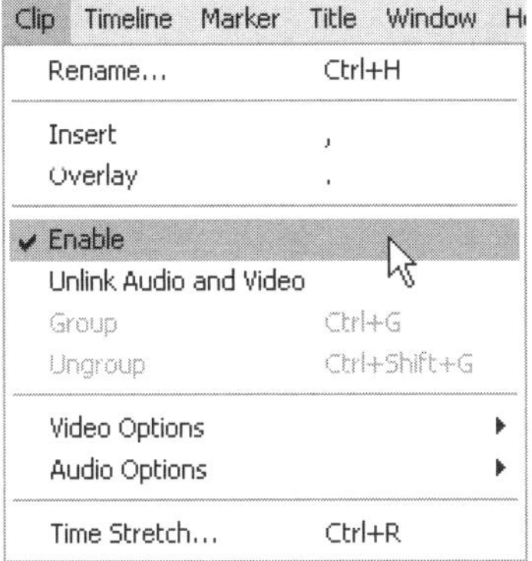

Figure 6.40 Choose Clip > Enable to uncheck it.

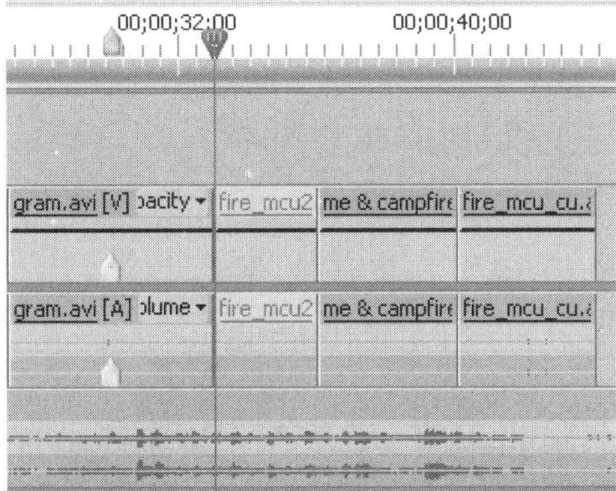

Figure 6.41 Disabled clips appear dimmed in the Timeline panel and don't appear in the Timeline view or in exported movies.

Enabling and Disabling Clips

Disabling a clip in the sequence prevents it from appearing during playback and when you preview or export the sequence. Disabling a clip is useful if you want to keep the clip in the sequence but exclude it temporarily. You might want to disable a single audio clip to hear what the program sounds like without it, for example. You can still move and make other changes to a disabled clip.

To disable or enable clips:

1. Select one or more clips in the timeline (**Figure 6.39**).
2. Choose Clip > Enable (**Figure 6.40**).

   A checkmark indicates that the clip is enabled. No checkmark indicates that the clip is disabled. Disabled clips appear dimmed in the timeline panel (**Figure 6.41**).

Grouping Clips

Even though you can select and move any number of clips (even a noncontiguous range of clips), at times it may be more convenient to group them. *Grouping* clips allows you to select and move them as a single clip.

You can adjust the outer edges—the In point of the first clip or the Out point of the last clip—of the group, but not the interior In and Out points. As opposed to individual clips, you can't apply clip-based commands (like speed changes) or effects to the group. However, you can select individual members of the group and apply effects to them without ungrouping the clips. And, of course, you can ungroup the clips at any time.

To group clips:

1. Select more than one clip in the Timeline panel (**Figure 6.42**).
2. Right-click the selected clips, and choose Group in the context menu (**Figure 6.43**).

   The clips are grouped together. Clicking any member of the group selects the entire group.

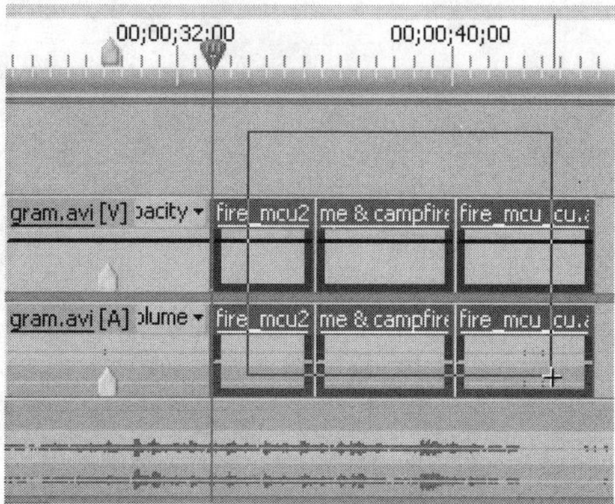

Figure 6.42 Select more than one clip in the sequence.

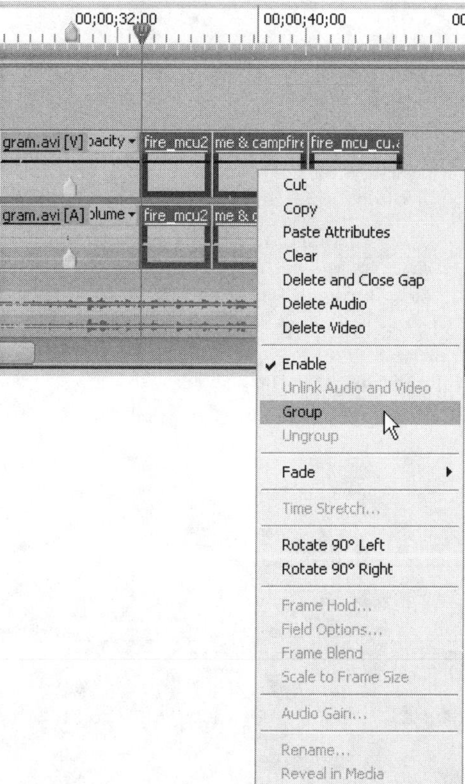

Figure 6.43 Right-click the selected clips and choose Group in the context menu.

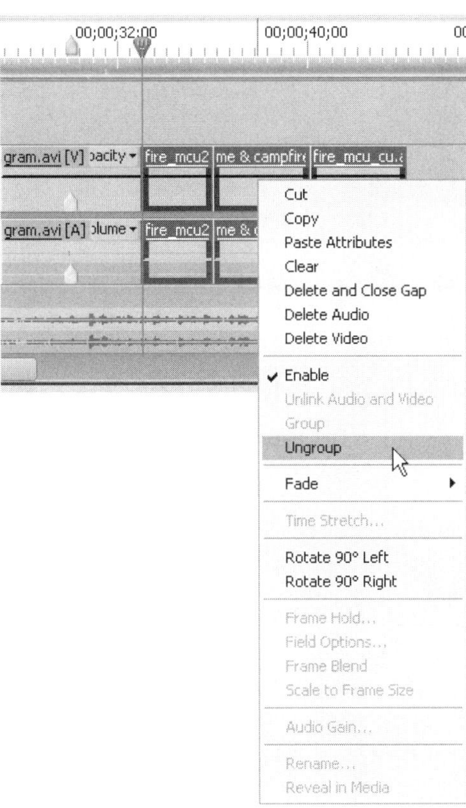

Figure 6.44 To ungroup clips, right-click any member of a clip group, and choose Ungroup in the context menu.

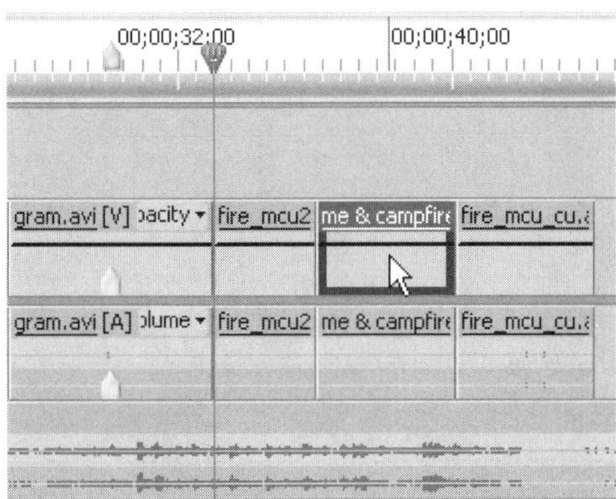

Figure 6.45 You can Alt-click to select members of a group clip without ungrouping them. Here, the video portion of the center clip in a group of three clips is selected.

To ungroup clips:

- In the Timeline panel, right-click a grouped clip, and choose Ungroup in the context menu (**Figure 6.44**).

  The clips are ungrouped, so that you can select and manipulate each clip independently.

To select individual clips in a group:

- *Do either of the following:*
  - Alt-click individual clips in a group (**Figure 6.45**).
  - Shift+Alt-click to add to or subtract from the selection.

Splitting Clips

Sometimes you need to cut a clip in the timeline into two or more pieces. You may want to apply an effect to one part of a shot but not to another, for example. When you split a clip, each piece becomes an independent sequence clip or clip instance. When you split a linked clip, both the video and audio tracks are split.

To split a clip with the Razor tool:

1. In the tools area of the Timeline panel, select the Razor tool (**Figure 6.46**).
2. Position the mouse at the point where you want to split the clip (**Figure 6.47**).
   The mouse pointer becomes a razor icon.
3. Click the clip in the timeline at the point where you want to split it.
   The clip is split into two individual clips at that point (**Figure 6.48**).

Figure 6.46 In the Timeline panel, select the Razor tool.

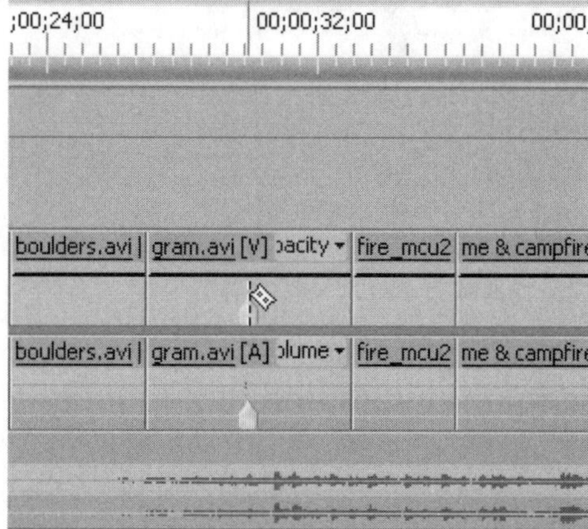

Figure 6.47 Clicking a clip with the Razor tool...

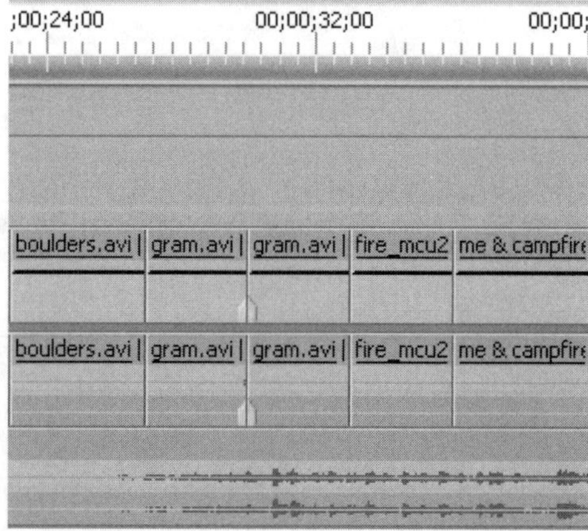

Figure 6.48 ...splits it into two clips at the point you click.

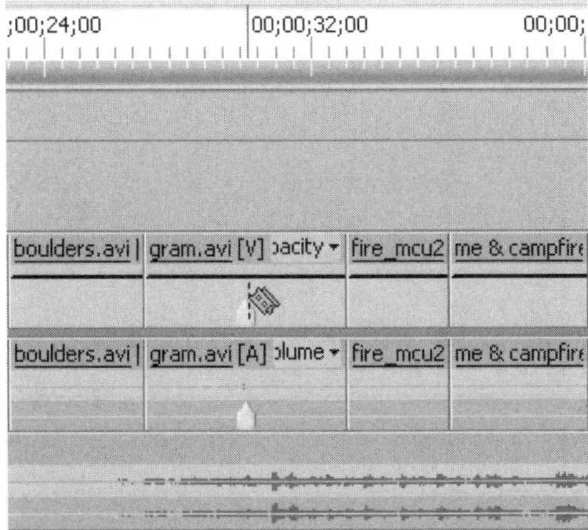

Figure 6.49 Pressing Shift toggles the razor tool to the Multirazor icon. Clicking with the Multirazor tool...

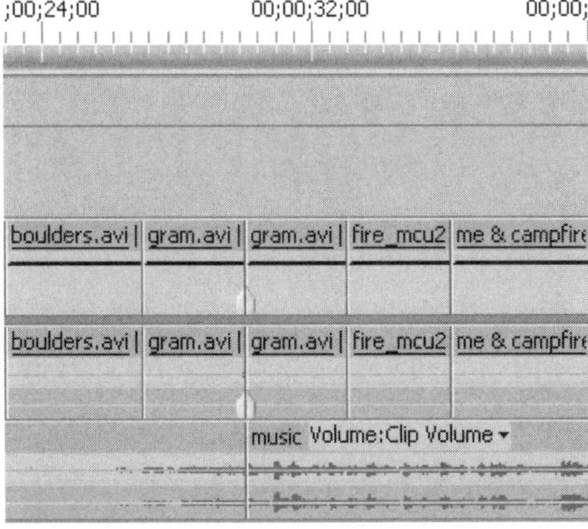

Figure 6.50 ...splits clips in all tracks.

To split clips in multiple tracks:

1. In the tools area of the Timeline panel, select the Razor tool.

2. Shift-click the point in the timeline where you want to split the clips in all tracks (**Figure 6.49**).

   Pressing Shift toggles changes the razor icon to the Multirazor icon. Shift-clicking splits all clips in all unlocked tracks at the same point in time (**Figure 6.50**).

To split clips at the CTI:

1. Using controls in the Timeline or timeline view of the Monitor panel, cue the CTI to the point you want to split clips in the sequence (**Figure 6.51**).
2. In the tools are of the Timeline panel, click the Split Clips at CTI button Split Clip (**Figure 6.52**).

   Clips in all unlocked tracks are split at the current time.

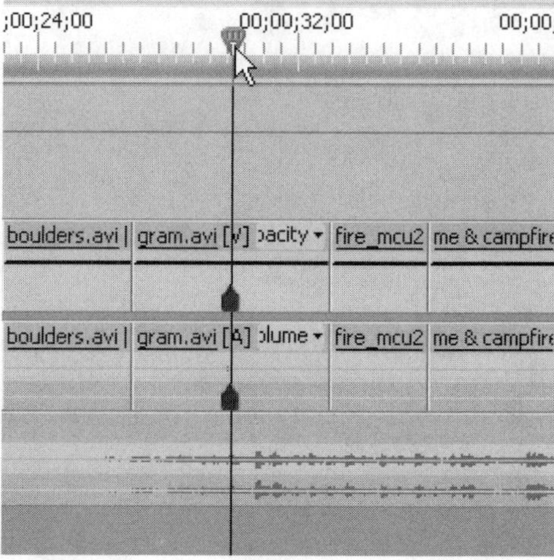

Figure 6.51 Or you can set the CTI to the point you want to split clips (here, aligned with the clip marker)...

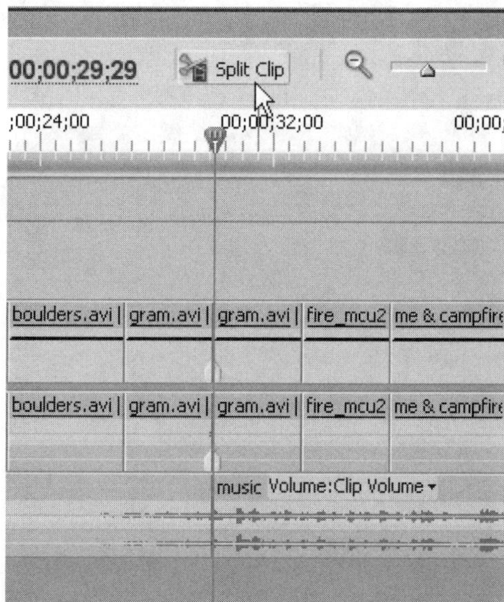

Figure 6.52 ...and click the Split Clips at CTI button.

Playing Clips at a Different Speed or in Reverse

In Premiere Elements, you can change the speed of a clip by choosing a menu command or by dragging directly in the timeline. A clip's speed correlates inversely with duration: increasing speed reduces duration; decreasing speed increases duration. The clip's In and Out points, however, remain intact. In other words, if the clip shows a 10-second countdown, increasing the speed won't cut out any of the shot. You'll still see all 10 numbers—they'll just go by in less than 10 seconds. You can also use the Time Stretch command to reverse playback at the specified speed, which would make the 10-second countdown in the example count *up*.

Note that a speed change applies to the entire clip. If you want to affect only part of a clip, split the clip and apply the speed change to one part only. If you want the speed to change over the course of the clip—making its playback accelerate or decelerate—you'll need to use a program like Adobe After Effects.

Unlike some editing programs, Premiere Elements doesn't create a new media file at the new speed; it merely plays back the clip at the specified speed in the project. The source media is unaffected. (If you want a new media file, you can change the clip's speed and then export it as a new movie file. See Chapter 11, "Export," to learn about exporting movie files.)

Match-Frame Edits

Splitting a clip creates a cut that is visible in the Timeline panel but invisible during playback. This kind of cut is called a *match-frame edit*. In Premiere Elements, match-frame edits can be useful if you want to add an effect or speed change in one part of a shot but not another. Because the viewer can't detect a match-frame edit, the effect appears to be seamless.

To change the speed of a clip by using the Time Stretch command:

1. Select a source clip in the Media panel or a sequence clip in the Timeline panel (**Figure 6.53**).
2. Choose Clip > Time Stretch (**Figure 6.54**).
   The Time Stretch dialog box appears (**Figure 6.55**).
3. Click the chain icon so that speed and duration values are linked.
   A Link icon indicates that speed and duration are linked; an Unlink icon indicates that speed and duration operate independently.
4. *Enter a value for either of the following*:
   Speed—A speed for the clip, expressed as a percentage of the normal speed. A value less than 100 percent decreases the clip's speed; a value greater than 100 percent increases the clip's speed.
   Duration—A total duration for the clip. Durations shorter than the original increase the clip's speed; durations longer than the original decrease the clip's speed.

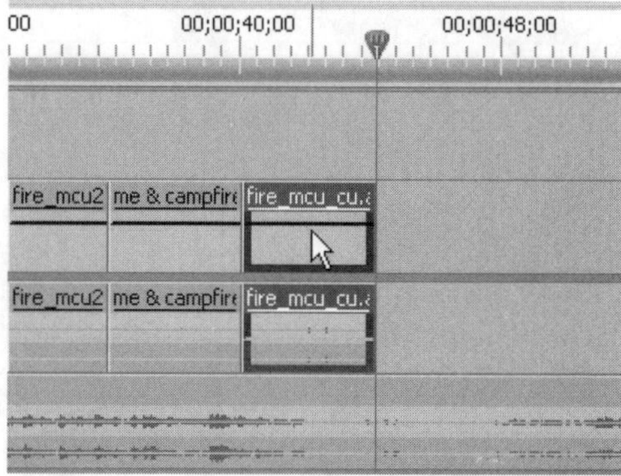

Figure 6.53 Select a source clip in the Media panel or a sequence clip in the Timeline panel (shown here).

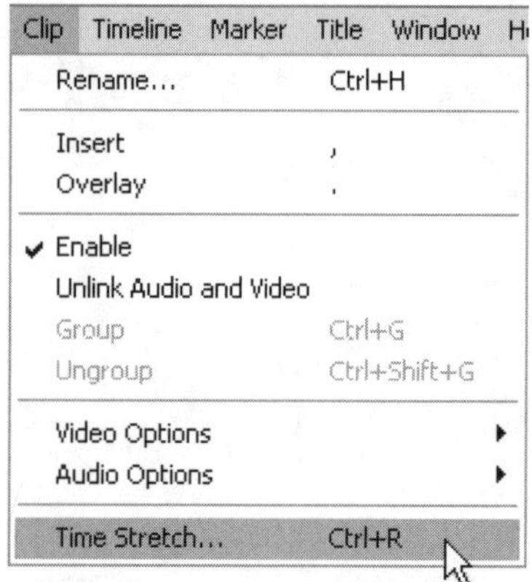

Figure 6.54 Choose Clip > Time Stretch.

Figure 6.55 In the Time Stretch dialog box, make sure the chain icon shows that speed and duration values are linked. Enter a value for Speed, and check the other options you want.

Figure 6.56 The clip's speed (and, consequently, its duration) changes according to your choices. In this example, the clip's speed is 50 percent, and therefore the clip is twice as long as it was in Figure 6.53.

5. *Select the options you want:*

   Reverse Speed—Plays the clip in reverse at the speed you specify.

   Maintain Audio Pitch—Shifts an audio clip's pitch to compensate for pitch changes caused by speed adjustments.

6. Click OK to close the Time Stretch dialog box.

   In the timeline, the clip's speed—and therefore its duration—change according to the values you specified (**Figure 6.56**). The source In and Out points are not changed, only the speed of the clip.

To change the speed of a clip by using the Time Stretch tool:

1. In the tools area of the Timeline panel, select the Time Stretch tool (**Figure 6.57**).
2. Position the Time Stretch tool at the edge of a clip in the timeline, and drag the edge (**Figure 6.58**).

   Dragging the edge to shorten the clip increases its speed; dragging the clip to lengthen it decreases its speed. The clip's In and Out points are not changed, only its speed. You can view the clip's speed by hovering the mouse over the clip until a tooltip appears (**Figure 6.59**).

✔ Tips

- Reversing a clip allows you to reverse camera moves: a tilt up becomes a tilt down, or a pan right becomes a pan left. Just be sure there's no movement in the frame (such as cars or pedestrians) that will give away the trick.
- You can unlink the speed and duration values to change the clip's speed or duration independent of each other. However, it's harder to predict the results.
- You can also use the Time Stretch command to change a clip's duration without affecting its speed. Doing so changes the clip's Out point so that the clip becomes the length you specify. Because there are numerous (and better) ways to change a clip's duration, this section doesn't cover this option.

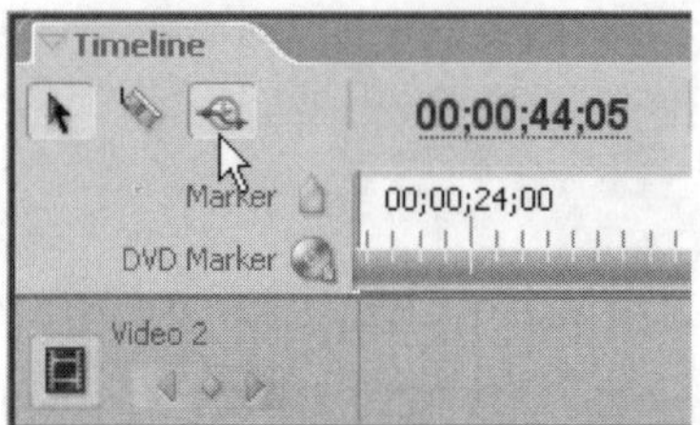

Figure 6.57 In the Timeline panel, select the Time Stretch tool.

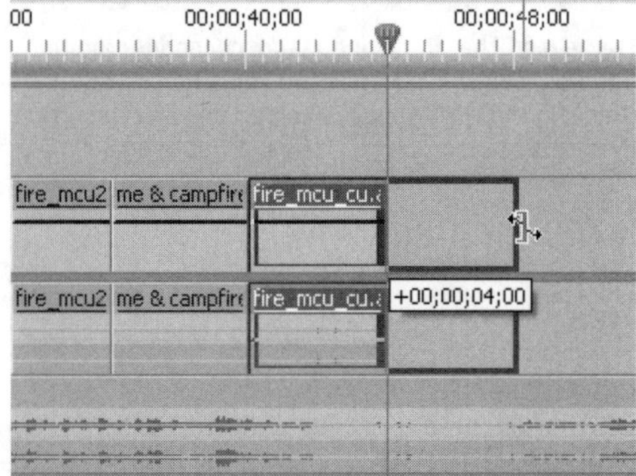

Figure 6.58 With the Time Stretch tool, drag the edge of a clip in the Timeline panel. A tooltip indicates how much you're stretching the clip, in minutes; seconds; frames.

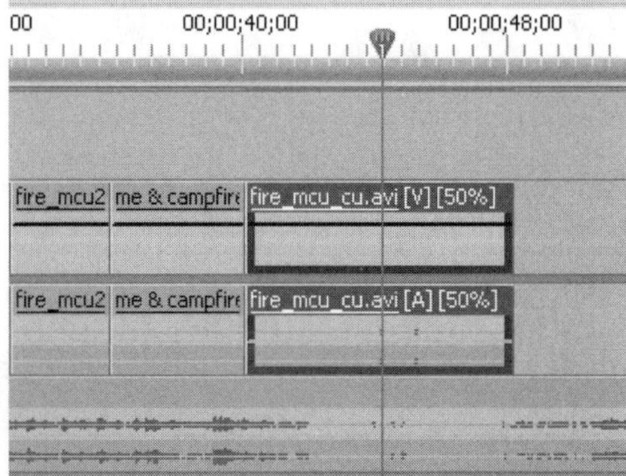

Figure 6.59 In this example, the clip's duration has been stretched by 04:01—twice as long and half as fast as the original. Hover the mouse over the clip to view a tooltip and learn the clip's speed as a percentage (50%).

Creating a Freeze Frame

Using the Frame Hold command, you can specify any frame of a clip to display for the entire duration of the clip. Because the held frame is based on the clip's current In point, Out point, or zero marker, it's easy to change the held frame. On the other hand, you have to be careful not to change the held frame inadvertently.

The corollary to how Frame Hold works is that you may need to take extra steps to achieve certain effects. For example, if you want the frame to hold longer than the clip's duration, you'll have to use more than one copy of the clip with the same Frame Hold effect. Creating what is commonly known as a *freeze frame*—playing the video at normal speed, and then halting the motion and holding on that frame—also requires two copies of the clip. The Out point of the first clip must match the held frame of the second clip. Because the match-frame edit is undetectable, it appears as though a single clip plays and freezes on a frame. (See the sidebar, "Match-Frame Edits," earlier in this chapter.)

If you find that the way the Frame Hold command works is more of a liability than an advantage, you should use a still image instead. Just export a frame as a still image file and import the still. See Chapter 11, "Export," for more about exporting a frame of the sequence as a still image file.

Slow-Mo Mojo

The quality of a slow-motion effect is limited by your source material. When shooting film, you can create a slow-motion effect in the camera by *overcranking*. Overcranking sets the frame rate higher than the film's standard frame rate, thereby capturing more images per second. When the film is played back at the normal frame rate, the image appears to move in slow motion. Most video cameras, on the other hand, can't increase their frame rate, so you must use a program such as Premiere Elements to create a slow-motion effect by repeating the existing frames. Because overcranked film captures a greater number of unique frames, the slow-motion image appears to be much smoother than in video, which merely duplicates frames.

To use the Frame Hold command:

1. In the Timeline panel, right-click a video clip, and choose Frame Hold from the context menu (**Figure 6.60**).

   The Frame Hold Options dialog box appears.

2. Select Hold On, and *choose an option* from the drop-down menu (**Figure 6.61**):

   In Point—Displays only the clip's current In point frame

   Out Point—Displays the clip's current Out point frame

   Marker 0—Displays the frame with Marker number 0, if present

3. *Select other options* you want:

   Hold Filters—Uses the effect settings (if present) at the held frame; otherwise, keyframed effects animate

   Deinterlace—Removes one field from an interlaced video frame and doubles the remaining field, in order to remove interlace artifacts (such as combing)

4. Click OK to close the dialog box.

   The specified frame displays for the duration of the clip. Changing the specified frame (In point, Out point, or zero marker) changes the held frame.

✔ Tips

- Speed changes, freeze frames, and other effects can sometimes result in *field artifacts*—defects in the image caused by the way video fields (the alternating lines of every frame) are processed. See the sidebar "Interlaced Video," in Chapter 11.
- If the freeze frame you want consists of more than one clip—the result of layering clips using transparency and compositing techniques—you must export the frame of the sequence as a still image and cut it into the sequence at the proper point.

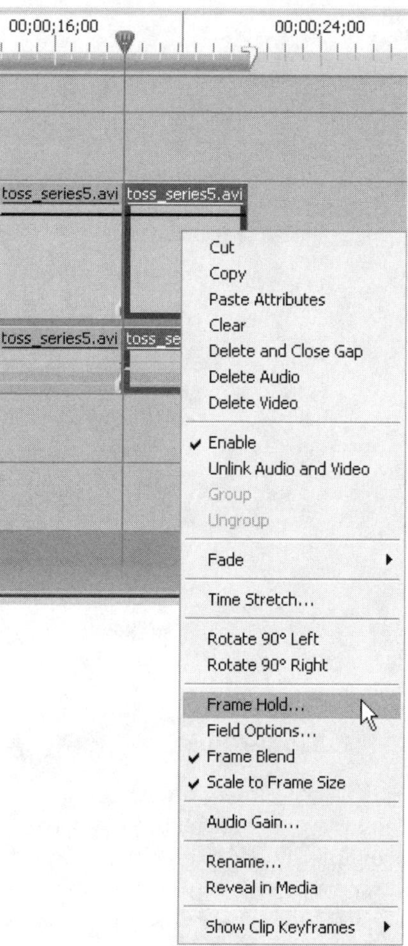

Figure 6.60 Right-click a video clip, and choose Frame Hold from the context menu.

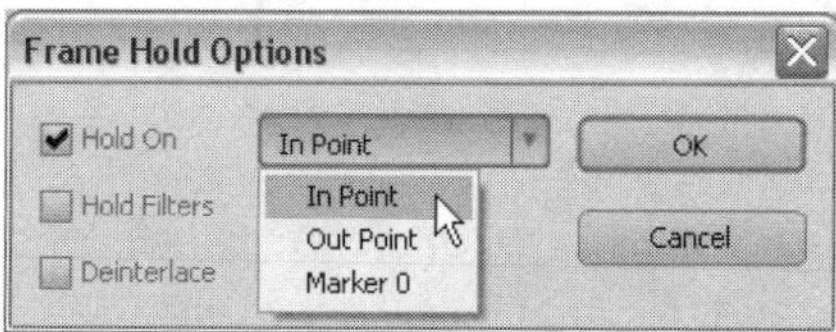

Figure 6.61 In the Frame Hold Options dialog box, select Hold On and choose the frame you want to hold. Specify other options you want and click OK.

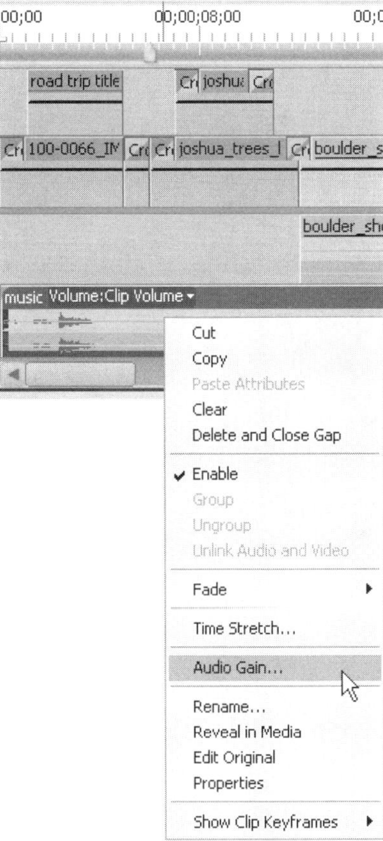

Figure 6.62 Right-click an audio clip, and choose Audio Gain.

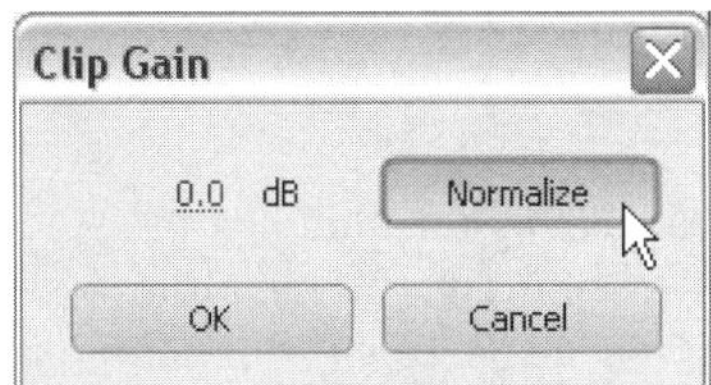

Figure 6.63 In the Clip Gain dialog box, either enter a gain value in dB or click Normalize to have Premiere Elements calculate the gain automatically.

Adjusting a Clip's Gain

You can adjust the overall volume, or *gain*, of a clip in the timeline by using a menu command. You can think of gain as the clip's input levels—the volume the clip starts with. The Gain command is a good way to bring a clip's levels in line with other clips before making adjustments to its output levels. Adjusting gain doesn't affect the initial position of a clip's volume level value graph. To learn about adjusting a value graph, see Chapter 10, "Adding Effects."

To adjust a clip's gain:

1. In the Timeline panel, right-click an audio clip, and choose Audio Gain (**Figure 6.62**).

   The Clip Gain dialog box appears (**Figure 6.63**).

2. To adjust the gain, *do either of the following:*
   - ▲ Enter a value for the gain, in decibels.

     A value of more than 0 amplifies the audio; a value of less than 0 attenuates the audio, making it quieter.
   - ▲ Click Normalize to have Premiere Elements calculate a gain value automatically.

     Normalizing audio boosts the volume where it's too quiet and limits it where it's too loud.

3. Click OK.

   The audio clip's overall gain is adjusted by the amount you specified.

✔ Tips

- Certain audio effects let you boost or attenuate (reduce) gain in particular frequencies.
- Changes you make using the Clip Gain command aren't apparent by looking at the clip, its waveform, or its keyframes. You can only see the amount of gain applied in the Clip Gain dialog box itself.

Using the Snapping Feature

When you move clips in the timeline, you usually want to align them precisely. When assembling a sequence, for example, you want to drag clips so that they butt up against one another without overlapping with another clip or leaving a gap. When you're placing a sound effect, you may want to align a marker in a video clip with a marker in an audio clip. Or you may want to move a clip to exactly where you placed the CTI.

The timeline provides an easy way to align clips through a feature called *snapping*. When you activate snapping, clips behave as though they're magnetized; they tend to snap to the edge of another clip, to a marker, and to the CTI. A vertical line with black arrows, or *snap line*, confirms that elements are flush (**Figure 6.64**).

Snapping also works when you're trimming clips in the timeline. When snapping is off, clips move smoothly past one another as you drag them in the timeline. Because snapping is so convenient, you'll probably leave it on most of the time.

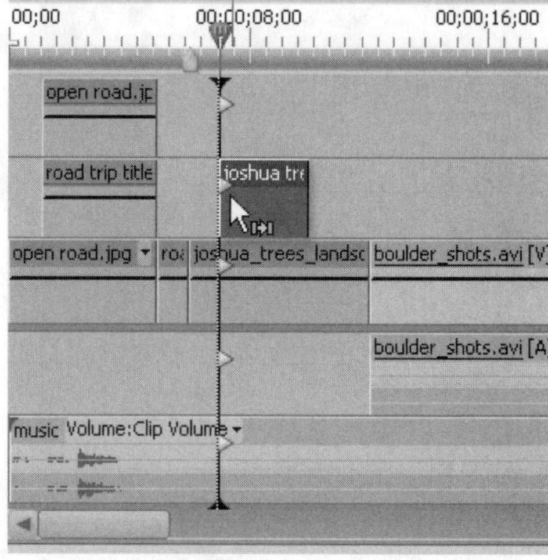

Figure 6.64 When snapping is on, a vertical line appears when you move clip edges, markers, or the CTI into alignment with one another.

Decibels

A decibel (dB) is the standard measure of acoustical power used by audio professionals everywhere. To double the volume, increase the level by +6 dB.

Technically speaking, a decibel is one-tenth of a bel, which measures the ratio of two audio power levels—usually, an audio signal and a reference (such as the threshold of hearing). And yes, it's bel as in Alexander Graham Bell, the telephone guy.

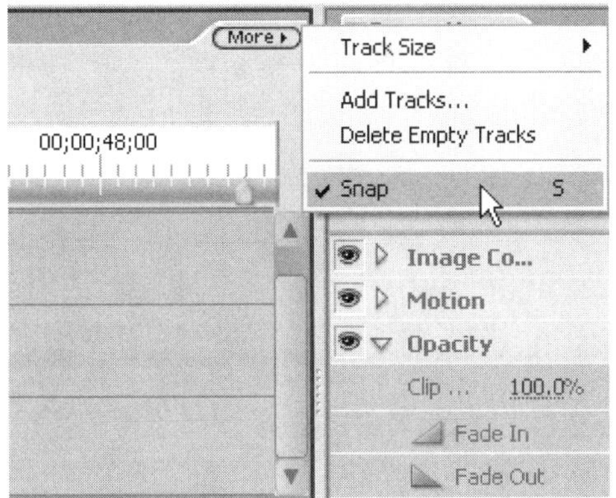

Figure 6.65 In the Timeline panel's More pull-down menu, choose Snap to toggle it on and off.

To toggle snapping on and off:

- In the Timeline panel's More pull-down menu, choose Snap to toggle it on and off (**Figure 6.65**).

✔ Tips

- When snapping is on, it's easy to use clip markers to cut video to the beat of music or to sync sound effects to video.
- Occasionally, several edges are so close together that snapping makes it difficult to place the clip properly. In these infrequent cases, you should zoom in to the timeline so that competing edges appear farther apart. Alternatively, you can turn off snapping and disable its magnetic effect.
- By default, you can toggle snapping by pressing the S key. It even works while you're dragging a clip.

Editing by Dragging

You can drag and move each clip in the timeline almost as though it were a physical object, just as editors used to rearrange clips of film. But, obviously, clips aren't bits of celluloid, so they aren't constrained by the laws of the physical world. In Premiere Elements, you aren't limited to rearranging clips like so many building blocks. Moving a clip from its current position either clears the clip or removes it and closes the gap, also known as a *ripple delete*; placing it somewhere new performs an overlay or insert edit (**Figures 6.66, 6.67, 6.68, 6.69, 6.70**). When you exchange or swap the positions of two clips, it's known as a *recycle edit* or *rearrange edit*. (See "Comparing Overlay and Insert Edits," in Chapter 5, and "Removing Clips and Gaps from the Sequence," earlier in this chapter.)

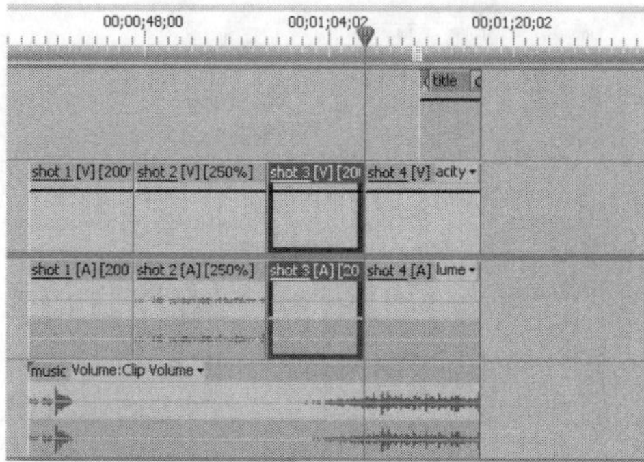

Figure 6.66 This figure shows the sequence before the edit. The selected clip will be moved back in time.

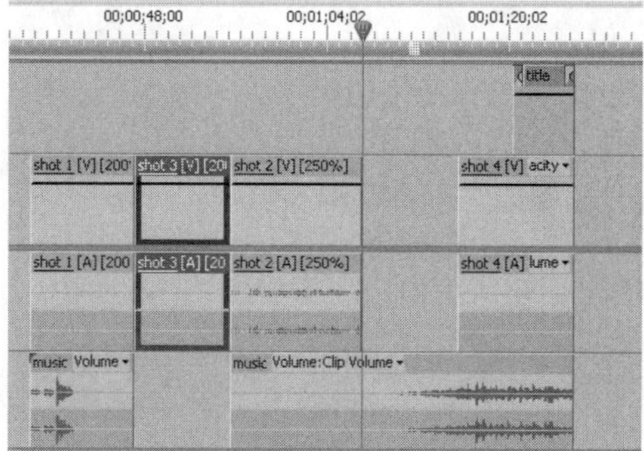

Figure 6.67 The selection made in Figure 6.66 has been cleared (lifted) and dropped into its new position using an insert edit.

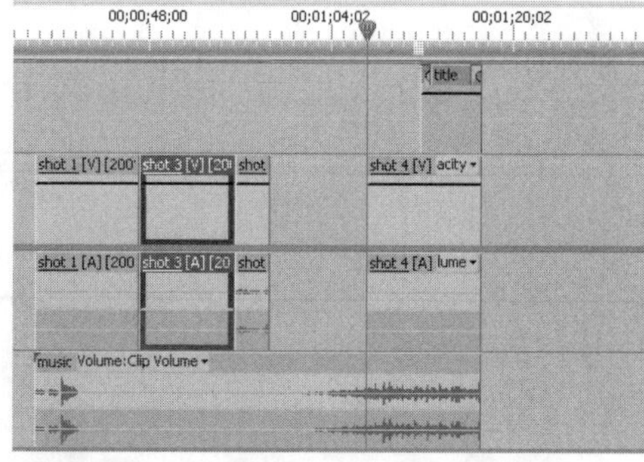

Figure 6.68 Here it has been cleared (lifted) and overlayed...

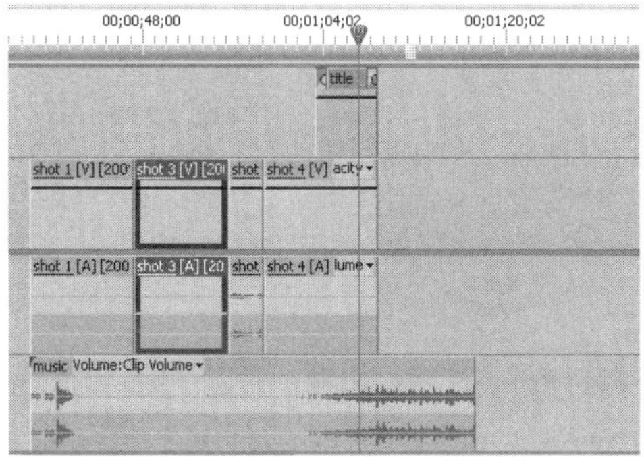

Figure 6.69 ...ripple-deleted (extracted) and overlayed...

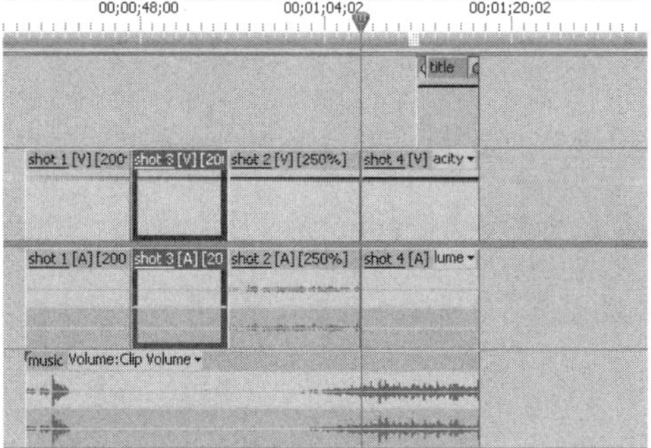

Figure 6.70 ...and finally, ripple-deleted (extracted) and inserted. These examples use linked clips.

Table 6.1

Editing by Dragging		
FUNCTION	ACTION	ICON
Clear/Lift	Click	no icon
Extract	Ctrl-click	
Overlay	Ctrl-drop	
Insert	Drop	
Rearrange/Recycle	Alt-drop	

To perform edits by dragging, you need to learn a simple set of *keyboard modifiers*, keys you press to toggle editing functions—in fact, you've already applied them in the previous chapter.

As you discovered in Chapter 5, an icon associated with each type of edit accompanies the mouse pointer, confirming that you're pressing the correct keys for the edit you want (**Table 6.1**). In addition, the Monitor panel's Timeline view provides helpful visual feedback, displaying the frames involved in the edit as you make it. And when you drag a clip in the timeline, a tooltip tells you how many frames the clip has traveled from its starting point.

As usual, if you want to limit the edit to either the video or audio portion of a linked clip, first Alt-click either the video or audio portion to select it, and then perform the edit.

To perform an edit by dragging:

1. In the Timeline panel, select one or more clips to move (**Figure 6.71**).

   Alt-click the video or audio portion of a linked clip to affect only that part of the clip.

2. *Do one of the following:*
   - ▲ To clear the selection (leaving a gap), click it and drag (**Figure 6.72**).
   - ▲ To extract the selection (closing the gap), Ctrl-click the selection before dragging it (**Figure 6.73**).

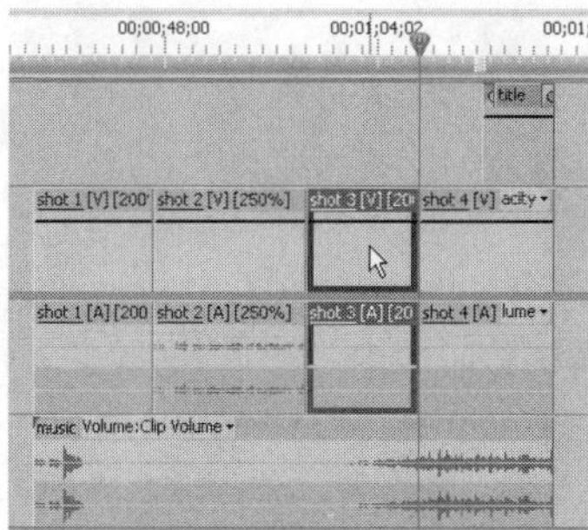

Figure 6.71 Select the clips you want to move. You must make a selection first if you want to move multiple clips at once.

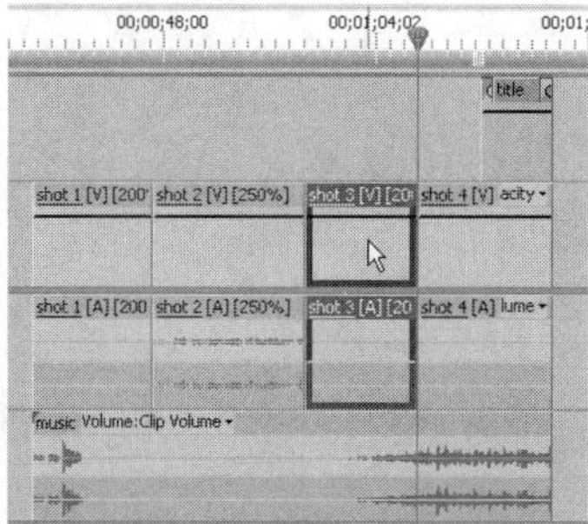

Figure 6.72 Click and then drag the selection to clear (lift) it from its original position.

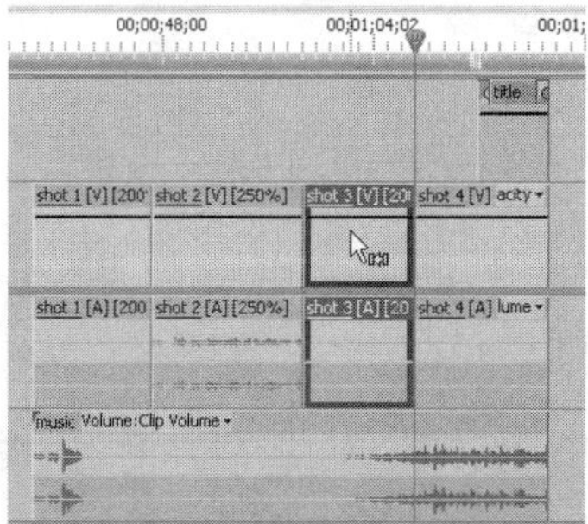

Figure 6.73 Ctrl-click and then drag the selection to ripple-delete (extract) it. Note the differences between the mouse icons.

Figure 6.74 The Timeline view helps you position the clip by showing the frame preceding the selection on the left and the frame after the selection on the right.

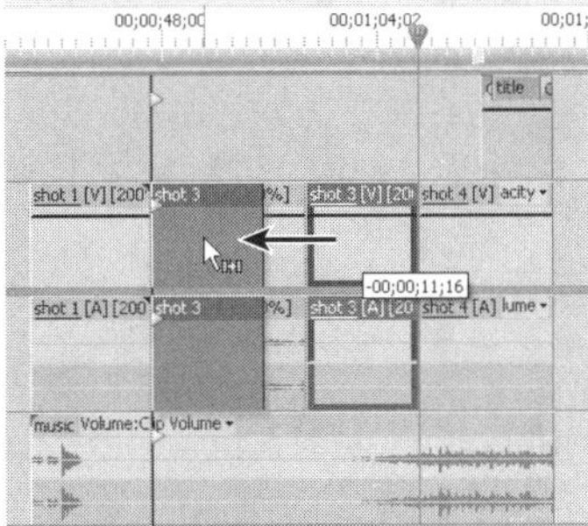

Figure 6.75 Dropping the selection inserts it, as the icon indicates.

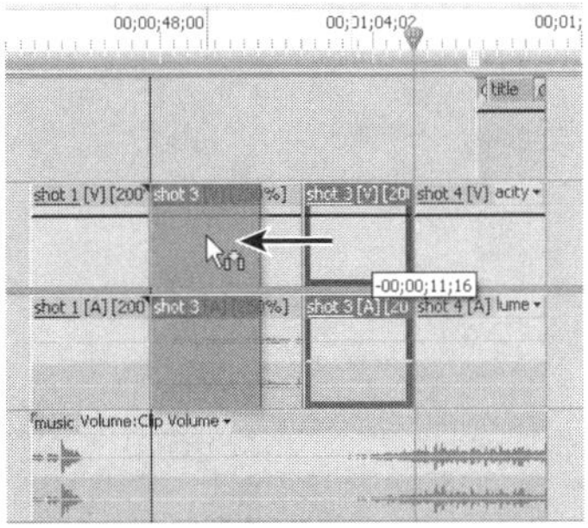

Figure 6.76 Pressing Ctrl as you drop the selection overlays it in the new location. Again, note the icon.

3. Drag the clip to its new position, using the visual feedback in the Timeline view as a reference (**Figure 6.74**).

   You don't have to hold down any modifier keys as you drag. Note that the tooltip indicates the number of frames the clip has moved.

4. *Do one of the following:*
   - To insert the selection, drop the clip at any point in an appropriate track (**Figure 6.75**).
   - To overlay the selection, Ctrl-drop the clip at any point in an appropriate track (**Figure 6.76**).

The selection is repositioned according to the methods you used. Insert edits shift all material in unlocked tracks by the duration of the selection, splitting clips if necessary (refer back to Figures 6.66–6.70).

To perform a recycle edit:

1. In the Timeline panel, select one or more clips you want to move (**Figure 6.77**).

   Alt-click the video or audio portion of a linked clip to affect only that part of the clip.

2. Click and drag the selection to its new position, using the visual feedback in the program view as a reference.

   You don't have to use a keyboard modifier until you're ready to drop the selection.

3. Press Alt so that the recycle icon appears, and drop the selection (**Figure 6.78**).

   The selection is extracted from its original position and inserted into its new position (**Figure 6.79**). The edit only affects material in the destination tracks. Because the extracted material and the inserted material are of equal duration, the total duration of the sequence remains the same.

✔ Tips

- You can change keyboard modifiers as you drag; just make sure you have the correct combination before you drop the clip.
- The figures in this section illustrate the result of one clip being moved to the previous edit point. Naturally, you can drop a clip in the middle of another clip. An insert edit splits the clip where you drop it.

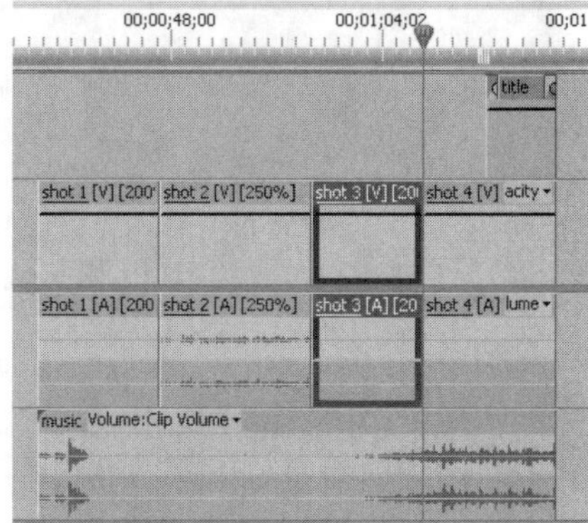

Figure 6.77 Select the clips you want to move.

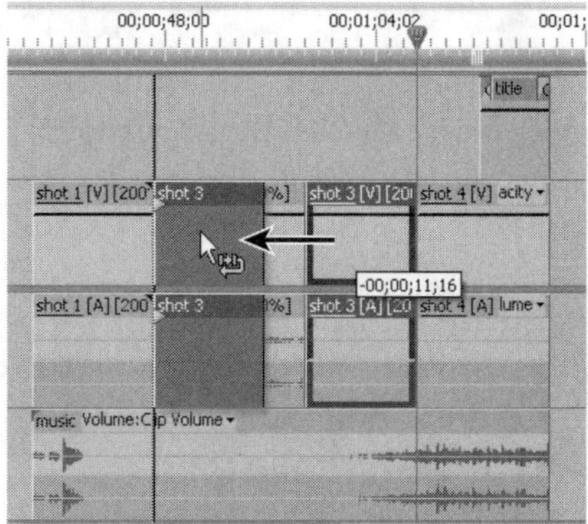

Figure 6.78 Press Alt as you drop the selection in its new location. Note the icon.

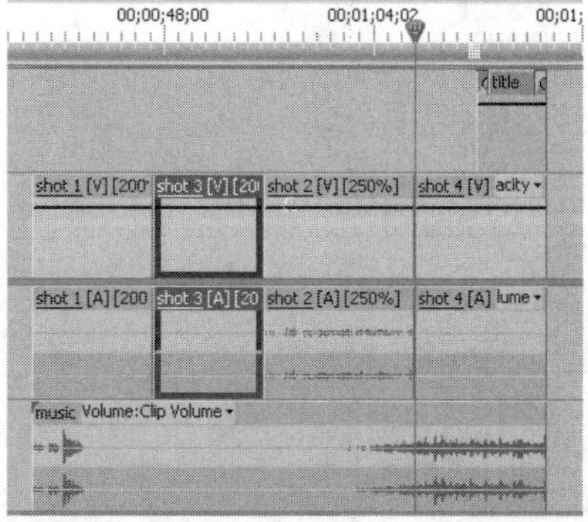

Figure 6.79 The selection is extracted from its original position and inserted into its new position. This figure illustrates how you can use this method to quickly exchange the order of clips—in this case, clips 2 and 3.

Understanding Trimming

Making an adjustment to a clip's In or Out point—particularly a small adjustment—is called *trimming*. Trimming in the timeline relies on using the mouse to move the edges of a program's clips, thereby changing their In or Out point. Like all timeline editing, trimming in the timeline is graphically clear and intuitive. The precision of the edit, however, depends partly on the detail of your view of the timeline.

By default, trimming a clip shifts clips in time, resulting in what's called a *ripple edit*. In other words, extending a clip works like an insert edit; shortening it works like a ripple delete (**Figures 6.80** and **6.81**). Consistent with other editing techniques, pressing the Ctrl key lets you extend a clip into an empty gap without causing a ripple effect, or to shorten a clip and leave a gap (**Figures 6.82** and **6.83**).

continues on next page

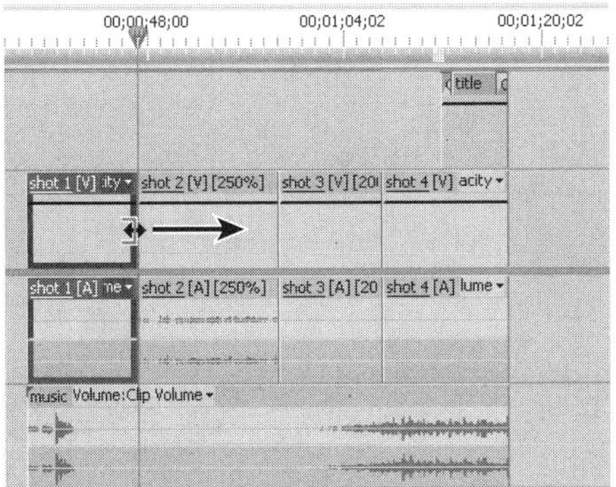

Figure 6.80 By default, extending a clip's edge by dragging...

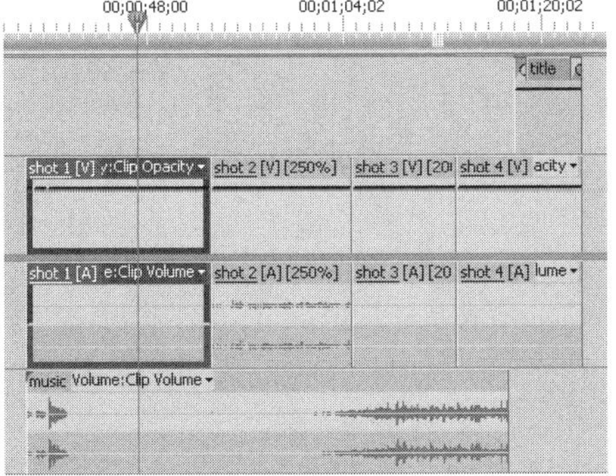

Figure 6.81 ...is comparable to an insert edit. When you're trimming, it's called a ripple edit, because it shifts subsequent clips in time, in a ripple effect.

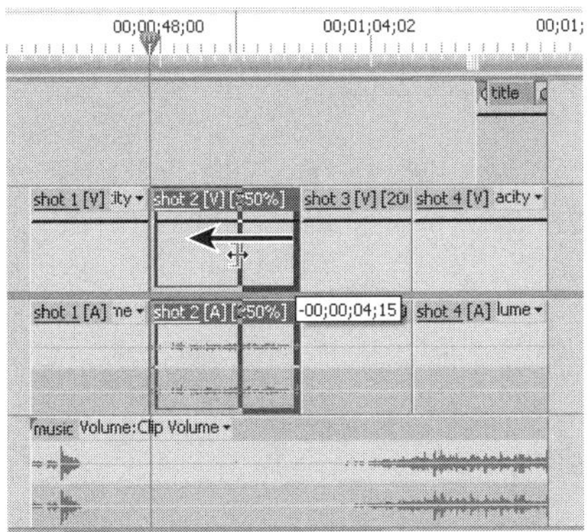

Figure 6.82 Pressing the Ctrl key as you trim...

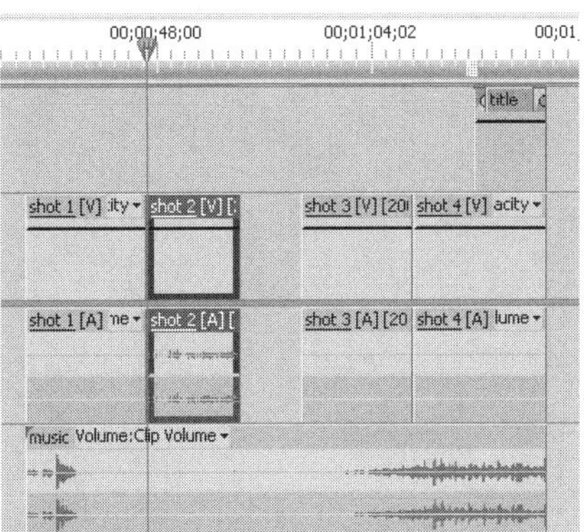

Figure 6.83 ...disables the ripple effect. Here, the clip has been shortened, leaving an empty gap. Subsequent clips remain unaffected.

Naturally, you can't extend a clip beyond the limits of its source media—that is, the amount of video you captured. When a clip's edge reaches the end of the source media, the top corner of that edge appears curved (**Figure 6.84**).

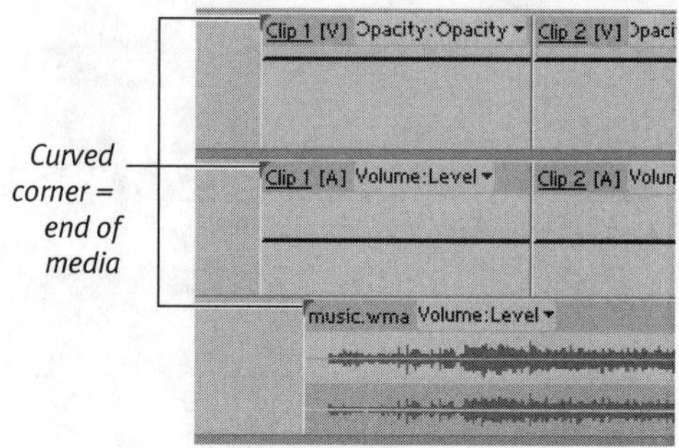

Figure 6.84 When a clip's edge has been extended to the limit, it appears with a curved corner.

✔ Tips

- Because the Timeline panel represents clips graphically, a clip's In and Out points are also called *edges*. The beginning of a clip is also known as the *head*, and the end is also known as the *tail*.
- You can also trim a sequence clip by opening it in the Clip view. This works well when you want to shorten a clip in the sequence; but subsequent clips in the sequence will prevent you from extending the clip.

Split Edits

In a *split edit* (aka *L-cut* or *J-cut*), the video and audio have different In points or Out points. A dialogue scene serves as a good example. First you see and hear a person talking, in sync. Then you hear the person's voice but see the person being addressed. In this case, the video Out point occurs earlier than the audio Out point. In the timeline, the video and audio form an L shape—hence the name *L-cut*. (When the situation is reversed, it's called a *J-cut*.) Split edits are a great way to make your edits feel much smoother. Watch a movie closely, and you'll find that split edits far outnumber *straight cuts*, in which the video and audio share the same In and Out points.

You can create split edits in a few different ways:

- Alt-click the video or audio portion of a clip, and then Ctrl-trim to shorten it. Alt-click and Ctrl-trim the adjacent clip to close the gap.
- Use the Unlink Audio and Video command to break the link between a clip's audio and video tracks, and then edit them separately (setting a clip marker beforehand provides a visible sync point).
- Set split edit points in the Clip view of the Monitor panel, and then Ctrl-trim adjacent clips to match.

Trimming Clips in the Timeline

To perform simple trimming in the timeline, you don't need to select a special tool. The default tool, the Selection tool, automatically switches to a trimming icon when you position it at a clip edge in the timeline.

By default, trimming is analogous to insert edits and ripple-delete edits (the Delete and Remove Gap command). In a *ripple edit*, you change the duration of one clip but don't affect the duration of the adjacent clips. After you ripple-edit the edge of a clip, all subsequent clips shift in the timeline to compensate for the change, in a ripple effect. Therefore, the total length of the sequence changes.

Pressing Ctrl disables the ripple/insert effect. Shortening a clip leaves an empty gap. However, pressing Ctrl won't let you trim and overwrite an adjacent clip. In other words, you can extend the edge of a clip into an adjacent gap without affecting other clips, but you can't continue trimming past the gap and over the adjacent clip.

The Monitor panel's Timeline view displays the edge frame as you trim. To gain more precise control, you can zoom in to the sequence before you start trimming.

To perform a ripple edit:

1. Using the selection tool, *do either of the following:*

   ▲ To trim the In point, position the pointer on the left edge of a clip in the timeline.

   The pointer becomes the Ripple Edit Head tool (**Figure 6.85**).

   ▲ To trim the Out point, position the pointer on the right edge of a clip in the timeline.

   The pointer becomes the Ripple Edit Tail tool (**Figure 6.86**).

2. Drag to the left or right to change the clip's In or Out point (**Figure 6.87**).

   The program view displays the edge frame (In point or Out point) as you adjust it. Lengthening a clip shifts subsequent clips forward in time accordingly; shortening a clip shifts clips back in time.

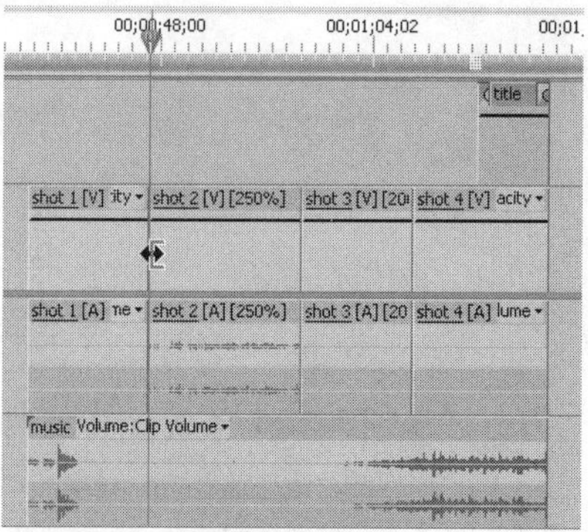

Figure 6.85 Position the mouse over a clip's left edge to ripple-edit its In point...

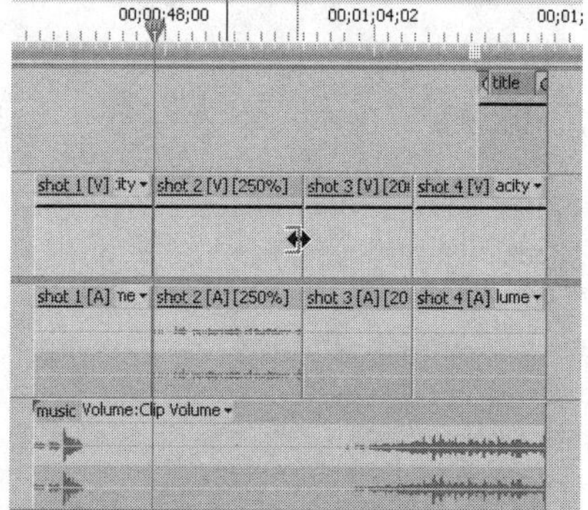

Figure 6.86 ...or position the mouse over a clip's right edge to ripple-edit its Out point.

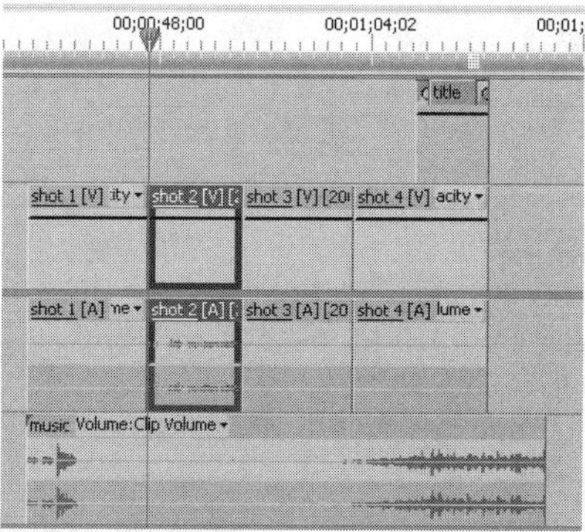

Figure 6.87 In this example, a ripple edit has been used to shorten the duration of the clip and shift subsequent clips back in time.

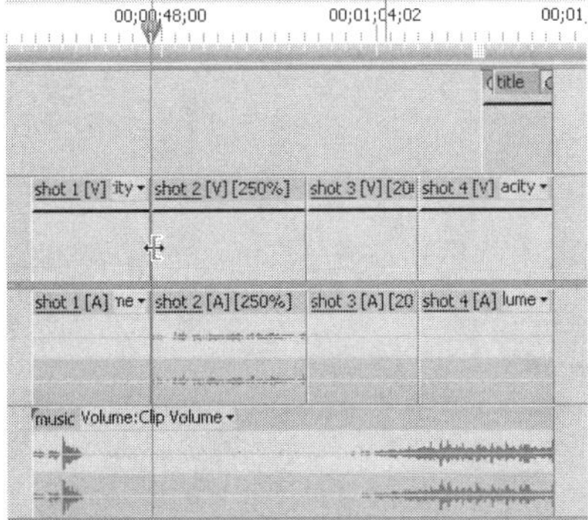

Figure 6.88 Pressing Ctrl, position the mouse at the left edge of the clip to trim its In point, or head...

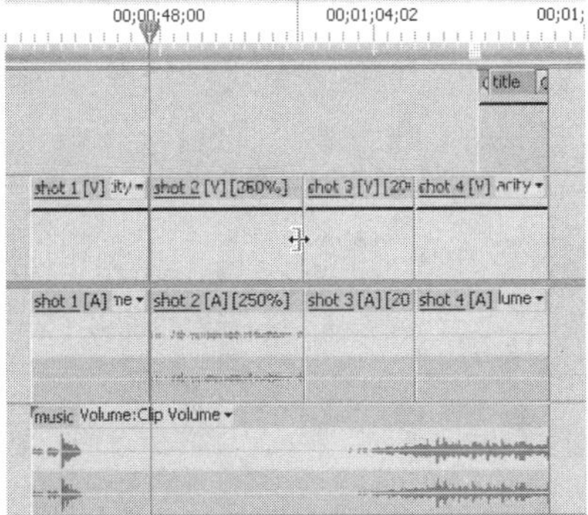

Figure 6.89 ...or with Ctrl pressed, position the mouse at the right edge to trim the Out point, or tail.

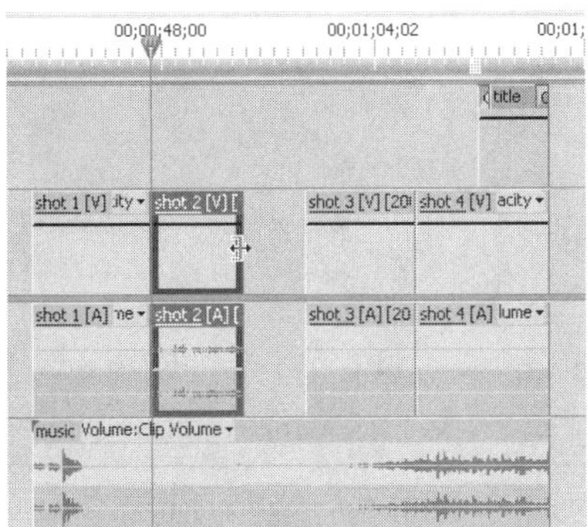

Figure 6.90 Ctrl-drag to shorten (trim in) or lengthen (trim out) the clip—without causing a ripple effect, which would shift clips after the edit point.

To trim without rippling:

1. Using the selection tool , *do either of the following:*
   - ▲ To trim the In point, position the pointer on the left edge of a clip in the timeline while pressing Ctrl.

     The pointer becomes the Trim Head tool (**Figure 6.88**).
   - ▲ To trim the Out point, position the pointer on the right edge of a clip in the timeline.

     The pointer becomes the Trim Tail tool (**Figure 6.89**).
2. Ctrl-drag to the left or right to change the clip's In or Out point (**Figure 6.90**).

   The program view displays the edge frame (In point or Out point) as you adjust it. Lengthening a clip overwrites subsequent clips forward in time accordingly; shortening a clip leaves an empty gap in the track.

✔ Tip

- If snapping is on, edges snap to other edges, markers, or the CTI as you trim. This setting is often advantageous, but if it prevents you from trimming to the frame you want, turn off snapping. (See "Using the Snapping Feature," earlier in this chapter.)

Breaking and Creating Links

As you know, a linked clip contains both video and audio. Although the video and audio portions of the clip appear in different tracks of the timeline, a link between the two portions of the clip helps maintain their synchronized relationship. (See "Understanding the Link Between Video and Audio," earlier in this chapter.)

As you've learned, you can use the Alt key to select the video or audio portion of a linked clip to manipulate them separately. But sometimes, you want to break the link altogether, so you can manipulate the video and audio independently. Note that although you can break or create links in the timeline, the links of the source clips and their associated media files on the drive remain unaffected.

To unlink audio and video:

1. In the timeline, select a linked clip.

   Both the video and audio tracks of the linked clip are selected (**Figure 6.91**).

2. Choose Clip > Unlink Audio and Video (**Figure 6.92**).

   The video and audio portions unlink, becoming two independent clips. In the Timeline panel, the names of the clips are no longer underlined, and they don't include *[V]* or *[A]* (**Figure 6.93**).

✔ Tips

- You can use the Link Audio and Video command to sync previously unrelated video and audio clips.
- Now you know why filmmakers use a *slate*, or clapperboard. They match the frame where the slate closes with the sound of the slate to synchronize the video and the audio.

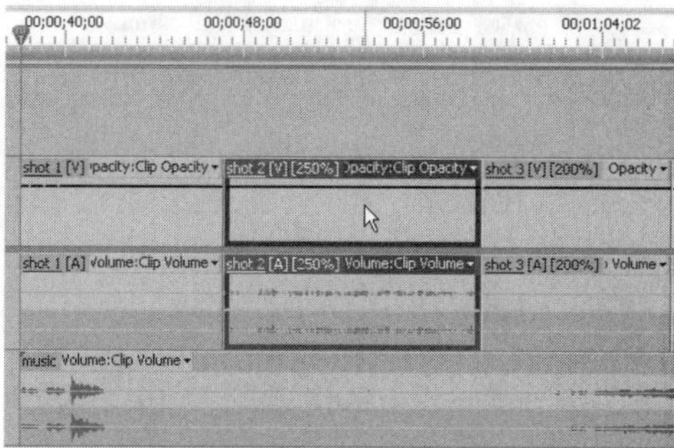

Figure 6.91 Select a linked clip. Note that the name of the video portion contains [V] and the name of the audio portion contains [A], and that both names are underlined.

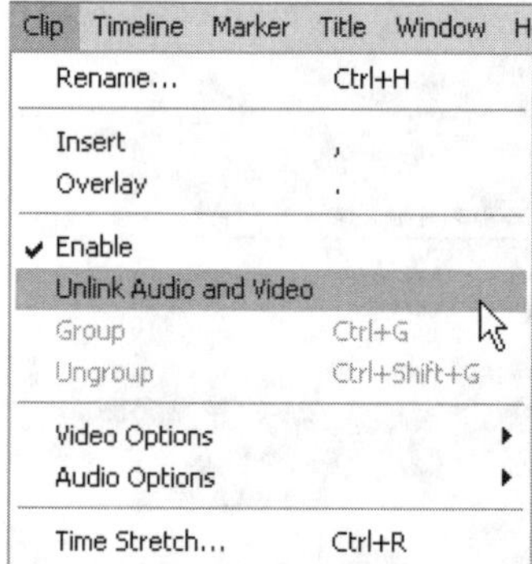

Figure 6.92 Choose Clip > Unlink Audio and Video.

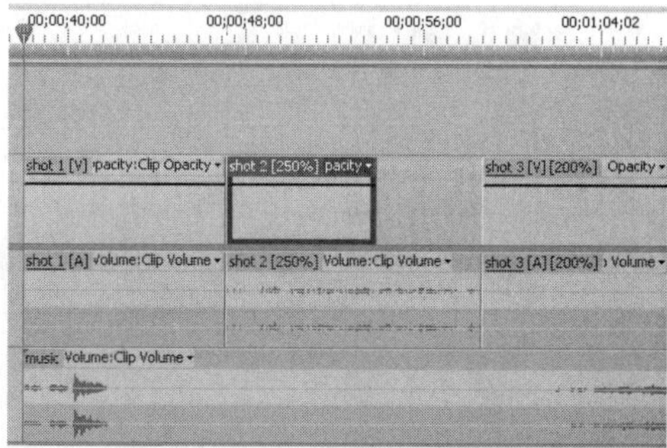

Figure 6.93 The video and audio are unlinked. The names are no longer underlined and don't contain [V] or [A]. Here, the video portion has been trimmed back to demonstrate that the link is broken.

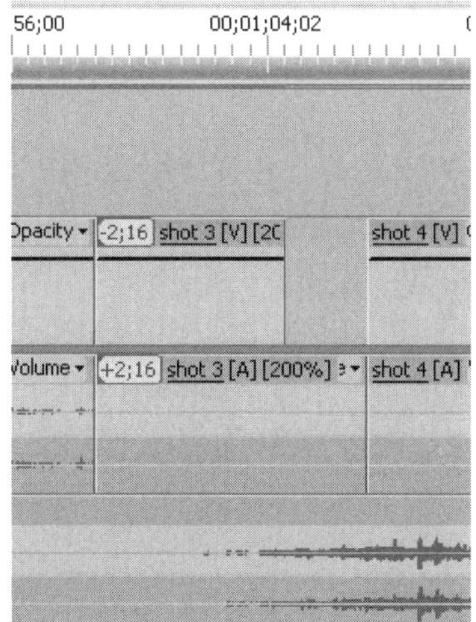

Figure 6.94 A number indicates the amount that linked video and audio have shifted out of sync.

Keeping Sync

During the course of editing, you may inadvertently lose sync between linked video and audio. Fortunately, Premiere Elements alerts you when linked clips are out of sync, and it provides a simple way to correct the problem.

To detect a loss of sync:

- A timecode number appears at the left edge of linked video and audio that are out of sync (**Figure 6.94**).

To restore sync automatically:

◆ Right-click the out-of-sync time display in either the video or audio portion of the clip, and *choose an option in the context menu* (**Figure 6.95**):

Move into Sync—Shifts the selected portion of the clip in time to restore sync, overwriting other clips if necessary (**Figure 6.96**)

Slip into Sync—Performs a slip edit on the selected portion of the clip to restore sync (**Figure 6.97**)

If space is available in the track, the clip shifts in the timeline to resynchronize with the linked portion. Otherwise, you'll have to create space in the track before resyncing the clips.

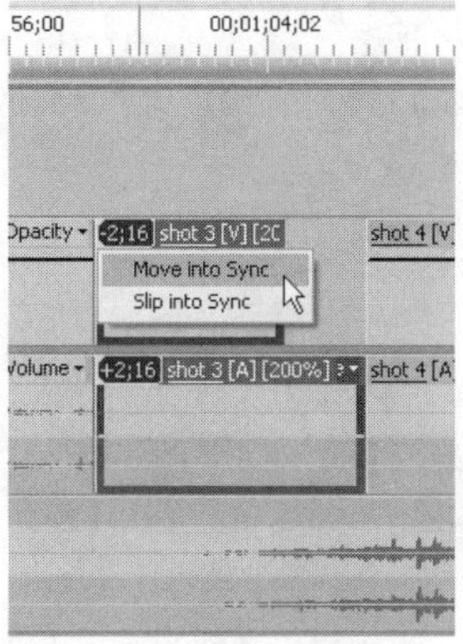

Figure 6.95 Right-click the number, and choose an option in the context menu.

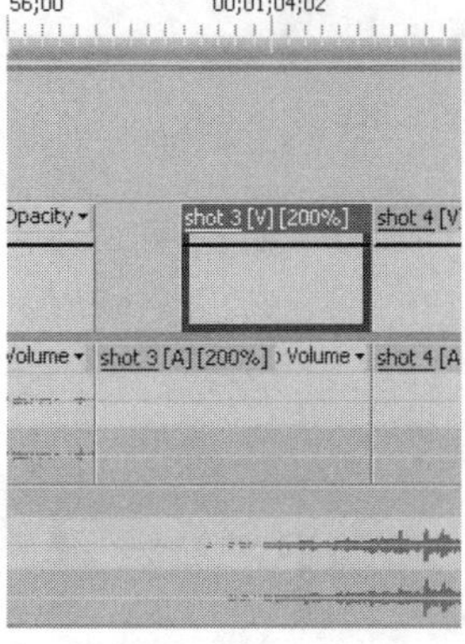

Figure 6.96 Depending on your choice, the clips move into sync...

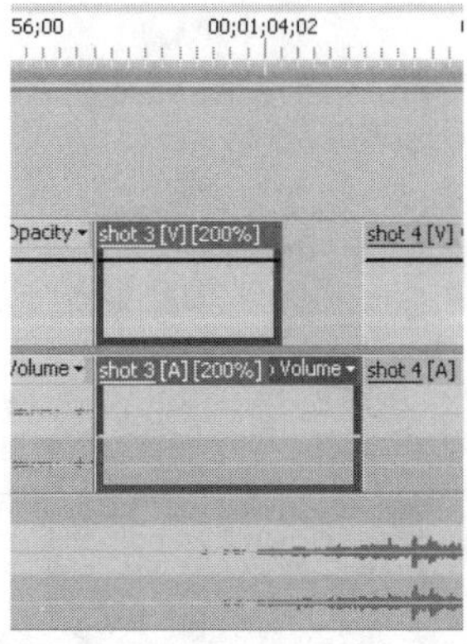

Figure 6.97 ...or slip into sync. A slip edit restores sync by changing the In and Out points of the clip's video or audio track without moving the clip's duration or position in the timeline.

✔ Tips

- A *slip edit* restores sync by changing the In and Out points of the clip's video or audio track without moving the clip's duration or position in the timeline.
- You can perform a slip edit manually by opening a sequence clip in the Monitor panel and dragging the dark area between the In and Out points, changing both by the same amount.

7

Adding Transitions

In editing, a *transition* is the way one clip replaces the last. Although the cut is the most basic transition, the term *transition* usually refers to a more gradual change from one clip to another. Adobe Premiere Elements 2 ships with loads of customizable video transitions, including an array of dissolves, wipes, and special effects. You can also transition between audio clips using two types of crossfade.

You select the transition you want from the *Effects and Transitions panel*, which lists not only video and audio transitions, but also video and audio filters in categorized folders.

Adding a transition is as simple as dragging it to a cut in the Timeline panel. You can even make adjustments to the transition's duration and placement by dragging it in the Timeline panel, much the same way you would move and trim a clip. But to really fine-tune a transition, use the *Properties panel.* The main area of the Properties panel describes the effect and includes an animated thumbnail demonstration. It also lets you control attributes common to all transitions—duration and placement—as well as settings specific to the transition. The Properties panel can also include an area that illustrates the selected transition in an *A/B roll* style timeline, which depicts the transition between two overlapping clips. This alternative way to visualize a transition can be easier to understand and adjust than the Timeline panel's version.

As you may have guessed, you'll use both the Effects and Transitions panel and Properties panel to add and adjust other types of effects—including motion, transparency, and filters. These techniques are covered in Chapter 10, "Adding Effects." This chapter explains how to create and modify transitions, and the following chapter, "Previewing a Sequence," covers how to render them for playback.

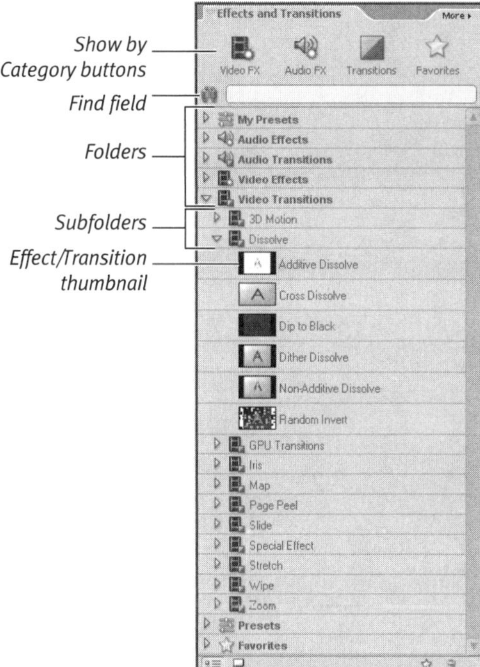

Figure 7.1 The Effects and Transitions panel lists and organizes items in a manner similar to (but not identical to) the Media panel.

Working with the Effects and Transitions Panel

The Effects and Transitions panel lists and organizes all effects, including audio and video transitions (**Figure 7.1**). The following sections address how to use the Effects and Transitions panel in general, and transitions in particular. You'll learn more about using effects in Chapter 10.

By default, the Effects and Transitions panel contains six folders: My Presets, Audio Effects, Audio Transitions, Video Effects, Video Transitions, and Presets. You can't rename these folders or remove items from them. However, you can add and name custom folders, which can contain copies of your favorite items or effect presets you save (see Chapter 10).

The Video Transitions folder includes 11 subfolders; the Audio Transitions folder contains just one subfolder. But technically speaking, the number and type of effects and transitions available in the Effects and Transitions panel is determined by the contents of Premiere Elements' Plug-Ins folder. You can add effects and filters from Adobe and third-party developers by adding plug-in files to the Plug-Ins folder.

Viewing Items in the Effects and Transitions Panel

As in the Media panel, you can expand folders in the Effects and Transitions panel to reveal their contents in list or icon view. You can't *open* a folder the way you can in the Media panel, but you can limit the visible items to the category you choose. You can also sift the items by entering the name of an item you want in a search field.

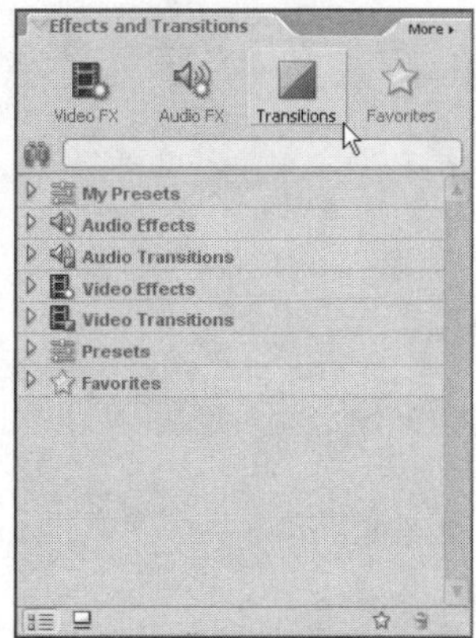

Figure 7.2 Selecting a category at the top of the Effects and Transitions panel...

To sift items by category:

- In the Effects and Transitions panel, select the button corresponding to the type of items you want to view (**Figure 7.2**):

  Video FX

  Audio FX

  Transitions

  Favorites

  The items that appear in the Effects and Transitions panel's main viewing area are limited to the category you select (**Figure 7.3**).

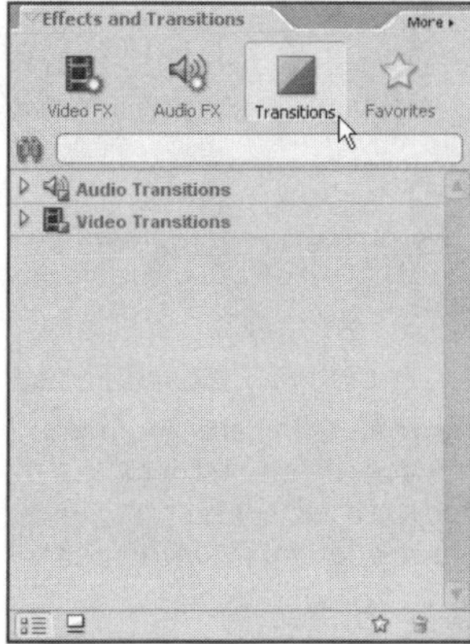

Figure 7.3 ...shows only items in that category—in this case, transitions.

To unsift the list:

- In the Effects and Transitions panel, click in the Find field (next to the Find icon).

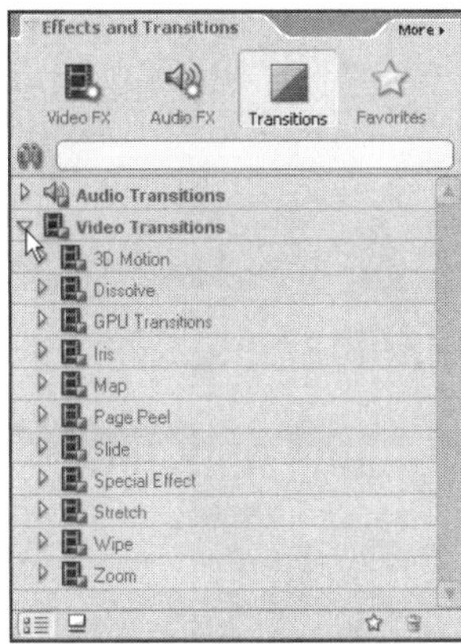

Figure 7.4 Click the triangle to expand or collapse a folder.

Figure 7.5 Clicking the list view icon displays items as small thumbnails in an outline fashion.

Figure 7.6 Clicking the icon view button displays items as large thumbnails tiled under an expanded folder.

To expand and collapse folders:

- In the Effects and Transitions panel, click the triangle next to a folder to expand or collapse it (**Figure 7.4**).

  A folder expands to reveal subfolders; a subfolder expands to reveal individual effects or transitions. Double-clicking a folder has no effect.

To set the view:

- At the bottom of the Effects and Transitions panel, click the button that corresponds to the view you want to use:

  List

  Icon

  The items in expanded folders are displayed according to your choice (**Figures 7.5** and **7.6**).

To find an item in the Effects and Transitions panel:

◆ In the Effects and Transitions panel, type the name of the item you're looking for in the Find field next to the Find icon (**Figure 7.7**).

As you type, the panel displays items that match what you type and hides other items. To unsift the list, clear the Find field.

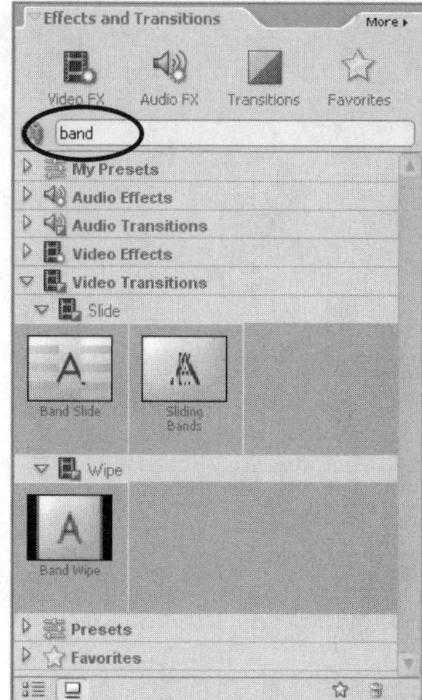

Figure 7.7 As you type the name of the item you're looking for in the Find field, the list is sifted to show only matching items.

✔ Tip

■ When you select a transition, its thumbnail image animates to demonstrate how the transition will look.

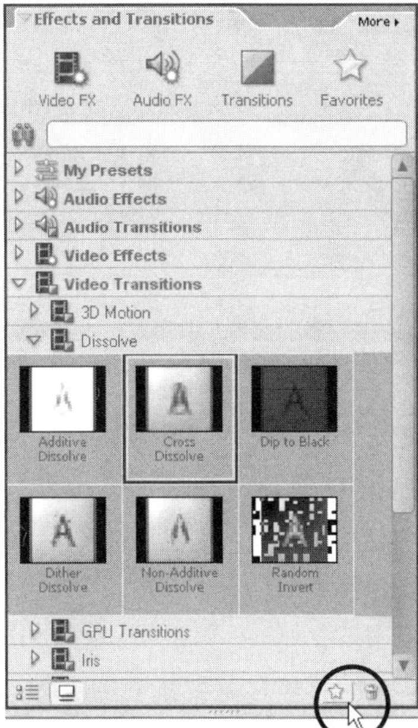

Figure 7.8 Select the item you want and click the Add to Favorites button.

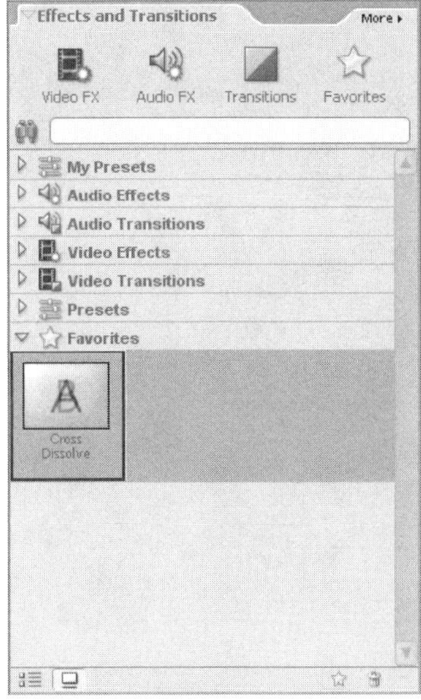

Figure 7.9 If necessary, Premiere Elements creates a Favorites folder, and adds the item to the folder. You'll have to select the Favorites button to view the Favorites folder, shown here.

Specifying Favorite Transitions

If you use a transition frequently, you can designate it a favorite. That is, you can easily make a copy of the transition that appears in a separate "Favorites" folder which, as you learned earlier, you can access quickly using the button at the top of the Effects and Transitions panel. You can delete the Favorites folder or any item it contains without affecting the original item. (You can specify customized effects in a similar manner, and save them in custom Presets folders. Saving and organizing custom effect presets is covered in Chapter 10.)

To specify a favorite effect or transition:

1. In the Effects and Transitions panel, select the item you want to set as a favorite.

   The Add to Favorites button becomes active.

2. Click the Add to Favorites button (**Figure 7.8**).

   The selected item is added to the Favorites folder. If this is the first item you specified as a favorite, Premiere Elements creates a Favorites folder automatically. You must click the Favorites button to see the Favorites folder (**Figure 7.9**). See the task "To sift items by category," earlier in this chapter.

To delete custom items:

1. *Do either of the following:*
   - ▲ Click to select the Favorites folder, a custom presets folder, or an item contained within them.
   - ▲ Ctrl-click to add items to or subtract items from your selection.
2. Click the Effects and Transitions panel's Delete Custom Items button (**Figure 7.10**).

   The selected custom items are removed from the Effects and Transitions panel (**Figure 7.11**).

✔ Tip

- Typically, you add transitions and effects after you complete a rough cut. Because you don't usually need both panels at once, docking the Effects and Transitions panel with the Media panel optimizes screen space; just select the tab of the panel you want to use. Refer to Chapter 1 for more about using panels.

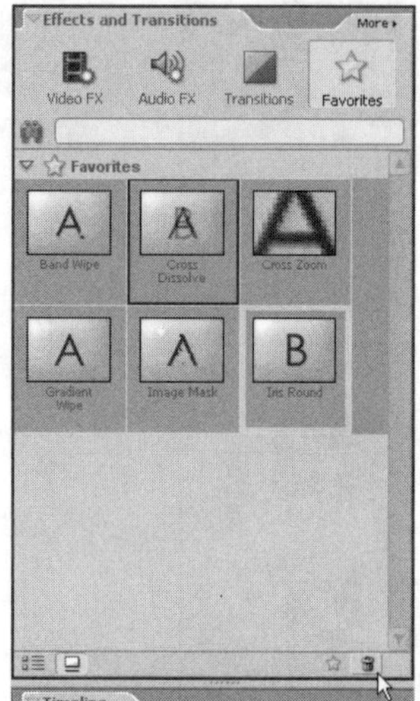

Figure 7.10 Select the items you want to remove from a custom folder, and click the Effects and Transitions panel's trashcan icon...

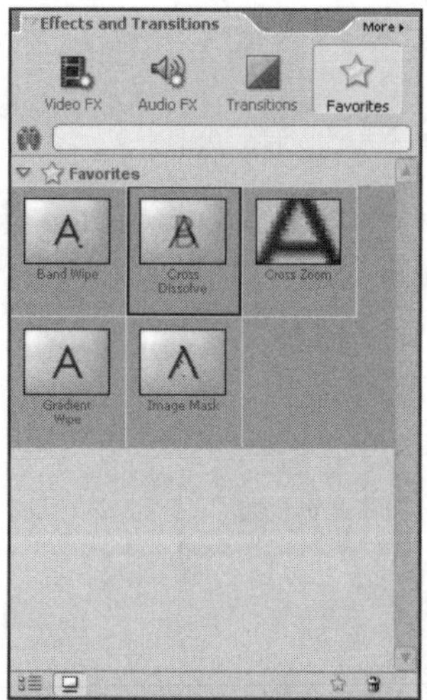

Figure 7.11 ...to remove the items from the list.

Figure 7.12 This figure depicts two clips in a sequence. Successive frames are represented by numbers in the first clip, and by letters in the second clip.

Figure 7.13 A transition utilizes frames beyond the cut point. In this case, a cross-dissolve involves frames after the first clip's Out point, and before second clip's In point.

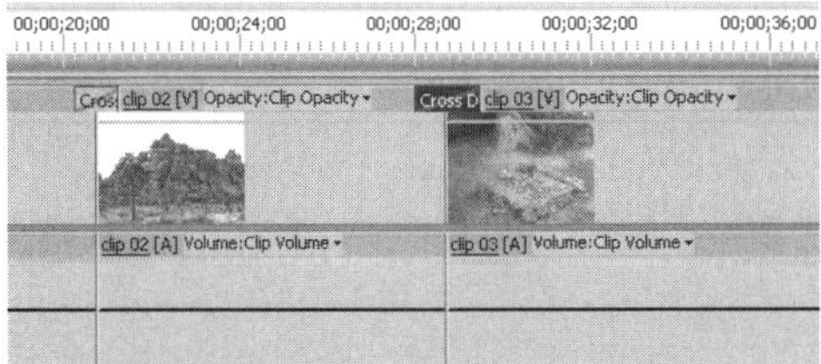

Figure 7.14 In the Timeline panel, the frames involved in a transition are hidden from view: You can only see when the transition begins and ends.

Understanding Transitions

If you're an experienced editor and already know the concepts behind transitions, feel free to skip ahead to the tasks (cut to the chase, as the old editing expression goes). But if you're new to editing, the inner workings of transitions can seem a little mysterious at first.

When you cut from one clip to another, the transition is instantaneous: The Out point of the first clip is immediately followed by the In point of the second clip (**Figure 7.12**). To switch from one clip to another more gradually, however, transitions must use frames *beyond* the cut point. In other words, the transition must mix some of the frames you previously trimmed away: frames after the first clip's Out point, before the second clip's In point, or, most often, a combination of both (**Figure 7.13**). (Remember, because editing in Premiere Elements is nondestructive, the frames you trimmed away are always available for use.)

But in the Timeline panel, these frames are hidden from view; you can only see when the transition begins and ends (**Figure 7.14**). For many, this layout makes it difficult to plan for the transition beforehand and to adjust it afterward.

continues on next page

Transitions are depicted more explicitly in the Properties panel. In the Properties panel's timeline area, each clip occupies a separate track—the first in track A, the second in track B. The transition appears between the two clips in its own track. As in the Timeline panel, the area where the transition and the clips overlap represents the duration of the transition's effect. A vertical line represents the cut point before the transition was applied. But because this view shows each clip in its own track, you can see the otherwise hidden material beyond the cut point—all the available material beyond the first clip's Out point and before the second clip's In point. This way, you can adjust the transition not only relative to the cut point, but also in terms of the footage available in each clip (**Figure 7.15**).

If there isn't enough footage to create the transition, Premiere Elements repeats the first clip's Out point frame or the second clip's In point frame. Of course, repeating frames results in a freeze-frame effect that you may find unacceptable. You can adjust the transition or trim the clips to avoid repeating frames, which are marked with a pattern of slashes (**Figures 7.16** and **7.17**). (See "Adjusting a Transition's Duration and Alignment," later in this chapter.)

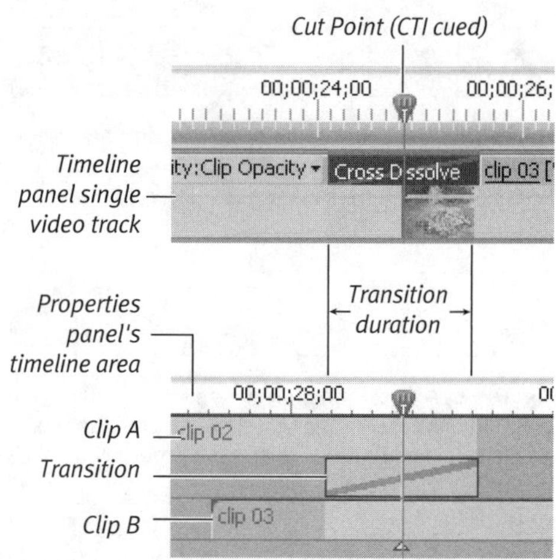

Figure 7.15 This figure contrasts how a transition looks in the Timeline with how it's represented in the Properties panel's timeline pane. The A/B roll layout lets you see the footage hidden in the Timeline panel's single-track layout.

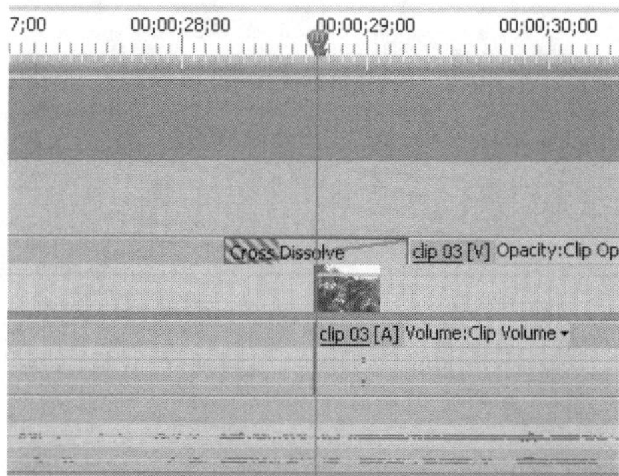

Figure 7.16 When there isn't enough footage for the transition, Premiere Elements repeats the edge frames. The affected area appears marked with a pattern of slashes both in the Timeline panel...

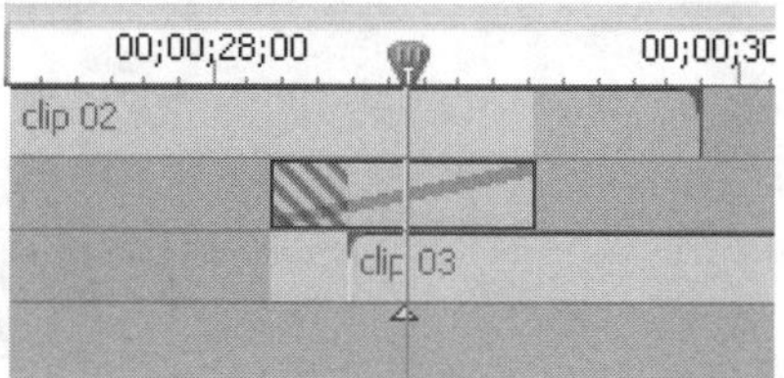

Figure 7.17 ...and in the corresponding area of the Properties panel's timeline pane.

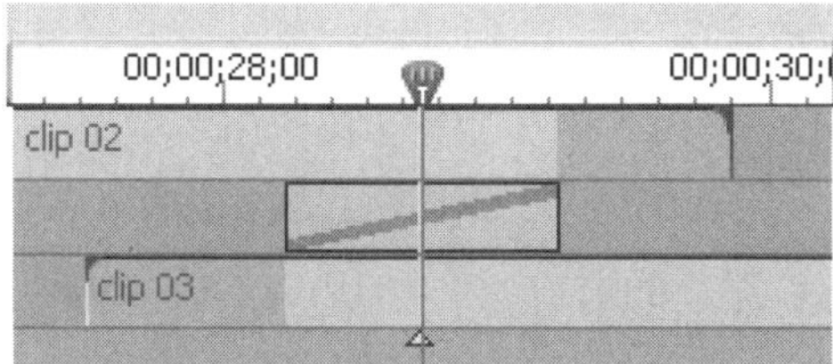

Figure 7.18 When a 1-second transition is centered on the cut, it looks like this in the Properties panel.

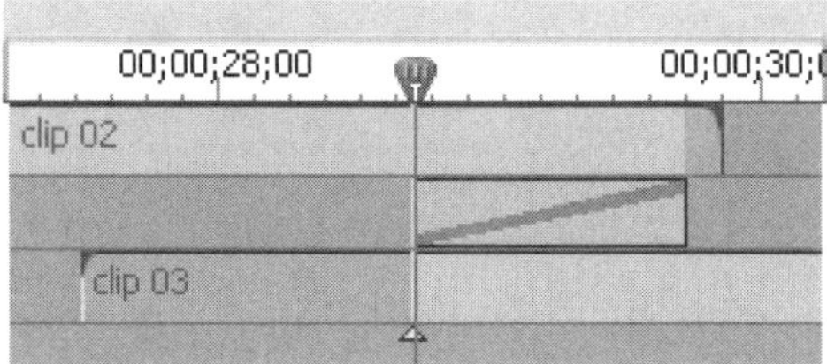

Figure 7.19 Here's the same transition as in the previous figure, except that it starts on the cut.

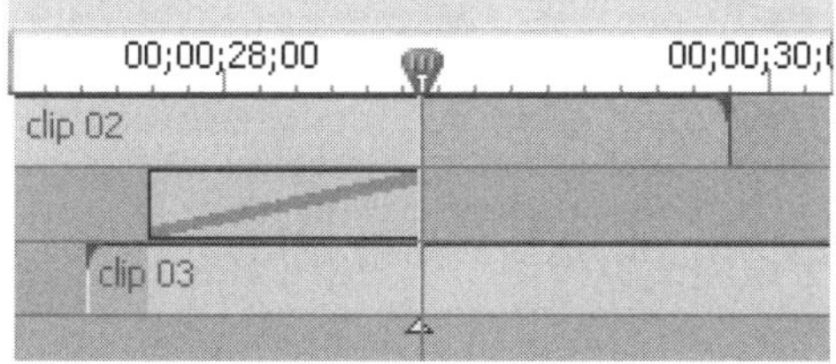

Figure 7.20 And here, the transition ends on the cut.

Understanding Transition Duration and Alignment

In the Timeline panel, transitions appear as clip-like objects. The width of the transition corresponds to its *duration*; its position relative to the cut point corresponds with its *alignment*. Once you add a transition, you can adjust its duration and alignment freely. However, its initial settings are more limited. A transition's initial duration is determined by a default setting you specify; its initial alignment is limited to three options, depending on where you drop it relative to the cut: center of cut, start of cut, or end of cut. Understanding these options makes it easier to plan for a transition beforehand and to adjust it afterward:

Center of Cut—Centers the transition over the cut so that an equal number of hidden frames on each side of the edit are used to create the transition. A 1-second transition centered on the cut would use 15 frames of footage after the Out point of footage of the first clip and 15 frames before the In point of the second clip (**Figure 7.18**).

Start of Cut—Starts the transition at the cut, so that the hidden frames of the first clip are combined with the frames of the second clip that were visible before the transition was applied. Using the same example as before, the transition would combine 30 frames of footage after the first clip's Out point (hidden frames) with the first 30 frames of the second clip (**Figure 7.19**).

End of Cut—Ends the transition at the cut, so that the hidden frames of the second clip are combined with the frames of the first clip that were visible before you added the transition. Continuing the same example, the transition would combine the last 30 frames of the first clip with 30 frames of the footage before the second clip's In point (hidden frames) (**Figure 7.20**).

Setting the Default Transition Duration

Initially, transitions are 1 second in duration. However, you can specify any default duration for video and audio transitions.

To specify the default duration for transitions:

1. In the Effects and Transitions panel's More menu, choose Default Transition Duration (**Figure 7.21**).

   The General pane of the Preferences dialog box opens.

2. *Do either of the following* (**Figure 7.22**):

   ▲ For Video Transition Default Duration, enter a value in frames.

   ▲ For Audio Transition Default Duration, enter a value in seconds.

   For audio, you can enter a value to two decimal points.

3. Click OK to close the dialog box.

   From this point on, video and audio transitions will use the duration you specified.

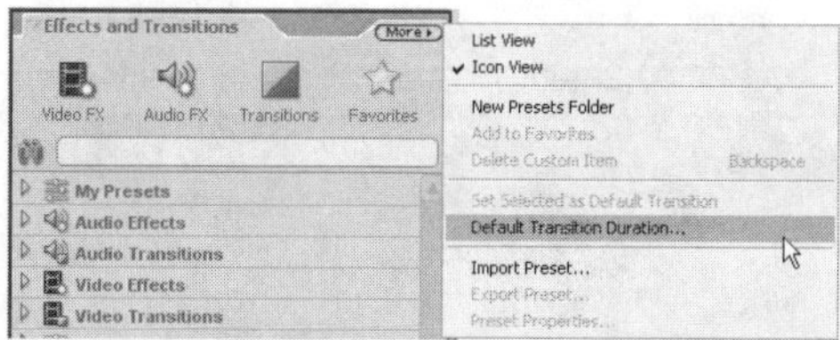

Figure 7.21 Choose Default Transition Duration.

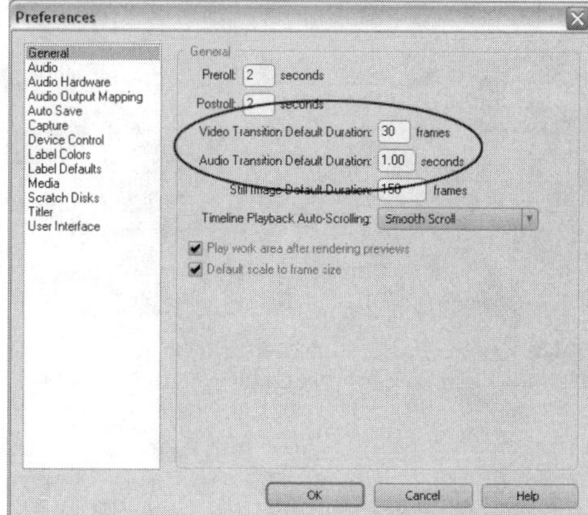

Figure 7.22 In the General pane of the Preferences dialog box, enter a duration for video transitions in frames, and a duration for audio transitions in seconds (to two decimal points).

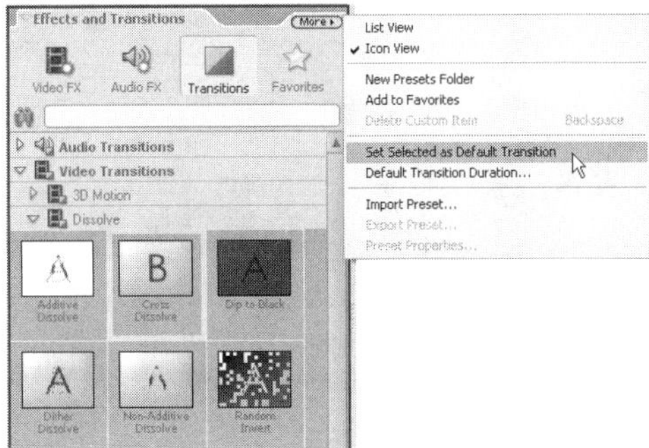

Figure 7.23 Select the transition you want to be the default, and choose Set Selected as Default Transition.

Specifying a Default Transition

The default duration can be applied automatically to a sequence created with the Automate to Timeline feature (explained in Chapter 5, "Editing Clips into a Sequence").

To specify the default transition:

1. In the Effects and Transitions panel, select the transition you want to set as the default.
2. In the Effects and Transitions panel's More menu, choose Set Selected as Default Transition (**Figure 7.23**).

   The selected transition becomes the default transition.

Applying a Transition

You can apply a video transition to any cut in a video track, and you can apply any audio transition to any cut in an audio track. Furthermore, video transitions aren't limited to video track 1. This way, it's possible to layer video tracks, complete with transitions. (See Chapter 10, "Adding Effects," for more about transparency.)

In addition to adding transitions between clips, you can add a transition to the end of a clip adjacent to an empty area in the track. Doing so automatically aligns the clip using End at Cut and is useful when you want to create an audio fade out or a video fade to black (the empty track acts as silence or black video).

To add a transition:

- Drag a transition from the Effects and Transitions panel to a cut point in the Timeline panel, and position the mouse so that its icon indicates the alignment option you want:

  Center at Cut —Centers the transition on the cut so that an equal number of hidden frames from each clip are used (**Figure 7.24**)

  Start at Cut —Aligns the beginning of the transition with the cut (**Figure 7.25**)

  End at Cut —Aligns the end of the transition with the cut (**Figure 7.26**)

  When you release the mouse, the transition appears over the clips. It uses the alignment you specified and the default duration (**Figure 7.27**).

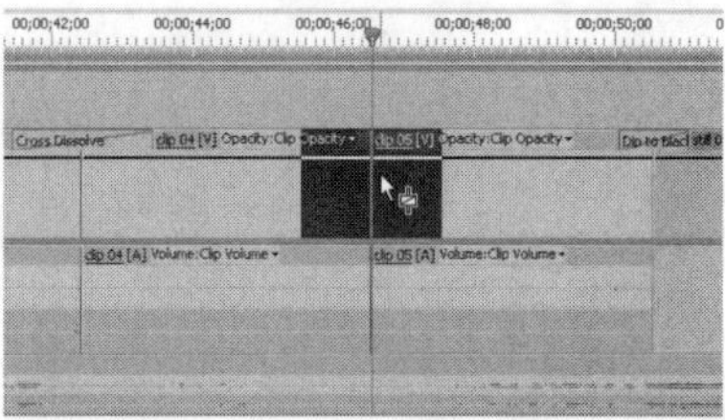

Figure 7.24 Depending on where you drop the transition, the icon indicates whether it's centered on the cut...

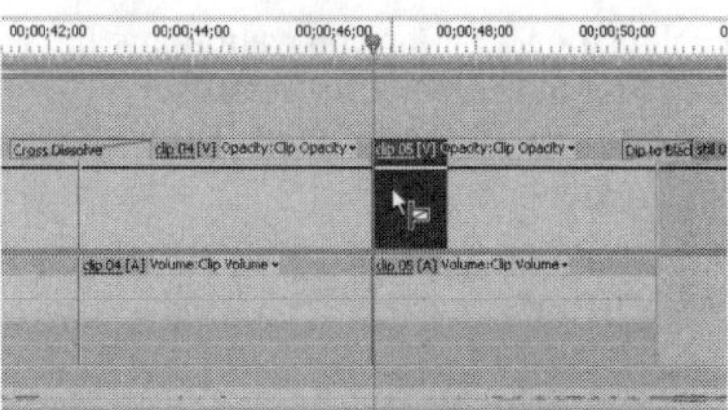

Figure 7.25 ...at the start of the cut...

Figure 7.26 ...or at the end of the cut.

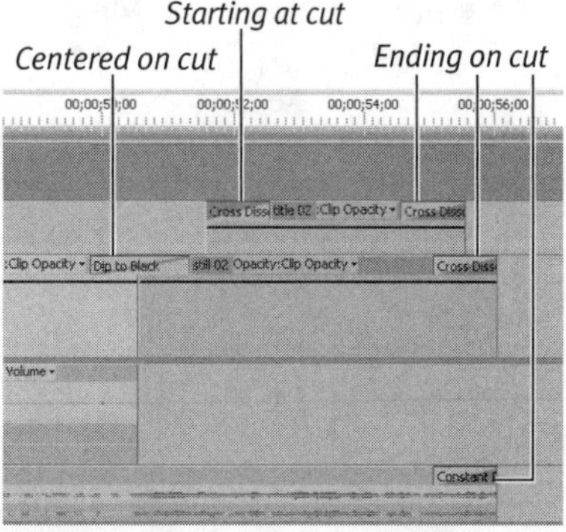

Figure 7.27 In this figure, the first transition is centered on the cut. A cross-dissolve starting on the cut makes the title fade up; a cross-dissolve ending on the cut makes it fade out. Similarly, the cross-dissolve on the audio clip ends on the cut; because the clip is followed by an empty area, it works as an audio fade out.

To force a Start at Cut or End at Cut alignment:

- Press Ctrl as you drag a transition from the Effects and Transitions panel to a cut point in the Timeline panel.

  Depending on which side of the cut you drag the transition to, the icon indicates either of only two alignment options: Start at Cut or End at Cut placement.

✔ Tips

- You can replace a transition by dropping a new transition on top of the old one.
- The default duration can be applied automatically to a sequence created with the Automate to Timeline feature (explained in Chapter 5, "Editing Clips into a Sequence").

Using the Properties Panel with Transitions

Although you can adjust a transition directly in the Timeline panel, you'll need to use the Properties panel to adjust the transition in an A/B layout or to customize the transition's settings. However, you must select the transition in the Timeline panel to make its controls appear in the Properties panel. (Selecting a clip lets you use the Properties panel to adjust its audio and video effects, or filters. See Chapter 10 for more information.)

The Properties panel's main pane contains information about the transition, a thumbnail preview, and controls for adjusting its duration, alignment, and various custom settings. You can also reveal a timeline pane, which lets you view and adjust the selected transition in its own timeline using an A/B roll layout. The timeline pane's CTI and scroll bar work just like those in the Monitor panel (covered in Chapter 5).

To show or hide the Properties panel's timeline pane:

- In the upper-right corner of the Properties panel's main pane, click the Show/Hide Timeline Panel button.

  The button's label and icon toggles depending on whether the Properties panel's timeline is concealed (**Figure 7.28**) or revealed (**Figure 7.29**).

Figure 7.28 Clicking the Show Timeline button...

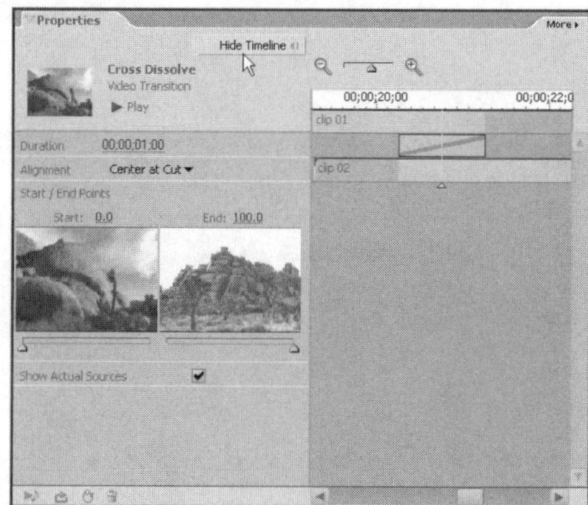

Figure 7.29 ...toggles the Properties panel's timeline open or closed.

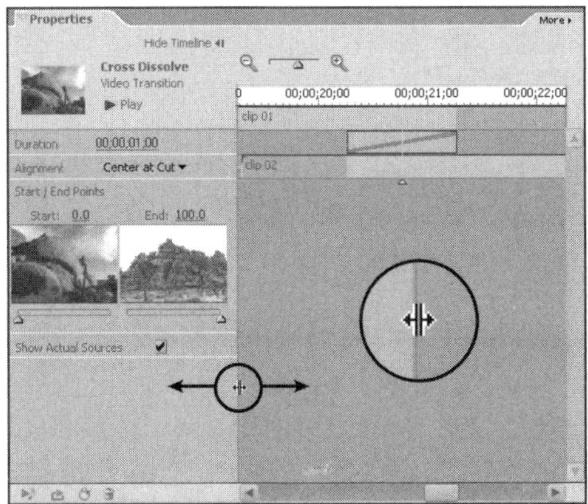

Figure 7.30 Drag the border between the two panels to change their relative sizes.

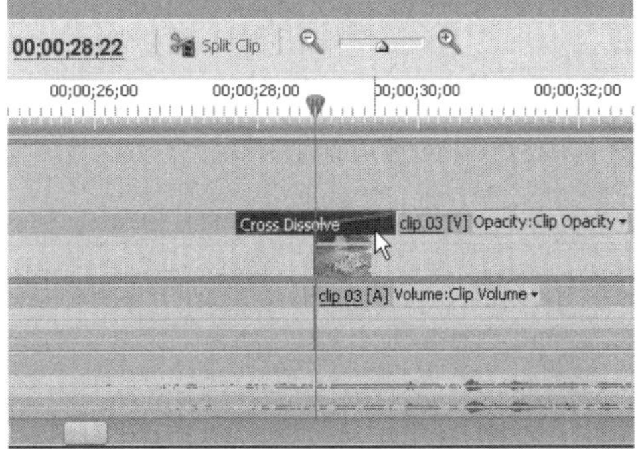

Figure 7.31 Selecting a transition in the timeline ...

Figure 7.32 ...makes its settings appear in the Properties panel.

To change the relative size of the timeline pane:

◆ Position the mouse pointer between the Properties panel's main pane and timeline pane so that the mouse pointer changes to the Width Adjustment icon, and drag left or right to change the relative widths of the two areas (**Figure 7.30**).

To view a transition in the Properties panel:

1. Click a transition in the Timeline panel to select it (**Figure 7.31**).

   The selected transition's thumbnail animates to demonstrate the transition. The Properties panel displays settings for the selected transition (**Figure 7.32**).

2. Adjust the transition by *doing either of the following:*
   - ▲ Use controls in the Properties panel's main pane to adjust the transition's settings.
   - ▲ Use the Properties panel's timeline pane to adjust the transition's duration and placement manually or to adjust the cut point between clips.

To show actual sources in thumbnail images:

- In the main pane of the Properties panel, select Show Actual Sources (**Figure 7.33**).

  When the check box is selected, the A and B sample images are replaced by the clips of the transition (**Figure 7.34**).

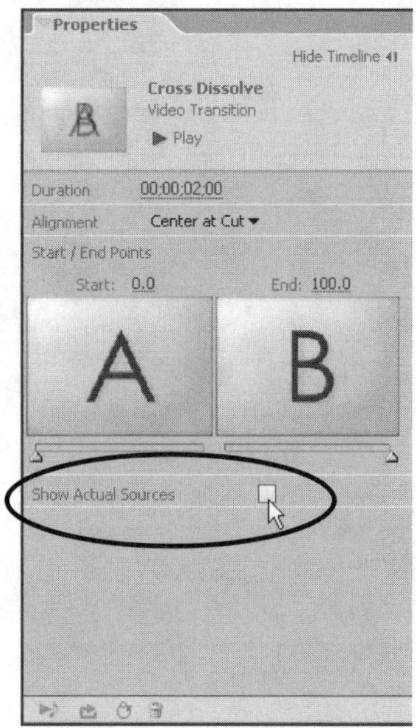

Figure 7.33 Select Show Actual Sources to replace the A and B sample images...

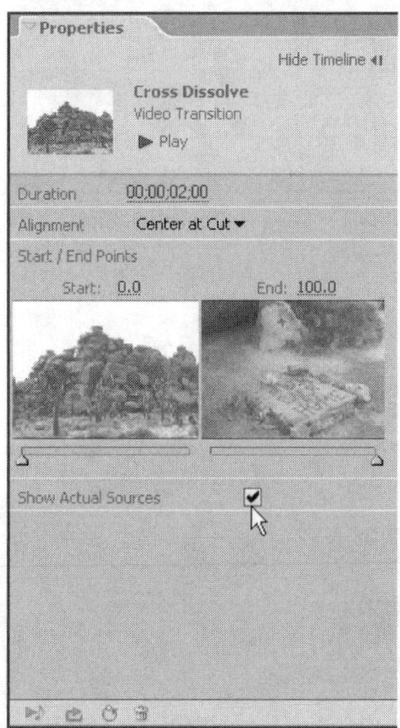

Figure 7.34 ...with the actual footage.

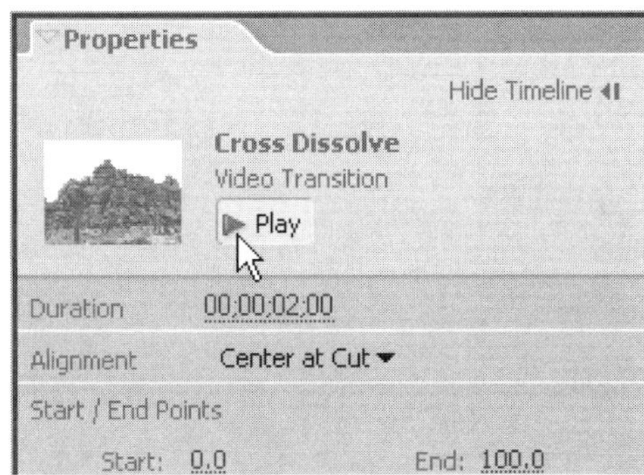

Figure 7.35 Click the Play button to preview the transition.

To play a thumbnail preview of a transition:

- Click the Play button ▶ Play in the upper-left corner of the Properties panel (next to the transition's description; **Figure 7.35**).

  The Play button toggles to a Stop button. The small thumbnail image demonstrates the transition, including any adjustments you make to the transition's settings. If Show Actual Sources is selected, the A and B sample images are replaced by the clip images.

✔ Tip

- When not all of a transition's customizable settings fit in the available vertical space of the Properties panel, a scroll bar appears. But when the Properties panel's timeline area is visible, the scroll bar appears to the right of the timeline, not the main pane. If some settings seem to be missing, look for the scroll bar at the far right.

Adjusting a Transition's Duration and Alignment

Sometimes, a transition's initial duration and alignment work perfectly, and you can move on to other edits. But chances are, you'll want to make small adjustments. You might even need to trim the clips involved in the transition. You can make these adjustments using controls in the Properties panel's main pane. Or, you can make manual adjustments by dragging in either the Timeline panel or the Properties panel's timeline area.

Figure 7.36 You can adjust the transition's duration by changing the Duration value in the Properties panel's main pane.

To adjust a transition's duration numerically:

- In the main panel of the Properties panel, *do either of the following:*
  - ▲ Drag the Duration display to change the value (**Figure 7.36**).
  - ▲ Click the Duration display, type a new duration, and press Enter.

  The selected transition reflects the duration you specify in the Timeline panel and in the timeline pane of the Properties panel.

To adjust a transition's alignment automatically:

- In the main pane of the Properties panel, choose an option in the Alignment drop-down menu (**Figure 7.37**):

  Center at Cut centers the transition on the cut.

  Start at Cut aligns the beginning of the transition with the cut.

  End at Cut aligns the end of the transition with the cut.

  Custom Start is dimmed, unless the transition is already positioned at a custom alignment.

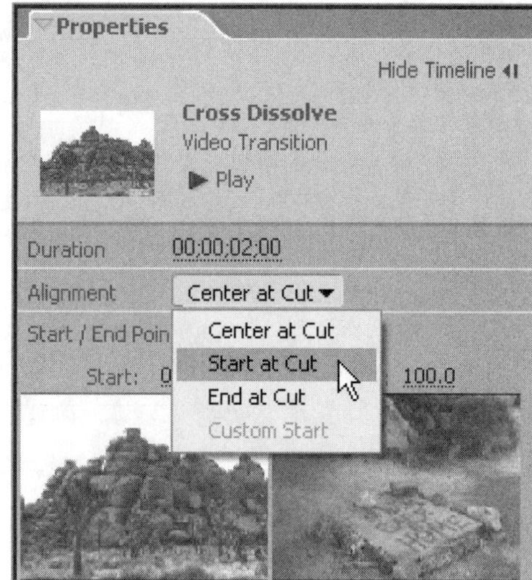

Figure 7.37 You can move the transition by choosing an option from the Alignment drop-down menu.

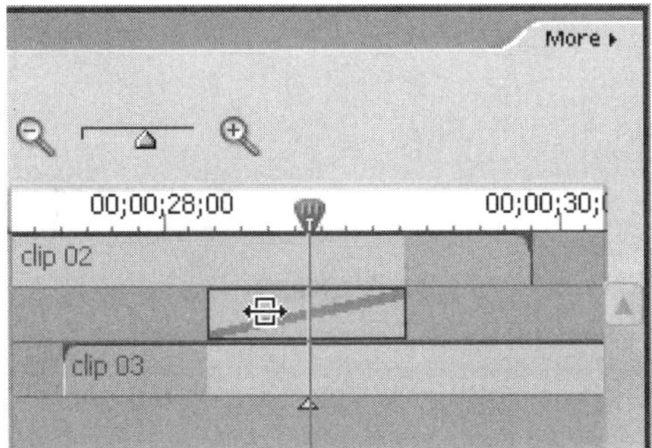

Figure 7.38 Drag the transition from the center to change its position relative to the cut.

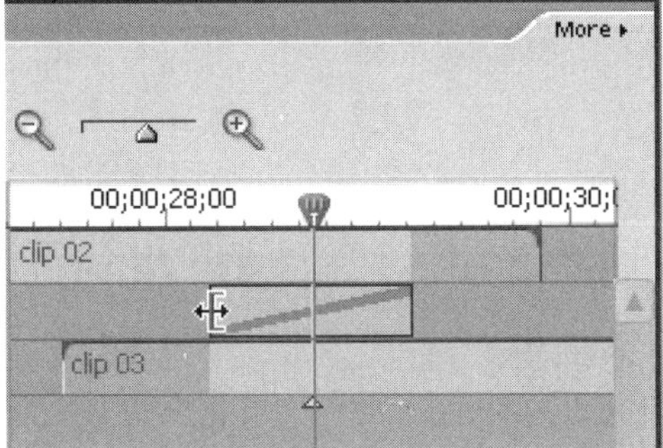

Figure 7.39 You can change the transition's duration by trimming its left edge...

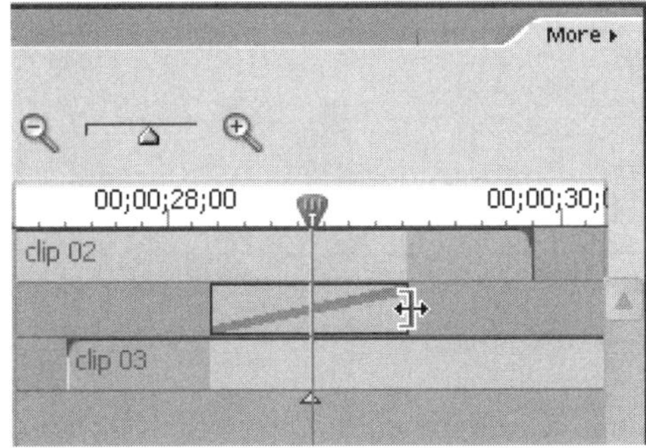

Figure 7.40 ...or by trimming its right edge.

To adjust a transition manually:

1. In either the Timeline panel or the Properties panel's timeline pane, *do any of the following:*
   - ▲ To change the alignment of the transition without changing its duration, position the mouse pointer on the center of the transition so that the pointer changes into a Move Transition icon (**Figure 7.38**).
   - ▲ To change the duration of the transition by changing its starting point, position the mouse on the transition's left edge, so that the pointer changes into a Trim Head icon (**Figure 7.39**).
   - ▲ To change the duration of the transition by changing where it ends, position the mouse on the transition's right edge, so that the pointer changes into a Trim Tail icon (**Figure 7.40**).

   The Trim Head or Trim Tail tool also appears if you position the mouse at the transition's edge in track A or track B.
2. Drag left or right to move or trim the transition.

To trim clips of a transition in the timeline pane:

1. In the Properties panel's timeline pane, *do any of the following:*
   - ▲ To change the edit point, position the mouse pointer at the cut point between clips, so that the pointer becomes the Rolling Edit icon (**Figure 7.41**).
   - ▲ To ripple-edit the first clip's Out point, position the mouse pointer on the clip in the A track, so that the pointer becomes the Ripple Tail icon (**Figure 7.42**).
   - ▲ To ripple-edit the first clip's In point, position the mouse pointer on the clip in the B track, so that the pointer becomes the Ripple Head icon (**Figure 7.43**).

   If you position the mouse at the edge of the transition, the mouse changes to the Trim Head or Trim Tail tool, which changes the duration of the transition.
2. Drag left or right to trim the clip.

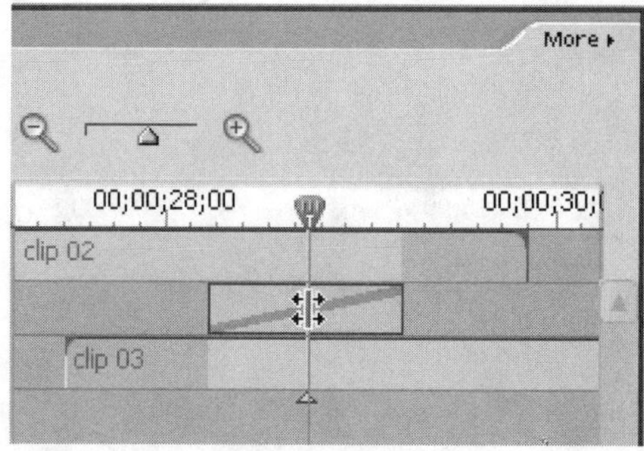

Figure 7.41 In the Properties panel's timeline area, drag the cut point to change the first clip's In point and the second clip's Out point by the same amount...

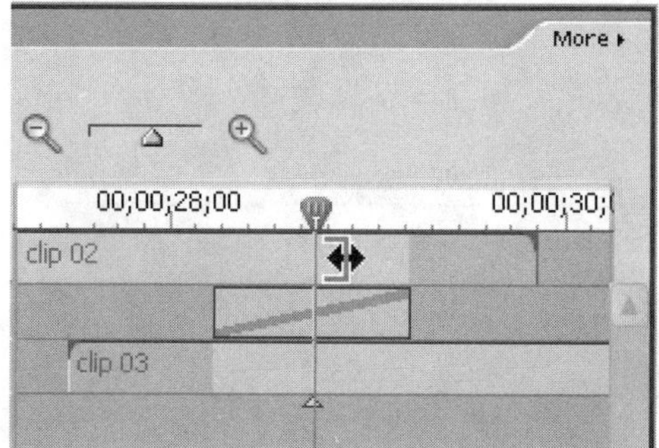

Figure 7.42 ...or drag the clip in the A track to ripple-edit its Out point...

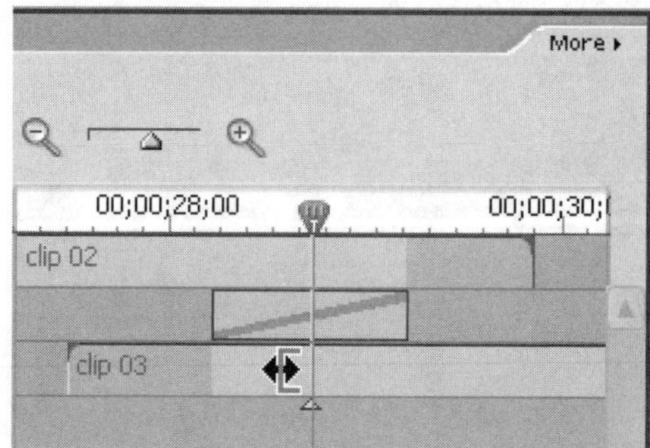

Figure 7.43 ...or drag the clip in the B track to ripple-edit its In point.

✔ Tips

- As you make adjustments to a transition, the Monitor panel's Timeline view displays the frames that are affected.
- Changing the edit point by dragging (changing the first clip's Out point and the second clip's In point by the same amount, and in a single step) is also called a *rolling edit.* You can perform a rolling edit in the Properties panel but not in the Timeline panel.

Direction button (diagonal)

Figure 7.44 Click one of the small arrows to set the direction of a transition. Here, a wipe is set to progress from the top-left corner of the image.

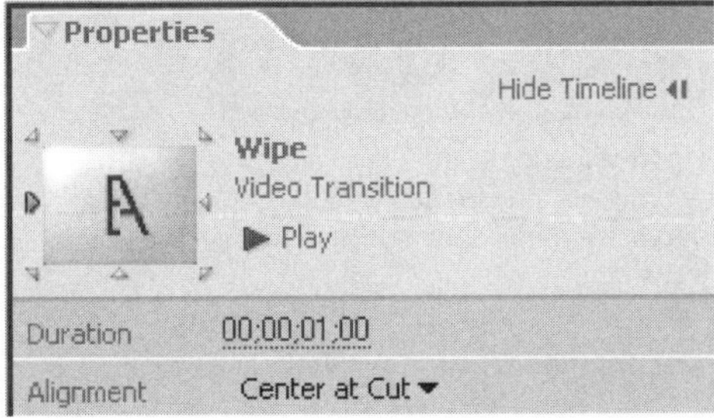

Figure 7.45 Here, the wipe is set to begin from the left side.

Customizing Transition Settings

Each transition has its own collection of customizable settings. The available options depend on the transition you're modifying. By modifying these settings, you can effectively expand your list of transitions. You can, for example, set the Wipe transition to wipe in any of eight directions; you can make it hard-edged or soft-edged; and you can add a border of any color or thickness.

As usual, you have to add the transition to a cut first and then select it to modify its settings in the Properties panel.

To set the direction of the transition:

- In the Properties panel, click the small arrows, or edge selectors, around the transition thumbnail to select the orientation of the transition (**Figure 7.44**).

  The movement of the transition, such as the direction of a wipe, progresses in the direction you specify (**Figure 7.45**).

To adjust the start and end of the transition:

- In the Properties panel, *do any of the following:*
  - ▲ Adjust the Start and End values by dragging or by entering a value between 0 and 100.
  - ▲ Drag the start and end sliders under the A and B thumbnail images, respectively (**Figures 7.46** and **7.47**).
  - ▲ Shift-drag either slider to set the start and end to the same value.

  A standard transition starts at 0 and ends at 100.

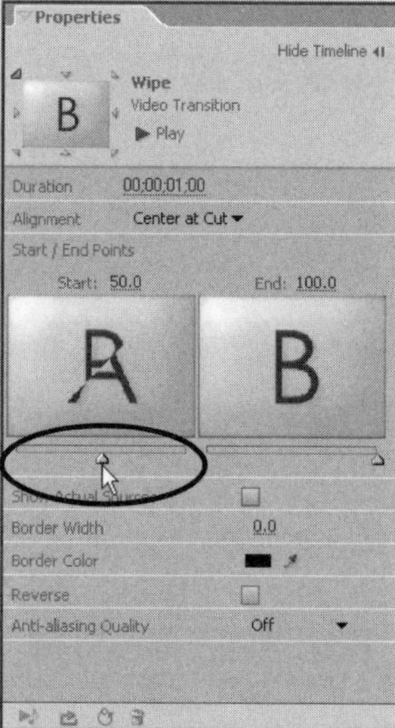

Figure 7.46 Adjust the Start value or drag the corresponding slider to define the initial appearance of the transition.

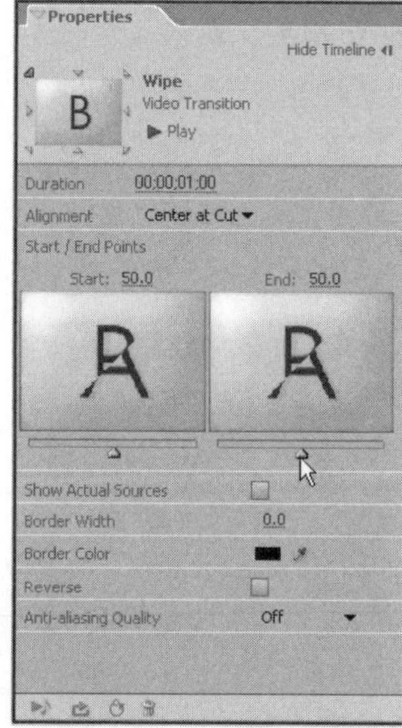

Figure 7.47 Adjust the End value or use the slider to define the transition's final appearance. Instead of wiping from shot A to shot B, this transition is set to show a mix of the two shots for the duration of the transition.

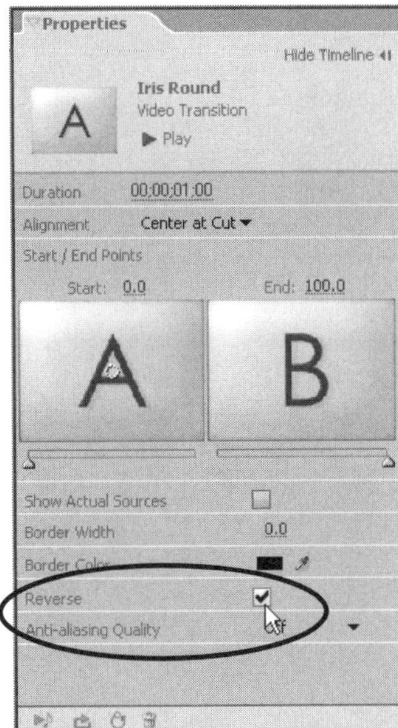

Figure 7.48 Clicking Reverse makes the transition progress in the opposite way. For example, reversing an iris round transition makes the iris close to reveal the second shot, rather than open to reveal it.

To reverse a transition:

- In the Properties panel, select Reverse.

  The transition is reversed. For example, reversing an iris round transition makes the iris close to reveal the next shot rather than open (**Figure 7.48**).

✔ Tips

- You can use the sliders to get a preview of the transition, but make sure you reset the transition to the position you want before you finish.
- You can't keyframe a transition; you can only set a start and an end state. (For more about keyframing effects, see Chapter 10.)

To set the center point of the transition:

- In the Properties panel, drag the handle in the Start (A) or End (B) image to set the center point of the transition (**Figures 7.49** and **7.50**).

  The handle represents the center of an iris transition, for example.

Figure 7.49 Drag the round handle in the Start thumbnail image to set the center point of transitions, such as iris transitions.

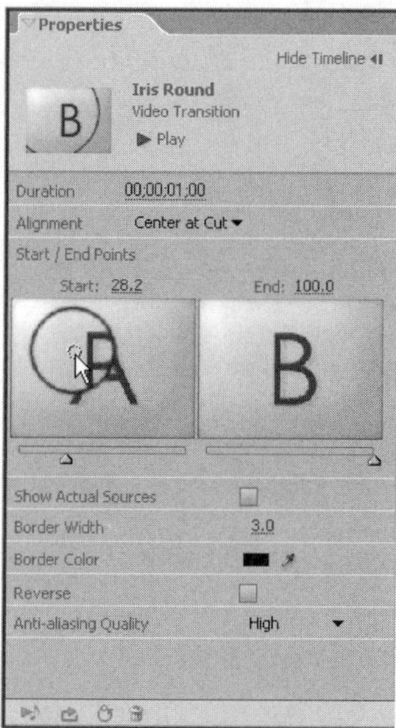

Figure 7.50 Here, the center point, or origin, has been moved off center. To better illustrate the effect, the Start slider has been moved, and a border has been added.

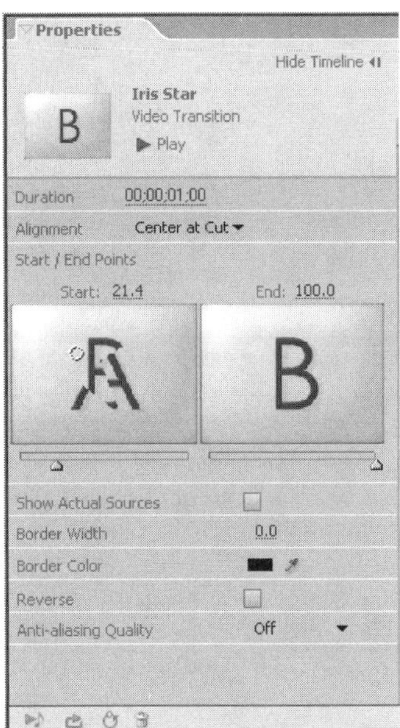

Figure 7.51 When the Border Width is set to 0, no border appears at the transition's edge (the Start setting has been increased so you can see the edge).

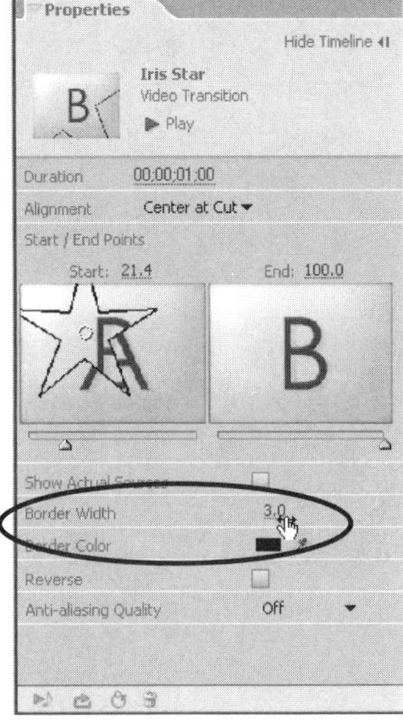

Figure 7.52 Increasing the value adds a border to the transition's edge.

To set the border thickness:

- To set the Border Width value, drag the underlined number, or click it and enter a new value (**Figure 7.51**).

  The edges of the transition appear with a border of the thickness you specified (**Figure 7.52**).

To set the border color:

- To set the Border Color value, *do either of the following:*
  - ▲ Click the color swatch to select a color using the color picker (**Figure 7.53**).
  - ▲ Click the Eyedropper tool, and, holding the mouse, position the tool over any color on the screen. Release the mouse to set the current color.

  The edges of the transition use the border color you specified.

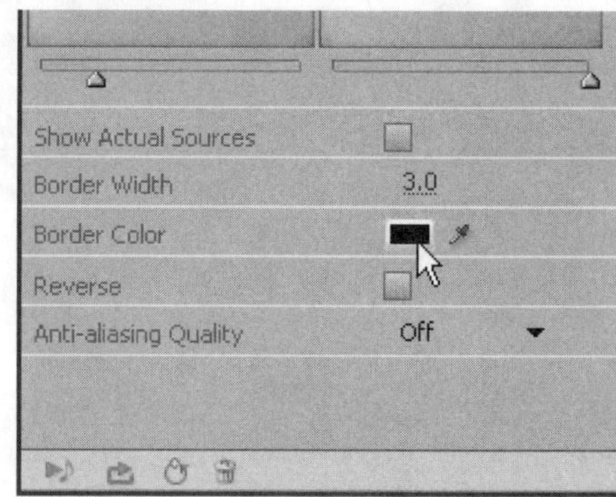

Figure 7.53 Change the color of the border by clicking the color swatch or using the Eyedropper tool.

To specify the smoothness of edges:

- To set the Anti-aliasing Quality value, choose an option from the drop-down menu (**Figure 7.54**).

  Settings range from Off to High. Off applies no anti-aliasing; High applies the maximum amount of smoothing.

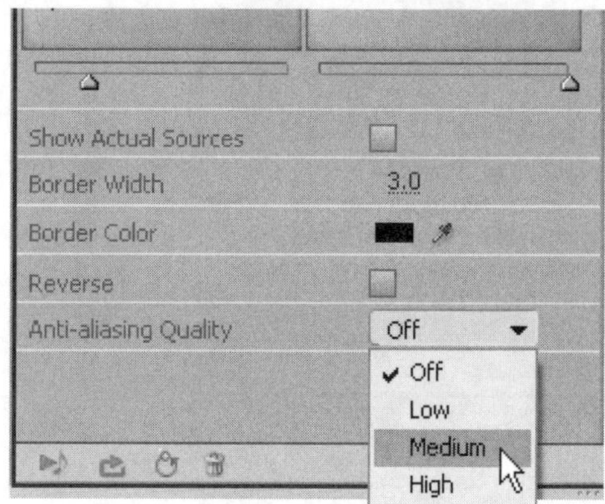

Figure 7.54 Choose an option from the Anti-aliasing Quality drop-down menu.

✔ Tips

- To see the border, you have to play the thumbnail preview or the actual transition. You can also set the Start slider to a higher number (such as 50) to help you adjust the border. Make sure you set the Start slider back to 0, though.
- Border thickness and anti-aliasing can only be approximated in the thumbnail images. The effect is more evident in the Monitor panel's Timeline view and especially in the output video on a television screen.

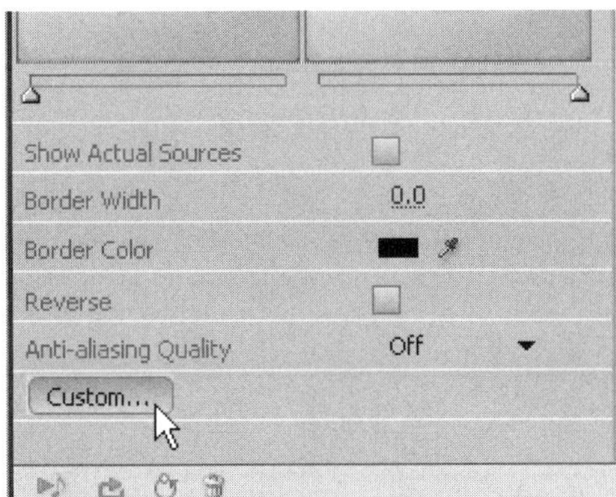

Figure 7.55 Some transitions have additional settings you can access by clicking the Custom button.

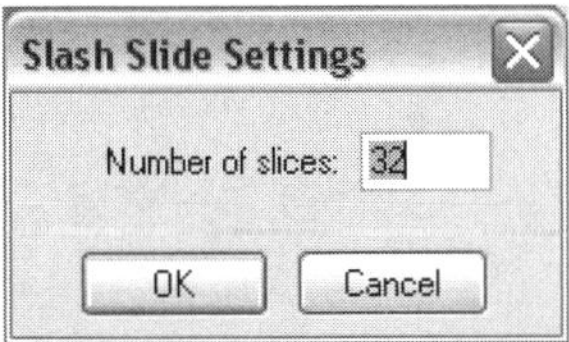

Figure 7.56 The Custom button opens a dialog box for the transition's special settings, such as the number of slices in the Slash Slide transition.

To set custom settings:

- In the Properties panel, click the Custom button to define settings specific for that transition (**Figure 7.55**).

  You can define the number of bands in the Slash Slide transition, for example (**Figure 7.56**).

✔ Tip

- Although the cross-dissolve transition is the best way to create a simple transition from one clip to the next, blending images for longer periods or blending multiple clips is best achieved by using the video fade controls on a superimposed clip. See Chapter 10 for more information.

Special Transitions

Most transitions included with Premiere Elements operate along the same lines and use similar settings. However, a few transitions work a little differently from the rest. Because these transitions can't all be covered in the limited scope of this book, the following list describes a few to which you should give special attention:

Displace and **Texturize**—To shift pixels in an image based on the luminance values of a clip or other image

Gradient Wipe and **Image Mask**—To transition between clips using a separate image as a matte or mask

These transitions are explained in detail in the Adobe Premiere Elements User Guide.

8 Previewing a Sequence

As you know, you can watch a sequence in the Monitor panel's Timeline view by just hitting its play button (or the keyboard equivalent). But for the most accurate view, you need to output the video to a television monitor via a digital video (DV) camera or deck.

Premiere Elements 2 utilizes your system's resources to render the frames of a sequence on the fly. Naturally, segments with transitions and other effects require more processing than those without. That's because effects force Premiere Elements to generate new material. To create a cross-dissolve transition, for example, the system must digitally combine the first shot with the next. But with the proper system configuration, Premiere Elements can play back even layered clips, transitions, and other effects in *real time*—that is, right away and at the full frame rate. Even when a complex segment exceeds your system's ability to deliver the effect at the full frame rate, Premiere Elements can still display the effect by reducing the image quality, the frame rate, or both.

To see these segments at the full frame rate, you'll have to forego on-the-fly processing and create a *render file* instead. Initially, rendering takes time—how much time depends on the complexity of the effect and your system's processing speed. But once rendered, the area should play back as easily as any other clip, and at the full frame rate.

In the past, the need to render effects was the Achilles' heel of nonlinear editing systems (NLEs). But technical developments—such as DV's ability to encode high-quality video at modest data rates, and ever-increasing storage and processing power—have made real-time editing accessible without the need for special hardware.

Using Real-Time Rendering

If your system meets the minimum requirements for DV (listed in the book's introduction), it should be able to render many transitions and effects on the fly and still play them back at the DV's normal playback speed.

When an effect is too complex for your system to deliver frames at full playback speed, Premiere Elements automatically degrades the Timeline view's image quality as needed. This way, you can see the video right away at normal speed, albeit at a lower quality. To have your cake and eat it too, create a render file, as explained in the section "Rendering the Work Area," later in this chapter.

✔ Tip

- Although it's an odd turn of phrase, the term *real time* makes sense to DV editors, who are necessarily obsessed with rendering times. Rendering times are often measured in multiples of real time. For example, if compressing a movie file to a particular codec on a particular system takes seven times real time, then a 10-second clip will take 70 seconds to compress.

Viewing a Sequence via a DV Device

As long as real-time rendering isn't burdened by effects, the image in the Monitor panel plays at highest quality. But even at highest quality, it's still inferior to the video output on a television.

When you're editing DV, you can output the video signal through your DV camera or deck and to a television monitor. This way, you can see (and evaluate) the video as your audience will see it.

The DV Playback settings let you specify whether to play video and audio through your DV device or in the Monitor panel only.

To use these options, your IEEE 1394 interface must be connected to a DV camcorder (set to VTR mode) or DV deck, which in turn must be connected to an NTSC (television) monitor.

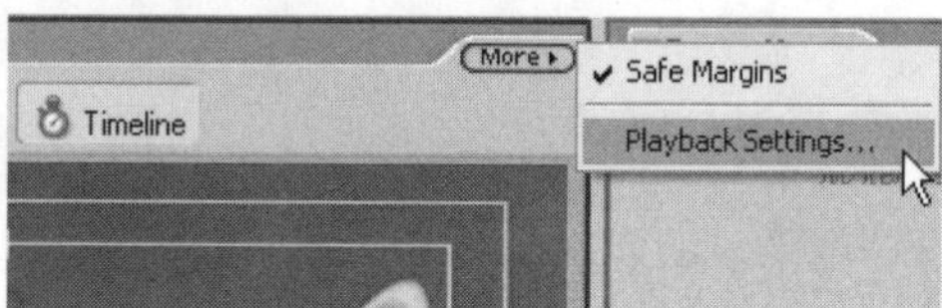

Figure 8.1 In the Monitor panel's More pull-down menu, choose Playback Settings.

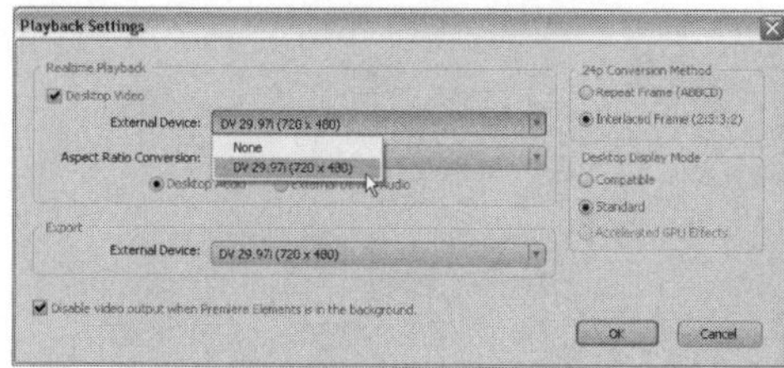

Figure 8.2 Choose the appropriate option in the Realtime Playback's External Device pull-down menu.

To play back via a DV device:

1. Make sure a DV camera or deck is connected to your computer's Premiere Elements–certified IEEE 1394 controller card and to a television monitor. Also make sure the DV device is on and set to receive a signal.
2. In the Monitor panel's More pull-down menu, choose Playback Settings (**Figure 8.1**).

   The Playback Settings dialog box appears.
3. In the Realtime Playback area of the Playback Settings dialog box, choose the option in the External Device pull-down menu that matches your DV device (**Figure 8.2**).

   If you use DV in the NTSC standard, choose DV 29.97i (720x480). Choose None to disable video output to an external device and view video in the Monitor panel only.

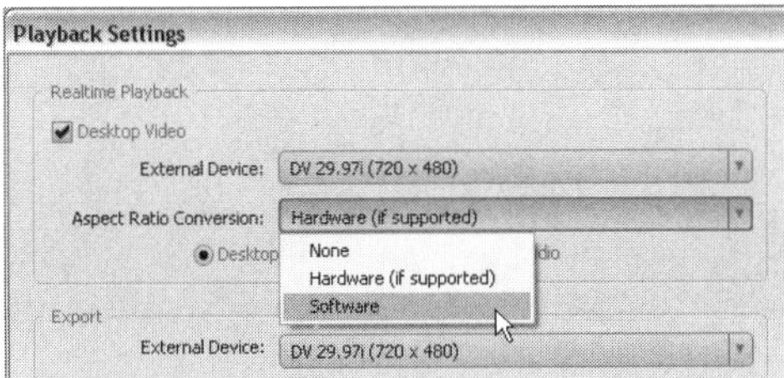

Figure 8.3 Select an Aspect Ratio Conversion method. Software is appropriate for most users.

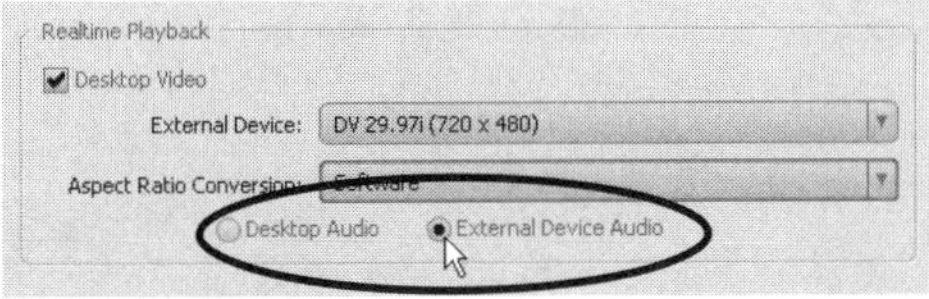

Figure 8.4 Specify whether audio will be output via your computer's speakers or through an external device.

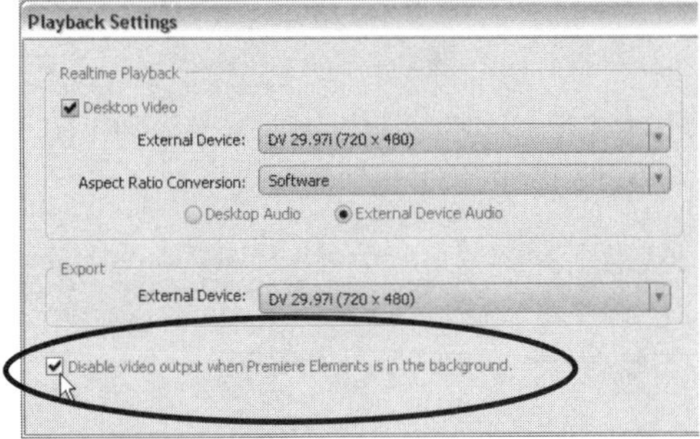

Figure 8.5 Specify whether you want to disable video output when Premiere Elements is in the background.

4. In the Aspect Ratio Conversion pull-down menu, choose whether you want hardware or software to correct distortion caused by differences between the video's and the display's pixel aspect ratio (**Figure 8.3**).

   For an explanation of pixel aspect ratio, see the sidebar "PAR Excellence: Pixel Aspect Ratios," in Chapter 3.

5. Select either of the following (**Figure 8.4**):

   Desktop Audio—To output audio through the speakers connected to your computer's audio card

   External Device Audio—To output audio through the speakers of an external device, such as a connected television

   Because the video and audio output on the computer isn't in sync with the signals output through an external device, it's usually best to watch and listen to the video on the same device.

6. If you want, select "Disable video output when Premiere Elements is in the background" (**Figure 8.5**).

   Selecting this option turns off output to the television whenever Premiere is minimized to the Windows taskbar or when another program is active and in the foreground.

To play audio while scrubbing:

1. Choose Edit > Preferences > Audio (**Figure 8.6**).

   The Audio panel of the Preferences dialog box appears.

2. Select "Play audio while scrubbing" (**Figure 8.7**).

   When the option is selected, you can hear audio as you drag the CTI in the time ruler of the source view, Timeline view, or Timeline panel.

✔ Tips

- Selecting an option from the External Device pull-down menu in the Export area of the Playback Settings dialog box determines whether video is output during export, as when you choose File > Export > Export to Tape.
- The 24p Conversion Method setting determines how Premiere Elements processes video captured at 24 progressive frames per second—a format not widespread among nonprofessionals. Consult the Adobe Premiere User Guide and your camera's documentation for more about 24p.

Figure 8.6 Choose Edit > Preferences > Audio.

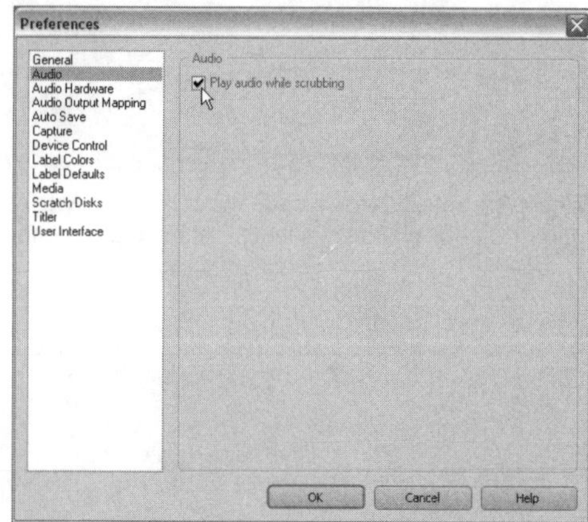

Figure 8.7 In the Audio panel of the Preferences dialog box, select "Play audio while scrubbing."

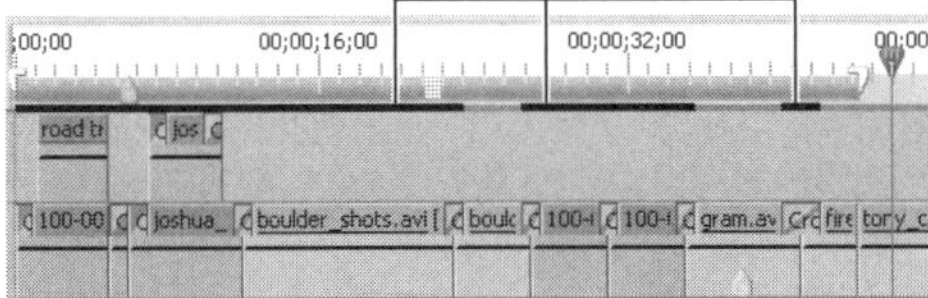

Figure 8.8 A thin red line appears over frames that require additional processing. Here, a line appears over each transition (the lines have been made darker to make them more visible).

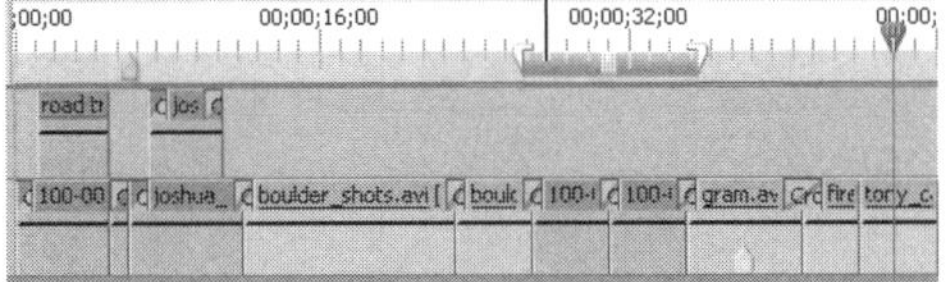

Figure 8.9 The work area bar defines the part of a sequence you can render. In this figure, the work area bar seen in Figure 8.8 has been resized to cover a smaller unrendered area, which includes three transitions.

Rendering the Work Area

At the bottom of the Timeline panel's time ruler, a thin red line appears above any frame that requires additional processing—such as the frames involved in a transition or a clip with effects (**Figure 8.8**). Premiere Elements' real-time rendering feature can process and play back most of these areas on the fly at the normal frame rate, assuming your system meets the minimum requirements to do so. If not, you can render these areas, creating new media on the hard drive called *render files* or *preview files*.

You can specify the area you want to render, called the *work area*, with (appropriately) the *work area bar*. The work area bar is the adjustable bar located near the bottom of the Timeline panel's time ruler (**Figure 8.9**). Premiere Elements automatically sets the work area bar over all the clips in the project, extending it as clips are added. However, you can reset the work area bar manually.

When you render the work area, Premiere Elements generates new media for all the transitions and effects under the work area bar and places them in a Preview Files folder on your hard disk. Once the frames have been rendered, the thin red line indicators become green. By default, Premiere Elements plays back the work area after the render is complete. You can change this setting to not play the work area, leaving the CTI in place.

continues on next page

When you make changes to a previewed area, Premiere Elements tries to utilize the rendered file as much as possible. However, significant changes make the preview file obsolete; the green line turns red, and you'll have to rerender the area or use the standard playback method, which may not be able to play complex effects at the full frame rate (see "Using Real-Time Rendering," earlier in this chapter).

This section explains how to set the work area bar and preview the part of the sequence it includes. However, you can also export the work area as explained in Chapter 11, "Export."

To preview the work area:

1. To set the work area bar over the part of the program that you want to preview, *do any of the following:*
   - ▲ Drag either end of the work area bar to shorten or lengthen it (**Figure 8.10**).
   - ▲ Drag the textured area at the center of the work area bar to move the bar without resizing it (**Figure 8.11**).
   - ▲ Double-click the dark gray area at the bottom of the Timeline panel's time ruler to resize the work area bar over a contiguous series of clips, or the current visible area of the time ruler, whichever is shorter.

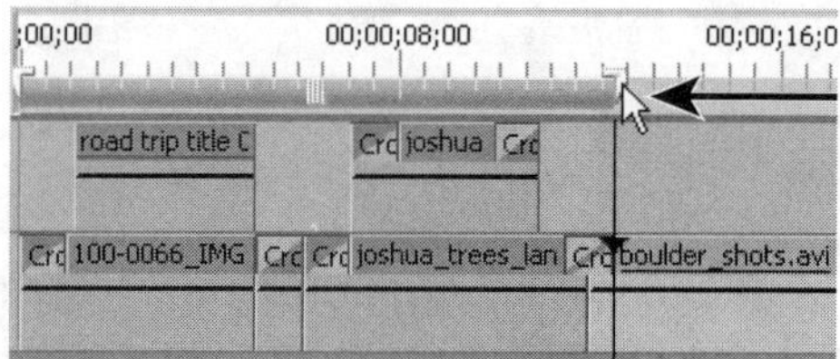

Figure 8.10 Drag either end to resize the work area bar. In this figure, snapping is on, so the start of the work area easily aligns with the beginning of the transition.

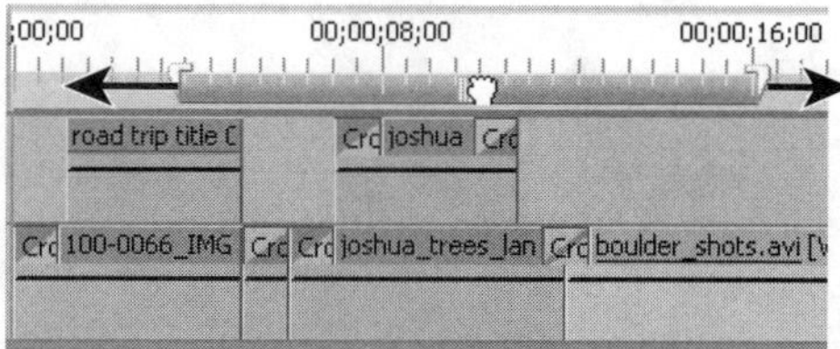

Figure 8.11 Drag the work area bar from the center to move it without changing its duration.

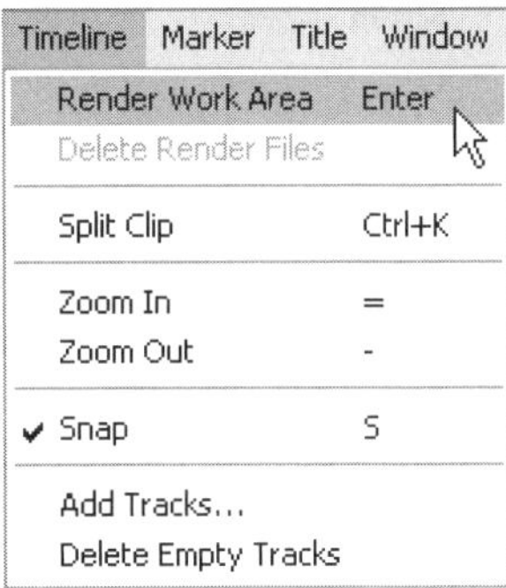

Figure 8.12 Choose Timeline > Render Work Area.

Figure 8.13 A Rendering dialog box estimates the approximate processing time.

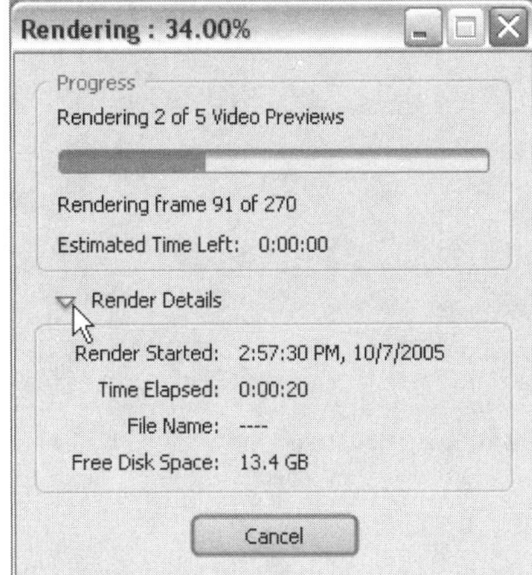

Figure 8.14 Clicking the triangle expands the dialog box and provides additional details.

2. *Do either of the following:*
   - ▲ Choose Timeline > Render Work Area (**Figure 8.12**).
   - ▲ Press Enter.

   A Rendering dialog box appears; a progress bar indicates the approximate time required to process the effects, based on the current operation (**Figure 8.13**). Click the triangle to expand the Render Details section to see additional details (**Figure 8.14**). When processing is complete, the red lines under the work area bar turn green, and the audio and video under the work area bar play back.

✔ Tips

- If snapping is on, the work area bar snaps to clip and transition edges, markers, and the CTI.
- Hover the mouse pointer over the work area bar to see a tooltip showing the bar's start, end, and duration.

To set whether the work area plays after rendering:

1. Choose Edit > Preferences > General (**Figure 8.15**).

   The General panel of the Preferences dialog box appears.

2. Select or deselect the "Play work area after rendering previews" check box (**Figure 8.16**).

   When the option is selected, the part of the sequence under the work area bar plays after rendering. When the option is unselected, the CTI remains where it was when rendering commenced.

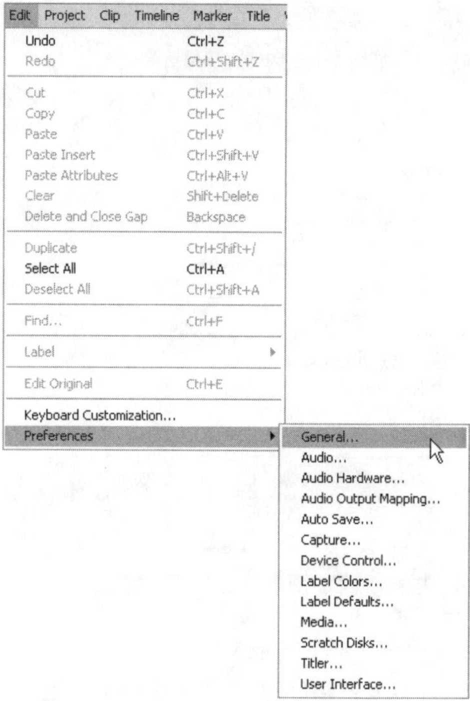

Figure 8.15 Choose Edit > Preferences > General.

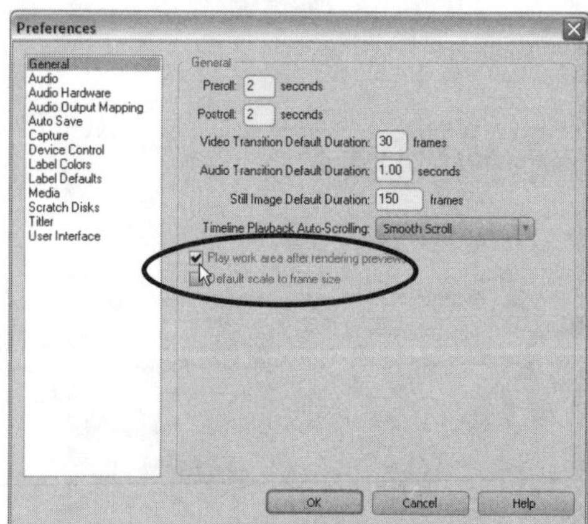

Figure 8.16 Select or deselect the "Play work area after rendering previews" check box.

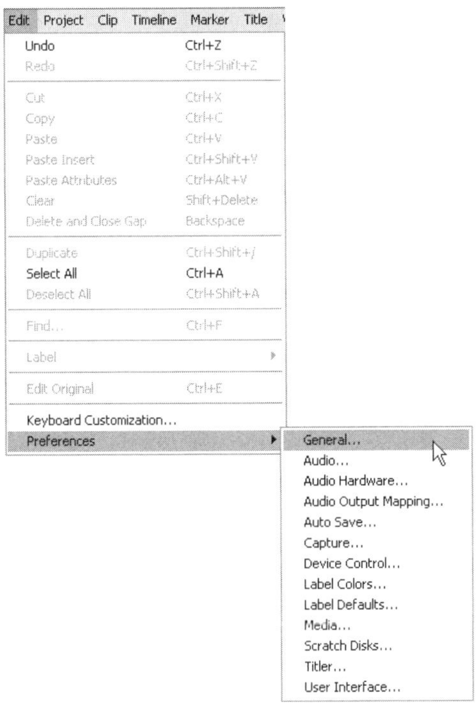

Figure 8.17 Choose Edit > Preferences > General.

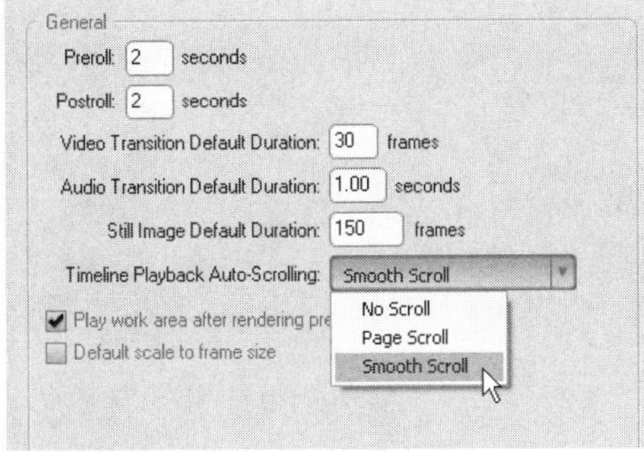

Figure 8.18 Choose how the timeline scrolls when the CTI moves across the timeline.

To set a timeline scrolling option:

1. Choose Edit > Preferences > General (**Figure 8.17**).

   The General panel of the Preferences dialog box appears.

2. For Timeline Playback Auto-Scrolling, choose one of the following (**Figure 8.18**):

   No Scroll—Scrolls the visible area of the timeline to show the CTI only when you pause playback

   Page Scroll—Scrolls by the width of the visible area of the timeline whenever the CTI reaches its edge

   Smooth Scroll—Continuously scrolls the timeline so that the CTI is always within the visible area

   During playback and previews, the timeline scrolls according to your choice.

3. Click OK to close the dialog box.

Storing Preview Files

By default, Premiere Elements stores rendered effects in a folder called Adobe Premiere Elements Preview Files. You can find this file by following the path My Documents/Adobe/Premiere Elements/1.0/Adobe Premiere Elements Preview Files. In this main folder, Premiere Elements stores each project's preview files in separate subfolders; the files use the naming convention *projectname*.PRV.

However, by specifying a scratch disk, you can designate any location for the video and audio preview files. This way, you can take a more active role in managing your files or ensure they're being played from a disk with adequate space and speed.

To choose scratch disks for preview files:

1. Choose Edit > Preferences > Scratch Disks (**Figure 8.19**).

   The Scratch Disks panel of the Preferences dialog box appears (**Figure 8.20**).

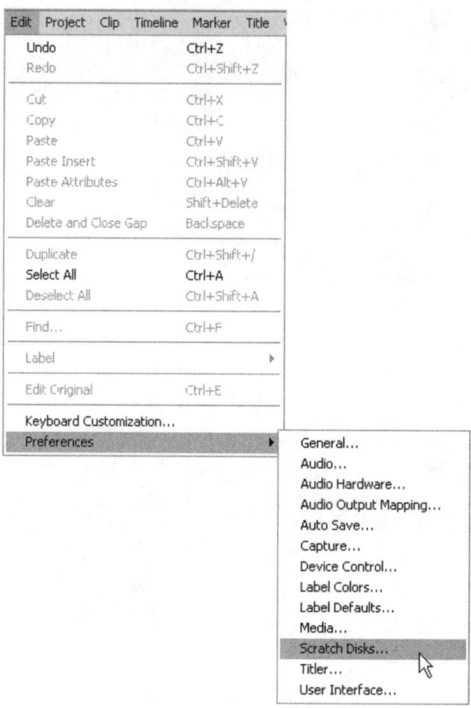

Figure 8.19 Choose Edit > Preferences > Scratch Disks.

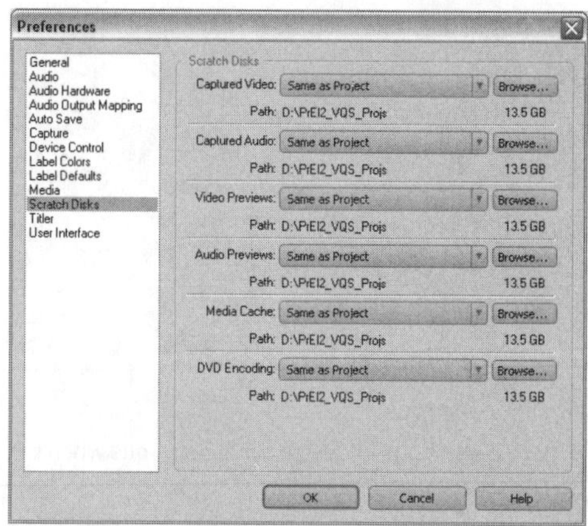

Figure 8.20 The Scratch Disks pane of the Preferences dialog box appears.

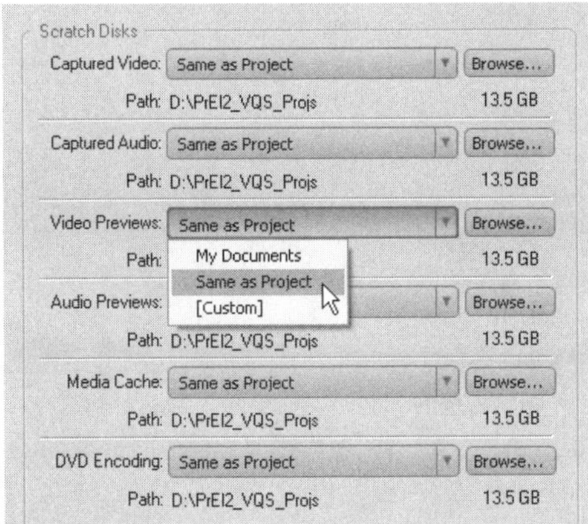

Figure 8.21 Choose a location for the video previews and audio previews from the appropriate drop-down menus, or choose a custom location by clicking the Browse buttons.

2. For the Video Previews and Audio Previews settings, *do any of the following* (**Figure 8.21**):

   Choose My Documents in the appropriate drop-down menu to store preview files in the My Documents folder.

   Choose Same as Project to store preview files in the same folder as the current project.

   Click Browse to specify a location for the Preview Files folder.

   The path for the folder appears for each type of scratch disk.

3. Click OK to close the Preferences dialog box.

✔ Tips

- Because the scratch disk plays back audio and video files, it should be a relatively large, fast disk. If you have several volumes, consider putting the Premiere Elements application, media files, and preview files on separate volumes.
- By default, the Premiere Elements Preview Files folder resides in the user's My Documents directory under \Adobe\Premiere Elements\2.0\.

Deleting Preview Files

You can delete preview files to free up drive space or for housekeeping purposes (to save a project just prior to archiving it, for example). In contrast to deleting the preview files by using the operating system, using Premiere Elements' Delete Render Files command ensures that the project no longer refers to the preview files and won't prompt you for them the next time you open the project.

Note that Premiere Elements can't distinguish between preview files made obsolete by editing changes and preview files that are still in use.

To delete preview files:

1. Choose Timeline > Delete Render Files (**Figure 8.22**).

   A dialog box prompts you to confirm your choice and warns you that the operation can't be undone.

2. In the Confirm Delete dialog box, click OK (**Figure 8.23**).

   The preview files associated with the current project are deleted from the hard disk. In the Timeline panel, the green lines that indicate rendered areas turn red.

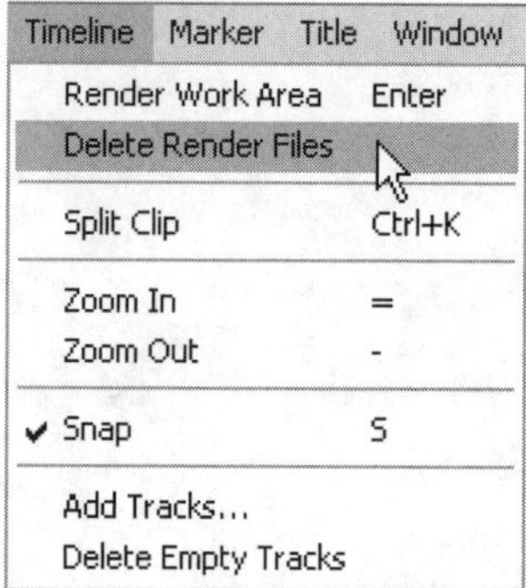

Figure 8.22 Choose Timeline > Delete Render Files.

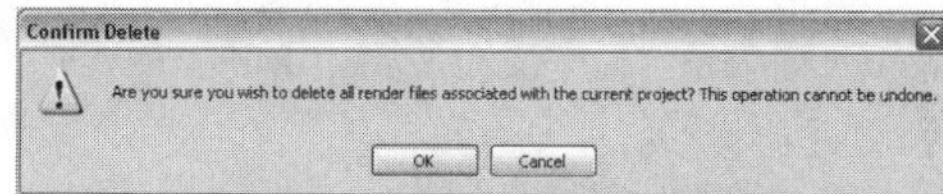

Figure 8.23 Click OK to confirm that you want to delete all render (aka preview) files for the project.

✔ Tips

- Premiere Elements keeps track of preview files in much the same way it references source media files. If you move or delete preview files using the operating system instead of within Premiere Elements, you're prompted to locate the files the next time you open the project. If so, direct Premiere Elements to the preview files' new location. Or, if you deleted the preview files, choose Skip Preview Files when prompted. See Chapter 2, "Starting a Project," for more about locating missing files.
- In Premiere Elements, the terms *render files* and *preview files* are used interchangeably.

Media Cache Files

To enhance playback performance, Premiere Elements creates several types of files, known collectively as *media cache files*. But although files in the media cache assist in playback, they aren't integral to a project. In other words, deleting them won't affect your project or associated media files, and you won't be prompted to find them when you reopen the project (as you would if you deleted preview files using the operating system).

Media cache files reside inside the same folder as their associated project, or in a folder you specify by choosing Edit > Preferences > Scratch Disks. Premiere Elements generates these files automatically, but if you want to remove them, you must do so manually. There's no command within Premiere Elements to remove media cache files (as there is with preview files).

In general, you don't have to worry about the media cache. You can specify a scratch disk to manage where they're stored, or delete them manually if you need to reclaim a little hard disk space. If you continue to work on the project, Premiere Elements will simply regenerate the necessary media cache files.

Creating Titles

No single aspect of a movie makes it seem as finished and polished as a simple title. An opening title fills viewers with anticipation; the closing credits give them a sense of satisfaction. But titles and graphics can serve a great many other uses. Titles can identify the onscreen speaker in a documentary, highlight the company logo, list important concepts in a presentation, or subtitle foreign-language footage. Even narrative projects may use titles within the program—for example, to identify a change of scene or time: "The City on the Moon," or "500 Years Later."

Sure, you can create titles in another program and add them to your project. But as usual, Premiere Elements 2 makes your life easier by including a built-in title-creation mode, the Titler. The Titler includes tools for creating text and graphics, title rolls, and crawls. Don't think of yourself as a graphic designer? Not to worry: The Titler comes with a collection of ready-made templates designed for occasions from "New Baby" to business presentations. Now, it's time to tackle the next button in the taskbar: Titles.

Using the Titler

Whenever you create or change a title clip, you invoke the Titles workspace, a "suite" of panels collectively known as the Titler (**Figure 9.1**). The Titler's main panel, called the Title Designer, consists of a large drawing area that corresponds to the television screen. It also includes a strip of buttons for creating a new title, and for various typesetting tasks. The Titler includes three more secondary panels: the Title Tools panel, which includes buttons to help you create and modify text, shapes, and images; the Title Actions panel, which helps you align and distribute selected items in a title; and

Figure 9.1 Premiere Elements' Titler consists of a suite of panels.

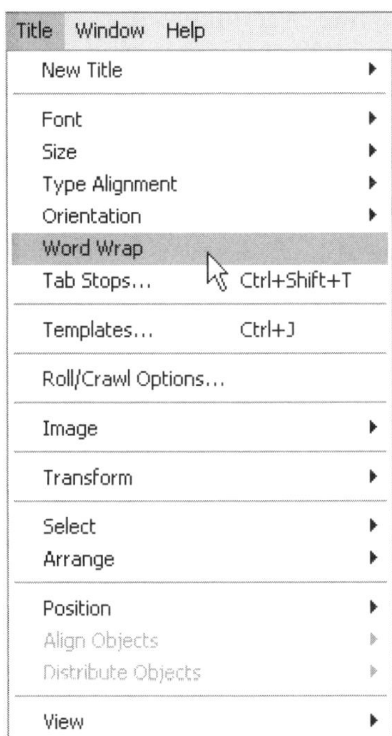

Figure 9.2 In the menu bar, a Title menu provides an alternative to controls found in the Titler's panels, as well as additional commands.

the Styles panel, a collection of preset and custom settings you can apply to objects in a title quickly and easily. In addition to (or as an alternative to) the functions found in the Titler's panels, you can use commands in the Titler menu, which become active whenever the Titler's main panel is present (**Figure 9.2**). Additional Titler settings can be found in the Preferences dialog box.

✔ Tip

- Note that titles are listed in the Window menu only when they're open, under Window > Titlers > *titlename*. Also, remember that the Title menu isn't in one of the Titler's panels; rather, it's on the main Premiere Elements menu bar.

Creating Titles

The Titler comes with an extensive list of preset templates—ready-made designs with generic text that you can replace with your own messages. Templates are organized into categories, such as Entertainment, Happy Birthday, Travel, and Wedding. Many contain photographic images that pertain to the selected topic.

You can also create a title from scratch, by choosing a menu command, by clicking the New Item button in the Media panel, or by using the handy Titles button in the taskbar. (Note that pressing and holding the Titles button reveals a pull-down menu of choices, but clicking the Titles button activates the menu's first choice: Template.)

When the title is added to the timeline's video track 2 or higher, empty areas in the title appear transparent, revealing the image contained by the track below. To help you visualize the final effect, you can set the Titler to show the current frame of the sequence in the Timeline. Otherwise, transparent areas appear as a checkerboard pattern in the Title Designer panel. For more information, see the section "Viewing the Video in the Background," later in this chapter.

In contrast to the previous version of Premiere Elements, version 2 saves all titles as part of the project—not as separate files. This way, saving your titles is as easy as saving your project, and you won't have to worry about losing track of your title files.

Figure 9.3 To customize a title template, click the taskbar's Titles button...

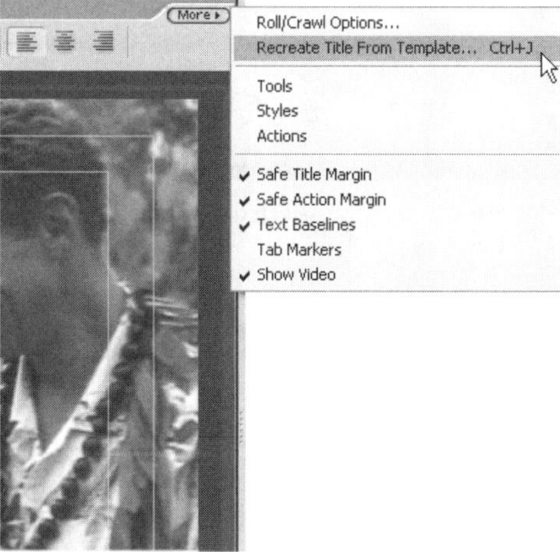

Figure 9.4 ...or, if the Title Designer panel is already open, choose Recreate Title From Template from the More pull-down menu.

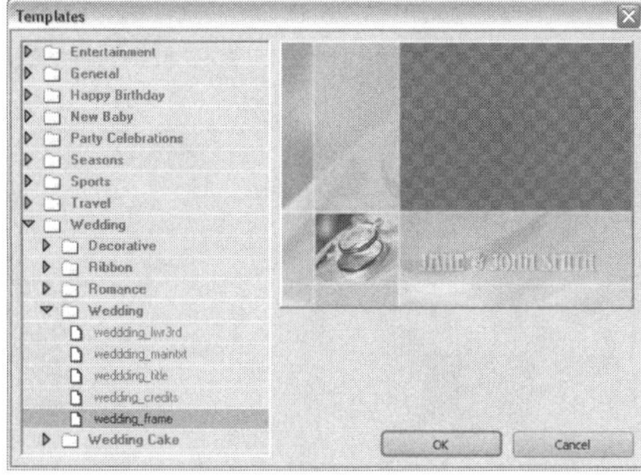

Figure 9.5 In the Templates dialog box, select a title template to preview it. Clicking OK...

To select a title template:

1. *Do either of the following:*
   - ▲ In the taskbar, click the Titles button (**Figure 9.3**).
   - ▲ To open a title template from within the Title Designer panel, choose Recreate Title From Template from the Title Designer's More pull-down menu (**Figure 9.4**).

   The Templates dialog box appears.
2. Select the title template you'd like to use.

   If necessary, click the triangle next to a folder or subfolder to reveal the templates it contains. A preview of the selected template appears in the Templates dialog box (**Figure 9.5**).

continues on next page

3. Click OK.

   If necessary, Premiere Elements switches to the Titles workspace. The title template is loaded into the Title Designer panel (**Figure 9.6**). By default, the current frame of the sequence in the Timeline serves as the background image (if the title contains transparent areas).

4. Modify the text or other objects (using methods described later in the chapter). For example, select the sample text, and type the appropriate message in its place (**Figure 9.7**).

5. When you've finished, you can create another title or switch to another workspace (such as the Editing workspace).

   The title appears in the selected bin of the Media panel automatically, and is saved whenever you save the project (**Figure 9.8**).

Figure 9.6 ...loads the selected title template into the Title Designer panel.

Figure 9.7 Customize the appropriate parts of the template to suit your needs.

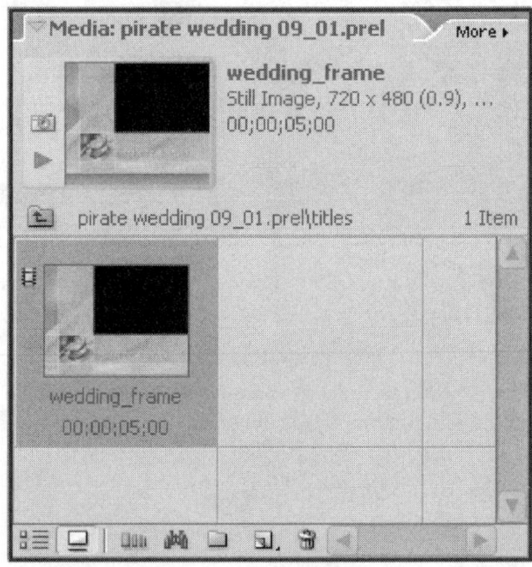

Figure 9.8 The title is added to the Media panel automatically, and is saved as part of the project when you save the project.

To create a new title using the taskbar:

1. In the taskbar, press and hold the Titles button, and select New Title from the pull-down menu (**Figure 9.9**).

   A New Title dialog box appears.

2. In the New Title dialog box, type a name for the title and click OK (**Figure 10**).

   If necessary, Premiere Elements switches to the Titles workspace. The Title Designer panel indicates the name you selected.

3. Modify the text or other objects (using methods described later in the chapter), and save the title (**Figure 9.11**).

4. When you've finished, you can create another title or switch to another workspace (such as the Editing workspace).

   The title appears in the selected bin of the Media panel automatically, and is saved whenever you save the project (**Figure 9.12**).

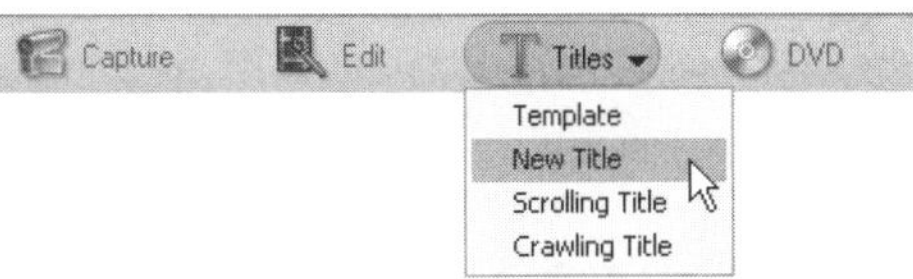

Figure 9.9 Press and hold the taskbar's Titles button, and select New Title.

Figure 9.10 Type a name in the New Title dialog box and click OK.

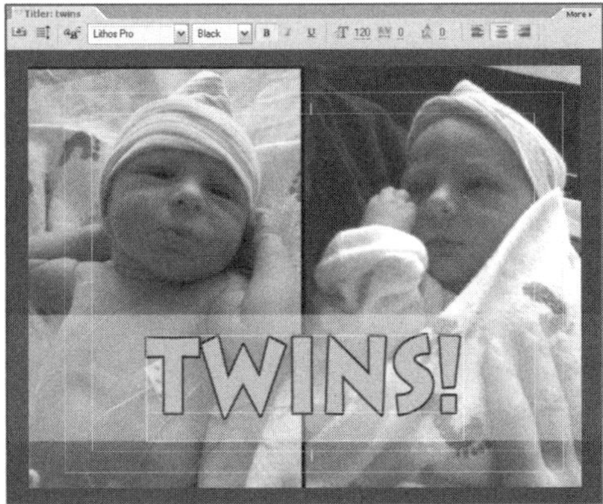

Figure 9.11 The Title Designer panel displays the new title, and its tab shows the name you entered. Create the title you want in the drawing area.

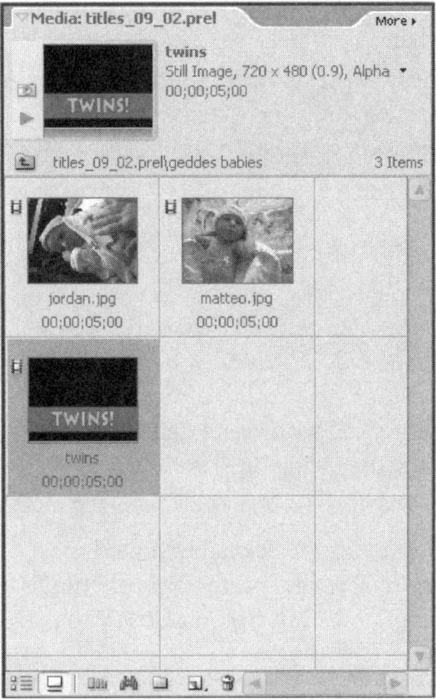

Figure 9.12 The title appears in the Media panel automatically, and is saved as part of the project when you save the project.

To create a title based on the current title:

1. In the Title Designer, click the New Title Based on Current Title button (**Figure 9.13**).

   A New Title dialog box appears.

2. In the New Title dialog box, type a name for the new title, and then click OK (**Figure 9.14**).

   The objects contained in the former title are copied into the current title. The Title Designer panel's tab indicates the new title name you entered, and the title is listed in the Media panel.

3. Modify the title's objects. For example, select text and type the appropriate message in its place (**Figure 9.15**).

4. When you've finished modifying the title, you can create other titles, or switch to the workspace best suited to the task at hand.

   The new title is added to the Media panel automatically, and saved with the project whenever you save the project.

✔ Tips

- Although titles are saved as part of the project, you can still export a title as a separate file. This way, you can import the title into another project, and share a title with Premiere Elements users. Exporting titles is covered in Chapter 11, "Export."
- You can use traditional keyboard shortcuts to copy and paste objects in the Title Designer: Ctrl+C to copy; Ctrl+V to paste.

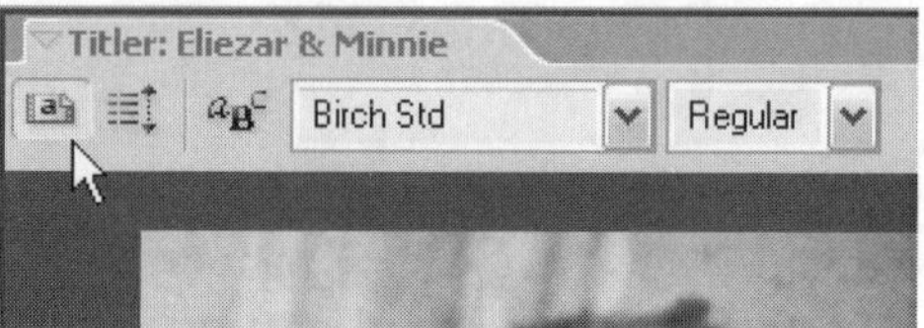

Figure 9.13 In the Title Designer panel, click the New Title Based on Current Title button.

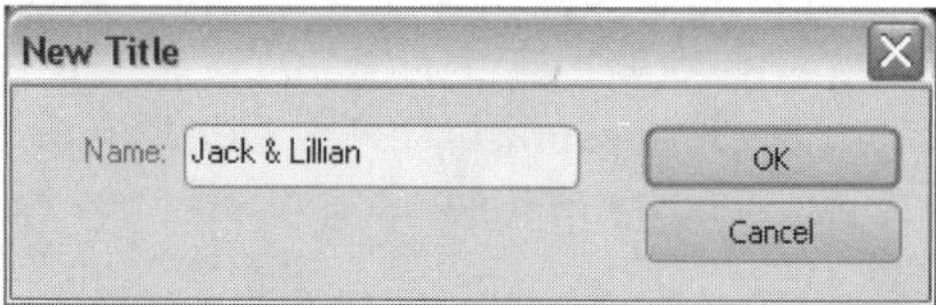

Figure 9.14 Enter a name for the title in the New Title dialog box, and then click OK.

Figure 9.15 The new title includes the objects contained by the previous title, which you can modify as necessary. Here, the names have been changed to match the photo.

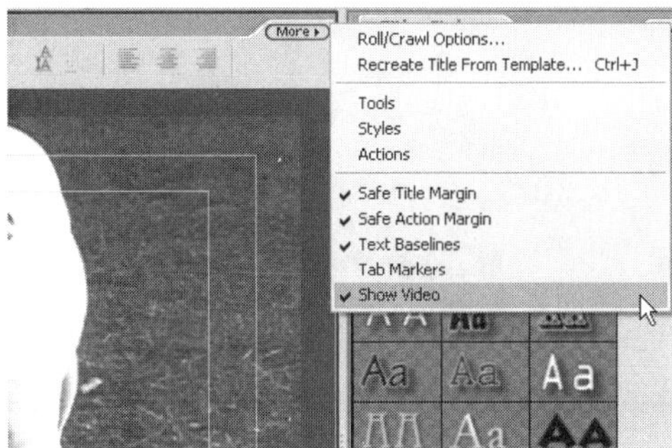

Figure 9.16 With Show Video selected, the video frame at the CTI serves as the background.

Viewing the Video in the Background

Because many titles are superimposed over video, the empty background areas of a title are transparent (see "Superimposing a Title Over Video," later in this chapter). By default, the empty area in the Title Designer panel's drawing area is filled with the sequence's current frame of video. The background frame isn't saved as part of the title; it's merely a helpful reference for positioning the title's elements, choosing colors, and the like. The actual video that appears behind the title depends on where you add the title to the sequence.

If you don't need the background frame (or find it distracting while you create the title), you can opt to view the transparent areas with a more neutral checkerboard pattern.

To toggle background video:

- In the Title Designer panel's More menu, select Show Video to display a frame of the program as the background of the drawing area (**Figure 9.16**).

  Deselect Show Video to view a checkerboard background in the drawing area.

To cue the background video frame:

◆ Cue the sequence time using the time controls in either the Timeline view of the Monitor panel or the Timeline panel (**Figure 9.17**).

The background frame in the Title Designer panel corresponds to the current frame in the sequence (**Figure 9.18**).

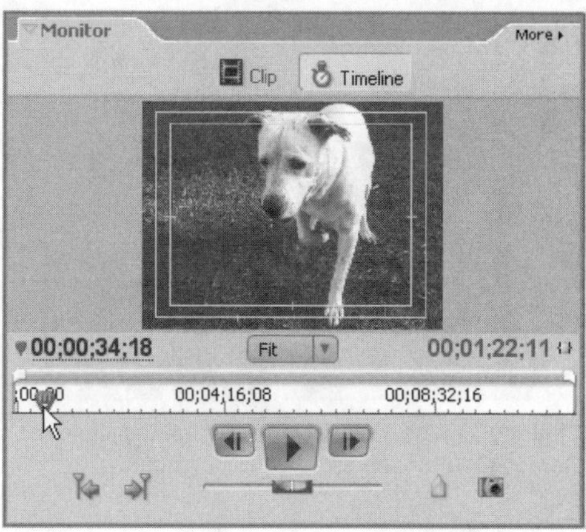

Figure 9.17 Cueing the current time in the sequence...

Figure 9.18 ...also sets the background image in the Title Designer panel.

✔ Tips

- When you're selecting colors for objects you create in the Titler, you can use an eyedropper tool to sample colors from the background video.
- If the composition of the background video changes over the course of a title, be sure to spot-check the title against several representative frames. This way, you avoid creating a title that gets in the way of the video.

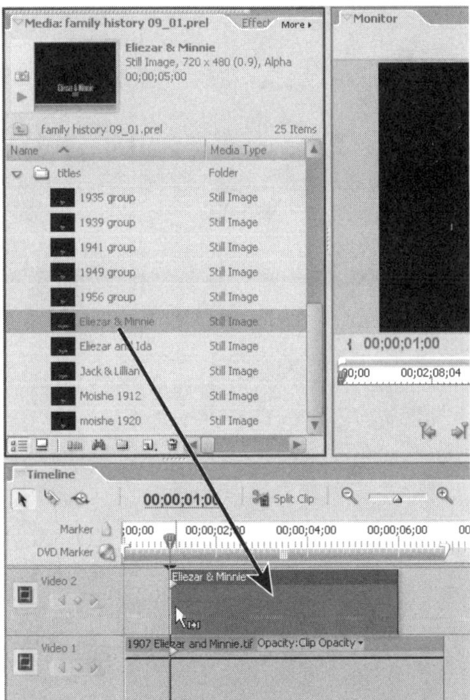

Figure 9.19 Drag the title from the Media panel to a video track above a video clip.

Superimposing a Title Over Video

As you saw in the previous section, you often design a title with a background image in mind. When you add the title to the timeline, the empty background areas of the title are interpreted as transparent, revealing the video image of clips in lower tracks.

Premiere Elements makes the background transparent automatically; you can make the visible parts of the title fade up and down with transitions. Although you learned all about transitions in Chapter 7, "Adding Transitions," the following task describes both how to superimpose a title and how to fade it up and down.

To superimpose a title over video:

1. Create a title, using any of the methods described in this chapter.

   The title appears in the Media panel.

2. Drag the title from the Media panel to a video track above a video clip (**Figure 9.19**).

   The title clip appears in the track using the default duration for still images you specified (see the task "To set the default duration for still images before you add them," in Chapter 3, "Capturing and Adding Footage").

3. Adjust the placement and duration of the title clip just as you would for other clips in the timeline.

   Use techniques you learned in Chapter 6, "Editing in the Timeline."

continues on next page

4. If you want, add transitions (such as a cross dissolve) to the title clip.

   Adding a cross dissolve to the beginning and end of the title clip fades the title up and down (**Figure 9.20**). See Chapter 7 for more about transitions.

5. To view the effect at high resolution and at the sequence's full frame rate, press Enter.

   The area of the sequence under the timeline's work area bar is rendered and played back (**Figure 9.21**). For more about rendering and previewing transitions and effects, see Chapter 8, "Previewing a Sequence."

✔ Tips

- You can also fade a title and adjust its opacity in more complex ways by manipulating its opacity property. See Chapter 10, "Adding Effects," to learn about manipulating a clip's opacity and other effects.
- Manipulating a title's opacity property or applying a transition affects the entire title's opacity level, including all the objects it contains. Note that you can set the maximum opacity of individual objects in a title in much the same way as you would set their color and so on. See "Transforming Objects," later in this chapter.

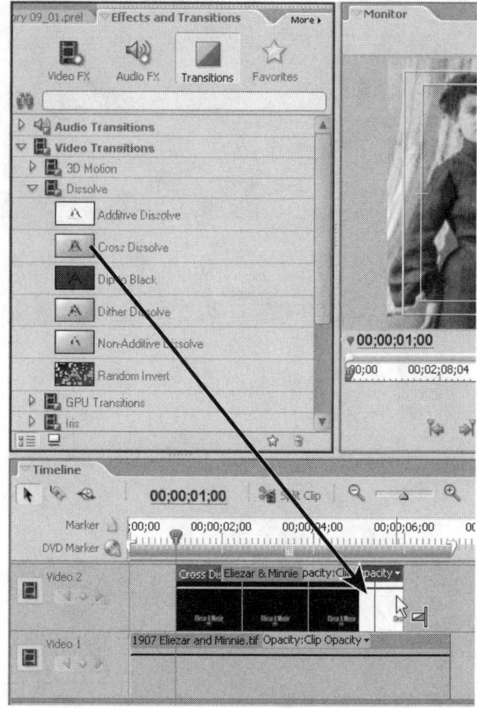

Figure 9.20 Adding a cross dissolve transition to the beginning and end of the title clip fades it up and down.

Figure 9.21 Setting the work area bar over the transition and pressing Enter renders the effect and plays it back.

Keying Effects

Generally speaking, any technique that makes parts of an image completely transparent is known as a *keying effect*, or a *key*. When you place a title in video track 2 or higher, Premiere Elements *keys out* the background automatically. In this case, Premiere Elements bases the key on the title's alpha channel, data that specifies opacity. (See Chapter 2, "Starting a Project," for more about alpha channels.) You can also apply keying effects to clips manually, to key out parts of any image based on other factors. For example, you can key out areas based on color (as in a bluescreen or greenscreen effect) or even on a separate image, or matte. See Chapter 10, "Adding Effects."

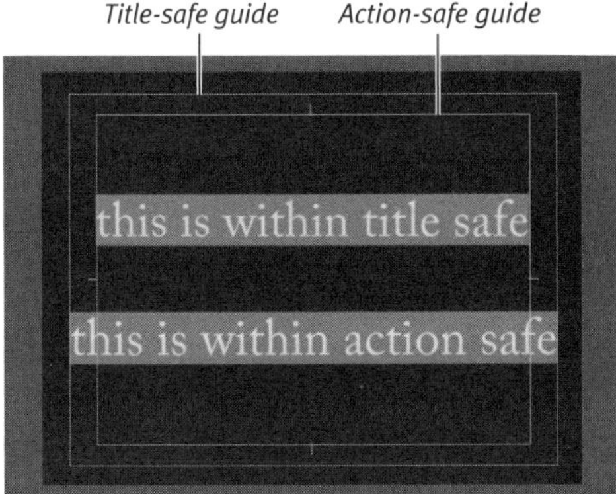

Figure 9.22 Reference marks can indicate the action-safe and title-safe zones.

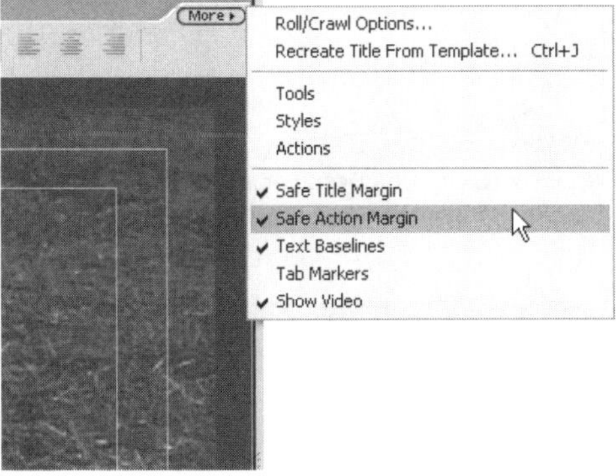

Figure 9.23 Choose the safe zone guides you want to display in the Title Designer's More pull-down menu.

Why *Key?*

Keying makes only certain parts of a clip transparent. The terms *key* and *keying* refer to their physical counterpart, the *keyhole.* This is because keying "cuts a hole" in an image, making it transparent. The hole is filled with another image—in this case, clips in lower tracks of the timeline.

Viewing the Video-Safe Zones

The Monitor panel displays the entire video frame, but television monitors are likely to crop off the outer edges of the image. Therefore, you may need to check whether certain parts of the image fall within the video *safe zones* (**Figure 9.22**).

In video, the inner 90 percent of the complete image is considered to be *action-safe*—that is, everything within that area is likely to appear on most television screens. The inner 80 percent is considered to be *title-safe.* Because you can't afford to let any of the title's content be lost, the title-safe area defines a necessary safety margin. The safe-zone guides are for your reference only; they aren't added to the source image and don't appear in the program output.

To view safe zones:

- In the Title Designer panel's More pull-down menu, select *either of the following* (**Figure 9.23**):

  Safe Title Margin—Displays guides for the inner 80 percent of the screen

  Safe Action Margin—Displays guides for the inner 90 percent of the screen

  Deselect an option to hide the safe-zone marks in the Title Designer panel.

Comparing Text Options

The Title Tools panel includes two tools for creating type: the Type tool and the Vertical Type tool (**Figure 9.24**). Depending how you use them, each tool can create either point text or paragraph text.

Horizontal and vertical type

As you'd guess, the Type tool creates standard text, which is oriented horizontally; the Vertical Type tool creates text that's oriented vertically (**Figure 9.25**). Because it's so much more common (at least in English), horizontally oriented text will be used in most examples in this chapter.

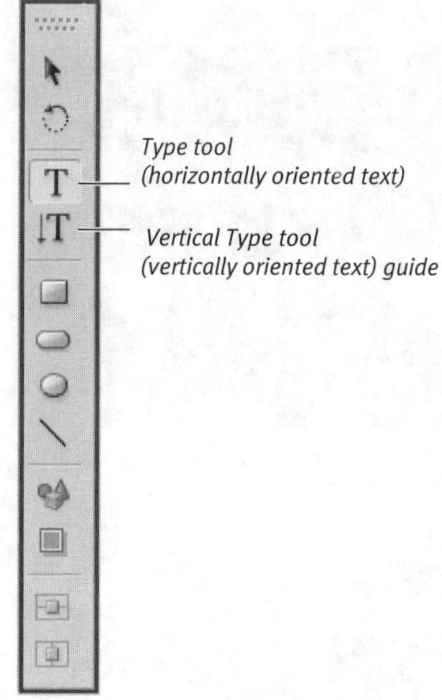

Figure 9.24 The Title Designer includes type tools for creating horizontally and vertically oriented text.

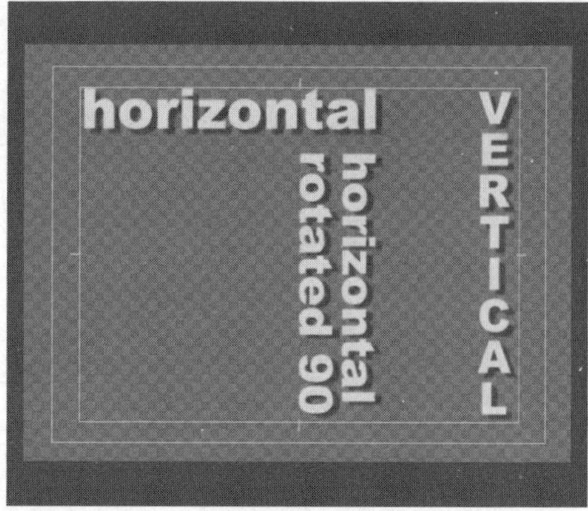

Figure 9.25 This example shows horizontally and vertically oriented text. Note the difference between vertically oriented text and horizontal text that has been rotated 90 degrees.

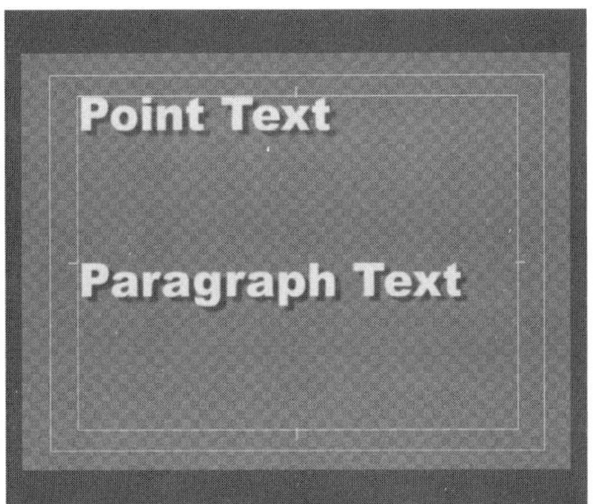

Figure 9.26 At first glance, creating text by clicking an insertion point and by dragging a text box yield similar results...

Figure 9.27 ...but resizing point text scales it, whereas resizing the text box reflows the text within the box.

Point text and paragraph text

Using either the Type or Vertical Type tool, you can create either point text or paragraph text. To create *point text*, click with a type tool and begin typing; to create *paragraph text*, click and drag with the tool to define a text box before you type.

At first glance, there seems to be little difference between the two approaches (**Figure 9.26**). But a big practical difference emerges after you create the text. Whereas changing a text box reflows the text it contains, changing the bounding box of text created with the type tool transforms the text—that is, it resizes or stretches it (**Figure 9.27**).

Therefore, it's best to use paragraph text to create larger blocks of text that may require tabs or margin changes. Use point text to create shorter messages that lend themselves to more expressive modifications.

✔ Tip

- In Premiere Elements, you can't create text that follows a curved path. However, you can do it in the companion program, Photoshop Elements.

Creating Point Text

In contrast to paragraph text, point text is unconstrained by a text box. However, whether typing continues on a single line or starts a new line depends on the *Word Wrap* setting.

When Word Wrap is on, point text automatically starts a new line when it reaches the edge of the title-safe area. If you turn off Word Wrap, text remains on a single line, continuing offscreen if necessary. To see the offscreen portions of the text, you'll just have to move or reflow the text to see it all at once.

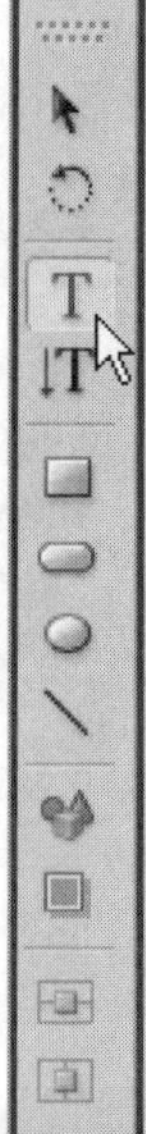

Figure 9.28 Select one of the type-creation tools.

To create point text:

1. In the Title Tools panel, *select either of the following* (**Figure 9.28**):

   Type tool T —Creates standard horizontal text

   Vertical Type tool ↓T —Creates vertical text

2. Click the mouse pointer in the drawing area where you want to begin typing.

   A blinking insertion point appears where you clicked.

3. Type the text you want (**Figure 9.29**).

   Whether the text starts on a new line when the edge of the title-safe area is reached depends on the Word Wrap option you specify.

Figure 9.29 Click to set an insertion point, and then type the text you want.

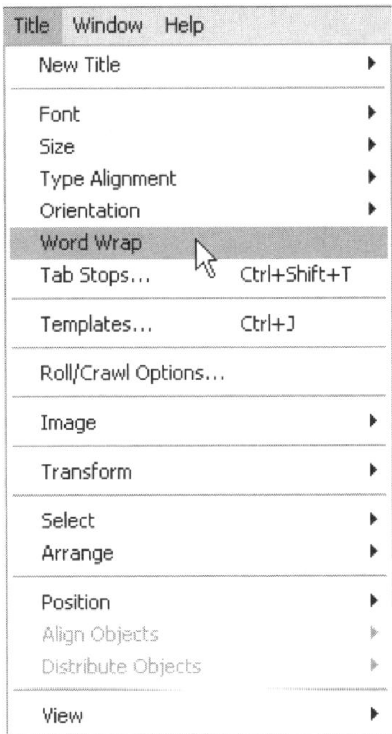

Figure 9.30 Select point text or set an insertion point, and choose Title > Word Wrap to toggle it on or off.

4. When you've finished typing, click the Selection tool in the Title Tools panel.

5. With the text still selected, modify any of its attributes, such as font, justification, and color.

   You can use options at the top of the Title Designer panel or Title menu, or select a style from the Title Styles panel (see the following sections for details).

To toggle Word Wrap for point text:

1. *Do either of the following:*
   - ▲ To set Word Wrap for existing point text, select it using the Title Tools panel's Selection tool.
   - ▲ To set Word Wrap for point text before you type, click in the drawing area with the Type or Vertical Type tool.

2. Choose Title > Word Wrap (**Figure 9.30**).

   When Word Wrap is selected, a new line of text begins when the type reaches the edge of the title-safe area. When Word Wrap is deselected, the feature is off, and text continues on a single line.

To scale point text:

1. In the Title Tools panel, select the Selection tool.
2. Click point text to select it.
3. *Do any of the following:*
   - ▲ To scale text horizontally, drag the left or right handle on the text's bounding box (**Figure 9.31**).
   - ▲ To scale text vertically, drag the top or bottom handle on the text's bounding box (**Figure 9.32**).
   - ▲ To scale text horizontally and vertically, drag a corner handle on the text's bounding box.
   - ▲ To maintain the text's proportions, press Shift as you drag a corner handle (**Figure 9.33**).

   The text scales according to your choice.

Figure 9.31 Dragging the selected text's left or right handle scales it horizontally...

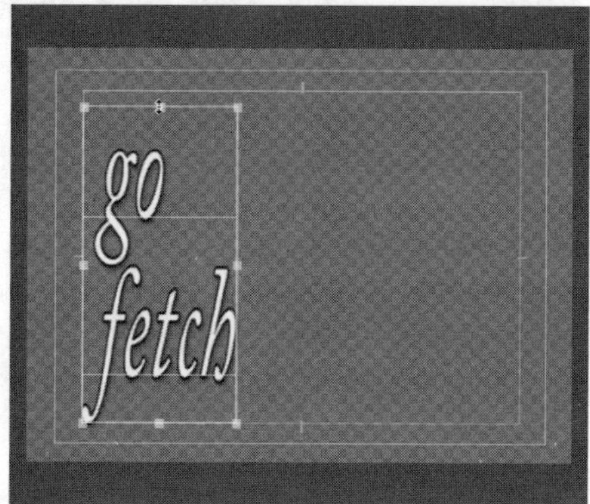

Figure 9.32 ...dragging the top or bottom handle scales it vertically...

Figure 9.33 ...and dragging a corner scales both aspects. Press Shift as you drag to constrain the proportions.

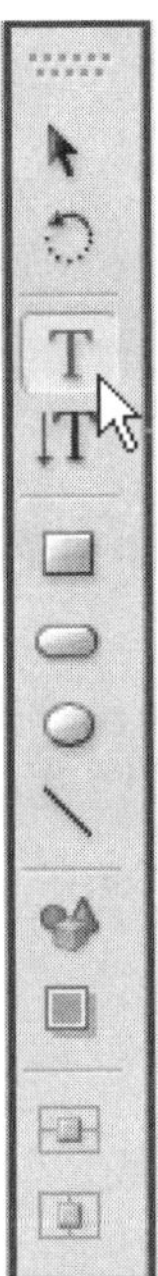

Figure 9.34 Select a type-creation tool.

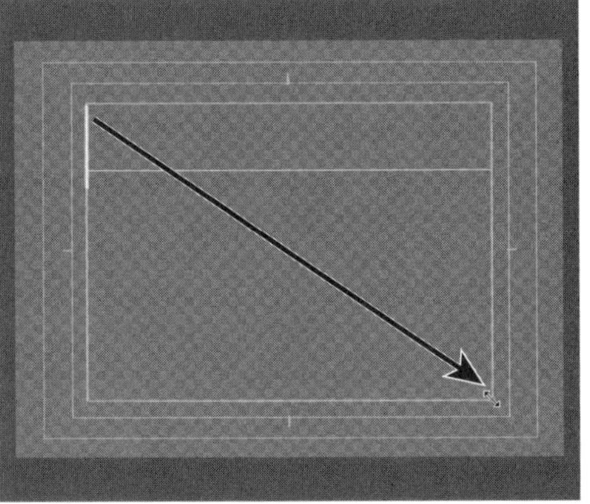

Figure 9.35 Click and drag diagonally in the drawing area to set the boundaries of the text box.

Creating Paragraph Text

Dragging with a type tool creates a text box that defines the margins for paragraph text. As its name implies, paragraph text is best suited for longer messages that may need to be reflowed to fit in the screen the way you want. Paragraph text may also use tabs. You can set tab stops much as you would in a word-processing program and view them in a text box.

For longer messages, such as a long list of credits, use a rolling title instead (see "Creating Scrolls and Crawls," later in this chapter).

To create paragraph text:

1. In the Title Tools panel, *select either of the following* (**Figure 9.34**):

   Type tool T —Creates standard horizontal text

   Vertical Type tool ↕T —Creates vertical text

2. Drag the mouse pointer diagonally in the drawing area to define a text box (**Figure 9.35**).

   When you release the mouse, a text box appears, with a blinking insertion point in the upper-left corner.

continues on next page

3. Type the text you want (**Figure 9.36**).

   You may type more than the text box can contain. To view the hidden text, resize the text box after you've entered all the text.

4. When you've finished typing, click the Selection tool in the Title Designer's tools area.

5. With the text still selected, modify any of its attributes, such as font, justification, and color.

   You can use options at the top of the Title Designer or Title menu, or select a style from the Style swatch panel (see the following sections for details).

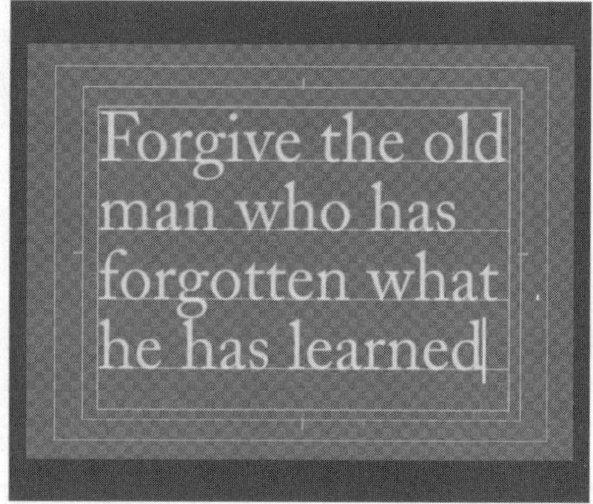

Figure 9.36 Type in the text box. If all the text doesn't fit in the box, you can resize it later.

✔ Tip

- Resizing a text box reflows only lines of text created with soft returns—new lines created by Word Wrap. Hard returns—new lines created by pressing Enter—aren't affected by resizing the bounding box.

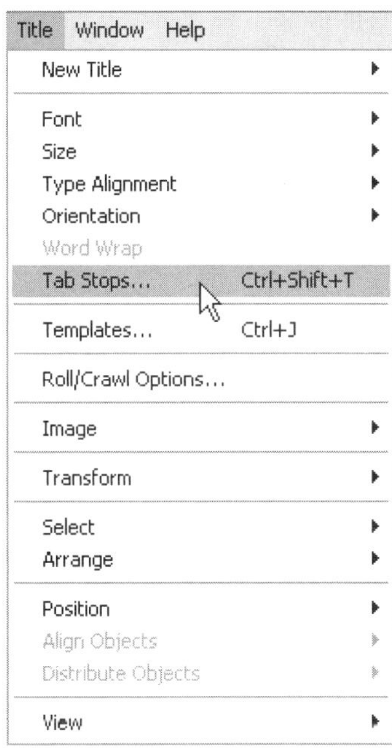

Figure 9.37 Choose Title > Tab Stops.

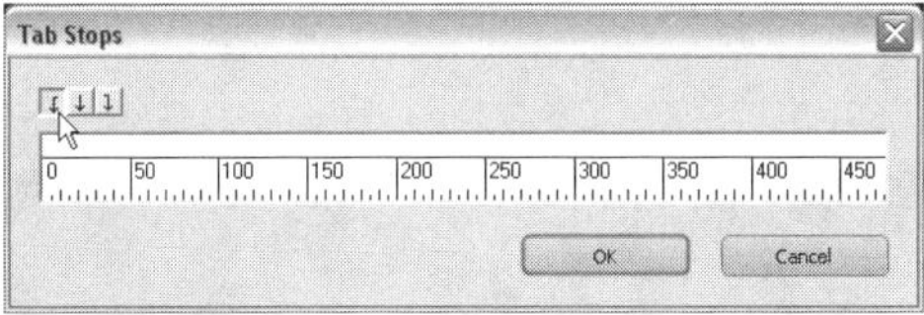

Figure 9.38 Select the kind of tab you want to use.

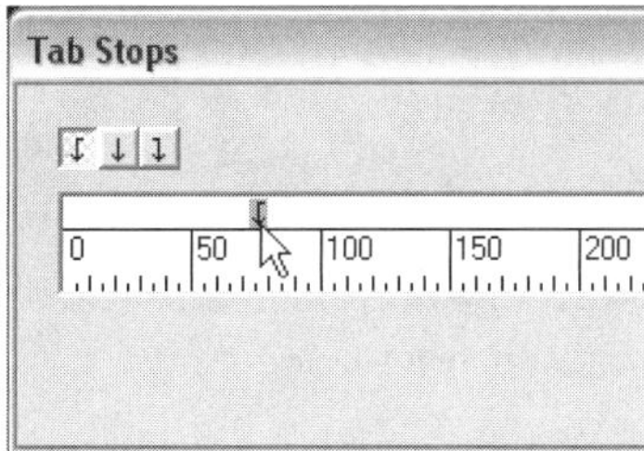

Figure 9.39 Click above the ruler to set the tab's position.

To set tabs in paragraph text:

1. Using either the Type tool T or Vertical Type tool ↓T, create a text box.
2. Choose Title > Tab Stops (**Figure 9.37**).
   The Tab Stops dialog box appears.
3. Select the type of tab you'd like to set (**Figure 9.38**):
   Left-aligned tab
   Center-aligned tab
   Right-aligned tab
4. Click above the ruler where you want to set the tab (**Figure 9.39**).
5. To delete a tab stop, drag it away from the ruler.
6. Click OK to close the Tab Stops dialog box.

To toggle tab markers:

1. Select a text box.
2. Choose Title > View > Tab Markers (**Figure 9.40**).

   A yellow line appears corresponding to each tab (**Figure 9.41**). Deselect Tab Markers to hide the reference lines.

✔ Tip

- Remember that it's hard to fit large amounts of text into the confines of a television screen—and still have the text be legible, that is. Consider cutting the amount of copy to the bare essentials or using a title scroll (aka a *roll*) instead (see "Creating Scrolls and Crawls," later in this chapter).

Figure 9.40 Choose Title > View > Tab Markers.

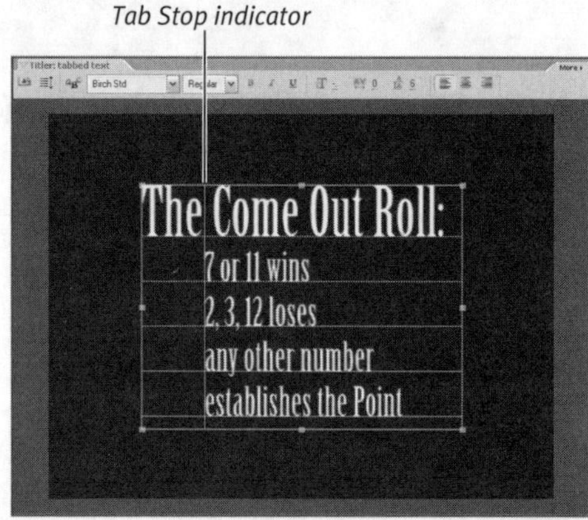

Figure 9.41 A yellow reference line corresponds to each tab you set.

Figure 9.42 Click text using the Selection tool to select it in its entirety.

Figure 9.43 Double-click with the Selection tool to set an insertion point...

Figure 9.44 ...and drag to select a range of characters.

Selecting Text

Whenever you want to edit or modify any of a text object's attributes, you must first select all or part of the object.

To select text for editing:

1. *Do one of the following:*
   - ▲ To select the entire text object, click the text with the Selection tool (**Figure 9.42**).
   - ▲ To set an insertion point, double-click the text object with the Selection tool (**Figure 9.43**).
   - ▲ To select a range of text, drag the insertion-point cursor (**Figure 9.44**).
2. Type to change the selected text or to insert text at the insertion point.

   You can also adjust other attributes of selected text, such as font, size, and fill color. (See the following sections to find out more about adjusting text attributes.)
3. When you finish making changes to the text, select the Selection tool.

   Click an empty part of the drawing area to deselect the text, or select another object-creation tool.

✔ Tip

- You can use the arrow keys to move the insertion point.

Formatting Text

You can assign numerous properties—color, drop shadow, and so on—to any object in the drawing area. However, some properties are exclusive to text. The next several sections focus on these text-only formatting options, which are represented by a majority of the buttons along the top of the Title Designer panel (**Figure 9.45**). Later sections cover attributes common to both text and shape objects.

Specifying a font, font style, and font size

You can set fonts using standard pull-down menus. Each font may include other style options, such as condensed or light, depending on the font. You can set the font's size using a pull-down menu of preset sizes or by entering the size numerically.

If you need help selecting a font, use the Font Browser feature. It not only lists fonts, it also shows what they look like and instantly changes the font of the selected text. This way, you can preview various fonts before you settle on one (and you won't have to contend with the Font pull-down menu, which can become long and unwieldy).

Figure 9.45 Most of the buttons along the top of the Title Designer are used to format text.

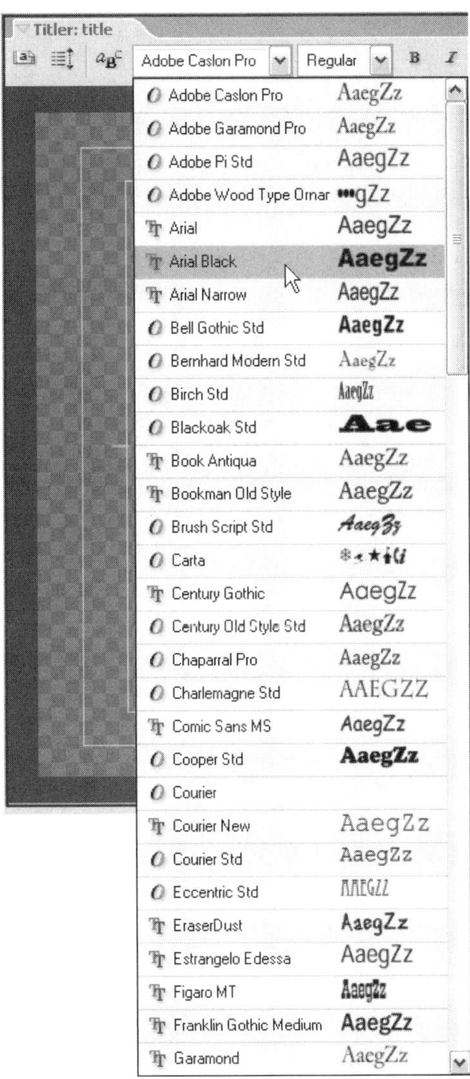

Figure 9.46 You can select a font in the Font pull-down menu...

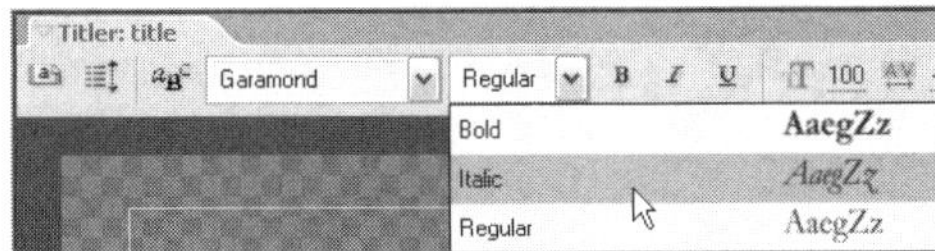

Figure 9.47 ...and choose style options in the Font Style pull-down.

To set the font, font style, and font size:

1. Select all or part of a text object.
2. Using the top row of buttons in the Title Designer panel, set *any of the following*:

   Font—Click to choose from a list of fonts in a pull-down menu (**Figure 9.46**).

   Font Style—Click to choose a style (regular, condensed, and so on) available for the selected font (**Figure 9.47**).

   Font Browser—Click the Browse button to open the Font Browser dialog box (explained in the next task, "To select a font using the Font Browser").

   Font Size—Specify a value to set the size of the text in points.

✔ Tip

- You can avoid scrolling through long lists of fonts by selecting More from the font list. Fonts are grouped in categories.

To select a font using the Font Browser:

1. *Do one of the following:*
   - ▲ Select one or more text objects.
   - ▲ Select a range of text.
   - ▲ Set an insertion point using one of the text tools.
2. In the Title Designer panel, click the Browse button (**Figure 9.48**).
   The Font Browser dialog box appears.
3. In the Font Browser dialog box, select a font you want to consider (**Figure 9.49**).
   The selected text reflects the font you choose in the Font Browser (**Figure 9.50**).
4. When you've found the font you want, click OK.

✔ Tips

- Not all fonts look like letters. Special fonts—often called symbols, ornaments, and dingbats—let you create useful graphic elements easily (**Figure 9.51**). You use these fonts just like other fonts, and you don't have to draw a thing.
- By default, the Font Browser presents a sample of each font consisting of six letters: *AaegZz*. You can change the letters by choosing Edit > Preferences > Titler and typing any other six letters you want.

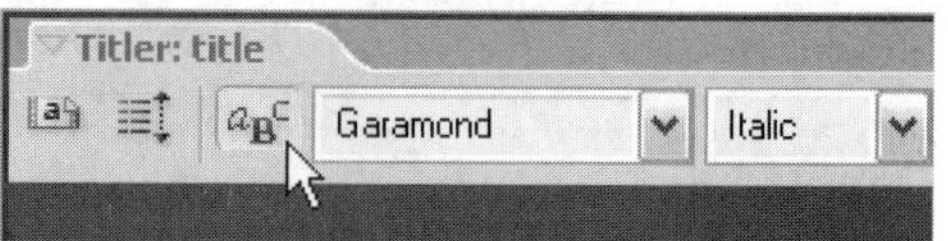

Figure 9.48 Click the Browse button.

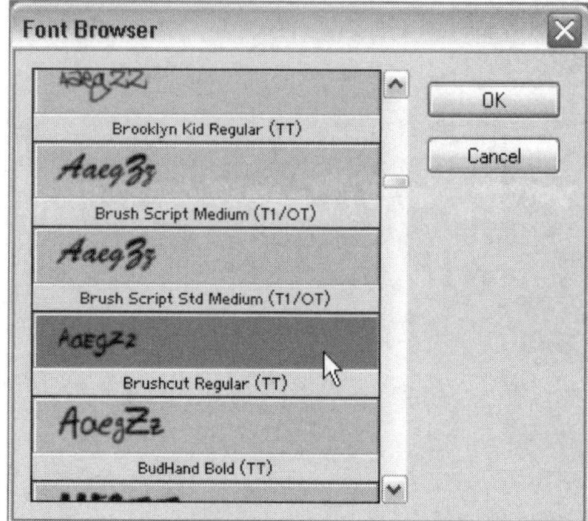

Figure 9.49 Select a font in the Font Browser dialog box.

Figure 9.50 The selected text reflects your choice.

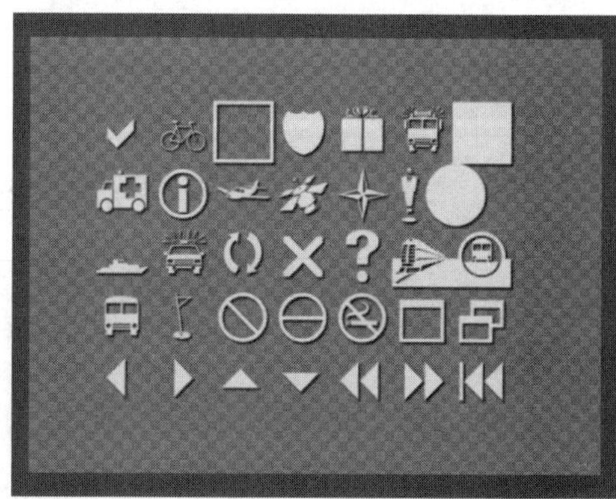

Figure 9.51 The font Webdings creates symbols instead of letters.

FORMATTING TEXT

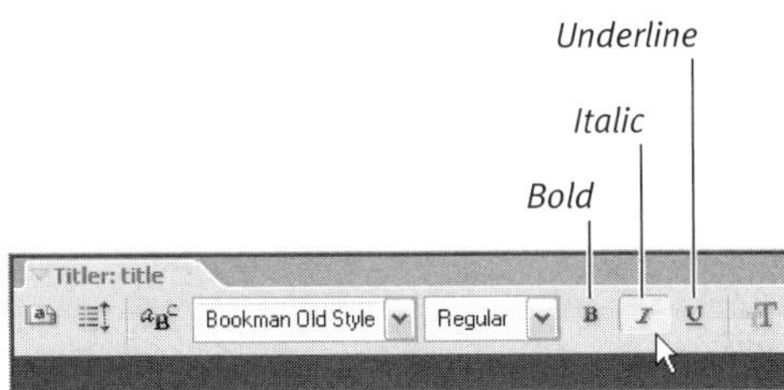

Figure 9.52 Select text you want to modify and click the appropriate button.

Figure 9.53 The selected characters reflect your choice.

Making text bold, italic, or underlined

Easy-to-use buttons in the Title Designer panel let you apply some of the most common typeface variations—boldface, italic, and underline. Note that not all fonts include these variations, and if you choose one of these options in the Style pull-down menu, the corresponding button appears dimmed.

To make text bold, italic, or underlined:

1. Select the text you want to make bold, italic, or underlined.
2. At the top of the Title Designer panel, click the button corresponding to the style you want to apply (**Figure 9.52**):

   Bold—Makes the selected characters boldface, a thicker version of the typeface

   Italic—Makes the selected characters italic, a more slanted version of the typeface

   Underline—Makes the selected characters underlined

   The style you specify is applied to the selected characters (**Figure 9.53**).

Setting text leading and kerning

Leading (which rhymes with *wedding)* defines the space between lines of text. The term *leading* refers to the literal strips of lead that typesetters of old placed between lines of metal type. Increasing leading expands the space between lines, whereas a negative leading value reduces the space.

Kerning describes the process of adjusting the value of *kern pairs*, spacing that the typeface's designer built into particular pairs of characters. This can be an important feature because automatic kerning is rarely perfect. You can kern between a pair of characters or across a range of characters.

Figure 9.54 At the top of the Title Designer panel, specify a Leading value.

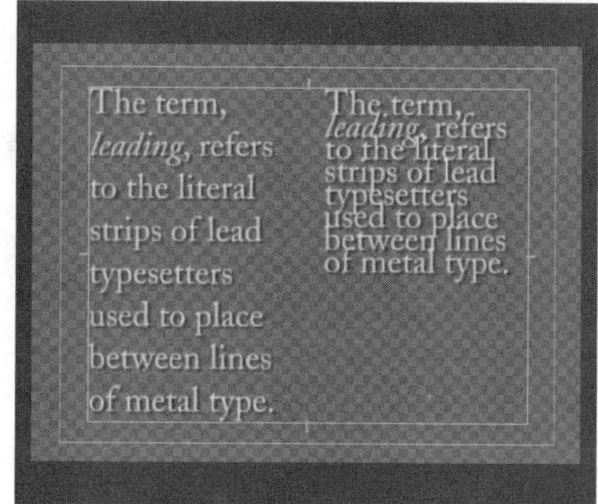

Figure 9.55 The text uses the leading you specify.

To set leading:

1. *Do either of the following:*
   - ▲ To specify leading for all lines in the text object, select the text object.
   - ▲ To specify leading between two lines, set an insertion cursor anywhere in the lower of the two lines.
2. At the top of the Title Designer panel, specify a Leading value (**Figure 9.54**).

   The text uses the leading you specify (**Figure 9.55**).

Figure 9.56 At the top of the Title Designer panel, specify a Kerning value.

To set kerning:

1. *Do either of the following:*
   - ▲ To specify kerning for a range of character pairs, select a range of characters.
   - ▲ To specify kerning between two characters, set an insertion cursor between the characters.
2. At the top of the Title Designer panel, specify a Kerning value (**Figure 9.56**).

   The text uses the kerning you specify (**Figure 9.57**).

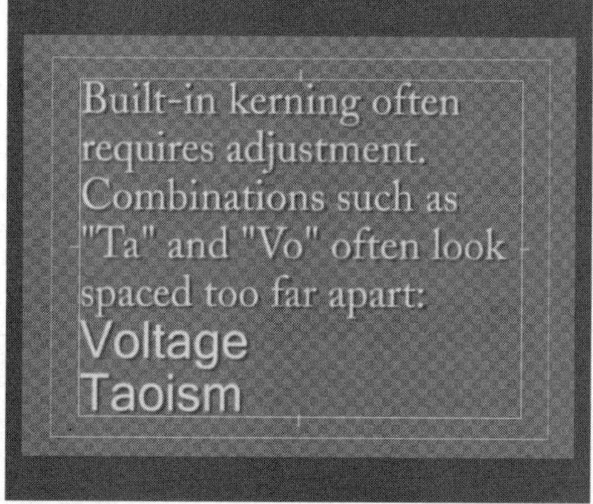

Figure 9.57 The text uses the kerning you specify.

Figure 9.58 Select the alignment option you want.

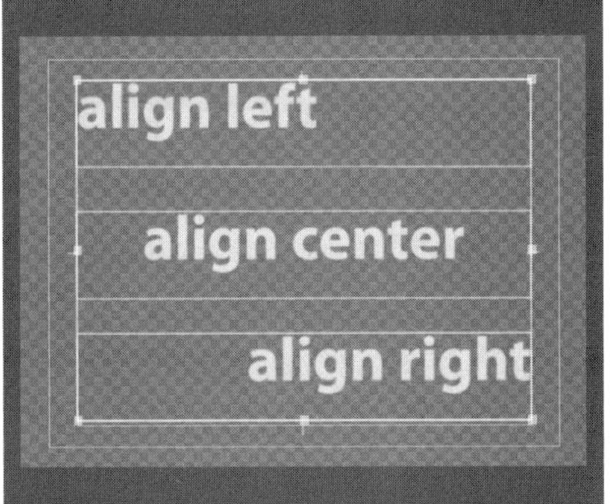

Figure 9.59 In this figure, all three text objects' bounding boxes are the same, but the text they contain are aligned differently.

Aligning text

Alignment determines how the lines in a paragraph are positioned relative to the margins (the left and right sides of the text box). As usual, you can set whether the lines align flush with the left or right or are centered horizontally in the box.

Although Premiere Elements refers to this feature as type "alignment," others may use the term "justification." Also, don't confuse aligning text within its text box with aligning multiple objects with one another—a separate feature discussed in the section "Aligning Objects," later in this chapter.

To align text:

1. Select all or part of a text object containing multiple lines of text.
2. At the top of the Title Designer panel, click the button that corresponds to the justification option you want (**Figure 9.58**):

   Align Left —Aligns text to the left side of its text box

   Align Center —Centers text horizontally within its text box

   Align Right —Aligns text to the right side of its text box

   The text uses the justification option you specify (**Figure 9.59**).

Using Styles

Besides conveying raw information, titles also contribute to the overall look of a project. So, it's common for all the titles in a project to share similar characteristics. Using the Styles feature, you can reapply your favorite attributes quickly, without adjusting attributes time and time again.

The Current Style swatch always reflects the current style of the text. Any modifications you make to the style of the text updates the Current Style swatch.

To assign a style to text:

1. Select a text object or a range of text (**Figure 9.60**).
2. In the Title Styles panel, click a style swatch (**Figure 9.61**).

   The selected text uses the style you selected (**Figure 9.62**).

Figure 9.60 Select a text object or a range of text.

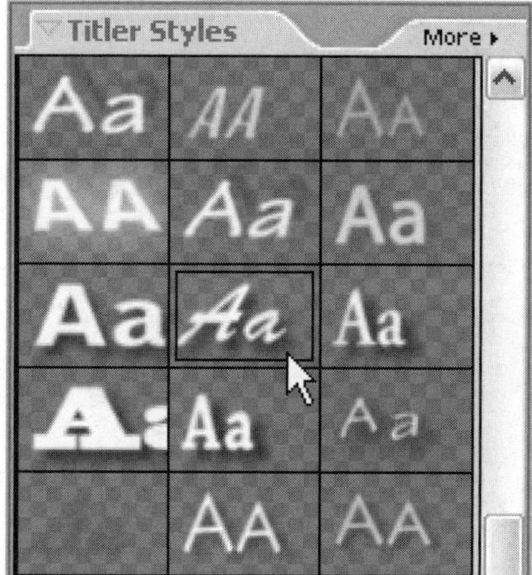

Figure 9.61 Click a style swatch in the Title Styles panel.

Figure 9.62 The style is applied to the selection.

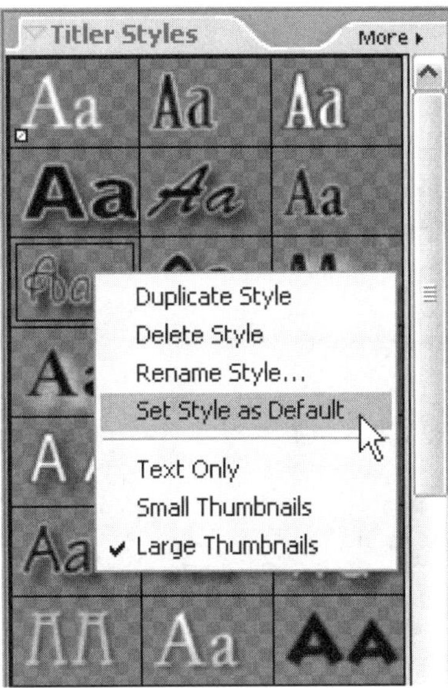

Figure 9.63 Right-click a style swatch, and choose Set Style as Default in the context menu.

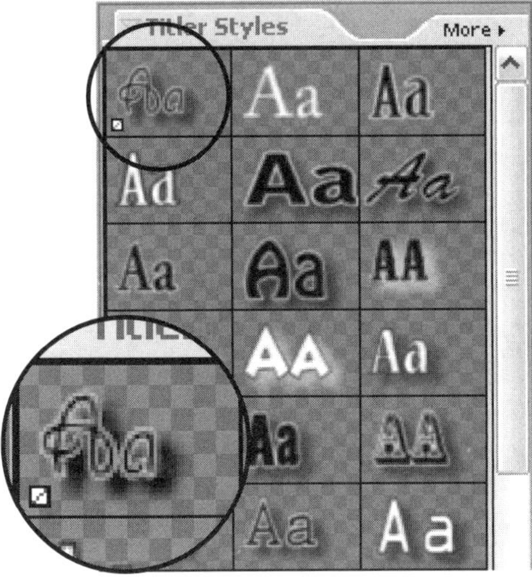

Figure 9.64 The default swatch always appears in the upper-left corner, with a small folded-corner (dog-ear) icon.

To set a style as the default:

1. Make sure no text objects in the drawing area are selected.
2. Right-click the style swatch you want to be the default, and choose Set Style as Default in the context menu (**Figure 9.63**).

   The swatch moves to the upper-left corner of the Styles panel. A dog-ear icon appears in the corner of the selected style swatch (**Figure 9.64**).

To save a custom style:

1. Select a text object or range of text that has the attributes you want to save as a style (**Figure 9.65**).
2. In the Title Styles panel's More menu, choose Save Style (**Figure 9.66**).
   A New Style dialog box appears.
3. Enter the name of the style, and click OK (**Figure 9.67**).
   The style is added to the style swatches (**Figure 9.68**).
4. To view the styles by name, choose Text Only from the Title Styles panel's More menu.

✔ Tips

- Commands in the Title Styles panel's menu also allow you to delete and rename styles and change how the style swatches look.
- By default, style swatches show how an uppercase and lowercase letter *A* look in the style. If you want to, you can choose Edit > Preferences > Titler and specify other letters.

Figure 9.65 Select text that uses the attributes you want to save as a style.

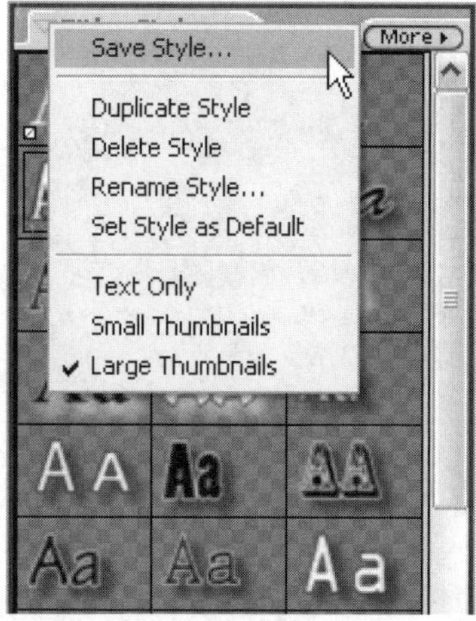

Figure 9.66 In the Title Styles panel's More menu, choose Save Style.

Figure 9.67 In the New Style dialog box, enter the name of the style, and click OK.

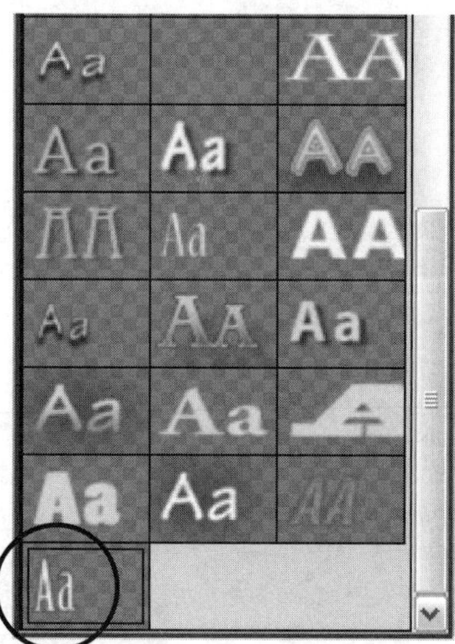

Figure 9.68 A swatch representing the style appears in the Title Styles panel.

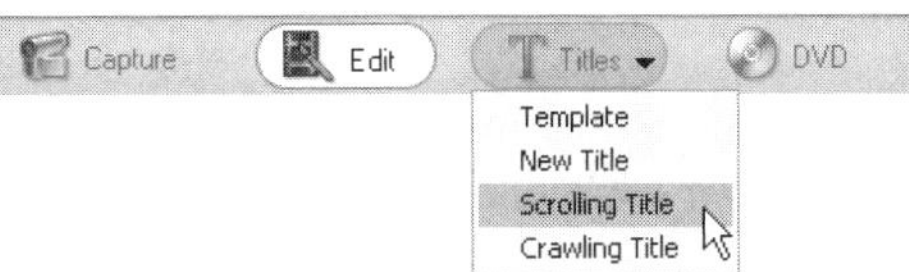

Figure 9.69 Click and hold the taskbar's Titles button, and choose the option you want.

Figure 9.70 Enter a name in the New Title dialog box.

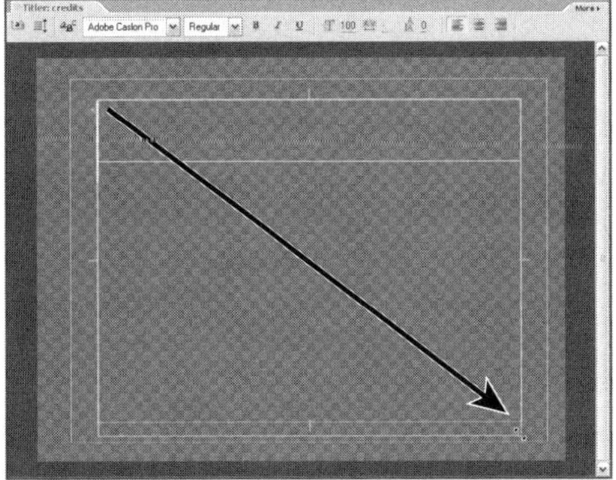

Figure 9.71 Drag in the drawing area to create a text box.

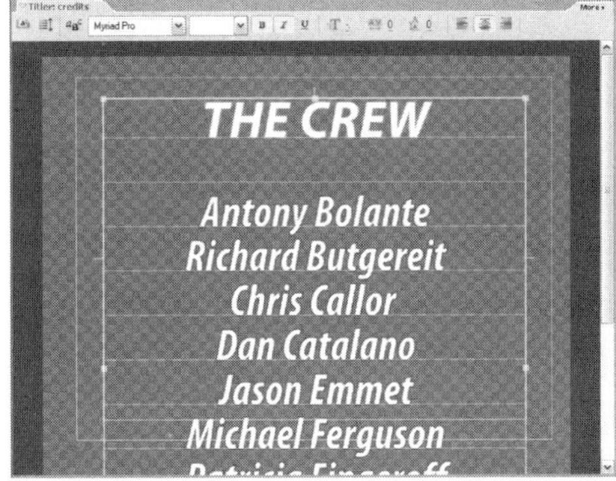

Figure 9.72 Type the text you want to scroll or crawl. A scroll bar appears.

Creating Scrolls and Crawls

In a title *scroll* (aka a *roll*), text appears to move from beyond the bottom of the screen to beyond the top of the screen. Title scrolls are frequently used in a final credit sequence or to present lengthy text onscreen.

A title *crawl* moves across the screen horizontally, typically from right to left. An emergency news bulletin is a classic example of a title crawl.

To create a roll or crawl:

1. In the taskbar, press and hold the Titles button, and choose an option from the pull-down menu (**Figure 9.69**):

   Scrolling Title—Creates scrolling text

   Crawling Title—Creates crawling text

   A New Title dialog box appears.

2. Type a name in the New Title dialog box and then click OK (**Figure 9.70**).

3. Select the Type tool.

   To create vertically oriented text, choose the Vertical Type tool.

4. Drag in the drawing area to create a text box (**Figure 9.71**).

   You should drag beyond the bottom edge for a roll or beyond the right edge for a crawl. Typically, you should keep title rolls between the left and right edges of the title-safe zone (see "Viewing the Video-Safe Zones," earlier in this chapter).

5. Type the text you want (**Figure 9.72**).

continues on next page

6. *Do one of the following:*
   - ▲ To make the text box larger, switch to the Selection tool, and drag one of the text box's control handles to resize the box.
   - ▲ To view other parts of the text box, drag the scroll bar (**Figure 9.73**).
7. Set the roll and crawl options, as explained in the next task.

   When you add the title clip to the timeline, it scrolls or crawls, according to your selections. The duration of the clip helps determine the speed of the scroll or crawl.

Figure 9.73 To make the text box larger, resize it with the Selection tool; use the scroll bar to view different parts of the box.

To set roll and crawl options:

1. With a scrolling or crawling text object selected, click the Roll/Crawl Options button in the Title Designer panel (**Figure 9.74**).

   The Roll/Crawl Options dialog box appears.

Figure 9.74 With the rolling or crawling object selected, click the Roll/Crawl Options button in the Title Designer panel.

2. Choose an option in the Motion pull-down menu (**Figure 9.75**):
   - ▲ Still
   - ▲ Roll
   - ▲ Crawl
3. *Choose one or more of the following options* (**Figure 9.76**):

   Start Off Screen—Positions the text box offscreen at the beginning of the roll or crawl

   End Off Screen—Positions the text box offscreen at the end of the roll or crawl

   Preroll—The number of frames to hold the title in its starting position before the roll or crawl begins (not available when Start Off Screen is selected)

   Ease-In—The number of frames during which the roll or crawl slowly accelerates before reaching full speed

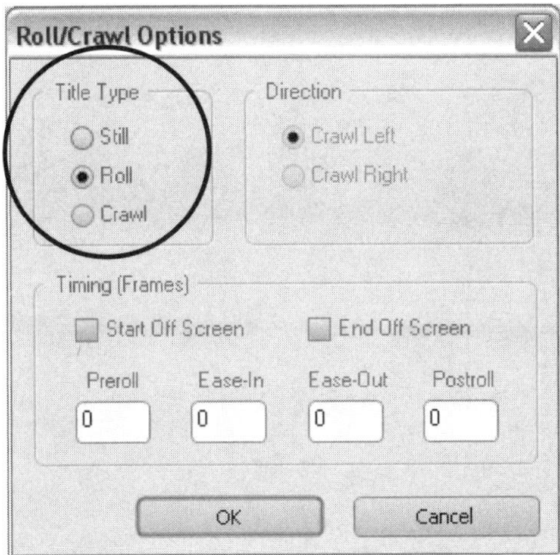

Figure 9.75 In the Roll/Crawl Options dialog box, specify whether you want a rolling (scrolling) title or crawling title.

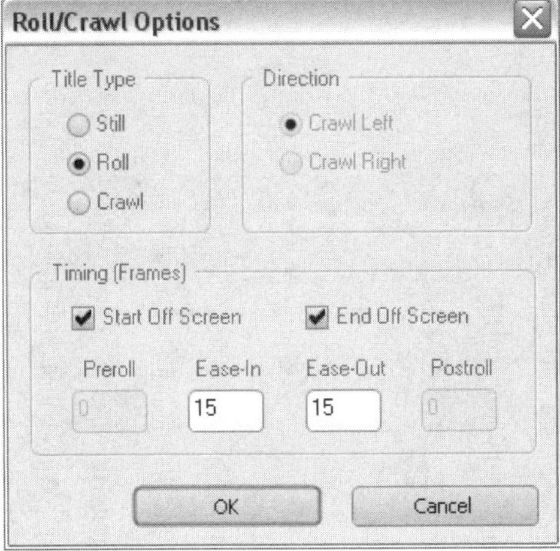

Figure 9.76 Specify timing options and, if you're creating a crawling title, a crawl direction.

Ease-Out—The number of frames during which the roll or crawl slowly decelerates before stopping

Postroll—The number of frames to hold the title in its ending position after the roll or crawl ends (not available when End Off Screen is selected)

4. If you specified Crawl in step 2, select an option for Crawl Direction:
   - ▲ Left to Right
   - ▲ Right to Left
5. Click OK to close the dialog box.

   The scrolling or crawling title obeys the settings you selected.

✔ Tips

- Although you can hold a title scroll (or roll) in its ending position by setting a Postroll value, getting the last lines to stop where you want might take some practice. For example, to get the text *copyright 2005* to end up alone in the center of the screen, you may have to experiment with adding blank lines or resizing the text box.
- In Premiere Elements, the terms *scrolling title* and *rolling title* (or *scroll* and *roll*) are used interchangeably. Don't be confused: They refer to the same thing. Chances are, Adobe will reconcile the terms and change Roll/Crawl Options to Scroll/Crawl Options in later versions.

Creating Shape Objects

When you create a shape, you define its dimensions by defining the size of an invisible, rectangular box called a *bounding box.* Whereas a rectangle fits exactly inside its bounding box, other shapes are circumscribed within theirs. When you select a shape, its bounding box appears with six *handles,* small squares you can grab and drag to change the dimensions of the box—and thereby the shape it contains.

You can also create open and closed polygons and Bezier shapes. These techniques are covered in later sections.

Figure 9.77 Select one of the shape tools. In this example, the Ellipse tool is selected.

To create a shape:

1. In the Title Tools panel, select a shape tool (**Figure 9.77**):
   - ▲ Rectangle
   - ▲ Rounded-Corner Rectangle
   - ▲ Ellipse
   - ▲ Line
2. *Do one of the following:*
   - ▲ Drag in the drawing area to define the size of the shape.
   - ▲ Shift-drag in the drawing area to make the shape's horizontal and vertical aspects the same (to create perfect circles and squares).
   - ▲ Alt-drag in the drawing area to define the shape from its center rather than its corners.

   The shape reflects the tool and technique you use (**Figure 9.78**).

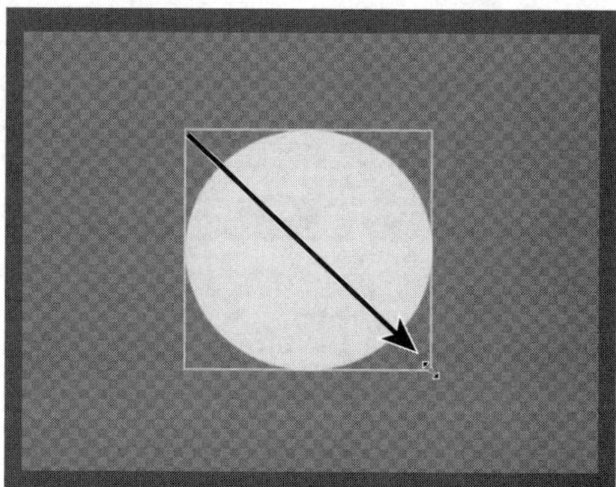

Figure 9.78 Drag in the drawing area to define the size of the shape. Hold Shift to constrain the aspect of the shape, and hold Alt to draw the shape from its center.

✔ Tip

- You can change the dimensions of a shape (or text created with a type tool) by selecting it and dragging a handle of its bounding box.

Setting Color Properties

Whether you're creating text or graphical objects, chances are you'll need to adjust their appearance—most notably, their color. You can access a number of color-related properties by clicking the (what else?) Color Properties button . This innocuous button opens the Color Properties dialog box, which controls several attributes:

Fill Color—The color within the object's contours

Stroke Color—The color of the object's outline, or contours

Stroke Weight—The thickness of the stroke

Color Gradient—A fill that transitions from one color to another, or between four colors

Drop shadow—A semitransparent, black duplicate of the object that appears to be behind the object. A drop shadow sets an object apart from the background, implying a sense of dimensionality and making text more legible.

Each option is explained in detail in the sections to follow.

To open the Color Properties dialog box:

1. In the Title Designer panel's drawing area, select the objects for which you want to specify a fill and stroke color.
2. To specify a stroke, make sure the current style includes a stroke, and, if necessary, click a style swatch that does (**Figure 9.79**).

   You can select a style with a single stroke or six strokes. If the current style doesn't have a stroke, the Color Properties dialog box's Stroke options appear dimmed.
3. In the Title Tools panel, click the Color Properties button ▣ (**Figure 9.80**).

   The Color Properties dialog box appears.

✔ Tip

- As you may have noticed, the Titler has a notable idiosyncrasy. To apply a stroke, you must first apply a preset style that has a stroke. You can set multiple strokes by first applying a preset style that has multiple strokes. If the current style uses no stroke, the Stroke options in the Color Properties dialog box appear dimmed. We hope Adobe will make the process more intuitive in future versions.

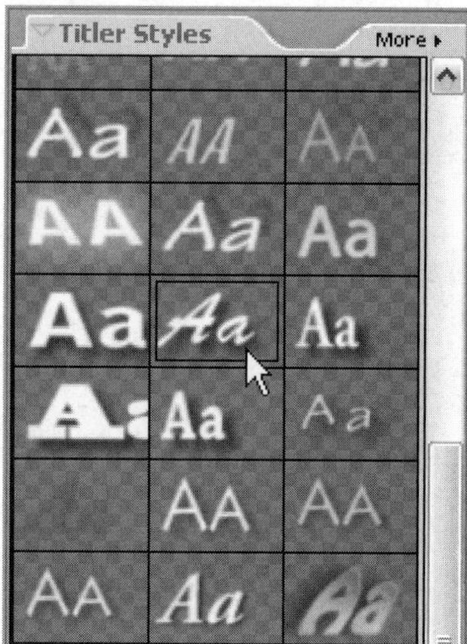

Figure 9.79 Select the objects you want to format, and, if you want to set strokes, make sure the current style includes one or more strokes.

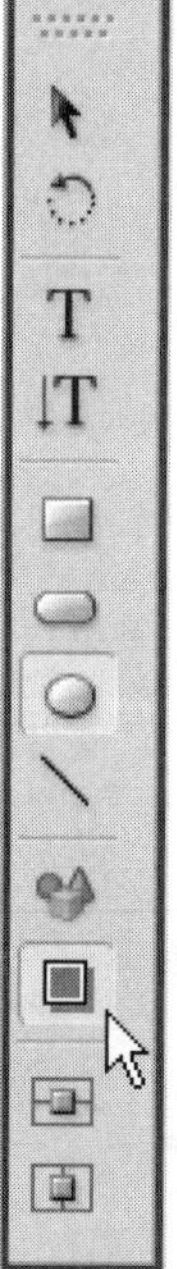

Figure 9.80 Click the Color Properties button.

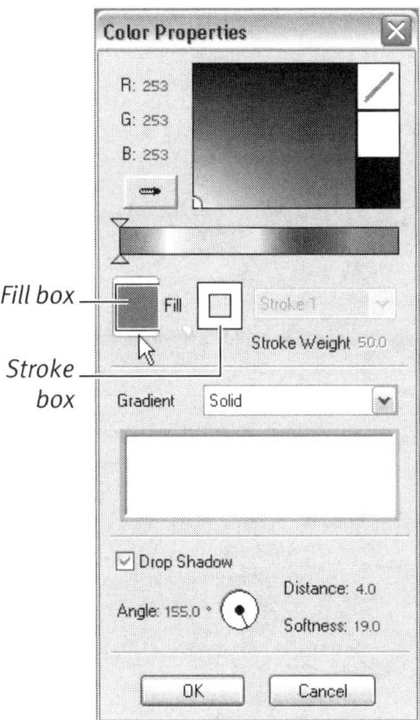

Figure 9.81 Select either the Fill box or Stroke box.

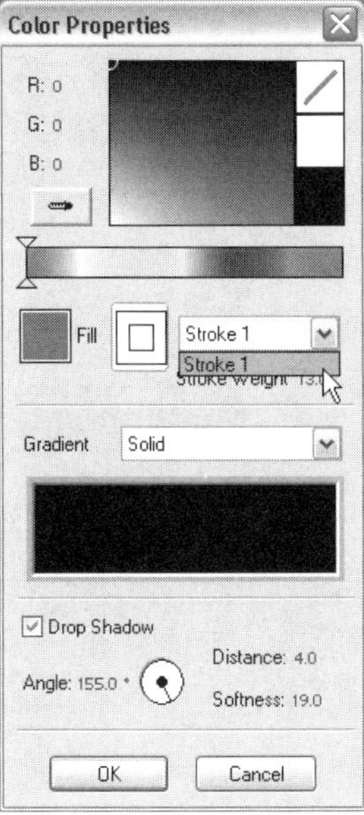

Figure 9.82 If you selected the Stroke box, specify the stroke you want to modify in the pull-down menu. Here, only one stroke is available; other styles include six strokes.

Setting the fill and stroke

Each object has two possible color attributes: fill and stroke. Not surprisingly, the *fill color* is the color of the character: the color within its contours. The *stroke color* is the color of the object's contours: its outlines. Naturally, you can detect the stroke color only if the stroke has a thickness greater than zero. Conversely, you can create an object that has a stroke but no fill color. The result is an object that resembles an empty frame.

When you set a color, you can opt to use a single solid color, or you can transition from one color to another, using a gradient. When a stroke is specified, you can specify the width, or thickness, of the stroke.

To specify a fill or stroke:

1. In the Color Properties dialog box, *do either of the following* (**Figure 9.81**):
   - ▲ To specify a fill color, click the Fill box to select it.
   - ▲ To specify a stroke color, click the Stroke box to select it.
2. If you selected the Stroke box in step 1, specify the stroke you want to affect in the Stroke pull-down menu (**Figure 9.82**).

   If the Stroke box and pull-down are dimmed, then you didn't specify a style that includes a stroke in the previous task, "To open the Color Properties dialog box." Close the Color Properties dialog box, and start again.
3. Specify the fill or stroke's color, stroke weight, and gradient option, as explained in the following sections.

To specify a color:

- In the Color Properties dialog box, select the fill or stroke you want, and *do any of the following* (**Figure 9.83**):
  - ▲ To leave the fill or stroke empty, click the No Color button.
  - ▲ To set the color to white, click the white color swatch.
  - ▲ To set the color to black, click the black color swatch.
  - ▲ To set the hue manually, drag the Hue slider to the color you want.
  - ▲ To set the saturation manually, click in the Saturation box.
  - ▲ To match the color to a color on the screen, click the Eyedropper, and then click on the color you want on the screen.

  The selected color (fill or stroke) becomes the color you specify, and its RGB values are displayed in the Color Properties dialog box. To set whether the fill or stroke uses a color gradient, see the section "Using color gradients," later in this chapter.

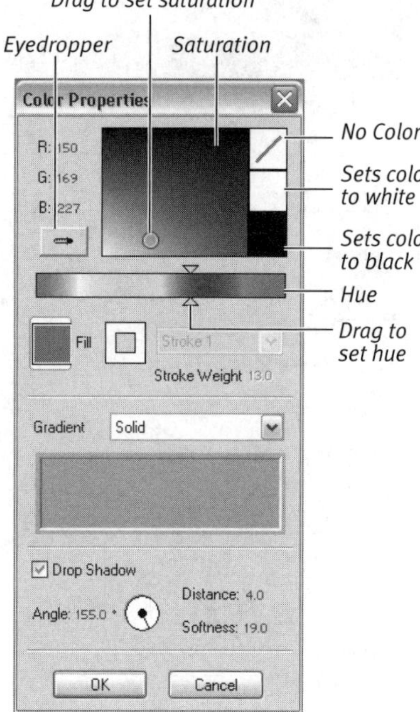

Figure 9.83 Set the color using one of the color controls.

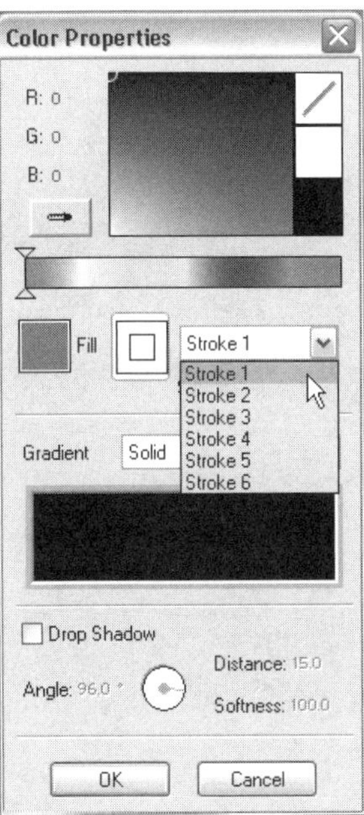

Figure 9.84 Select the Stroke box, and choose a stroke from the Stroke pull-down menu.

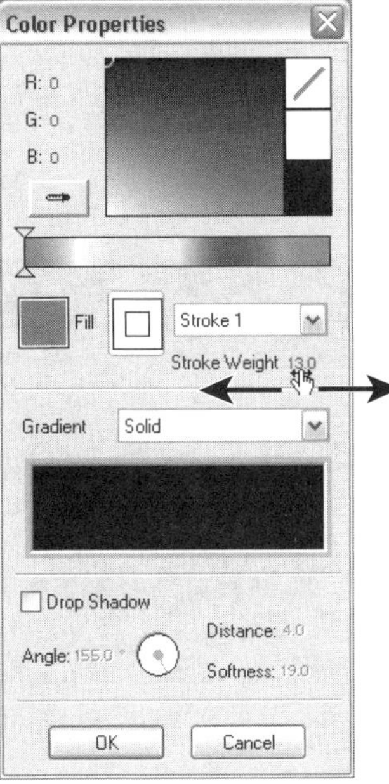

Figure 9.85 Set the Stroke Weight.

To set the stroke weight:

1. In the Color Properties dialog box, click the Stroke box to select it.

   The Stroke pull-down menu appears selected.

2. Choose the Stroke you want to affect in the Stroke pull-down menu (**Figure 9.84**).

3. For Stroke Weight, set a value in pixels (**Figure 9.85**).

   The selected object's stroke uses the thickness you specify (**Figure 9.86**).

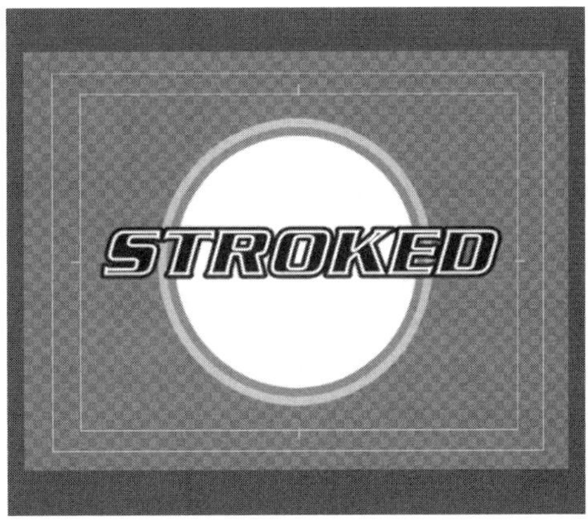

Figure 9.86 The selected object's stroke uses the thickness you specify.

To set a gradient option:

1. In the Color Properties dialog box, *select an option* from the Gradient pull-down menu (**Figure 9.87**):

   Solid—Sets a uniform color fill

   Linear Gradient—Sets a fill that gradually changes from one color to another in a linear pattern

   Radial Gradient—Sets a fill that gradually changes from one color to another in a circular pattern

   4 Color Gradient—Sets a gradient composed of four colors, each starting from a different corner of the object's bounding box

   Bevel—Highlights the object's edges with a color you specify, giving it a beveled appearance

   Eliminate—Makes the fill transparent and unable to cast a shadow

   Ghost—Makes the fill transparent yet capable of casting a shadow

   In the Color Properties dialog box, the gradient color box reflects your choice (**Figure 9.88**).

2. If you chose a gradient or bevel, specify a color for each color stop (see the task "To set gradient options," later in this chapter).

✔ Tips

- Setting the fill color to Ghost lets you create semitransparent, soft-edged objects (by using the object's soft drop shadow). Try arranging a ghost shape behind text or other objects to set them apart from the background.
- Naturally, choosing Eliminate as the fill type is useful only if you add a stroke to the object.

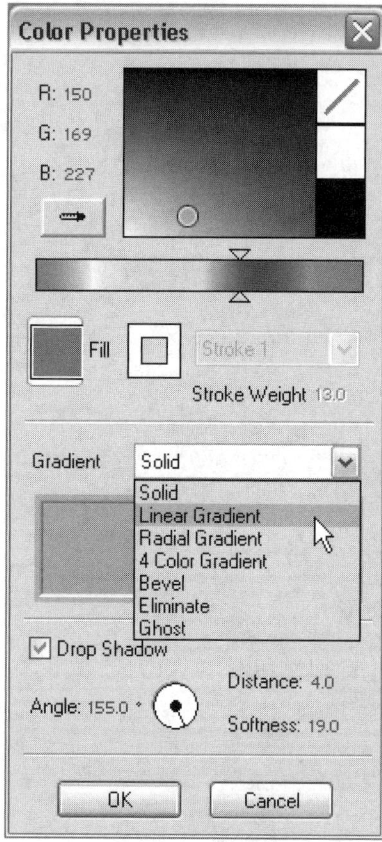

Figure 9.87 To set a gradient, select an option in the Gradient pull-down menu.

Figure 9.88 This figure shows text and shapes using different options for their fill color. The Ghost option makes the objects invisible, but their drop shadows still appear.

Using color gradients

As you saw in the previous section, three of the seven fill types are gradients: linear gradient, radial gradient, and four-color gradient. Because the gradients change from one color to another, they use special controls.

Under the Fill property heading, each color used in a gradient is represented by a *color stop*—a small box alongside a sample image of the gradient. For linear and radial gradients, the left color stop shows the starting color; the right color stop shows the ending color (**Figure 9.89**). Four-color gradients have a color box for each corner of the object (**Figure 9.90**).

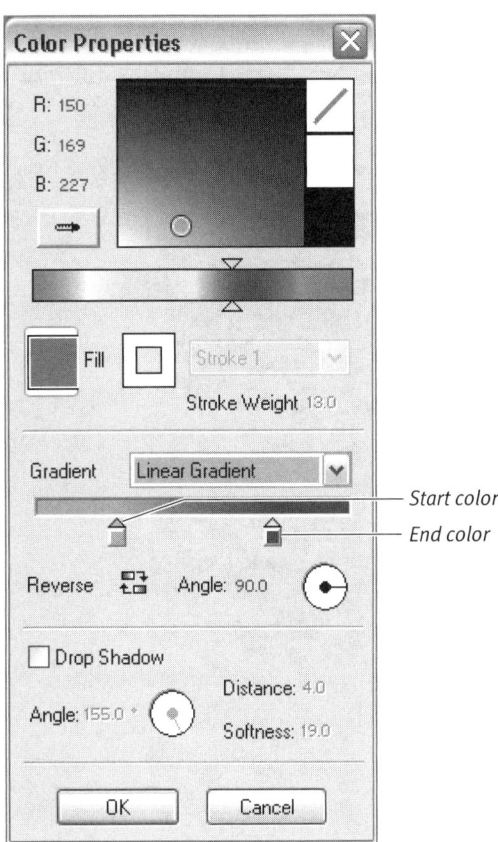

Figure 9.89 Color stops represent the starting and ending colors of a linear or radial gradient.

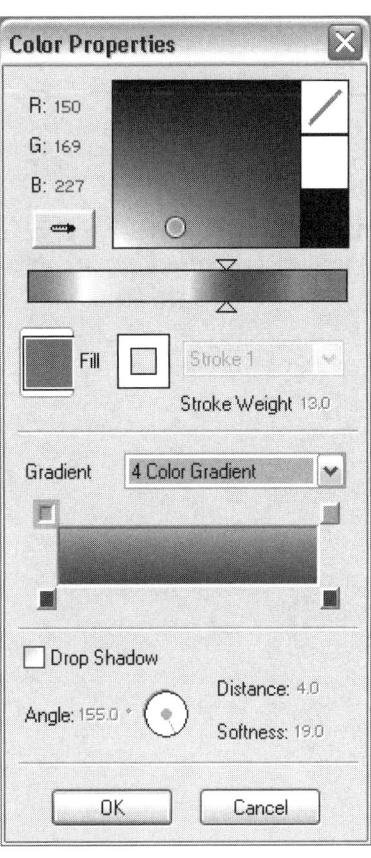

Figure 9.90 Four-color gradients have a color stop in each corner of the gradient sample.

To set gradient options:

1. In the Color Properties dialog box, specify a linear, radial, or four-color gradient, or a bevel.
2. Click the color stop you want to adjust (**Figure 9.91**).
3. To set the color stop's color, *do one of the following:*
   - ▲ Specify a color using the Hue slider and saturation box.
   - ▲ Click the Eyedropper tool to sample a color from the screen.

   See the task "To specify a color," earlier in this chapter.
4. Repeat steps 2–3 for other color stops, as needed.
5. To adjust the transition, or *ramp,* between colors in the gradient, drag the color swatches along the gradient sample (**Figure 9.92**).

   The relative spacing of the color swatches along the gradient sample affects the transition between colors.
6. To adjust the angle of a linear gradient, drag the angle control (**Figure 9.93**).

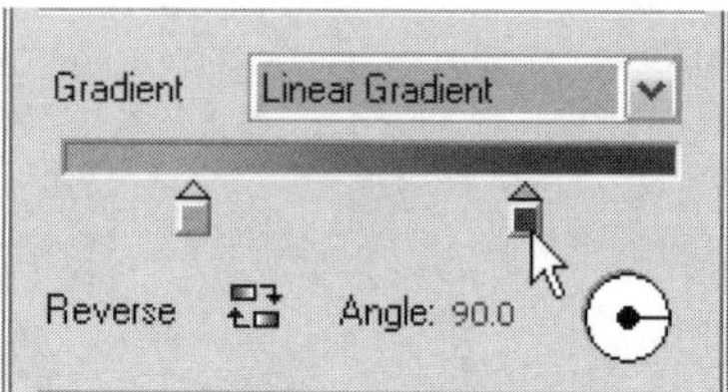

Figure 9.91 Select a color stop.

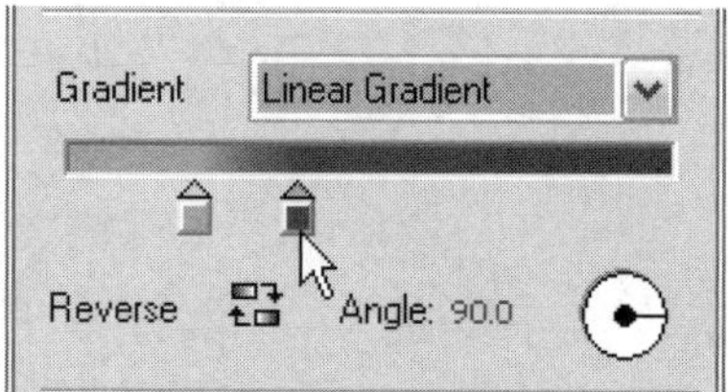

Figure 9.92 Drag the color swatches along the gradient sample to adjust the gradient's ramp—how quickly it transitions from one color to the other.

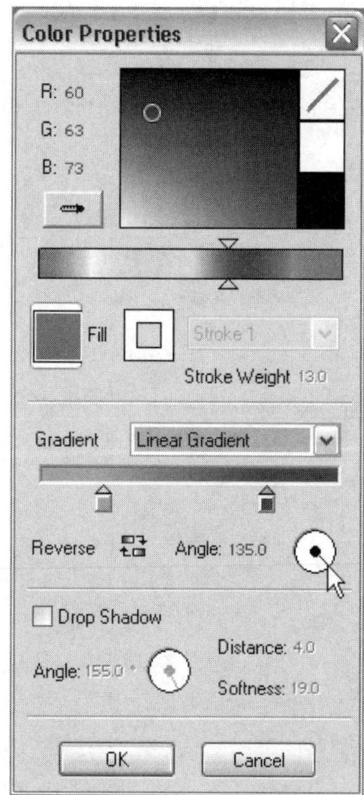

Figure 9.93 For linear gradients, set the direction using the angle control.

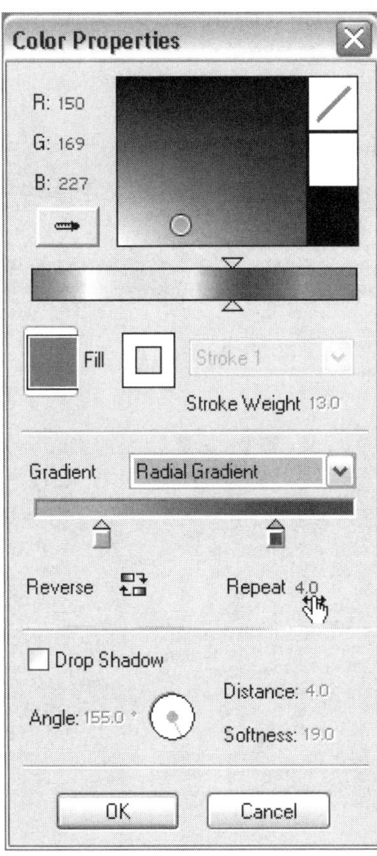

Figure 9.94 For radial gradients, specify the number times to repeat the gradient.

7. To repeat the pattern of a radial gradient, specify a value for Repeat (**Figure 9.94**).

   The gradient transitions between the start and end colors the number of times you specify.

8. Click OK to close the Color Properties dialog box.

   The selected objects use the gradient you specified (**Figures 9.95** and **9.96**).

✔ Tips

- To quickly swap a gradient's start and ending colors, click the Reverse button.
- When you're applying gradients to text, the gradient is applied to each character separately. In other words, gradient colors start and end within each letter, not in the text box as a whole.
- The Render category of the Video Effects folder in the Effects and Transitions panel includes an After Effects filter called Ramp. You can apply this filter to a clip to create a full-screen linear or radial gradient.

Figure 9.95 In this example, the circle uses a linear gradient...

Figure 9.96 ...whereas in this example, a rectangle filling the screen uses a radial gradient that repeats.

Adding drop shadows

A drop shadow can set an object apart from the background or impart a sense of depth. You can apply a drop shadow to any object. In Premiere Elements, shadows are always semitransparent black.

To apply a shadow:

1. In the Title Designer panel's drawing area, select the objects to which you want to apply a drop shadow, and click the Color Properties button.
2. In the Color Properties dialog box, select Drop Shadow.
3. Set the shadow's properties (**Figure 9.97**):

   Angle—The direction, in degrees, from the object in which the shadow falls

   Distance—How far, in pixels, the shadow falls from the object

   Softness—Blurs the edges of the shadow by the number of pixels you specify

   The shadow uses the settings you specified (**Figures 9.98** and **9.99**).

✔ Tips

- You can see a shadow through a semitransparent object (as long as the fill type isn't set to Eliminate). If a stroke or fill seems darker than it should be, the drop shadow may be showing through.
- A fill or stroke set to Ghost is transparent, but it can still cast a shadow.

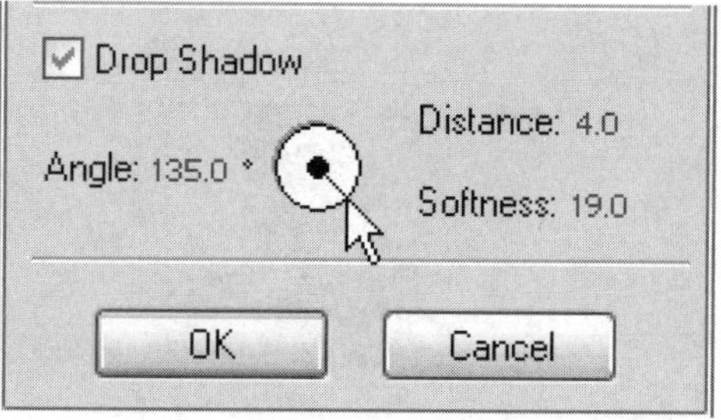

Figure 9.97 In the Color Properties dialog box, select Drop Shadow, and set the shadow's angle, distance, and softness.

Figure 9.98 Text without a drop shadow can be more difficult to read...

Figure 9.99 ...than when it has a drop shadow.

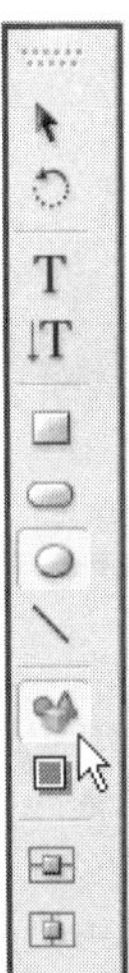

Figure 9.100 Click the Add Image button.

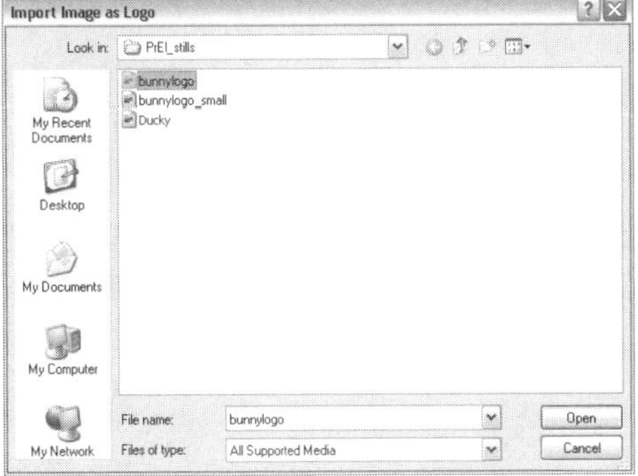

Figure 9.101 Locate the image file you want to use, and click Open.

Adding Images to Titles

As you've learned by working with title templates, titles can include imported still image files. With the Titler, you can place a picture directly in the drawing area along with the other objects you create. This way, it's easy to add design elements, create a theme, or incorporate a logo into your title designs.

To add a picture:

1. In the Title Tools panel, click the Add Image button (**Figure 9.100**).

   An Import Image as Logo dialog box appears. By default, the Import Image as Logo dialog box opens the Logos folder, which is located in Premiere Elements' Presets folder.

2. In the Import Image as Logo dialog box, locate the image file you want to use, and click Open (**Figure 9.101**).

   The image appears in the drawing area at full size (**Figure 9.102**).

3. If necessary, adjust the logo's properties, such as position, opacity, and scale (**Figure 9.103**).

   See "Transforming Objects," later in this chapter.

Figure 9.102 Initially, the image appears in the drawing area at full size...

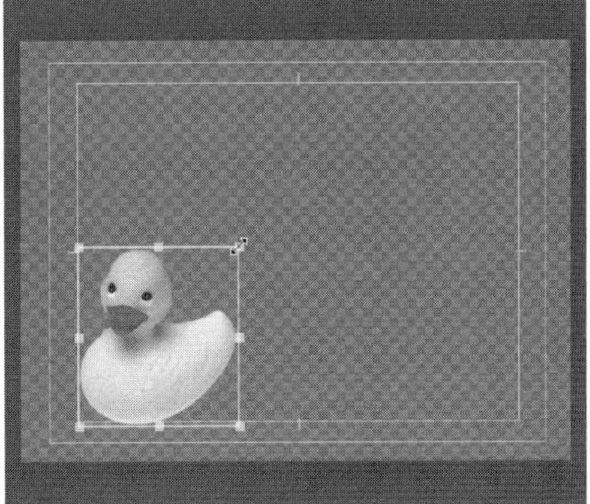

Figure 9.103 ...but you can adjust it using techniques described in the section "Transforming Objects."

To add a picture into a text box:

1. In the Title Designer panel's drawing area, select a text object, and position the insertion point where you want to add an image (**Figure 9.104**).
2. Choose Title > Image > Insert Image into Text (**Figure 9.105**).
3. An Import Image as Logo dialog box appears.
   By default, it opens the Logos folder.
4. Locate the image file you want to use, and click Open (**Figure 9.106**).
   The image appears at the insertion point, scaled to fit into the line of text. Changing the font size also scales the inserted image (**Figure 9.107**).

✔ Tips

- The Insert Image into Text command can be a great way to simulate a special character that you can't get with a font.
- Remember, you can always superimpose a title over any clip. Whether you superimpose a title over a clip or add a still image to the title itself depends on the effect you want.

Figure 9.105 Choose Title > Image > Insert Image into Text.

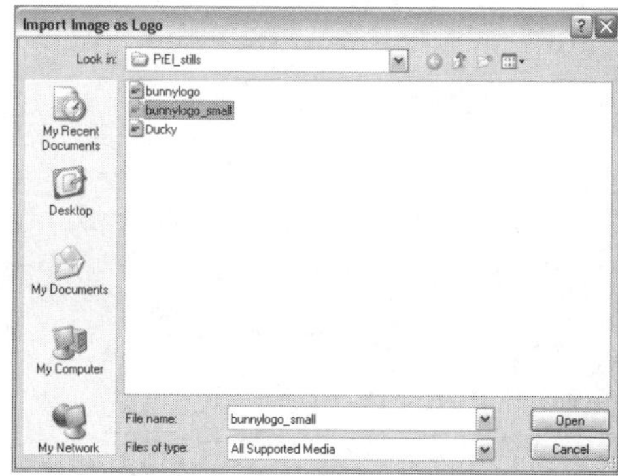

Figure 9.106 Select the image file you want to insert.

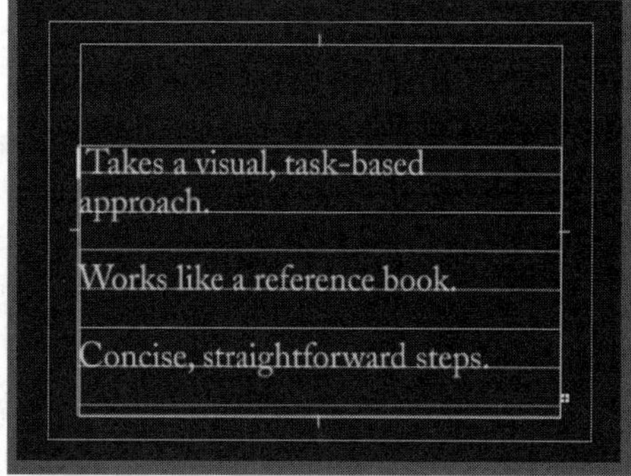

Figure 9.104 Set the insertion point.

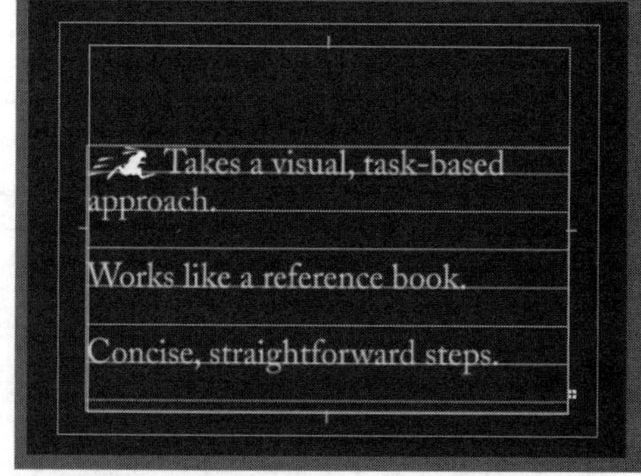

Figure 9.107 When you add the picture, it appears at the insertion point as part of the text. Here, the QuickStart bunny appears in the line of text.

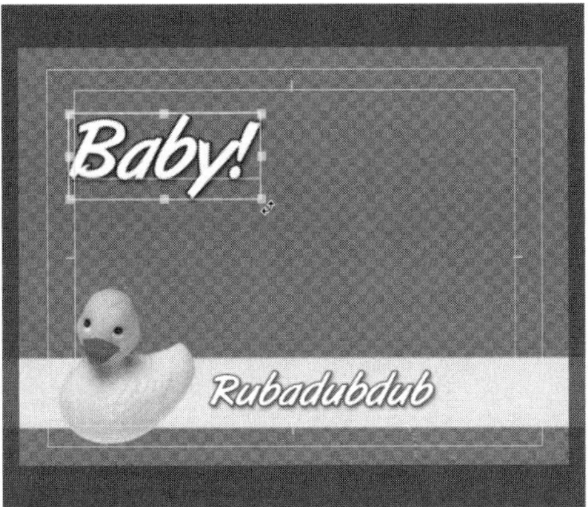

Figure 9.108 Drag an object to move it; drag a handle to scale it; or drag at the corner to rotate it (shown here).

Figure 9.109 Here, the text has been rotated.

Transforming Objects

An object's *transform* properties include its position, scale, rotation, and opacity. With the exception of opacity, you can control these properties by dragging the object in the drawing area. (Scaling any object works just like scaling point text; see the task "To scale point text," earlier in this chapter.) You can set opacity and the other transformations using menu commands (or context menus).

When you use a menu command, you set the value numerically. The following tasks cover how to transform objects by dragging and how to set opacity using a menu command.

To transform an object by dragging:

1. In the Title Designer panel's drawing area, select an object.

   The object's bounding box appears, which includes dots, or *handles*, you can move using the mouse.

2. *Do any of the following:*
   - ▲ To move an object, drag the object by dragging anywhere inside its bounding box.
   - ▲ To scale an object, drag any of the bounding box's handles.
   - ▲ To scale an object and retain its proportions, press Shift as you drag a handle.
   - ▲ To rotate an object, position the mouse near a corner handle so that the mouse icon becomes a Rotate icon, and drag (**Figure 9.108**).

   The object is transformed accordingly (**Figure 9.109**).

To set an object's opacity or other transform property numerically:

1. In the Title Designer panel's drawing area, select an object.
2. Choose Title > Transform, and select a transform property (**Figure 9.110**):

   Position—Sets the position, measured from the center of the object

   Scale—Sets the object's horizontal and vertical aspects

   Rotation—Sets the object's angle in degrees, where its upright vertical position is zero degrees

   Opacity—Sets the object's opacity: 100% is completely opaque, and 0% is completely transparent

   A dialog box appears. The type of dialog box depends on the property you selected.
3. In the dialog box, specify the property's value (**Figure 9.111**).

   The object is transformed according to the settings you specify (**Figure 9.112**).

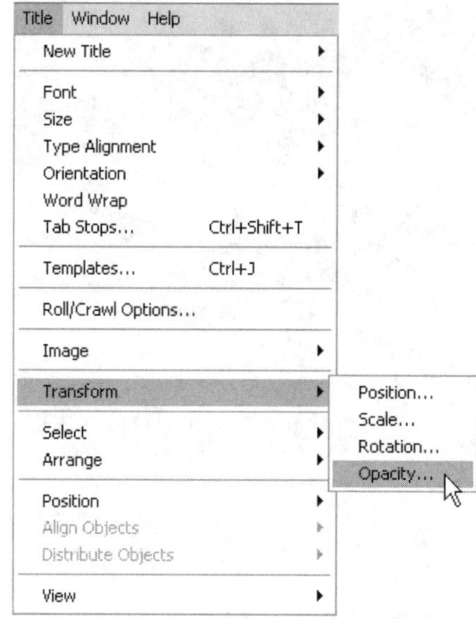

Figure 9.110 Choose Title > Transform, and then choose an option from the submenu.

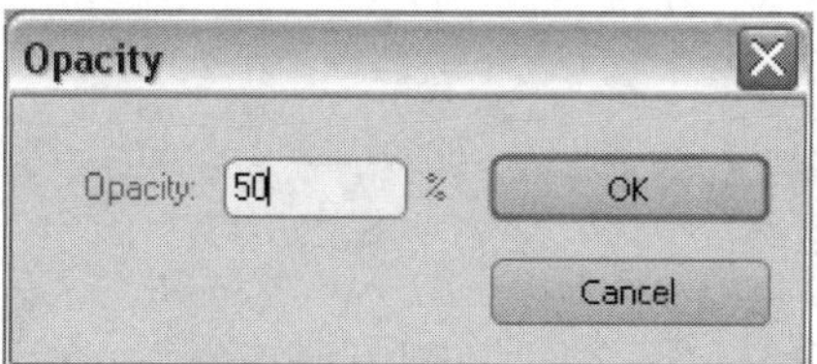

Figure 9.111 Specify a value in the dialog box.

Figure 9.112 The object uses the property value you specified. Here, the box's (behind the text) Opacity is set to 50 percent.

✔ Tips

- Transformations—such as scaling and rotation—are calculated from the center of an object's bounding box. There's no way to change the center point (also called an *anchor point*) of objects in titles.
- Just as you can control the overall opacity of any clip using the clip's opacity effect. Similarly, you can scale, rotate, or reposition any clip using its motion effect. You can even animate opacity and motion. These and other effects are covered in Chapter 10.
- You can *nudge*, or move a selected object by one-pixel increments, by using arrow keys.
- The Title Tools include a Rotate tool, but it's usually easier to position the mouse pointer near a bounding box's corner so it becomes a Rotate icon.

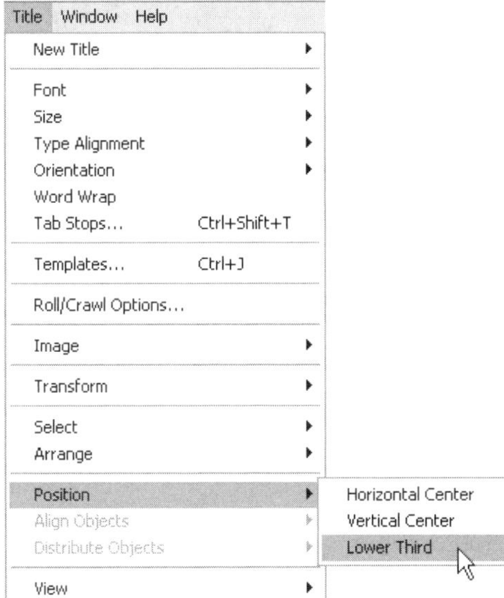

Figure 9.113 Choose Title > Position, and then choose an option from the submenu.

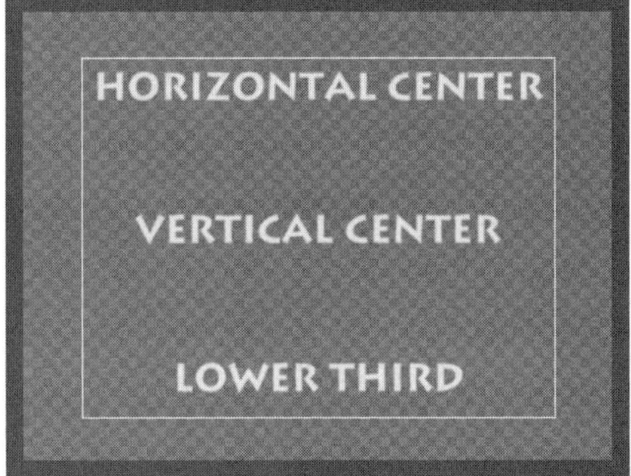

Figure 9.114 These three text objects illustrate the Position command options. All of them are centered horizontally.

Positioning Objects Automatically

You can move selected objects by dragging them with the mouse or pressing the arrow keys. But menu commands can quickly center objects or align objects with the bottom edge of the title-safe zone.

To position objects using menu commands:

1. Select one or more objects in the drawing area.
2. Choose Title > Position, and then choose an option from the submenu (**Figure 9.113**).

   The selected objects are positioned according to your choice (**Figure 9.114**).

✔ Tips

- The Title Tools panel includes buttons for centering objects horizontally and centering objects vertically. However, there's no button equivalent to the menu command Title > Position > Lower Third.
- Note that the position commands place the bounding box, not the object within the box. If a text object doesn't look centered even after you've used the Horizontal Center command, make sure you've centered the text within the box using the Type Alignment command.
- You can copy a selected object by Alt-dragging it. A double arrow icon (like the one you'd see in Adobe Illustrator) appears when you use this keyboard shortcut.

Arranging Objects

In addition to controlling the position of objects, you can control how they're layered. Initially, the most recently created object appears in front of the others, but you can change the stacking order at any time.

To change the stacking order:

1. Select an object in the drawing area (**Figure 9.115**).
2. Choose Title > Arrange, and *select one of the following options* (**Figure 9.116**):

   Bring to Front—Makes the selected object first in the stack

   Bring Forward—Moves the selected object one step up in the stack

   Send to Back—Makes the selected object last in the stack

   Send Backward—Moves the selected object back one step in the stack

   The object's placement in the stacking order changes according to your selection (**Figure 9.117**).

✔ Tip

- Some templates include an empty space to reveal the background video or an image you add (see "Adding Images to Titles," earlier in this chapter). After you import an image and position it, choose Arrange > Send Backward to place the picture in its "frame."

Figure 9.115 Select an object in the drawing area.

Figure 9.116 Choose Title > Arrange, and select the appropriate option...

Figure 9.117 ...to change the object's relative position in the stacking order. Here, Send to Back makes the rectangle last in the stacking order, so it appears behind the text.

Arranging Objects

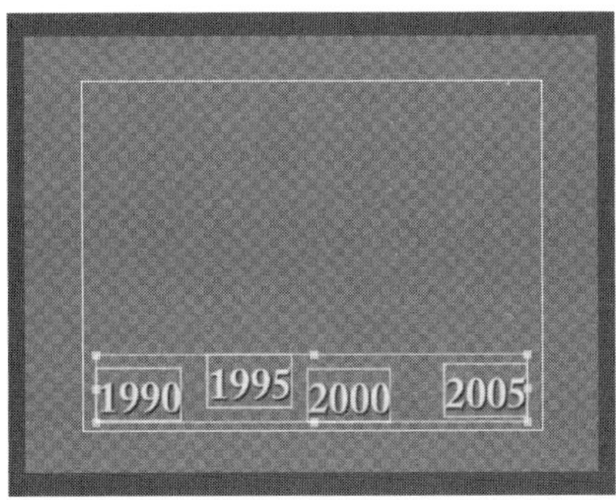

Figure 9.118 Select two or more objects in the drawing area.

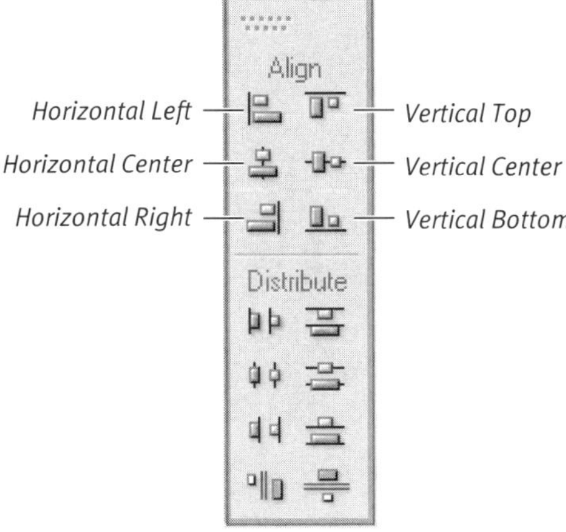

Figure 9.119 Click the alignment option you want in the Title Actions panel.

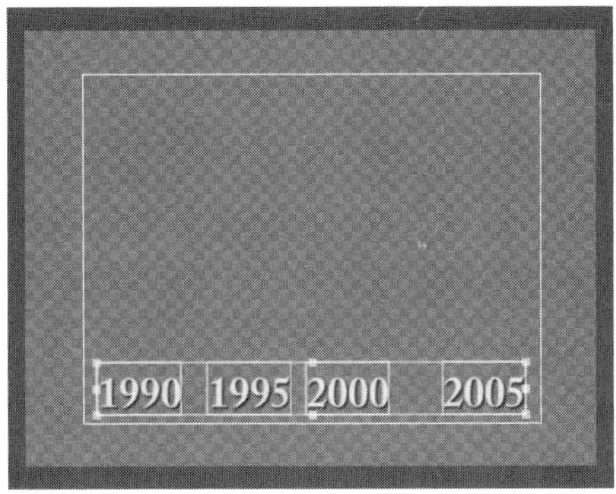

Figure 9.120 The objects are aligned according to your choice. Here, the objects are aligned using the Vertical Bottom option.

Aligning Objects

Other commands allow you to align multiple objects with one another. The Align area in the Title Actions panel uses helpful icons that illustrate your options.

To align objects:

1. Select two or more objects in the drawing area (**Figure 9.118**).
2. In the Title Actions panel, click the button that corresponds to the alignment option you want (**Figure 9.119**).

   The objects are aligned according to your choice (**Figure 9.120**).

✔ Tips

- By default, the Title Actions panel doesn't open when you invoke the Titles workspace. If you anticipate using the Align and Distribute options, choose Window > Title Actions, and then add the panel to the rest of the interface, as described in Chapter 1, "Basic Elements." You might find the Title Actions panel fits nicely under the Title Tools panel.
- Don't confuse aligning multiple objects with the Type Alignment command, discussed in the section "Aligning text," earlier in this chapter.

Distributing Objects

Other commands allow you to evenly distribute multiple objects, saving you meticulous placement or—*gulp!*—even math. As with alignment options, the Distribute area of the Title Actions panel uses helpful icons that illustrate your options. (If the Title Actions panel isn't visible, you can open it using the Window menu, or choose the comparable command in the Title menu instead.)

To distribute objects:

1. Select multiple objects in the drawing area.
2. In the Title Actions panel, click the button that corresponds to the distribution option you want (**Figure 9.121**).

   The objects are spaced according to your selection (**Figure 9.122**).

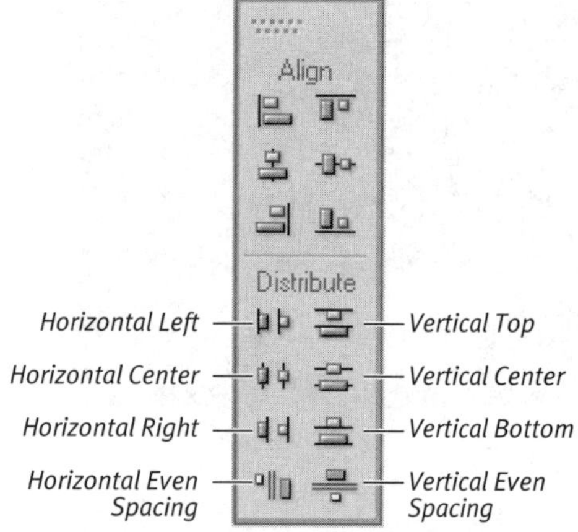

Figure 9.121 Click the distribution option you want in the Title Actions panel.

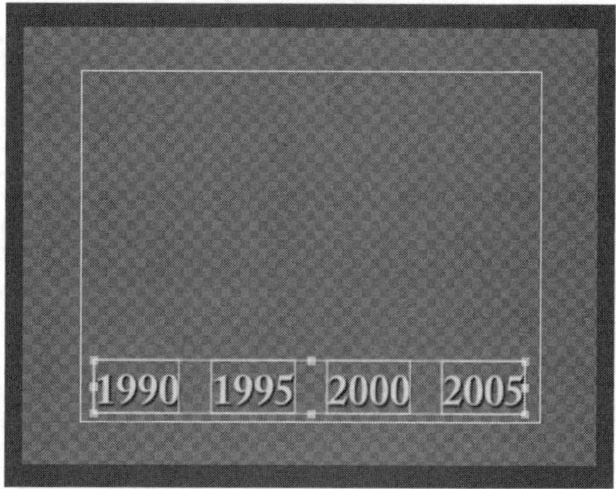

Figure 9.122 Here, objects are distributed using the Horizontal Even Spacing option.

10

Adding Effects

Although it's possible that the clips in your sequence require no alteration, chances are you need to modify them in some way, using effects. In Premiere Elements, the rubric *effects* encompasses any means by which you adjust a clip's audio or video characteristics, or properties.

Effects are categorized by function: image control, motion, opacity, volume, and filters. By changing a clip's motion properties, for example, you can resize the clip for use as a picture-in-picture effect or simulate a camera move over a large image. Altering a clip's opacity lets you superimpose one clip over another. And although you may not think of changing a clip's volume as an effect, per se, you fade audio up and down in much the same way as you raise and lower its opacity.

You can also apply any combination of audio and video filters. Apply an equalization filter to enhance a voice-over, or use reverb to imply certain acoustics. Similarly, video filters can alter an image in countless ways, from subtle color correction, to fantastic distortions, to combining (or *compositing*) parts of an image with a background.

Befitting moving media, nearly all effect settings can change over time, using a technique called *keyframing*. This allows you to animate motion, fade a clip's opacity or volume, or vary the character or intensity of any video or audio filter. You can even specify whether the change is constant, accelerates, or decelerates. For example, you can simulate the way the camera starts to move in slowly, comes up to full speed, and then slows to a stop.

Despite their diversity, you apply, adjust, and animate effects using only a few methods. This chapter reflects Premiere Elements' unified approach. First you'll learn to distinguish effects not only by function but also by methodology. Then you'll learn ways to view and adjust effect properties. You'll find that by first focusing on techniques common to *all* effects, you'll be prepared to tackle *any* effect.

Summarizing the Chapter

Because Premiere Elements takes a unified approach to adding and animating effects, this chapter tackles a range of interrelated topics. But despite its length, it's easy to navigate the chapter once you know the big picture.

Understanding effects

The first part of the chapter includes these sections:

Comparing Effect Types explains how effects are categorized.

Understanding Properties and Animation describes how an effect's qualities can be adjusted globally, or animated over time.

Viewing Effect Property Values explains different areas in which you view and adjust effects.

Choosing a Keyframing Method explores the two methods for animating effects.

Animating effects in the timeline

Next, the chapter includes these sections:

Understanding Opacity and Volume Graphs explains how effect values appear as a graph in each clip in the timeline.

Rubberbanding Opacity and Volume describes how to animate video opacity and audio levels by manipulating the property graph.

Adjusting Keyframes in the Timeline explains how to adjust effect animation in a property graph.

Adding effects and setting properties

This part of the chapter includes these sections:

Adding Standard Effects explains how to add filters to clips.

Using Preset Effects discusses how to add built-in preset effects.

Viewing Properties in the Properties panel describes how to view and adjust effects in the Properties panel.

Viewing Motion Effects explains how to view motion effects in the Monitor panel.

Setting Spatial Properties in the Timeline View shows how to adjust motion effects by dragging in the Monitor panel.

Disabling and Removing Effects explains how to temporarily disable or permanently remove effects.

Resetting an Effect to Its Default Values describes how to return an effect's property values to their default.

Specifying Custom Settings explains how to adjust special settings included with certain effects.

Using Multiple Effects explores how the number and order of effects influence a clip.

Animating effects

The chapter's next sections are as follows:

Keyframing in the Properties Panel explains how to animate effects in the Properties panel.

Using Keyframes in the Properties Panel examines how to adjust an animation using the Properties panel.

Understanding Interpolation explains how Premiere Elements calculates changes between the effect values you specify, temporally and spatially.

Interpolation Types describes the methods for interpolating keyframe values.

Reshaping a Motion Path explains how to adjust a motion effect using Bézier curves.

Specifying a Spatial Interpolation Method explores how to apply a spatial interpolation method to a keyframe.

Specifying a Temporal Interpolation Method explains how to apply a temporal interpolation method to a keyframe.

Standard effect categories

Sections at the end of the chapter provide an overview of filters, by category.

Comparing Effect Types

Although the previous section describes effects by what they do, it's just as useful to classify them by how they're applied. In Premiere Elements, effects fall into two major categories: fixed effects and standard effects.

Fixed/inherent effects

Motion effects, opacity, and volume are called *fixed effects*. This isn't meant to imply that you can't adjust or animate the settings over time; you can. *Fixed* refers to the fact that these effects let you control attributes that are inherent to the clip: its overall appearance, position on the screen, its level of opacity, and its volume. A better term might be *built-in effects*, *inherent effects*, or *intrinsic effects*. The upshot is that you don't have to actively apply these effects to a clip; they're always listed in the Properties panel (which you'll learn more about soon) (**Figure 10.1**).

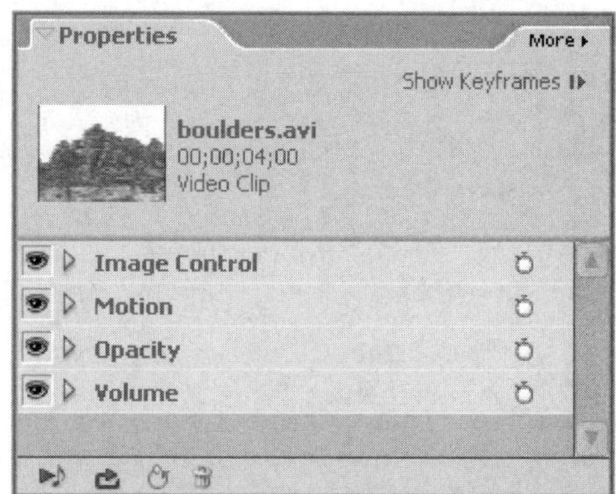

Figure 10.1 Motion, opacity, and volume are inherent to clips and are always listed in the Properties panel.

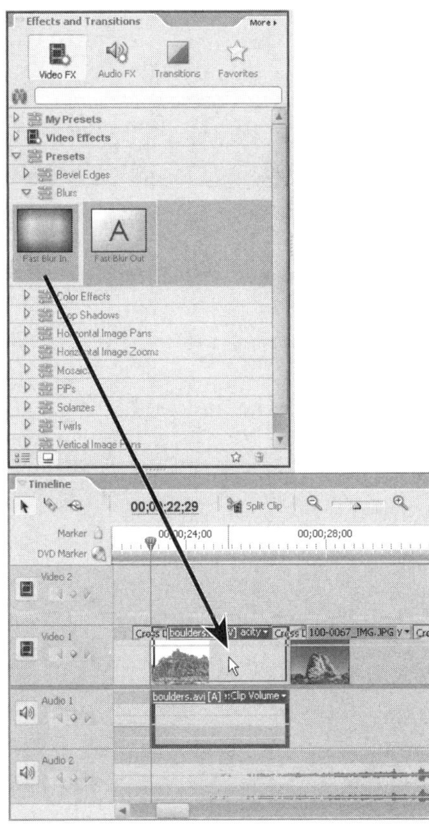

Figure 10.2 You add standard effects by dragging them from the Properties panel to a clip in the Timeline panel.

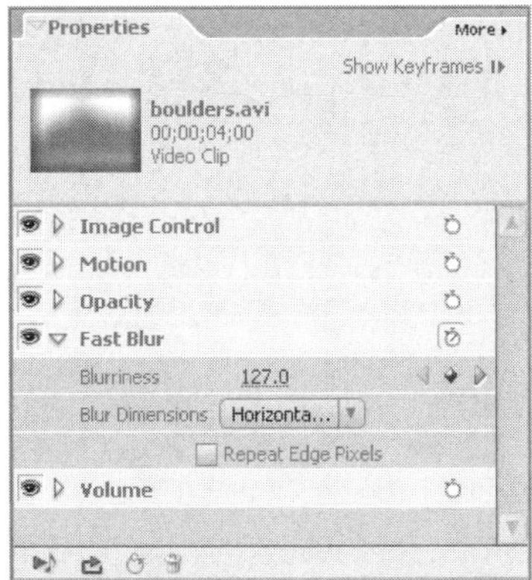

Figure 10.3 Once standard effects are applied, they appear in the Properties panel in the order they were added.

Standard effects/filters

Effects you actively apply to clips are known as *standard effects*. You apply a standard effect by dragging it from the Effects and Transitions panel to a clip in the timeline (**Figure 10.2**). Once the effect has been applied, you can view and adjust its parameters using the same methods you use for fixed effects (**Figure 10.3**).

Standard effects are also called *filters*, after the filters you place in front of a camera lens to filter light or distort an image. Of course, digital filters can modify both images and sound in countless ways. You can make subtle adjustments—such as color correction or audio equalization—or create more dramatic distortions and stylizations. Note that standard effects include *keying effects*, which are used to composite layers of images. On the other hand, standard effects are listed separately from transitions (which operate differently and are explained in Chapter 7, "Adding Transitions").

Standard effects are stored in Premiere Elements' Plug-Ins folder. You can add compatible filters created by other software developers to expand your collection.

Understanding Properties and Animation

A *property* refers to any effect parameter to which you can assign a value. For example, you can specify a clip's Opacity property value from 0 percent (completely transparent) to 100 percent (completely opaque), or you can determine the intensity of the Gaussian Blur filter by adjusting its Blur value. You can set any property to a *global* value, a single value for the duration of the clip. You can also animate a property, varying its values over time.

To produce animation, you change a clip's properties over time—for example, you create motion by changing a clip's position over time. In Premiere Elements (as in other programs), you use keyframes to define and control these changes.

A *keyframe* defines a property's value at a specific point in time. When you create at least two keyframes with different values, Premiere Elements *interpolates* the value for each frame in between. In other words, Premiere Elements calculates how to progress smoothly from one keyframe value to another—or, in terms of motion, how to get from Point A to Point B (**Figure 10.4**).

As you adjust any effect, you can view it right away in the Timeline view of the Monitor panel. But as you learned in Chapter 8, "Previewing a Sequence," whether you can play it at the project's full frame rate depends on both the complexity of the effect and your system's resources.

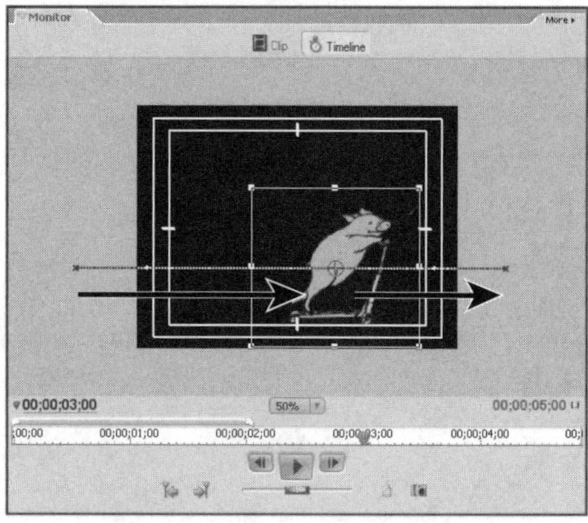

Figure 10.4 You can vary any property's value over time using keyframes. In this example, Premiere Elements calculates the position of a clip between two keyframes to create movement.

Keyframes

Keyframe is a term borrowed from traditional animation. In a traditional animation studio, a senior animator might draw only the keyframes—what the character looks like at key moments in the animation (these poses are also called the *extremes*). The junior animators then drew the in-betweens (a process sometimes called *tweening*). The same principle applies to animating effects in Premiere Elements: If you supply the keyframes for a property, the program calculates the values in between. And you can keyframe any property, not just movement.

In Premiere Elements, you're always the senior animator, so you should supply only the keyframes—just enough to define the animation. Premiere Elements does the tedious tweening. Setting too many keyframes defeats the purpose of this division of labor.

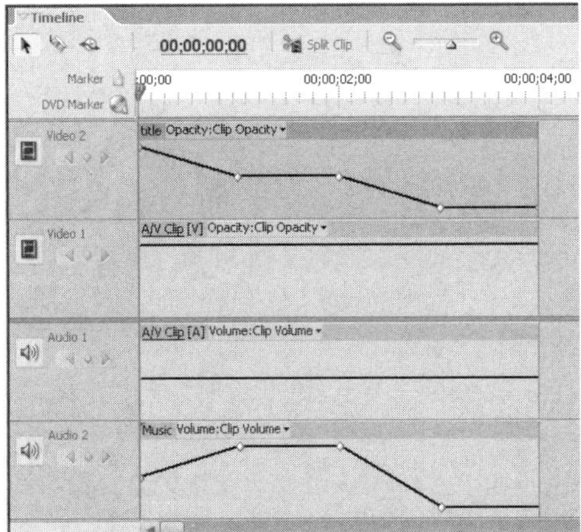

Figure 10.5 In the Timeline, each clip contains a graph that represents the selected effect's property values over the course of the clip.

Viewing Effect Property Values

You can view and adjust each clip's effect properties in the Timeline panel, in the Properties panel, and (in the case of motion effect properties) in the Timeline view of the Monitor panel.

Effects in the Timeline panel

In the Timeline panel, each clip contains a property graph, a thin line in the bottom part of the video and audio tracks of a clip (**Figure 10.5**). Although each clip contains fixed and any number of standard effects, you can display only one property graph at a time (one for video and one for audio).

Diamond-shaped icons on the graph represent values you specify, or keyframes. Dragging a keyframe horizontally changes its position in time, whereas dragging it vertically changes the property's value at that time. The line connecting keyframes represents interpolated values.

In the property graph—particularly when it represents opacity or volume—keyframes are also known as *handles*. The graph itself is often referred to as a *rubberband* view, and the keyframing process is called *rubberbanding*.

Effects in the Properties panel

You can also view and control effect property values in a window optimized for the task: the Properties panel (**Figure 10.6**). The Properties panel lists all the effects contained in a selected clip. You can expand each effect heading to reveal controls for each property value. To vary values over time, you can reveal a *property keyframe area*. The property keyframe area's time ruler corresponds to the sequence's timeline and includes familiar controls, such as a CTI, zoom slider, and zoom buttons.

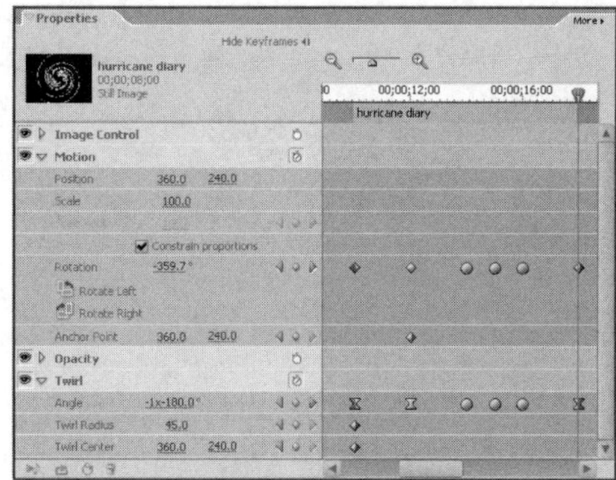

Figure 10.6 In the Properties panel, you can view all of the selected clip's effects at once.

In contrast to the Timeline panel, the Properties panel's Timeline area shows the selected clip in isolation. Under the clip, keyframes for each property appear in vertically stacked rows, or *property tracks*. Instead of a property graph, the Properties panel shows property values numerically. You can drag keyframes horizontally in time, but you change their value using numerical controls. For each animated property, you can add, delete, and cue to keyframes using a set of buttons called a *keyframe navigator*.

Note that when you select a clip, the Properties panel's Timeline pane looks and functions differently than when you select a transition. (See Chapter 7, "Adding Transitions.")

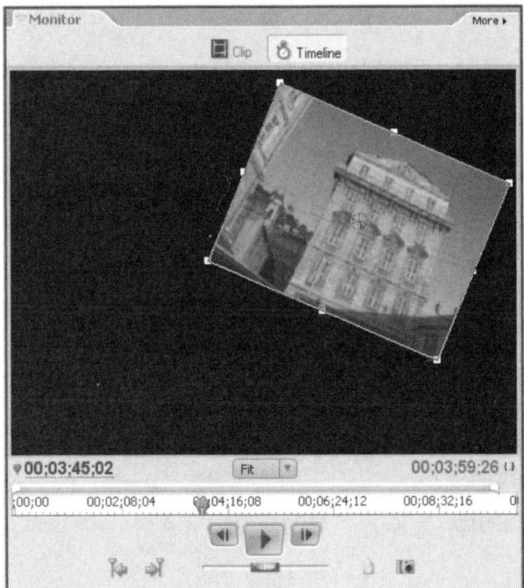

Figure 10.7 In the Monitor panel's Timeline view, you can manipulate a clip's spatial properties—position, scale, rotation, and anchor point—at the current frame.

Motion effects in the Monitor panel's Timeline view

Because they're spatial in nature, Premiere Elements lets you view and control motion effect properties—position, rotation, scale, and anchor point—by dragging in the Monitor panel's Timeline view, a method Adobe likes to call *direct manipulation* (**Figure 10.7**). In the Timeline view, animated motion appears as keyframe icons connected by a *motion path*. Direct manipulation controls complement the Properties panel's controls. You use the former to control the spatial properties at a keyframe; you use the latter to control the timing. Certain filters also offer direct manipulation controls, including Crop, Corner Pin, Lightning, Mirror, Ramp, and Transform.

Choosing a Keyframing Method

As you learned earlier in this chapter, you can animate any effect using a process called keyframing. In general, there are two methods for keyframing an effect property: rubberbanding, and in the Properties panel. Although you can switch among keyframing methods freely, you'll find that each is better suited for certain types of effects.

Opacity and volume in the property graph

Rubberbanding (adjusting keyframes in a clip's property graph in the timeline) is ideal for making adjustments to opacity and volume values—not only because this approach is time-tested and familiar to many users, but because these values are easy to understand in graph form (**Figure 10.8**). When the graph goes up, the opacity or volume value increases; when the graph goes down, the value decreases. Properties like rotation, for instance, don't translate to a vertical graph nearly as well (). Moreover, adjusting opacity and volume requires only a single property graph, whereas motion effects and many filters include several parameters you need to adjust.

The graph's appearance changes depending on the track's display mode. The graph is black when the track's display mode is set to Name Only; it's colored when set to any other display mode. (See Chapter 6, "Editing in the Timeline.")

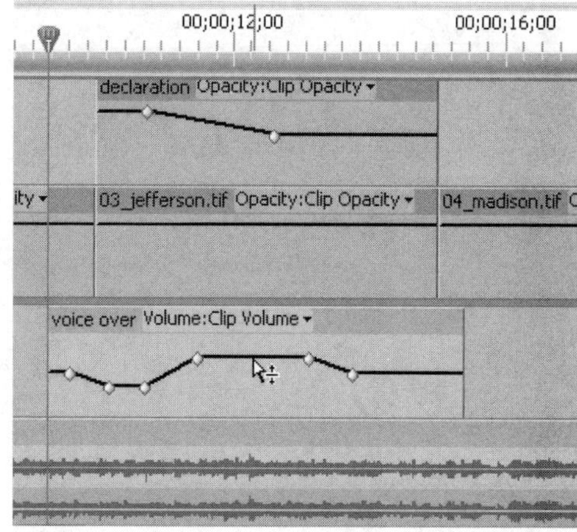

Figure 10.8 Keyframing in the timeline—sometimes called rubberbanding—is best suited for controlling clip volume and opacity (shown here)...

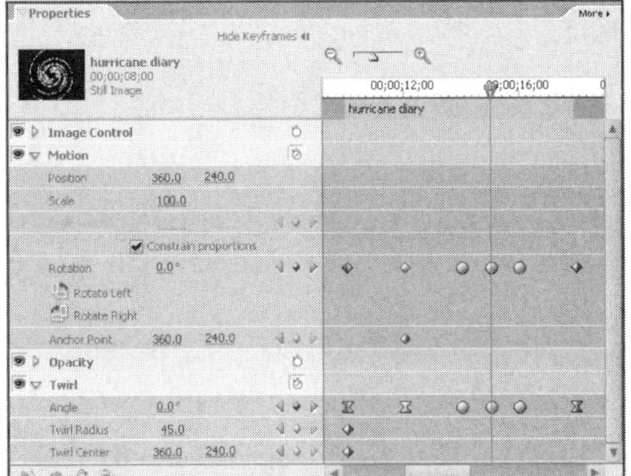

Figure 10.9 ...whereas motion and standard effects (filters) are more easily controlled in the Properties panel.

Motion and filters in the Properties panel

For all other effects, focus on the Properties panel. It lets you adjust both the value and timing of several properties at once with numerical precision (**Figure 10.9**). By comparison, the graphical clarity of a single property graph provides little benefit for many filters.

For motion effects (and other effects you can manipulate in the Monitor panel's Timeline view), use the Properties panel to activate the direct manipulation controls in the Timeline view, and to control the timing of keyframes for the various spatial properties (such as position, rotation, scale, and anchor point).

Understanding Opacity and Volume Graphs

As explained in "Choosing a Keyframing Method" earlier in this chapter, keyframing in the timeline, or rubberbanding, is ideally suited to controlling opacity and volume.

Rubberbanding opacity

You can keyframe the opacity of clips in video track 2 and higher to blend them with clips in lower tracks. Lowering the opacity of clips in track 1 blends the image with black.

An Opacity property graph appears for the clips in the track. The height of the property graph corresponds to clip opacity levels, so that near the top of the clip is 100 percent opaque, and near the bottom of the clip is 0 percent opaque (completely transparent) (**Figure 10.10**).

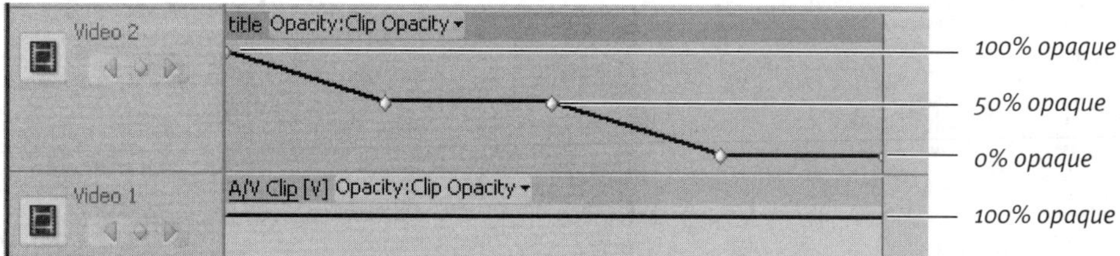

Figure 10.10 In a video clip's opacity graph, the clip is 100 percent opaque when the graph is at the top; the clip is completely transparent when the graph is at the bottom.

Rubberbanding volume

A Volume property graph appears for the clips in the track (not for the track as a whole). The height of the property graph corresponds to clip volume levels, so that levels are adjusted 0 dB when the graph is in the center of the clip, +6 dB near the top of the clip, and becomes completely silent when the graph is near the bottom (**Figure 10.11**).

✔ Tips

- Remember: to create simple video dissolves and audio fades, use a video or audio transition instead of keyframes (see Chapter 7, "Adding Transitions").
- If you prefer to use keyframes for simple fades of opacity or volume, you can select the clip and then use the Fade In and Fade Out buttons in the Properties panel.
- If you want to make only parts of the clip transparent, use a keying effect. Premiere Elements applies an alpha key to title clips in video track 2 or higher automatically. (See Chapter 9, "Creating Titles," for more information.)
- Naturally, you can combine keying with fading—for example, when you want to make a superimposed title semitransparent.

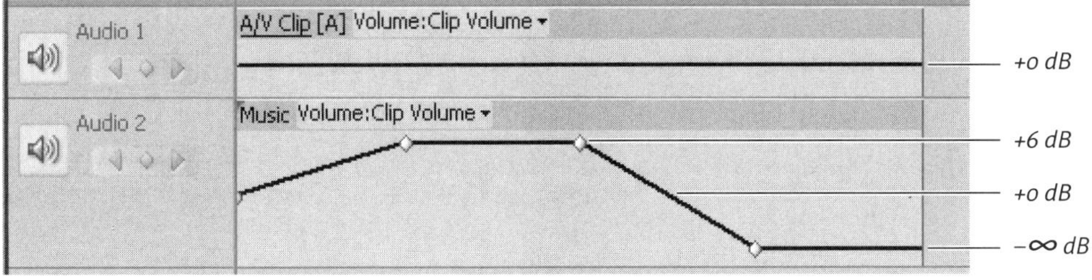

Figure 10.11 In an audio clip's Volume graph, levels are adjusted 0 dB when the graph is in the center of the clip, +6 dB at the top of the clip, and silent at the bottom.

Rubberbanding Opacity and Volume

This task summarizes the keyframing process; later tasks cover ways to adjust keyframes.

To rubberband opacity or volume:

1. Arrange clips in the timeline so that the clip you want to superimpose is in video track 2 or higher and the background image is in lower tracks (**Figure 10.12**).
2. *Do either of the following:*
   - ▲ To animate opacity, click the video clip's keyframes pull-down menu, and choose Opacity > Clip Opacity (**Figure 10.13**).
   - ▲ To animate volume, click the audio clip's keyframes pull-down menu, and choose Volume > Clip Volume (**Figure 10.14**).

   The pull-down menu lists inherent effects as well as any filters you add. The clip's property graph represents the property you select.
3. Press Ctrl as you position the mouse pointer over the property graph, so that the mouse changes into an Add Keyframe icon, and click at the point where you want to add a keyframe (**Figure 10.15**).

   A keyframe appears in the selected property graph where you click (**Figure 10.16**).
4. To adjust the keyframe, *do any of the following:*
   - ▲ To increase the property's value at the keyframe, drag the keyframe up.
   - ▲ To decrease the property's value at the keyframe, drag the keyframe down (**Figure 10.17**).
   - ▲ To move the keyframe later in time, drag it right.

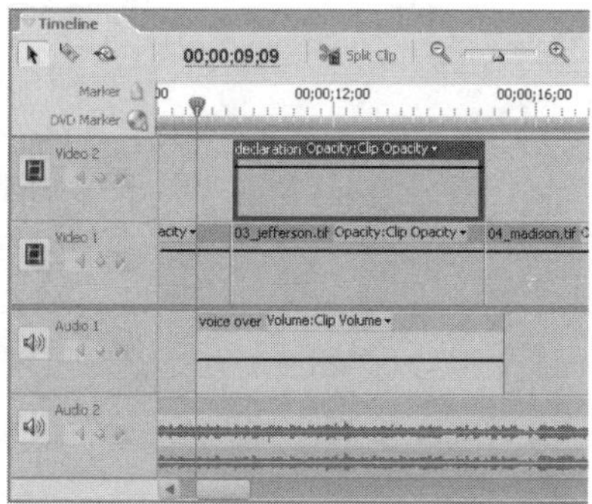

Figure 10.12 To adjust opacity, make sure the clip is positioned above the clip (or clips) that will serve as the underlying image. (Otherwise, the clip will be blended with black video.)

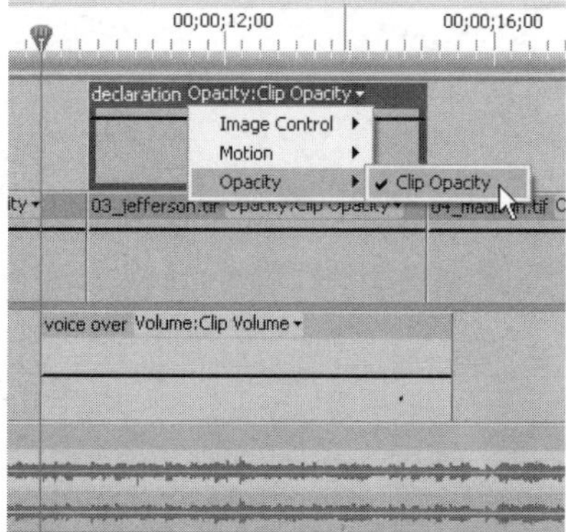

Figure 10.13 To rubberband a video clip's opacity, choose Opacity > Clip Opacity in its effect pull-down menu.

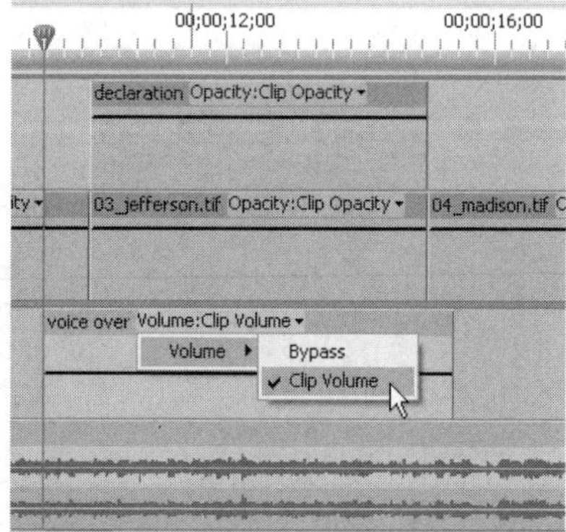

Figure 10.14 To rubberband an audio clip's volume, choose Volume > Clip Volume in its effect pull-down menu.

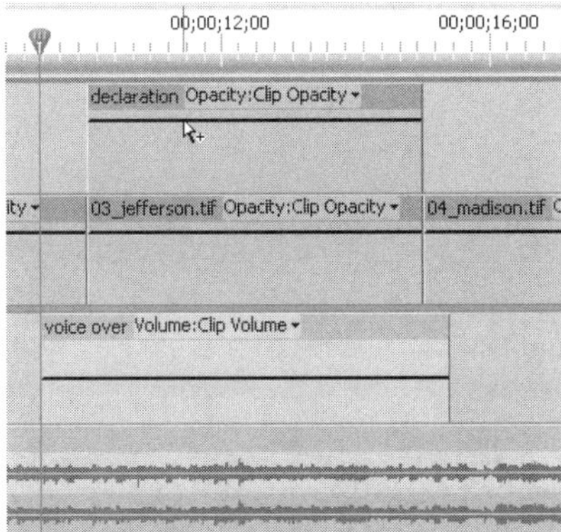

Figure 10.15 Pressing Ctrl as you click on the property graph makes the mouse become an Add Keyframe icon. Click on the graph's line...

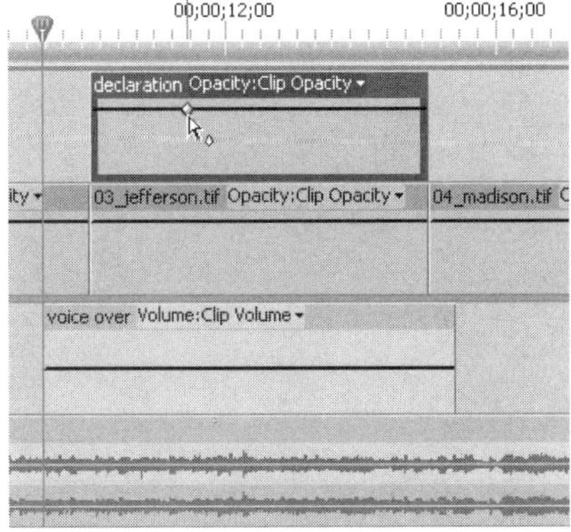

Figure 10.16 ...to add a keyframe (handle) for the selected property.

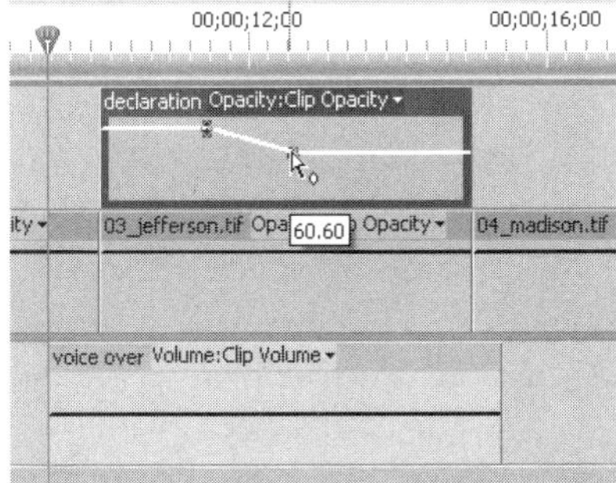

Figure 10.17 Drag the keyframe up to increase the property's value or down to decrease its value at the keyframe (shown here).

- ▲ To move the keyframe earlier in time, drag it left (**Figure 10.18**).
- ▲ To constrain the keyframe to vertical or horizontal movement only, press Shift after you start dragging.

5. Repeat steps 3 and 4 as needed, in any order you choose.
6. To see or hear the animation, play back or preview the clip in the timeline.

✔ Tips

- When your view of the timeline is zoomed out for a wider view, a clip may appear too narrow to show its keyframe pulldown menu. To access the menu, you can zoom into the timeline until the clip appears large enough to accommodate the menu. Alternatively, you can right-click the clip and in the context menu choose Show Clip keyframes, and then choose the option you want from the submenu.
- An audio clip's effect keyframe pull-down menu includes a Bypass option. Activating Bypass allows you to disable, or *bypass*, audio filters you add to a clip.
- Once you add a keyframe to the property graph, don't Ctrl-click it again. Doing so changes the mouse pointer to a Convert icon and changes the keyframe's interpolation method. See "Understanding Interpolation," later in this chapter.

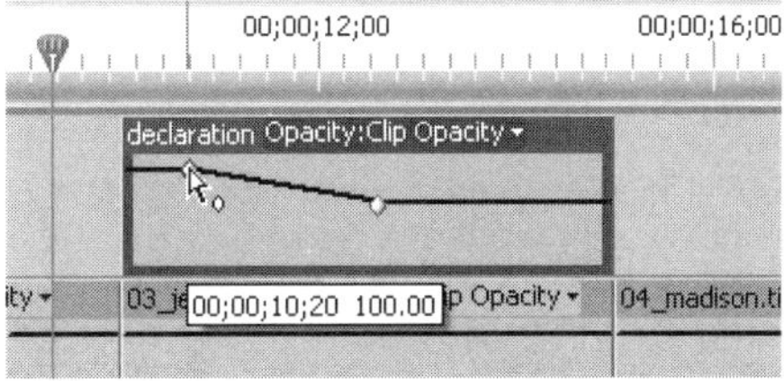

Figure 10.18 Drag the keyframe right to move the keyframe later in time or left to move the keyframe earlier in time (shown here). Pressing Shift after you start dragging constrains movement either vertically or horizontally.

Adjusting Keyframes in the Timeline

At any time, you can add, delete, or adjust the value and timing of keyframes in a clip's selected property graph.

You can select multiple keyframes and, by dragging any keyframe in the selection, adjust them all by the same amount.

To select keyframes:

- In a property graph of a clip in the timeline, position the Selection tool over a keyframe so that the mouse pointer becomes the Select Keyframe icon.

  Do one of the following:

  ▲ To select a keyframe, click it (**Figure 10.19**).

  ▲ To add keyframes to and subtract them from your selection, Shift-click them (**Figure 10.20**).

  Selected keyframes appear shaded yellow; unselected keyframes appear gray. Dragging one selected keyframe adjusts all selected keyframes by the same amount (**Figure 10.21**).

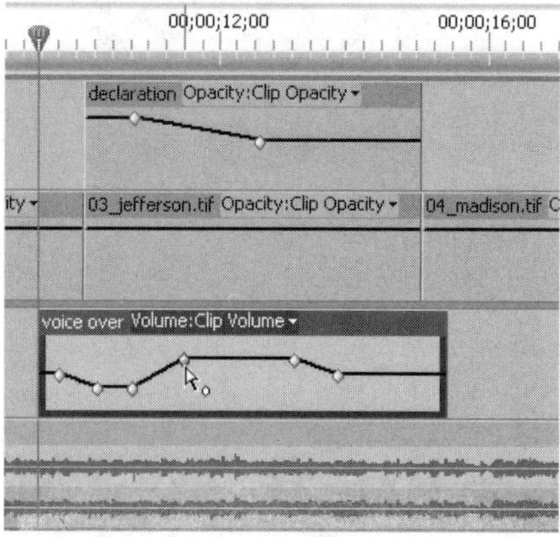

Figure 10.19 Click a keyframe to select it...

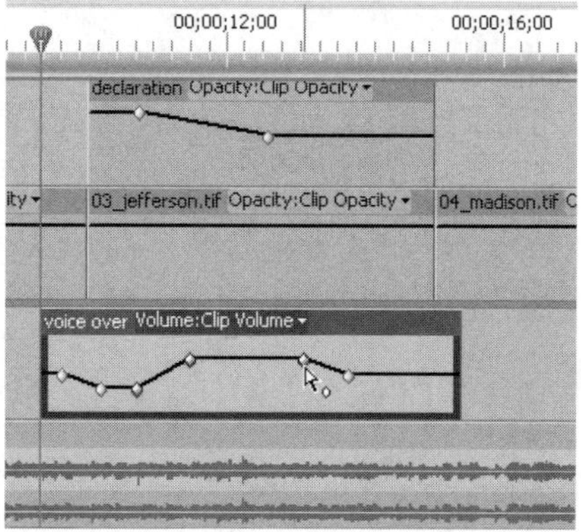

Figure 10.20 ...and Shift-click keyframes to add them to or subtract them from the selection.

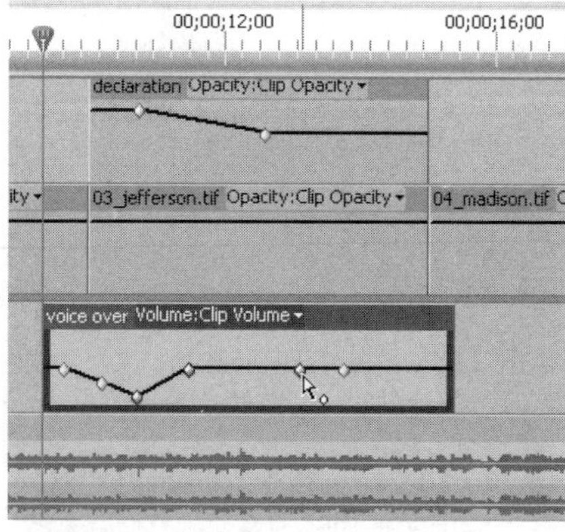

Figure 10.21 Dragging any of the selected keyframes moves all of them.

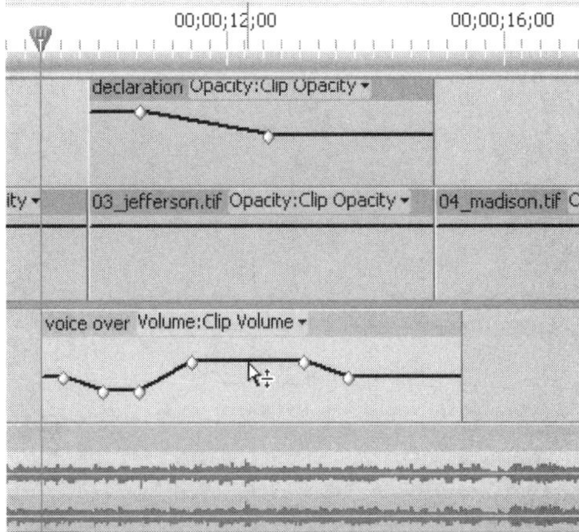

Figure 10.22 Positioning the mouse over the line connecting keyframes changes the mouse icon to the graph editing icon...

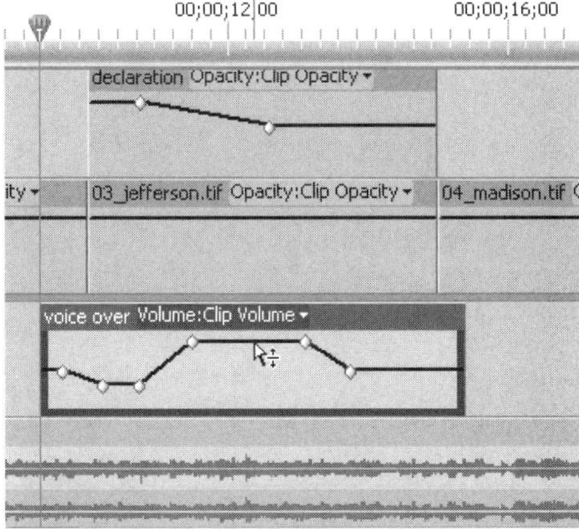

Figure 10.23 ...and dragging changes adjacent keyframe values by the same amount.

To move two keyframes simultaneously:

1. Position the mouse pointer over the line connecting two keyframes so that the mouse pointer's icon becomes a graph editing icon (**Figure 10.22**).
2. Drag up to increase both keyframes' values; drag down to decrease both keyframes' values.

   Dragging changes both keyframes' values by the same amount, and interpolated values before and after the keyframes adjust accordingly (**Figure 10.23**).

To remove keyframes:

- In a clip's property graph, right-click a keyframe and choose Delete from the context menu (**Figure 10.24**).

  The keyframe is removed from the property graph. The line between remaining keyframes (representing interpolated values) adjusts accordingly (**Figure 10.25**).

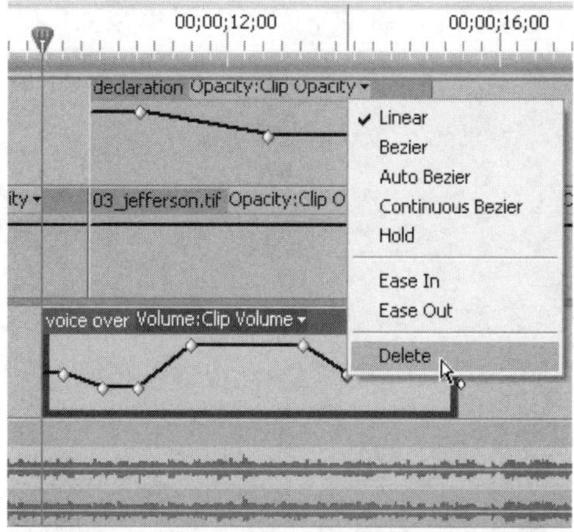

Figure 10.24 Right-clicking a keyframe and choosing Delete...

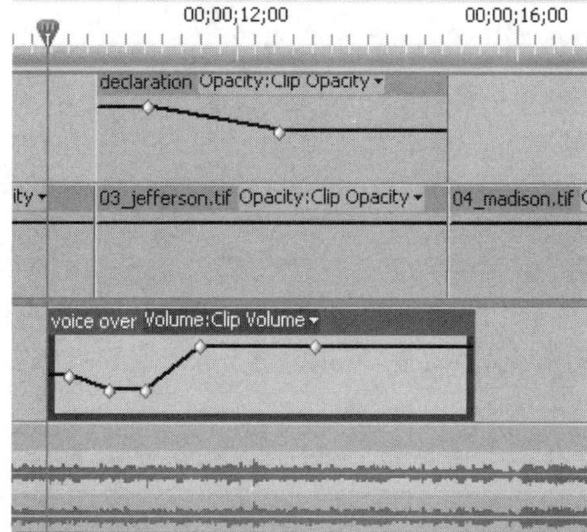

Figure 10.25 ...removes the keyframe.

✔ Tips

- You can also use a track's keyframe navigator to add, delete, and cue to the keyframes for a clip's selected property graph. A track's keyframe navigator works the same way as the keyframe navigator controls in the Properties panel, as explained later in this chapter.
- In the property graph, the line connecting keyframes is straight, implying that property values between keyframes are calculated using a linear progression. However, a different interpolation method makes the line appear curved. See "Specifying a Temporal Interpolation Method," later in this chapter.

Adding Standard Effects

The procedure for adding a standard effect (or filter) to a clip is nearly self-explanatory: You simply drag a filter from the Effects and Transitions panel directly to a compatible (video or audio) clip in the timeline. Clips with effects applied appear with a thin colored line under the clip's name.

On the Effects and Transitions panel, video and audio are contained in separate folders and are further organized into categorized subfolders. (You already learned how to organize and find items on the Effects and Transitions panel in Chapter 7, "Adding Transitions," so that information won't be repeated here.)

Nearly all filters have one or more properties that you can adjust either by using a value graph in the Timeline panel or by using the Properties panel. But as explained in "Choosing a Keyframing Method" earlier in this chapter, using the Properties panel is the most appropriate method for most filters. Some filters also include a Settings dialog box that opens automatically when you apply the filter. You can also reopen the dialog box from the Properties panel.

This task summarizes the basic process of adding an effect to a clip. You'll discover that each effect has a unique set of parameters, or *properties,* that you can customize.

In the following sections, you'll first learn how to apply an effect and specify *global* property values—a single set of property values for the duration of the clip. Then you'll learn how to animate any effect—fixed or standard—using the Properties panel.

To add an effect to a clip:

1. In the Effects and Transitions panel, locate the video or audio effect you want to apply.

   For more about organizing and locating effects, see Chapter 7.

2. Drag the effect to the appropriate clip in the Timeline panel (**Figure 10.26**).

   The effect is applied to the clip, indicated by a thin colored line under the clip's name. When the clip is selected, it's listed in the Properties panel (when open).

3. To adjust the effect's settings, *do one of the following* (depending on the particular effect):

   ▲ If a Settings dialog box appears automatically, specify values for the effect's parameters, and click OK (**Figure 10.27**).

   ▲ Select the clip in the timeline, and adjust its effect properties in the Properties panel (**Figure 10.28**).

4. To vary effect properties over time, specify keyframes as explained in the task "To set keyframes in the Properties panel," later in this chapter.

Figure 10.26 Drag an effect from the Effects and Transitions panel to the appropriate clip in the Timeline panel.

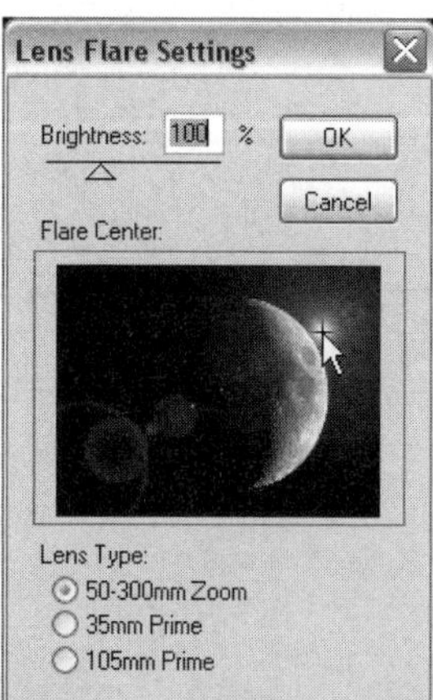

Figure 10.27 If a Settings dialog box appears automatically, specify values for the effect's parameters and click OK...

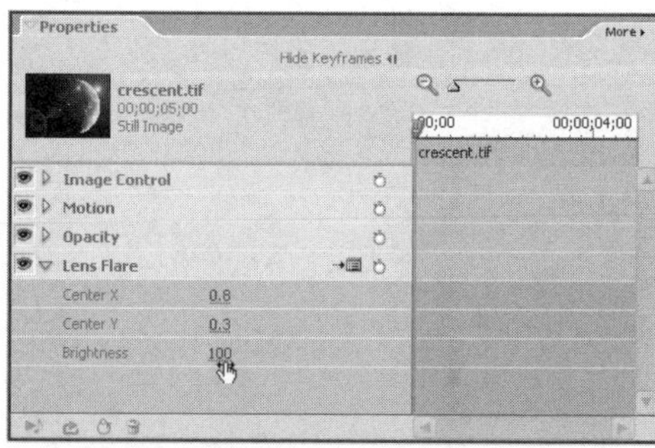

Figure 10.28 ...otherwise, select the clip and adjust the effect's property values in the Properties panel. Property values are global (the same throughout the clip) unless you keyframe the effect.

Figure 10.29 Premiere Elements comes with a number of preset effects, contained in the Presets folder of the Effects and Transitions panel.

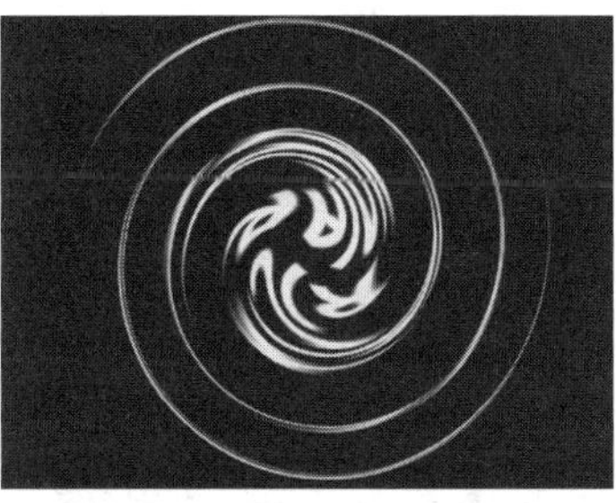

Figure 10.30 Here, a preset Twirl effect has been applied to a title clip and modified to taste.

Using Preset Effects

Adobe has supplied a number of presets to get you started. Many of the most common tasks, such as creating a Picture-in-Picture (PIP) effect or using different effects to transition in to and out of a clip, are already available in the Effects and Transitions panel's Presets folder (**Figures 10.29** and **10.30**).

You can use an existing preset, as well as modify, save, and import a preset. And because presets are saved as small files on your hard disk, it's easy to share presets with other editors. When you change the parameters of an effect in the Properties panel, you have the option to save the effect as a preset in the Properties panel's More pull-down menu.

To save an effect as a preset:

1. Apply an effect to a clip in the timeline, and (if you want) animate it (**Figure 10.31**).
2. With the clip selected, select the effect you want to save in the Properties panel.
3. In the Properties panel's More pull-down menu, choose Save Preset (**Figure 10.32**).

   The Save Preset dialog box appears.
4. Enter a unique name for your preset effect.
5. To determine the spacing of keyframes when applying the effect to clips of different durations, *specify an option* for Type:

   Scale—Places keyframes in proportion to the clip's duration

   Anchor to In Point—Applies the keyframes at the spacing they were saved with, starting at the clip's In point

   Anchor to Out Point—Applies the keyframes at the spacing they were saved with, placing the last keyframe at the clip's Out point

Figure 10.31 Here, a still photo clip's motion property has been animated to zoom out, an effect that will be applied to other photos.

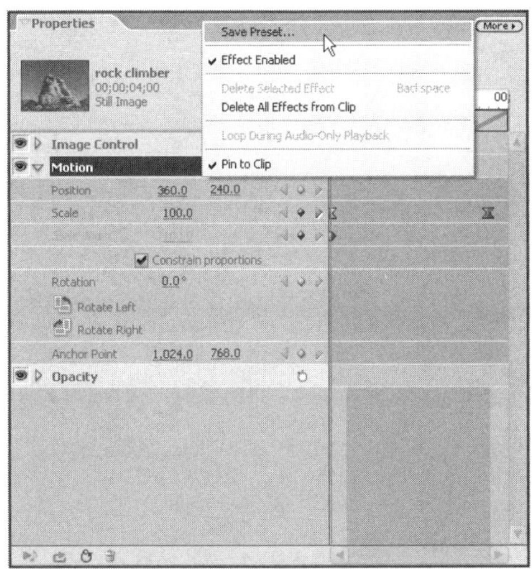

Figure 10.32 With the clip containing the effect selected, select the effect in the Properties panel, and choose Save Preset in the More pull-down menu.

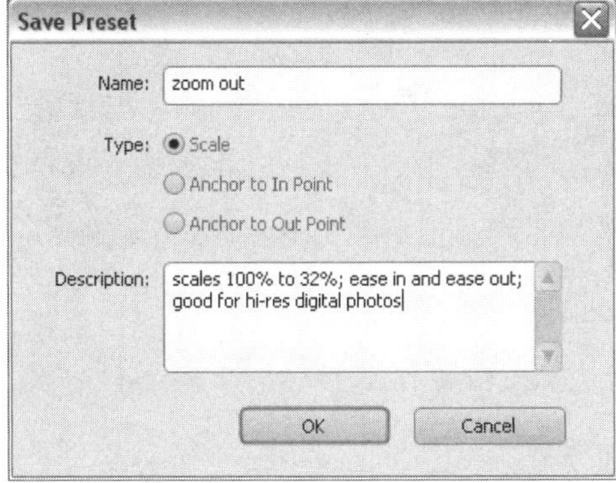

Figure 10.33 In the Save Preset dialog box, specify how you want keyframes to be spaced when applying the preset, and enter a name and description.

6. If you want, enter a description of your preset (**Figure 10.33**).
7. Click OK to close the dialog box and save the preset.

   The preset you created appears listed in the My Presets folder of the Effects and Transitions panel. You can move and apply the preset as you would any other effect in the Effects and Transitions panel.

✔ Tip

- You can also import effect preset files. This makes it easy to share effect presets between systems or users.

Viewing Effects in the Properties panel

The Properties panel lists all the effects for a selected clip and provides controls for adjusting each property's value (**Figure 10.34**). Fixed video and audio effects are listed by default; standard effects are listed in the order they're applied (see the section "Adding Standard Effects," earlier in this chapter). To see and adjust the timing of keyframes, use the Properties panel's property keyframe area.

You can control each effect property using familiar numerical controls that you set by dragging or by selecting and entering a value. Most property value controls can also be expanded to reveal a slider control, knob, or color picker. You'll also notice that the main area of the Properties panel includes playback and zoom controls; its keyframe area includes a time ruler, zoom controls, and CTI. By now, all these controls should be familiar to you, and they won't be reviewed here.

To view effect properties in the Properties panel:

1. Make sure the Properties panel is open.
2. In the Timeline panel, select the clip that contains the effect properties you want to adjust (**Figure 10.35**).

   The selected clip's effects appear in the Properties panel (**Figure 10.36**).

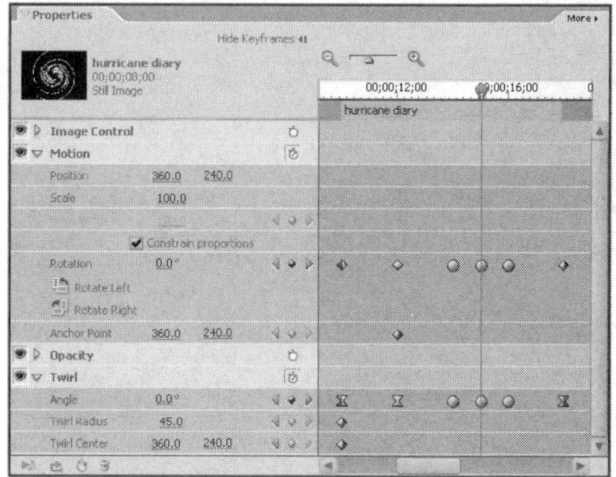

Figure 10.34 The Properties panel lists all the effects for the selected clip and provides controls for adjusting their values over time.

Figure 10.35 Selecting the clip containing the effects you want to adjust...

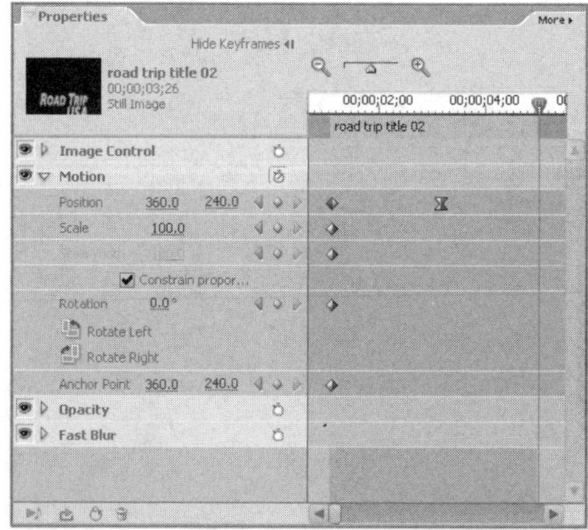

Figure 10.36 ...makes the clip and its effects appear in the Properties panel.

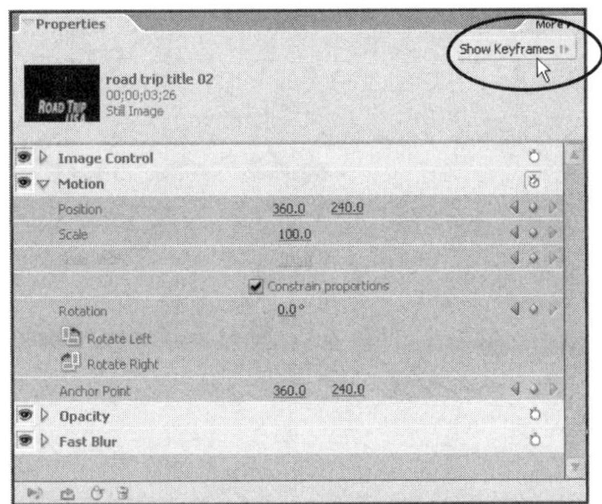

Figure 10.37 Clicking the Show Keyframes button toggles between hiding the keyframes area...

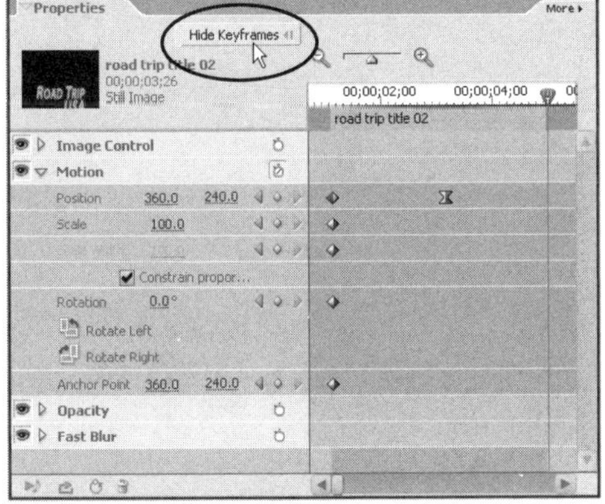

Figure 10.38 ...and showing the keyframes area.

To show and hide the Properties panel's keyframes area:

◆ In the Properties panel, click the Show Keyframes/Hide Keyframes button.

Clicking the button toggles the keyframes area of the Properties panel open and closed (**Figures 10.37** and **10.38**). The name of the button changes accordingly.

To set the zoom range of the Properties panel's time ruler:

- In the Properties panel's More pull-down menu, *do either of the following:*
  - ▲ Select Pin to Clip to make the maximum visible area of the timeline panel's time ruler correspond to the selected clip (**Figures 10.39** and **10.40**).
  - ▲ Deselect Pin to Clip to make the maximum visible area of the time ruler correspond to the duration of the sequence (**Figure 10.41**).

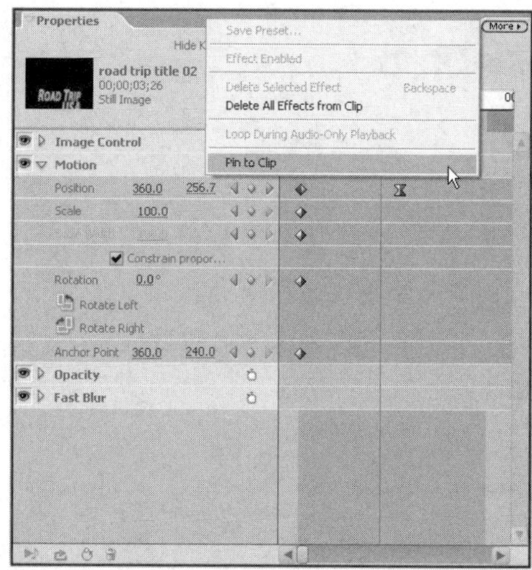

Figure 10.39 In the Properties panel's More pull-down menu, choose Pin to Clip.

✔ Tips

- If you've used the previous version of Premiere Elements, you'll notice that there's no longer a button to set the workspace for effects editing automatically. But you can still adjust the arrangement of panels manually (using the methods you learned back in Chapter 1, "Basic Elements").
- To optimize the workspace for effects, try modifying the default editing workspace so that the Effects and Transitions panel occupies the top left, the Monitor panel is top center, and the Properties panel is top right. The Timeline panel can span the bottom of the screen. Resize the Properties panel so that there's plenty of room to view keyframes; set the Timeline panel's track size to Large for rubberbanding.

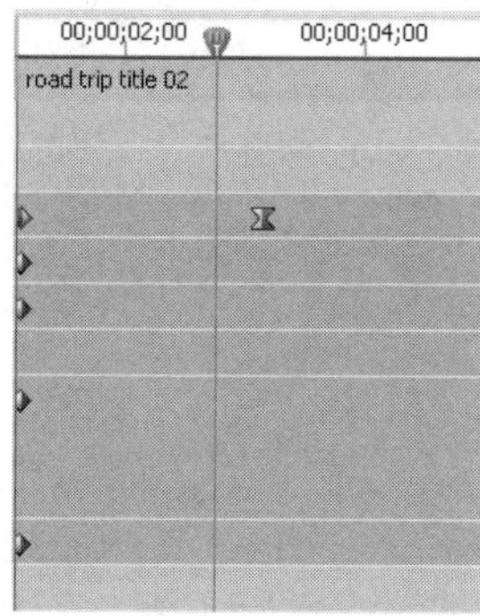

Figure 10.40 When Pin to Clip is selected, the maximum visible area of the time ruler corresponds to the selected clip.

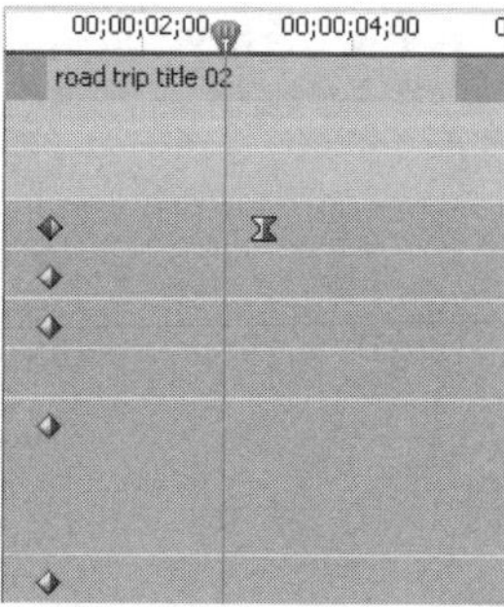

Figure 10.41 When Pin to Clip is deselected, the maximum visible area of the time ruler corresponds to the sequence's duration.

Viewing Motion Effects

Motion effects include the inherent spatial properties of a video clip: position, scale, rotation, and anchor point. You can adjust these properties as you would any other property, using controls in the Properties panel.

But because these properties are spatial in nature, it's more convenient to change them by dragging the clip in the Monitor panel's Timeline view, using what are called *direct manipulation controls* (**Figure 10.42**). When these controls are enabled, the selected clip appears with a bounding box and control handles. A circle with an X indicates the clip's anchor point. Dragging the clip changes its position, whereas dragging the control handles can alter the clip's scale or rotation.

When you animate the clip's position, the keyframed positions appear as small x icons in the program view. The clip's route (its interpolated position values) is represented by a dotted line, or *motion path,* connecting the x icons. The spacing of the motion path's dots indicates speed: closely spaced dots correspond to slower movement, and widely spaced dots correspond to faster movement. You can change a clip's position at a keyframe by dragging the keyframe's X icon in the Monitor panel's Timeline view.

Whereas you can control position, scale, and rotation using direct manipulation controls, you must set the clip's anchor point using controls in the Properties panel. You must also use the Properties panel (or, if you prefer, the clip's property graph in the timeline) to adjust the timing of keyframes.

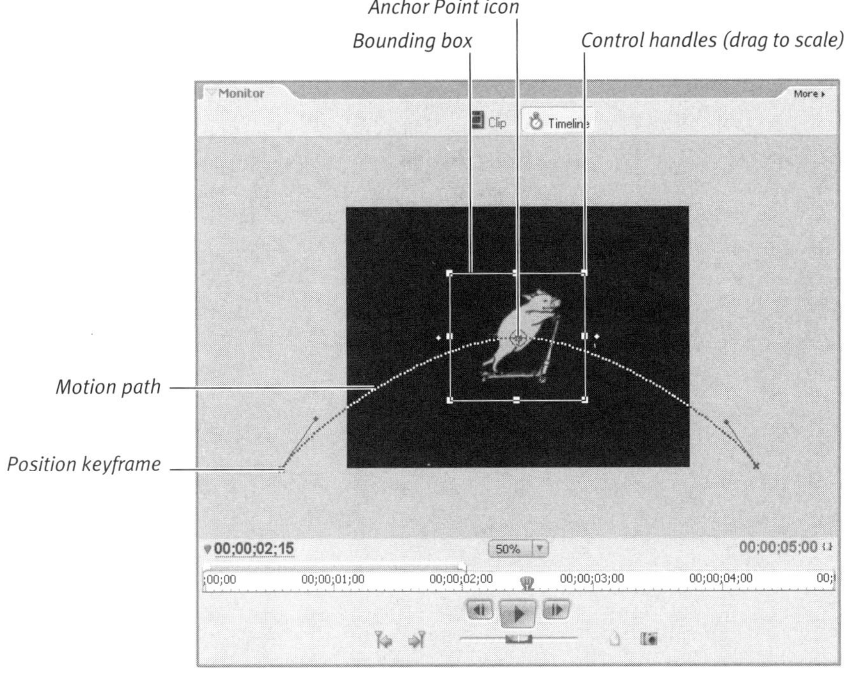

Figure 10.42 You can manipulate a clip's position, scale, and rotation directly in the Monitor panel's Timeline view. Here, the Timeline view's magnification has been reduced so it's easier to see the controls.

To view Motion controls in the Monitor panel's Timeline view:

1. Select a clip in the timeline so that its effects appear in the Properties panel.
2. Cue the sequence time to anywhere within the selected clip's duration, so that it appears in the Monitor panel's Timeline view.
3. *Do either of the following:*
   - ▲ In the Properties panel, select the Motion category (**Figure 10.43**).
   - ▲ Click the image in the Monitor panel's Timeline view (**Figure 10.44**).

   In the Timeline view, the selected clip appears with a bounding box and handles, and its anchor point is represented by a circle with an X. When the clip's position is animated, keyframes and a motion path are visible also.

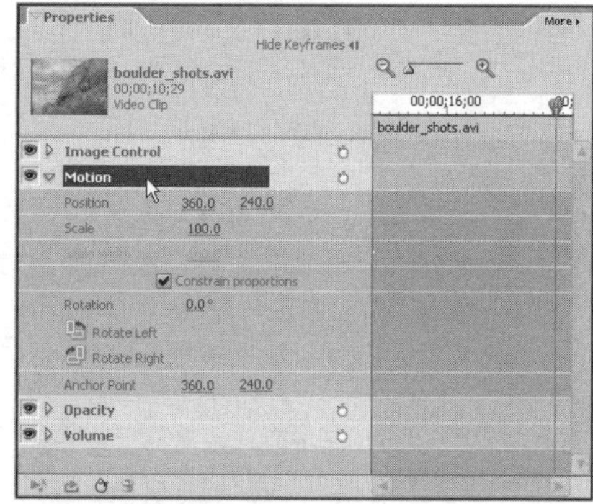

Figure 10.43 Set the sequence's current time to the frame you want, and either select the Motion category heading in the Properties panel...

Figure 10.44 ...or click the image in the Monitor panel's Timeline view so that its bounding box and anchor point appear. In this figure, the clip has been scaled down so it's easier to see its bounding box.

Setting Spatial Properties in the Timeline View

Once you enable the selected clip's direct manipulation controls, you can adjust its position, scale, and rotation in the Monitor panel's timeline view.

Be aware that Premiere Elements calculates the position, scale, and rotation of a clip based on its anchor point. In other words, the anchor point defines the position of a layer, the point around which a layer is scaled, and the pivot point of the layer's rotation. By default, a layer's anchor point is positioned in the center of the layer. In the Timeline view, a clip's anchor point is represented by a circle with an X.

For now, you'll learn how to set spatial properties. Later, you'll learn how to keyframe any property, animating its values over time—and, in the case of spatial properties, creating motion.

Setting the position

Setting a layer's position places its anchor point anywhere inside or outside the viewable area of the Monitor panel's Timeline view (which corresponds to the television screen). The exact position of a layer is expressed in *x*, *y* coordinates, where the upper-left corner of the program view is 0, 0. When the clip image doesn't fill the screen, the empty areas of the screen reveal either clips in lower tracks or (when there is no video in lower tracks) black video.

Rotational Values

Rotation is expressed as an absolute, not relative, value. You might even think of it as a rotational position. A clip's default rotation is 0 degrees; setting its rotation to 0 degrees always restores it to its original upright angle. This is true when you keyframe rotational values as well. For example, if you want to rotate a layer 180 degrees clockwise (upside down) and back again, the rotation values at each keyframe would be 0, 180, and 0. Mistakenly setting values of 0, 180, and −180 would cause the layer to turn clockwise 180 degrees and then turn counterclockwise—past its original position—until it was upside down again.

To position a clip in the Monitor panel's Timeline view:

◆ In the Monitor panel's Timeline view, drag the clip to the position you want (**Figure 10.45**).

The Position property values in the Properties panel change accordingly. If the property's Stopwatch icon is selected, then changing the position creates a keyframe at the current time.

Figure 10.45 Drag a clip to change its position.

✔ Tip

- When you change the anchor point, it may appear that you've also changed the clip's position. Actually, the layer's Position property remains the same; you changed the spot in the clip's image that determines its position on the screen.

Setting the scale

By default, a layer is set to 100 percent of its original size, or scale. You scale a layer around its anchor point. In other words, the anchor point serves as the mathematical center of a change in size. When you scale a layer by dragging, you'll notice that the handles of the layer seem to expand or contract from the anchor point.

✔ Tip

- Remember that bitmapped images look blocky and pixelated when they're scaled much beyond 100 percent.

Figure 10.46 In the Properties panel, deselect Constrain Proportions to scale the clip's vertical and horizontal aspects separately.

Figure 10.47 Drag the center-left or center-right handle to scale horizontally.

Figure 10.48 Drag the center-top or center-bottom handle to scale vertically.

To scale a clip in the Monitor panel's Timeline view:

1. In the Properties panel, deselect Constrain Proportions under the Scale Width property (**Figure 10.46**).

   If you select Uniform Scale, dragging any handle maintains the clip's proportions, or aspect ratio.

2. In the program view, *do one of the following:*
   - ▲ To scale the clip's horizontal aspect, drag the center-left or center-right handle (**Figure 10.47**).
   - ▲ To scale the clip's vertical aspect, drag the center-top or center-bottom handle (**Figure 10.48**).
   - ▲ To scale the clip horizontally and vertically, drag a corner handle (**Figure 10.49**).
   - ▲ To scale the layer while maintaining its proportions, press Shift as you drag a corner handle (or click Uniform Scale in the Properties panel).

Figure 10.49 Drag a corner handle to scale both aspects, or Shift-drag a corner handle to maintain the clip's aspect ratio as you scale.

Setting the rotation

When you rotate a clip, it pivots around the clip's anchor point. Therefore, make sure the anchor point is where you want it before you adjust rotation.

To rotate a clip in the Monitor panel's Timeline view:

1. Position the mouse pointer near, but not on, a corner handle, so that the mouse becomes the Rotate icon.

   The angle of the icon depends on which corner you position the mouse.
2. With the Rotate icon visible, drag to rotate the clip (**Figure 10.50**).

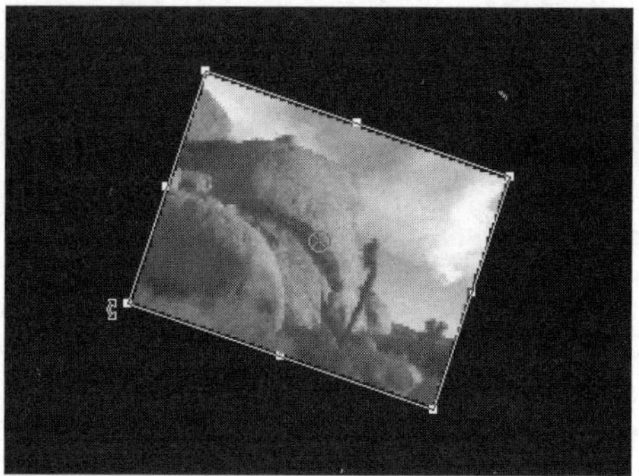

Figure 10.50 Position the mouse just off the clip's corner handle, so that the Rotate icon appears, and then drag to rotate.

✔ Tips

- The Properties panel includes handy buttons for rotating a selected clip in 90-degree increments, both clockwise (right) and counterclockwise (left). This can be a real timesaver when you're using a lot of imported photos that were taken with the camera turned sideways.
- You can't flip a clip's image by changing its horizontal or vertical scale. However, you can achieve this effect with the Horizontal Flip or Vertical Flip filter. You can animate a flipping movement with the Transform filter or the Basic 3D filter.
- In contrast to other programs, you can't use the Shift key to constrain rotational movement to 45-degree angles. To rotate the clip to exact angles, use the Rotation property controls in the Properties panel.

Superimposing Motion

As you saw in Chapter 9, "Creating Titles," empty areas of a title become transparent when you add the title clip to video track 2 or higher. Similarly, a clip that has been moved with a motion effect can leave an empty space in the visible area of the screen. If you place the clip in video track 2 or higher, the empty spaces are filled with the image from clips in lower tracks automatically. This way, it's easy to create a picture-in-picture effect or video collage (**Figure 10.51**).

Figure 10.51 When a clip is in video track 2 or higher, empty areas caused by motion effects become transparent automatically. This way, it's easy to create effects like this picture-in-picture effect.

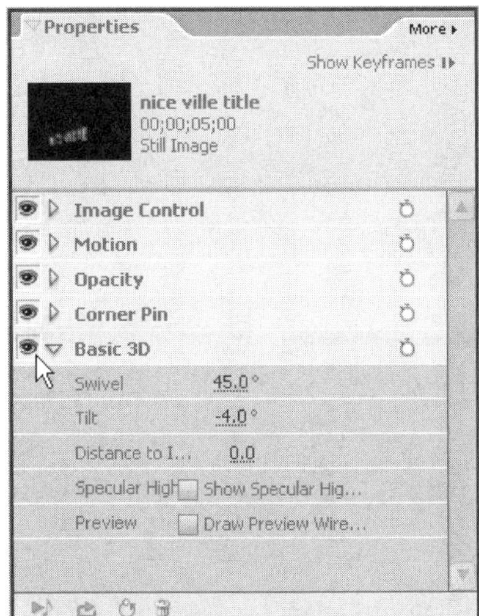

Figure 10.52 In the Properties panel, clicking an effect's Eye Icon...

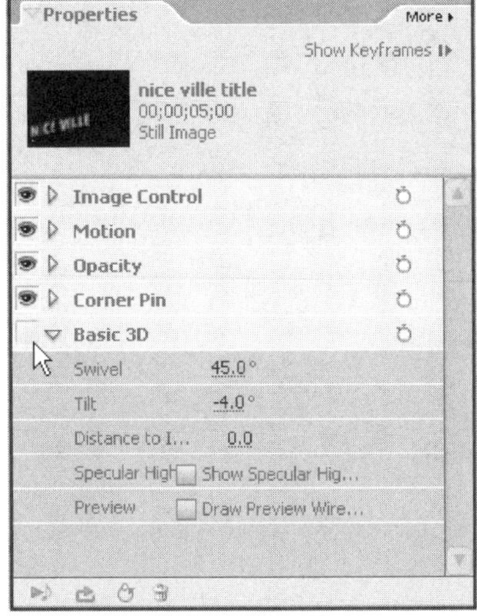

Figure 10.53 ...makes the icon disappear and disables the effect.

Disabling and Removing Effects

Whereas you can view effect values in either the Timeline panel or the Properties panel, you can disable effects only in the Properties panel. Disabling an effect doesn't delete your settings; it turns off the effect until you toggle it back on.

You can also completely remove one or all effects from a clip. Naturally, you can't remove the fixed (aka inherent) effects: image control, motion, opacity, and volume.

To disable or enable an effect:

1. Select the clip containing effects you want to disable.

   The Properties panel lists the clip's effects.

2. In the Properties panel, click the effect's Eye icon next to the effect you want to disable (**Figure 10.52**).

   The icon disappears, and the effect is disabled (**Figure 10.53**). Clicking the empty box makes the icon reappear and enables the effect.

Disabling and Removing Effects

To remove effects from a clip:

1. Select the clip containing effects you want to remove.

   The Properties panel lists the clip's effects.

2. To remove a particular effect, select the effect's name in the Properties panel (**Figure 10.54**).

3. In the Properties panel's More pull-down menu, *do either of the following:*

   ▲ To remove the selected standard effect, choose Delete Selected Effect, or press Backspace.

   ▲ To remove all standard effects (filters), choose Delete All Effects from Clip (**Figure 10.55**).

   Effects are removed from the clip according to your selection.

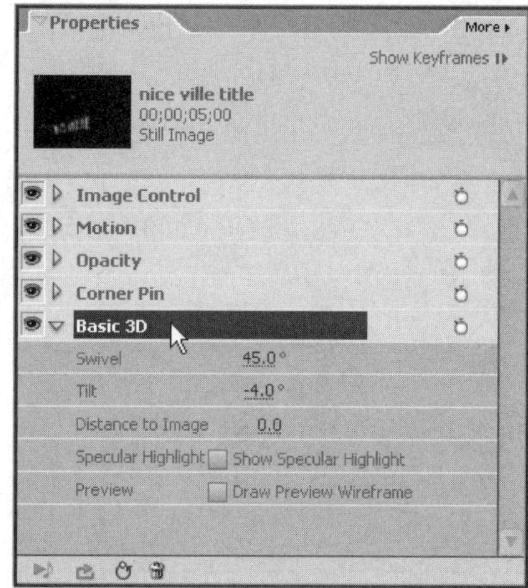

Figure 10.54 Select a clip so that its effects are listed in the Properties panel. To remove a particular effect, select it.

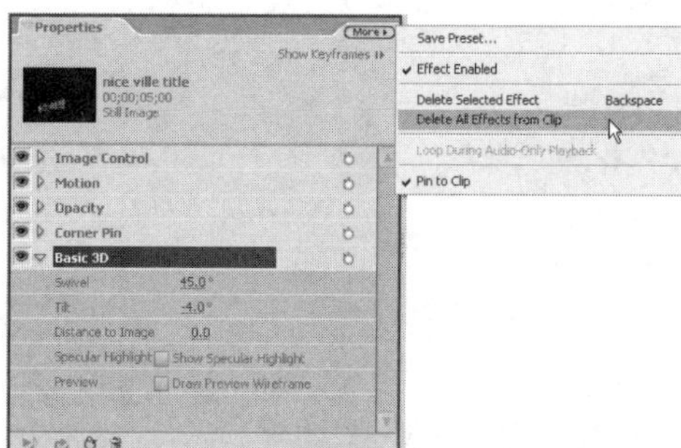

Figure 10.55 Press Backspace to remove the selected effect; or, to remove all of the clip's effects, choose Delete All Effects from Clip from the More pull-down menu (shown here).

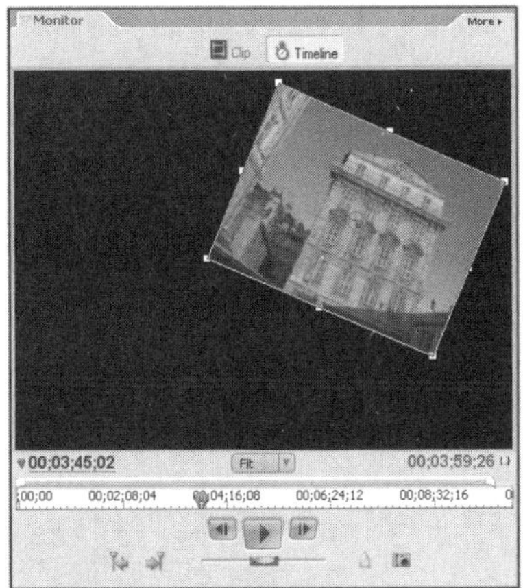

Figure 10.56 Here, the clip's motion effects have been set globally (they don't animate over time).

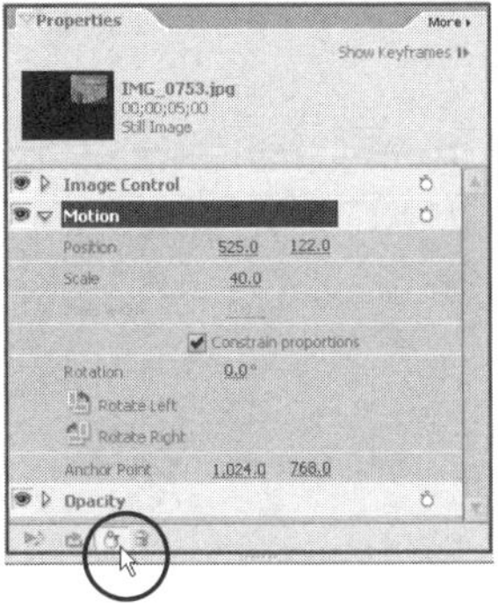

Figure 10.57 Selecting the effect and then clicking the Reset button...

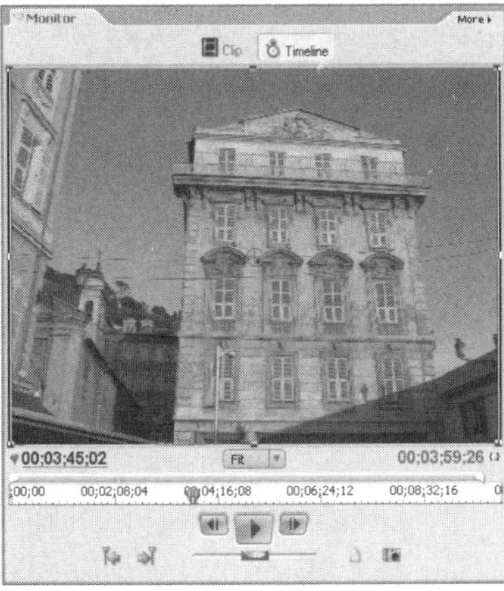

Figure 10.58 ...returns its values to their default. In this case, the clip is returned to its default position, scale, and rotation. (If the effect is keyframed, it sets or resets the current keyframe to the default values.)

Resetting an Effect to Its Default Values

Resetting an effect sets its property values to their defaults. When keyframing is inactive (and the property's Stopwatch icon is off), this is a good way to start over. For example, resetting the Motion effect puts the clip back in its original position: centered and full-screen.

But when keyframing is active (and the Stopwatch icon is on), the same button only resets the values at the current keyframe or creates a keyframe using the default values.

This task covers resetting the effect's property values globally, not its keyframed values. For more about keyframing, proceed through the chapter.

To reset an effect's property values to their defaults:

1. Select the clip containing effects you want to reset (**Figure 10.56**).

   The Properties panel lists the clip's effects.

2. In the Properties panel, select the heading of the property you want to reset and then click the Reset button (**Figure 10.57**).

   The effect's properties are reset to their default values (**Figure 10.58**). If the effect is keyframed, the values are reset only at the current time, either resetting the current keyframe's values or creating a keyframe.

Specifying Custom Settings

Immediately after you add them to a clip, some effects prompt you to specify custom settings in a special dialog box. And though they may not prompt you automatically, other effects also contain custom settings in a dialog box separate from the Properties panel. The options contained by custom dialog boxes tend to be ill suited for the Properties panel's standard layout. However, the Properties panel makes it easy for you to revisit or open custom settings.

To use a standard effect's custom settings:

- In the Properties panel, click a standard effect's Setup button (**Figure 10.59**).

  Depending on the effect, a Settings dialog box may open, or (in the case of effects like the Image Matte filter) a dialog box for choosing a file to serve as an effect source may appear (**Figure 10.60**).

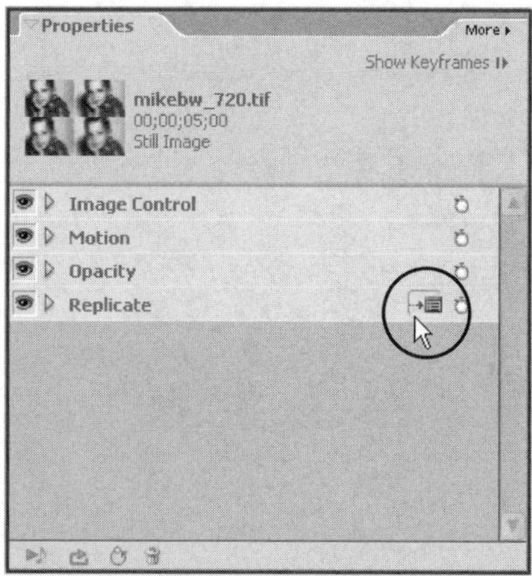

Figure 10.59 In the Properties panel, clicking an effect's Setup button...

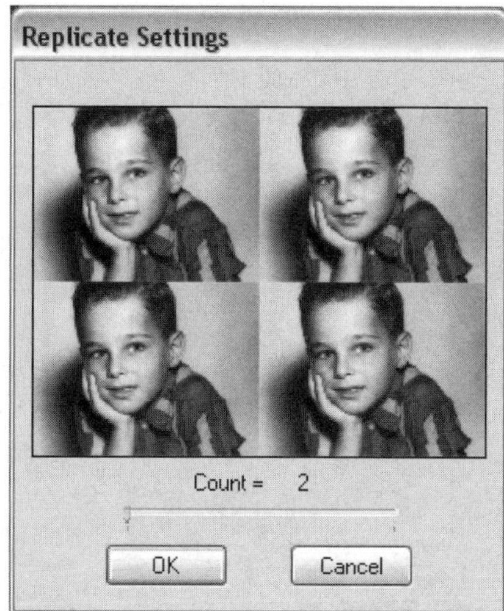

Figure 10.60 ...opens the effect's custom settings in a dialog box. Because these options don't lend themselves to the Properties panel, they appear in a separate dialog box.

Figure 10.61 The Mirror filter followed by the Replicate filter results in this image.

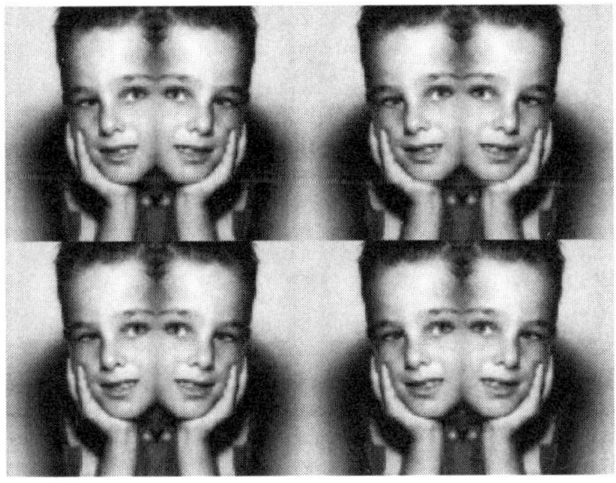

Figure 10.62 Reversing the order of the filters results in this image.

Using Multiple Effects

You can add any number of effects to a clip. You can layer different effects onto a single clip or apply the same effect more than once, specifying different settings each time.

Because each filter adds to the effect of the preceding one, the order of the filters determines the cumulative effect. Changing the order of filters can change the final appearance of the clip (**Figures 10.61** and **10.62**).

To set the order of standard effects:

◆ In the Effect Controls palette, drag an effect up or down to change its position in the list (**Figure 10.63**).

The effect name appears in the new position (**Figure 10.64**). You can't drag a standard effect (filter) above the fixed effects (Image Control, Motion, and Opacity for video, or Volume for audio effects).

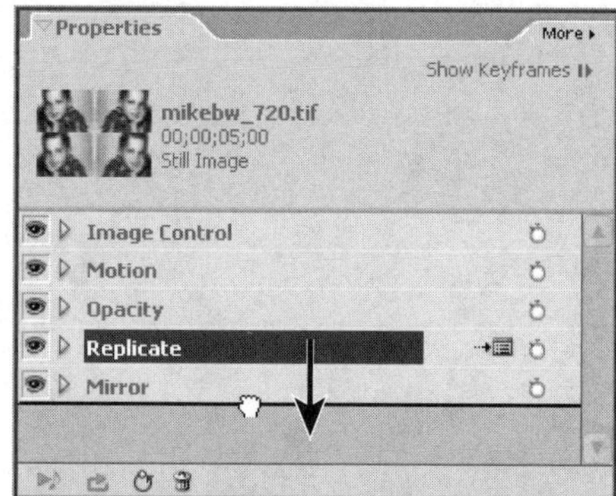

Figure 10.63 In the Properties panel, drag a filter's name up or down to change its position in the list.

Figure 10.64 The filter appears in the new position, and the filters are rendered accordingly.

Subverting the Render Order

At times, the rendering order prevents you from achieving the result you want. For example, you might want to use the Replicate filter to create numerous copies of a rotating image. However, the rendering order dictates that the Replicate filter is applied before rotation. This causes the image to be replicated before it's rotated, making it appear as though all the images are rotated as a group—*not* the effect you desire. To solve the problem, you need to defy the rendering order so that the effect is applied after rotation.

Although you can't alter the rendering order, you can subvert it by using standard effects that emulate fixed effects. One such effect is the Transform filter. Its properties match those of fixed effects: anchor point, position, scale, rotation, and opacity. It also includes skew and shutter angle. By applying the Transform filter after the Replicate filter, you can adjust the properties in the order you want. The same principle can be applied to using the Volume filter instead of adjusting the Volume fixed effect.

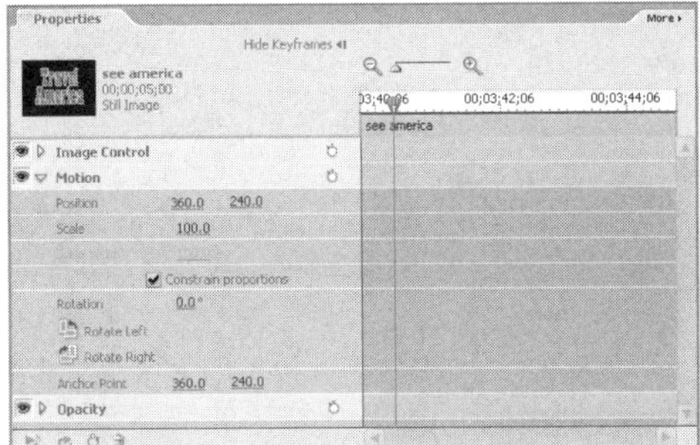

Figure 10.65 Select the clip containing the effect you want to animate, and set the CTI to the frame at which you want to set a keyframe.

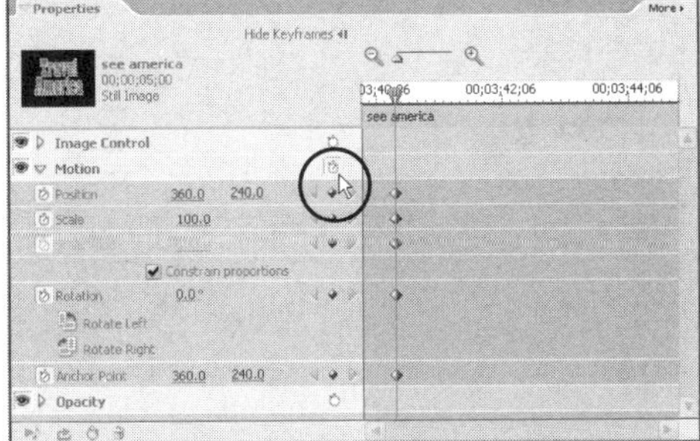

Figure 10.66 In the Properties panel, click the effect's Stopwatch icon to activate it (and the keyframe process). A Keyframe icon appears at the CTI.

Keyframing in the Properties Panel

Essentially, keyframing is nothing more than repeating a two-step process: setting the current frame, and setting the property value for that frame. The specific steps are outlined in this section.

If you're new to animating with keyframes, you might want to start with a simple effect property that yields results that are easy to see. For starters, try the Scale property (under the Motion category), or add a standard effect such as Fast Blur.

In later sections, you'll learn to gain greater control over your animations by manipulating both keyframes themselves and the interpolation method used between keyframes.

To set keyframes in the Properties panel:

1. In the Properties panel, make sure the timeline area is visible.
2. In the Timeline panel, select the clip that contains effect properties you want to adjust.

   The selected clip's effect properties appear in the Properties panel.
3. Set the sequence CTI to the frame where you want to specify a keyframed property value (**Figure 10.65**).
4. Click the Stopwatch icon next to the property you want to keyframe, to activate the icon and the keyframing process (**Figure 10.66**).

   The property's Stopwatch icon appears on. To the right of the property name, a keyframe navigator appears; a selected diamond indicates that the CTI is cued to a keyframe. In the property's track in the Timeline view, a Keyframe icon appears at the CTI.

continues on next page

5. Set the value for the keyframe (**Figure 10.67**).
6. Set the CTI to another frame.
7. *Do one of the following:*
   - ▲ To create a keyframe with a new value, change the property's value (**Figure 10.68**).

   In the property's track of the Timeline panel, a new keyframe appears, and the diamond at the center of the keyframe navigator is highlighted.
   - ▲ To create a keyframe without changing the property's value at that frame, click the center diamond of the keyframe navigator (**Figure 10.69**).

   If the new keyframe becomes the last keyframe for the property, it has the same value as the previous keyframe. Otherwise, the new keyframe's value is based on the previously interpolated value for that frame.

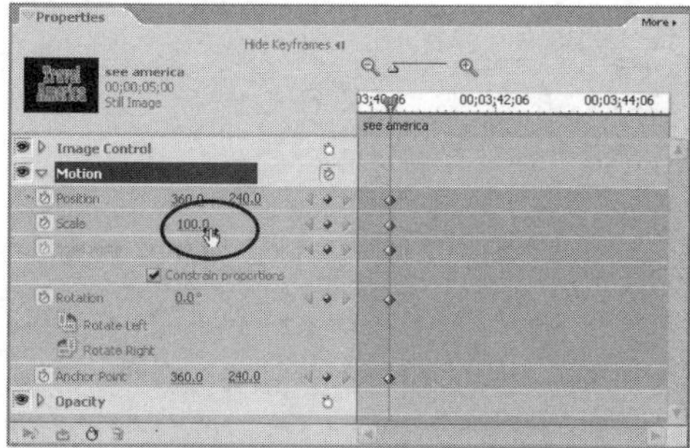

Figure 10.67 Use the property value controls to set the keyframe's value.

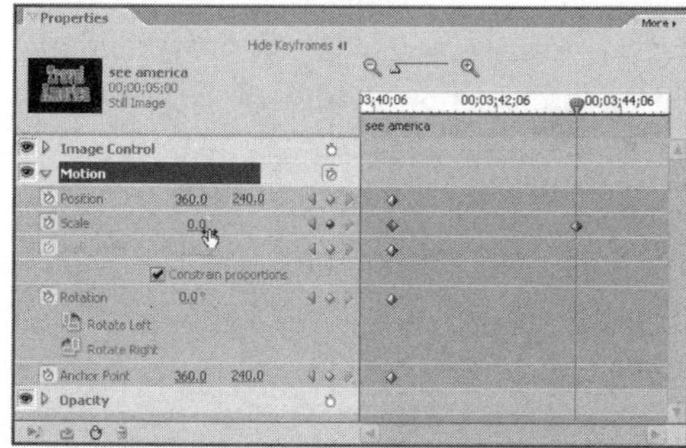

Figure 10.68 Set the CTI to a new frame, and change the property's value to set a keyframe with a new value...

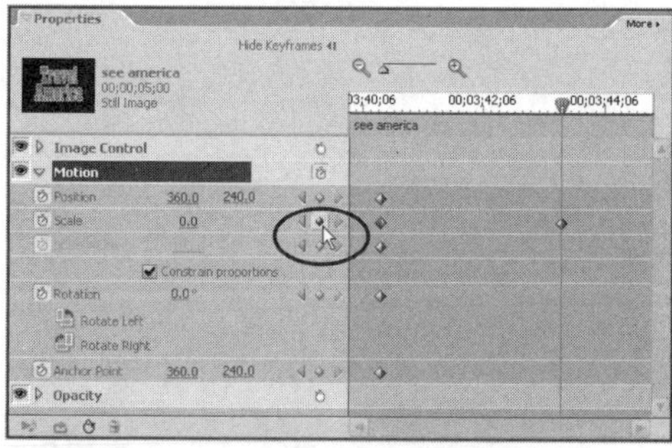

Figure 10.69 ...or click the keyframe navigator's diamond icon to set a keyframe using the value already calculated for that frame.

Figure 10.70 Use the playback controls or render a preview file to see the effect in motion. Here, a title clip is scaled down over time, making it appear to shrink, or disappear into the distance.

8. To create additional keyframes, repeat steps 6 and 7.

   To modify the keyframe values or to change the keyframes' position in time, use the methods explained in the following sections.

9. To see the effect property values vary over time in the Monitor panel's Timeline view, use the playback controls in the Properties panel or any of the sequence playback controls you've learned about so far.

   You may need to render a preview file to see the effect play back at the project's full frame rate (see Chapter 8, "Previewing a Sequence") (**Figure 10.70**).

To create fades automatically:

1. In the Timeline panel, select the clip that you want to fade (**Figure 10.71**).
2. In the Properties panel, expand the property you want to fade.

   You can fade a clip's opacity or volume automatically.
3. Under the appropriate property, click the button that corresponds to the fade you want (**Figure 10.72**):

   Fade In—Creates a keyframe at the selected clip's In point set to 0% opacity or –∞ dB, and another keyframe 1 second later at 100% opacity or +0dB (normal volume).

   Fade Out—Creates a keyframe at 1 second before the clip's Out point set to 100% opacity or +0dB (normal volume), and another keyframe at the clip's Out point set to 0% opacity or –∞ dB.

   Premiere Elements applies the keyframes to the selected clip's property (**Figure 10.73**).

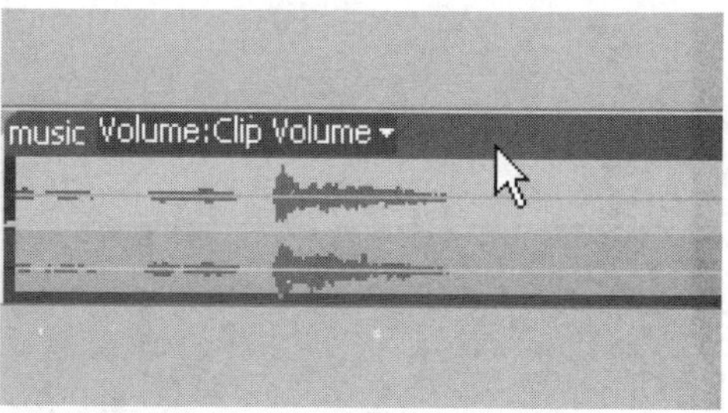

Figure 10.71 Select the clip you want to fade.

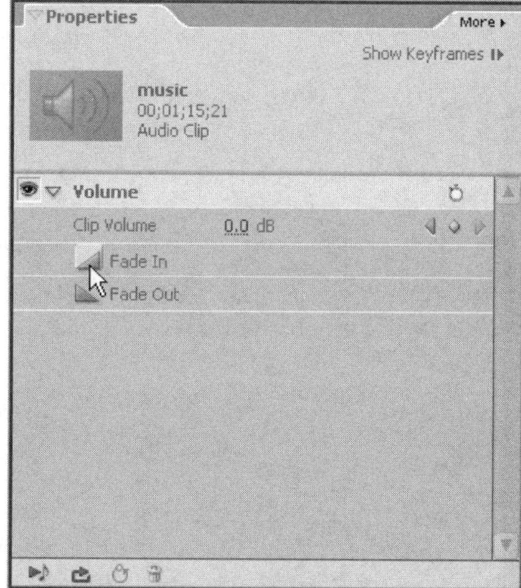

Figure 10.72 Click the type of fade you want in the Properties panel—in this case, a one-second audio fade up.

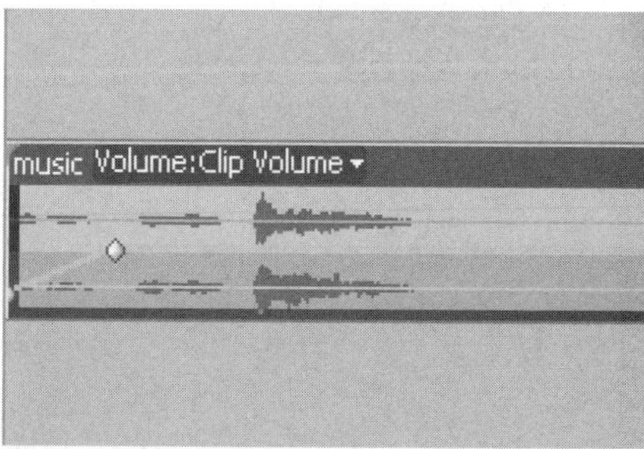

Figure 10.73 Keyframes are added to the clip to create the fade. Here, two keyframes have been applied to the beginning of an audio clip to fade it up.

✔ Tips

- Although it's possible to set a keyframe beyond the duration of the clip, doing so is usually unnecessary and will prevent you from seeing the keyframe in the Timeline panel of the Properties panel when Pin to Clip is selected.
- There's more than one way to make a property pause, or hold, at a certain value. You can create two consecutive keyframes that use the same value, or you can apply a hold interpolation method to a keyframe (explained later in this chapter). And naturally, a value is also maintained after the last keyframe.
- Property values before the first keyframe use the first keyframe's values; values after the last keyframe use the last keyframe's values. Therefore, setting the first keyframe after the beginning of the clip delays the animation, and setting the last keyframe before the end of the clip makes the value hold until the clip's Out point.
- It's often better to animate an effect "in reverse," setting the last keyframe first, and working backward in time.

Using Keyframes in the Properties Panel

After you animate a property, the keyframes aren't set in stone. In the Properties panel's Timeline area, you can select, move, delete, copy, and paste keyframes using the mouse. To change the property value at a keyframe, you must cue the sequence's CTI to the keyframe and then change the value using controls in the left side of the window. (In the case of the position, you can also drag the keyframe's x icon in the motion path; see "Reshaping a Motion Path," later in this chapter.)

To select keyframes:

- *Do one of the following:*
  - ▲ To select a keyframe, click it in the Timeline view (**Figure 10.74**).
  - ▲ To add or subtract from your selection, Shift-click a keyframe.
  - ▲ To select a range of keyframes, drag a marquee around them (**Figure 10.75**).
  - ▲ To select all the keyframes for a property, click the name of the property (**Figure 10.76**).

  Selected keyframes appear blue.

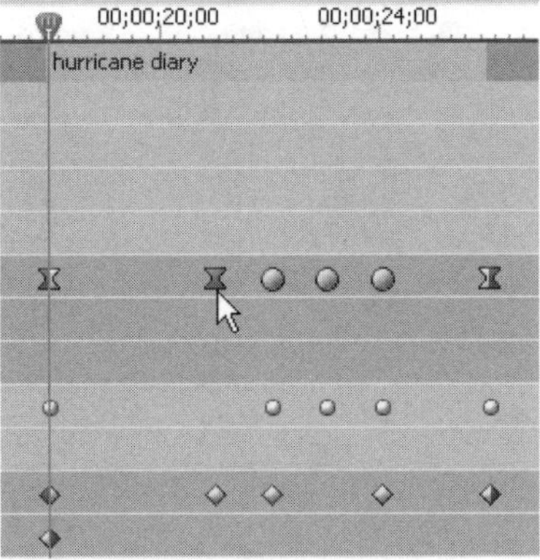

Figure 10.74 In the Properties panel's Timeline pane, click a keyframe to select it, or Shift-click to add to or subtract from the selection.

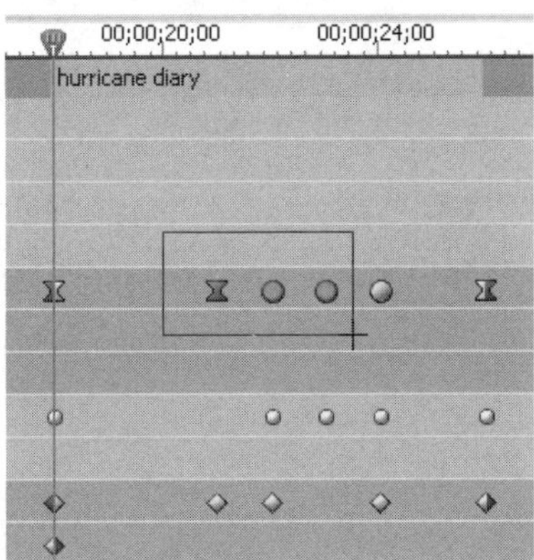

Figure 10.75 You can select contiguous keyframes by dragging a marquee around them.

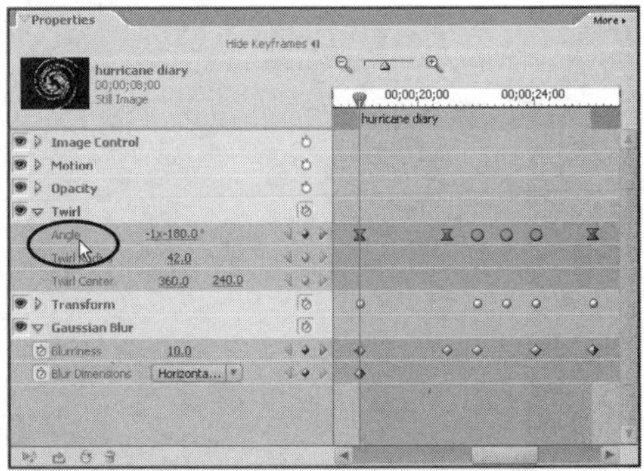

Figure 10.76 Select the property's name to select all of its keyframes.

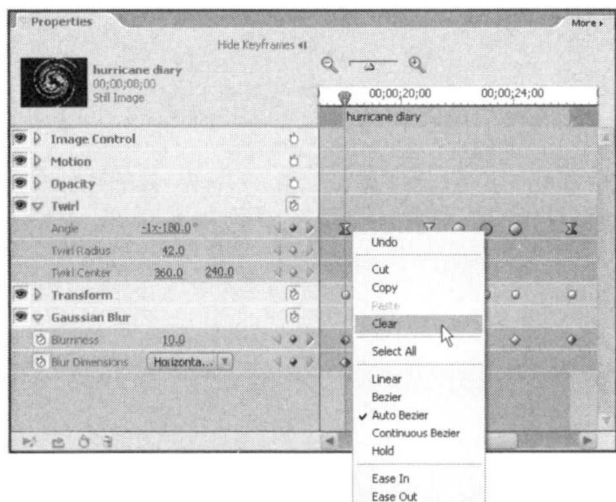

Figure 10.77 To delete a keyframe, select it and press Delete, or context-click it and choose Clear from the menu.

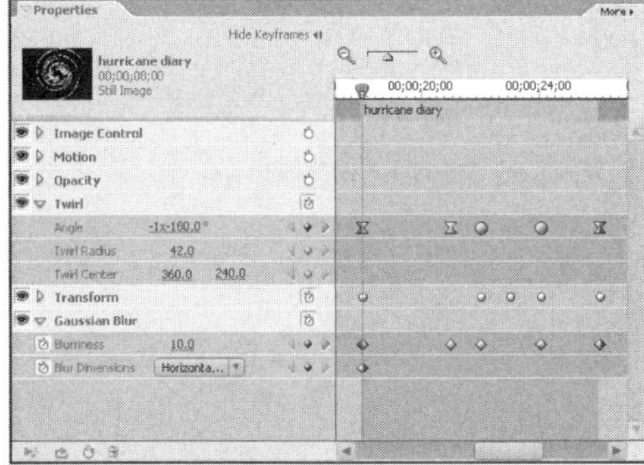

Figure 10.78 The keyframe is removed, and the property's values between the remaining keyframes are recalculated.

To delete keyframes:

- In the Properties panel's Timeline pane, *do one of the following:*
  - ▲ Select one or more keyframes, and press Delete.
  - ▲ Context-click a keyframe, and choose Clear from the menu (**Figure 10.77**).

  The keyframes are removed, and the property's interpolated values are recalculated accordingly (**Figure 10.78**).

To delete all keyframes for a property:

- Deactivate the Stopwatch icon for the property (**Figure 10.79**), and confirm your choice when prompted.

  All keyframes disappear (**Figure 10.80**). You can't restore the keyframes by reactivating the Stopwatch (doing this only starts a new keyframe process).

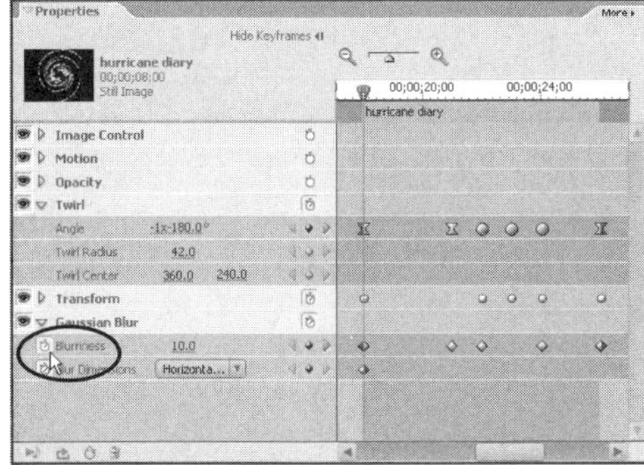

Figure 10.79 Click the Stopwatch to deactivate it...

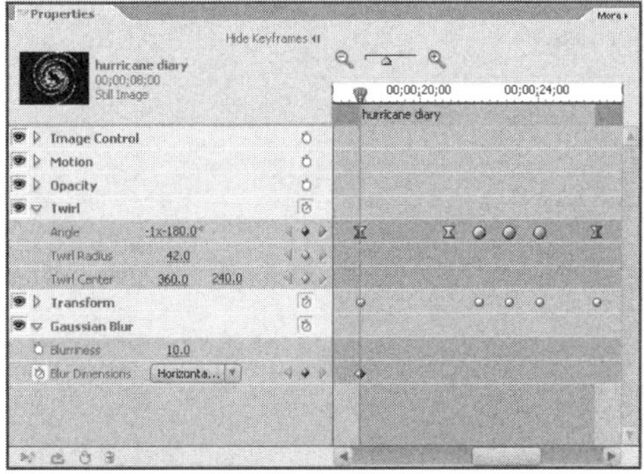

Figure 10.80 ...and remove all the keyframes. Here all keyframes for the Blurriness property have been removed.

To move keyframes in time:

1. Select one or more keyframes (as explained earlier in this chapter).
2. Drag the selected keyframes left or right, to a new position in time (**Figure 10.81**).

To copy and paste keyframed values:

1. Select one or more keyframes (as explained earlier in this chapter) (**Figure 10.82**).
2. Choose Edit > Copy, or press Ctrl-C (**Figure 10.83**).
3. Set the CTI to the time at which you want the pasted keyframes to begin.
4. Choose Edit > Paste, or press Ctrl-V (**Figure 10.84**).

   The keyframes are pasted into the property, starting at the CTI (**Figure 10.85**).

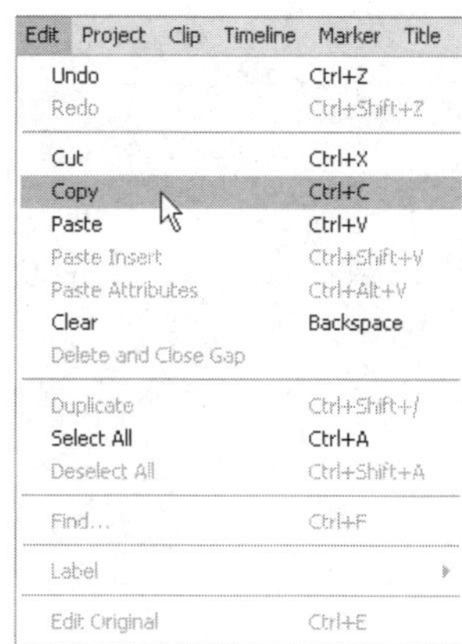

Figure 10.83 Choose Edit > Copy.

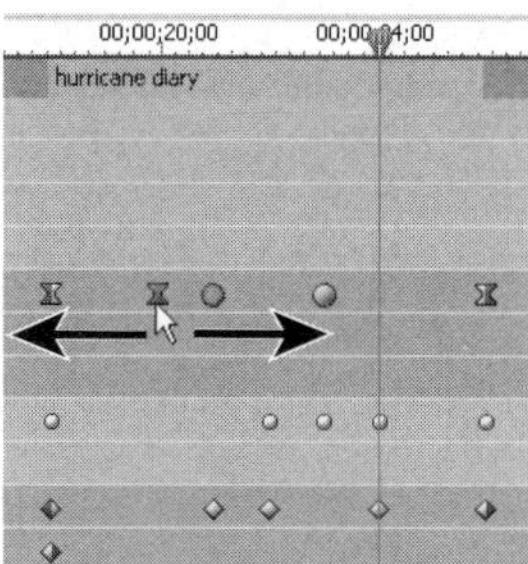

Figure 10.81 Drag keyframes right or left to change their position in time.

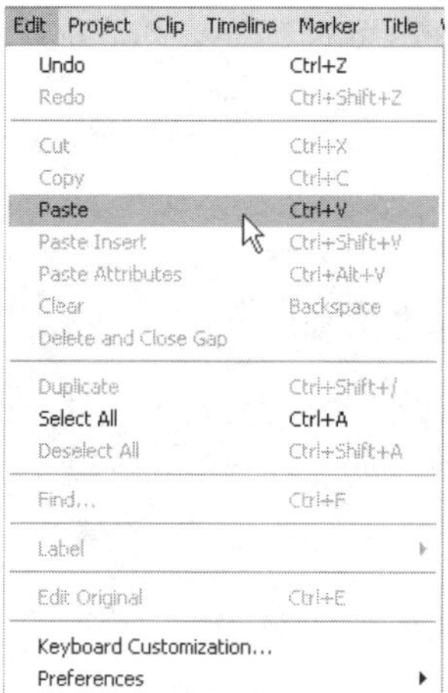

Figure 10.84 Setting the CTI and choosing Edit > Paste...

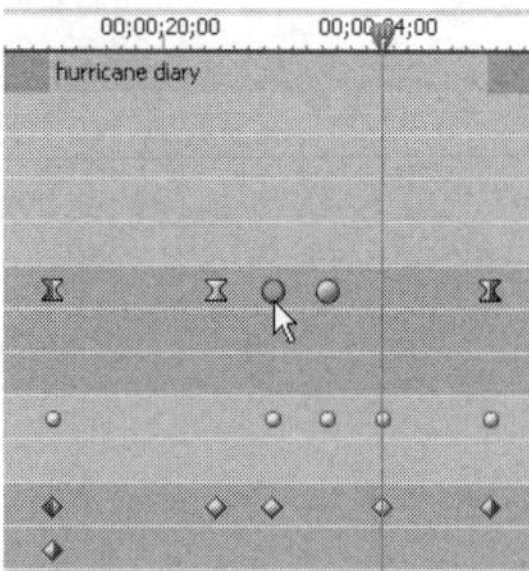

Figure 10.82 Select one or more keyframes.

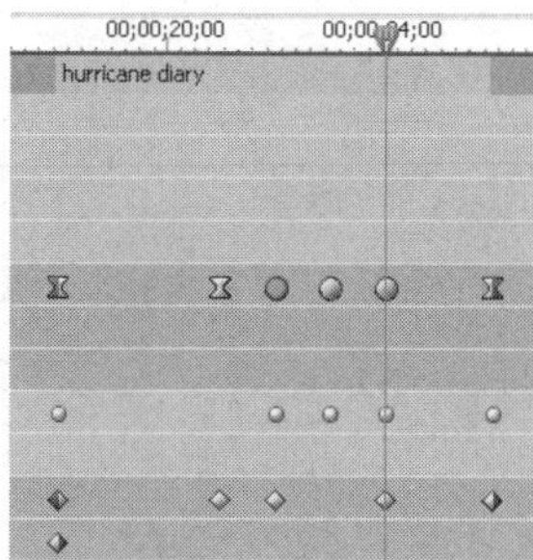

Figure 10.85 ...pastes the copied keyframes, starting at the CTI.

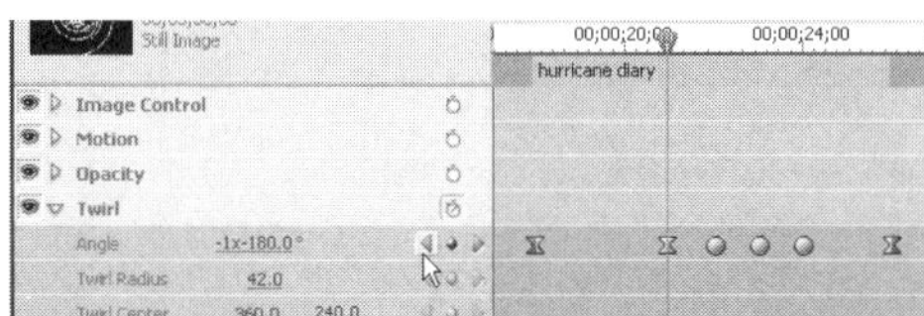

Figure 10.86 Use the keyframe navigator's left and right arrow buttons to cue the CTI. In this example, clicking the left button...

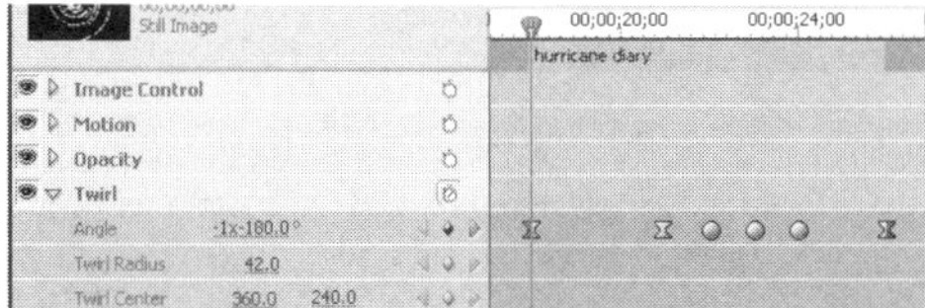

Figure 10.87 ...cues the CTI to the previous keyframe.

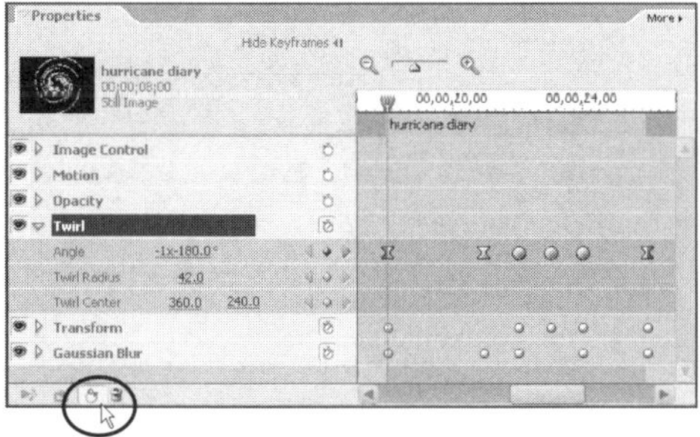

Figure 10.88 Cuing to a keyframe and clicking the Reset button...

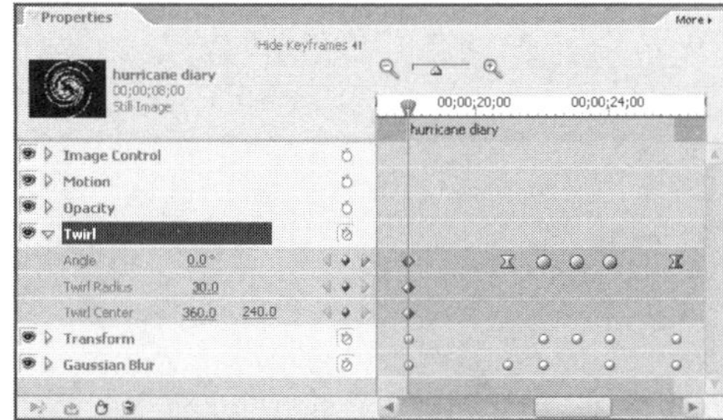

Figure 10.89 ...resets the keyframe's values to their defaults. In this figure, note how the angle value returns to zero degrees. (Note also how keyframes at default values are added to other properties in the effect.)

To cue to keyframes in the Properties panel:

1. Make sure the property with the keyframes you want to see is visible in the Properties panel.
2. In the keyframe navigator for the property, *do one of the following:*
   - ▲ To cue the current time to the previous keyframe, click the left arrow (**Figure 10.86**).
   - ▲ To cue the current time to the next keyframe, click the right arrow.

   The sequence's CTI moves to the keyframe you specify (**Figure 10.87**). If no keyframe exists beyond the current keyframe, the appropriate arrow appears dimmed.

To reset a keyframe to its default settings:

1. In the Properties panel, select the property and use the property's keyframe navigator to cue to the keyframe you want to reset.
2. In the Properties panel, click the Reset icon for the effect you want to reset to its default property values (**Figure 10.88**).

   The values at the keyframe return to their default values. If the CTI isn't cued to a keyframe, clicking the Reset button creates a keyframe that uses the default values (**Figure 10.89**).

✔ Tips

- Use one effect property's keyframe navigator to help you synchronize its keyframes with another property's keyframes.
- You can use the Properties panel's current time display to cue the CTI. Remember, you can enter plus (+) or minus (-) to cue to a relative time (for example, to move the CTI one second later and set a keyframe there).

Keyframe Icons

A property's keyframes appear in its corresponding row, or *property track*, in the Properties panel's Timeline pane. When the property heading is expanded, its keyframes appear as large icons (**Figure 10.90**). When the property heading is collapsed, the keyframes of the properties in that category appear as smaller circles, known as *summary keyframes*, that can't be modified (**Figure 10.91**).

The full-sized keyframe icons vary according to the interpolation method used by the keyframe (see "Specifying a Temporal Interpolation Method," later in this chapter). Regardless of method, shading indicates that the property value either before or after the keyframe hasn't been interpolated.

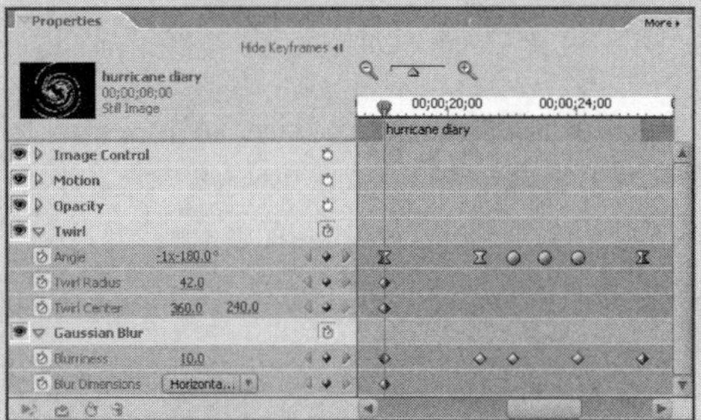

Figure 10.90 When the property is expanded, its keyframe icons appear full-sized and reflect interpolation methods.

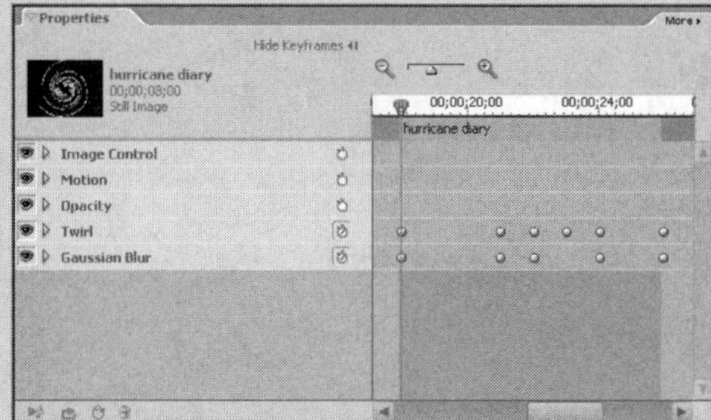

Figure 10.91 When the property heading is collapsed, the keyframes of the properties in that category appear as smaller circles (known as summary keyframes) that can't be modified.

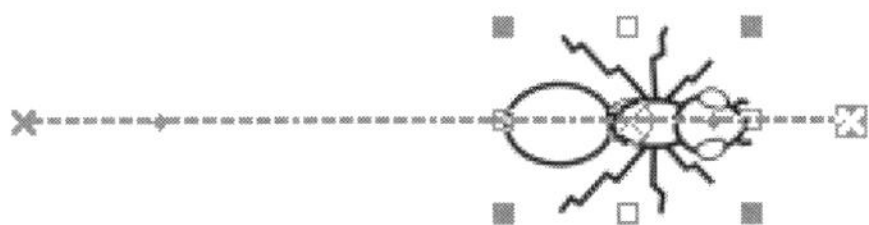

Figure 10.92 Spatial interpolation determines the motion path between position keyframes. Does the clip proceed directly from one keyframe to the next...

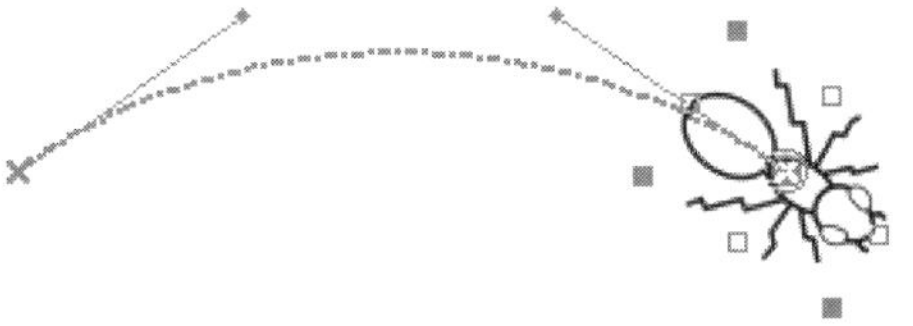

Figure 10.93 ...or does it take a curved route?

Understanding Interpolation

The beauty of keyframes is that they save you work. If you set the keyframes, Premiere Elements calculates the values for the frames in between, a process known as *interpolation*. Controlling the interpolation between keyframes allows you to set fewer keyframes than you could otherwise—without sacrificing precise control over your animation. Premiere Elements interpolates values in terms of both space and time:

Spatial interpolation

Spatial interpolation refers to the way Premiere Elements calculates changes in position. Does a clip proceed directly from one keyframe to the next, or does it take a curved route (**Figures 10.92** and **10.93**)?

As you've seen, spatial interpolation is represented in the Timeline view as a motion path, a dotted line connecting keyframes. By default, Premiere Elements calculates the values between spatial keyframes—the motion path—using a curved progression called an *auto Bézier* curve. This means that there is a smooth rate of change through the keyframe. In other words, there aren't any sharp changes in direction.

Temporal interpolation

Temporal interpolation refers to any property value's rate of change between keyframes. Does the value change at a constant rate from one keyframe to the next, or does it accelerate or decelerate?

For example, **Figure 10.94** shows two familiar rabbits. They both travel the same distance in the same amount of time. However, one proceeds from the first keyframe to the last keyframe at a constant rate. The other gradually accelerates, starting slowly and then speeding up. As a result, the second rabbit falls behind at first and then gradually catches up. Both reach their destination simultaneously.

By default, Premiere Elements calculates the values between temporal keyframes using a linear progression, or *linear interpolation* method. This means that property values change at a constant rate. However, you can set the rate of change to accelerate or decelerate. You can even specify no interpolation, so that a keyframe value holds until the next keyframe value is reached (in terms of the example, this rabbit would magically appear at the finish line at the moment the others reach it by foot).

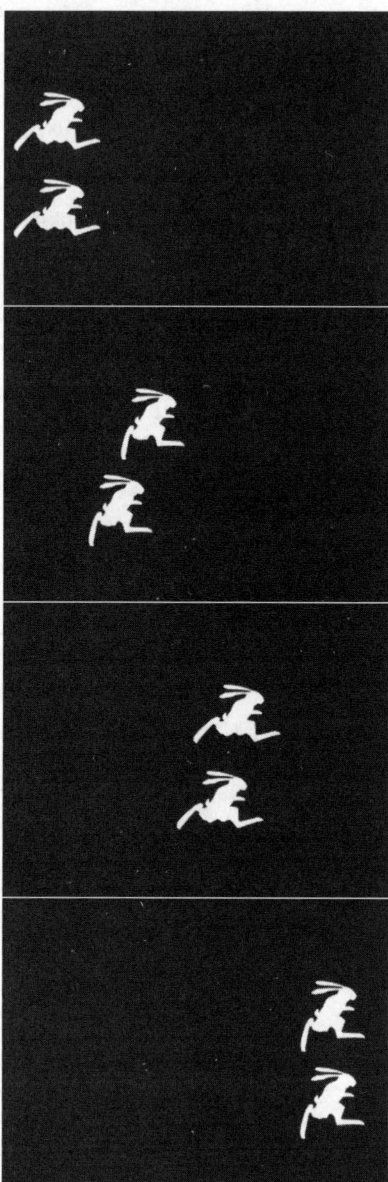

Figure 10.94 Both rabbits run the same distance in the same amount of time. However, the top rabbit moves at a steady pace (linear interpolation), whereas the bottom rabbit accelerates as it nears the final position.

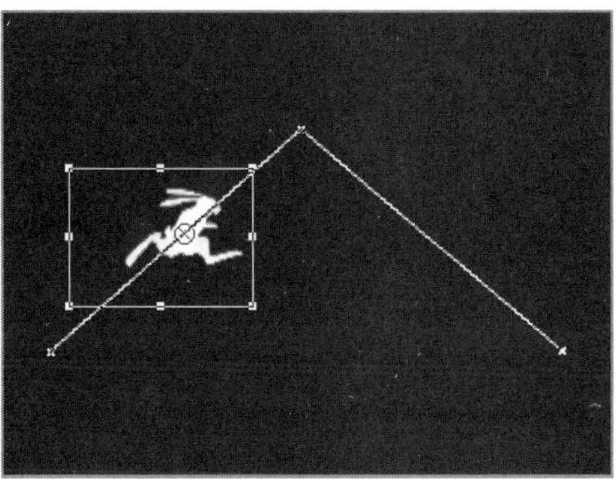

Figure 10.95 Linear interpolation calculates changes in a linear progression. Spatially, linear interpolation defines a straight path.

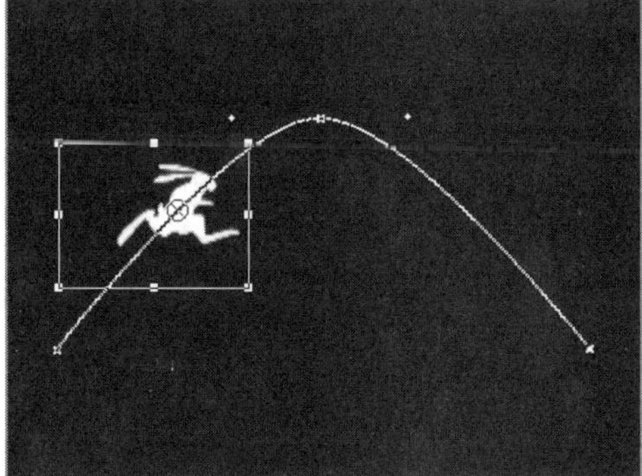

Figure 10.96 Auto Bézier interpolation smoothes incoming and outgoing value changes equally; spatially, it creates an even, curved path.

Interpolation Types

You can apply the following interpolation methods to calculate both spatial and temporal interpolation. But for the sake of clarity, the following figures illustrate them spatially. (Later, you'll learn about methods unique to temporal interpolation: hold interpolation and the Ease In and Ease Out options.)

Linear interpolation dictates a constant rate of change from one keyframe to the next. Spatially, linear interpolation defines a straight path from one keyframe to the next (**Figure 10.95**); temporally, linear interpolation results in a constant speed between keyframes.

Auto Bézier interpolation automatically reduces the rate of change equally on both sides of a keyframe. Spatially, a keyframe set to auto Bézier results in a smooth, symmetrical curve in a motion path (**Figure 10.96**). Temporally, auto Bézier interpolation reduces the rate of change equally before and after a keyframe, creating a gradual deceleration that eases into and out of the keyframe.

Adjusting an auto Bézier keyframe's direction handles manually make it a continuous Bézier keyframe.

continues on next page

Continuous Bézier interpolation, like auto Bézier, reduces the rate of change on both sides of a keyframe. But because continuous Bézier interpolation is set manually, it does not affect the incoming and outgoing rates of change equally. In the motion path, continuous Bézier interpolation results in a smooth and continuous but asymmetrical curve (**Figure 10.97**). Temporally, continuous Bézier interpolation reduces the rate of change before and after a keyframe unequally.

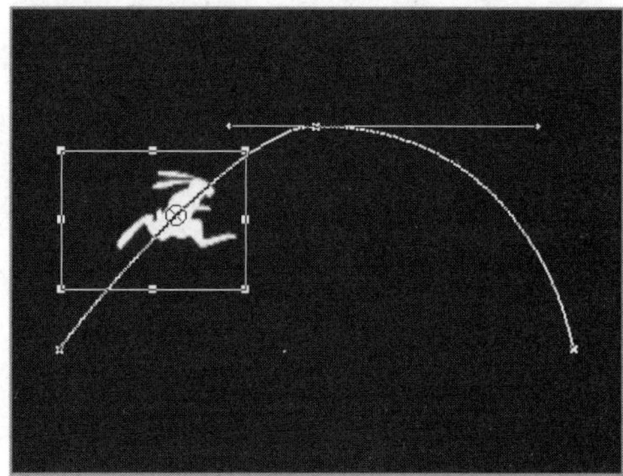

Figure 10.97 Continuous Bézier interpolation works like auto Bézier but affects incoming and outgoing interpolation unevenly. Spatially, it produces an asymmetrically curved path.

Ctrl-clicking a continuous Bézier keyframe's handles makes it a Bézier keyframe.

Bézier interpolation is set manually, like continuous Bézier. Bézier interpolation can either decrease or increase the rate of change on either or both sides of a keyframe. In a motion path, Bézier interpolation creates a discontinuous curve, or *cusp*, at the keyframe (**Figure 10.98**). Temporally, Bézier interpolation can reduce or increase the rate of change before and after a keyframe.

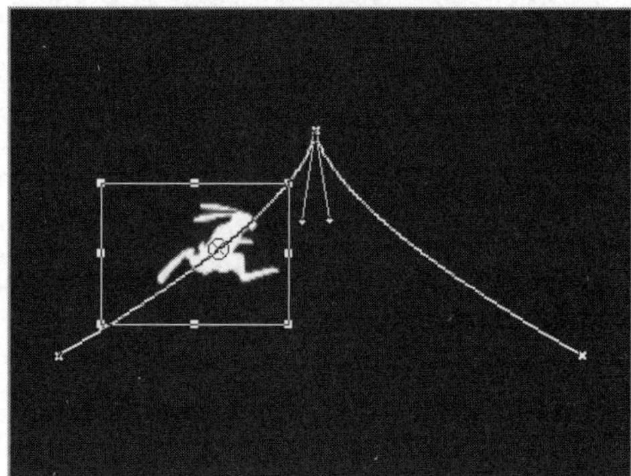

Figure 10.98 Bézier interpolation allows both an uneven and a discontinuous change before and after the keyframe. Spatially, this can be expressed as a discontinuous curve, or cusp, in the path.

Bézier Curves and the Motion Path

Motion paths work like Bézier curves you find in other programs—particularly programs that include drawing tools, such as Photoshop, Illustrator, and After Effects.

Instead of drawing a shape freehand, you can define a shape using a *Bézier curve*. In a Bézier curve, you define control points, which are connected by line segments automatically. (It already sounds a lot like keyframes and interpolation, doesn't it?)

The curves of the line segments are defined and controlled by *direction lines*. Two direction lines can extend from each control point. The length and angle of one direction line influences the shape of the curve preceding the control point; the other influences the curve following the control point. (Imagine that the direction lines exert a gravitational pull on the line that enters and exits a control point.) Dragging the end of a direction line alters the line and thus its corresponding curve (**Figure 10.99**).

Just as a Bézier curve consists of control points connected by line segments, a *motion path* consists of position keyframes connected by line segments (albeit dotted lines). The same techniques you use to draw shapes in a drawing program can be applied to creating motion paths in Adobe Premiere Elements (**Figure 10.100**).

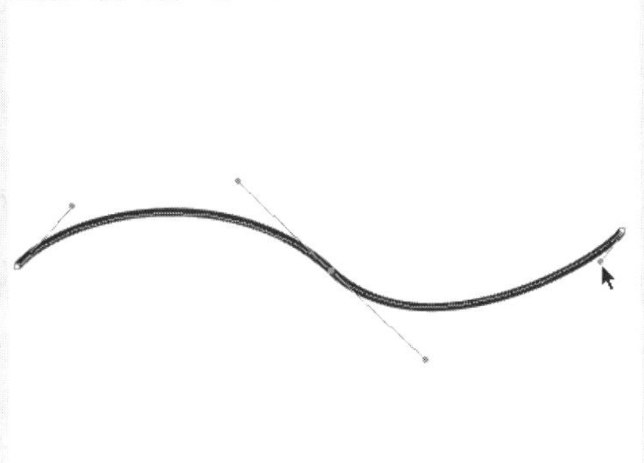

Figure 10.99 Bézier curves in a drawing program...

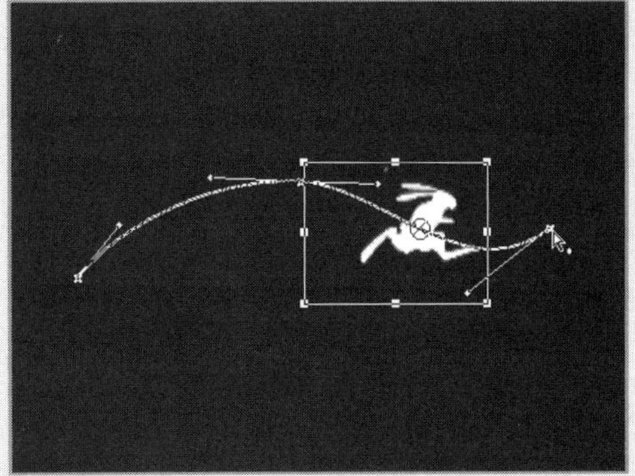

Figure 10.100 ...work essentially the same as motion paths in Premiere Elements.

Reshaping a Motion Path

When you make adjustments to a motion path, you alter either a clip's position keyframes or the spatially interpolated values between them. Like the keyframed position values themselves, you can alter the interpolated values by dragging in the Monitor panel's Timeline view. Reshaping a motion path works just like reshaping a Bézier curve in a drawing program (see the sidebar "Bézier Curves and the Motion Path").

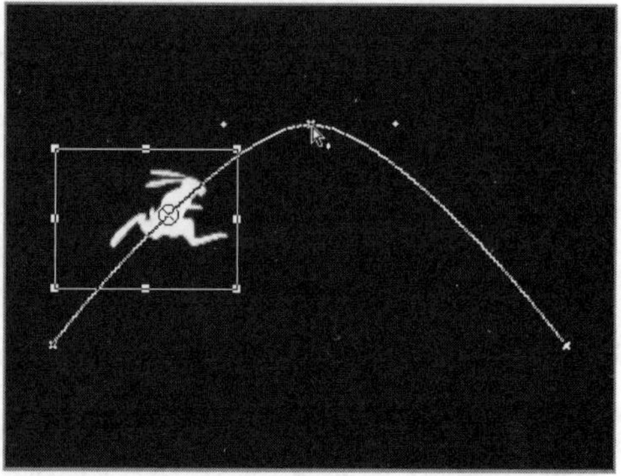

Figure 10.101 Position the mouse over a position keyframe so the pointer becomes a Move Keyframe icon...

To move a position keyframe:

1. In a clip's motion path, position the mouse pointer over a position keyframe (an x in the path) so that the pointer changes into a Move Keyframe icon (**Figure 10.101**).
2. Drag the keyframe to a new position (**Figure 10.102**).

   The clip's Position property value at the keyframe changes accordingly.

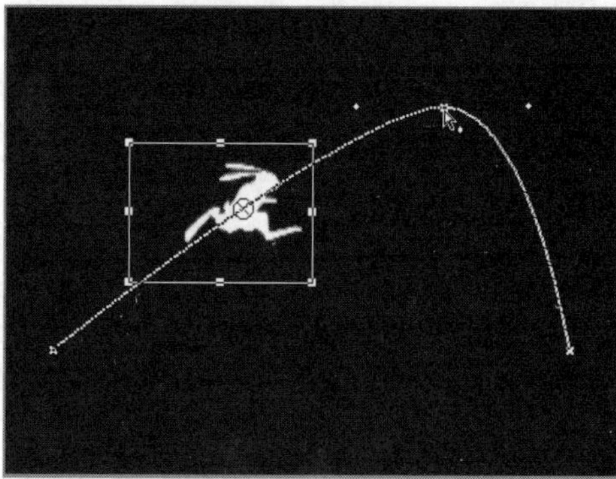

Figure 10.102 ...and drag the keyframe to the position you want.

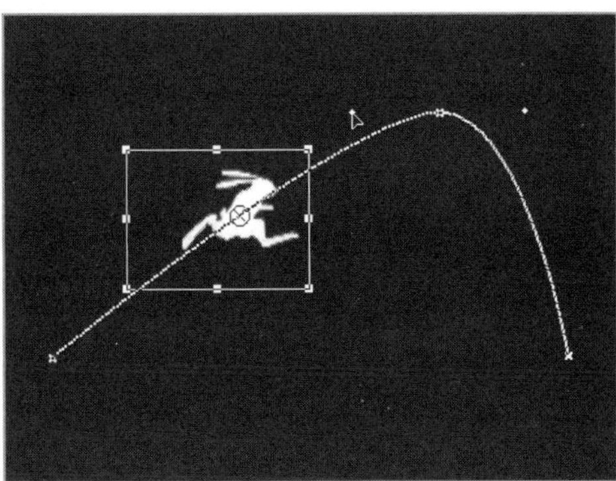

Figure 10.103 Dragging the direction line of an auto Bézier keyframe...

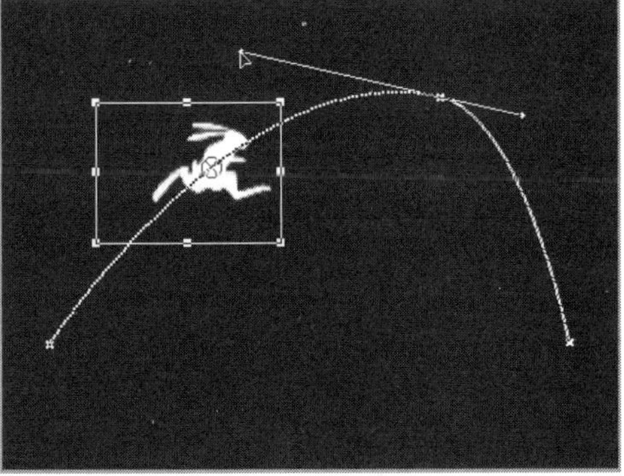

Figure 10.104 ...converts it to a continuous Bézier keyframe, allowing you to change the angle of both lines but the length of only one.

To convert auto Bézier to continuous Bézier:

- In a clip's motion path, drag the end handle of any keyframe's direction line.

  If the keyframe's direction lines are continuous (auto Bézier or continuous Bézier), dragging changes the angle of both direction lines, but the length of only the line you grab (continuous Bézier) (**Figures 10.103** and **10.104**). If the direction lines are split (Bézier), dragging moves the line you grab independently.

To toggle between continuous Bézier and Bézier (and vice versa):

- In a clip's motion path, Ctrl-drag the end handle of any keyframe's direction line.

  The mouse pointer becomes a Convert icon (**Figure 10.105**). If the keyframe's direction lines are continuous (auto Bézier or continuous Bézier), the line's length and angle change independently of the other direction line (**Figure 10.106**).

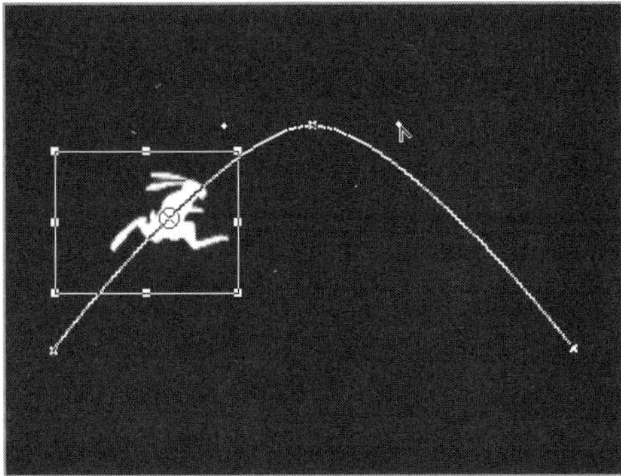

Figure 10.105 Ctrl-dragging changes the mouse into a Convert icon...

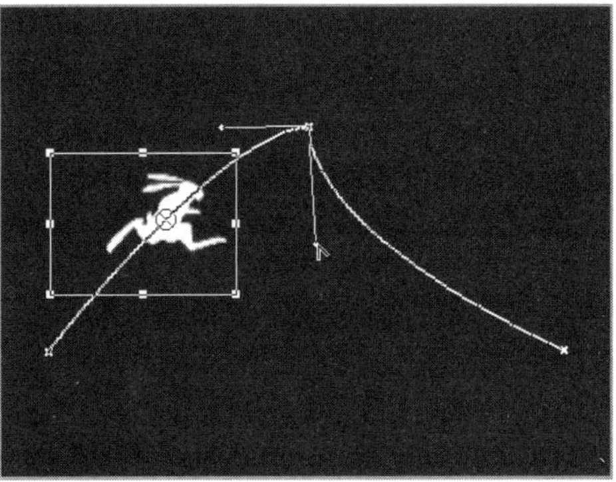

Figure 10.106 ...converting the keyframe (in this case) from continuous Bézier to Bézier, breaking the relationship between direction lines.

To toggle between auto Bézier and linear interpolation:

1. In a clip's motion path, press Ctrl, and position the mouse pointer over a position keyframe (an x in the path) so that the pointer changes into a Convert Keyframe icon (**Figure 10.107**).
2. Click the keyframe.

   The keyframe toggles from having two equal and continuous direction lines and a curved path (auto Bézier interpolation) to having no direction lines and a straight path (linear interpolation) (**Figure 10.108**).

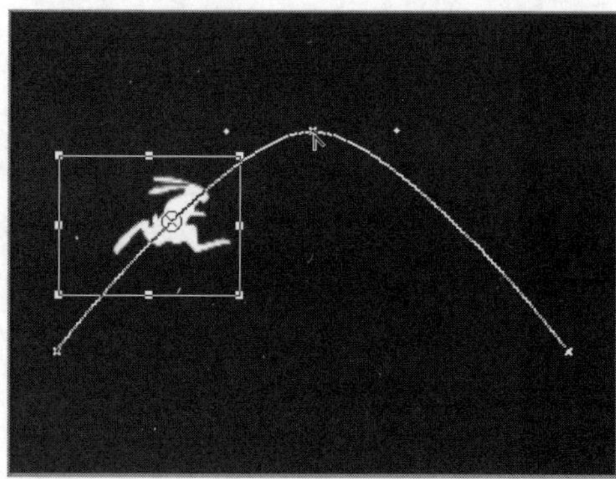

Figure 10.107 Pressing Ctrl as you position the mouse over a position keyframe changes the mouse into a Convert Keyframe icon...

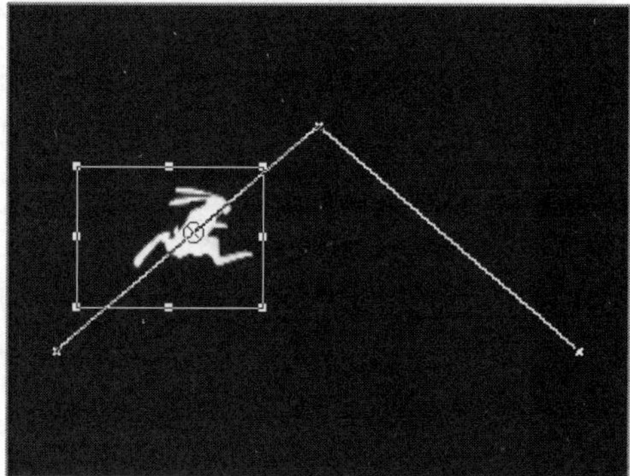

Figure 10.108 ...and clicking toggles the keyframe from (in this case) auto Bézier to linear.

✔ Tip

- Technically speaking, direction lines define the spatial interpolation between position keyframes. See the section "Understanding Interpolation," earlier in this chapter, for more information.

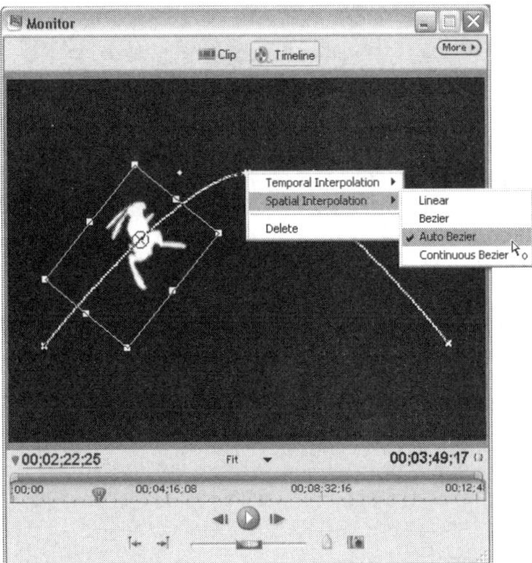

Figure 10.109 Right-click a selected keyframe and choose an option from the context menu.

Specifying a Spatial Interpolation Method

As you've seen, you can reshape a motion path—in effect, its spatial interpolation— by dragging. You can also use commands to set a keyframe's interpolation type.

To specify a spatial interpolation method:

1. In either the Properties panel or the Monitor panel, right-click a keyframe; in the context menu, choose Spatial Interpolation, and select an option (**Figure 10.109**):
   - ▲ Linear
   - ▲ Bézier
   - ▲ Auto Bézier
   - ▲ Continuous Bézier
2. Drag the Bézier handles in the Monitor panel's Timeline view.

✔ Tip

- You can also right-click a position keyframe in the Monitor panel's Timeline view to choose an interpolation method in a context menu.

Specifying a Temporal Interpolation Method

As discussed earlier, you can specify how interpolated values are calculated spatially (position values) or temporally (any property values) using the same set of interpolation methods.

You can also specify an interpolation method unique to temporal interpolation: *hold interpolation*. In addition, you can quickly ease the incoming or outgoing interpolation of a keyframe using the Ease In or Ease Out option. These options let you achieve these common effects without having to adjust the interpolation manually:

Hold: Although you can observe its effects both spatially and temporally, hold interpolation is a strictly temporal type of interpolation, halting changes in a property's value at the keyframe. The value remains fixed until the current frame of the sequence reaches the next keyframe, where the property is set to a new value instantly (**Figure 10.110**). For example, specifying hold keyframes for a layer's Position property can cause the layer to disappear suddenly and then reappear in different places. When hold interpolation is applied to position keyframes, no motion path connects the keyframes displayed in the Timeline view.

Ease In: The property value's rate of change accelerates from, or eases out of, the previous keyframe and then decelerates into, or eases into, the selected keyframe (**Figure 10.111**). Contrast this to the auto or continuous Bézier option, which affects both the incoming and outgoing interpolation.

Figure 10.110 Hold interpolation suspends calculations, retaining the current keyframe's property values until the next keyframe is reached. Here, the title clip "GO!" will appear instantly at each keyframe (x in the Monitor panel).

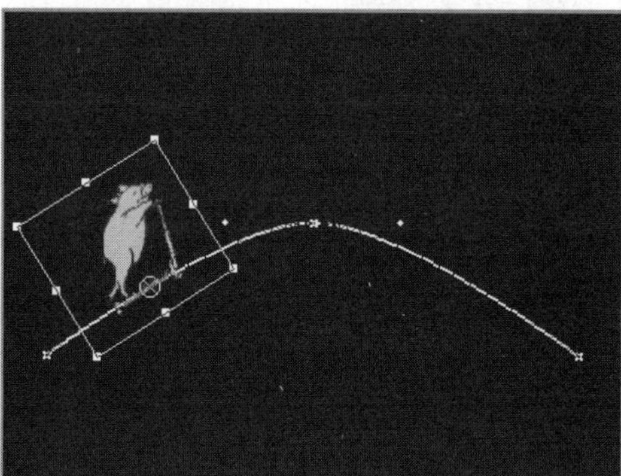

Figure 10.111 Ease In smoothes the incoming rate of change. You can use it to simulate gradual deceleration into a keyframe. Setting the second keyframe to Ease In makes the pig decelerate as it approaches the keyframe.

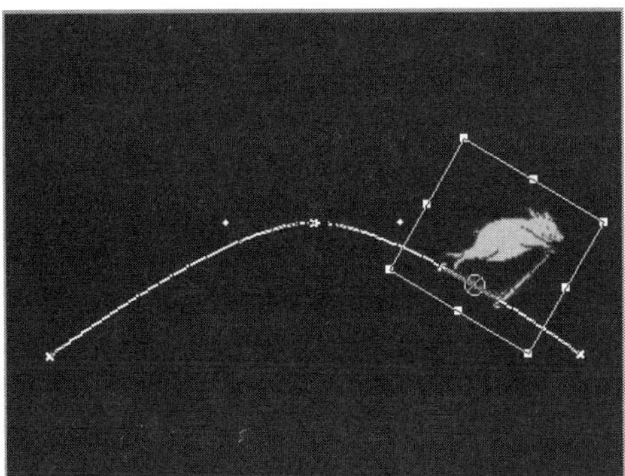

Figure 10.112 Ease Out smoothes the outgoing rate of change. You can use it to simulate gradual acceleration out of a keyframe. Setting the second keyframe to Ease Out makes the pig gradually accelerate as it leaves the keyframe.

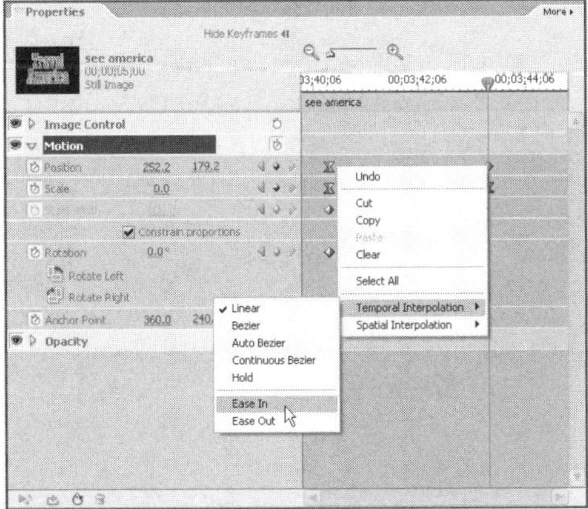

Figure 10.113 Right-click a selected keyframe, and choose an option from the context menu.

Ease Out: The property value's rate of change accelerates from, or eases out of, the selected keyframe and then decelerates into, or eases into, the following keyframe (**Figure 10.112**). Contrast this to the auto or continuous Bézier option, which affects both the incoming and outgoing interpolation.

To set a keyframe's interpolation method:

- In either the Properties panel or the Monitor panel, right-click a selected keyframe; in the context menu, choose Temporal Interpolation, and select an option (**Figure 10.113**):
  - Linear
  - Bézier
  - Auto Bézier
  - Continuous Bézier
  - Hold
  - Ease In
  - Ease Out

✔ Tips

- Only spatial effect properties include both Spatial and Temporal interpolation options. Other property values have Temporal interpolation options only. Therefore, the context menu omits the Spatial Interpolation and Temporal Interpolation options, and lists the Temporal Interpolation options in the main context menu.
- It's possible to view and adjust a property value's interpolation in a clip's property graph in the timeline (its rubberband). You can learn more about this advanced set of techniques in the Adobe Premiere Elements User Guide and Help System.

Standard Effect Categories

Standard effects, or filters, are organized into categorized folders. The following sections summarize the types of filters you'll find in each folder.

Adjust filters

You may already be familiar with the effects in this category from working with Adobe Photoshop or similar image-editing software. One critical difference between these programs and Premiere Elements is that Premiere Elements' Adjust filters are nondestructive. As you learned at the beginning of the book, nothing you do in Premiere Elements alters source files.

Blur and Sharpen filters

Blur filters cause an image to appear softer and out of focus, whereas Sharpen filters make an image appear crisper, with more defined edges.

Channel filters

Channel filters manipulate the individual channels of an image (R, G, B, and alpha) or their resulting color values (hue, saturation, and luminance).

Distort filters

Filters in the Distort category are designed to shift pixels to deform images. But as usual, don't let the category's name limit the way you use these filters; often, a distortion may appear quite natural.

Note that the Transform effect resides in this folder—not the Transform folder. The Transform filter allows you to apply fixed effects (position, rotation, and so on) to a clip at the effect stage of rendering. See the sidebar "Subverting the Render Order" for details.

GPU

Filters in the GPU category depend on their namesake, your computer's Graphics Processing Unit, to process particularly complex effects (such as 3D effects). To find out the minimum system requirements for GPU effects, see Adobe's documentation.

Image Control filters

Image Control filters change the color values in a clip's image. Most of them will be familiar to you from other programs, and their controls are fairly straightforward.

Keying filters

Keying filters let you *key out* parts of an image, or make them transparent, based on the clip's existing alpha channel, on its luminance, on its chrominance, or on a separate image that defines the alpha channel's matte. You can also make these keying filters more effective by employing a *garbage matte*—a filter that crops out extraneous edges of an image.

Perspective filters

Perspective filters imply dimensionality in clips (or elements within a clip). Although the Perspective filters give the impression of three dimensions, they aren't true 3D effects (which are processed according to a 3D spatial model).

Pixelate filters

Videographers and editors often seek to conceal or diminish the blocky, pixilated nature of the video image. Pixelate filters, on the other hand, emphasize pixels and reduce detail in order to create a stylized effect.

Render filters

Unlike filters that modify existing pixels, effects in this category generate their own elements.

Stylize filters

The Stylize category encompasses a range of filters used to make images abstract or to impart a distinctive visual character.

Time filters

The Time category contains effects that manipulate the playback timing of a clip's frames. The Echo filter retains video frames, causing moving objects in a clip—or a moving clip itself—to leave a trail of images. The Posterize Time filter reduces a clip's frame rate, making motion look choppier (as in an old movie or time-lapse footage).

Transform filters

A clip's—opacity and motion properties are often referred to collectively as *transform properties*. In the case of filters, however, *transform* is used more loosely and includes filters like Camera View, which simulates the viewfinder data in a camcorder; and Vertical Hold, which resembles a badly adjusted television set. Oddly enough, the Transform filter resides in the Distort folder.

Keying

In contrast to fading, *keying* makes only certain parts of a clip transparent. You encountered one form of keying in Chapter 9, "Creating Titles," where you learned that empty areas in a title become transparent automatically. Similarly, any areas of the screen left empty when you move a clip using a motion effect also become transparent automatically. This way, it's easy to create a picture-in-picture or split-screen effect. In both cases, Premiere Elements generates an alpha channel for the empty areas and applies an *alpha key* to make areas corresponding with the alpha channel transparent. Premiere Elements also applies an alpha key to imported clips that contain an alpha channel.

Other key types must be added manually. They make parts of an image transparent based on other factors, such as brightness or color.

11

Export

At last: it's time to share your creation with the world.

When you're shooting video, miniDV is the format of choice; but when you watch movies, most people prefer DVD. With Premiere Elements and a DVD burner, you can present your movies on a DVD, and they can even have a fully functional menu with scene selections.

Of course, you can also export video from Premiere Elements *to* a DV tape just as easily as you captured footage *from* a DV tape. Use the result as your project's master tape for dubbing to other formats or for safekeeping.

In addition, you can export a stand-alone movie file for use on a CD-ROM, for viewing on the Web, or to incorporate into a multimedia presentation. In this case, the format options are as varied as the presentation media. Moreover, the options controlling the movie file's characteristics and compatibility can be daunting. But again, Premiere Elements simplifies the process by providing a number of presets, allowing you to pick the format designed for your needs with the click of a mouse.

Finally, you can export other useful files—most notably, audio and still-image files.

This chapter guides you through each of these options and closes with your movie's premiere.

Export Options

This chapter covers the most common export goals. Here's an overview of the options.

DVD

If you have a DVD burner attached to or installed in your computer, you can record your project to a DVD that plays on a standard DVD player. Premiere Elements' DVD Layout panel includes templates that make creating interactive DVD menus a breeze.

Videotape

You can record your masterpiece to a DV tape just as easily as you captured footage from a DV tape. The same IEEE 1394 (FireWire, iLink) or USB 2 cable will deliver audio and video—this time *from* your computer *to* your camcorder.

Movie files

If you want to export a movie file, your choices become more varied and complex. You choose the combination of options best suited for the purpose you have in mind. Do you want to play the movie from a CD-ROM, present it on the Web, or use it in another program (such as a presentation or multimedia program)? Fortunately, Premiere Elements offers a number of preset settings tailored to the most common output goals.

Still images and audio-only files

In addition to exporting the entire edited sequence to DVD or tape, users commonly use a few other export options.

You can export a still image from any frame of the video. An Export button is conveniently located in the Monitor panel—in both the Clip and the Timeline views. This makes it easy to export a still for use as a freeze frame in the sequence or for printing.

You can also export an audio-only file. For example, you might want to use just the audio track of an interview to use as a voiceover; an audio file without the video track is significantly smaller than the original.

About Creating DVDs

Using Premiere Elements and a DVD burner, you can create DVDs that play in just about any DVD player. Before getting to the tasks, let's overview the process.

Autoplay and menus

The DVD you create in Premiere Elements can work in either of two ways, depending on the choice you specify:

AutoPlay DVD creates a DVD that plays from the beginning when you insert the DVD into the player. It contains no navigational menus for cuing to scenes; but naturally, you can use your player's standard playback controls, such as Play, Stop, Rewind, and Fast Forward.

DVD with Menus creates a more full-featured DVD, including a menu with buttons that cue to the scenes you specify. In Premiere Elements, you specify scenes (also called *chapters*) by setting DVD markers in the timeline; you create the DVD menu by customizing one of the numerous DVD menu templates in the DVD Layout panel.

DVD menus

Making a DVD that includes a scene menu involves two simple procedures, which you can perform in any order:

Add DVD Markers—DVD markers work a lot like timeline markers (see Chapter 6, "Editing in the Timeline"). But rather than designate important points in the sequence for editing, they specify points in the sequence used in the DVD's menu. Specifically, they assign the location of the main menu, scenes (chapters), or points at which the DVD returns to the main menu. You can specify DVD markers manually in the Timeline panel. Or, you can have Premiere Elements set scene markers automatically, either from the main menu bar or from the DVD Layout panel.

Customize a DVD Template—Using Premiere Elements' DVD Layout panel, you can select from a wide variety of DVD menu layouts designed with numerous themes in mind: Entertainment, Birthday, New Baby, and so on. DVD scene markers are translated into DVD menu buttons automatically, but you can adjust them as needed. Before burning, you can test-drive the DVD using the Preview DVD window, to ensure that everything looks and works just right.

DVD

DVD stands for *Digital Versatile Disc* or *Digital Video Disc*. A typical DVD is single-sided and single-layered. That is, its data is encoded on one side of the disk and on a single layer, or at a proscribed depth from its surface. Such DVDs can contain up to 4.7 GB of data, or about 2 hours of high-quality video in a DVD-compatible format. (Contrast that to a CD, which holds up to 650 or 700 MB, depending on the disk). For most folks, that data is in the form of a copy-protected movie you buy or rent from a video store.

With a DVD burner and the proper software, you can record any kind of data to a recordable DVD. Premiere Elements helps get your movies on a DVD in the form that can be understood by just about any DVD player.

DVD Markers

DVD markers work something like the timeline markers you learned about in Chapter 6. You can set, clear, and cue to them using comparable menu commands (**Figure 11.1**). Therefore, those procedures won't be reviewed here.

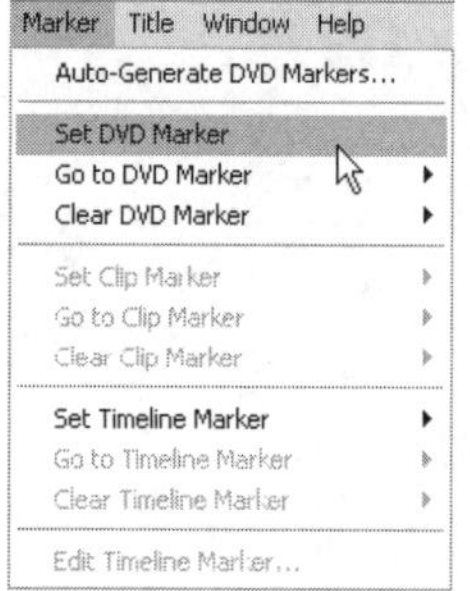

Figure 11.1 You can set, clear, and cue to DVD markers using menu commands comparable to those for timeline markers.

Unlike timeline markers, DVD markers don't appear in the time ruler of the Monitor panel's Timeline view; they only appear in the Timeline panel's time ruler. DVD markers look similar to timeline markers, but instead of appearing in the upper half of the Timeline panel's time ruler, they appear in the lower half, in the same area as the work area bar (**Figure 11.2**).

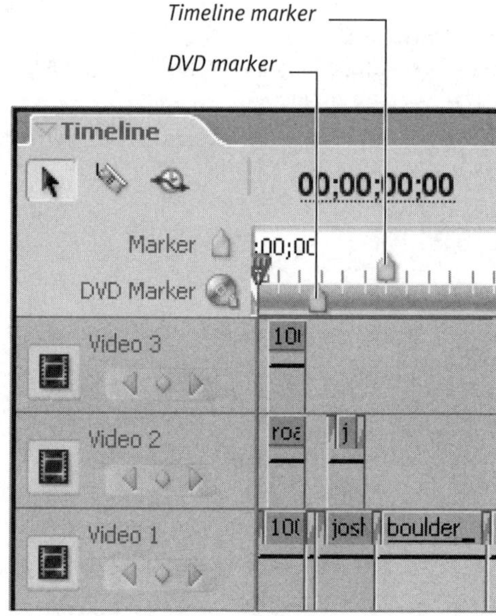

Figure 11.2 DVD markers are similar in appearance to timeline markers, but are lower in the timeline's time ruler and are color coded according to function. They don't appear in the Monitor panel's time ruler.

In contrast to timeline markers, DVD markers create links to buttons in a DVD menu you create using Premiere Elements' DVD Layout panel. The color of a DVD marker corresponds to its function:

Green—Scene marker

Blue—Main menu marker

Red—Stop marker

Figure 11.3 Position the timeline's CTI, and click the DVD Marker button.

Setting DVD markers

You can add DVD markers in the Timeline panel manually, using the DVD Marker button. Alternatively, Premiere Elements can set scene markers automatically, placing them at points that correspond to cuts in the sequence, or at the interval you specify. The Auto-Generate DVD Scene Markers command is available in the Timeline panel and in the DVD Layout panel.

To add DVD markers manually:

1. Set the timeline's CTI to the frame you want to mark.
2. In the Timeline panel, click the DVD Marker button (**Figure 11.3**).

   The DVD Marker dialog box appears. The video frame at the marker appears as a thumbnail image in the dialog box.
3. Enter a name for the marker.

   DVD scene markers' names are transferred to chapter button names automatically.

continues on next page

4. In the Marker Type pull-down menu, specify the type of marker you want to set (**Figure 11.4**):

   Scene Marker—Creates a Scene button in the DVD's scene menu, and appears as a green marker in the Timeline panel

   Main Menu Marker—Creates a button on the DVD's main menu, and appears as a blue marker in the Timeline panel

   Stop Marker—Causes the DVD to return to the main menu at the specified time, and appears as a red marker in the Timeline panel

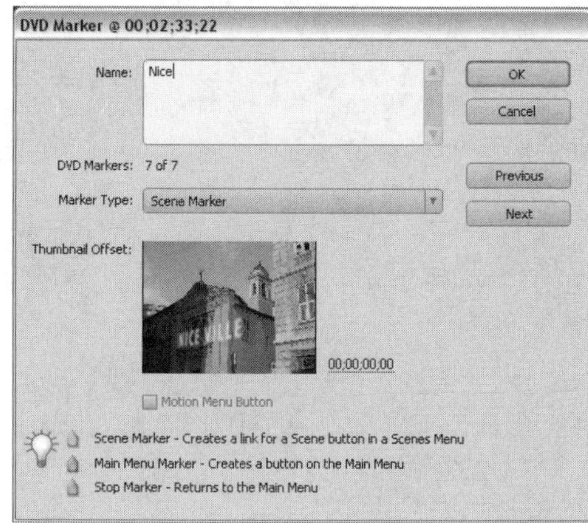

Figure 11.4 In the DVD Marker dialog box, name the marker and specify its type.

5. If the video frame at the marker isn't representative of the scene it's meant to designate, adjust the value for Thumbnail Offset.

   You can scrub the value under the thumbnail image or select it and enter a new value, so that the thumbnail image shows the frame you want (**Figure 11.5**).

6. Click OK to close the dialog box.

   The specified type of marker appears at the CTI in the timeline.

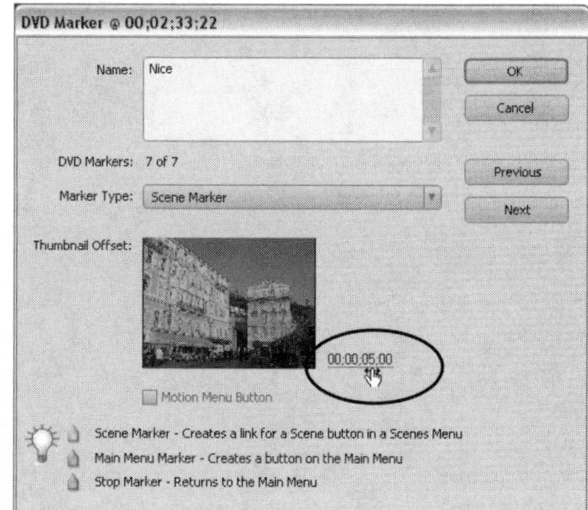

Figure 11.5 Adjusting the Thumbnail Offset changes the image used for the scene marker in the DVD menu.

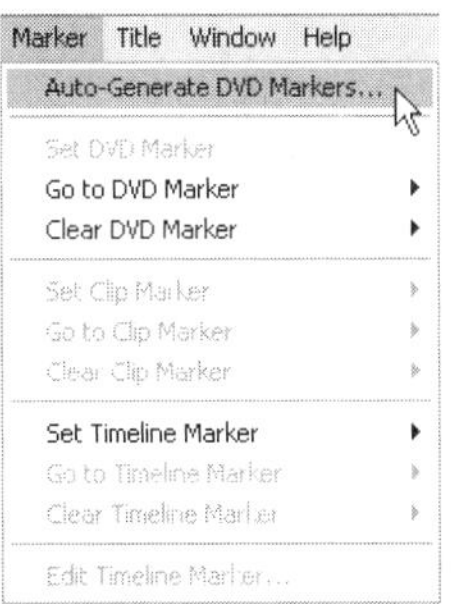

Figure 11.6 You can set DVD scene markers automatically by selecting the timeline and choosing Marker › Auto-Generate DVD Markers...

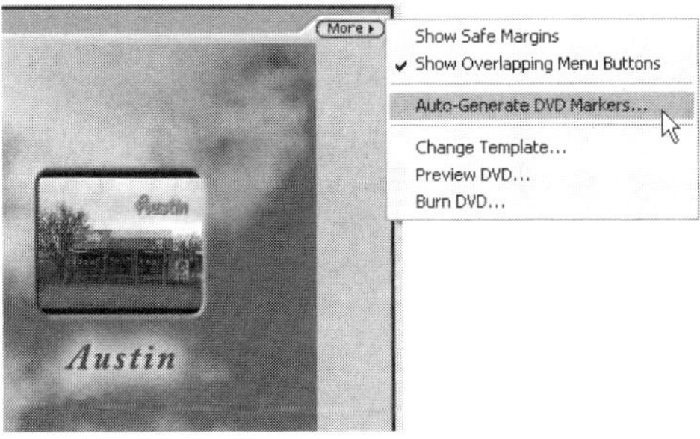

Figure 11.7 ...or by choosing the same command in the DVD Layout panel's More pull-down menu.

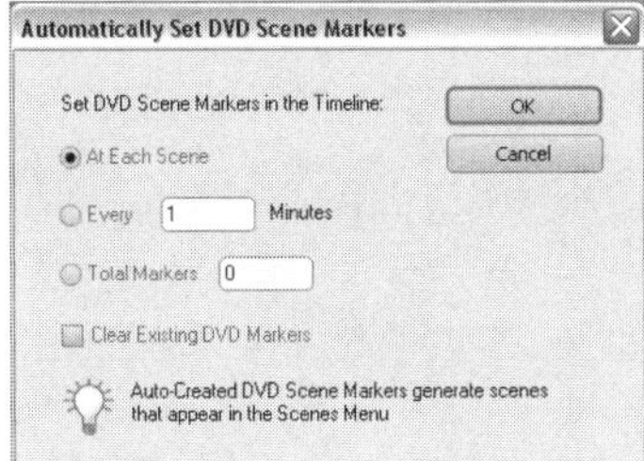

Figure 11.8 In the Automatically Set DVD Scene Markers dialog box, specify how often scene markers appear.

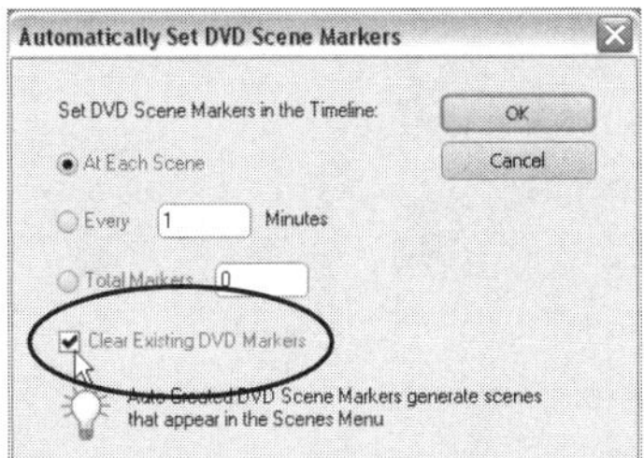

Figure 11.9 Check Clear Existing DVD Markers to remove DVD markers already in the timeline.

To add DVD scene markers automatically:

1. *Do either of the following:*
   - ▲ With the Timeline panel selected, choose Marker > Auto-Generate DVD Markers (**Figure 11.6**).
   - ▲ In the DVD Layout panel, choose Auto-Generate DVD Markers in the More pull-down menu (**Figure 11.7**).

   The Automatically Set DVD Scene Markers dialog box appears.
2. *Select one of the following* (**Figure 11.8**):

   At Each Scene—Sets a scene marker at each cut in the sequence

   Every *x* Minutes—Sets a scene marker at intervals of the number of minutes you specify

   Total Markers—Sets the number of scene markers you specify, spacing them evenly over the total duration of the sequence
3. To remove scene markers already in the timeline, check Clear Existing DVD Markers (**Figure 11.9**).
4. Click OK to close the dialog box.

   The DVD scene markers appear in the timeline according to the options you specified and dictate chapter breaks when you use the DVD Layout panel.

Selecting a DVD Template

In Premiere Elements, you base your DVD menu on one of any number of templates, much like the title templates you use to create titles in the Titler (see Chapter 9, "Creating Titles"). Some DVD menu templates even include moving elements, animated backgrounds, and buttons.

Each template includes a layout for the DVD's main menu page and for the pages that contain buttons for skipping to scenes (aka *chapters*).

You can switch to another DVD menu template any time before you burn the DVD. Or if you want to depart from the template's preset designs, you can completely customize it, as explained in later sections.

To select a DVD template:

1. In the taskbar, click the DVD button DVD (**Figure 11.10**).

   The DVD Templates window appears.

2. Select "Apply a Template for a DVD with Menus."

3. In the Theme pull-down menu, select a category of templates to choose from (**Figure 11.11**).

   Templates in the selected category appear in the main panel of the DVD Templates dialog box.

Figure 11.10 Click the taskbar's DVD button.

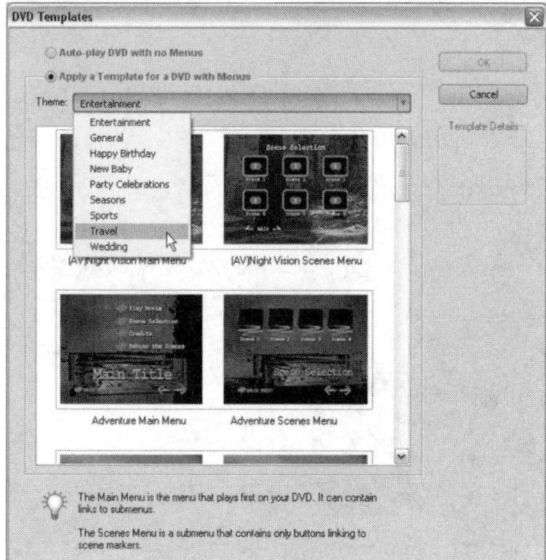

Figure 11.11 In the DVD Templates window, select "Apply a Template for a DVD with Menus," and choose a category in the Theme pull-down menu.

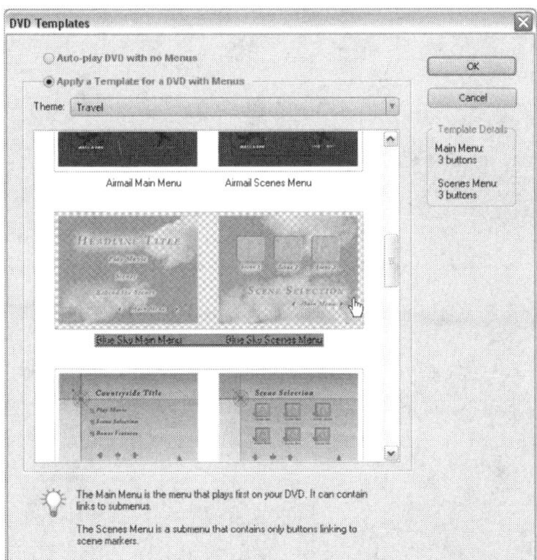

Figure 11.12 Select the particular template you want from among the templates in the theme category.

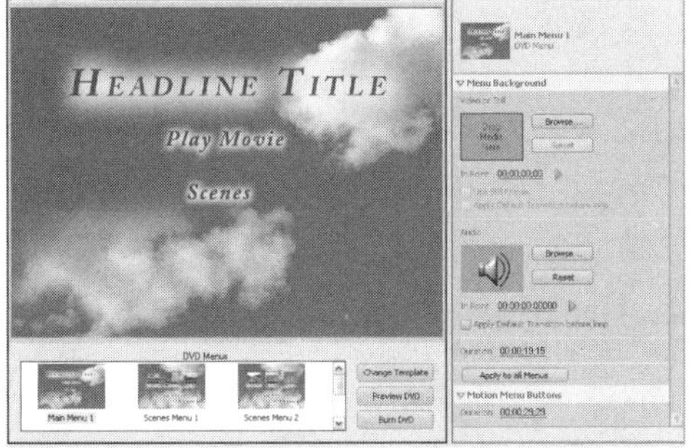

Figure 11.13 The template you select appears in the DVD Layout panel, and controls appear in the Properties panel.

Figure 11.14 You can change the template at any time by clicking the DVD Layout panel's Change Template button.

4. Use the scroll bar to review the templates in the selected category.

   The thumbnail image on the left shows the template's main menu; the image on the right depicts a Scenes menu.

5. Select the menu template you want (**Figure 11.12**).

   The Template Details area of the dialog box describes the number of buttons on each page of the template.

6. Click OK to close the dialog box.

   The DVD Layout menu appears and controls appear in the Properties panel (**Figure 11.13**). Scenes in the Scenes Menu pages of the template use the name and thumbnail images of DVD scene markers in the sequence. Otherwise, they use generic scene names, such as "scene 1," "scene 2," and so on.

To change the current DVD template:

1. In the DVD Layout panel, click the Change Template button (**Figure 11.14**).

2. In the DVD Templates dialog box, specify the theme and template you want to use, and click OK.

   For a full explanation, see the previous task, "To select a DVD template."

✔ Tip

- If you set DVD scene markers ahead of time, they'll be linked to the scene buttons once you select the template you want. Otherwise, you can use the Auto-Generate DVD Scene Marker command, and name the buttons in the DVD Layout panel.

Customizing a DVD Menu

Premiere Elements creates a DVD menu according to the template you select, using the DVD scene markers you set to name the buttons and create corresponding thumbnail images. If you like the template and if you named the buttons ahead of time, then you're ready to preview and burn a DVD (and you can skip this section). But if you want to customize the DVD menu, read on.

The DVD Layout panel allows you to select and modify text and images, in much the same way the Titler does. And as usual, the Properties panel automatically switches to the controls you need for the task at hand—in this case, setting a DVD menu's background image, audio, and text attributes.

You can specify a still image or video clip as the background image. The menu can use a video background's linked audio or no audio, or you can specify a separate audio file. Video and audio loops for the duration you specify, up to a maximum of 30 seconds. You can even specify whether menu buttons use a static thumbnail image or play a video loop at the scene marker.

To view DVD menu pages:

- In the DVD Layout panel, click the page in the DVD Menus area (**Figure 11.15**).

  If necessary, use the scroll bars to make later pages visible.

To edit text in DVD menu pages:

1. In the DVD Menus area of the DVD Layout panel, select the page you want to view.

   The selected page appears in the main image area of the DVD Layout panel.

2. Double-click the text you want to edit (**Figure 11.16**).

   A Change Text dialog box appears; in it, the current text message is highlighted.

Figure 11.15 Clicking the thumbnail of a menu page makes it appear in the window's large image area.

Figure 11.16 In the large image area, double-click the text you want to edit.

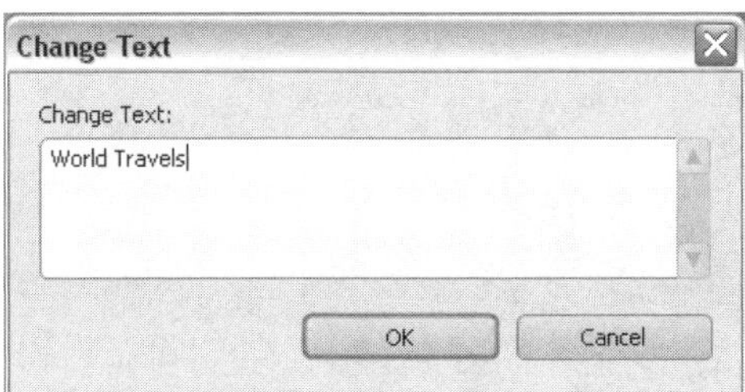

Figure 11.17 In the Change Text dialog box, enter the text you want, and click OK.

Figure 11.18 In the DVD Layout panel, the menu button uses the text you entered.

3. Enter the text you want, and click OK (**Figure 11.17**).

   The edited text appears in the DVD Layout panel (**Figure 11.18**).

4. To change text attributes, such as font, font size, color, etc., specify the options you want in the text (**Figure 11.19**).

✔ Tips

- You can reopen a DVD scene marker's dialog box and edit its settings by double-clicking the marker's icon in the Timeline panel.
- Generally, DVD menu buttons can only accommodate relatively short labels. Long labels tend to overlap with other objects on screen (and prevent buttons from operating properly); reducing the text size can render it illegible. So, instead of labeling a DVD scene, say, "Traveling Around Europe," try simply "Europe" or "Eurotrip."

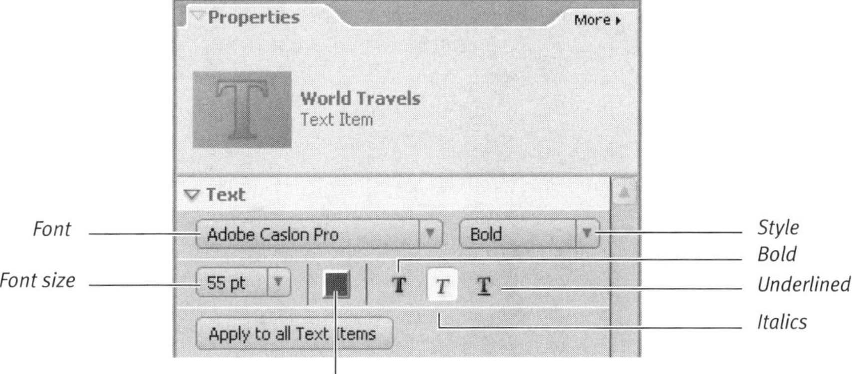

Figure 11.19 Specify any changes to the text attributes you want.

To specify a custom menu background:

1. Set DVD markers and select a DVD template.

   For detailed instructions, consult tasks in the sections "DVD Markers," "Selecting a DVD Template," and "Customizing a DVD Menu," earlier in this chapter.

2. In the DVD Layout panel, select the menu you want to customize (**Figure 11.20**).

3. In the Properties panel, *do any of the following*:

   ▲ To specify a background image, click the Browse button in the Video or Still area of the Properties panel (Figure 11.21).

   ▲ To specify an audio loop, click the Browse button in the Audio area of the Properties panel.

   A Select Background Media dialog box appears.

Figure 11.20 Select the menu page you want to modify in the DVD Layout panel.

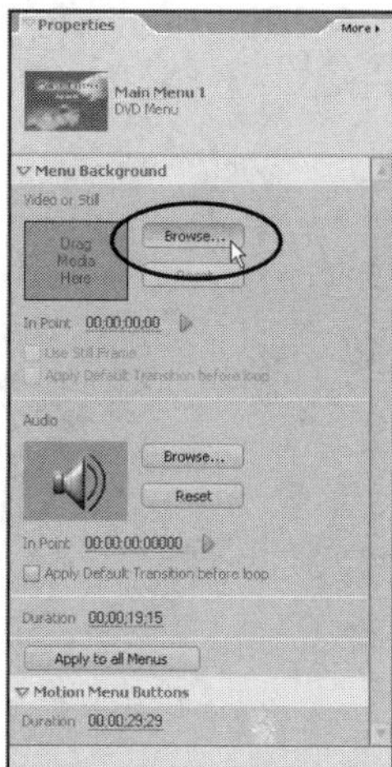

Figure 11.21 In the Properties panel, click the Browse button for the type of file you want.

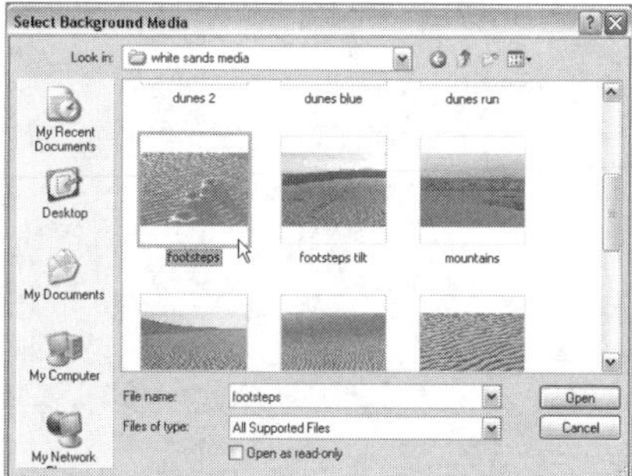

Figure 11.22 Select the file you want in the Select Background Media dialog box.

Figure 11.23 The selected file replaces the template's background image or audio for the selected menu page. A linked file inserts both video and audio into the template (shown here).

Figure 11.24 Click Apply to all Menus to make the background appear in all menu pages.

4. In the Select Background Media dialog box, select the media file you want to use and then click Open (**Figure 11.22**).

   The selected file's image or audio is applied to the selected menu page. Selecting a video file with a linked audio track adds both tracks to the menu page (**Figure 11.23**).

5. To apply the custom file to all menus, click the Apply to all Menus button (**Figure 11.24**).

   Video or still images appear as the menu background for all menus in the DVD layout, and when you preview or burn the DVD.

6. If you select a video or audio file (or a file with linked video and audio), specify options explained in the task "To set video and audio menu background options," later in this chapter.

To reset the menu background to the default:

1. Choose a DVD template and specify a custom background image.
2. In the Properties panel, *do any of the following*:
   - ▲ To reset a custom image background, click Reset in the panel's Video or Still area (**Figure 11.25**).
   - ▲ To reset a custom audio file, click Reset in the panel's Audio area.

   Depending on your choice, the menu's reverts to the template's initial image background or audio loop.

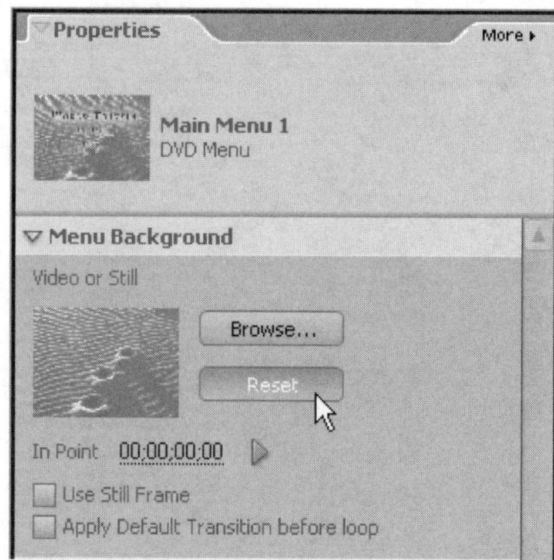

Figure 11.25 Click Reset to revert to the template's original image background or audio.

Figure 11.26 Set a video or audio background's starting point by setting the In point or by using the Play/Pause button.

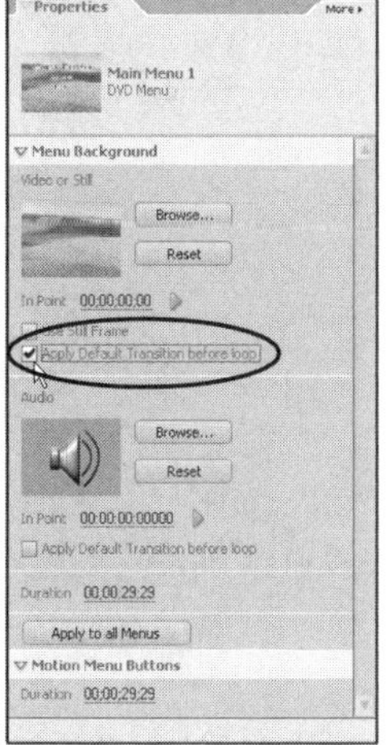

Figure 11.27 Selecting Apply Default Transition Before Loop can make a video or audio loop seem less abrupt.

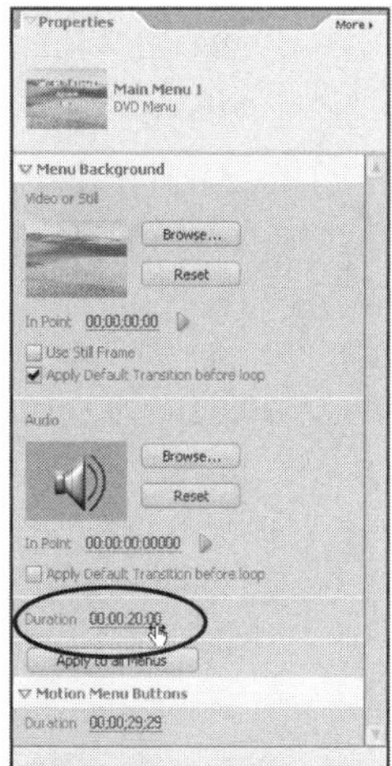

Figure 11.28 For Duration, set the duration of the looping background, up to 30 seconds.

To set video and audio menu background options:

1. Select a DVD menu template and specify a custom video or audio file for a menu background.

2. To set the video or audio file's starting point, do any of the following in the corresponding area of the Properties panel:
   - ▲ Set a value for the media file's In point.
   - ▲ Click the Play button to play the video thumbnail or audio file, and then click the Pause button when the file reaches the starting point you want (**Figure 11.26**).

   The button toggles between Play and Pause. Setting a starting point for a video file with linked audio sets the linked audio's starting point.

3. To add a transition at the beginning of the video or audio background, select Apply Default Transition Before Loop (**Figure 11.27**).

   See the task "To specify the default transition," in Chapter 7.

4. Specify a value for Duration (**Figure 11.28**).

   The video and audio loops after playing for the duration you specified. The maximum value is 30 seconds.

To use a single video frame as a menu background:

1. Select a DVD menu template and specify a custom video file for a menu background.
2. In the Video or Still area of the Properties panel, *do any of the following:*
   - ▲ Set a value for the media file's In point.
   - ▲ Click the Play button to play the video thumbnail or audio file, and then click the Pause button when the file reaches the starting point you want.

   The button toggles between Play and Pause. Setting a starting point for a video file with linked audio sets the linked audio's starting point.
3. Select Use Still Frame (**Figure 11.29**).

   The frame at the In point you specified is used as the menu background.
4. To use the specified frame for all menu backgrounds, click Apply to all Menus.

Figure 11.29 To use a single frame of a video clip as the background image, set the In point and select Use Still Frame.

Figure 11.30 Select the menu containing the buttons you want to customize in the DVD Layout panel.

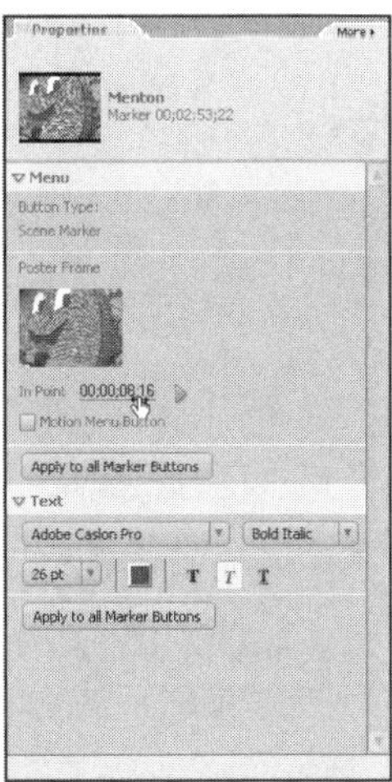

Figure 11.31 Set the button's starting point by setting an In point value or by using the Play/Pause button.

To customize DVD menu buttons:

1. Set DVD markers and select a DVD template.

   For detailed instructions, consult tasks in the sections, "DVD Markers," "Selecting a DVD Template," and "Customizing a DVD Menu," earlier in this chapter.

2. In the DVD Layout panel, select the menu containing the menu you want to customize and then select the menu button (**Figure 11.30**).

   The Properties panel includes controls for customizing menu buttons.

3. Specify the button's thumbnail image or starting frame to *do either of the following* (**Figure 11.31**):

   ▲ Set a value for the media file's In point.

   ▲ Click the Play button to play the video thumbnail or audio file, and then click the Pause button when the file reaches the frame you want.

   The frame becomes the button thumbnail (for still menu buttons) or the starting frame (for motion menu buttons).

continues on next page

4. To make the thumbnail play as a video loop, select Motion Menu Button (**Figure 11.32**).

5. To apply the same In Point and Motion Menu Button setting to all buttons in the DVD menus, click Apply to all Marker Buttons.

   The In point setting is expressed as an offset from each button's initial frame, as determined by the position of its corresponding DVD marker.

6. To deselect the menu button, click an empty area in the DVD Layout panel.

7. If you specified a motion menu in Step 4, specify a Duration in the Motion Menu Buttons area of the Properties panel (**Figure 11.33**).

   The button's thumbnail video plays for duration you specify (up to 30 seconds) before looping.

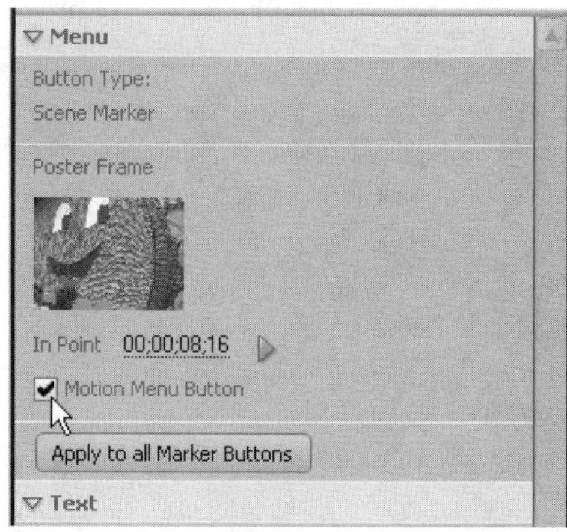

Figure 11.32 Select Motion Menu Button to have the menu button's thumbnail play as a video loop.

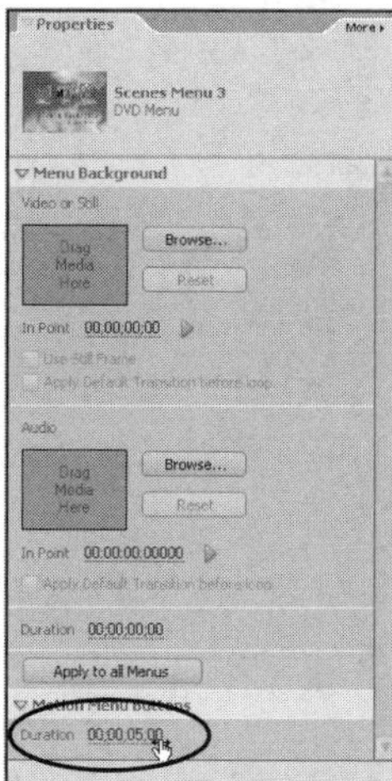

Figure 11.33 With no buttons selected, specify a Duration for Motion Menu Buttons in the Properties panel.

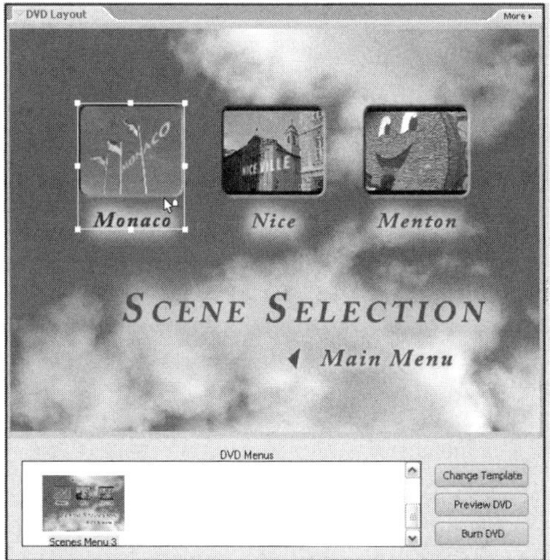

Figure 11.34 Select the menu page and menu button you want to modify.

To modify menu button text attributes:

1. Set DVD markers and select a DVD template.

   For detailed instructions, consult tasks in the sections, "DVD Markers," "Selecting a DVD Template," and "Customizing a DVD Menu," earlier in this chapter.

2. In the DVD Layout panel, select the menu containing the menu you want to customize and then select the menu button (**Figure 11.34**).

   The Properties panel includes controls for customizing menu buttons.

continues on next page

3. To modify the text attributes of marker buttons, *do any of the following* (**Figure 11.35**):
   - ▲ Specify a font in the font pull-down menu.
   - ▲ Specify a style in the type style pull-down menu.
   - ▲ Specify a font size in the font size pull-down menu.
   - ▲ Specify a font color by clicking the color swatch to open a color picker dialog box.
   - ▲ Make the text bold, italic, or underlined by selecting the corresponding button.
4. To apply the text attributes you specified to all marker buttons, click Apply to all Marker Buttons.

   The options you specified in Step 3 are applied to all menu buttons (**Figure 11.36**).

Figure 11.35 Specify the text attributes you want in the Properties panel.

Figure 11.36 The text attributes you selected are reflected in the DVD Layout panel.

✔ Tips

- Consider using Premiere Elements to edit a clip especially for a motion menu background or audio loop. If you're feeling ambitious, you can try creating a "seamless" video loop by animating graphics in Premiere Elements or a program like After Effects. Or try recording or editing a seamless audio loop.
- Like other kinds of stock footage, seamless video and audio loops are also available through third-party vendors.

Figure 11.37 In the DVD Layout panel, click the Preview DVD button.

Figure 11.38 The Preview DVD window appears.

Previewing a DVD

Before you record, or *burn*, a DVD, you should confirm that the menu is working the way you want: scene buttons are named correctly, use the proper name, and jump to the proper point in the sequence when you click them. The Preview DVD window emulates how the finished DVD will play on a standard DVD player and includes a comparable set of playback and navigational controls.

To preview a DVD:

1. In the DVD Layout panel, click the Preview DVD button (**Figure 11.37**).

   The Preview DVD window appears (**Figure 11.38**).

2. Use the controls to test the menu's operation before creating the DVD (**Figure 11.39**).

3. Close the Preview DVD window to return to the DVD Layout panel.

   In the DVD Layout panel, you can edit the button names or the placement of markers, change the template, or continue to burn the sequence to DVD (as explained in the following section).

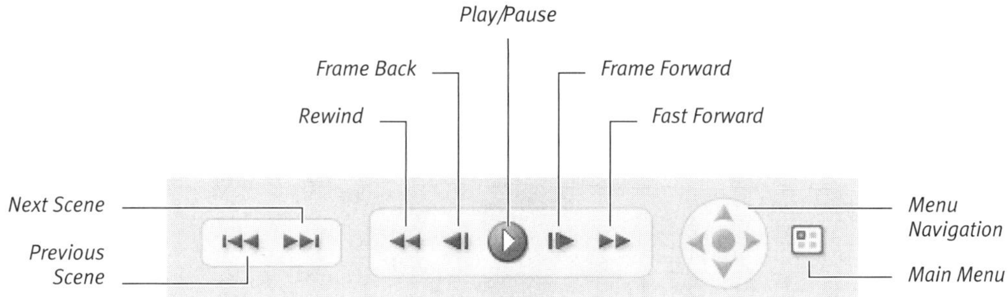

Figure 11.39 The Preview DVD window's controls emulate those on a standard DVD player.

Burning to DVD

If your system is equipped with a DVD burner, you can export your sequence to DVD much as you'd export to tape.

As you learned in the section "About Creating DVDs," earlier in this chapter, you can burn a no-frills DVD that plays when you insert it into a DVD player, or a DVD complete with a navigational menu. Either way, the process is the same when burning from the DVD Layout panel.

This section covers how to burn to DVD recordable media directly, using a connected DVD burner. You can also "burn" to a folder, creating a DVD-compatible file (in the MPEG-2 format) that can be burned to a DVD using any DVD authoring software (say, Adobe Encore DVD). But this chapter sticks to using the simple, preset method—which, after all, is one of the nice things about using Premiere Elements.

To burn a DVD:

1. In the DVD Layout panel, click the Burn DVD button (**Figure 11.40**).

   The Burn DVD dialog box appears.

2. Choose the appropriate "Burn to" option (**Figure 11.41**):

   Disc—Records the DVD to blank DVD recordable media, using a connected burner

   Folder—Creates a DVD-compatible MPEG2 file on your hard disk

3. Enter a name for the DVD.

4. For Burner Location, choose the DVD burner you want to use (**Figure 11.42**).

   If your DVD burner doesn't appear in the pull-down menu, click the Rescan button.

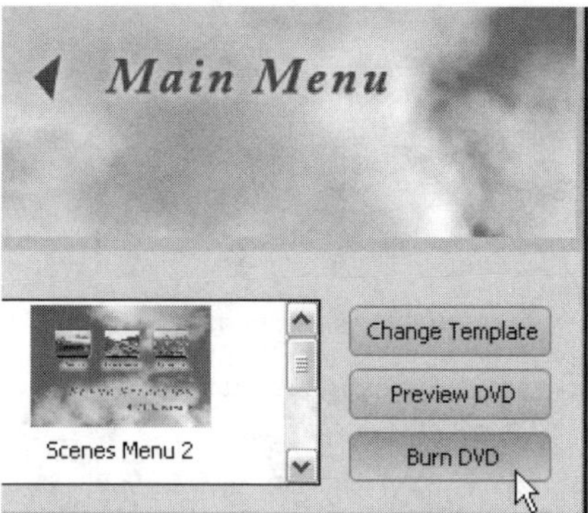

Figure 11.40 In the DVD Layout panel, click the Burn DVD button.

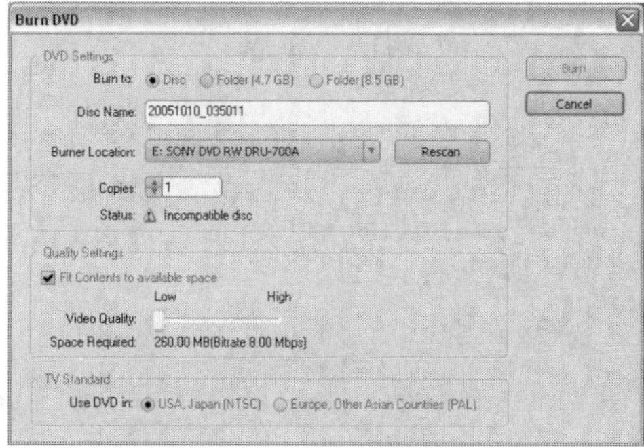

Figure 11.41 In the Burn DVD dialog box, select Disc to burn to a connected DVD burner. Otherwise, you can select one of the Folder options to create a file on your hard drive.

Figure 11.42 Choose the DVD burner you want to use in the Burner Location pull-down menu.

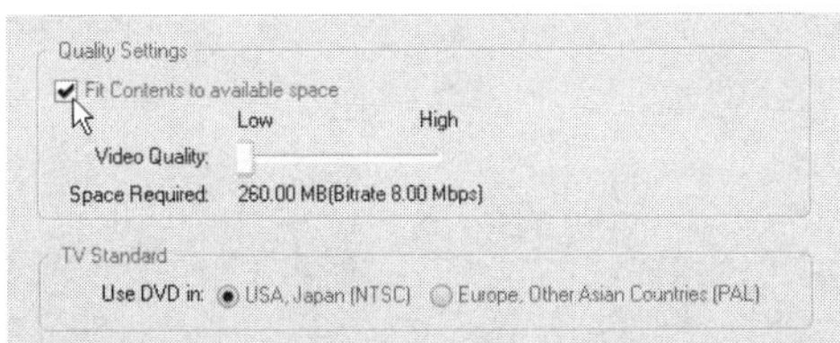

Figure 11.43 Check "Fit Contents to available space" to have Premiere Elements adjust the exported file's quality—and thereby its size—automatically.

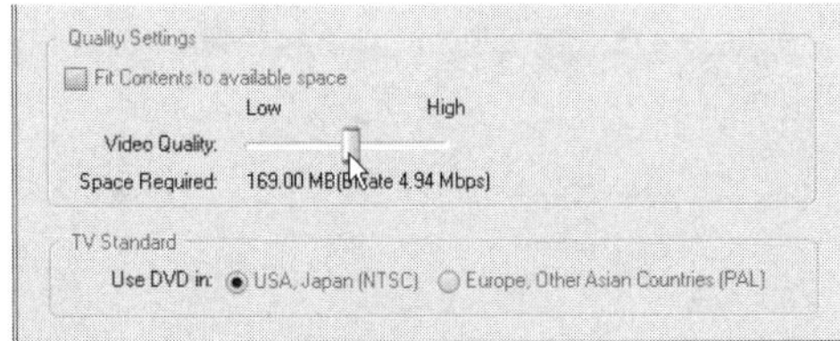

Figure 11.44 Alternatively, uncheck the option, and adjust the quality and file size manually.

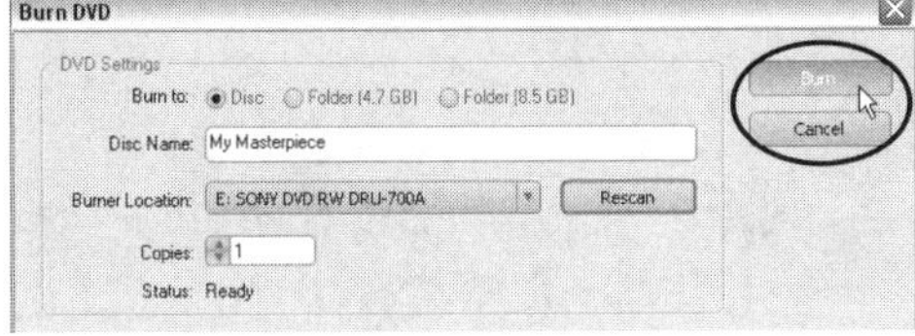

Figure 11.45 Click Burn to start.

5. To scan the DVD recordable media for errors before burning data onto it, check Test Media Before Burning.
6. For Copies, specify the number of DVDs you want to record during this export session.

   Premiere Elements prompts you to insert a new, blank DVD when necessary.
7. For Quality Settings, *do one of the following:*
   - ▲ Check "Fit Contents to available space" to set the compression quality automatically so that the data fits onto the DVD media (**Figure 11.43**).
   - ▲ Uncheck "Fit Contents to available space," and use the Video Quality slider to set the compression manually (**Figure 11.44**).

   As you drag the Video Quality slider, note the value displayed for Space Required. Standard (single-layer) DVD-recordable media holds 4.7 GB of data.
8. Select the TV Standard compatible with the players on which you want to play the DVD:
   - ▲ USA, Japan (NTSC)
   - ▲ Europe, Other Asian Countries (PAL)
9. Click the Burn button to record the DVD (**Figure 11.45**).

   If you're burning to a DVD, first make sure there is a blank recordable DVD in the burner.

continues on next page

✔ Tips

- Unless you really need to take manual control over video quality, checking "Fit Contents to available space" should yield good results.
- If the sequence runs much over 90 minutes or so, the video quality must be reduced to fit the data onto a standard DVD recordable disk. Consider splitting an extremely long sequence into two projects and burning two DVDs instead of one.
- The File > Export menu also contains DVD and other export options not covered in this chapter. This method doesn't employ presets, requiring you to specify numerous settings. As relatively advanced options, they won't be covered here.
- As with capture, preview, and media cache files, you can specify a scratch disk for DVD encoding. As usual, choose Edit > Preferences > Scratch Disks and specify a relatively fast, capacious hard disk.

More or Less the Same? DVD+R and DVD–R

You may have noticed that DVD burners and DVD blank media (discs) come in two varieties: DVD–R and DVD+R. DVD–R (pronounced *DVD minus R*) was the first recordable DVD standard that's compatible with set-top (or stand-alone) DVD players. DVD+R (*DVD plus R*) was introduced later. Both standards have the same 4.7 GB storage capacity, share similar features, and are compatible with most DVD players. However, the DVD–R format is compatible with a slightly greater percentage of the players out there. Many manufacturers of DVD burners solve the problem of competing formats by supporting both in a single burner: DVD+/–R. Whatever format you go with, make sure your burner and your media match.

Figure 11.46 Click the taskbar's Export button, and choose To Tape.

Figure 11.47 The Export to Tape dialog box appears.

Exporting to Tape

Using the Export to Tape command, you can output video to a connected camera or deck through your IEEE 1394 or other capture device. You can export any clip you open in the Clip view or, more likely, the sequence in the Timeline view and Timeline panel. Using IEEE 1394 or add-on device control, Premiere Elements can activate your deck automatically (see the task "To set up device control" in Chapter 3).

You can even choose where on the tape to start recording, if you can provide a timecode number at the start time. To do so, however, your tape must have timecode on it, at least at the beginning of the tape. You can provide timecode by recording a little footage (say, a minute or two) with the lens cap on (if you can, disable the microphone, too). This way, Premiere Elements has some timecode to latch onto when cuing the tape automatically. (For more about timecode, see the sidebar "Timecode," in Chapter 3.)

To export to tape:

1. *Do one of the following:*
   - ▲ To export a sequence, select the Timeline panel or Monitor panel's Timeline view.
   - ▲ To export a clip, select it in the Media panel, or open a clip in the Monitor panel's Clip view.
2. In the taskbar, click the Export button, and choose To Tape in the pull-down menu (**Figure 11.46**).

   The Export to Tape dialog box opens (**Figure 11.47**).

continues on next page

3. To have Premiere Elements automatically trigger recording using device control, select Activate Recording Device, and then *specify any of the following options* (**Figure 11.48**):

   Assemble at timecode—The timecode number on the tape where you want recording to start. To use this option, the tape must already have a timecode signal. Therefore, you can't use a blank tape.

   Delay movie start by—The number of frames to delay playback after you click the OK button. Some recording devices require time between receiving the record command and the video playback from the computer.

   Preroll—The number of frames the camera or deck will rewind before the start time (the timecode you specified for the "Assemble at timecode" setting, or the tape's current position), to ensure the tape is up to speed when recording begins.

4. In the Options area of the Export to Tape dialog box, *specify any of the following* (**Figure 11.49**):

   Abort after *x* **dropped frames**—Allows you to set the minimum number of frames that fail to record before Premiere Elements halts recording. For most users, even one dropped frame is unacceptable.

   Report dropped frames—Generates a report in the event frames are dropped during export.

Figure 11.48 Select Activate Recording Device to have Premiere Elements trigger recording automatically; then specify related options.

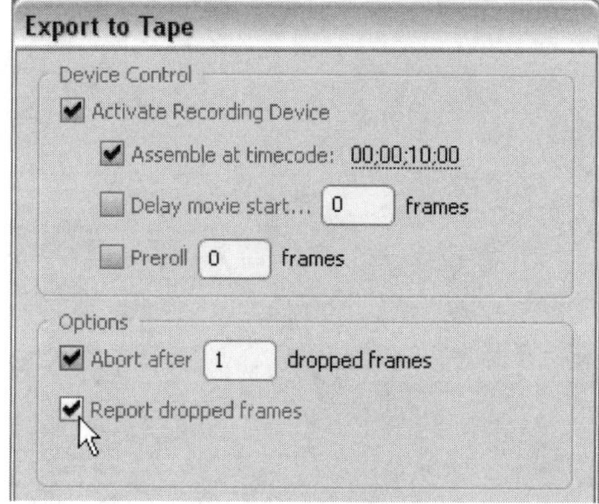

Figure 11.49 In the Options area, specify how Premiere Elements deals with dropped frames during export and whether to render audio before exporting to tape.

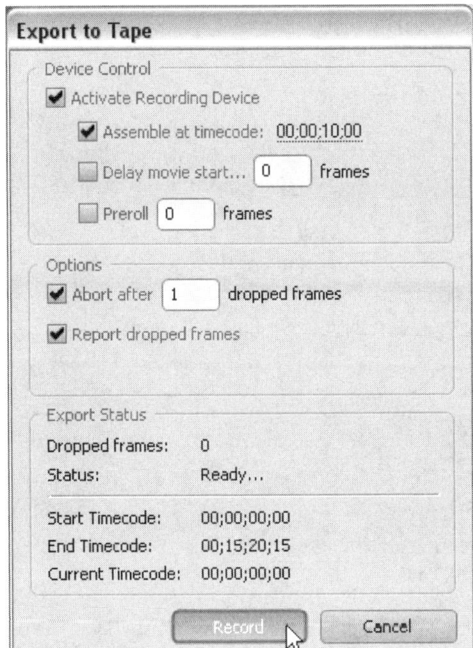

Figure 11.50 Click Record to start the export to tape, and monitor its progress in the Export Status area.

5. Click Record.

   If you're controlling the recording device manually, make sure you trigger record mode. If you selected Activate Recording Device, Premiere Elements triggers the recording device automatically. You can monitor the progress of the export in the Export Status area of the Export to Tape dialog box (**Figure 11.50**).

✔ Tips

- It's highly unlikely that you'll need to adjust the "Delay movie start by" setting, unless you're specifically directed to do so by your hardware documentation or Adobe has notified users of a known issue with your hardware.
- Even though you can leave the export process unattended, it's wise to keep an eye on it. This way, you can spot problems as they occur and export again if necessary. In addition to problems with the export, you might notice problems in the sequence itself. In any case, always double-check the tape after export, especially if you're going to show it off to family and friends (not to mention clients and colleagues) right away.

Codecs

Codec stands for *compressor/decompressor. Compressor* refers to encoding a file and is synonymous with capture and rendering. *Decompressor* refers to decoding a file and is associated with playback. *Codec* denotes a particular compression scheme—a method of compressing and decompressing a file.

Exporting for the Web

When you optimize movies for Web delivery, file size (and its conjoined twin, data rate) is the primary concern. To stream a movie, you need to limit the movie's data rate to the slowest anticipated connection speed. Even for fast Internet connections, that's a big limitation. You'll have to decide whether the loss in quality is worth the immediate playback capability.

The limitations are more forgiving for movies that can be downloaded. In this case, file size influences how long the viewer will have to wait before watching your movie. Although a *progressive download* format begins playing before the movie is fully downloaded to the viewer's hard drive, file size remains an impediment—especially if the movie is more than, say, one minute in duration.

Export for Other Programs

If you're exporting footage from Premiere Elements to use in another program, the factors you should consider depend on the format and the program. Nevertheless, you should bear in mind several common issues.

Make sure you know the file formats and compression types the program accepts. If you want to retain transparency, choose a codec that supports an alpha channel (such as Uncompressed in Windows Media, or None or Animation when exporting QuickTime). When you're exporting still frames acquired on video, be aware that video resolution translates into a mere 72 dpi, which is appropriate only for relatively small, low-quality printouts. You should also know how to deal with other aspects of translating video to other formats: color, interlacing, and image and pixel aspect ratios.

Exporting a Movie Using a Preset

You can create a single, independent file from all or part of the sequence in the timeline. You can also create a movie from a clip. Exporting from a clip is useful if you want to make a movie from only one portion of a clip or create a version that uses a different format or compression type.

To export a movie using a preset:

1. *Do one of the following:*
   - ▲ To export the edited sequence in the timeline, select the Monitor panel's Timeline view or the Timeline panel.
   - ▲ To export a clip, open a video clip in the Monitor panel's Clip view.
2. To define the footage you want to export, *do one of the following:*
   - ▲ In the timeline, set the work area bar over the range in the timeline you want to export.
   - ▲ In a clip, set the In and Out points to define the frames you want to export.

continues on next page

Exporting for CD-ROM

When you optimize a movie to play from a CD-ROM, your primary goal is compatibility. You also should answer the following questions:

- Does the movie need to be cross-platform compatible?
- What movie-player software will be used?
- What is the slowest possible CD drive that will be playing the movie?
- Will the movie be copied from CD to play back from a hard drive? If so, what is the slowest hard drive that will be playing back the movie?
- What image quality do you require?
- What is the total running time of the movie, and will you be able to reduce the file size to fit onto a typical CD-ROM?

3. In the taskbar, click the Export button, and choose the movie format you want (**Figure 11.51**):
   - ▲ MPEG
   - ▲ QuickTime
   - ▲ Windows Media

   The Export Format dialog box appears. The name and content of the dialog box depend on the format you chose (**Figure 11.52**).

Figure 11.51 Click the taskbar's Export button, and choose the movie format you want to use.

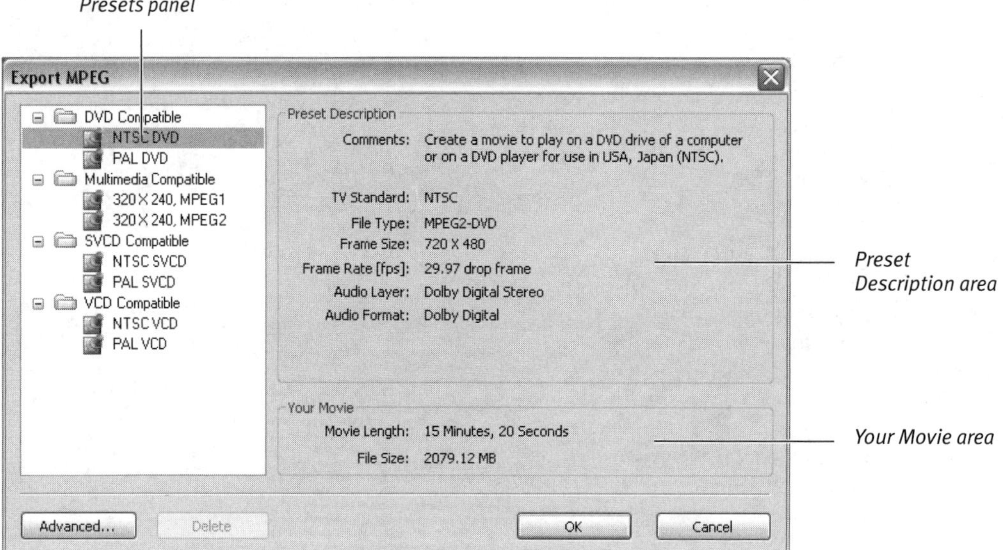

Figure 11.52 An Export dialog box appears; the name of the dialog box matches the export format you selected.

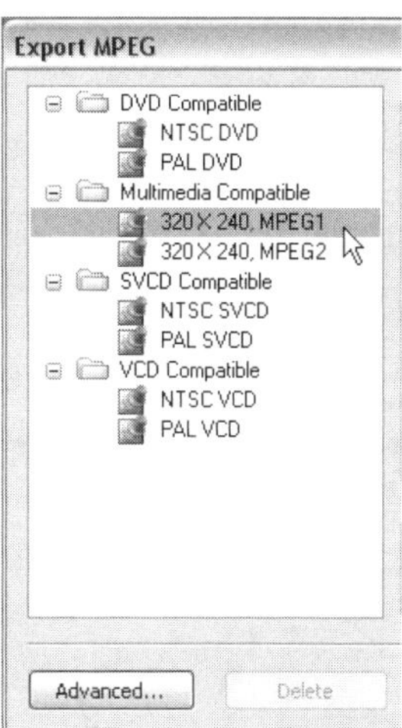

Figure 11.53 In the left panel of the dialog box, select the preset designed for your output goal.

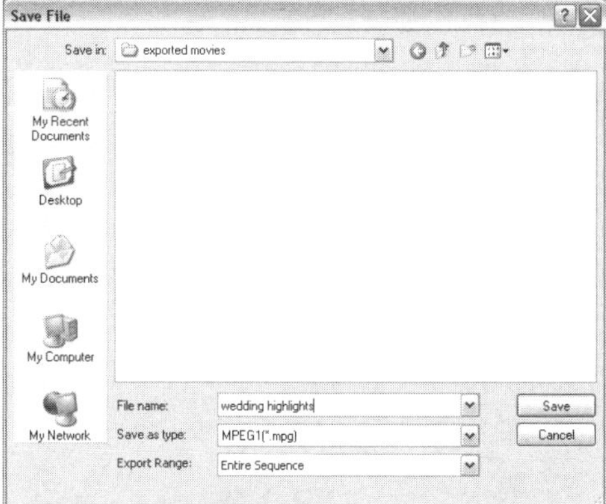

Figure 11.54 In the Save File dialog box, specify the name and destination for the exported movie file.

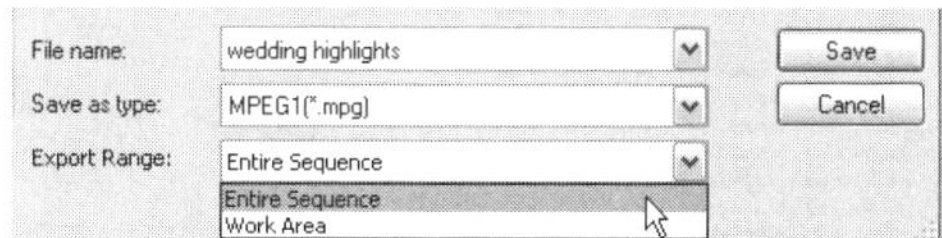

Figure 11.55 Choose whether to export the entire clip or sequence, or only the frames between the In and Out point (when exporting a clip) or under the work area (when exporting a sequence).

4. In the left panel of the dialog box, select the preset designed for your output goal (**Figure 11.53**).

   The summary of the selected preset's settings appears in the Preset Description area of the dialog box. The estimated size of the exported file appears in the Your Movie area.

5. Click OK to close the dialog box.

   A Save File dialog box appears.

6. Specify a name and destination for the exported movie file (**Figure 11.54**).

7. In the Export Range pull-down menu, *do either of the following:*

   ▲ When exporting a clip, specify whether you want to export the entire clip or the frames between its specified In point and Out point.

   ▲ When exporting a sequence, specify whether you want to export the entire sequence or the frames under the Timeline panel's work area bar (**Figure 11.55**).

8. Click Save to render and export the file.

   Premiere Elements renders the file according to the preset. The file's size and software compatibility depend on the preset you selected.

✔ Tips

- Although the reasons for exporting a movie file are varied, they usually share one goal: to make a large movie file smaller. DV movie files are small in terms of video, but they're still too large for media other than DVD, particularly for CD-ROM or delivery over the Web.
- You can also export a movie file by choosing File > Export > Movie. However, this method requires that you take a more active role in specifying the characteristics of the exported movie, such as frame size, frame rate, compression, and audio quality.

Formats

MPEG1—A set of compression standards (developed by the Moving Picture Experts Group) designed to yield results comparable to VHS tape quality at relatively low data rates. This format is typically used for Web download, CD-ROM, or video CD (VCD).

MPEG1-VCD—Preset MPEG1 settings that conform to VCD specifications. The VCD format supports lower quality than DVD but can be played using a standard CD-ROM player and appropriate software.

MPEG2—Another set of standards developed by the Moving Picture Experts Group, intended to produce high-quality, full-screen interlaced video.

MPEG2-DVD—Preset MPEG2 settings that conform to DVD specifications.

MPEG2-SVCD—Preset MPEG2 settings that conform to Super Video CD (SVCD) specifications. SVCD supports higher quality video and more advanced features than the VCD format.

QuickTime—Apple Computer's multimedia architecture, which includes a wide variety of codecs designed for various applications.

RealMedia—Real Networks' standard for low-data-rate applications, particularly for downloading and streaming audio and video over the Web.

Windows Media—Microsoft's standard for low-data rate applications, particularly for downloading streaming audio and video over the Web.

Figure 11.56 Cue to the frame you want to export either in the Clip view (shown here) or in the Timeline view.

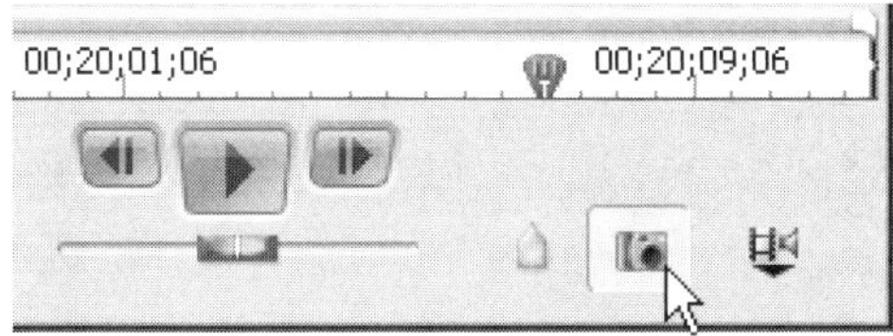

Figure 11.57 In the Monitor panel, click the Export Frame button.

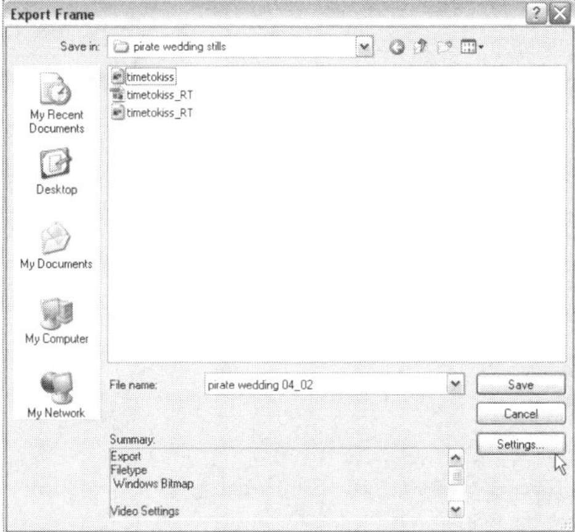

Figure 11.58 Click the Settings button.

Exporting Single Still Images

You can export the current frame of video from the sequence or source clip as a single still-image file.

To export a single frame:

1. *Do one of the following:*
   - ▲ To export a frame from the sequence, cue the Monitor panel's Timeline view to the frame you want to export.
   - ▲ To export a frame from a clip, cue the Monitor panel's Clip view to the frame you want to export (**Figure 11.56**).
2. In the Monitor panel, click the Export Frame button (**Figure 11.57**).

   The Export Frame dialog box appears.
3. Click Settings (**Figure 11.58**).

   The General panel of the Export Frame Settings dialog box appears.

continues on next page

4. Choose a still-image format from the File Type pull-down menu (**Figure 11.59**).
5. *Do one of the following:*
   - ▲ To open the exported still image automatically, click Open When Finished.
   - ▲ To specify options for CompuServe GIF images, click Compile Settings.
6. To specify video options, select Video in the left side of the Export Frame Settings dialog box (**Figure 11.60**).

   Usually, you don't need to change these settings. However, if you want to retain alpha channel information in the still, choose "Millions+ of colors" in the Color Depth drop-down menu (**Figure 11.61**).
7. To deinterlace the exported frame, select Keyframe and Rendering from the left side of the Export Frame Settings dialog box, and then select Deinterlace Video Footage (**Figure 11.62**).

   This option removes one field from an interlaced image, which can remove the combing effect sometimes apparent in still frames taken from video containing objects in motion. For more about interlacing, see the sidebar "Interlaced Video."

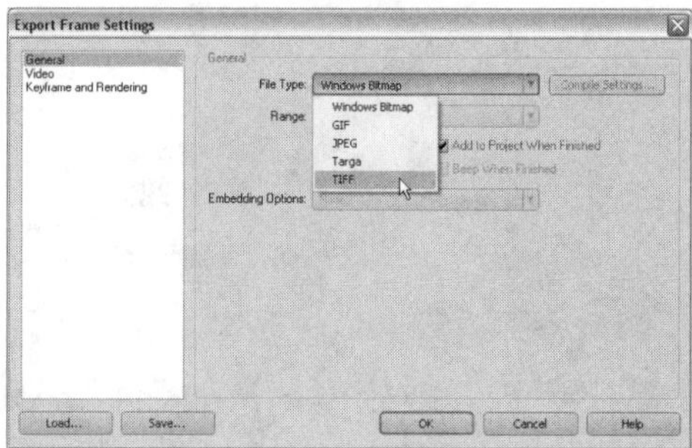

Figure 11.59 Choose a still-image format from the File Type drop-down menu.

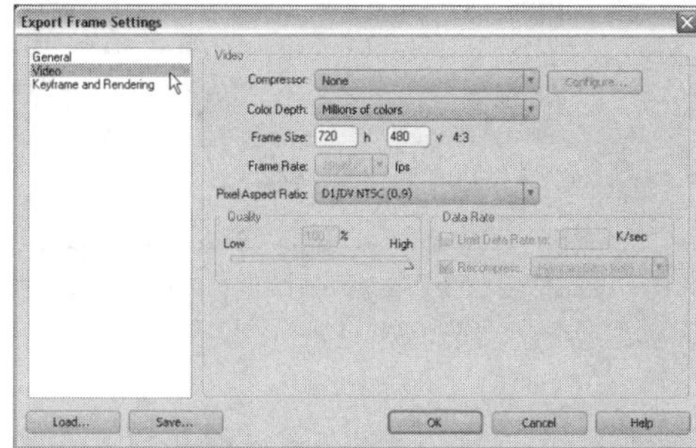

Figure 11.60 To specify video options, select Video in the left side of the Export Frame Settings dialog box.

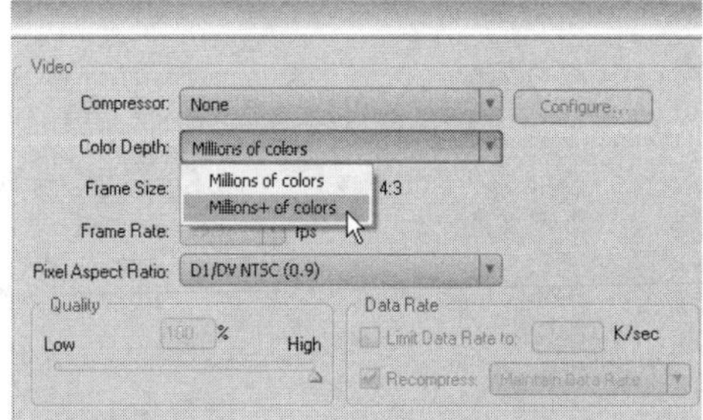

Figure 11.61 If you want to retain alpha channel information, choose "Millions+ of colors" in the Color Depth drop-down menu.

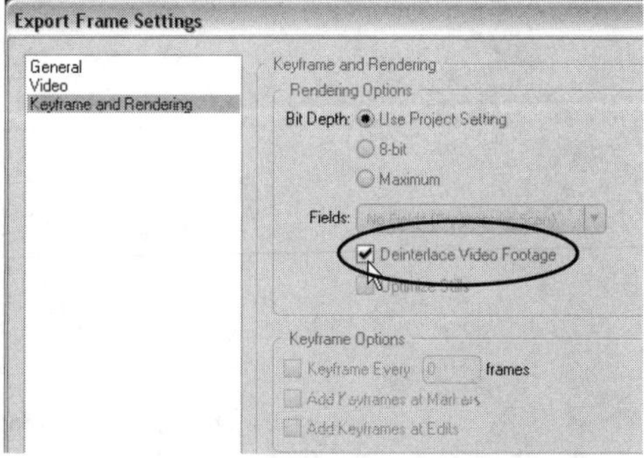

Figure 11.62 To deinterlace the exported frame, select Keyframe and Rendering from the left side of the Export Frame Settings dialog box, and then select Deinterlace Video Footage.

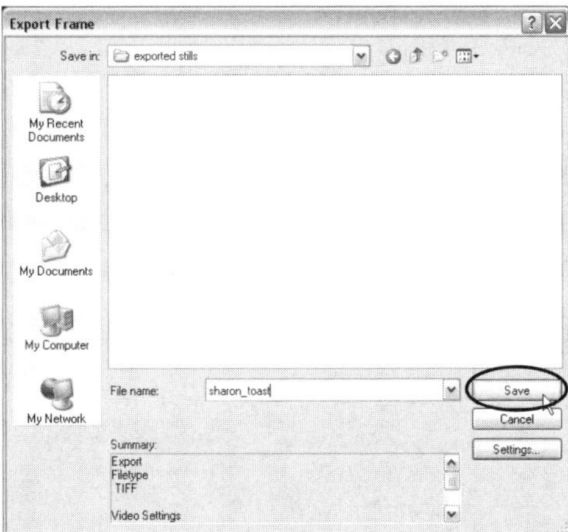

Figure 11.63 Specify a name and destination for the still image, and click Save.

8. Click OK.

   The Export Frame Settings dialog box closes, and you return to the Export Frame dialog box.

9. Specify a name and destination for the still image, and click Save (**Figure 11.63**).

   The frame you specified is exported as a still-frame file in the format and location you set.

✔ Tips

- If you plan to print the still image, you should know that standard-resolution video always translates to 72 dpi, regardless of the camera's tape format. This is fine for small, low-resolution printouts. But if you want to create a photo album or other printed materials, be sure to take stills with a film camera or a high-quality (multiple mega-pixel) digital still camera.
- Most stills taken from DV must be deinterlaced and resized to compensate for differences in pixel aspect ratios. In Photoshop, deinterlace first (the order of steps matters), and then reduce the video frame's width by 10 percent to remove distortion.
- You can export an Animated GIF as you would any other movie file (using File > Export > Movie) or a CompuServe GIF like any other single still-image or still-image sequence file. However, these formats have a few special options (accessed via the Export dialog box's Compile Settings button). Consult your Premiere Elements User Guide or Help system for more guidance.

Interlaced Video

Each video frame consists of horizontal lines. (The number of lines depends on the video standard: NTSC or PAL.) In contrast to a motion picture frame—which is instantly displayed in its entirety—each line of a video frame is displayed over time, in an interlaced pattern.

Interlaced video divides each frame into two fields. Each field includes every other horizontal line (scan line) in the frame. A television displays one field first, drawing alternating scan lines from the top of the image to the bottom (**Figure 11.64**). Returning to the top, it then displays the alternate field, filling in the gaps to complete the frame (**Figure 11.65**). In NTSC video, each frame displays approximately $^1/_{30}$ of a second; each field displays every $^1/_{60}$ of a second.

The field that contains the topmost scan line is called *field 1*, the *odd field*, or the *upper field*. The other field is known as *field 2*, the *even field*, or the *lower field*. DV footage is almost always lower-field dominant.

Figure 11.64 Interlaced displays present a single field that includes every other line of the image...

Figure 11.65 ...and then interlaces the other field to create a full frame.

Interlacing Problems and Solutions

Because video cameras capture each field of a frame at different moments in time, moving objects may be in one position in one field and in a different position in the next field. You'd never notice the difference as the video is playing, but it becomes apparent when you view a single interlaced frame. The way interlacing makes a moving object look when viewed as a still frame is described as *combing* or *field artifacts*. Interlacing can also become apparent when you make a clip play in slow motion.

If you intend to export interlaced video to a noninterlaced format or to a still frame, you should deinterlace it. *Deinterlacing* converts two fields into a single frame, either by duplicating one field or blending the two.

Deinterlacing is an option when exporting (in the Keyframe and Rendering panel of the Export Frame Settings dialog box), when creating a freeze frame (in the Frame Hold dialog box), and when you choose Clip > Video Options > Field Options.

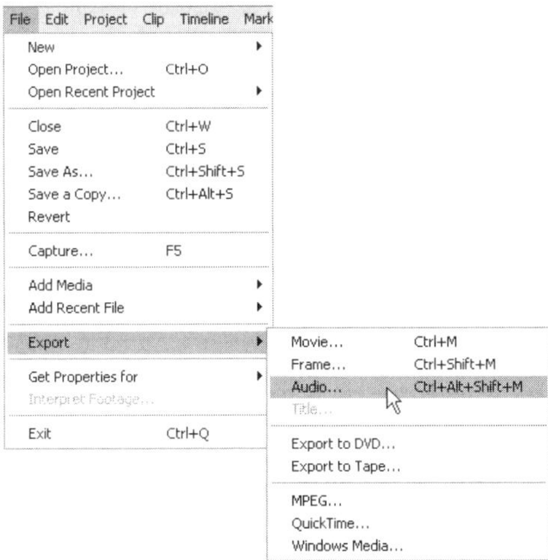

Figure 11.66 Choose File › Export › Audio.

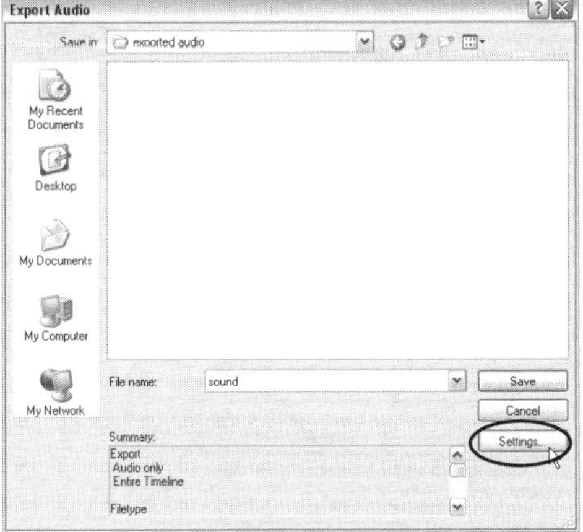

Figure 11.67 To change the current export settings, click the Settings button.

Exporting Audio-Only Files

The process for exporting audio is similar to exporting a movie with video and audio, except that you're limited to audio-only file formats.

To export an audio file:

1. *Do one of the following:*
   - ▲ To export audio from the timeline, select the sequence's tab in the Timeline panel or the program view of the Monitor panel.
   - ▲ To export a clip's audio, open a clip in the source view.
2. To define the footage you want to export, *do one of the following:*
   - ▲ In the timeline, set the work area bar over the range you want to export.
   - ▲ In a clip, set the In and Out points to define the frames you want to export.
3. Choose File > Export > Audio (**Figure 11.66**).

   The Export Audio dialog box appears. The bottom of the dialog box summarizes the current export settings.
4. To change the current export settings, click the Settings button (**Figure 11.67**).

   The General panel of the Export Audio Settings dialog box appears.

continues on next page

5. To change the current export settings, specify settings in the other panels of the Export Audio Settings dialog box by *choosing a category from the left side of the dialog box*:

   General—To specify the audio file's file type, the range of the timeline to export, and whether to embed a project link (**Figure 11.68**)

   Audio—To specify settings that control aspects of the audio, such as sample rate and bit depth (**Figure 11.69**)

6. Click OK to exit the Export Audio Settings dialog box.

   You return to the Export Audio dialog box.

7. Specify a name and destination for your file, and click Save (**Figure 11.70**).

   A progress bar appears, indicating the processing time required to make the movie.

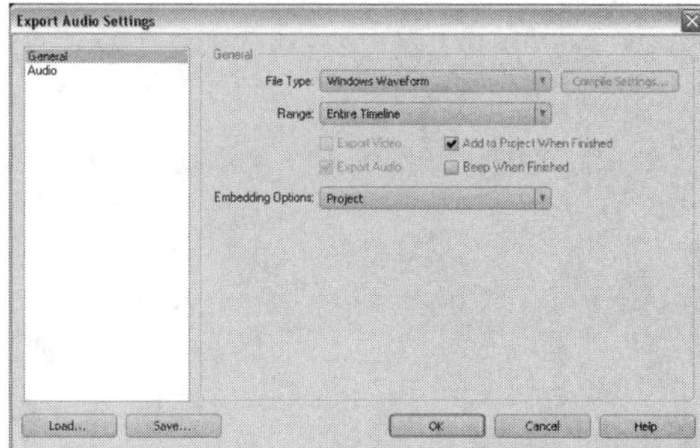

Figure 11.68 Specify the General settings.

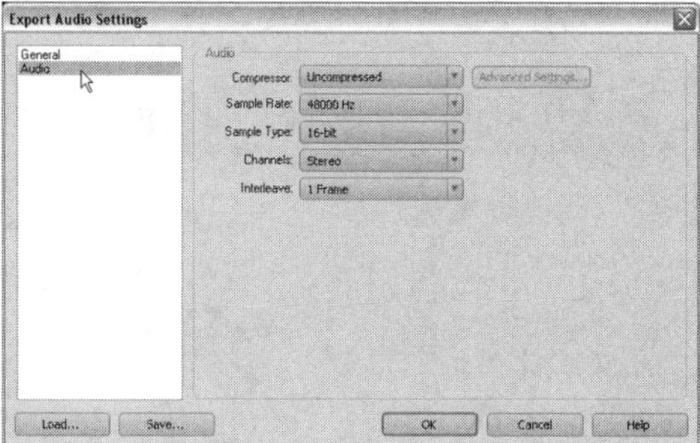

Figure 11.69 Specify the Audio settings.

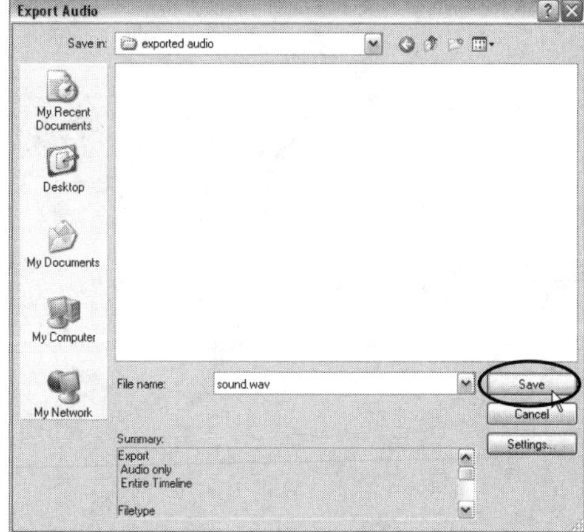

Figure 11.70 Specify a name and location for your file, and click Save.

Audio Bit Depth

Audio bit depth refers to the number of bits used to describe each audio sample. Bit depth affects the range of sound the audio file can reproduce, from silence to the loudest sound. This range is known as the *signal-to-noise ratio* (s/n), which can be measured in decibels (dB).

In general, higher bit depths are desirable when you're importing and editing, because processing audio requires the extra precision to minimize errors. When you're exporting audio, it can be useful to specify a lower bit depth to reduce the size of the exported file.

INDEX

Symbols and numbers

A

INDEX

D

E

F

INDEX

N

O

P

Q

R

S

T

INDEX